Oxford Dictionary of
Modern Quotations

Oxford Dictionary of
Modern
Quotations

THIRD EDITION

Edited by **Elizabeth Knowles**

OXFORD
UNIVERSITY PRESS

OXFORD
UNIVERSITY PRESS

Great Clarendon Street, Oxford OX2 6DP

Oxford University Press is a department of the University of Oxford.
It furthers the University's objective of excellence in research, scholarship,
and education by publishing worldwide in

Oxford New York

Auckland Cape Town Dar es Salaam Hong Kong Karachi
Kuala Lumpur Madrid Melbourne Mexico City Nairobi
New Delhi Shanghai Taipei Toronto

With offices in Argentina Austria Brazil Chile Czech Republic
France Greece Guatemala Hungary Italy Japan Poland
Portugal Singapore South Korea Switzerland Thailand
Turkey Ukraine Vietnam

Oxford is a registered trade mark of Oxford University Press
in the UK and in certain other countries

Published in the United States
by Oxford University Press Inc., New York

First published 1991
Second edition published 2002
Third edition published 2007

British Library Cataloguing in Publication Data

Data available

Library of Congress Cataloging-in-Publication Data

Data available

Typeset by Interactive Sciences Ltd, Gloucester
Printed in Great Britain
on acid-free paper by
Clays Ltd, St Ives plc

ISBN 978-0-19-920-8951

1 3 5 7 9 10 8 6 4 2

Contents

Introduction

The third edition of the *Oxford Dictionary of Modern Quotations*, like its predecessor, shows us the world of today against a background of the preceding century. All quotations are from the 20th or 21st century, and the book concentrates on authors who were alive in or after 1914 (taking the First World War as the cultural watershed of the modern period). The *Dictionary* at once reflects the interests and concerns of today, and records key utterances and events of the past which still have resonance for us.

Affairs of today are inevitably dominated by events in Iraq, but as with any dictionary of quotations, the range of material covered here stretches from the deeply serious to the lighthearted (not to say surreal, as in Stephen Colbert's straight-faced definition of 'truthiness' as Truth that comes from the gut, not books, and Linda Smith's assertion that she played all her country and western music backwards: Your lover returns, your dog comes back to life and you cease to be an alcoholic).

Current issues often prompt comparison with earlier periods, especially when considering shifts in public opinion. In 1968 the American broadcaster and journalist Walter Cronkite said in a special television report, having returned from the country: It now seems more certain than ever that the bloody experience of Vietnam is to end in a stalemate. Hearing of it, President Lyndon Johnson commented grimly, If I've lost Walter Cronkite, I've lost Mr Average Citizen.

Considerations of the war in Iraq, and President Bush's role, brought up a wry quotation from the American jurist Francis Biddle, advisor to Franklin Roosevelt: The Constitution has never greatly bothered any wartime President. Discussions of British involvement prompted a comparison with T. E. Lawrence's view of Mesopotamia in 1920: The people of England have been led in Mesopotamia into a trap from which it will be hard to escape with dignity and honour. A *Times* leader from the same year was similarly quoted: How much longer are valuable lives to be sacrificed in the vain endeavour to impose upon the Arab population an elaborate and expensive administration which they never asked for and do not want?

Over 70 years ago, Kemal Atatürk addressed a group of Australians at Anzac Cove, Gallipoli. In one passage of his speech he said: There is no difference between the Johnnies and the Mehmets to us where they lie side by side in this country of ours. You, the mothers, who sent their sons from faraway countries, wipe away your tears. Your sons are now lying in our bosom and are in peace. After having lost their lives on this land, they have become our sons as well. His words, subsequently inscribed on the memorial at Gallipoli, appear also on memorials at Canberra and Wellington, and are read on Anzac Day, but today the reference to war dead in a foreign land has fresh resonance.

Words of today often echo the past. Indira Gandhi, asked in 1982 by a Washington reporter why India 'always tilted towards the Soviet Union' responded: We do not tilt on either side . . . we walk upright. Following the bombings in Mumbai in 2006, the

Indian Prime Minister Manmohan Singh declared, No one can make India kneel. Sometimes the link is an explicit one. I should love to think of a black Archbishop of York . . . telling a future generation of the scandal and glory of the Church said Archbishop Michael Ramsey in 1960. Well, here I am said Archbishop John Sentamu in 2006. The film director Peter Jackson, announcing that his company would not be following the success of *The Lord of the Rings* by making *The Hobbit*, used Tolkien's own subtitle when he said ruefully We got to go there—but not back again.

Quotations from the march of events inevitably feature the powerful, but there are also reminders of the role of the individual. Thurgood Marshall, first African-American Justice of the US Supreme Court, warned We must never forget that the only real source of power that we as judges can tap is the respect of the people. It is an observation that chimes neatly with a comment attributed to the anthropologist Margaret Mead: Never doubt that a small group of thoughtful committed citizens can change the world. In fact, it's the only thing that ever has. The philosophy of Cicely Saunders, founder of the hospice movement, is summed up in the words You matter because you are you, and you matter to the last moment of your life. When the civil rights campaigner Rosa Parks died, Jesse Jackson commented: She sat down in order that we might stand up—and the walls of segregation came down.

Advertising slogans open a window on lifestyle preferences. In the 1940s, fashion tips included Revlon's offer of Matching lips and fingertips, although in today's climate it may be hard to believe that there was ever a cigarette advertisement which ran More doctors smoke Camels than any other cigarette. Mr Kipling's Exceedingly good cakes from Britain in the 1960s were followed in 1970s America by General Food's invention of 'Stove Top Stuffing'—to be offered with the question, Stuffing instead of potatoes? By the 1990s, more radical changes were heralded by Ikea's instruction to Chuck out the chintz, and perhaps most memorably by Apple's Think different. Slogans for Australian tourism have morphed from Paul Hogan, in the persona of Crocodile Dundee, promising to slip another shrimp on the barbie of 1984 to the more challenging So where the bloody hell are you? of 2006. (A choice of language that was defended by the Tourism Minister, Fran Bailey: This is a great Australian adjective. It's plain speaking and friendly. It is our vernacular.)

Quotations from the sporting world can offer a view of changing culture. After the World Cup of 2006, the Brazilian football coach Felipe Scolare commented Now there is so much professionalism, we have to revert to urging players to like the game, love it, do it with joy. The Dutch athlete Fanny Blankers-Koen, looking back at the end of her life to outstanding success in the 1948 Olympics, reflected that When I competed, no one ever thought it would be possible to make money from doing something you enjoyed so much. And fame in sport brings its own pressures. The footballer Alan Ball, part of the English World Cup-winning squad of 1966, told an interviewer I tell you what made us what we were. We had this wonderful feeling that we were still part of the people. Freddie Trueman, asked whether he thought anyone would beat his record-breaking capture of Test wickets, responded dryly, If anyone beats it, they'll be bloody tired.

The world of fashion, like that of sport, naturally provides words reflecting cultural change. The daring is gone. No one can dream any more said Elsa Schiaparelli after her last collection in 1954. The word 'daring' might have been coined for a creation of a few years before, the bikini. A bikini is not a bikini unless it can be pulled through a wedding ring said its creator Louis Reard. The fashion editor Diana Vreeland put it in a slightly different way, commenting that it revealed everything about a girl except her mother's maiden name. But there were, of course, further fashion icons to come. The couturier Yves Saint Laurent had regrets where one of them was concerned, saying simply I wish I had invented blue jeans.

Famous people are not necessarily impressed by the adulation given to them. Celebrity can go hand-in-hand with a wry self-awareness, as in Alice Cooper's I am past writing angst songs for kids. My angst is when I can't get my Porsche roof up and when I can't get my golf handicap down. The American jockey Eddie Arcaro commented that When a jockey retires, he becomes just another little man. The Algonquin wit George Kaufman recognized ruefully that his revision of a Broadway play, staged during the influenza epidemic of 1918, was unsuccessful. His suggestion for a line to attract the public ran: Beware of flu. Avoid crowds. See *Someone in the House*.

Marlene Dietrich had a clear-eyed view of her allure: Glamour is what I sell in my act, and it costs plenty. It's my stock-in-trade. Pamela Anderson saw some advantages in being considered 'a dumb blonde': When you have nothing to live up to, you can't disappoint anybody . . . When you form a sentence, you're a genius. Dawn French pointed out: If I were alive in Rubens's time, I'd be celebrated as a model. Kate Moss would be used as a paint brush. Even the Queen, on her 80th birthday, was alert to the dangers of being too easily impressed: As Groucho Marx once said, 'Anyone can get old —all you have to do is live long enough.'

As before, a number of special category sections, including **Borrowed titles** (His dark materials—Philip Pullman's use of Milton's words), **Film lines** (Even the smallest person can change the course of the future—Galadriel's encouragement to Frodo in *The Fellowship of the Ring*), and **Misquotations** (Hug a hoodie) have been incorporated into the main author sequence. (A full list of these can be found on p. v.) There is also a selective thematic index, to guide readers to quotations on such topics as **Language** and **Success**.

Each author entry has a direction to any quotations about that author elsewhere in the *Dictionary*. For example, at the entry for J. K. Rowling, there is a cross-reference to Lemony Snicket's reason for not choosing to advise her on how to close her Harry Potter saga: I wouldn't stoop to giving advice to anyone who lives in a castle in Scotland. I think the last people to give someone like that advice were the witches in Macbeth and they didn't come out so well. The entry for Bob Dylan includes a direction to Joan Baez's comment that He always had a rainbow pen.

As with other central titles in our Oxford Quotations family, we have built on the foundation of earlier editions, augmented by material from our bank of new quotations. This is fed by our reading programme, and further enhanced through suggestions, questions, and comments received from the general public, as from colleagues in the Reference and Dictionaries Departments, and on the staff of the *Oxford English Dictionary*. We have also benefited enormously from exploitation of the Corpus resources developed by our English Dictionaries colleagues.

As before, it has been fascinating for the editorial staff to see how quotations illuminate the history of modern times. We hope that our readers will again share in the interest and absorption felt in compiling the book.

Acknowledgements

Thanks are due all those who have contributed to this new edition, in particular Ralph Bates for library research, Jean Harker and Verity Mason for contributions to the Quotations reading programme, Robert E. Blackburn for suggestions for the music coverage, Susanne Charlett for data capture, Nick Clarke for text design, Sarah O'Connor for controlling the various stages of production, and Carolyn Garwes for proofreading. We have again benefited from James McCracken's work on the Oxford Corpus, and we are most grateful for the generous support and skilled assistance of Michael Proffitt, Melinda Babcock, and Pamela Wagner of the *Oxford English Dictionary*. Ben Harris read and commented fruitfully on earlier versions of the text, and I have very much appreciated his support and that of Ruth Langley. Finally, as always, Susan Ratcliffe has given generously of her expertise: I am more than grateful for her meticulous work and wise advice.

ELIZABETH KNOWLES

Oxford 2007

How to Use the Dictionary

Finding a quotation . . .

. . . if you know the author

If you know the author of a quotation you can go straight to that entry in the dictionary: authors are in alphabetical order (see **Author entry order** below). Unless the entry is very large you should be able to spot the quotation you want.

. . . if you know the words but not the author

If you know some words from the quotation but not who wrote it, look in the Keyword Index. The most significant words from each quotation are indexed with a reference to the author, the page on which the quotation appears, and the number of the quotation within the page (see **Keyword Index** below).

. . . on a subject

If you want to find a quotation on a specific subject, the subject may be included in the Thematic Index. A list of these subjects is given on the Contents pages. If the subject is not listed there, try looking for the word and related terms in the Keyword Index.

Authors

Author entry order

The entries are in alphabetical order of author, usually by surname but with occasional exceptions such as members of royal families (for example **Diana, Princess of Wales** and **Elizabeth II**) and Popes (**John Paul II**). In general authors' names are given in the form by which they are best known, so that we have **George Orwell** (not Eric Blair), **Harold Macmillan** (not Lord Stockton), and **H. G. Wells** (not Herbert George Wells). If the medium in which a quotation originally appeared is commonly multi-authored or anonymous, it may be included in a special entry box (see **Special Categories** below).

Author information

The name of each author is followed by their dates of birth and death (where known) and a brief biography. Where appropriate, cross-references are then given to quotations about that author elsewhere in the text (*on Blair: see* **Cameron** 73:4). Cross-references are also made to other entries or quotations in which the author appears, e.g. '*see also* **Lennon and McCartney**' and '*see also* **Epitaphs** 109:2'.

Special Categories

Within the author sequence there are a number of special entries, such as **Advertising slogans**, **Catchphrases**, **Film lines**, **Misquotations**, and **Newspaper headlines and leaders**. Quotations in these sections are arranged alphabetically according to the first word of the quotation (ignoring 'a' and 'the'). A full list of the special categories is given on the Contents pages.

Quotations

Quotation order

Within each author entry, quotations are separated by literary form (novels, plays, or poems) and within each group arranged by alphabetical order of title. Quotations from diaries, letters, and speeches are given in chronological order. The form for which the author is best known is given first. Thus in the case of political figures, speeches appear first, just as poetry quotations come second for an author regarded primarily as a novelist.

Quotations from secondary sources such as biographies and other writer's works, to which a date in the author's lifetime can be assigned, are arranged within the chronological sequence. Other quotations from secondary sources and attributed quotations which cannot be so dated are arranged in alphabetical order of quotation text. Foreign-language text is given where the quotation is likely to be encountered in the language of origin.

Information about quotations

Background information regarded as essential to a full appreciation of the quotation precedes the text in an italicized note; information seen as providing useful amplification follows in an italicized note.

Each quotation is accompanied by a bibliographical note of the source from which the quotation is taken. Titles of published volumes (*Fever Pitch* by Nick Hornby and *Wild Swans* by Jung Chang) appear in italics; titles of short stories and poems not published as volumes in their own right, and individual song titles, are given in roman type inside inverted commas ('Dis Poetry' by Benjamin Zephaniah and 'Candle in the Wind' by Elton John). Dates of publication are given in brackets.

Looking elsewhere in the book

Cross-references are used to direct the reader to another related quotation. In each case a reference is given to an author's name or to the title of a special category entry, followed by the page number and then the unique quotation number on that page ('see **Blair** 37:6', 'see **Film lines** 115:11'). In descriptions, context notes, or source notes, authors who have their own entries are indicated by the use of bold ('*of Margaret* **Thatcher**', '*by Philip* **Pullman**')

Indexes

Keyword Index

The most significant words from each quotation appear in the keyword index, allowing individual quotations to be traced. Each instance of a keyword is given with a short section of the surrounding text, to help identify it. Both the keywords and the sections of text, including those in foreign languages, are in strict alphabetical order. Singular and plural nouns are grouped separately. To simplify searching, words are indexed in standard British English form, regardless of spelling in the original.

References are to the author's name (usually in abbreviated form, for instance CHUR for Winston Churchill) followed by the page number and the number of the unique quotation on the page. So looking up **tears** will show

tears blood, toil, t. and sweat   CHUR 66:8

This means the quotation about 'blood, toil, tears and sweat' can be found as quotation number 8 on page 66, in the entry for Churchill.

Thematic Index

In addition, a selection of quotations on designated subjects can be traced through the
thematic index. Each subject heading is followed by a line from each of the selected
quotations on the theme. References are to the author's name, with page and
quotation number, as in the keyword index. Thus, under **Art**, the first entry reads

active line on a walk   KLEE 184:19

This means a quotation about art including the words 'active line on a walk' can be
found as quotation number 19 on page 184, in the entry for Klee.

a

Diane Abbott 1953–
British Labour politician and first black woman MP, elected to Parliament in 1987

1 Being an MP is the sort of job all working-class parents want for their children—clean, indoors and no heavy lifting.
in Independent 18 January 1994

Dannie Abse 1923–
Welsh-born doctor and poet

2 I know the colour rose, and it is lovely,
But not when it ripens in a tumour;
And healing greens, leaves and grass, so springlike
In limbs that fester are not springlike.
'Pathology of Colours' (1968)

Bella Abzug 1920–98
American lawyer, feminist leader, and Democratic politician

3 Richard Nixon impeached himself. He gave us Gerald Ford as his revenge.
in Rolling Stone; quoted in Linda Botts *Loose Talk* (1980)

4 When I was a young lawyer . . . working women wore hats. It was the only way they would take you seriously.
the origin of her custom of wearing wide-brimmed hats
in American National Biography (online edition) 'Bella Abzug'

Goodman Ace 1899–1982
American humorist

5 TV—a clever contraction derived from the words Terrible Vaudeville . . . we call it a medium because nothing's well done.
letter, to Groucho Marx, in The Groucho Letters (1967)

Chinua Achebe 1930–
Nigerian novelist

6 The world is like a Mask dancing. If you want to see it well you do not stand in one place.
Arrow of God (1988)

7 In such a regime, I say, you died a good death if your life had inspired someone to come forward and shoot your murderer in the chest—without asking to be paid.
A Man of the People (1966)

Dean Acheson 1893–1971
American lawyer and Democratic politician, US Secretary of State 1949–53, instrumental in the formation of NATO

8 Great Britain has lost an empire and has not yet found a role.
speech at the Military Academy, West Point, 5 December 1962

9 The Soviet Union was playing one of the greatest gambles in history at minimal cost. It did not need to win all the possibilities. Even one or two offered immense gain. We and we alone were in a position to break up the play.
of the Soviet Union's role in the Eastern Mediterranean in 1947
Present at the Creation (1969)

10 A memorandum is written not to inform the reader but to protect the writer.
in Wall Street Journal 8 September 1977

Giuseppe Adami 1878–1946
and Renato Simoni 1875–1952
Italian librettists

1 *Nessun dorma.*

None shall sleep.
sung by the Prince who has challenged Princess Turandot to discover his name; she and her court must do so before dawn
   Turandot (1926 opera, music by Puccini) closing lines (after Gozzi's drama, 1762); as sung by Luciano Pavarotti, the song was the anthem for the 1990 Football World Cup in Italy

Douglas Adams 1952–2001
English science fiction writer

2 Don't panic.
   The Hitch Hiker's Guide to the Galaxy (1979) preface

3 The Answer to the Great Question Of . . . Life, the Universe and Everything . . . [is] Forty-two.
   The Hitch Hiker's Guide to the Galaxy (1979)

4 Time is an illusion. Lunchtime doubly so.
   The Hitch Hiker's Guide to the Galaxy (1979) ch. 2

Franklin P. Adams 1881–1960
American journalist and humorist

5 Years ago we discovered the exact point, the dead centre of middle age. It occurs when you are too young to take up golf and too old to rush up to the net.
   Nods and Becks (1944)

6 Elections are won by men and women chiefly because most people vote against somebody rather than for somebody.
   Nods and Becks (1944); see **Fields 111:15**

Gerry Adams 1948–
Northern Irish politician; President of Sinn Féin

7 Peace cannot be built on exclusion. That has been the price of the past 30 years.
   of the Good Friday peace agreement
   in *Daily Telegraph* 11 April 1998

Phillip Adams 1939–
Australian film director and producer

8 Adams' first law of television: the weight of the backside is greater than the force of the intellect.
   in 1970; attributed, Stephen Murray-Smith (ed.) *The Dictionary of Australian Quotations* (1984)

Harold Adamson 1906–80
American songwriter

9 Comin' in on a wing and a pray'r.
   derived from the contemporary comment of a war pilot, speaking from a disabled plane to ground control
   title of song (1943)

Alfred Adler 1870–1937
Austrian psychologist and psychiatrist, who held the view that society and culture were significant factors in mental illness

10 The truth is often a terrible weapon of aggression. It is possible to lie, and even to murder, for the truth.
   The Problems of Neurosis (1929)

11 It is always easier to fight for one's principles than to live up to them.
   Phyllis Bottome *Alfred Adler* (1939); quoted by Adlai **Stevenson** in a speech to the American Legion Convention, New York, 27 August 1952

Theodor Adorno 1903–69
German philosopher, sociologist, and musicologist

12 It is barbarous to write a poem after Auschwitz.
   attributed; I. Buruma *Wages of Guilt* (1994)

Advertising slogans
see box opposite
see also **Taglines for films**

Herbert Agar 1897–1980
American poet and writer

13 The truth which makes men free is for the most part the truth which men prefer not to hear.
   A Time for Greatness (1942); referring to the *Bible* St John: 'And ye shall know the truth, and the truth shall make you free'

Advertising slogans

1 Access—your flexible friend.
Access credit card, 1981 onwards

2 An ace caff with quite a nice museum attached.
the Victoria and Albert Museum, February 1989

3 All human life is there.
the *News of the World*, used by Maurice Smelt in the late 1950s; earlier, Henry James wrote in *The Madonna of the Future* (1879): 'Cats and monkeys—monkeys and cats—all human life is there!'

4 American Express? . . . That'll do nicely, sir.
American Express credit card, 1970s

5 And all because the lady loves Milk Tray.
Cadbury's Milk Tray chocolates, 1968 onwards

6 Australians wouldn't give a XXXX for anything else.
Castlemaine lager, 1986 onwards

7 Beanz meanz Heinz.
Heinz baked beans, *c.*1967; coined by Maurice Drake

8 Bovril . . . Prevents that sinking feeling.
Bovril, 1920; coined by H. H. Harris

9 . . . But I know a man who can.
Automobile Association, 1980s

10 Can you tell Stork from butter?
Stork margarine, from *c.*1956

11 Chuck out the chintz.
IKEA, 1990s

12 Cool as a mountain stream.
Consulate menthol cigarettes, early 1960s onwards

13 A diamond is forever.
De Beers Consolidated Mines, 1940s onwards; coined by Frances Gerety; see **Loos 202:10**

14 Does she . . . or doesn't she?
Clairol hair colouring, 1950s

15 Don't be vague, ask for Haig.
Haig whisky, *c.*1936

16 Don't forget the fruit gums, Mum.
Rowntree's fruit gums, 1958–61; coined by Roger Musgrave

17 Drinka Pinta Milka Day.
National Dairy Council, 1958; coined by Bertrand Whitehead

18 Even your closest friends won't tell you.
Listerine mouthwash, US, in *Woman's Home Companion* November 1923

19 Exceedingly good cakes.
Mr Kipling cakes, 1967 onwards

20 Full of Eastern promise.
Fry's Turkish Delight, 1950s onwards

21 The future's bright, the future's Orange.
slogan for Orange telecom company, mid 1990s

22 Go to work on an egg.
British Egg Marketing Board, from 1957; perhaps written by Fay **Weldon** or Mary Gowing

23 Guinness is good for you.
reply universally given to researchers asking people why they drank Guinness
adopted by Oswald Greene, *c.*1929; see **Advertising slogans 4:16**

24 Happiness is a cigar called Hamlet.
Hamlet cigars; see **Ephron 106:1, Lennon 196:9, Schulz 288:7**

25 Have a break, have a Kit-Kat.
Rowntree's Kit-Kat, from *c.*1955

26 Heineken refreshes the parts other beers cannot reach.
Heineken lager, 1975 onwards; coined by Terry Lovelock

27 Hello boys.
Wonderbra, 1994 onwards

28 Horlicks guards against night starvation.
Horlicks malted milk drink, 1930s

29 If you want to get ahead, get a hat.
the Hat Council, 1965

30 I liked it so much, I bought the company!
Remington Shavers, 1980; spoken by the company's new owner Victor Kiam (1926–2001)

▶

► Advertising slogans continued

1 I'm only here for the beer.
Double Diamond beer, 1971 onwards; coined by Ros Levenstein

2 It beats as it sweeps as it cleans.
Hoover vacuum cleaners, devised in 1919 by Gerald Page-Wood

3 It's finger lickin' good.
Kentucky fried chicken, from 1958

4 It's good to talk.
British Telecom, from 1994

5 It's tingling fresh. It's fresh as ice.
Gibbs toothpaste; the first advertising slogan heard on British television, 22 September 1955

6 I was a seven-stone weakling.
Charles Atlas body-building, originally in US

7 Keep that schoolgirl complexion.
Palmolive soap, from 1917; coined by Charles S. Pearce

8 Kills all known germs.
Domestos bleach, 1959

9 Let the train take the strain.
British Rail, 1970 onwards

10 Let your fingers do the walking.
Bell system Telephone Directory Yellow Pages, 1960s

11 A Mars a day helps you work, rest and play.
Mars bar, c.1960 onwards; coined by Norman Gaff (d. 1988)

12 Matching lips and fingertips.
Revlon cosmetics, 1940

13 Maybe, just maybe.
British national lottery, from 1998

14 The mint with the hole.
Life-Savers, US, 1920; and Rowntree's Polo mints, UK, from 1947

15 More doctors smoke Camels than any other cigarette.
Camel cigarettes, 1940s-50s

16 My Goodness, My Guinness.
Guinness stout, 1935; coined by Dicky Richards; see **Advertising slogans 3:23**

17 Naughty but nice.
fresh cream cakes for the National Dairy Council, 1980s; sometimes said to have been coined by Salman **Rushdie** when a copywriter, although the phrase itself goes back to the late 19th century (and was also the title of two films, in 1927 and 1939)

18 Never knowingly undersold.
motto of the John Lewis Partnership, from c.1920; coined by John Spedan Lewis (1885–1963)

19 Nice one, Cyril.
taken up by supporters of Cyril Knowles, Tottenham Hotspur footballer; the Spurs team later made a record featuring the line
Wonderloaf, 1972

20 No manager ever got fired for buying IBM.
IBM

21 Oxo gives a meal man-appeal.
Oxo beef extract, c. 1960

22 People take pictures of people they love.
Polaroid, 1954; slogan devised by the Doyle Dane Bernbach agency co-founded by Bill **Bernbach**

23 Persil washes whiter—and it shows.
Persil washing powder, 1970s

24 Probably the best lager in the world.
Carlsberg lager, 1970s

25 Put a tiger in your tank.
Esso petrol, 1964

26 Say it with flowers.
Society of American Florists, 1917; coined by Patrick O'Keefe (1872–1934)

27 Sch . . . you know who.
Schweppes mineral drinks, 1960s

28 Slip another shrimp on the barbie.
Tourism Australia, 1984, spoken by Paul Hogan as Crocodile Dundee

29 Someone, somewhere, wants a letter from you.
British Post Office, 1960s

►

▶ Advertising slogans continued

1 So where the bloody hell are you?
   Tourism Australia, 2006, promoting
   Australia as a destination; this was the
   punchline to such opening lines as 'We've
   poured you a beer', 'We've had the camels
   shampooed', and 'We've got the sharks out
   of the pool'; see also **Bailey 20:11**

2 Stop me and buy one.
   Wall's ice cream, from spring 1922; coined
   by Cecil Rodd

3 Stuffing instead of potatoes?
   General Foods' Stove Top Stuffing, 1974,
   invented by the home economist Ruth M.
   Siems (1931–2005)

4 Tell Sid.
   privatization of British Gas, 1986

5 Things go better with Coke.
   Coca-Cola, 1963

6 Think different.
   Apple Computers, 1997

7 Top people take *The Times*.
   The Times newspaper, from January 1959

8 *Vorsprung durch Technik.*
   Progress through technology.
   Audi cars, from 1986

9 We are the Ovaltineys,
   Little [*or* Happy] girls and boys.
   'We are the Ovaltineys' (song from *c.*1935);
   Ovaltine drink

10 We're number two. We try harder.
   Avis car rentals, 1960s; slogan devised by
   the Doyle Dane Bernbach agency co-
   founded by Bill **Bernbach**

11 We won't make a drama out of a crisis.
   Commercial Union insurance

12 Where's the beef?
   Wendy's Hamburgers, from January 1984;
   coined by Cliff Freeman; see **Mondale
   226:12**

13 The world's favourite airline.
   British Airways, from 1983

14 You don't have to be Jewish to love
   Levy's.
   Henry S. Levy Bakery of Brooklyn, 1950s;
   slogan devised by the Doyle Dane Bernbach
   agency co-founded by Bill **Bernbach**

15 You're never alone with a Strand.
   Strand cigarettes, 1960; coined by John May;
   the image of loneliness conveyed by the
   advertisement was in fact damaging to the
   product

James Agate 1877–1947
British drama critic and novelist

16 A professional is a man who can do his job
   when he doesn't feel like it. An amateur is
   a man who can't do his job when he does
   feel like it.
   diary, 19 July 1945

17 Shaw's plays are the price we pay for
   Shaw's prefaces.
   diary, 10 March 1933

Spiro T. Agnew 1918–96
American Republican politician, Vice-President
1969–73 (he resigned office after being charged
with tax evasion, and was replaced by Gerald **Ford**)

18 I didn't say I wouldn't go into ghetto areas.
   I've been in many of them and to some
   extent I would have to say this: If you've
   seen one city slum you've seen them all.
   in *Detroit Free Press* 19 October 1968; echoing
   Robert Burton (1577–1640) *The Anatomy of
   Melancholy* (1621–51): 'See one promontory
   (said Socrates of old), one mountain, one sea,
   one river, and see all'

19 In the United States today, we have more
   than our share of the nattering nabobs of
   negativism.
   speech in San Diego, 11 September 1970

Bertie Ahern 1951–
Irish Fianna Fáil statesman, Taoiseach since 1997

20 It is a day we should treasure. Today is
   about the promise of a bright future, a day
   when we hope a line will be drawn under
   the bloody past.
   on the signing of the Good Friday agreement
   in *Guardian* 11 April 1998

Jonathan Aitken 1942–
British Conservative politician

1 If it falls to me to start a fight to cut out the cancer of bent and twisted journalism in our country with the simple sword of truth and the trusty shield of British fair play, so be it.
after press reports that as Minister of State for Defence he had violated the ministerial code of conduct; a libel action started by him collapsed in 1997, and he was later convicted of perjury
statement, London, 10 April 1995

Anna Akhmatova 1889–1966
Russian poet

2 It was a time when only the dead smiled, happy in their peace.
Requiem (1935–40)

3 Stars of death stood over us,
and innocent Russia squirmed
under the bloody boots,
under the wheels of black Marias.
Requiem (1935–40)

Zoë Akins 1886–1958
American poet and dramatist

4 The Greeks had a word for it.
when the play was produced in London in 1933, the Times *reviewer wrote, 'the Greek word was probably an unpleasant one, for the three girls who are the heroines—if the word may be allowed—of this extremely Transatlantic comedy have tendencies which can best be described by the Transatlantic expression "gold-diggers"'*
title of play (1930); later filmed as *The Greeks Had a Word for Them* (1932)

Alain (Émile-Auguste Chartier)
1868–1951
French poet and philosopher

5 *Rien n'est plus dangereux qu'une idée, quand on n'a qu'une idée.*
Nothing is more dangerous than an idea, when you have only one idea.
Propos sur la religion (1938) no. 74

Edward Albee 1928–
American dramatist

6 Who's afraid of Virginia Woolf?
title of play (1962); see **Churchill 66:10**

Richard Aldington 1892–1962
English poet, novelist, and biographer

7 Patriotism is a lively sense of collective responsibility. Nationalism is a silly cock crowing on its own dunghill.
The Colonel's Daughter (1931) pt. 1, ch. 6

Brian Aldiss 1925–
English science fiction writer

8 Keep violence in the mind
Where it belongs.
Barefoot in the Head (1969) 'Charteris'

Buzz Aldrin 1930–
American astronaut; second man on the moon, following Neil **Armstrong**

9 Beautiful! Beautiful! Magnificent desolation.
of the lunar landscape
on the first moon walk, 20 July 1969

Nelson Algren 1909–
American novelist

10 A walk on the wild side.
title of novel (1956)

11 Never play cards with a man called Doc. Never eat at a place called Mom's. Never sleep with a woman whose troubles are worse than your own.
in *Newsweek* 2 July 1956

Muhammad Ali (Cassius Clay) 1942–
American boxer

12 I'm the greatest.
catchphrase used from 1962, in *Louisville Times* 16 November 1962

13 Float like a butterfly, sting like a bee.
summary of his boxing strategy
G. Sullivan *Cassius Clay Story* (1964); probably originated by Drew 'Bundini' Brown

14 I ain't got no quarrel with the Viet Cong.
refusing to be drafted to fight in Vietnam
at a press conference in Miami, Florida, February 1966

Iyad Allawi 1945–
Iraqi statesman, Prime Minister 2004–5

1 If this is not civil war, then God knows what civil war is.
interview on BBC Television *Sunday AM*, 19 March 2006

Fred Allen 1894–1956
American humorist

2 California is a fine place to live—if you happen to be an orange.
in *American Magazine* December 1945

3 Committee—a group of men who individually can do nothing but as a group decide that nothing can be done.
attributed

Lewis Allen (Abel Meeropol) *fl.* 1939
American teacher

4 Southern trees bear strange fruit,
Blood on the leaves and blood at the root,
Black bodies swinging in the Southern breeze,
Strange fruit hanging from the poplar trees.
'Strange Fruit' (1939), adapted and sung by Billie **Holiday**

Woody Allen 1935–
American film director, writer, and actor
on Allen: see **Farrow 109:9**; see also **Film titles 117:13**

5 That [sex] was the most fun I ever had without laughing.
Annie Hall (1977 film, with Marshall Brickman)

6 Don't knock masturbation. It's sex with someone I love.
Annie Hall (1977 film, with Marshall Brickman)

7 Is sex dirty? Only if it's done right.
Everything You Always Wanted to Know about Sex (1972 film)

8 My brain? It's my second favourite organ.
Sleeper (1973 film, with Marshall Brickman)

9 It's not that I'm afraid to die. I just don't want to be there when it happens.
Death (1975)

10 More than any other time in history, mankind faces a crossroads. One path leads to despair and utter hopelessness. The other, to total extinction. Let us pray we have the wisdom to choose correctly.
Side Effects (1980) 'My Speech to the Graduates'

11 A fast word about oral contraception. I asked a girl to go to bed with me and she said 'no'.
at a nightclub in Chicago, March 1964, recorded on *Woody Allen Volume Two*

12 Not only is there no God, but try getting a plumber on weekends.
in *New Yorker* 27 December 1969 'My Philosophy'

13 If only God would give me some clear sign! Like making a large deposit in my name at a Swiss bank.
'Selections from the Allen Notebooks' in *New Yorker* 5 November 1973

14 On bisexuality: It immediately doubles your chances for a date on Saturday night.
in *New York Times* 1 December 1975

15 I don't want to achieve immortality through my work . . . I want to achieve it through not dying.
Eric Lax *Woody Allen and his Comedy* (1975)

16 I recently turned sixty. Practically a third of my life is over.
in *Observer* 10 March 1996

Robert Altman 1922–2006
American film director

17 What's a cult? It just means not enough people to make a minority.
in *Guardian* 11 April 1981

Lord Altrincham
see **John Grigg**

Luis Walter Alvarez 1911–88
American physicist

18 There is no democracy in physics. We can't say that some second-rate guy has as much right to opinion as Fermi.
D. S. Greenberg *The Politics of Pure Science* (1969)

Leo Amery 1873–1955
British Conservative politician

1 Speak for England.
   to Arthur Greenwood in the House of
   Commons, 2 September 1939: see **Boothby
   39:4**

2 I will quote certain other words. I do it with
   great reluctance, because I am speaking of
   those who are old friends and associates of
   mine, but they are words which, I think,
   are applicable to the present situation. This
   is what Cromwell said to the Long
   Parliament when he thought it was no
   longer fit to conduct the affairs of the
   nation: 'You have sat too long here for any
   good you have been doing. Depart, I say,
   and let us have done with you. In the name
   of God, go.'
   speech, House of Commons, 7 May 1940;
   recalling Oliver Cromwell (1599–1658)
   addressing the Rump Parliament, 20 April
   1653 (oral tradition)

Hardy Amies 1909–2003
English couturier, who from the 1950s was royal
dressmaker to the Queen

3 A man should look as if he bought his
   clothes with intelligence, put them on with
   care, then forgot about them.
   in *Mail on Sunday* 27 May 2001

Kingsley Amis 1922–95
English novelist and poet, father of Martin **Amis**. He
achieved popular success with his first novel *Lucky
Jim* (1954), a satiric comedy set in a provincial
university
see also **Cope 77:2**

4 His mouth had been used as a latrine by
   some small creature of the night, and then
   as its mausoleum.
   Jim Dixon wakes with a hangover
   Lucky Jim (1954)

5 Outside every fat man there was an even
   fatter man trying to close in.
   One Fat Englishman (1963); see **Orwell 245:5**

6 Should poets bicycle-pump the human
   heart
   Or squash it flat?
   Man's love is of man's life a thing apart;

Girls aren't like that.
   'A Bookshop Idyll' (1956); referring to Lord
   Byron (1788–1824) *Don Juan* (1819–24):
   'Man's love is of man's life a thing apart, / 'Tis
   woman's whole existence'

7 The delusion that there are thousands of
   young people about who are capable of
   benefiting from university training, but
   have somehow failed to find their way
   there, is . . . a necessary component of the
   expansionist case . . . More will mean
   worse.
   in *Encounter* July 1960

8 If you can't annoy somebody with what
   you write, I think there's little point in
   writing.
   in *Radio Times* 1 May 1971

9 No pleasure is worth giving up for the sake
   of two more years in a geriatric home in
   Weston-super-Mare.
   in *Times* 21 June 1994; attributed

Martin Amis 1949–
English novelist, son of Kingsley **Amis**

10 Weapons are like money; no one knows
   the meaning of *enough*.
   Einstein's Monsters (1987)

Maxwell Anderson 1888–1959
American dramatist

11 But it's a long, long while
   From May to December;
   And the days grow short
   When you reach September.
   'September Song' (1938 song)

Maxwell Anderson 1888–1959
and **Lawrence Stallings** 1894–1968
American dramatists

12 What price glory?
   title of play (1924), a black comedy depicting
   US Marines in the First World War

Pamela Anderson 1967–
Canadian actress

13 When you have nothing to live up to, you
   can't disappoint anybody . . . When you

form a full sentence, you're a genius.
looking on the bright side of being universally considered a 'dumb blonde'
quoted in *Entertainment Briefs* (online edition) 2 October 2005

Robert Anderson 1917–
American dramatist

1 All you're supposed to do is every once in a while give the boys a little tea and sympathy.
Tea and Sympathy (1953), said by Bill

Benny Andersson 1946–
and Björn Ulvaeus 1945–
Swedish musicians and songwriters, members of the group Abba

2 Money, money, money
Must be funny
In the rich man's world.
'Money, Money, Money' (1976 song)

Maya Angelou 1928–
American novelist and poet

3 I know why the caged bird sings.
title of book (1969), the autobiographical account of her experiences as a black child in the American South; see **Dunbar 94:1**

4 Children's talent to endure stems from their ignorance of alternatives.
I Know Why The Caged Bird Sings (1969) ch.17

5 Lift up your eyes
Upon this day breaking for you.
Give birth again
To the dream.

Here, on the pulse of this new day,
You may have the grace to look up and out
And into your sister's eyes,
And into your brother's face,
Your country,
And say simply
Very simply
With hope
Good morning.
'On the Pulse of Morning' (1993); the poem was read at the inauguration of President **Clinton**, January 1993

6 You may shoot me with your words,
You may cut me with your eyes,
You may kill me with your hatefulness,

But still, like air, I'll rise.
'Still I Rise' (1978); see also **Borrowed titles 40:2**

7 The sadness of the women's movement is that they don't allow the necessity of love. See, I don't personally trust any revolution where love is not allowed.
in *California Living* 14 May 1975

8 In all my work what I try to say is that as human beings we are more alike than we are unlike.
interview in *New York Times* 20 January 1993

Paul Anka 1941–
Canadian singer and composer

9 I've lived a life that's full, I've travelled each and ev'ry highway
And more, much more than this. I did it my way.
'My Way' (1969 song); adapted for the singer Frank Sinatra (1915–98), it became his signature tune

Kofi Annan 1938–
Ghanaian diplomat, Secretary General of the United Nations 1997–2006

10 The peace we seek in Iraq, as everywhere, is one that reflects the lessons of our terrible century: that peace is not true or lasting if it is bought at any cost; that only peace with justice can honour the victims of war and violence; and that, without democracy, tolerance and human rights for all, no peace is truly safe.
speech to the Council on Foreign Relations, New York, January 1999

Anne, Princess Royal 1950–
British princess; daughter of **Elizabeth II**

11 I don't work that way . . . The very idea that all children want to be cuddled by a complete stranger, I find completely amazing.
on her work for Save the Children
in *Daily Telegraph* 17 January 1998

Anonymous

see also **Advertising slogans, Newspaper headlines, Official advice, Political sayings and slogans, Sayings and slogans, Taglines for films**

1 An abomination unto the Lord, but a very present help in time of trouble.
definition of a lie
an amalgamation of the *Bible* Proverbs 12.22 and Psalms 46.1, often attributed to Adlai **Stevenson**

2 All human beings are born free and equal in dignity and rights.
Universal Declaration of Human Rights (1948) article 1

3 *Arbeit macht frei.*
Work liberates.
words inscribed on the gates of Dachau concentration camp, 1933, and subsequently on those of Auschwitz

4 The best defence against the atom bomb is not to be there when it goes off.
contributor to *British Army Journal*, in *Observer* 20 February 1949

5 Bigamy is having one husband too many. Monogamy is the same.
Erica Jong *Fear of Flying* (1973) epigraph

6 A bigger bang for a buck.
description of Charles E. **Wilson**'s defence policy, in *Newsweek* 22 March 1954

7 Can't act. Slightly bald. Also dances.
studio official's comment on Fred Astaire
Bob Thomas *Astaire* (1985)

8 A community in which power, wealth and opportunity are in the hands of the many not the few, where the rights we enjoy reflect the duties we owe ... in which the enterprise of the market and the rigour of competition are joined with the forces of partnership and cooperation.
new Clause Four of the Labour Party constitution, passed at a special conference 29 April 1995; see **Anonymous 12:15**

9 Expletive deleted.
*frequent editorial amendment of transcripts of Richard **Nixon** during the Watergate inquiry*
Submission of Recorded Presidential Conversations ... by President Richard M. Nixon 30 April 1974

10 Exterminate ... the treacherous English, walk over General French's contemptible little army.
annexe to British Expeditionary Force Routine Orders, 24 September 1914 (allegedly quoting Kaiser Wilhelm II but probably fabricated by the British)
A. Ponsonby *Falsehood in Wartime* (1928)

11 The first and only thing they have to do is to decide how a resigned commission behaves.
unidentified British official in Brussels of the European Commission
in *Daily Telegraph* 18 March 1999

12 For ours is the harbour, the bridge and the Bradman for ever and ever.
Australian parody of the Lord's Prayer, 1930s, referring to Sydney Harbour, its bridge, and the cricketer Donald **Bradman**

13 [A] frozen flash of history.
*Pulitzer Prize (1945) citation on the photograph by Joe **Rosenthal** of US Marines raising the flag at Iwo Jima*
quoted in *New York Times* 9 May 1945

14 God is not dead but alive and working on a much less ambitious project.
graffito quoted in *Guardian* 26 November 1975; see **Anonymous 11:8**

15 Hark the herald angels sing
Mrs Simpson's pinched our king.
children's rhyme at the time of the Abdication in 1936, quoted in letter from Clement Attlee, 26 December 1938; referring to George Whitefield's version, in *Hymns for Social Worship* (1753), of Charles Wesley's 'Hymn for Christmas' (1739): 'Hark! the herald-angels sing / Glory to the new born king'

16 Here we go, here we go, here we go.
song sung especially by football supporters, 1980s

17 Hey, Jardine, you leave our flies alone.
called by a spectator to the English captain Douglas Jardine as he brushed the flies away, during the 1932–3 MCC tour of Australia, when England's controversial technique of 'bodyline' bowling resulted in injuries to several of the home batsmen
Jack Fingleton *Cricket Crisis: bodyline and other lines* (1946)

1 Hip young gunslinger.
New Musical Express *advertisement for a journalist in 1976, answered by Julie **Burchill**; the phrase was coined by the assistant editor Tony Tyler (1943–2006)*
Julie Burchill *I Knew I Was Right* (1998)

2 The idea that the PM gets integrated advice is nonsense. You could not see a more *unjoined* system. To say they have imported the White House to No. 10—Washington to Downing Street—is absolutely right.
a senior Whitehall figure on the Blair administration, January 2000
Peter Hennessy *The Prime Minister: the Office and its Holders since 1945* (2000)

3 If I should die and leave you here awhile,
Be not like others, sore undone, who keep
Long vigils by the silent dust, and weep.
For my sake—turn again to life and smile,
Nerving thy heart and trembling hand
    to do
Something to comfort other hearts than
    thine.
Complete those dear unfinished tasks of
    mine
And I, perchance, may therein comfort
    you.
*read at the funeral of **Diana**, Princess of Wales; variously attributed (origins discussed in Nigel Rees 'Quote . . . Unquote' Newsletter October 1997)*

4 If you really want to make a million . . . the quickest way is to start your own religion.
previously attributed to L. Ron Hubbard 1911–86 in B. Corydon and L. Ron Hubbard Jr. L. Ron Hubbard (1987), but attribution subsequently rejected by L. Ron Hubbard Jr., who also dissociated himself from this book;
*see also **Orwell 246:10***

5 The iron lady.
*name given to Margaret **Thatcher**, then Leader of the Opposition, by the Soviet defence ministry newspaper* Red Star, *which accused her of trying to revive the cold war*
in *Sunday Times* 25 January 1976

6 It became necessary to destroy the town to save it.
statement issued by US Army, referring to Ben Tre in Vietnam; in New York Times 8 February 1968

7 It is becoming difficult to find anyone in the Commission who has even the slightest

sense of responsibility.
report on the European Commission; in Guardian 17 March 1999

8 Jacques Brel is alive and well and living in Paris.
*title of musical entertainment (1968–72) which triggered numerous imitations; see **Anonymous 10:14***

9 *Jedem das Seine.*
To each his own.
often quoted as 'Everyone gets what he deserves'
*inscription on the gate of Buchenwald concentration camp, c. 1937; see **Bold 38:9***

10 *Je suis Marxiste—tendance Groucho.*
I am a Marxist—of the Groucho tendency.
slogan found at Nanterre in Paris, 1968

11 Kilroy was here.
graffito popularized by American servicemen in the Second World War

12 Liberty is always unfinished business.
title of 36th Annual Report of the American Civil Liberties Union, 1 July 1955–30 June 1956

13 Life is a sexually transmitted disease.
graffito found on the London Underground; D. J. Enright (ed.) Faber Book of Fevers and Frets (1989)

14 Lloyd George knew my father,
My father knew Lloyd George.
sung to the tune of 'Onward, Christian Soldiers'; possibly by Tommy Rhys Roberts (1910–75)

15 Mademoiselle from Armenteers,
Hasn't been kissed for forty years,
Hinky, dinky, parley-voo.
song of the First World War, variously attributed to Edward Rowland and to Harry Carlton

16 The most famous picture nobody's ever seen.
of the photograph (taken by the American photographer Richard Drew) of an unidentified man falling from the World Trade Center, 11 September 2001, which after initial publication has been regarded as too horrific to be shown
*quoted in New York Times 5 October 2003; see also **Drew 93:3***

1 The noise, my dear! And the people!
of the retreat from Dunkirk, May 1940
A. Rhodes *Sword of Bone* (1942)

2 Nostalgia isn't what it used to be.
graffito, taken as title of book by Simone
Signoret, 1978

3 Not so much a programme, more a way of
life!
title of satirical BBC television series, 1964

4 O Death, where is thy sting-a-ling-a-ling,
O grave, thy victory?
The bells of Hell go ting-a-ling-a-ling
For you but not for me.
'For You But Not For Me', song of the First
World War, in S. Louis Guiraud (ed.) *Songs
That Won the War* (1930); with allusion to the
biblical verse 1 Corinthians 15:55, 'O death,
where is thy sting?'

5 The plan is called 'Shock and Awe', and its
goal is 'the psychological destruction of the
enemy's will to fight'.
in *New Yorker* 10 February 2003; see also
Ullman 321:1

6 Prudence is the other woman in Gordon's
life.
of Gordon **Brown**
unidentified aide, quoted in BBC News online
(Budget Briefing), 20 March 1998

7 Psychological flaws.
*on which, according to an unnamed source,
Gordon* **Brown** *needed to 'get a grip'*
in *Observer* 18 January 1998; attributed to
Alastair **Campbell** by Bernard **Ingham** in
minutes of the Parliamentary Select
Committee on Public Administration, 2 June
1998, but denied by Campbell in evidence to
the Committee, 23 June 1998

8 Science finds, industry applies, man
conforms.
subtitle of guidebook to 1933 Chicago World's
Fair

9 She was poor but she was honest
Victim of a rich man's game.
First he loved her, then he left her,
And she lost her maiden name . . .
It's the same the whole world over,
It's the poor wot gets the blame,
It's the rich wot gets the gravy.
Ain't it all a bleedin' shame?
'She was Poor but she was Honest' (sung by
British soldiers in the First World War)

10 Some television programmes are so much
chewing gum for the eyes.
*John Mason Brown quoting a friend of his young
son, interview, 28 July 1955*
J. B. Simpson *Best Quotes* (1957)

11 There shall be a Scottish parliament.
first clause of the Scotland Act, 1998; see
Dewar 89:12

12 [This film] is so cryptic as to be almost
meaningless. If there is a meaning, it is
doubtless objectionable.
banning Jean **Cocteau***'s film* The Seashell and
the Clergyman (*1929*)
The British Board of Film Censors, in
J. C. Robertson *Hidden Cinema* (1989)

13 This is a rotten argument, but it should be
good enough for their lordships on a hot
summer afternoon.
*annotation to a ministerial brief, said to have
been read out inadvertently in the House of
Lords*
Lord Home *The Way the Wind Blows* (1976)

14 Though I yield to no one in my admiration
for Mr Coolidge, I do wish he did not look
as if he had been weaned on a pickle.
anonymous remark, in Alice Roosevelt
Longworth *Crowded Hours* (1933)

15 To secure for the workers by hand or by
brain the full fruits of their industry and
the most equitable distribution thereof that
may be possible upon the basis of the
common ownership of the means of
production, distribution, and exchange.
Clause Four of the Labour Party's Constitution
of 1918 (revised 1929); the commitment to
common ownership of services was largely
removed in 1995; see **Anonymous 10:8**

16 We do not need a loose cannon like her.
*an unidentified junior minister commenting on
the intervention into the campaign against
landmines by* **Diana***, Princess of Wales*
in *Times* 15 January 1997

17 We're here
Because
We're here.
sung to the tune of 'Auld Lang Syne' by British
soldiers in the First World war, in John Brophy
and Eric Partridge *Songs and Slang of the
British Soldier 1914–18* (1930)

18 We trained hard . . . but it seemed that
every time we were beginning to form up

into teams we would be reorganized. I was to learn later in life that we tend to meet any new situation by reorganizing; and a wonderful method it can be for creating the illusion of progress while producing confusion, inefficiency, and demoralization.

   modern saying, frequently (and wrongly) attributed to Petronius Arbiter

1 We value excellence as well as fairness, independence as dearly as mateship.
   draft preamble to the Australian constitution, made public 23 March 1999

2 When cult is added to power
even the chairman makes mistakes.
Xiaoping suffered criticism (in the Cultural Revolution)
and the people raised him up.
Now he represents bureaucracy
and official corruption.
The country does not want him,
the people do not want him.
poem put up in the Forbidden City in 1989, shortly before the tanks moved into Tiananmen Square
   quoted in obituary of **Deng** Xiaoping, in *Guardian* 20 February 1997

3 Winston is back.
Board of Admiralty signal to the Fleet on Winston Churchill's reappointment as First Sea Lord, 3 September 1939
   Martin Gilbert *Winston S. Churchill* (1976)

4 Writing about music is like dancing about architecture.
also found in the form 'Talking about music . . . '
   attributed to Elvis Costello, David Bowie, Frank Zappa, and many others, but of unknown origin

5 You should make a point of trying every experience once, excepting incest and folk-dancing.
   Arnold Bax (1883–1953), quoting 'a sympathetic Scot' in *Farewell My Youth* (1943)

6 You were a premature anti-Fascist.
interviewer for Yale Classics Department in 1946, on hearing that the young Bernard Knox had fought with the International Brigade in the Spanish Civil War
   Bernard Knox 'Premature Anti-Fascist' (Bill Susman Lecture Series, New York, 1998)

Jean Anouilh 1910–87
French dramatist

7 The spring is wound up tight. It will uncoil of itself. That is what is so convenient in tragedy. The least little turn of the wrist will do the job. Anything will set it going.
   Antigone (1944, tr. L. Galantiere, 1957)

8 Tragedy is clean, it is restful, it is flawless.
   Antigone (1944, tr. L. Galantiere, 1957)

9 There will always be a lost dog somewhere that will prevent me from being happy.
   La Sauvage (1938)

Guillaume Apollinaire 1880–1918
French poet

10 *Les souvenirs sont cors de chasse*
   Dont meurt le bruit parmi le vent.

   Memories are hunting horns
   Whose sound dies on the wind.
   'Cors de Chasse' (1912)

11 When man wanted to make a machine that would walk he created the wheel, which does not resemble a leg.
   Les Mamelles de Tirésias (1918)

Yasser Arafat 1929–2004
Palestinian statesman, President from 1996

12 Palestine is the cement that holds the Arab world together, or it is the explosive that blows it apart.
   in *Time* 11 November 1974

Diane Arbus 1923–71
American photographer

13 I really believe there are things which nobody would see unless I photographed them.
   Diane Arbus (1972)

14 Most people go through life dreading they'll have a traumatic experience. Freaks are born with their trauma. They've already passed it. They're aristocrats.
   Diane Arbus (1972)

15 A photograph is a secret about a secret. The more it tells you the less you know.
   Patricia Bosworth *Diane Arbus: a Biography* (1985)

Eddie Arcaro 1916–97
American jockey

1 When a jockey retires, he becomes just
another little man.
attributed; A. J. Maikovich and M. Brown
(eds.) *Sports Quotations* (2000)

Elizabeth Arden *c.*1880–1966
Canadian-born American beautician and
businesswoman
on Arden: see **Rubinstein 277:1, Rubinstein 277:2**

2 Nothing that costs only a dollar is worth
having.
attributed; in *Fortune* October 1973

Robert Ardrey 1908–80
American dramatist and evolutionist, who believed
in the essentially aggressive nature of human
beings

3 Not in innocence, and not in Asia, was
mankind born.
African Genesis (1961)

4 We are born of risen apes, not fallen
angels, and the apes were armed killers
beside.
African Genesis (1961)

Hannah Arendt 1906–75
American political philosopher

5 It was as though in those last minutes he
was summing up the lessons that this long
course in human wickedness had taught
us—the lesson of the fearsome, word-and-
thought-defying *banality of evil*.
of Adolf **Eichmann**
Eichmann in Jerusalem (1963)

6 The most radical revolutionary will
become a conservative on the day after the
revolution.
in *New Yorker* 12 September 1970

7 Under conditions of tyranny it is far easier
to act than to think.
W. H. Auden *A Certain World* (1970)

Lance Armstrong 1971–
American cyclist

8 This is a hard tour and hard work wins it.
Vive Le Tour.
*on winning his seventh consecutive Tour de
France*
in *Independent* 25 July 2005

Louis Armstrong 1901–71
American singer and jazz musician
see also **Misquotations 224:12**

9 All music is folk music, I ain't never heard
no horse sing a song.
in *New York Times* 7 July 1971

Neil Armstrong 1930–
American astronaut; first man on the moon,
followed by Buzz **Aldrin**

10 Houston, Tranquillity Base here. The Eagle
has landed.
*radio message as the lunar module touched
down*
in *Times* 21 July 1969

11 That's one small step for a man, one giant
leap for mankind.
landing on the moon
in *New York Times* 21 July 1969; interference in
transmission obliterated 'a'

Robert Armstrong 1927–
British civil servant; Head of the Civil Service,
1981–7

12 It contains a misleading impression, not a
lie. It was being economical with the truth.
*referring to a letter during the 'Spycatcher' trial,
Supreme Court, New South Wales; the
expression 'over-economical with the truth' had
been applied to Harold* **Wilson** *by the Earl of
Dalkeith in the House of Commons, 4 July 1968*
in *Daily Telegraph* 19 November 1986; earlier,
Edmund Burke (1729–97) wrote in *Two letters
on Proposals for Peace* (1796): 'Falsehood and
delusion are allowed in no case whatsoever:
But, as in the exercise of all the virtues, there
is an economy of truth'; see also **Clark 70:6**

Peter Arno 1904–68
American cartoonist
see also **Cartoons 56:13**

13 It must be done rapidly, with careless care,
so it doesn't look like work.
quoted in *American National Biography*
(online edition) 'Peter Arno'

George Asaf 1880–1951
British songwriter

14 What's the use of worrying?
It never was worth while,

So, pack up your troubles in your old kit-
bag,
And smile, smile, smile.
'Pack up your Troubles' (1915 song)

Isaac Asimov 1920–92
Russian-born biochemist and science fiction writer

1 The three fundamental Rules of Robotics
... One, a robot may not injure a human
being, or, through inaction, allow a
human being to come to harm ... Two ...
a robot must obey the orders given it by
human beings except where such orders
would conflict with the First Law ... three,
a robot must protect its own existence as
long as such protection does not conflict
with the First or Second Laws.
I, Robot (1950) 'Runaround'

2 Science fiction writers foresee the
inevitable, and although problems and
catastrophes may be inevitable, solutions
are not.
'How Easy to See the Future' in *Natural History*
April 1975

3 When, however, the lay public rallies
around an idea that is denounced by
distinguished but elderly scientists and
supports that idea with great fervour and
emotion—the distinguished but elderly
scientists are then, after all, probably right.
*corollary to Arthur C. **Clarke**'s law; see **Clarke**
70:10*
Arthur C. Clarke 'Asimov's Corollary' in
K. Frazier (ed.) *Paranormal Borderlands of
Science* (1981)

4 The first law of dietetics seems to be: if it
tastes good, it's bad for you.
attributed

Elizabeth Asquith (Princess Antoine Bibesco) 1897–1945
British daughter of Herbert Henry **Asquith** and
Margot **Asquith**

5 Kitchener is a great poster.
More Memories (1933); see **Military sayings**
221:11

Herbert Henry Asquith 1852–1928
British Liberal statesman, Prime Minister 1908–16;
husband of Margot **Asquith**

6 We had better wait and see.
*referring, in 1910, to the rumour that the House
of Lords was to be flooded with new Liberal
peers to ensure the passage of the Finance Bill*
Roy Jenkins *Asquith* (1964)

7 Happily there seems to be no reason why
we should be anything more than
spectators.
of the approaching war
letter to Venetia Stanley, 24 July 1914

8 It is fitting that we should have buried the
Unknown Prime Minister [Bonar Law] by
the side of the Unknown Soldier.
R. Blake *The Unknown Prime Minister* (1955)

9 [The War Office kept three sets of figures:]
one to mislead the public, another to
mislead the Cabinet, and the third to
mislead itself.
A. Horne *Price of Glory* (1962)

Margot Asquith 1864–1945
British political hostess; wife of Herbert **Asquith**

10 The *t* is silent, as in *Harlow*.
*to Jean Harlow, who had mispronounced her
name*
T. S. Matthews *Great Tom* (1973)

Nancy Astor 1879–1964
American-born British Conservative politician
on Astor: see **Churchill 69:11**

11 One reason why I don't drink is because I
wish to know when I am having a good
time.
in *Christian Herald* June 1960

12 I married beneath me, all women do.
in *Dictionary of National Biography* (1917–)

Kemal Atatürk 1881–1938
Turkish general and statesman, commander of
Turkish forces at Gallipoli, President of the Turkish
Republic 1923–38

13 There is no difference between the Johnnies
and the Mehmets to us where they lie side
by side in this country of ours. You, the
mothers, who sent their sons from faraway
countries, wipe away your tears. Your sons
are now lying in our bosom and are in

peace. After having lost their lives on this land, they have become our sons as well.

address to a group of visiting Australians at Anzac Cove, Gallipoli, 1934; subsequently inscribed on the memorial there, and on the Atatürk memorials in Canberra and Wellington

Brooks Atkinson 1894–1984
American journalist and critic

1 After each war there is a little less democracy to save.

Once Around the Sun (1951) 7 January

2 In every age 'the good old days' were a myth. No one ever thought they were good at the time. For every age has consisted of crises that seemed intolerable to the people who lived through them.

Once Around the Sun (1951) 8 February; see also **Binchy 34:9**

Jacques Attali 1943–
French economist and writer

3 Machines are the new proletariat. The working class is being given its walking papers.

Millenium: Winners and Losers in the Coming World Order (1991)

Clement Attlee 1883–1967
British Labour statesman, Party Leader 1935–55 and Prime Minister 1945–51. Elected on a landslide in 1945 in the closing months of the Second World War, his term of office saw the creation of the modern welfare state and the nationalization of major industries

on Attlee: see **Churchill 68:14**, **Churchill 69:14**, **de Gaulle 87:7**

4 I must remind the Right Honourable Gentleman that a monologue is not a decision.

*to Winston **Churchill**, who had complained that a matter had been raised several times in Cabinet, c.1945*

Francis Williams *A Prime Minister Remembers* (1961)

5 A period of silence on your part would be welcome.

letter to Harold Laski, 20 August 1945

6 Few thought he was even a starter
There were many who thought themselves
   smarter

But he ended PM
CH and OM
An earl and a knight of the garter.
describing himself
   letter to Tom Attlee, 8 April 1956

7 [Russian Communism is] the illegitimate child of Karl Marx and Catherine the Great.
   speech at Aarhus University, 11 April 1956

8 Democracy means government by discussion, but it is only effective if you can stop people talking.
   speech at Oxford, 14 June 1957

9 Often the 'experts' make the worst possible Ministers in their own fields. In this country we prefer rule by amateurs.
   speech at Oxford, 14 June 1957

Margaret Atwood 1939–
Canadian novelist

10 The threshold of a new house is a lonely place.
   The Handmaid's Tale (1985)

11 To live without mirrors is to live without the self.
   Two-Headed Poems (1978) 'Marrying the Hangman'

W. H. Auden 1907–73
British-born poet and critic, resident in America from 1939

12 Sob, heavy world,
   Sob as you spin
   Mantled in mist, remote from the happy.
   The Age of Anxiety (1947) pt. 4 'The Dirge'

13 Blessed Cecilia, appear in visions
   To all musicians, appear and inspire:
   Translated Daughter, come down and
      startle
   Composing mortals with immortal fire.
   Anthem for St Cecilia's Day (1941) pt. 1; set to music by Benjamin Britten, to whom it was dedicated, as *Hymn to St Cecilia* op. 27 (1942)

14 I'll love you, dear, I'll love you
   Till China and Africa meet
   And the river jumps over the mountain
   And the salmon sing in the street,

   I'll love you till the ocean
   Is folded and hung up to dry
   And the seven stars go squawking
   Like geese about the sky.
   'As I Walked Out One Evening' (1940)

1 The glacier knocks in the cupboard,
   The desert sighs in the bed,
   And the crack in the tea-cup opens
   A lane to the land of the dead.
   'As I Walked Out One Evening' (1940)

2 The desires of the heart are as crooked as
     corkscrews
   Not to be born is the best for man.
   'Death's Echo' (1937); referring to Sophocles
   (c.496–406 BC) *Oedipus Coloneus* (tr.
   R. C. Jebb): 'Not to be born is, past all prizing,
   best'; see **Yeats 345:3**

3 Happy the hare at morning, for she cannot
     read
   The Hunter's waking thoughts.
   Dog beneath the Skin (with Christopher
   Isherwood, 1935)

4 To save your world you asked this man to
     die:
   Would this man, could he see you now, ask
     why?
   'Epitaph for the Unknown Soldier' (1955)

5 When he laughed, respectable senators
     burst with laughter,
   And when he cried the little children died
     in the streets.
   'Epitaph on a Tyrant' (1940); compare John
   Lothrop Motley (1814–77) on William of
   Orange in *The Rise of the Dutch Republic*
   (1856): 'As long as he lived, he was the
   guiding-star of a whole brave nation, and
   when he died the little children cried in the
   streets'

6 Stop all the clocks, cut off the telephone,
   Prevent the dog from barking with a juicy
     bone,
   Silence the pianos and with muffled drum
   Bring out the coffin, let the mourners
     come.
   'Funeral Blues' (1936)

7 He was my North, my South, my East and
     West,
   My working week and my Sunday rest,
   My noon, my midnight, my talk, my song;
   I thought that love would last for ever: I
     was wrong.
   'Funeral Blues' (1936)

8 To us he is no more a person
   now but a whole climate of opinion.
   'In Memory of Sigmund Freud' (1940)

9 You were silly like us; your gift survived it
     all:
   The parish of rich women, physical decay,
   Yourself. Mad Ireland hurt you into poetry.
   'In Memory of W. B. Yeats' (1940)

10 For poetry makes nothing happen: it
     survives
   In the valley of its saying where executives
   Would never want to tamper.
   'In Memory of W. B. Yeats' (1940)

11 Earth, receive an honoured guest:
   William Yeats is laid to rest.
   Let the Irish vessel lie
   Emptied of its poetry.
   'In Memory of W. B. Yeats' (1940)

12 In the nightmare of the dark
   All the dogs of Europe bark,
   And the living nations wait,
   Each sequestered in its hate;

   Intellectual disgrace
   Stares from every human face,
   And the seas of pity lie
   Locked and frozen in each eye.
   'In Memory of W. B. Yeats' (1940)

13 Time that with this strange excuse
   Pardoned Kipling and his views,
   And will pardon Paul Claudel,
   Pardons him for writing well.
   'In Memory of W. B. Yeats' (1940)

14 Look, stranger, at this island now.
   title of poem (1936)

15 Lay your sleeping head, my love,
   Human on my faithless arm.
   'Lullaby' (1940)

16 About suffering they were never wrong,
   The Old Masters: how well they
     understood
   Its human position; how it takes place
   While someone else is eating or opening a
     window or just walking dully along.
   'Musée des Beaux Arts' (1940)

17 Even the dreadful martyrdom must run its
     course
   Anyhow in a corner, some untidy spot
   Where the dogs go on with their doggy life
     and the torturer's horse
   Scratches its innocent behind on a tree.
   'Musée des Beaux Arts' (1940)

18 To the man-in-the-street, who, I'm sorry to
     say,

Is a keen observer of life,
The word 'Intellectual' suggests straight
   away
A man who's untrue to his wife.
   New Year Letter (1941)

1 This is the Night Mail crossing the Border,
Bringing the cheque and the postal order,
Letters for the rich, letters for the poor,
The shop at the corner, the girl next door.
   'Night Mail' (1936)

2 Private faces in public places
Are wiser and nicer
Than public faces in private places.
   Orators (1932) dedication

3 Out on the lawn I lie in bed,
Vega conspicuous overhead.
   'Out on the lawn I lie in bed' (1936)

4 Some thirty inches from my nose
The frontier of my Person goes,
And all the untilled air between
Is private *pagus* or demesne.
Stranger, unless with bedroom eyes
I beckon you to fraternize,
Beware of rudely crossing it:
I have no gun, but I can spit.
   'Prologue: the Birth of Architecture' (1966)

5 Once we had a country and we thought it
   fair,
Look in the atlas and you'll find it there:
We cannot go there now, my dear, we
   cannot go there now.
   'Refugee Blues' (1940)

6 I and the public know
What all schoolchildren learn,
Those to whom evil is done
Do evil in return.
   'September 1, 1939' (1940)

7 But who can live for long
In an euphoric dream;
Out of the mirror they stare,
Imperialism's face
And the international wrong.
   'September 1, 1939' (1940)

8 All I have is a voice
To undo the folded lie,
The romantic lie in the brain
Of the sensual man-in-the-street
And the lie of Authority
Whose buildings grope the sky:
There is no such thing as the State
And no one exists alone;

Hunger allows no choice
To the citizen or the police;
We must love one another or die.
   'September 1, 1939' (1940)

9 A shilling life will give you all the facts.
   title of poem (1936)

10 Each year brings new problems of Form
   and Content,
new foes to tug with: at Twenty I tried to
vex my elders, past Sixty it's the young
   whom
I hope to bother.
   'Shorts I' (1969)

11 A poet's hope: to be,
like some valley cheese,
local, but prized elsewhere.
   'Shorts II' (1976)

12 Sir, no man's enemy.
   title of poem (1930)

13 Harrow the house of the dead; look
   shining at
New styles of architecture, a change of
   heart.
   'Sir, No Man's Enemy' (1930)

14 To-morrow for the young the poets
   exploding like bombs,
The walks by the lake, the weeks of perfect
   communion;
To-morrow the bicycle races
Through the suburbs on summer
   evenings: but to-day the struggle.
   'Spain 1937' (1937)

15 History to the defeated
May say Alas but cannot help or pardon.
   'Spain 1937' (1937)

16 To ask the hard question is simple.
   title of poem (1933)

17 Was he free? Was he happy? The question
   is absurd:
Had anything been wrong, we should
   certainly have heard.
   'The Unknown Citizen' (1940)

18 Of course, Behaviourism 'works'. So does
torture. Give me a no-nonsense, down-
to-earth behaviourist, a few drugs, and
simple electrical appliances, and in six
months I will have him reciting the
Athanasian Creed in public.
   A Certain World (1970) 'Behaviourism'

1 It is a sad fact about our culture that a poet can earn much more money writing or talking about his art than he can by practising it.
   The Dyer's Hand (1963) foreword

2 Man is a history-making creature who can neither repeat his past nor leave it behind.
   The Dyer's Hand (1963) 'D. H. Lawrence'

3 When I find myself in the company of scientists, I feel like a shabby curate who has strayed by mistake into a drawing room full of dukes.
   The Dyer's Hand (1963) 'The Poet and the City'

4 Some books are undeservedly forgotten; none are undeservedly remembered.
   The Dyer's Hand (1963) 'Reading'

5 Art is born of humiliation.
   Stephen Spender *World Within World* (1951)

6 LSD? Nothing much happened, but I did get the distinct impression that some birds were trying to communicate with me.
   George Plimpton (ed.) *The Writer's Chapbook* (1989)

7 My face looks like a wedding-cake left out in the rain.
   Humphrey Carpenter *W. H. Auden* (1981)

8 Nothing I wrote in the thirties saved one Jew from Auschwitz.
   attributed

Stan Augarten *fl.* 1983
American writer on the history of computing

9 Computers are composed of nothing more than logic gates stretched out to the horizon in a vast numerical irrigation system.
   State of the Art: A Photographic History of the Integrated Circuit (1983)

Aung San Suu Kyi 1945–
Burmese political leader

10 In societies where men are truly confident of their own worth, women are not merely tolerated but valued.
   videotape speech at NGO Forum on Women, China, early September 1995

Revd W. Awdry 1911–97
English writer of children's books, creator of 'Thomas the Tank Engine'
see also **Epitaphs 107:10**

11 You've a lot to learn about trucks, little Thomas. They are silly things and must be kept in their place. After pushing them about here for a few weeks you'll know almost as much about them as Edward. Then you'll be a Really Useful Engine.
   the Fat Controller's advice
   Thomas the Tank Engine (1946)

12 Railways and the Church have their critics, but both are the best ways of getting a man to his ultimate destination.
   in *Daily Telegraph* 22 March 1997; obituary

Alan Ayckbourn 1939–
English dramatist

13 This place, you tell them you're interested in the arts, you get messages of sympathy.
   Chorus of Disapproval (1986)

A. J. Ayer 1910–89
English philosopher

14 No moral system can rest solely on authority.
   Humanist Outlook (1968) introduction

15 It seems that I have spent my entire time trying to make life more rational and that it was all wasted effort.
   in *Observer* 17 August 1986

16 Even logical positivists are capable of love.
   Kenneth Tynan *Profiles* (1989)

17 If I had been someone not very clever, I would have done an easier job like publishing. That's the easiest job I can think of.
   attributed

18 Why should you mind being wrong if someone can show you that you are?
   attributed

Pam Ayres 1947–
English writer of humorous verse

19 Medicinal discovery,
   It moves in mighty leaps,
   It leapt straight past the common cold
   And gave it us for keeps.
   'Oh no, I got a cold' (1976)

b

Isaac Babel 1894–1940
Russian short-story writer. He died in a
concentration camp in Siberia as a result of one of
Stalin's purges

1 No iron can stab the heart with such force
as a full stop put just at the right place.
Guy de Maupassant (1932)

2 The bee of sorrow had stung his heart.
Red Cavalry (1926) 'Pan Apolek' (translated by
Walter Morison)

3 They didn't let me finish.
to his wife, on the day of his arrest by the
NKVD, 16 May 1939

Lauren Bacall 1924–
American actress, wife of Humphrey Bogart
see also **Film lines 115:11**

4 I think your whole life shows in your face
and you should be proud of that.
in *Daily Telegraph* 2 March 1988

Francis Bacon 1909–92
Irish painter

5 What I see is a marvellous painting. But
how are you going to make it? And, of
course, as I don't know how to make it, I
rely then on chance and accident making it
for me.
David Sylvester (ed.) *Interviews with Francis
Bacon* (ed. 3, 1987)

Lord Baden-Powell 1857–1941
English soldier; founder of the Boy Scouts, 1908

6 The scouts' motto is founded on my
initials, it is: BE PREPARED.
Scouting for Boys (1908)

Joan Baez 1941–
American singer and songwriter

7 His songs were brilliant; people have never
been able to copy them. He always had a
rainbow pen.
*on Bob **Dylan***
in *Independent* 19 January 2004

David Bailey 1938–
English photographer, a prominent figure of 1960s
pop culture
see also **Sayings and slogans 286:20**

8 It takes a lot of imagination to be a good
photographer. You need less imagination
to be a painter, because you can invent
things. But in photography everything is so
ordinary; it takes a lot of looking before
you learn to see the ordinary.
interview in *The Face* December 1984

9 I never cared for fashion much. Amusing
little seams and witty little pleats. It was
the girls I liked.
in *Independent* 5 November 1990

10 Fashion often starts off beautiful and
becomes ugly, whereas art starts off ugly
sometimes and becomes beautiful.
in *Observer* 20 November 2005

Fran Bailey 1946–
Australian Liberal politician

11 This is a great Australian adjective. It's
plain speaking and friendly. It is our
vernacular.
*as Minister for Tourism, defending the use of
'bloody' in Tourism Australia's 2006 travel
slogan (see **Advertising slogans 5:1**)*
in *Sydney Morning Herald* 24 February 2006

Ewen Bain
see **Cartoons 56:9**

Beryl Bainbridge 1933–
English novelist

1 Some people like being burdened. It gives
them an interest.
An Awfully Big Adventure (1989)

Bruce Bairnsfather
see **Cartoons 57:2**

James Baldwin 1924–87
American novelist and essayist

2 Children have never been very good at
listening to their elders, but they have
never failed to imitate them. They must,
they have no other models.
Nobody Knows My Name (1961) 'Fifth Avenue,
Uptown: a letter from Harlem'

3 Anyone who has ever struggled with
poverty knows how extremely expensive it
is to be poor.
Nobody Knows My Name (1961) 'Fifth Avenue,
Uptown: a letter from Harlem'

4 At the root of the American Negro problem
is the necessity of the American white man
to find a way of living with the Negro in
order to be able to live with himself.
in *Harper's Magazine* October 1953 'Stranger
in a Village'

5 Money, it turned out, was exactly like sex,
you thought of nothing else if you didn't
have it and thought of other things if you
did.
in *Esquire* May 1961 'Black Boy looks at the
White Boy'

6 It comes as a great shock around the age of
5, 6 or 7 to discover that the flag to which
you have pledged allegiance, along with
everybody else, has not pledged allegiance
to you. It comes as a great shock to see
Gary Cooper killing off the Indians and,
although you are rooting for Gary Cooper,
that the Indians are you.
*speaking for the proposition that 'The American
Dream is at the expense of the American Negro'*
speech at the Cambridge Union, England, 17
February 1965

7 If they take you in the morning, they will
be coming for us that night.
in *New York Review of Books* 7 January 1971
'Open Letter to my Sister, Angela Davis'

Stanley Baldwin 1867–1947
British Conservative statesman, Prime Minister
1923–4, 1924–9, 1935–7
on Baldwin: see **Churchill 68:11, Curzon 82:2**; see
also **Kipling 183:10, Mary 216:8, Misquotations
224:14**

8 They [parliament] are a lot of hard-faced
men who look as if they had done very well
out of the war.
J. M. Keynes *Economic Consequences of the
Peace* (1919)

9 A platitude is simply a truth repeated until
people get tired of hearing it.
speech, House of Commons, 29 May 1924

10 The bomber will always get through. The
only defence is in offence, which means
that you have to kill more women and
children more quickly than the enemy if
you want to save yourselves.
speech, House of Commons, 10 November
1932

11 Since the day of the air, the old frontiers
are gone. When you think of the defence of
England you no longer think of the chalk
cliffs of Dover; you think of the Rhine. That
is where our frontier lies.
speech, House of Commons, 30 July 1934

*of the advice he had given to **Edward VIII** on the
possibility of marriage with Mrs Simpson:*
12 I pointed out to him that the position of the
King's wife was different from the position
of any other citizen in the country; it was
part of the price which the King has to
pay. His wife becomes Queen; the Queen
becomes Queen of the country; and,
therefore, in the choice of a Queen, the
voice of the people must be heard.
speech, House of Commons, 10 December
1936

13 This House today is a theatre which is
being watched by the whole world. Let us
conduct ourselves with that dignity which
His Majesty is showing in this hour of his
trial.
speech, House of Commons, 10 December
1936

1 Do not run up your nose dead against the Pope or the NUM!

> Lord Butler *The Art of Memory* (1982); see **Macmillan 209:8**

Arthur James Balfour 1848–1930
British Conservative statesman, Prime Minister 1902–5

2 His Majesty's Government view with favour the establishment in Palestine of a national home for the Jewish people, and will use their best endeavours to facilitate the achievement of this object, it being clearly understood that nothing shall be done which may prejudice the civil and religious rights of existing non-Jewish communities in Palestine, or the rights and political status enjoyed by Jews in any other country.

> *known as the 'Balfour Declaration'; see* **Weizmann 330:9**
> letter to Lord Rothschild 2 November 1917

3 I make it a rule never to stare at people when they are in obvious distress.

> *on being asked what he thought of the behaviour of the German delegation at the signing of the Treaty of Versailles*
> Max Egremont *Balfour* (1980)

Alan Ball 1945–
English footballer, member of the winning World Cup team in 1966

4 I tell you what made us what we were. We had this wonderful feeling that we were still part of the people.

> Simon Hattenstone *The Best of Times: What became of the heroes of '66?* (2006)

J. G. Ballard 1930–
British writer

5 A car crash harnesses elements of eroticism, aggression, desire, speed, drama, kinaesthetic factors, the stylizing of motion, consumer goods, status—all these in one event. I myself see the car crash as a tremendous sexual event really: a liberation of human and machine libido (if there is such a thing).

> interview in *Penthouse* September 1970; the theme of his novel *Crash* (1973)

6 Some refer to it as a cultural Chernobyl. I think of it as a cultural Stalingrad.

> *of Euro Disney*
> in *Daily Telegraph* 2 July 1994; see **Mnouchkine 226:10**

Whitney Balliett 1926–
American jazz critic and writer

7 A critic is a bundle of biases held loosely together by a sense of taste.

> *Dinosaurs in the Morning* (1962) introductory note

8 The sound of surprise.

> title of book on jazz (1959)

Pierre Balmain 1914–82
French couturier

9 The trick of wearing mink is to look as though you were wearing a cloth coat. The trick of wearing a cloth coat is to look as though you are wearing mink.

> in *Observer* 25 December 1955

E. Digby Baltzell 1915–96
American educationist and sociologist

10 There is a crisis in American leadership in the middle of the twentieth century that is partly due, I think, to the declining authority of an establishment which is now based on an increasingly castelike White-Anglo Saxon-Protestant (WASP) upper class.

> *The Protestant Establishment* (1964)

Tallulah Bankhead 1903–68
American actress

11 Cocaine habit-forming? Of course not. I ought to know. I've been using it for years.

> *Tallulah* (1952)

12 There is less in this than meets the eye.

> *describing a revival of Maeterlinck's play* Aglavaine and Selysette
> Alexander Woollcott *Shouts and Murmurs* (1922)

13 I'm as pure as the driven slush.

> in *Saturday Evening Post* 12 April 1947

14 I read Shakespeare and the Bible and I can shoot dice. That's what I call a liberal education.

> attributed

1 They used to shoot her through gauze. You should shoot me through linoleum.
on Shirley Temple
attributed

Imamu Amiri Baraka (Everett LeRoi Jones) 1934–
American poet and dramatist

2 God has been replaced, as he has all over the West, with respectability and air conditioning.
Midstream (1963)

3 A man is either free or he is not. There cannot be any apprenticeship for freedom.
in *Kulchur* Spring 1962 'Tokenism'

Joel Arthur Barker
American futurist

4 Vision without action is merely a dream. Action without vision just passes the time. Vision with action can change the world.
The Power of Vision (1991 video)

Pat Barker 1943–
English novelist

5 Another person's life, observed from outside, always has a shape and definition that one's own life lacks.
The Ghost Road (1995)

6 The Somme is like the Holocaust. It revealed things about mankind that we cannot come to terms with and cannot forget. It can never become the past.
on winning the 1995 Booker Prize for her First Word War novel The Ghost Road
in *Athens News* 9 November 1995

Ronnie Barker 1929–2005
English comedian
see also **Catchphrases 60:7**

7 The marvellous thing about a joke with a double meaning is that it can only mean one thing.
Sauce (1977)

Frederick R. Barnard *fl.* 1920s
American advertising agency executive

8 One picture is worth ten thousand words.
in *Printers' Ink* 10 March 1927

Clive Barnes 1927–
British journalist and critic

9 This is the kind of show to give pornography a dirty name.
of the theatrical revue Oh, Calcutta!, *devised and produced by Kenneth* **Tynan**
in *New York Times* 18 June 1969

Julian Barnes 1946–
English novelist

10 The land of embarrassment and breakfast.
of Britain
Flaubert's Parrot (1984)

11 Do not imagine that Art is something which is designed to give gentle uplift and self-confidence. Art is not a *brassière*. At least, not in the English sense. But do not forget that *brassière* is the French for life-jacket.
Flaubert's Parrot (1984)

12 Books say: she did this because. Life says: she did this. Books are where things are explained to you; life is where things aren't.
Flaubert's Parrot (1984)

13 Does history repeat itself, the first time as tragedy, the second time as farce? No, that's too grand, too considered a process. History just burps, and we taste again that raw-onion sandwich it swallowed centuries ago.
A History of the World in 10½ Chapters (1989); referring to Karl Marx (1818–83) *The Eighteenth Brumaire of Louis Bonaparte* (1852): 'Hegel says somewhere that all great events and personalities in world history reappear in one fashion or another. He forgot to add: the first time as tragedy, the second as farce'

14 If you want to get to know someone better, you shouldn't take them out for a candlelit dinner, you should watch them at work. When they're full of concentration, only not concentrating on you.
Love, Etc. (2000)

15 Love is just a system for getting someone to call you darling after sex.
Talking It Over (1991)

J. M. Barrie 1860–1937

Scottish writer and dramatist, creator of 'Peter Pan'
on Barrie: see **Hope 157:8**

1 His lordship may compel us to be equal
upstairs, but there will never be equality in
the servants' hall.
The Admirable Crichton (performed 1902)

2 To die will be an awfully big adventure.
Peter Pan (1928); see **Last words 191:10**

3 Do you believe in fairies? Say quick that
you believe! If you believe, clap your
hands!
Peter Pan (1928)

4 There are few more impressive sights in the
world than a Scotsman on the make.
What Every Woman Knows (performed 1908)

5 Someone said that God gave us memory so
that we might have roses in December.
Rectorial Address at St Andrews, 3 May 1922

6 Courage is the thing. All goes if courage
goes!
Rectorial Address at St Andrews, 3 May 1922;
see **Lewis 199:8**

John Barrymore 1882–1942

American actor

7 My only regret in the theatre is that I could
never sit out front and watch me.
Eddie Cantor *The Way I See It* (1959)

Karl Barth 1886–1968

Swiss Protestant theologian

8 Men have never been good, they are not
good and they never will be good.
Christian Community (1948)

Roland Barthes 1915–80

French writer and critic, a leading exponent of
structuralism and semiology in literary criticism

9 The birth of the reader must be at the cost
of the death of the Author.
The Death of the Author (1968)

10 All domination begins by prohibiting
language.
S/Z (1974) tr. Richard Miller

Vernon Bartlett 1894–1983

British journalist and writer

11 I believe the British would have acted in
much the same way as Germany has acted
if they had been in the same position.
*when Germany left the League of Nations in
1933*
in a BBC radio broadcast (which caused a
storm of protest); quoted in *Oxford Dictionary
of National Biography* (online edition) 'Vernon
Bartlett'

12 I, and many others who had interviews
with him, were at first impressed by his
sincerity, and later realized that he was
sincere only in his belief that he was
destined to rule the world.
of Adolf **Hitler**
I Know What I Liked (1974)

Bernard Baruch 1870–1965

American financier and presidential adviser,
especially to Franklin **Roosevelt** in the Second World
War

13 We are today in the midst of a cold war.
'cold war' was suggested to him by H. B. **Swope,**
former editor of the New York World
speech to South Carolina Legislature 16 April
1947

14 To me old age is always fifteen years older
than I am.
in *Newsweek* 29 August 1955

15 Vote for the man who promises least; he'll
be the least disappointing.
M. Berger *New York* (1960)

16 A political leader must keep looking over
his shoulder all the time to see if the boys
are still there. If they aren't still there, he's
no longer a political leader.
in *New York Times* 21 June 1965

Jacques Barzun 1907–

American historian and educationist

17 If it were possible to talk to the unborn, one
could never explain to them how it feels to
be alive, for life is washed in the speechless
real.
The House of Intellect (1959)

H. M. Bateman
see **Cartoons 56:8**

Jean Baudrillard 1929–
French sociologist and cultural critic

1 The microwave, the waste disposal, the orgasmic elasticity of the carpets, this soft resort-style civilization irresistibly evokes the end of the world.
America (1986)

Yehuda Bauer 1926–
Czech-born Israeli historian

2 I come from a people who gave the ten commandments to the world. Time has come to strengthen them by three additional ones, which we ought to adopt and commit ourselves to: thou shalt not be a perpetrator; thou shalt not be a victim; and thou shalt never, but never, be a bystander.
speech to the German Bundestag, 1998, quoted in his own speech to the Stockholm International Forum on the Holocaust, 26 July 2000

L. Frank Baum
American writer
see **Film lines 116:6, Harburg 144:9**

Buzzie Bavasi 1914–
American baseball manager

3 We live by the Golden Rule. Those who have the gold make the rules.
attributed; A. J. Maikovich and M. D. Brown (eds.) *Sports Quotations* (2000)

Todd Beamer
see **Last words 190:6**

Lord Beatty 1871–1936
British sailor and Admiral of the Fleet, 1916–19

4 There's something wrong with our bloody ships today.
at the Battle of Jutland, 1916
Winston Churchill *The World Crisis 1916–1918* (1927)

Lord Beaverbrook 1879–1964
Canadian-born British newspaper proprietor and Conservative politician
on Beaverbrook: see **Kipling 183:10**

5 Our cock won't fight.
of Edward VIII, during the abdication crisis of 1936, to Winston Churchill, another supporter, after the King had told his Prime Minister, Stanley Baldwin, that he was prepared to abdicate
F. Donaldson *Edward VIII* (1974)

6 Now who is responsible for this work of development on which so much depends? To whom must the praise be given? To the boys in the back rooms. They do not sit in the limelight. But they are the men who do the work.
in *Listener* 27 March 1941

7 I ran the paper [*Daily Express*] purely for propaganda, and with no other purpose.
evidence to Royal Commission on the Press, 18 March 1948, in A. J. P. Taylor *Beaverbrook* (1972)

8 Who's in charge of the clattering train?
habitual question about an organization
A. Chisholm and M. Davie *Beaverbrook* (1992); a modification of '*Who* is in charge of the clattering train?', the first line of 'Death and his Brother Sleep', an anonymous poem about a railway crash at Eastleigh in June 1890, which appeared in *Punch* 4 October 1890

Samuel Beckett 1906–89
Irish dramatist, novelist, and poet

9 We could have saved sixpence. We have saved fivepence. (*Pause*) But at what cost?
All That Fall (1957)

10 CLOV: Do you believe in the life to come?
HAMM: Mine was always that.
Endgame (1958)

11 Where I am, I don't know, I'll never know, in the silence you don't know, you must go on, I can't go on, I'll go on.
The Unnamable (1959)

12 Nothing to be done.
Waiting for Godot (1955)

13 There's a man all over for you, blaming on his boots the faults of his feet.
Waiting for Godot (1955)

1 One of the thieves was saved. (*Pause*) It's a reasonable percentage.
Waiting for Godot (1955)

2 ESTRAGON: Charming spot. Inspiring prospects. Let's go.
VLADIMIR: We can't.
ESTRAGON: Why not?
VLADIMIR: We're waiting for Godot.
Waiting for Godot (1955)

3 Nothing happens, nobody comes, nobody goes, it's awful!
Waiting for Godot (1955)

4 He can't think without his hat.
Waiting for Godot (1955)

5 VLADIMIR: That passed the time.
ESTRAGON: It would have passed in any case.
VLADIMIR: Yes, but not so rapidly.
Waiting for Godot (1955)

6 Habit is a great deadener.
Waiting for Godot (1955)

7 Ever tried. Ever failed. No matter. Try again. Fail again. Fail better.
Worstward Ho (1983)

8 I couldn't have done it otherwise, gone on I mean. I could not have gone on through the awful wretched mess of life without having left a stain upon the silence.
Deirdre Bair *Samuel Beckett* (1978)

9 Even death is unreliable: instead of zero it may be some ghastly hallucination, such as the square root of minus one.
attributed

10 INTERVIEWER: You are English, Mr Beckett?
BECKETT: *Au contraire.*
attributed

Harry Bedford and Terry Sullivan
British songwriters

11 I'm a bit of a ruin that Cromwell knocked about a bit.
'It's a Bit of a Ruin that Cromwell Knocked about a Bit' (1920 song, written for Marie Lloyd)

Thomas Beecham 1879–1961
English conductor

12 Good music is that which penetrates the ear with facility and quits the memory with difficulty.
speech, *c.*1950, in *New York Times* 9 March 1961

13 The English may not like music, but they absolutely love the noise it makes.
in *New York Herald Tribune* 9 March 1961

14 Too much counterpoint; what is worse, Protestant counterpoint.
of J. S. Bach
in *Guardian* 8 March 1971

15 Two skeletons copulating on a corrugated tin roof.
describing the harpsichord
H. Atkins and A. Newman *Beecham Stories* (1978)

Max Beerbohm 1872–1956
English critic, essayist, and caricaturist

16 She was one of the people who say 'I don't know anything about music really, but I know what I like.'
Zuleika Dobson (1911)

Brendan Behan 1923–64
Irish dramatist

17 PAT: He was an Anglo-Irishman.
MEG: In the blessed name of God what's that?
PAT: A Protestant with a horse.
The Hostage (1958)

18 When I came back to Dublin, I was courtmartialled in my absence and sentenced to death in my absence, so I said they could shoot me in my absence.
The Hostage (1958)

on being asked 'What was the message of your play' after a performance of The Hostage:
19 Message? Message? What the hell do you think I am, a bloody postman?
Dominic Behan *My Brother Brendan* (1965); see **Goldwyn 135:9**

20 There's no such thing as bad publicity except your own obituary.
Dominic Behan *My Brother Brendan* (1965)

Clive Bell 1881–1964
English art critic

1 I will try to account for the degree of my
aesthetic emotion. That, I conceive, is the
function of the critic.
Art (1914)

2 Only reason can convince us of those three
fundamental truths without a recognition
of which there can be no effective liberty:
that what we believe is not necessarily
true; that what we like is not necessarily
good; and that all questions are open.
Civilization (1928)

George Bell 1883–1958
English clergyman, Bishop of Chichester

3 The policy is obliteration, openly
acknowledged. This is not a justifiable act
of war.
*of the saturation bombing of Berlin; the
bombing of Dresden took place in the following
year*
speech, House of Lords, 9 February 1944

Gertrude Bell 1868–1926
English traveller, archaeologist, and government
servant

4 I feel at times like the Creator about the
middle of the week. He must have
wondered what it was going to be like, as I
do.
*creating Iraq, at the Cairo Conference 1921;
attributed*

Hilaire Belloc 1870–1953
British poet, essayist, historian, novelist, and
Liberal politician

5 Believing Truth is staring at the sun.
title of poem (1938); see also **Borrowed titles
41:5**

6 And always keep a-hold of Nurse
For fear of finding something worse.
Cautionary Tales (1907) 'Jim'

7 Sir! you have disappointed us!
We had intended you to be
The next Prime Minister but three:
The stocks were sold; the Press was
squared;
The Middle Class was quite prepared.
But as it is! . . . My language fails!

Go out and govern New South Wales!
Cautionary Tales (1907) 'Lord Lundy'

8 Matilda told such Dreadful Lies,
It made one Gasp and Stretch one's Eyes.
Cautionary Tales (1907) 'Matilda'

9 For every time She shouted 'Fire!'
They only answered 'Little Liar!'
Cautionary Tales (1907) 'Matilda'

10 I said to Heart, 'How goes it ?' Heart
replied:
'Right as a Ribstone Pippin!' But it lied.
'The False Heart' (1910)

11 I'm tired of Love: I'm still more tired of
Rhyme.
But Money gives me pleasure all the time.
'Fatigued' (1923)

12 Remote and ineffectual Don
That dared attack my Chesterton.
'Lines to a Don' (1910)

13 Lord Finchley tried to mend the Electric
Light
Himself. It struck him dead: And serve him
right!
It is the business of the wealthy man
To give employment to the artisan.
More Peers (1911) 'Lord Finchley'

14 Like many of the Upper Class
He liked the Sound of Broken Glass.
New Cautionary Tales (1930) 'About John'; see
Waugh 329:1

15 The accursed power which stands on
Privilege
(And goes with Women, and Champagne,
and Bridge)
Broke—and Democracy resumed her
reign:
(Which goes with Bridge, and Women and
Champagne).
'On a Great Election' (1923)

16 I am a sundial, and I make a botch
Of what is done far better by a watch.
'On a Sundial' (1938)

17 When I am dead, I hope it may be said:
'His sins were scarlet, but his books were
read.'
'On His Books' (1923)

18 Pale Ebenezer thought it wrong to fight,

But Roaring Bill (who killed him) thought
    it right.
  'The Pacifist' (1938)

1 Do you remember an Inn,
    Miranda?
    Do you remember an Inn? . . .
    And the fleas that tease in the High
        Pyrenees
    And the wine that tasted of the tar?
    'Tarantella' (1923)

2 Be content to remember that those who
    can make omelettes properly can do
    nothing else.
    A Conversation with a Cat (1931)

Saul Bellow 1915–2005
Canadian-born American novelist

3 Sitting tight is power.
    The Adventures of Augie March (1953)

4 If I am out of my mind, it's all right with
    me, thought Moses Herzog.
    Herzog (1961), opening line

5 New York makes one think of the collapse
    of civilization, about Sodom and
    Gomorrah, the end of the world. The end
    wouldn't come as a surprise here. Many
    people already bank on it.
    Mr Sammler's Planet (1970)

Robert Benchley 1889–1945
American humorist
see also **Film lines 115:3, Telegrams 311:8**

6 The surest way to make a monkey of a man
    is to quote him.
    My Ten Years in a Quandary (1936)

7 In America there are two classes of
    travel—first class, and with children.
    Pluck and Luck (1925)

8 It took me fifteen years to discover that I
    had no talent for writing, but I couldn't
    give it up because by that time I was too
    famous.
    Nathaniel Benchley *Robert Benchley* (1955)

9 One square foot less and it would be
    adulterous.
    of the cramped office he shared with Dorothy
    Parker
    in *New Yorker* 5 January 1946

Julien Benda 1867–1956
French philosopher and novelist

10 *La trahison des clercs.*
    The treachery of the intellectuals.
    title of book (1927)

Pope Benedict XVI (Joseph Ratzinger)
1927–
German cleric, Pope from 2005

11 Love is free; it is not practised as a way of
    achieving other ends.
    Deus Caritas Est (God is Love, 2005)

Stephen Vincent Benét 1898–1943
American poet and novelist

12 I have fallen in love with American names,
    The sharp, gaunt names that never get fat,
    The snakeskin-titles of mining-claims,
    The plumed war-bonnet of Medicine Hat,
    Tucson and Deadwood and Lost Mule Flat.
    'American Names' (1927)

13 Bury my heart at Wounded Knee.
    the village of Wounded Knee in South Dakota
    was the site (in 1890) of the last major
    confrontation between the US Army and
    American Indians
    'American Names' (1927)

Tony Benn 1925–
British Labour politician
see also **Epitaphs 107:8**

14 Not a reluctant peer but a persistent
    commoner.
    a few days after the death of his father, Viscount
    Stansgate; his protest at automatically
    succeeding to the title resulted in the 1963
    Peerage Act, which made possible the
    renunciation of a hereditary peerage
    at a Press Conference, 23 November 1960

15 A faith is something you die for; a doctrine
    is something you kill for: there is all the
    difference in the world.
    in *Observer* 16 April 1989

    questions habitually asked by Tony Benn on
    meeting somebody in power:
16 What power have you got? Where did you
    get it from? In whose interests do you

exercise it? To whom are you accountable? How do we get rid of you?
'The Independent Mind', lecture at Nottingham, 18 June 1993

1 If you file your waste-paper basket for 50 years, you have a public library.
in *Daily Telegraph* 5 March 1994

2 She taught us how to live and she taught us how to die—and you can't ask more than that.
oration at memorial service for his wife Caroline, 6 March 2001
in *Daily Telegraph* 7 March 2001

Alan Bennett 1934–
English dramatist and actor

3 I go to the theatre to be entertained, I want to be taken out of myself, I don't want to see lust and rape and incest and sodomy and so on, I can get all that at home.
Beyond the Fringe (1963) 'Man of Principles'

4 Outside Shakespeare the word treason to me means nothing. Only, you pissed in our soup and we drank it.
Coral Browne to Guy Burgess
  An Englishman Abroad (1989)

5 I have never understood this liking for war. It panders to instincts already catered for within the scope of any respectable domestic establishment.
Forty Years On (1969)

6 Sapper, Buchan, Dornford Yates, practitioners in that school of Snobbery with Violence that runs like a thread of good-class tweed through twentieth-century literature.
Forty Years On (1969)

7 To be Prince of Wales is not a position. It is a predicament.
The Madness of King George (1995 film); in the 1992 play *The Madness of George III* the line was 'To be heir to the throne . . .'

8 Brought up in the provinces in the forties and fifties one learned early the valuable lesson that life is generally something that happens elsewhere.
introduction to *Talking Heads* (1988)

Arnold Bennett 1867–1931
English novelist

9 'What great cause is he identified with?' 'He's identified . . . with the great cause of cheering us all up.'
The Card (1911) ch. 12

10 A cause may be inconvenient, but it's magnificent. It's like champagne or high heels, and one must be prepared to suffer for it.
The Title (1918)

A. C. Benson 1862–1925
English writer

11 Land of Hope and Glory, Mother of the Free,
How shall we extol thee who are born of thee?
Wider still and wider shall thy bounds be set;
God who made thee mighty, make thee mightier yet.
'Land of Hope and Glory' written to be sung as the Finale to Elgar's *Coronation Ode* (1902)

Stella Benson 1892–1933
English novelist

12 Call no man foe, but never love a stranger.
This is the End (1917)

Edmund Clerihew Bentley 1875–1956
English writer, inventor of the comic verse form the clerihew

13 The Art of Biography
Is different from Geography.
Geography is about Maps,
But Biography is about Chaps.
Biography for Beginners (1905) introduction

14 George the Third
Ought never to have occurred.
One can only wonder
At so grotesque a blunder.
'George the Third' (1929)

15 Sir Christopher Wren
Said, 'I am going to dine with some men.
If anybody calls
Say I am designing St Paul's.'
'Sir Christopher Wren' (1905)

Eric Bentley 1916–
American dramatist and writer

1 Ours is the age of substitutes: instead of language, we have jargon; instead of principles, slogans; and, instead of genuine ideas, Bright Ideas.
  in *New Republic* 29 December 1952

Lloyd Bentsen 1921–2006
American Democratic politician, vice-presidential nominee in the 1988 campaign

*responding to Dan **Quayle**'s claim to have 'as much experience in the Congress as Jack **Kennedy** had when he sought the presidency':*
2 Senator, I served with Jack Kennedy. I knew Jack Kennedy. Jack Kennedy was a friend of mine. Senator, you're no Jack Kennedy.
  in the vice-presidential debate, 5 October 1988

Irving Berlin 1888–1989
American songwriter

3 Anything you can do, I can do better, I can do anything better than you.
  'Anything You Can Do' (1946 song)

4 Heaven—I'm in Heaven—And my heart beats so that I can hardly speak; And I seem to find the happiness I seek When we're out together dancing cheek-to-cheek.
  'Cheek-to-Cheek' (1935 song)

5 God bless America, Land that I love, Stand beside her and guide her Thru the night with a light from above. From the mountains to the prairies, To the oceans white with foam, God bless America, My home sweet home.
  'God Bless America' (1939 song)

6 There may be trouble ahead, But while there's moonlight and music and love and romance, Let's face the music and dance.
  'Let's Face the Music and Dance' (1936 song)

7 A pretty girl is like a melody That haunts you night and day.
  'A Pretty Girl is like a Melody' (1919 song)

8 The song is ended (but the melody lingers on).
  title of song (1927)

9 There's no business like show business.
  title of song (1946)

10 I'm puttin' on my top hat, Tyin' up my white tie, Brushin' off my tails.
  'Top Hat, White Tie and Tails' (1935 song)

11 I'm dreaming of a white Christmas, Just like the ones I used to know.
  'White Christmas' (1942 song)

12 Listen, kid, take my advice, never hate a song that has sold half a million copies.
  *to Cole **Porter**, of the song 'Rosalie'*
  Philip Furia *Poets of Tin Pan Alley* (1990)

Isaiah Berlin 1909–97
British philosopher

13 There exists a great chasm between those, on one side, who relate everything to a single central vision . . . and, on the other side, those who pursue many ends, often unrelated and even contradictory . . . The first kind of intellectual and artistic personality belongs to the hedgehogs, the second to the foxes.
  The Hedgehog and the Fox (1953); referring to a fragment by Archilochus (7th century BC): 'The fox knows many things—the hedgehog one *big* one'

14 Liberty is liberty, not equality or fairness or justice or human happiness or a quiet conscience.
  Two Concepts of Liberty (1958)

15 Few new truths have ever won their way against the resistance of established ideas save by being overstated.
  Vico and Herder (1976)

16 Rousseau was the first militant lowbrow.
  in *Observer* 9 November 1952

J. D. Bernal 1901–71
Irish-born physicist

17 Men will not be content to manufacture life: they will want to improve on it.
  The World, the Flesh and the Devil (1929)

Cassie Bernall
see **Last words 191:12**

Georges Bernanos 1888–1948
French novelist and essayist

1 The wish for prayer is a prayer in itself.
   Journal d'un curé de campagne (1936)

Bill Bernbach 1911–82
American advertising executive

2 A great ad campaign will make a bad
   product fail faster. It will get more people to
   know it's bad.
   Bill Bernbach said (1989)

3 Word of mouth is the best medium of all.
   Bill Bernbach said (1989)

4 In this very real world, good doesn't drive
   out evil. Evil doesn't drive out good. But
   the energetic displaces the passive.
   Bill Bernbach said (1989)

5 Don't be slick. Tell the truth.
   habitual advice on advertising
      quoted in *American National Biography*
      (online edition) 'William Bernbach'

Eric Berne 1910–70
American psychiatrist

6 Games people play: the psychology of
   human relationships.
   title of book (1964)

Lord Berners 1883–1950
English composer, artist, and writer

7 He's always backing into the limelight.
   of T. E. **Lawrence**
      oral tradition; see also **Shaw 293:13**

Tim Berners-Lee 1955–
English computer scientist

8 The Web is a tremendous grassroots
   revolution. All these people coming from
   very different directions achieved a
   change. There's a tremendous message of
   hope for humanity in that.
   in *Independent* 17 May 1999

Carl Bernstein 1944–
and Bob Woodward 1943–
American journalists, whose investigations on
behalf of their paper, the *Washington Post*, brought
the Watergate affair to public notice

9 All the President's men.
   title of book (1974) on the Watergate scandal;
   see also **Film lines 113:10**

Yogi Berra 1925–
American baseball player

10 It ain't over till it's over.
   comment on National League pennant race,
   1973, quoted in many versions

11 The future ain't what it used to be.
   attributed

12 If people don't want to come out to the ball
   park, nobody's going to stop 'em.
   of baseball games
   attributed

13 It was déjà vu all over again.
   attributed

Chuck Berry 1931–
American rock and roll singer

14 Roll over, Beethoven, and tell Tchaikovsky
   the news.
   'Roll Over, Beethoven' (1956 song)

John Berryman 1914–72
American poet

15   People will take balls,
   Balls will be lost always, little boy,
   And no one buys a ball back.
   'The Ball Poem' (1948)

16 We must travel in the direction of our fear.
   'A Point of Age' (1942)

17 Life, friends, is boring. We must not say so
         . . .
   And moreover my mother told me as a boy
   (repeatingly) 'Ever to confess you're bored
   means you have no
   Inner Resources.'
   77 Dream Songs (1964) no. 14

18 I seldom go to films. They are too exciting,
   said the Honourable Possum.
   77 Dream Songs (1964) no. 53

Pierre Berton 1920–2004
Canadian writer

1 Somebody who knows how to make love in a canoe.
definition of a Canadian
   in *Toronto Star, Canadian Magazine*
   22 December 1973

Theobald von Bethmann Hollweg
1856–1921
German statesman, Chancellor 1909–17

2 Just for a word 'neutrality'—a word which in wartime has so often been disregarded—just for a scrap of paper, Great Britain is going to make war on a kindred nation who desires nothing better than to be friends with her.
   summary of a report by Sir Edward Goschen to Sir Edward Grey in *British Documents on Origins of the War 1898–1914* (1926)

John Betjeman 1906–84
English poet, Poet Laureate from 1972
on Betjeman: see **Newspaper headlines 237:4**

3 He sipped at a weak hock and seltzer
   As he gazed at the London skies
   Through the Nottingham lace of the curtains
   Or was it his bees-winged eyes?
   'The Arrest of Oscar Wilde at the Cadogan Hotel' (1937)

4 And girls in slacks remember Dad,
   And oafish louts remember Mum,
   And sleepless children's hearts are glad,
   And Christmas-morning bells say 'Come!'
   'Christmas' (1954)

5 And is it true? And is it true,
   This most tremendous tale of all,
   Seen in a stained-glass window's hue,
   A Baby in an ox's stall?
   'Christmas' (1954)

6 Oh! Chintzy, Chintzy cheeriness,
   Half dead and half alive!
   'Death in Leamington' (1931)

7 Spirits of well-shot woodcock, partridge, snipe
   Flutter and bear him up the Norfolk sky.
   'Death of King George V' (1937)

8 Old men who never cheated, never doubted,
   Communicated monthly, sit and stare
   At the new suburb stretched beyond the run-way
   Where a young man lands hatless from the air.
   'Death of King George V' (1937)

9 Phone for the fish-knives, Norman
   As Cook is a little unnerved;
   You kiddies have crumpled the serviettes
   And I must have things daintily served.
   'How to get on in Society' (1954)

10 It's awf'lly bad luck on Diana,
   Her ponies have swallowed their bits;
   She fished down their throats with a spanner
   And frightened them all into fits.
   'Hunter Trials' (1954)

11 The Church's Restoration
   In eighteen-eighty-three
   Has left for contemplation
   Not what there used to be.
   'Hymn' (1931)

12 Think of what our Nation stands for,
   Books from Boots' and country lanes,
   Free speech, free passes, class distinction,
   Democracy and proper drains.
   'In Westminster Abbey' (1940)

13 Gaily into Ruislip Gardens
   Runs the red electric train,
   With a thousand Ta's and Pardon's
   Daintily alights Elaine;
   Hurries down the concrete station
   With a frown of concentration,
   Out into the outskirt's edges
   Where a few surviving hedges
   Keep alive our lost Elysium—rural Middlesex again.
   'Middlesex' (1954)

14 Come, friendly bombs, and fall on Slough!
   It isn't fit for humans now,
   There isn't grass to graze a cow.
   Swarm over, Death!
   'Slough' (1937)

15 Miss J. Hunter Dunn, Miss J. Hunter Dunn,
   Furnish'd and burnish'd by Aldershot sun.
   'A Subaltern's Love-Song' (1945)

1 Love-thirty, love-forty, oh! weakness of
   joy,
  The speed of a swallow, the grace of a boy,
  With carefullest carelessness, gaily you
   won,
  I am weak from your loveliness, Joan
   Hunter Dunn.
    'A Subaltern's Love-Song' (1945)

2 Ghastly good taste, or a depressing story of
  the rise and fall of English architecture.
    title of book (1933)

Aneurin Bevan 1897–1960

British Labour politician, who as Minister of Health
in the post-war Labour government was responsible
for the introduction of the National Health Service
on Bevan: see **Bevin 34:3, Churchill 68:7**

3 This island is made mainly of coal and
  surrounded by fish. Only an organizing
  genius could produce a shortage of coal
  and fish at the same time.
    speech at Blackpool, 24 May 1945

4 No amount of cajolery, and no attempts at
  ethical or social seduction, can eradicate
  from my heart a deep burning hatred for
  the Tory Party . . . So far as I am concerned
  they are lower than vermin.
    speech at Manchester, 4 July 1948

5 He is still fighting Blenheim all over again.
  His only answer to a difficult situation is
  send a gun-boat.
  *of Winston **Churchill***
    speech at Labour Party Conference, 2 October
    1951

6 We know what happens to people who
  stay in the middle of the road. They get run
  down.
    in *Observer* 6 December 1953

7 Damn it all, you can't have the crown of
  thorns *and* the thirty pieces of silver.
  on his position in the Labour Party, c.1956; his
  role as a left-wing critic from within the party
  had frequently brought him into collision with
  the official leadership
    Michael Foot *Aneurin Bevan* vol. 2 (1973)

8 I am not going to spend any time
  whatsoever in attacking the Foreign
  Secretary . . . If we complain about the
  tune, there is no reason to attack the

monkey when the organ grinder is present.
on the Suez crisis, referring to Selwyn Lloyd
(1904–78), then Foreign Secretary, and the Prime
*Minister, Anthony **Eden***
    speech, House of Commons, 16 May 1957

9 If you carry this resolution you will send
  Britain's Foreign Secretary naked into the
  conference chamber.
  on a motion proposing unilateral nuclear
  disarmament by the UK
    speech at Labour Party Conference, 3 October
    1957

10 I know that the right kind of leader for the
   Labour Party is a desiccated calculating
   machine who must not in any way permit
   himself to be swayed by indignation. If he
   sees suffering, privation or injustice he
   must not allow it to move him, for that
   would be evidence of the lack of proper
   education or of absence of self-control. He
   must speak in calm and objective accents
   and talk about a dying child in the same
   way as he would about the pieces inside an
   internal combustion engine.
   *generally taken as referring to Hugh **Gaitskell**,*
   although Bevan specifically denied it
    Michael Foot *Aneurin Bevan* vol. 2 (1973)

11 This so-called affluent society is an ugly
   society still. It is a vulgar society. It is a
   meretricious society. It is a society in which
   priorities have gone all wrong.
    speech in Blackpool, 29 November 1959; see
    Galbraith 128:6

12 I read the newspapers avidly. It is my one
   form of continuous fiction.
    in *Times* 29 March 1960

13 I stuffed their mouths with gold.
   on his handling of the consultants during the
   establishment of the National Health Service
    B. Abel-Smith *The Hospitals 1800–1948* (1964)

William Henry Beveridge 1879–1963

British economist

14 Ignorance is an evil weed, which dictators
   may cultivate among their dupes, but
   which no democracy can afford among its
   citizens.
    Full Employment in a Free Society (1944)

15 Want is one only of five giants on the road
   of reconstruction . . . the others are

Disease, Ignorance, Squalor and Idleness.
Social Insurance and Allied Services (1942)

Ernest Bevin 1881–1951

British Labour politician and trade unionist, Minister of Labour during the Second World War, and Foreign Secretary from 1945 in **Attlee**'s government
on Bevin: see **Foot 119:7**

1 My [foreign] policy is to be able to take a ticket at Victoria Station and go anywhere I damn well please.
in *Spectator* 20 April 1951

2 If you open that Pandora's Box, you never know what Trojan 'orses will jump out.
on the Council of Europe
Roderick Barclay *Ernest Bevin and the Foreign Office* (1975)

*on the observation that Aneurin **Bevan** was sometimes his own worst enemy:*
3 Not while I'm alive 'e ain't!
*also attributed to Bevin of Herbert **Morrison***
Roderick Barclay *Ernest Bevin and Foreign Office* (1975)

Benazir Bhutto 1953–

Pakistani stateswoman; Prime Minister 1988–90 and 1993–96

4 Every dictator uses religion as a prop to keep himself in power.
interview on *60 Minutes*, CBS-TV, 8 August 1986

Francis Biddle 1886–1968

American lawyer and judge, Attorney-General 1941–7, senior American judge at the Nuremberg Trials

5 The Constitution has never greatly bothered any wartime President.
In Brief Authority (1962)

Steve Biko 1946–77

South African anti-apartheid campaigner

6 The liberal must understand that the days of the Noble Savage are gone; that the blacks do not need a go-between in this struggle for their own emancipation. No true liberal should feel any resentment at the growth of black consciousness. Rather, all true liberals should realize that the place for their fight for justice is within their white society. The liberals must realize that

they themselves are oppressed if they are true liberals and therefore they must fight for their own freedom and not that of the nebulous 'they' with whom they can hardly claim identification. The liberal must apply himself with absolute dedication to the idea of educating his white brothers.
'Black Souls in White Skins?' (written 1970), in *Steve Biko—I Write What I Like* (1978)

7 The most potent weapon in the hands of the oppressor is the mind of the oppressed.
statement as witness, 3 May 1976

Maeve Binchy 1940–

Irish novelist

8 People don't come in my size until they're old . . . I used to think people were born with big bones and large frames, but apparently these grow when you're about sixty-eight.
Circle of Friends (1990)

9 It's not perfect, but to me on balance Right Now is a lot better than the Good Old Days.
in *Irish Times* 15 November 1997; see also **Atkinson 16:2**

Laurence Binyon 1869–1943

English poet

10 They shall grow not old, as we that are left grow old.
Age shall not weary them, nor the years condemn.
At the going down of the sun and in the morning
We will remember them.
regularly recited as part of the ritual for Remembrance Day parades; see **Epitaphs 108:10**
'For the Fallen' (1914)

Nigel Birch 1906–81

British Conservative politician
on Birch: see **Macmillan 209:4**

11 My God! They've shot our fox!
on hearing of the resignation of Hugh Dalton (1887–1962), Labour Chancellor of the Exchequer, after the leak of Budget secrets
comment, 13 November 1947

John Bird 1936–
English actor and satirist

1 That was the week that was.
title of satirical BBC television series, 1962–3

Elizabeth Bishop 1911–79
American poet

2 The state with the prettiest name,
the state that floats in brackish water,
held together by mangrove roots.
'Florida' (1946)

3 Topography displays no favourites;
    North's as near as West.
More delicate than the historians' are the
    map-makers' colours.
'The Map' (1946)

4 If she speaks of a chair you can practically
sit on it.
of Marianne **Moore**
notebook, *c.*1934/5; D. Kalstone *Becoming a
Poet* (1989)

5 I am sorry for people who can't write
letters. But I suspect also that you and I . . .
love to write them because it's kind of like
working without really doing it.
letter to Kit and Ilse Barker, 5 September 1953

Björk 1965–
Icelandic pop star

6 Icelandic peoples were the ones who
memorized sagas . . . We were the first
rappers of Europe.
attributed, January 1996

Conrad Black 1944–
Canadian-born British businessman and newspaper
proprietor

7 We can't spend ourselves rich; we can't
drink ourselves sober; and we will pay an
unbearable price if we don't remember that
the power to tax is the power to destroy.
in *Report on Business Magazine* January 1987

8 Since when was greed a criminal offence?
in January 2003; in *Guardian* 18 December
2004

James Black 1924–
British analytical pharmacologist; winner of the
Nobel prize for medicine

9 In the culture I grew up in you did your
work and you did not put your arm around
it to stop other people from looking—you
took the earliest possible opportunity to
make knowledge available.
on modern scientific research
in *Daily Telegraph* 11 December 1995

Otis Blackwell 1931–
and **Jack Hammer**
American songwriter

10 Goodness gracious great balls of fire.
'Great Balls of Fire' (1957 song)

Cherie Blair
see **Misquotations 225:6**

Tony Blair 1953–
British Labour statesman, Prime Minister since 1997
on Blair: see **Cameron 51:8**; see also **Bush 49:9**

11 Labour is the party of law and order in
Britain today. Tough on crime and tough
on the causes of crime.
as Shadow Home Secretary
speech at the Labour Party Conference, 30
September 1993

12 Those who seriously believe we cannot
improve on words written for the world of
1918 when we are now in 1995 are not
learning from our history but living it.
on the proposed revision of Clause IV
in *Independent* 11 January 1995; see
Anonymous 10:8, Anonymous 12:15

13 Ask me my three main priorities for
Government, and I tell you: education,
education and education.
speech at the Labour Party Conference,
1 October 1996

14 We are not the masters. The people are the
masters. We are the servants of the people
. . . What the electorate gives, the
electorate can take away.
*addressing Labour MPs on the first day of the
new Parliament, 7 May 1997*
in *Guardian* 8 May 1997; see **Misquotations
225:5**

15 She was the People's Princess, and that is
how she will stay . . . in our hearts and in

our memories forever.
*on hearing of the death of **Diana**, Princess of Wales*
     in *Times* 1 September 1997

1 I am a pretty straight sort of guy.
     interviewed on the government's exemption of Formula One racing from the tobacco advertising ban
          interviewed on *On the Record* (BBC TV), 17 November 1997

2 We need two or three eye-catching initiatives . . . I should be personally associated with as much of this as possible.
     leaked memorandum, 29 April 2000; in *Times* 18 July 2000

3 This is not a battle betweeen the United States and terrorism, but between the free and democratic world and terrorism. We therefore here in Britain stand shoulder to shoulder with our American friends in this hour of tragedy and we, like them, will not rest until this evil is driven from our world.
     in Downing Street, London, 11 September 2001

4 The state of Africa is a scar on the conscience of the world.
     speech to Labour Party Conference, 2 October 2001

5 I can only go one way. I've not got a reverse gear.
     speech, Labour Party Conference, Bournemouth, 30 September 2003; see also **Kinnock 181:11**

6 However much the right hon. gentleman may dance around the ring beforehand, at some point, he will come within the reach of a big clunking fist.
     to David **Cameron**, the House of Commons, 15 November 2006

Eubie Blake 1883–1983
American ragtime pianist

     at the age of ninety-seven, Blake was asked at what age the sex drive goes:
7 You'll have to ask somebody older than me.
     attributed

8 If I'd known I was gonna live this long, I'd have taken better care of myself.
     on reaching the age of 100
          in *Observer* 13 February 1983

Lesley Blanch 1907–
British writer

9 She was an Amazon. Her whole life was spent riding at breakneck speed towards the wilder shores of love.
     of the adventuress Jane Digby El Mezrab (1807–81)
          The Wilder Shores of Love (1954)

Danny Blanchflower 1926–93
British footballer and journalist

10 The great fallacy is that the game is first and last about winning. It is nothing of the kind. The game is about glory, it is about doing things in style and with a flourish, about going out and beating the lot, not waiting for them to die of boredom.
     attributed, 1972

Fanny Blankers-Koen 1918–2004
Dutch athlete who won four gold medals at the London Olympics in 1948

11 When I competed, no one ever thought it would be possible to make money from doing something you enjoyed so much.
     quoted in *Independent* 27 January 2004 (obituary)

Hans Blix 1928–
Swedish diplomat, head of the United Nations Monitoring, Verification and Inspection Commission 2000–3

12 In the Middle Ages people were convinced there were witches. They looked for them and they certainly found them.
     on British and American claims that Iraq had weapons of mass destruction
          interviewed on BBC Radio Four, Today programme, in *BBC News* (online edition) 18 September 2003

13 Advertisers will advertise a refrigerator in terms they do not quite believe in but you expect governments to be more serious and have more credibility.
     interviewed on *Today* (BBC Radio 4); in *BBC News* (online edition) 18 September 2003

Karen Blixen
see **Isak Dinesen**

Judy Blume 1938–
American writer

1 Are you there God? It's me, Margaret.
I just told my mother I want a bra.
Please help me grow God. You know
where.
I want to be like everyone else.
Are You There God? It's Me, Margaret (1970)

Edmund Blunden 1896–1974
English poet

2 I am for the woods against the world,
But are the woods for me?
'The Kiss' (1931)

3 I have been young, and now am not too
old;
And I have seen the righteous forsaken,
His health, his honour and his quality
taken.
This is not what we were formerly told.
'Report on Experience' (1929); an echo of
Psalm 37 in the *Book of Common Prayer*: 'I
have been young, and now am old, and yet
saw I never the righteous forsaken'

David Blunkett 1947–
British Labour politician, Minister for Education,
1997–2001, Home Secretary 2001–5

4 Let me say this very slowly indeed. Watch
my lips: no selection by examination or
interview under a Labour government.
in *Daily Telegraph* (electronic edition) 5
October 1995

5 I was parodying George Bush . . . Watch
my lips was a joke. If I were doing it again I
would say 'no more selection'.
in *Sunday Telegraph* 12 March 2000; see **Bush
48:16**

6 I don't use or recognize the term 'bog
standard' but what I do recognize is the
critical importance of honesty about what
some children, in some schools, have had
to put up with over the years.
at Labour spring conference, 17 February
2001; see **Campbell 51:11**

Alfred Blunt 1879–1957
English Protestant cleric, Bishop of Bradford

7 The benefit of the King's Coronation
depends, under God, upon two elements:
First, on the faith, prayer, and self-
dedication of the King himself, and on that
it would be improper for me to say
anything except to commend him, and ask
you to commend him, to God's grace,
which he will so abundantly need . . . if he
is to do his duty faithfully. We hope that he
is aware of his need. Some of us wish that
he gave more positive signs of his
awareness.
referring to **Edward VIII**'s *relationship with Mrs
Simpson, which until then had not been publicly
mentioned; see also* **Anonymous 10:15**
speech to Bradford Diocesan Conference, 1
December 1936

Robert Bly 1926–
American poet

8 Every modern male has, lying at the
bottom of his psyche, a large, primitive
being covered with hair down to his feet.
Making contact with this Wild Man is the
step the Eighties male or the Nineties male
has yet to take.
Iron John (1990)

Ronald Blythe 1922–
English writer

9 With full-span lives having become the
norm, people may need to learn how to be
aged as they once had to learn how to be
adult.
The View in Winter (1979)

David Boaz 1953–
American lawyer

10 Alcohol didn't cause the high crime rates
of the '20s and '30s, Prohibition did. Drugs
don't cause today's alarming crime rates,
but drug prohibition does.
*quoted by Judge James C. Paine, addressing the
Federal Bar Association in Miami, 1991*
'The Legalization of Drugs' 27 April 1988

Ivan F. Boesky 1937–
American businessman; in 1986 he was charged
with insider trading and subsequently convicted

1 Greed is all right . . . Greed is healthy. You
   can be greedy and still feel good about
   yourself.
   > commencement address, Berkeley, California,
   > 18 May 1986; see **Film lines 113:13**

Louise Bogan 1897–1970
American poet

2 Women have no wilderness in them,
   They are provident instead,
   Content in the tight hot cell of their hearts
   To eat dusty bread.
   > 'Women' (1923)

Dirk Bogarde 1921–99
British actor and writer

3 I realised I was looking at Dante's Inferno.
   of Belsen during the liberation
   > in *Daily Telegraph* 10 May 1999; obituary

4 You haven't cracked me yet!
   to the interviewer Russell Harty
   > in *Daily Telegraph* 10 May 1999; obituary

Humphrey Bogart
see **Film lines 113:14, Film lines 114:3, Film lines 115:16**

John B. Bogart 1848–1921
American journalist

5 When a dog bites a man, that is not news,
   because it happens so often. But if a man
   bites a dog, that is news.
   > F. M. O'Brien *Story of the* [New York] *Sun*
   > (1918); often attributed to the American
   > newspaper editor Charles A. Dana
   > (1819–1897)

Niels Bohr 1885–1962
Danish physicist

6 Of course not, but I am told it works even if
   you don't believe in it.
   when asked whether he really believed a
   horseshoe hanging over his door would bring
   him luck, c.1930
   > A. Pais *Inward Bound* (1986)

7 Anybody who is not shocked by this
   subject has failed to understand it.
   of quantum mechanics
   > attributed; *Nature* 23 August 1990

Eavan Boland 1944–
Irish poet

8 I think of what great art removes:
   Hazard and death, the future and the past.
   > 'From the painting *Back from Market* by
   > Chardin' (1967)

Alan Bold 1943–
Scottish poet

9 This happened near the core
   Of a world's culture. This
   Occurred among higher things.
   This was a philosophical conclusion.
   Everybody gets what he deserves.

   The bare drab rubble of the place.
   The dull damp stone. The rain.
   The emptiness. The human lack.
   > 'June 1967 at Buchenwald' (1969); see
   > **Anonymous 11:9**

10 Our job is to try
   To change things.
   After Hiroshima
   You ask a poet to sing.
   > 'Recitative' (1965)

Robert Bolt 1924–95
English dramatist
see also **Borrowed titles 40:17**

11 Morality's *not* practical. Morality's a
   gesture. A complicated gesture learned
   from books.
   > *A Man for All Seasons* (1960)

12 It profits a man nothing to give his soul for
   the whole world . . . But for Wales—!
   > *A Man for All Seasons* (1960); referring to the
   > *Bible* St Mark: 'For what shall it profit a man, if
   > he shall gain the whole world, and lose his
   > own soul?'

Erma Bombeck 1927–96
American humorist

13 If a man watches three games of football in
   a row, he should be declared legally dead.
   > attributed; A. J. Maikovich and M. Brown
   > (eds.) *Sports Quotations* (2000)

1 I do not participate in any sport with ambulances at the bottom of the hill.
attributed; A. J. Maikovich and M. Brown (eds.) *Sports Quotations* (2000)

Violet Bonham Carter
see **Telegrams 311:4**

Dietrich Bonhoeffer 1906–45
German Lutheran theologian and martyr, executed by the Nazis

2 It is the nature, and the advantage, of strong people that they can bring out the crucial questions and form a clear opinion about them. The weak always have to decide between alternatives that are not their own.
Widerstand und Ergebung (1951)

Christopher Booker 1937–
and **Richard North** 1946–
British writers

3 Castle of lies: why Britain must get out of Europe.
title of book (1996)

Connie Booth
see **John Cleese and Connie Booth**

Robert Boothby 1900–86
British Conservative politician

4 *You* speak for Britain!
*to Arthur Greenwood, acting Leader of the Labour Party, after Neville **Chamberlain** had failed to announce an ultimatum to Germany; perhaps taking up an appeal already voiced by Leo **Amery***
Harold Nicolson diary, 2 September 1939; see **Amery 8:1**

Betty Boothroyd 1929–
British Labour politician; Speaker of the House of Commons, 1992–2000

5 The level of cynicism about Parliament and the accompanying alienation of many of the young from the democratic process is troubling. Let's make a start by remembering that the function of Parliament is to hold the executive to account.
in her valedictory statement as Speaker in the House of Commons, 26 July 2000

6 Time's up!
concluding her valedictory statement in the House of Commons, 26 July 2000

James H. Boren 1925–
American bureaucrat

7 Guidelines for bureaucrats: (1) When in charge, ponder. (2) When in trouble, delegate. (3) When in doubt, mumble.
in *New York Times* 8 November 1970

Jorge Luis Borges 1899–1986
Argentinian writer

8 I come from a vertiginous country where the lottery forms a principal part of reality.
Fictions (1956) 'The Babylon Lottery'

9 The original is unfaithful to the translation.
of Samuel Henley's translation of Vathek, *the oriental romance (1786, originally written in French) by the writer and collecter William Beckford (1759–1844)*
Sobre el 'Vathek' de William Beckford; in *Obras Completas* (1974)

10 The Falklands thing was a fight between two bald men over a comb.
application of a proverbial phrase in *Time* 14 February 1983

Borrowed titles
see box overleaf

Horatio Bottomley 1860–1933
British newspaper proprietor and financier

11 What poor education I have received has been gained in the University of Life.
speech at the Oxford Union, 2 December 1920

reply to a prison visitor who asked if he were sewing:
12 No, reaping.
S. T. Felstead *Horatio Bottomley* (1936)

Pierre Bourdieu 1930–2002
French sociologist

13 Artists and writers, and more generally intellectuals, are a dominated fraction of the dominant class.
In Other Words: essays towards a reflexive sociology (1990) 'The Intellectual Field: A World Apart'

Borrowed titles

1 Across the river and into the trees.
   novel (1950) by Ernest **Hemingway**, from the
   last words of Thomas Jonathan 'Stonewall'
   Jackson (1824–63): 'Let us cross over the
   river and rest under the shade of the trees'

2 And still I rise.
   autobiography (2006) of Doreen Wallace
   (1952–), mother of the black teenager
   Stephen Lawrence murdered in 1993, from a
   poem by Maya Angelou (see **Angelou 9:6**)

3 Anyone here been raped and speaks
   English?
   shouted by a British TV reporter in a crowd of
   Belgian civilians waiting to be airlifted out of
   the Belgian Congo, c.1960
   book (1981) by Edward Behr on being a
   foreign correspondent

4 Appointment in Samarra.
   novel (1934) by John **O'Hara**, from the play
   Sheppey by W. Somerset Maugham (see
   Maugham 217:4)

5 Brave new world.
   novel (1932) by Aldous **Huxley**, from William
   Shakespeare (1564–1616) *The Tempest*
   (1611): 'How beauteous mankind is! O brave
   new world, / That has such people in't'

6 By Grand Central Station I sat down and
   wept.
   book (1945) by Elizabeth Smart (1913–86),
   from *Book of Common Prayer* Psalm 137: 'By
   the waters of Babylon we sat down and
   wept: when we remembered thee, O Sion'

7 The catcher in the rye.
   novel (1951) by J. D. **Salinger**, ultimately
   from Robert Burns (1759–96) 'Comin thro'
   the rye' (1796): 'Gin a body meet a body /
   Comin thro' the rye'; see **Salinger 282:8**

8 A dance to the music of time.
   novel sequence (1951–75) by Anthony
   Powell, after *Le 4 stagioni che ballano al*
   suono del tempo (title given by Giovanni
   Pietro Bellori to a painting by Nicolas
   Poussin)

9 An evil cradling.
   book (1992) by Brian Keenan (1950–); from
   the Koran: 'Say to the unbelievers: "You
   shall be / overthrown, and mustered into
   Gehenna— / an evil cradling!"'

10 For whom the bell tolls.
   novel (1940) by Ernest **Hemingway**, from
   John Donne (1572–1631) *Devotions upon*
   Emergent Occasions (1624): 'And therefore
   never send to know for whom the bell tolls;
   it tolls for thee'

11 The glittering prizes.
   novel (1976) by Frederic **Raphael**; see **Smith**
   64:5

12 Good night, and good luck.
   film (2005), directed by George **Clooney** and
   written by George Clooney and Grant Heslov
   (1963–) about the broadcaster Edward R.
   Murrow and his attack on Joseph **McCarthy**
   (the title comes from Murrow's habitual
   sign-off); see **Catchphrases 59:6**

13 The grapes of wrath.
   novel (1939) by John **Steinbeck**, from Julia
   Ward Howe (1819–1910) 'Battle Hymn of the
   Republic' (1862): 'He is trampling out the
   vintage where the grapes of wrath are
   stored'

14 The heart is a lonely hunter.
   novel (1940) by the American writer Carson
   McCullers (1917–67); from Fiona McLeod
   (1855–1905) 'The Lonely Hunter' (1896): 'My
   heart is a lonely hunter that hunts on a
   lonely hill'

15 His dark materials.
   overall title for the fantasy trilogy
   (1996–2001) for young people by Philip
   Pullman, from Milton's *Paradise Lost* (1667)
   bk 2: 'Unless th'Almighty Maker them ordain
   / His dark materials to create more worlds'

16 The last enemy.
   book (1942) by Battle of Britain pilot
   Richard Hillary (1919–43), from the Bible I
   Corinthians: 'The last enemy that shall be
   destroyed is death'. Hillary, though badly
   burned, had survived being shot down in
   1940; he was killed on a training flight as a
   night fighter in 1943

17 A man for all seasons.
   play (1960) by Robert **Bolt**, from Robert
   Whittington (c.1480–1553?) *Vulgaria* (1521):
   'As time requireth, a man of marvellous
   mirth and pastimes, and sometime of as sad

▶

▶ **Borrowed titles** continued

gravity, as who say: a man for all seasons';
Erasmus had applied the idea earlier, saying
that More played: 'A man of all hours'

1 Remembrance of things past.
English title of the translation by C. K. Scott-
Moncrieff and S. Hudson of the novel *À la
recherche du temps perdu* (1913–27) by
Marcel **Proust**, from William Shakespeare
(1564–1616) sonnet 30: 'When to the
sessions of sweet silent thought / I summon
up remembrance of things past'

2 Ring of bright water.
book (1960) by Gavin Maxwell (1914–69),
from Kathleen Raine (1908–2003) 'The
Marriage of Psyche' (1952): 'He has married
me with a ring, a ring of bright water'

3 The seven pillars of wisdom.
book (1926) by T. E. **Lawrence**, from the
Bible Proverbs: 'Wisdom hath builded her
house, she hath hewn out her seven pillars'

4 The singer not the song.
novel (1959) by Audrey Erskine Lindop, from
a West Indian calypso

5 Staring at the sun.
title of a novel (1986) by Julian Barnes, from
a poem by Hilaire Belloc; see **Belloc 27:5**

6 A summer bird-cage.
novel (1963) by Margaret **Drabble**, from John
Webster (c.1580–c.1625) *The White Devil*
(1612) act 1, scene 2: ''Tis just like a summer
birdcage in a garden; the birds that are
without despair to get in, and the birds
that are within despair, and are in a
consumption, for fear they shall never
get out'

7 Two solitudes.
novel (1945) by Hugh MacLennan (1907–90);
see **Rilke 271:5**

8 We wish to inform you that tomorrow we
will be killed with our families.
an account (1998) by the journalist Philip
Gourevitch of the Rwanda genocide of 1994;
the title comes from a letter from seven
Christian pastors to their religious leader, 15
April 1994, 'We wish to inform you that we
have heard that tomorrow we will be killed
with our families.' The massacre of Tutsi
refugees at Mugonero took place the
following day

Louis Bousquet *fl.* 1914
French songwriter

9 *Nous en rêvons la nuit, nous y pensons le jour,
Ce n'est que Madelon, mais pour nous, c'est
l'amour.*
We dream of her by night, we think of her
by day,
It's only Madelon, but for us, it's love.
'Quand Madelon' (1914), French soldiers' song
of the First World War

Elizabeth Bowen 1899–1973
British novelist and short-story writer, born in
Ireland

10 It is about five o'clock in an evening that
the first hour of spring strikes—autumn
arrives in the early morning, but spring at
the close of a winter day.
The Death of the Heart (1938)

11 The heart may think it knows better: the
senses know that absence blots people out.
We have really no absent friends.
The Death of the Heart (1938)

12 I suppose art is the only thing that can go
on mattering once it has stopped hurting.
Heat of the Day (1949)

13 There is no end to the violations committed
by children on children, quietly talking
alone.
The House in Paris (1935)

14 Jealousy is no more than feeling alone
against smiling enemies.
The House in Paris (1935)

15 A high altar on the move.
*of Edith **Sitwell***
V. Glendinning *Edith Sitwell* (1981)

David Bowie 1947–
English rock musician

1 We can be heroes
Just for one day.
'Heroes' (1977 song)

2 Ground control to Major Tom.
'Space Oddity' (1969 song)

3 What the music says may be serious, but
as a medium it should not be questioned,
analysed, or taken so seriously. I think it
should be tarted up, made into a prostitute,
a parody of itself.
in *Rolling Stone* 1 April 1971

4 We have created a child who will be so
exposed to the media that he will be lost to
his parents by the time he is 1 2.
in *Melody Maker* 22 January 1972

Charles Boyer
see **Misquotations 224:2**

Boy George 1961–
English pop singer and songwriter

5 She's a gay man trapped in a woman's
body.
of Madonna
Take It Like a Man (1995)

6 Sex has never been an obsession with me.
It's just like eating a bag of crisps. Quite
nice, but nothing marvellous. Sex is not
simply black and white. There's a lot of
grey.
in *Sun* 21 October 1982

7 New York is so clean now you could eat
your dinner off its streets. I'll do London
next, but I'll charge this time.
*after five days cleaning the streets of New York
as community service for wasting police time*
in *Independent* 8 September 2006

Benjamin C. Bradlee 1921–
American journalist, former Editor of the
Washington Post

8 Maybe not all of you are familiar with what
it takes to make a great newspaper. It takes
a great owner. Period.
at the funeral of Katherine Graham, owner of the
Washington Post *during his Editorship*
in *Daily Telegraph* 24 July 2001

Omar Bradley 1893–1981
American general, in command of American ground
forces for the Normandy landings, chairman of the
Joint Chiefs of Staff 1949–53

9 The way to win an atomic war is to make
certain it never starts.
speech on Armistice Day, 1948

10 We have grasped the mystery of the atom
and rejected the Sermon on the Mount.
speech on Armistice Day, 1948

11 The world has achieved brilliance without
wisdom, power without conscience. Ours
is a world of nuclear giants and ethical
infants.
speech on Armistice Day, 1948

12 Red China is not the powerful nation
seeking to dominate the world. Frankly, in
the opinion of the Joint Chiefs of Staff, this
strategy would involve us in the wrong
war, at the wrong place, at the wrong
time, and with the wrong enemy.
*US Congress Senate Committee on Armed
Services* (1951)

Don Bradman 1908–2001
Australian cricketer, who holds the record for the
highest Australian Test score against England (334
in 1930); his Test match batting average of 99.94 is
also well above that of any other cricketer of any era
on Bradman: see **Anonymous 10:12**

13 When you play Test cricket you don't give
Englishmen an inch. Play it tough, all the
way.
telling Keith Miller to 'bowl faster'
Jack Fingleton *Batting from Memory* (1981)

14 Every ball is for me the first ball.
attributed; Colin Jarman (ed.) *Guinness
Dictionary of Sports Quotations* (1990)

Louis Brandeis 1856–1941
American lawyer, US Supreme Court justice

15 Publicity is justly commended as a remedy
for social and industrial diseases. Sunlight
is said to be the best of disinfectants;
electric light the most efficient policeman.
Other People's Money (1914)

16 Our government is the potent, the
omnipresent teacher. For good or ill, it

teaches the whole people by its example.
quoted by the Oklahoma bomber, Timothy McVeigh, just prior to being sentenced to death, 14 August 1997

    dissenting opinion in *Olmstead v. United States* (1928)

Marlon Brando
see **Film lines 113:16**; see also **Glass 134:1**

Georges Braque 1882–1963
French painter

1 Art is meant to disturb, science reassures.
Le Jour et la nuit: Cahiers 1917–52

2 Truth exists; only lies are invented.
Le Jour et la nuit: Cahiers 1917–52

John W. Bratton
British songwriters
see **James B. Kennedy and John W. Bratton**

Werner von Braun 1912–77
German-born American rocket engineer

3 Don't tell me that man doesn't belong out there. Man belongs wherever he wants to go—and he'll do plenty well when he gets there.
on space
    in *Time* 17 February 1958

4 Basic research is what I am doing when I don't know what I am doing.
    R. L. Weber *A Random Walk in Science* (1973)

Bertolt Brecht 1898–1956
German dramatist, producer, and poet, whose later plays were written in exile after Hitler's rise to power

5 Terrible is the temptation to be good.
The Caucasian Chalk Circle (1948)

6 ANDREA: Unhappy the land that has no heroes! ...
GALILEO: No. Unhappy the land that needs heroes.
The Life of Galileo (1939)

7 The aim of science is not to open the door to infinite wisdom, but to set a limit to infinite error.
The Life of Galileo (1939)

8 The finest plans are always ruined by the littleness of those who ought to carry them out, for the Emperors can actually do nothing.
Mother Courage (1939)

9 Don't tell me peace has broken out, when I've just bought fresh supplies.
Mother Courage (1939)

10 The resistible rise of Arturo Ui.
title of play (1941)

11 Oh, the shark has pretty teeth, dear,
And he shows them pearly white.
Just a jack-knife has Macheath, dear
And he keeps it out of sight.
The Threepenny Opera (1928)

12 Food comes first, then morals.
The Threepenny Opera (1928)

13 What is robbing a bank compared with founding a bank?
The Threepenny Opera (1928)

14 Who built Thebes of the seven gates?
In the books you will find the names of kings.
Did the kings haul up the lumps of rock?
    . . .
Where, the evening that the wall of China was finished
Did the masons go?
'Questions From A Worker Who Reads' (1935)

15 Would it not be easier
In that case for the government
To dissolve the people
And elect another?
on the uprising against the Soviet occupying forces in East Germany in 1953
'The Solution' (1953)

16 Truly, I'm living in a time of darkness.
'To Those Born Later' (1939)

17 Yes, we went, as often changing countries as changing shoes
Through the wars of the classes, despairing
Each time we found an abuse, and no sense of outrage.
'To Those Born Later' (1939)

William J. Brennan Jr. 1906–97
American lawyer and judge, US Supreme Court justice, a leading proponent of the view that the Constitution needed to be adapted to the needs of each generation

18 The genius of the Constitution rests not in any static meaning it might have had in a

world that is dead and gone, but in the adaptability of its great principles to cope with current problems and needs.
  address to the Text and Teaching Symposium, Georgetown University, 12 October 1985

1 The nation's future depends upon leaders trained through wide exposure to that robust exchange of ideas which discovers truth 'out of a multitude of tongues'.
  Supreme Court decision on *Keyishian v. Board of Regents of the University of the State of New York et al.* (1967); see **Hand 143:15**

Sydney Brenner 1927–
British scientist

2 A modern computer hovers between the obsolescent and the nonexistent.
  attributed in *Science* 5 January 1990

Aristide Briand 1862–1932
French radical statesman, Prime Minister of France 11 times between 1909 and 1929

3 The high contracting powers solemnly declare . . . that they condemn recourse to war and renounce it . . . as an instrument of their national policy towards each other . . . The settlement or the solution of all disputes or conflicts of whatever nature or of whatever origin they may be which may arise . . . shall never be sought by either side except by pacific means.
  later incorporated into the Kellogg Pact, a treaty renouncing war as an instrument of national policy, signed in Paris in 1928 by representatives of fifteen nations
  draft text, 20 June 1927

Edward Bridges 1892–1969
British civil servant, Cabinet Secretary and Head of the Civil Service

4 I confidently expect that we shall continue to be grouped with mothers-in-law and Wigan Pier as one of the recognized objects of ridicule.
  of civil servants
  Portrait of a Profession (1950)

Vera Brittain 1893–1970
English writer

5 Politics are usually the executive expression of human immaturity.
  Rebel Passion (1964)

Benjamin Britten 1913–76
English composer, pianist, and conductor

6 It is better to be a bad composer writing for society than to be a bad composer writing against it. At least your work can be of *some* use.
  interview, *New York Times*, 1969, quoted in Humphrey Carpenter *Benjamin Britten* (1992)

Russell Brockbank
see **Cartoons 56:3**

Joseph Brodsky 1940–96
Russian-born American poet

7 There is no other antidote to the vulgarity of the human heart than doubt and good taste, which one finds fused in works of great literature.
  'Letter to a President [Václav Havel]' (1993), in *On Grief and Reason* (1996)

Tom Brokaw 1940–
American journalist

8 We don't just have egg on our face. We have omelette all over our suits.
  on the networks' premature calls of a win in Florida in the presidential election, first to Al **Gore** *and then to George W.* **Bush**
    in *Atlanta Constitution-Journal* 9 November 2000 (online edition)

Jacob Bronowski 1908–74
Polish-born mathematician and humanist

9 The world can only be grasped by action, not by contemplation . . . The hand is the cutting edge of the mind.
  The Ascent of Man (1973)

10 The essence of science: ask an impertinent question, and you are on the way to a pertinent answer.
  The Ascent of Man (1973)

11 The wish to hurt, the momentary intoxication with pain, is the loophole through which the pervert climbs into the minds of ordinary men.
  The Face of Violence (1954)

Rupert Brooke 1887–1915
English poet
see also **Opening lines 45:5**

12 Blow out, you bugles, over the rich Dead!

There's none of these so lonely and poor of
    old,
But, dying, has made us rarer gifts than
    gold.
These laid the world away; poured out the
    red
Sweet wine of youth.
    'The Dead' (1914)

1 Unkempt about those hedges blows
    An English unofficial rose.
    'The Old Vicarage, Grantchester' (1915)

2 For Cambridge people rarely smile,
    Being urban, squat, and packed with guile.
    'The Old Vicarage, Grantchester' (1915)

3 Stands the Church clock at ten to three?
    And is there honey still for tea?
    'The Old Vicarage, Grantchester' (1915)

4 Now, God be thanked Who has matched us
    with His hour,
    And caught our youth, and wakened us
    from sleeping,
    With hand made sure, clear eye, and
    sharpened power,
    To turn, as swimmers into cleanness
    leaping.
    'Peace' (1914)

5 If I should die, think only this of me:
    That there's some corner of a foreign field
    That is for ever England.
    'The Soldier' (1914)

Peter Brookes
see **Cartoons 56:2**

Anita Brookner 1928–
British novelist and art historian

6 Good women always think it is their fault
    when someone else is being offensive. Bad
    women never take the blame for anything.
    Hotel du Lac (1984)

7 Dr Weiss, at forty, knew that her life had
    been ruined by literature.
    A Start in Life (1981)

Gwendolyn Brooks 1917–2000
American poet

8 Exhaust the little moment. Soon it dies.
    And be it gash or gold it will not come

Again in this identical disguise.
    'Exhaust the little moment' (1949)

9 Abortions will not let you forget.
    You remember the children you got that
    you did not get . . .
    'The Mother' (1945)

10 The time
    cracks into furious flower. Lifts its face
    all unashamed. And sways in wicked
    grace.
    'The Second Sermon on the Warpland' (1968)

J. Brooks 1912–71
British-born American songwriter

11 A four-legged friend, a four-legged friend,
    He'll never let you down.
    sung by Roy Rogers about his horse Trigger
    'A Four Legged Friend' (1952)

Heywood Broun 1888–1939
American journalist

12 Everybody favours free speech in the slack
    moments when no axes are being ground.
    in *New York World* 23 October 1926

13 Just as every conviction begins as a whim
    so does every emancipator serve his
    apprenticeship as a crank. A fanatic is a
    great leader who is just entering the room.
    in *New York World* 6 February 1928

Christy Brown 1932–81
Irish writer

14 Painting became everything to me . . .
    Through it I made articulate all that I saw
    and felt, all that went on inside the mind
    that was housed within my useless body
    like a prisoner in a cell.
    My Left Foot (1954)

Gordon Brown 1951–
British Labour politician, Chancellor of the
Exchequer from 1997
see also **Blair 225:6**

15 Ideas which stress the growing importance
    of international cooperation and new
    theories of economic sovereignty across a

wide range of areas—macroeconomics, the environment, the growth of post neo-classical endogenous growth theory and the symbiotic relationships between growth and investment in people and infrastructure.

New Labour Economics speech, September 1994, 'winner' of the ironic Plain English No Nonsense Award for 1994

1 It is about time we had an end to the old Britain, where all that matters is the privileges you were born with, rather than the potential you actually have.

speech, 25 May 2000

2 I stand with people like Mrs Thatcher, who believed that the Union was important to the Conservatives. I believe the Union is important to the Labour Party.

interview with *Sky News*, 14 September 2006, quoted in *Scotsman* (online edition) 15 September 2006

3 It will not be a surprise to you to learn I'm more interested in the future of the Arctic circle than the future of the Arctic Monkeys.

speech to Labour Party Conference, 25 September 2006

H. Rap Brown 1943–
American Black Power leader

4 I say violence is necessary. It is as American as cherry pie.

speech, 27 July 1967

Lew Brown 1893–1958
American songwriter
see also **De Sylva 89:6**

5 Life is just a bowl of cherries.

title of song (1931)

Cecil Browne 1932–
American businessman

6 But not so odd
As those who choose
A Jewish God,
But spurn the Jews.

reply to verse by William Norman Ewer; see **Ewer 106:7**

Frederick 'Boy' Browning 1896–1965
British soldier

7 I think we might be going a bridge too far.

expressing reservations about the Arnhem 'Market Garden' operation
on 10 September 1944; R. E. Urquhart *Arnhem* (1958)

Lenny Bruce 1925–66
American comedian

8 The liberals can understand everything but people who don't understand them.

John Cohen (ed.) *The Essential Lenny Bruce* (1967)

9 People should be taught what is, not what should be. All my humour is based on destruction and despair. If the whole world were tranquil, without disease and violence, I'd be standing in the breadline.

John Cohen (ed.) *The Essential Lenny Bruce* (1967)

10 I'll die young, but it's like kissing God.

on his drug addiction
attributed

Gro Harlem Brundtland 1939–
Norwegian stateswoman; Prime Minister 1981, 1986–89, and 1990–96

11 I do not know of any environmental group in any country that does not view its government as an adversary.

in *Time* 25 September 1989

Frank Bruno 1961–
English boxer

12 Boxing's just show business with blood.

in *Guardian* 20 November 1991

13 Know what I mean, Harry?

supposed to have been said in interview with sports commentator Harry Carpenter, possibly apocryphal

Anita Bryant 1940–
American singer

14 If homosexuality were the normal way, God would have made Adam and Bruce.

in *New York Times* 5 June 1977

Bill Bryson 1951–
American travel writer

1 I had always thought that once you grew
up you could do anything you wanted—
stay up all night or eat ice-cream straight
out of the container.
The Lost Continent (1989)

2 What an odd thing tourism is. You fly off to
a strange land, eagerly abandoning all the
comforts of home, and then expend vast
quantities of time and money in a largely
futile attempt to recapture the comforts
that you wouldn't have lost if you hadn't
left home in the first place.
Neither Here Nor There (1991)

Zbigniew Brzezinski 1928–
American politician, National Security Adviser to
President **Carter**, 1977–81

3 Russia can be an empire or a democracy,
but it cannot be both.
in *Foreign Affairs* March/April 1994 'The
Premature Partnership'

Martin Buber 1878–1965
Austrian-born religious philosopher and Zionist

4 Through the Thou a person becomes I.
Ich und Du (1923)

John Buchan 1875–1940
Scottish novelist and brother of O. **Douglas**;
Governor-General of Canada, 1935–40
on Buchan: see **Bennett 29:6**

5 It's a great life if you don't weaken.
Mr Standfast (1919)

6 An atheist is a man who has no invisible
means of support.
H. E. Fosdick *On Being a Real Person* (1943)

Frank Buchman 1878–1961
American evangelist; founder of the Moral
Re-Armament movement

7 There is enough in the world for
everyone's need, but not enough for
everyone's greed.
Remaking the World (1947)

8 I thank heaven for a man like Adolf Hitler,
who built a front line of defence against the
anti-Christ of Communism.
in *New York World-Telegram* 26 August 1936

Gene Buck 1885–1957
and **Herman Ruby** 1891–1959
American songwriters

9 That Shakespearian rag,—
Most intelligent, very elegant.
'That Shakespearian Rag' (1912 song); see
Eliot 103:2

Warren Buffett 1930–
American businessman, stock investor, and
philanthropist

10 It's only when the tide goes out that you
learn who's been swimming naked.
at Berkshire Hathaway annual meeting,
Omaha, 1993; *Warren Buffet Speaks* (1997)

11 A very rich person should leave his kids
enough to do anything but not enough to
do nothing.
quoted in *Fortune Magazine* (online edition)
25 June 2006

Arthur Buller 1874–1944
British botanist and mycologist

12 There was a young lady named Bright,
Whose speed was far faster than light;
She set out one day
In a relative way
And returned on the previous night.
'Relativity' in *Punch* 19 December 1923

Luis Buñuel 1900–83
Spanish film director
see also **Film titles 117:4**

13 Science doesn't interest me much. I find it
analytical, pretentious, and superficial—
largely because it doesn't address itself to
dreams, chance, laughter, feelings, or
paradox—in other words, all the things I
love the most.
*My Last Sigh: The Autobiography of Luis
Buñuel* (1983)

14 Thanks to God, I am still an atheist.
in *Le Monde* 16 December 1959

Julie Burchill 1960–
English journalist and writer
see also **Anonymous 11:1**

15 Now, at last, this sad, glittering century
has an image worthy of it: a wandering,
wondering girl, a silly Sloane turned

secular saint, coming home in her coffin to
RAF Northolt like the good soldier she was.
*of **Diana**, Princess of Wales*
  in *Guardian* 2 September 1997

Anthony Burgess 1917–93
English novelist and critic

1 A clockwork orange.
  title of novel (1962)

2 It was the afternoon of my eighty-first
birthday, and I was in bed with my
catamite when Ali announced that the
archbishop had come to see me.
  Earthly Powers (1980), opening line

3 He said it was artificial respiration, but
now I find I am to have his child.
  Inside Mr Enderby (1963)

4 The US presidency is a Tudor monarchy
plus telephones.
  George Plimpton (ed.) *Writers at Work* (4th
  Series, 1977)

Johnny Burke 1908–64
American songwriter

5 Every time it rains, it rains
Pennies from heaven.
Don't you know each cloud contains
Pennies from heaven?
  'Pennies from Heaven' (1936 song); see
  Thatcher 312:6

6 Like Webster's Dictionary, we're Morocco
bound.
  'The Road to Morocco' (1942 song)

Thomas E. Burnett Jnr d. 2001
American businessman

7 I love you, honey. I know we're all going to
die—but there's three of us who are going
to do something about it.
  *final phone call to his wife from the hijacked
  Flight 93, which crashed south of Pittsburgh*
  in *Independent* 13 September 2001; see **Last
  words 190:15**

William S. Burroughs 1914–97
American novelist; his best-known writing deals
with life as a drug addict in a unique, surreal style
see also **Last words 191:3**

8 Kerouac opened a million coffee bars and
sold a million pairs of Levis to both sexes.

Woodstock rises from his pages.
  The Adding Machine (1985) 'Remembering
  Jack Kerouac'

9 Junk is the ideal product . . . the ultimate
merchandise. No sales talk necessary. The
client will crawl through a sewer and beg
to buy.
  The Naked Lunch (1959) introduction

10 The face of 'evil' is always the face of total
need.
  The Naked Lunch (1959)

Benjamin Hapgood Burt 1880–1950
American songwriter

11 'You can tell a man who "boozes" by the
  company he chooses'
And the pig got up and slowly walked
  away.
  'The Pig Got Up and Slowly Walked Away'
  (1933 song)

12 When you're all dressed up and no place to
go.
  title of song (1913)

Nat Burton
British songwriter

13 There'll be bluebirds over the white cliffs of
  Dover,
Tomorrow, just you wait and see.
  'The White Cliffs of Dover' (1941 song),
  associated particularly with the popular
  singer Vera Lynn (1917–)

George Bush 1924–
American Republican statesman, 41st President of
the US 1989–93; father of George W. **Bush**
on Bush: see **Richards 270:12**

14 Oh, the vision thing.
  *responding to the suggestion that he turn his
  attention from short-term campaign objectives
  and look to the longer term*
  in *Time* 26 January 1987

15 What's wrong with being a boring kind of
guy?
  during the campaign for the Republican
  nomination; in *Daily Telegraph* 28 April 1988

16 Read my lips: no new taxes.
  campaign pledge on taxation
  in *New York Times* 19 August 1988; see
  Blunkett 37:5

1 I'm President of the United States, and I'm not going to eat any more broccoli!
in *New York Times* 23 March 1990

2 And now, we can see a new world coming into view. A world in which there is the very real prospect of a new world order.
speech, in *New York Times* 7 March 1991

George W. Bush 1946–
American Republican statesman, 43rd President of the US from 2001; son of George **Bush**
see also **Gore 136:1**

3 We will make no distinction between terrorists who committed these acts and those who harbour them.
after the terrorist attacks of 11 September
televised address, 12 September 2001

4 Today we feel what Franklin Roosevelt called the warm courage of national unity. This unity against terror is now extending across the world.
address in Washington National Cathedral, 14 September 2001, at the day of mourning for those killed in the terrorist attacks of 11 September
in *Times* 15 September 2001; see **Roosevelt 273:14**

5 This crusade, this war on terrorism is going to take a while.
the President later retracted his use of the word 'crusade'
at a White House press conference, 16 September 2001; see **Kennedy 176:9**

6 States like these . . . constitute an axis of evil, arming to threaten the peace of this world.
of Iraq, Iran, and North Korea
State of the Union address, in *Newsweek* 11 February 2002

7 Brownie, you're doing a heck of a job.
to Michael Brown, then Director of the Federal Emergency Managemenet Agency, in the aftermath of Hurricane Katrina's devastation of New Orleans
quoted in *New York Times* 3 September 2005

8 I'm the decider, and I decide what's best. And what's best is for Don Rumsfeld to remain as the secretary of defence.
in *New York Times* (online edition) 19 April 2006

9 Yo, Blair. How are you doing?
*the President addresses Tony **Blair** during a break in the G8 summit in St Petersburg, Russia, 17 July 2006; a microphone had been left on*
in *Guardian* 18 July 2006

Nicholas Murray Butler 1862–1947
American President of Columbia University, 1901–45

10 An expert is one who knows more and more about less and less.
Commencement address at Columbia University; attributed

R. A. ('Rab') Butler 1902–82
British Conservative politician

11 REPORTER: Mr Butler, would you say that this [Anthony Eden] is the best Prime Minister we have?
R. A. BUTLER: Yes.
interview at London Airport, 8 January 1956

12 Politics is the Art of the Possible. That is what these pages show I have tried to achieve—not more—and that is what I have called my book.
The Art of the Possible (1971); from Bismarck (1815–98) conversation with Meyer von Waldeck, 11 August 1867: 'Politics is the art of the possible'; see also **Galbraith 128:12, Medawar 218:6**

A. S. Byatt 1936–
English novelist, sister of Margaret **Drabble**

13 What literature can and should do is change the people who teach the people who don't read the books.
interview in *Newsweek* 5 June 1995

C

James Branch Cabell 1879–1958
American novelist and essayist

1 The optimist proclaims that we live in the
best of all possible worlds; and the
pessimist fears this is true.
The Silver Stallion (1926); referring to Voltaire
(1694–1778) *Candide* (1759): 'In this best of
possible worlds . . . all is for the best'

Irving Caesar 1895–1996
American songwriter

2 Picture you upon my knee,
Just tea for two and two for tea.
'Tea for Two' (1925 song), written for the show
No, No, Nanette

3 Sometimes I write lousy, but always I write
fast.
habitual comment, quoted in *American
National Biography* (online edition) 'Irving
Caesar'

John Cage 1912–
American composer, pianist, and writer; his
experimental approach included the use of periods
of silence

4 I have nothing to say
and I am saying it and that is
poetry.
'Lecture on nothing' (1961)

James Cagney
see **Film lines 113:1, Misquotations 225:9**

James M. Cain 1892–1977
American novelist

5 The postman always rings twice.
title of novel (1934)

LeRoy Cain
American flight director for the space shuttle
Columbia, which disintegrated shortly before its
scheduled landing, 1 February 2003, with the loss of
all on board

6 Lock the doors.
*instruction to his staff, meaning that nobody
could leave until all mission control records were
completed (a tacit recognition that there was no
more hope for Columbia)*
from transcript of final Columbia radio
transmissions released by Nasa; in *Guardian*
13 February 2003

Michael Caine 1933–
English film actor

7 Not many people know that.
title of book (1984)

Charles Calhoun 1897–1972
American songwriter

8 Shake, rattle and roll.
title of song (1954)

James Callaghan 1912–2005
British Labour statesman, Prime Minister 1976–9
see also **Misquotations 224:3**

9 Leaking is what you do; briefing is what *I*
do.
*when giving evidence to the Franks Committee
on Official Secrecy in 1971*
Franks Report (1972); oral evidence

10 You cannot now, if you ever could, spend
your way out of a recession.
speech at Labour Party Conference, 28
September 1976

1 You never reach the promised land. You can march towards it.
> in a television interview, 20 July 1978

2 I had known it was going to be a 'winter of discontent'.
> television interview, 8 February 1979; in *Daily Telegraph* 9 February 1979; quoting William Shakespeare (1564–1616) *Richard III* (1591): 'Now is the winter of our discontent / Made glorious summer by this sun of York'; see **Newspaper headlines 238:9**

3 It's the first time in recorded history that turkeys have been known to vote for an early Christmas.
> *in the debate resulting in the fall of the Labour government, when the pact between Labour and the Liberals had collapsed, and the Scottish and Welsh Nationalists had also withdrawn their support*
> in the House of Commons, 28 March 1979

4 There are times, perhaps once every thirty years, when there is a sea-change in politics. It then does not matter what you say or what you do. There is a shift in what the public wants and what it approves of. I suspect there is now such a sea-change— and it is for Mrs Thatcher.
> *during the election campaign of 1979*
> Bernard Donoughue *Prime Minister* (1987)

Italo Calvino 1923–85
Italian novelist and short-story writer

5 Everything has already begun before, the first line of the first page of every novel refers to something that has already happened outside the book.
> *If on a Winter's Night a Traveller* (1979)

Helder Camara 1909–99
Brazilian priest

6 When I give food to the poor they call me a saint. When I ask why the poor have no food they call me a communist.
> attributed

David Cameron 1966–
British Conservative politician, Party Leader from 2005

7 It's where you are going to, not where you have come from that matters.
> interview in *Sunday Times* 22 May 2005

8 I want to talk about the future. He was the future once.
> of Tony **Blair** at Prime Minister's Questions, in House of Commons, 7 December 2005

9 You'll interrupt yourself in a minute.
> *being interviewed by John Humphrys on the* Today *programme, BBC Radio 4, 1 March 2006*
> in *Mail on Sunday* 5 March 2006

10 We—the people in suits—often see hoodies as aggressive, the uniform of a rebel army of gangsters. But hoodies are more defensive than offensive. They're a way to stay invisible in the street.
> speech to Centre for Social Justice, 10 July 2006, in BBC News (online edition) 10 July 2006; see **Coaker 72:10**, **Misquotations 224:9**

Alastair Campbell 1957–
British journalist, Press Secretary to the Prime Minister, Tony **Blair**, 1997–2003
see also **Anonymous 12:7**

11 The day of the bog-standard comprehensive is over.
> press briefing, 12 February 2001; see **Blunkett 37:6**

Mrs Patrick Campbell 1865–1940
English actress
on Campbell: see **Woollcott 342:7**

12 I'm out of a job. London wants flappers, and I can't flap.
> *of the theatre of 1927*
> Margot Peters *Mrs Pat* (1984)

13 The deep, deep peace of the double-bed after the hurly-burly of the chaise-longue.
> *on her recent marriage*
> Alexander Woollcott *While Rome Burns* (1934)
> 'The First Mrs Tanqueray'

14 It doesn't matter what you do in the bedroom as long as you don't do it in the street and frighten the horses.
> Daphne Fielding *The Duchess of Jermyn Street* (1964)

Roy Campbell 1901–57
South African poet

15 You praise the firm restraint with which they write—
I'm with you there, of course:
They use the snaffle and the curb all right,

But where's the bloody horse?
'On Some South African Novelists' (1930)

1 South Africa, renowned both far and wide
For politics and little else beside.
The Wayzgoose (1928)

Albert Camus 1913–60
Algerian-born French novelist, dramatist, and
essayist

2 You know what charm is: a way of getting
the answer yes without having asked any
clear question.
The Fall (1957)

3 We are all special cases. We all want to
appeal against something! Everyone insists
on his innocence, at all costs, even if it
means accusing the rest of the human race
and heaven.
The Fall (1957)

4 I'll tell you a big secret, *mon cher*. Don't
wait for the last judgement. It takes place
every day.
The Fall (1957)

5 Poor people's memory is less nourished
than that of the rich; it has fewer
landmarks in space because they seldom
leave the place where they live, and fewer
reference points in time . . . Of course, there
is the memory of the heart that they say is
the surest kind, but the heart wears out
with sorrow and labour, it forgets sooner
under the weight of fatigue.
The First Man (1994)

6 The struggle itself towards the heights is
enough to fill a human heart. One must
imagine that Sisyphus is happy.
The Myth of Sisyphus (1942)

7 Politics and the fate of mankind are formed
by men without ideals and without
greatness. Those who have greatness
within them do not go in for politics.
Notebooks 1935–42 (1963)

8 An intellectual is someone whose mind
watches itself.
Notebooks 1935–42 (1963)

9 Mother died today. Or perhaps it was
yesterday, I don't know.
The Outsider (1942), opening line

10 In our society any man who doesn't cry at
his mother's funeral is liable to be
condemned to death.
'Afterword' (1955), to *The Outsider* (1942)

11 What we learn in a time of pestilence: that
there are more things to admire in men
than to despise.
The Plague (1947)

12 What is a rebel? A man who says no.
The Rebel (1951)

13 Kings were put to death long before 21
January, 1793, and before the regicides of
the nineteenth century. But regicides of
earlier times and their followers were
interesting in attacking the person, not the
principle, of the king. They wanted
another king, and that was all. It never
occurred to them that the throne could
remain empty for ever.
The Rebel (1951)

14 All modern revolutions have ended in a
reinforcement of the State.
The Rebel (1951)

15 Every revolutionary ends as an oppressor
or a heretic.
The Rebel (1951)

16 When the imagination sleeps, words are
emptied of their meaning.
Resistance, Rebellion and Death (1961)
'Reflections on the Guillotine'

17 What I know most surely about morality
and the duty of man I owe to sport.
often quoted as '. . . I owe to football'
Herbert R. Lottman *Albert Camus* (1979)

18 Without work, all life goes rotten, but
when work is soulless, life stifles and dies.
attributed; E. F. Schumacher *Good Work*
(1979)

Elias Canetti 1905–94
Bulgarian-born writer and novelist, winner of the
Nobel Prize for literature in 1981

19 The fear of burglars is not only the fear of
being robbed, but also the fear of a sudden
and unexpected clutch out of the darkness.
Crowds and Power (1960)

20 All the things one has forgotten scream for
help in dreams.
Die Provinz der Menschen (1973)

Eric Cantona 1966–
French footballer

1 When seagulls follow a trawler, it is
because they think sardines will be thrown
into the sea.
> to the media at the end of a press conference,
> 31 March 1995, after winning an appeal
> against a prison sentence for an assault on a
> hostile fan

Robert Capa 1913–54
Hungarian-born American photojournalist; he was
killed stepping on a landmine while covering the
French Indochina War

2 If your pictures aren't good enough, you
aren't close enough.
> Russell Miller *Magnum: Fifty years at the Front
> Line of History* (1997)

3 The nearest thing to journalism for anyone
who found himself without a language.
> *of photography*
> quoted in *American National Biography*
> (online edition)

Al Capone 1899–1947
American gangster, of Italian descent, who
dominated organized crime in Chicago in the 1920s

4 Once in the racket you're always in it.
> in *Philadelphia Public Ledger* 18 May 1929

5 Don't you get the idea I'm one of these
goddam radicals. Don't get the idea I'm
knocking the American system.
> interview, *c.*1929, with Claud Cockburn; Claud
> Cockburn *In Time of Trouble* (1956)

Truman Capote 1924–84
American writer and novelist
on Capote: see **Vidal 325:10**

6 Other voices, other rooms.
> title of novel (1948)

Al Capp 1907–79
American cartoonist, creator of the L'il Abner comic
strip about a family of hillbillies

7 A product of the untalented, sold by the
unprincipled to the utterly bewildered.
> *on abstract art*
> in *National Observer* 1 July 1963

Benjamin Cardozo 1870–1938
American lawyer and judge, US Supreme Court
Justice

8 Justice is not to be taken by storm. She is to
be wooed by slow advances.
> *The Growth of the Law* (1924)

*asked who among his colleagues was the
greatest living American jurist:*
9 The greatest living American jurist isn't *on*
the Supreme Court.
> *of Learned* **Hand**
> quoted in *American National Biography*
> (online edition)

George Carey 1935–
English Anglican churchman; Archbishop of
Canterbury 1991–2002

10 I see it as an elderly lady, who mutters
away to herself in a corner, ignored most of
the time.
> *on the Church of England*
> in *Readers Digest* (British ed.) March 1991

James B. Carey 1911–73
American labour leader

11 I don't think that makes any difference. A
door-opener for the Communist party is
worse than a member of the Communist
party. When someone walks like a duck,
swims like a duck, and quacks like a duck,
he's a duck.
> in *New York Times* 3 September 1948

Peter Carey 1943–
Australian writer

12 She understood, as women often do more
easily than men, that the declared
meaning of a spoken sentence is only its
overcoat, and the real meaning lies
underneath its scarves and buttons.
> *Oscar and Lucinda* (1989)

13 My fictional project has always been the
invention or discovery of my own country.
> interview in *Boldtype* (online journal) March
> 1999

14 Self-knowledge does not necessarily help a
novelist. It helps a human being a great

deal but novelists are often appalling human beings.
attributed; in *Times* 27 October 2001

Stokely Carmichael 1941–98
American Black Power leader

1 The only position for women in SNCC is prone.
response to a question about the position of women
at a Student Nonviolent Coordinating Committee conference, November 1964

Stokely Carmichael 1941–98 and Charles Vernon Hamilton 1929–
American Black Power leaders

2 The adoption of the concept of Black Power is one of the most legitimate and healthy developments in American politics and race relations in our time. . . . It is a call for black people in this country to unite, to recognize their heritage, to build a sense of community. It is a call for black people to begin to define their own goals, to lead their own organizations and to support those organizations. It is a call to reject the racist institutions and values of this society.
Black Power (1967)

Dale Carnegie 1888–1955
American writer and lecturer, teacher of public speaking

3 How to win friends and influence people.
title of book (1936)

Jimmy Carr 1972–
Irish comedian

4 On your way out be aware of women and children—they tend to slow you down.
advising his audience at the Edinburgh Festival on how to leave after a fire alarm sounded
in *Independent* (online edition) 23 August 2006

Lord Carrington 1919–
British Conservative politician, Foreign Secretary 1979–82

5 Q: If Mrs Thatcher were run over by a bus . . . ?

LORD CARRINGTON: It wouldn't dare.
during the Falklands War
Russell Lewis *Margaret Thatcher* (1984)

Edward Carson 1854–1935
British lawyer and politician, a key supporter of Ulster Unionism and opponent of Irish Home Rule

6 From the day I first entered parliament up to the present, devotion to the union has been the guiding star of my political life.
he became leader of the Irish Unionist MPs at Westminster in 1910
in *Dictionary of National Biography* (1917–)

Johnny Carson 1925–2005
American broadcaster and comedian

7 Happiness is . . . finding two olives in your martini when you're hungry.
Happiness is—a Dry Martini (1966)

Rachel Carson 1907–64
American zoologist

8 Over increasingly large areas of the United States, spring now comes unheralded by the return of the birds, and the early mornings are strangely silent where once they were filled with the beauty of bird song.
The Silent Spring (1962)

Angela Carter 1940–92
English novelist

9 Comedy is tragedy that happens to *other* people.
Wise Children (1991)

Howard Carter 1874–1939
English archaeologist, who discovered the tomb of Tutankhamen while excavating in the Valley of the Kings at Thebes in 1922

10 Yes, wonderful things.
when asked what he could see on first looking into the tomb of Tutankhamun, 26 November 1922; his notebook records the words as 'Yes, it is wonderful'
H. V. F. Winstone *Howard Carter and the discovery of the tomb of Tutankhamun* (1993)

Jimmy Carter 1924–
American Democratic statesman, 39th President of the US, 1977–81

1 I'm Jimmy Carter, and I'm going to be your next president.
to the son of a campaign supporter, November 1975
   I'll Never Lie to You (1976); see **Gore 136:1**

2 I've looked on a lot of women with lust. I've committed adultery in my heart many times. This is something that God recognizes I will do—and I have done it—and God forgives me for it.
   in *Playboy* November 1976

Sydney Carter 1915–2004
English folk-song and hymn writer

3 It's God they ought to crucify
Instead of you and me,
I said to the carpenter
A-hanging on the tree.
   'Friday Morning' (1967)

4 Dance then wherever you may be,
I am the Lord of the Dance, said he,
And I'll lead you all, wherever you may be
And I'll lead you all in the dance, said he.
   'Lord of the Dance' (1967)

5 One more step along the world I go.
   'One More Step'

Henri Cartier-Bresson 1908–2004
French photographer and artist

6 To me, photography is the simultaneous recognition, in a fraction of a second, of the significance of an event as well as of a precise organisation of forms which give that event its proper expression.
   The Decisive Moment (1952)

Barbara Cartland 1901–2000
English writer, author of light romantic fiction

7 After forty a woman has to choose between losing her figure or her face. My advice is to keep your face, and stay sitting down.
   Libby Purves 'Luncheon à la Cartland'; in *Times* 6 October 1993; similar remarks have been attributed to Cartland since *c.*1980

Cartoons
see box overleaf

Pablo Casals 1876–1973
Spanish cellist, conductor, and composer

8 It is like a beautiful woman who has not grown older, but younger with time, more slender, more supple, more graceful.
of the cello
   in *Time* 29 April 1957

Roger Casement 1864–1916
Irish nationalist; executed for treason in 1916

9 Self-government is our right, a thing born in us at birth, a thing no more to be doled out to us, or withheld from us, by another people than the right to life itself—than the right to feel the sun, or smell the flowers, or to love our kind.
   statement at the conclusion of his trial, the Old Bailey, London, 29 June 1916

10 Where all your rights become only an accumulated wrong; where men must beg with bated breath for leave to subsist in their own land, to think their own thoughts, to sing their own songs, to garner the fruits of their own labours . . . then surely it is a braver, a saner and truer thing, to be a rebel in act and deed against such circumstances as these than tamely to accept it as the natural lot of men.
   statement at the conclusion of his trial, the Old Bailey, London, 29 June 1916

Johnny Cash 1932–2003
American singer and songwriter

11 Many a good man I saw fall
And even now, every time I dream
I hear the men and the monkeys in the jungle scream.
Drive on, it don't mean nothin'
My children love me, but they don't understand
And I got a woman who knows her man.
   'Drive On' (1993)

12 It was a real slow walk in a real sad rain.
   'Drive On' (1993)

Cartoons

1 All right, have it your own way—you heard a seal bark!
showing a man and his wife in bed, with a seal looking over the headboard
caption in *New Yorker* 30 January 1932, by James **Thurber**

2 Does Bambi have teeth?
*when Tony **Blair** had begun to make his mark as Labour Leader of the Opposition; the smiling Bambi is depicted in a forest glade, blood dripping from his teeth, standing over the eviscerated body of a rabbit (John **Major**)*
front cover of the *Spectator* 1 October 1994, by Peter Brookes (1943–)

3 Fog in Channel—Continent isolated.
newspaper placard in cartoon, *Round the Bend with Brockbank* (1948) by the British cartoonist Russell Brockbank (1913–); the phrase 'Continent isolated' was quoted as already current by John Gunther *Inside Europe* (1938)

4 I feel like a fugitive from th' law of averages.
showing Willie and Joe, American GIs, under fire
caption in *Up Front* (1945), by Bill Mauldin (1921–2003)

5 I had a crash with a man, who had a crash with a lady, who had a crash with Camilla Parker Bowles.
alongside a front-page report of a woman driver whose car had been written off in a collision with Camilla Parker Bowles (now Duchess of Cornwall, wife of the Prince of Wales), a pocket cartoon showed a couple looking ruefully at a damaged car
in *Daily Telegraph* 13 June 1997, by Matthew Pritchett ('Matt', 1964–); see also **Farjeon 109:7**

6 It's a naive domestic Burgundy without any breeding, but I think you'll be amused by its presumption.
caption in *New Yorker* 27 March 1937, by James **Thurber**

7 MOTHER: It's broccoli, dear.
CHILD: I say it's spinach, and I say the hell with it.
caption in *New Yorker* 8 December 1928, by E. B. **White**

8 The man who . . .
illustrating social gaffes resulting from snobbery
opening words of the caption for a series of cartoons (first appearing in 1912) by H. M. Bateman (1887–1970)

9 No son—they're not the same—devolution takes longer.
father to his son, who is reading a book on evolution
caption in *Scots Independent* January 1978, by Ewen Bain (1925–89)

10 On the Internet, nobody knows you're a dog.
a large dog at a desk, paw on keyboard, enlightening a smaller friend
caption in *New Yorker*, July 1993, by the American cartoonist Peter Steiner

11 The price of petrol has been raised by a penny. Official.
a torpedoed sailor with oil-stained face lying on a raft; the message was intended to be a warning against wasting petrol, but it was taken by some as suggesting that lives were being put at risk for profit
caption in *Daily Mirror* 3 March 1942; cartoon by Philip Zec (1909–83) and caption by 'Cassandra' (William Connor, 1909–67).

12 We have met the enemy and he is us.
the cartoon-strip character, Pogo the opossum, looking at litter under a tree; used as an Earth Day poster in 1971
Pogo cartoon, 1970, by the American cartoonist Walt Kelly (1913–73); the comment is a modification of the message in which Commodore Perry (1785–1819) reported his victory over the British in the battle of Lake Erie, 1813, 'We have met the enemy, and they are ours'

13 Well, back to the old drawing board.
a civilian designer, plans under his arm, turns away from a crashed plane, as service personnel look on in horror or rush forward
caption to a cartoon in the *New Yorker*, 1 March 1941, by the American cartoonist Peter **Arno**

▶

▶ **Cartoons** continued

1 Well, if I called the wrong number, why did you answer the phone?
  in *New Yorker* 5 June 1937, by James **Thurber**

2 Well, if you knows of a better 'ole, go to it.
  Old Bill and a friend in a shellhole under fire
  caption in *Fragments from France* (1915), by the British cartoonist Bruce Bairnsfather (1888–1959)

3 You mean I'm supposed to stand on that?
  a reluctant elephant (symbol of the Republican Party) is propelled towards a small platform resting on an unstable tower of buckets beneath a tar-barrel; the label on the barrel introduced the term 'McCarthyism'
  caption in *Washington Post* 29 March 1950; by the American cartoonist 'Herblock' (Herbert Lawrence Block, 1910–2001)

Barbara Castle 1910–2002
British Labour politician

4 I will fight for what I believe in until I drop dead. And that's what keeps you alive.
  in *Guardian* 14 January 1998

Ted Castle 1907–79
British journalist

5 In place of strife.
  title of Government White Paper, 17 January 1969, suggested by Castle to his wife, Barbara Castle, then Secretary of State for Employment
  Barbara Castle diary, 15 January 1969

Fidel Castro 1927–
Cuban statesman, Prime Minister 1959–76 and President since 1976

6 Capitalism is using its money; we socialists throw it away.
  in *Observer* 8 November 1964

Catchphrases
see box overleaf
see also **Grenfell 138:13, Laurel 191:15**

Willa Cather 1873–1947
American novelist

7 Oh, the Germans classify, but the French arrange!
  Death Comes For the Archbishop (1927)

Mr Justice Caulfield 1914–
British lawyer

8 Remember Mary Archer in the witness box. Your vision of her will probably never disappear. Has she elegance? Has she fragrance? Would she have—without the strain of this trial—a radiance?
  summing up of court case between Jeffrey Archer and the Star, *July 1987*
  in *Times* 24 July 1987

Charles Causley 1917–2003
English poet and schoolmaster

9 Watch where he comes walking
Out of the Christmas flame,
Dancing, double-talking:
Herod is his name.
  'Innocents' Song' (1961)

10 Timothy Winters comes to school
With eyes as wide as a football-pool,
Ears like bombs and teeth like splinters:
A blitz of a boy is Timothy Winters.
  'Timothy Winters' (1957)

Constantine Cavafy 1863–1933
Greek poet

11 What are we waiting for, gathered in the market-place?
The barbarians are to arrive today.
  'Waiting for the Barbarians' (1904)

12 And now, what will become of us without the barbarians?
Those people were a kind of solution.
  'Waiting for the Barbarians' (1904)

Catchphrases

1 CECIL: After you, Claude.
CLAUDE: No, after you, Cecil.
ITMA (BBC radio programme, 1939–49), written by Ted Kavanagh (1892–1958)

2 Am I bovvered?
teenager Lauren, in *The Catherine Tate Show* (2004–), created by Catherine Tate (1968–)

3 And now for something completely different.
Monty Python's Flying Circus (BBC TV programme, 1969–74)

4 . . . and that's the way it is.
Walter **Cronkite**'s habitual sign-off as anchorman for CBS Evening News (1962–81)

5 Anyone for tennis?
said to be typical of drawing-room comedies, sometimes associated with the young Humphrey Bogart (1899–1957); perhaps from George Bernard Shaw 'Anybody on for a game of tennis?' *Misalliance* (1914)

6 Are yer courtin'?
Have a Go! (BBC radio quiz programme, 1946–67), used by Wilfred Pickles (1904–78)

7 Are you sitting comfortably? Then I'll begin.
sometimes 'Then we'll begin'
Listen with Mother (BBC radio programme for children, 1950–82), used by Julia Lang (1921–)

8 The butler did it!
a solution for detective stories
Nigel Rees, in *Sayings of the Century* (1984), quotes a correspondent who recalls hearing it at a cinema *c.*1916 but the origin of the phrase has not been traced

9 Can I do you now, sir?
spoken by 'Mrs Mopp'
ITMA (BBC radio programme, 1939–49), written by Ted Kavanagh (1892–1958)

10 Can you hear me, mother?
used by Sandy Powell (1900–82)

11 Come on! Come on!
habitual adjuration by Jeremy **Paxman** to contestants on *University Challenge* on BBC2 (1994–)

12 Confused? You won't be after this week's episode of 'Soap'
announcer, following a brief summary of the plot so far, at the beginning of each episode of the ABC television sitcom *Soap*, 1977–81

13 Crikey!
trademark exclamation of Australian naturalist and television presenter Steve Irwin (1962–2006), the 'Crocodile Hunter'

14 The day war broke out.
customary preamble to radio monologues in the role of a Home Guard, used by Robb Wilton (1881–1957); from *c.*1940

15 Didn't she [*or* he *or* they] do well?
used by Bruce Forsyth (1928–) in 'The Generation Game' on BBC Television, 1973 onwards

16 Don't forget the diver.
spoken by 'The Diver'; based on 'a memory of the pier at New Brighton where Tommy Handley used to go as a child . . . A man in a bathing suit . . . whined "Don't forget the diver, sir."'
ITMA (BBC radio programme, 1939–49), written by Ted Kavanagh (1892–1958)

17 Don't have nightmares. Do sleep well.
habitual closing words for BBC1's *Crimewatch* (1984–), spoken by Nick Ross

18 Eat my shorts!
The Simpsons (American TV series, 1990–), created by Matt **Groening**

19 Ee, it was agony, Ivy.
Ray's a Laugh (BBC radio programme, 1949–61), written by Ted Ray (1906–77)

20 Evening, all.
opening words spoken by Jack Warner as Sergeant Dixon in *Dixon of Dock Green* (BBC television series, 1956–76), written by Ted Willis (1918–)

21 Everybody wants to get inta the act!
used by Jimmy Durante (1893–1980)

22 An everyday story of country folk.
introduction to *The Archers* (BBC radio serial, 1950 onwards), written by Geoffrey Webb and Edward J. Mason

▶

▶ Catchphrases continued

1 Exterminate! Exterminate!
the Daleks in *Dr Who* (BBC television series, from 1963), written by Terry Nation

2 Faster than a speeding bullet! . . . Look! Up in the sky! It's a bird! It's a plane! It's Superman! Yes, it's Superman! . . . who—disguised as Clark Kent, mild-mannered reporter for a great metropolitan newspaper—fights a never ending battle for truth, justice and the American way!
Superman (US radio show, 1940 onwards) preamble

3 Good evening, Mr and Mrs North America and all the ships at sea. Let's go to press! Flash!
habitual introduction by American journalist Walter Winchell (1897–1972) to network radio spot, 1931–56

4 A good idea—son.
Educating Archie, 1950–3 BBC radio comedy series, written by Eric Sykes (1923–) and Max Bygraves (1922–)

5 Good morning, sir—was there something?
used by Sam Costa in radio comedy series *Much-Binding-in-the-Marsh*, written by Richard Murdoch (1907–90) and Kenneth Horne (1900–69), started 2 January 1947

6 Good night and good luck.
habitual sign-off by the broadcaster Ed **Murrow**; see also **Borrowed titles 40:12**

7 Goodnight, children . . . everywhere.
closing words normally spoken by 'Uncle Mac' in the 1930s and 1940s
on *Children's Hour* (BBC radio programme); written by Derek McCulloch (1892–1978)

8 Have you read any good books lately?
used by Richard Murdoch in radio comedy series *Much-Binding-in-the-Marsh*, written by Richard Murdoch (1907–90) and Kenneth Horne (1900–69), started 2 January 1947

9 Hello, good evening, and welcome.
used by David **Frost** (1939–) in 'The Frost Programme' on ITV Television, 1966 onwards

10 Here come de judge.
from the song-title 'Here comes the judge' (1968); written by Dewey 'Pigmeat' Markham, Dick Alen, Bob Astor, and Sarah Harvey

11 Here's one I made earlier.
culmination to directions for making a model out of empty yoghurt pots, coat-hangers, and similar domestic items
children's BBC television programme *Blue Peter*, 1963 onwards

12 I am not a number, I am a free man!
Number Six, in *The Prisoner* (TV series 1967–68), written by Patrick McGoohan 1928–, George Markstein, and David Tomblin; additional title sequence from the second episode onwards

13 I didn't get where I am today without . . . .
used by the manager C. J. in BBC television series *The Fall and Rise of Reginald Perrin* (1976–80); based on David Nobbs *The Death of Reginald Perrin* (1975)

14 I do not know the answer to this question, but I think we should be told.
used by John **Junor**; in *Sunday Express* and elsewhere

15 I don't like this game, let's play another game—let's play doctor and nurses.
phrase first used by Bluebottle in 'The Phantom Head-Shaver' in *The Goon Show* (BBC radio series) 15 October 1954, written by Spike **Milligan**; the catchphrase was often 'I do not like this game'

16 I don't mind if I do.
spoken by 'Colonel Chinstrap'
ITMA (BBC radio programme, 1939–49), written by Ted Kavanagh (1892–1958)

17 I go—I come back.
spoken by 'Ali Oop'
ITMA (BBC radio programme, 1939–49), written by Ted Kavanagh (1892–1958)

18 I have a cunning plan.
Baldrick's habitual over-optimistic promise in *Blackadder II* (1987 television series), written by Richard Curtis (1956–) and Ben Elton (1959–)

▶

▶ **Catchphrases** continued

1 I'm Bart Simpson: who the hell are you?
The Simpsons (American TV series, 1990–),
created by Matt **Groening**

2 I'm in charge.
used by Bruce Forsyth (1928–) in 'Sunday
Night at the London Palladium' on ITV, 1958
onwards

3 I'm worried about Jim.
frequent line in *Mrs Dale's Diary*, BBC radio
series 1948–69

4 It all depends what you mean by . . .
habitually used by the philosopher and
broadcaster C. E. M. Joad (1891–1953) when
replying to questions on 'The Brains Trust'
(formerly 'Any Questions'), BBC radio
(1941–8)

5 It's a good thing.
customary form of approbation in the areas
of home decorating and cooking from US
businesswoman Martha Stewart (1941–)

6 It's being so cheerful as keeps me going.
spoken by 'Mona Lott'
ITMA (BBC radio programme, 1939–49),
written by Ted Kavanagh (1892–1958)

7 CORBETT: It's goodnight from me.
BARKER: And it's goodnight from him.
Ronnie Corbett (1930–) and Ronnie Barker
(1929–2005) in *The Two Ronnies*, 1971–87
BBC television series

8 I've arrived and to prove it I'm here!
Educating Archie, 1950–3 BBC radio comedy
series, written by Eric Sykes (1923–) and
Max Bygraves (1922–)

9 I've started so I'll finish.
said when a contestant's time runs out while a
question is being put
Magnus Magnusson (1929–) *Mastermind*,
BBC television (1972–97)

10 Just like that!
used by Tommy Cooper (1921–84)

11 Keep on truckin'.
used by Robert Crumb (1943–) in cartoons
from *c.*1972

12 Left hand down a bit!
The Navy Lark (BBC radio series, 1959–77),
written by Laurie Wyman

13 Let's be careful out there.
Hill Street Blues (television series, 1981
onwards), written by Steven Bochco and
Michael Kozoll

14 Mind my bike!
used by Jack Warner (1895–1981) in the BBC
radio series *Garrison Theatre*, 1939 onwards

15 Nice to see you—to see you, nice.
used by Bruce Forsyth (1928–) in 'The
Generation Game' on BBC Television, 1973
onwards

16 Oh, calamity!
used by Robertson Hare (1891–1979)

17 Ohhh, I don't *believe* it!
Victor Meldrew in *One Foot in the Grave*
(BBC television series, 1989–), written by
David Renwick

18 Oh, titter ye not.
Frankie **Howerd**'s habitual adjuration to his
audience, first introduced in *The Frankie*
Howerd Variety Show 1978

19 Once again we stop the mighty roar of
London's traffic.
In Town Tonight (BBC radio series, 1933–60)
preamble

20 The only gay in the village.
Daffyd's boast
spoken by Matt Lucas in the BBC comedy
Little Britain (2003–), written and
performed by Matt Lucas and David
Walliams

21 Ooh, you are awful—but I like you.
Mandy's habitual protest
spoken by Dick Emery, in *The Dick Emery*
Show (1967–81)

22 Pass the sick bag, Alice.
used by John **Junor**; in *Sunday Express* and
elsewhere

23 Phone a friend.
advice to contestants by Chris Tarrant, host
of the ITV quiz show *Who Wants to be a*
Millionaire (1998–)

24 Seriously, though, he's doing a grand
job!
used by David **Frost** (1939–) in 'That Was
The Week That Was', on BBC Television,
1962-3

▶

▶ Catchphrases continued

1 Shome mishtake, shurely?
in *Private Eye* magazine, 1980s

2 Silly moo.
Alf Garnett to his wife Elsie
spoken by Warren **Mitchell** in the BBC
television comedy *Till Death Us Do Part*
(1966–74), written by Johnny Speight
(1920–98)

3 So farewell then . . .
frequent opening of poems by 'E. J. Thribb' in
Private Eye *magazine, usually as an obituary*
1970s onwards

4 Take me to your leader.
from science-fiction stories

5 That's all folks!
closing line of Warner Brothers *Looney
Tunes* cartoons, originally introduced in
Porky's Duck Hunt (1937)

6 Thunderbirds are go!
Thunderbirds (British television puppet
series 1965–6), created by Gerry Anderson

7 Time for bed, said Zebedee.
frequent ending to the BBC television series
The Magic Roundabout (1965–77), narrated
by Eric Thompson (1929–82)

8 The truth is out there.
The X Files (American television series,
1993–), created by Chris Carter

9 Very interesting . . . but stupid.
Rowan and Martin's Laugh-In (American
television series, 1967–73), written by Dan
Rowan (1922–87) and Dick Martin (1923–)

10 The weekend starts here.
Ready, Steady, Go, British television series,
*c.*1963

11 We have ways of making you talk.
perhaps originating in the line 'We have
ways of making men talk' in *Lives of a
Bengal Lancer* (1935 film), written by
Waldemar Young et al.

12 What do you think of the show so far?
Rubbish!
Eric Morecambe (1926–84), on *The
Morecambe and Wise Show* (BBC Television,
1968–78; Thames Television, 1978–83)

13 What's up, Doc?
Bugs Bunny cartoons, written by Tex Avery
(1907–80), from *c.*1940

14 Who loves ya, baby?
used by Telly Savalas (1926–94) in American
TV series *Kojak* (1973-8)

15 Without hesitation, deviation, or
repetition.
instruction for contestants' monologues on
the panel show *Just a Minute* (BBC Radio,
1967–)

16 Yeah but no but yeah but no.
Vicky Pollard's habitual protest
spoken by Matt Lucas, in the BBC comedy
Little Britain (2003–), written and
performed by Matt Lucas and David
Walliams

17 You are the weakest link . . . goodbye.
used by Anne Robinson (1944–) on the
television game-show *The Weakest Link*
(2000–)

18 You bet your sweet bippy.
Rowan and Martin's Laugh-In (American
television series, 1967–73), written by Dan
Rowan (1922–87) and Dick Martin (1923–)

19 You might very well think that. I
couldn't possibly comment.
*the Chief Whip's habitual response to
questioning*
House of Cards (televised 1990); written by
Michael Dobbs (1948–)

20 You're going to like this . . . not a lot . . .
but you'll like it!
used by Paul Daniels (1938–) in his
conjuring act, especially on television from
1981 onwards

21 You rotten swines. I told you I'd be
deaded.
phrase first used by Bluebottle in 'Hastings
Flyer' in *The Goon Show* (BBC radio series),
3 January 1956, written by Spike **Milligan**

22 Your starter for ten.
phrase often used by Bamber Gascoigne
(1935–) in *University Challenge* (ITV quiz
series, 1962–87)

▶

> ▶ **Catchphrases** continued

1 You silly twisted boy.
> phrase first used in 'The Dreaded Batter
> Pudding Hurler' in *The Goon Show* (BBC
> radio series) 12 October 1954, written by
> Spike **Milligan**

Edith Cavell 1865–1915
English nurse, executed by the Germans for
assisting in the escape of British soldiers from
occupied Belgium

2 Patriotism is not enough. I must have no
hatred or bitterness towards anyone.
on the eve of her execution
> in *Times* 23 October 1915

Paul Celan 1920–70
German poet

3 A man lives in the house he plays with his
vipers he writes
he writes when it grows dark to
Deutschland your golden hair
Margareta
Your ashen hair Shulamith we shovel a
grave in the air there you won't lie too
cramped.
> 'Deathfugue' (written 1944)

4 He shouts play death more sweetly this
Death is a master from Deutschland
he shouts scrape your strings darker you'll
rise then as smoke to the sky
you'll have a grave then in the clouds there
you won't lie too cramped.
> 'Deathfugue' (written 1944)

5 *Der Tod ist ein Meister aus Deutschland.*
Death is a master from Germany.
> 'Deathfugue' (written 1944)

6 There's nothing in the world for which a
poet will give up writing, not even when he
is a Jew and the language of his poems is
German.
> letter to relatives, 2 August 1948

Neville Chamberlain 1869–1940
British Conservative statesman, Prime Minister
1937–40; he was replaced in office by Winston
Churchill
on Chamberlain: see **Jenkins 167:12**; see also **Amery
8:1, Boothby 39:4**

7 How horrible, fantastic, incredible it is that
we should be digging trenches and trying
on gas-masks here because of a quarrel in a
far away country between people of whom
we know nothing.
*on Germany's annexation of the Sudetenland,
which after the First World War had been
allocated to Czechoslovakia*
> radio broadcast, 27 September 1938

8 This is the second time in our history that
there has come back from Germany to
Downing Street peace with honour. I
believe it is peace for our time.
> speech from 10 Downing Street, 30 September
> 1938; earlier, Benjamin Disraeli (1804–81) said
> in a speech on returning from the Congress of
> Berlin, 16 July 1878: 'Lord Salisbury and
> myself have brought you back peace—but a
> peace I hope with honour'

9 This morning, the British Ambassador in
Berlin handed the German government a
final Note stating that, unless we heard
from them by eleven o'clock that they were
prepared at once to withdraw their troops
from Poland, a state of war would exist
between us. I have to tell you now that no
such undertaking has been received, and
that consequently this country is at war
with Germany.
> radio broadcast, 3 September 1939

10 Whatever may be the reason—whether it
was that Hitler thought he might get away
with what he had got without fighting for
it, or whether it was that after all the
preparations were not sufficiently

complete—however, one thing is certain—
he missed the bus.
> speech at Central Hall, Westminster, 4 April
> 1940

Raymond Chandler 1888–1959
American writer of detective fiction

1 It was a blonde. A blonde to make a bishop
kick a hole in a stained glass window.
> *Farewell, My Lovely* (1940)

2 Crime isn't a disease, it's a symptom. Cops
are like a doctor that gives you aspirin for a
brain tumour.
> *The Long Good-Bye* (1953)

3 Down these mean streets a man must go
who is not himself mean, who is neither
tarnished nor afraid.
> in *Atlantic Monthly* December 1944 'The
> Simple Art of Murder'

4 If my books had been any worse, I should
not have been invited to Hollywood, and if
they had been any better, I should not
have come.
> letter to Charles W. Morton, 12 December 1945

5 Would you convey my compliments to the
purist who reads your proofs and tell him
or her that I write in a sort of broken-down
patois which is something like the way a
Swiss waiter talks, and that when I split an
infinitive, God damn it, I split it so it will
stay split.
> letter to Edward Weeks, 18 January 1947

6 When in doubt have a man come through
the door with a gun in his hand.
> attributed

Coco Chanel 1883–1971
French couturière, noted for simple but
sophisticated garments which were a radical
departure from stiff corseted styles

7 Look for the woman in the dress. If there is
no woman, there is no dress.
> in *New York Times* 23 August 1964

8 Clothes by a man who doesn't know
women, never had one, and dreams of
being one!
> *of Dior's New Look*
> attributed; in *Vanity Fair* June 1994

9 Youth is something very new: twenty
years ago no one mentioned it.
> Marcel Haedrich *Coco Chanel, Her Life, Her
> Secrets* (1971)

Henry ('Chips') Channon 1897–1958
American-born British Conservative politician and
diarist

10 What is more dull than a discreet diary?
One might just as well have a discreet soul.
> diary, 26 July 1935

Charlie Chaplin 1889–1977
English film actor and director, star of short silent
comedies, especially in his trademark character of a
bowler-hatted tramp

11 All I need to make a comedy is a park, a
policeman and a pretty girl.
> *My Autobiography* (1964)

12 Words are cheap. The biggest thing you
can say is 'elephant'.
> *on the universality of silent films*
> B. Norman *The Movie Greats* (1981)

Arthur Chapman 1873–1935
American poet

13 Out where the handclasp's a little stronger,
Out where the smile dwells a little longer,
That's where the West begins.
> *Out Where the West Begins* (1916)

John Jay Chapman 1862–1933
American essayist and poet

14 The present in New York is so powerful
that the past is lost.
> *Emerson and Other Essays* (rev. ed. 1909),
> preface

Charles, Prince of Wales 1948–
Heir apparent to the British throne; son of **Elizabeth
II** and former husband of **Diana**, Princess of Wales

when asked if he was 'in love':
15 Yes . . . whatever that may mean.
> *after the announcement of his engagement*
> interview, 24 February 1981; see **Duffy 93:8**

16 A monstrous carbuncle on the face of a
much-loved and elegant friend.
> *on the proposed extension to the National
> Gallery*
> speech in London, 30 May 1984; see also
> **Spencer 300:1**

1 I just come and talk to the plants, really—
very important to talk to them, they
respond I find.
    television interview, 21 September 1986

Jack Charlton 1935–
English footballer and manager

2 It was either work in the pit or play
football.
    Simon Hattenstone *The Best of Times: What
    became of the heroes of '66?* (2006)

Bruce Chatwin 1940–89
English writer and traveller

3 Finding in 'primitive' languages a dearth of
words for moral ideas, many people
assumed these ideas did not exist. But the
concepts of 'good' or 'beautiful', so
essential to Western thought, are
meaningless unless they are rooted to
things.
    In Patagonia (1977)

Hugo Chavez 1954–
Venezuelan statesman, President 1999–

4 Fatherland, socialism or death—I swear it.
    third inauguration speech, 10 January 2007, in
    New York Times (online edition) 11 January
    2007

G. K. Chesterton 1874–1936
English essayist, novelist, and poet
on Chesterton: see **Belloc 27:12**, **Epitaphs 108:3**;
see also **Telegrams 311:1**

5 Talk about the pews and steeples
And the Cash that goes therewith!
But the souls of Christian peoples . . .
Chuck it, Smith!
    satirizing F. E. **Smith**'s response to the Welsh
    Disestablishment Bill
    'Antichrist' (1915)

6 I tell you naught for your comfort,
Yea, naught for your desire,
Save that the sky grows darker yet
And the sea rises higher.
    The Ballad of the White Horse (1911)

7 For the great Gaels of Ireland
Are the men that God made mad,
For all their wars are merry,
And all their songs are sad.
    The Ballad of the White Horse (1911)

8 The strangest whim has seized me . . . .
    After all
I think I will not hang myself today.
    'Ballade of Suicide' (1915)

9 When fishes flew and forests walked
And figs grew upon thorn,
Some moment when the moon was blood
Then surely I was born.

With monstrous head and sickening cry
And ears like errant wings,
The devil's walking parody
On all four-footed things.
    'The Donkey' (1900)

10 Fools! For I also had my hour;
One far fierce hour and sweet:
There was a shout about my ears,
And palms before my feet.
    'The Donkey' (1900)

11 They died to save their country and they
only saved the world.
    'English Graves' (1922)

12 From all that terror teaches,
From lies of tongue and pen,
From all the easy speeches
That comfort cruel men,
From sale and profanation
Of honour and the sword,
From sleep and from damnation,
Deliver us, good Lord!
    'A Hymn' (1915)

13 Strong gongs groaning as the guns boom
    far,
Don John of Austria is going to the war.
    'Lepanto' (1915)

14 Before the Roman came to Rye or out to
    Severn strode,
The rolling English drunkard made the
    rolling English road.
A reeling road, a rolling road, that rambles
    round the shire,
And after him the parson ran, the sexton
    and the squire;
A merry road, a mazy road, and such as we
    did tread
The night we went to Birmingham by way
    of Beachy Head.
    'The Rolling English Road' (1914)

15 For there is good news yet to hear and fine
    things to be seen,

Before we go to Paradise by way of Kensal
  Green.
  'The Rolling English Road' (1914)

1 Smile at us, pay us, pass us; but do not
  quite forget.
  For we are the people of England, that
    never have spoken yet.
  'The Secret People' (1915)

2 Tea, although an Oriental,
  Is a gentleman at least;
  Cocoa is a cad and coward,
  Cocoa is a vulgar beast.
    'Song of Right and Wrong' (1914)

3 And Noah he often said to his wife when he
    sat down to dine,
  'I don't care where the water goes if it
    doesn't get into the wine.'
  'Wine and Water' (1914)

4 After the first silence the small man said to
  the other: 'Where does a wise man hide a
  pebble?'
  And the tall man answered in a low voice:
  'On the beach.'
  The small man nodded, and after a short
  silence said: 'Where does a wise man hide
  a leaf?'
  And the other answered: 'In the forest.'
    The Innocence of Father Brown (1911)

5 One sees great things from the valley; only
  small things from the peak.
    The Innocence of Father Brown (1911)

6 Thieves respect property. They merely
  wish the property to become their property
  that they may more perfectly respect it.
    The Man who was Thursday (1908)

7 The men who really believe in themselves
  are all in lunatic asylums.
    Orthodoxy (1908)

8 Tradition means giving votes to the most
  obscure of all classes, our ancestors. It is
  the democracy of the dead.
    Orthodoxy (1908)

9 All conservatism is based upon the idea
  that if you leave things alone you leave
  them as they are. But you do not. If you
  leave a thing alone you leave it to a torrent
  of change.
    Orthodoxy (1908)

10 It isn't that they can't see the solution. It is
  that they can't see the problem.
    The Scandal of Father Brown (1935)

11 They say travel broadens the mind; but
  you must have the mind.
  'The Shadow of the Shark' (1921)

12 The Christian ideal has not been tried and
  found wanting. It has been found difficult;
  and left untried.
    What's Wrong with the World (1910) pt. 1 'The
    Unfinished Temple'

13 The prime truth of woman, the universal
  mother . . . that if a thing is worth doing, it
  is worth doing badly.
    What's Wrong with the World (1910) pt. 4 'Folly
    and Female Education'

14 Journalism largely consists in saying 'Lord
  Jones Dead' to people who never knew that
  Lord Jones was alive.
    The Wisdom of Father Brown (1914)

15 When men stop believing in God they don't
  believe in nothing; they believe in
  anything.
    widely attributed, although not traced in his
    works; first recorded as 'The first effect of not
    believing in God is to believe in anything' in
    Emile Cammaerts *Chesterton: The Laughing
    Prophet* (1937)

Maurice Chevalier 1888–1972
French singer and actor

16 Considering the alternative, it's not too bad
  at all.
    *on being asked what he felt about the advancing
    years, on his seventy-second birthday*
    Michael Freedland *Maurice Chevalier* (1981)

Joseph Benedict 'Ben' Chifley
1885–1951
Australian Labor statesman, Prime Minister 1945–9

17 We have a great objective—the light on
  the hill—which we aim to reach by
  working for the betterment of mankind not
  only here but anywhere we may give a
  helping hand.
    speech to the Annual Conference of the New
    South Wales branch of the Australian Labor
    Party, 12 June 1949

Erskine Childers 1870–1922
British writer and Irish nationalist
see also **Last words 190:2**

1 The riddle of the sands.
    title of novel (1903) featuring German plans
    for an invasion of England

Jaques Chirac 1932–
French statesman, Prime Minister 1974–6 and
1986–8, President since 1995

2 For its part, France wants you to take part
in this great undertaking.
on European Monetary Union
    speech to both British Houses of Parliament,
    15 May 1996

Noam Chomsky 1928–
American linguistics scholar

3 Colourless green ideas sleep furiously.
illustrating that grammatical structure is
independent of meaning
    Syntactic Structures (1957)

4 The Internet is an élite organization; most
of the population of the world has never
even made a phone call.
on the limitations of the World Wide Web
    in *Observer* 18 February 1996

5 The best scientists aren't the ones who
know the most data; they're the ones who
know what they're looking for.
    in *Guardian* 31 October 2005

Jean Chrétien 1934–
Canadian Liberal statesman, Prime Minister
1993–2003

6 Leadership means making people feel good.
    in *Toronto Star* 7 June 1984

7 The art of politics is learning to walk with
your back to the wall, your elbows high,
and a smile on your face. It's a survival
game played under the glare of lights.
    Straight from the Heart (1985)

Agatha Christie 1890–1976
English writer of detective fiction
on Christie: see **Thomas 314:17**

8 He [Hercule Poirot] tapped his forehead.
'These little grey cells. It is "up to them".'
    The Mysterious Affair at Styles (1920)

9 I'm a sausage machine, a perfect sausage
machine.
    G. C. Ramsey *Agatha Christie* (1972)

Frank Edwin Churchill 1901–42
American composer

10 Who's afraid of the big bad wolf?
    title of children's song, written especially for
    Walt Disney's 1933 cartoon film *Three Little*
    Pigs; probably written in collaboration with
    Ann Ronell (1905–93)

Winston Churchill 1874–1965
British Conservative statesman, Prime Minister
1940–5 and 1951–5. A consistent opponent of
appeasement between the wars, he replaced Neville
Chamberlain as leader of the coalition government
in 1940 and led Britain throughout the war, until the
election of 1945 brought in the Labour government
of Clement **Attlee**
on Churchill: see **Anonymous 13:3**, **Attlee 16:4**,
Bevan 33:5, **Murrow 232:5**; see also **Misquotations**
225:3, **Spears 299:12**

11 It cannot in the opinion of His Majesty's
Government be classified as slavery in the
extreme acceptance of the word without
some risk of terminological inexactitude.
    speech in the House of Commons, 22
    February 1906

12 Business carried on as usual during
alterations on the map of Europe.
on the self-adopted 'motto' of the British people
    speech at Guildhall, 9 November 1914

13 The whole map of Europe has been
changed . . . but as the deluge subsides and
the waters fall short we see the dreary
steeples of Fermanagh and Tyrone
emerging once again.
    speech in the House of Commons, 16 February
    1922

14 Anyone can rat, but it takes a certain
amount of ingenuity to re-rat.
on rejoining the Conservatives twenty years
after leaving them for the Liberals, c.1924
    Kay Halle *Irrepressible Churchill* (1966)

15 I remember, when I was a child, being
taken to the celebrated Barnum's circus,
which contained an exhibition of freaks
and monstrosities, but the exhibit on the
programme which I most desired to see
was the one described as 'The Boneless

Wonder'. My parents judged that that spectacle would be too revolting and demoralizing for my youthful eyes, and I have waited 50 years to see the boneless wonder sitting on the Treasury Bench.
of Ramsay **MacDonald**
> speech in the House of Commons, 28 January 1931

1 Dictators ride to and fro upon tigers which they dare not dismount. And the tigers are getting hungry.
> letter, 11 November 1937

2 I cannot forecast to you the action of Russia. It is a riddle wrapped in a mystery inside an enigma.
> radio broadcast, 1 October 1939

3 I have nothing to offer but blood, toil, tears and sweat.
> speech in the House of Commons, 13 May 1940

4 What is our policy? . . . to wage war against a monstrous tyranny, never surpassed in the dark, lamentable catalogue of human crime.
> speech in the House of Commons, 13 May 1940

5 What is our aim? . . . Victory, victory at all costs, victory in spite of all terror; victory, however long and hard the road may be; for without victory, there is no survival.
> speech in the House of Commons, 13 May 1940

6 We shall not flag or fail. We shall go on to the end. We shall fight in France, we shall fight on the seas and oceans, we shall fight with growing confidence and growing strength in the air, we shall defend our island, whatever the cost may be. We shall fight on the beaches, we shall fight on the landing grounds, we shall fight in the fields and in the streets, we shall fight in the hills; we shall never surrender.
> speech in the House of Commons, 4 June 1940

7 What General Weygand called the 'Battle of France' is over. I expect that the Battle of Britain is about to begin. Upon this battle depends the survival of Christian civilization. Upon it depends our own British life and the long continuity of our institutions and our Empire. The whole fury and might of the enemy must very soon be turned on us. Hitler knows that he will have to break us in this island or lose the war. If we can stand up to him all Europe may be free and the life of the world may move forward into broad, sunlit uplands; but if we fail then the whole world, including the United States, and all that we have known and cared for, will sink into the abyss of a new dark age made more sinister, and perhaps more prolonged, by the lights of a perverted science. Let us therefore brace ourselves to our duty, and so bear ourselves that, if the British Empire and its Commonwealth lasts for a thousand years, men will still say, 'This was their finest hour.'
> speech in the House of Commons, 18 June 1940

8 Never in the field of human conflict was so much owed by so many to so few.
on the Battle of Britain
> speech in the House of Commons, 20 August 1940

9 As far as I can see you have used every cliché except 'God is Love' and 'Please adjust your dress before leaving'.
on a long-winded report from Anthony **Eden**
> in *Life* 9 December 1940; when this story was repeated in the *Daily Mirror*, Churchill denied that it was true

10 Give us the tools and we will finish the job.
addressing President **Roosevelt**
> radio broadcast, 9 February 1941

11 The British nation is unique in this respect. They are the only people who like to be told how bad things are, who like to be told the worst.
> speech in the House of Commons, 10 June 1941

12 The people of London with one voice would say to Hitler: 'You have committed every crime under the sun . . . We will have no truce or parley with you, or the grisly gang who work your wicked will. You do your worst—and we will do our best.'
> speech at County Hall, London, 14 July 1941

13 It becomes still more difficult to reconcile Japanese action with prudence or even with sanity. What kind of a people do they think we are?
> speech to US Congress, 26 December 1941

1 When I warned them [the French Government] that Britain would fight on alone whatever they did, their generals told their Prime Minister and his divided Cabinet, 'In three weeks England will have her neck wrung like a chicken.' Some chicken! Some neck!
speech to Canadian Parliament, 30 December 1941

2 We mean to hold our own. I have not become the King's First Minister in order to preside over the liquidation of the British Empire.
speech in London, 10 November 1942

3 Now this is not the end. It is not even the beginning of the end. But it is, perhaps, the end of the beginning.
on the Battle of Egypt
speech at the Mansion House, London, 10 November 1942

4 National compulsory insurance for all classes for all purposes from the cradle to the grave.
radio broadcast, 21 March 1943

5 There is no finer investment for any community than putting milk into babies.
radio broadcast, 21 March 1943

6 The empires of the future are the empires of the mind.
speech at Harvard, 6 September 1943

7 Unless the right hon. Gentleman changes his policy and methods and moves without the slightest delay, he will be as great a curse to this country in time of peace, as he was a squalid nuisance in time of war.
*of Aneurin **Bevan***
speech in the House of Commons, 6 December 1945

8 From Stettin in the Baltic to Trieste in the Adriatic an iron curtain has descended across the Continent.
*'iron curtain' previously had been applied by others to the Soviet Union or her sphere of influence, e.g. Ethel Snowden Through Bolshevik Russia (1920), Dr **Goebbels** Das Reich (25 February 1945), and by Churchill himself in a cable to President **Truman** (4 June 1945)*
speech at Westminster College, Fulton, Missouri, 5 March 1946; see also **Solzhenitsyn 298:9**

9 Democracy is the worst form of Government except all those other forms that have been tried from time to time.
speech in the House of Commons, 11 November 1947

10 This is the sort of English up with which I will not put.
Ernest Gowers *Plain Words* (1948) 'Troubles with Prepositions'

11 No, not dead. But the candle in that great turnip has gone out.
*in reply to the comment 'One never hears of **Baldwin** nowadays—he might as well be dead'*
Harold Nicolson diary, 17 August 1950

12 Naval tradition? Monstrous. Nothing but rum, sodomy, prayers, and the lash.
often quoted as 'rum, sodomy, and the lash', as in Peter Gretton Former Naval Person (1968)
Harold Nicolson diary, 17 August 1950

13 To jaw-jaw is always better than to war-war.
speech at White House, 26 June 1954

14 A modest man who has a good deal to be modest about.
*of Clement **Attlee***
in *Chicago Sunday Tribune Magazine of Books* 27 June 1954

15 I am prepared to meet my Maker. Whether my Maker is prepared for the great ordeal of meeting me is another matter.
at a news conference in Washington, 1954, in *New York Times* 25 January 1965

16 It was the nation and the race dwelling all round the globe that had the lion's heart. I had the luck to be called upon to give the roar. I also hope that I sometimes suggested to the lion the right place to use his claws.
speech at Westminster Hall, 30 November 1954

17 I have taken more out of alcohol than alcohol has taken out of me.
Quentin Reynolds *By Quentin Reynolds* (1964)

18 In defeat unbeatable: in victory unbearable.
*of Lord **Montgomery***
E. Marsh *Ambrosia and Small Beer* (1964)

19 I wrote my name at the top of the page. I wrote down the number of the question '1'. After much reflection I put a bracket

round it thus '(1)'. But thereafter I could not think of anything connected with it that was either relevant or true. . . . It was from these slender indications of scholarship that Mr Welldon drew the conclusion that I was worthy to pass into Harrow. It is very much to his credit.
My Early Life (1930)

1 By being so long in the lowest form [at Harrow] I gained an immense advantage over the cleverer boys. They all went on to learn Latin and Greek . . . . But I was taught English. . . . Thus I got into my bones the essential structure of the ordinary British sentence—which is a noble thing. . . . Naturally I am biased in favour of boys learning English. I would make them all learn English: and then I would let the clever ones learn Latin as an honour, and Greek as a treat.
My Early Life (1930)

2 It is a good thing for an uneducated man to read books of quotations.
My Early Life (1930)

3 In war: resolution. In defeat: defiance. In victory: magnanimity. In peace: goodwill.
The Second World War (1948) vol. 1 epigraph

4 I felt as if I were walking with destiny, and that all my past life had been but a preparation for this hour and this trial.
The Second World War (1948) vol. 1

5 The loyalties which centre upon number one are enormous. If he trips he must be sustained. If he makes mistakes they must be covered. If he sleeps he must not be wantonly disturbed. If he is no good he must be pole-axed. But this last extreme process cannot be carried out every day; and certainly not in the days just after he has been chosen.
The Second World War (1949) vol. 2

6 If Hitler invaded hell I would make at least a favourable reference to the devil in the House of Commons.
The Second World War (1950) vol. 3

7 It may almost be said, 'Before Alamein we never had a victory. After Alamein we never had a defeat.'
The Second World War (1951) vol. 4

8 Jellicoe was the only man on either side who could lose the war in an afternoon.
The World Crisis (1927)

9 The ability to foretell what is going to happen tomorrow, next week, next month, and next year. And to have the ability afterwards to explain why it didn't happen.
describing the qualifications desirable in a politician
B. Adler *Churchill Wit* (1965)

10 I am fond of pigs. Dogs look up to us. Cats look down on us. Pigs treat us as equals.
attributed, in M. Gilbert *Never Despair* (1988)

11 NANCY ASTOR: If I were your wife I would put poison in your coffee!
CHURCHILL: And if I were your husband I would drink it.
Consuelo Vanderbilt Balsan *Glitter and Gold* (1952)

12 A remarkable example of modern art. It certainly combines force with candour.
on the notorious 80th birthday portrait by Graham Sutherland, later destroyed by Lady Churchill
Martin Gilbert *Churchill: A Life* (1991)

13 The Prime Minister has nothing to hide from the President of the United States.
*on stepping from his bath in the presence of a startled President **Roosevelt***
recalled by Roosevelt's son in *Churchill* (BBC television series presented by Martin Gilbert, 1992)

14 A sheep in sheep's clothing.
*of Clement **Attlee***
Lord Home *The Way the Wind Blows* (1976)

15 BESSIE BRADDOCK: Winston, you're drunk.
CHURCHILL: Bessie, you're ugly. But tomorrow I shall be sober.
J. L. Lane (ed.) *Sayings of Churchill* (1992)

Count Galeazzo Ciano 1903–44
Italian fascist politician; son-in-law of **Mussolini**. He supported Mussolini's deposition in 1943, and was subsequently shot by fascist forces

16 Victory has a hundred fathers, but no-one wants to recognise defeat as his own.
often quoted as '. . . but defeat is an orphan'
diary, 9 September 1942

Santo Cilauro 1962–
Australian writer

recommendation for a successful tabloid story:
1 Add sex, and stir.
> episode title for *Frontline* Season 1 1994
> (written by Santo Cilauro, Tom Gleisner, Jane
> Kennedy, and Rob Sitch)

E. M. Cioran 1911–95
Romanian-born French philosopher

2 Without the possibility of suicide, I would
have killed myself long ago.
> in *Independent* 2 December 1989

3 I do nothing, granted. But I see the hours
pass—which is better than trying to fill
them.
> in *Guardian* 11 May 1993

Eric Clapton 1945–
English guitarist, singer, and songwriter

4 Rock is like a battery that must always go
back to blues to get recharged.
> attributed; M. Palmer *Small Talk, Big Names*
> (1993)

Alan Clark 1928–99
British Conservative politician, son of Kenneth **Clark**
see also **Epitaphs 107:1**

5 There are no true friends in politics. We are
all sharks circling, and waiting, for traces
of blood to appear in the water.
> diary, 30 November 1990

6 Our old friend economical . . . with the
actualité.
> *under cross-examination at the Old Bailey*
> *during the Matrix Churchill case*
> in *Independent* 10 November 1992; see
> **Armstrong 14:12**

Joe Clark 1939–
Canadian Conservative statesman, Prime Minister
1979–80

7 I'm not the greatest. I'm the best available.
> *of his election as Conservative leader*
> in *Maclean's* 21 February 1977

Kenneth Clark 1903–83
English art historian, father of Alan **Clark**

8 It's a curious fact that the all-male
religions have produced no religious
imagery—in most cases have positively
forbidden it. The great religious art of the
world is deeply involved with the female
principle.
> *Civilisation* (1969)

Arthur C. Clarke 1917–
English science fiction writer

9 Any sufficiently advanced technology is
indistinguishable from magic.
> *The Lost Worlds of 2001* (1972)

10 If an elderly but distinguished scientist says
that something is possible he is almost
certainly right, but if he says that it is
impossible he is very probably wrong.
> in *New Yorker* 9 August 1969; see **Asimov 15:3**

11 How inappropriate to call this planet Earth
when it is clearly Ocean.
> in *Nature* 8 March 1990

12 The only genuine consciousness-
expanding drug.
> *of science fiction*
> letter claiming coinage in *New Scientist* 2 April
> 1994

Kenneth Clarke 1940–
British Conservative politician, Chancellor of the
Exchequer 1993–7

13 Tell your kids to get their scooters off my
lawn.
> *allegedly said to the Party Chairman, Brian*
> *Mawhinney, of young Central Office personnel;*
> *see* **Wilson 338:11**
> television report, 5 December 1996; in
> *Guardian* 7 December 1996

Philip 'Tubby' Clayton 1885–1972
Australian-born British clergyman, founder of Toc H

14 CHAIRMAN: What is service?
CANDIDATE: The rent we pay for our room
on earth.
> *admission ceremony of Toc H, a society founded*
> *after the First World War to provide Christian*
> *fellowship and social service (the name came*
> *from the initials of* Talbot House, *a soldier's club*
> *established in Belgium in 1915,* toc *being former*
> *telegraphy code for T)*
> Tresham Lever *Clayton of Toc H* (1971)

Eldridge Cleaver 1935–98
American civil rights activist

1 You're either part of the solution or you're part of the problem.
  speech in San Francisco, 1968, in R. Scheer *Eldridge Cleaver, Post Prison Writings and Speeches* (1969)

John Cleese 1939–
and Connie Booth
British comedy writer and actor; British comedy actress
see also **Monty Python's Flying Circus**

2 They're Germans. Don't mention the war.
  Fawlty Towers 'The Germans' (BBC TV programme, 1975)

Georges Clemenceau 1841–1929
French statesman, Prime Minister 1906–9, 1917–20

3 My home policy: I wage war; my foreign policy: I wage war. All the time I wage war.
  speech to French Chamber of Deputies, 8 March 1918

4 What do you expect when I'm between two men of whom one [Lloyd George] thinks he is Napoleon and the other [Woodrow Wilson] thinks he is Jesus Christ?
  to André Tardieu, on being asked why he always gave in to **Lloyd George** *at the Paris Peace Conference, 1918*
  letter from Harold Nicolson to his wife, Vita Sackville-West, 20 May 1919

5 It is easier to make war than to make peace.
  speech at Verdun, 20 July 1919

6 Oh, to be seventy again!
  on seeing a pretty girl on his eightieth birthday
  James Agate diary, 19 April 1938

7 War is too serious a matter to entrust to military men.
  attributed to Clemenceau, e.g. in Hampden Jackson *Clemenceau and the Third Republic* (1946), but also to Aristide **Briand** and the earlier French statesman Talleyrand (1754–1838); see also **de Gaulle 87:7**

Harlan Cleveland 1918–
American government official

8 The revolution of rising expectations.
  phrase coined, 1950; Arthur Schlesinger *A Thousand Days* (1965)

Clarice Cliff 1899–1972
English ceramic artist

9 Women today want continual change, they will have colour and plenty of it. Colour seems to radiate happiness and the spirit of modern life and movement, and I cannot put too much of it into my designs to please women.
  in 1930; Leonard Griffin *Clarice Cliff: the Art of the Bizarre* (1999)

Hillary Rodham Clinton 1947–
American lawyer, wife of Bill **Clinton**, First Lady of the US 1993–2001

10 I am not standing by my man, like Tammy Wynette. I am sitting here because I love him, I respect him, and I honour what he's been through and what we've been through together.
  interview on *60 Minutes*, CBS-TV, 27 January 1992; see **Wynette 343:1**

11 I could have stayed home and baked cookies and had teas. But what I decided was to fulfil my profession, which I entered before my husband was in public life.
  comment on questions raised by rival Democratic contender Edmund G. Brown Jr.; in *Albany Times-Union* 17 March 1992

12 The great story here . . . is this vast right-wing conspiracy that has been conspiring against my husband since the day he announced for president.
  interview on *Today* (NBC television), 27 January 1998

13 A hard dog to keep on the porch.
  on her husband
  in *Guardian* 2 August 1999

14 I'm in. And I'm in to win.
  announcing her campaign for the Democratic nomination for the Presidency on her website, www.hillaryclinton.com, 20 January 2007

William Jefferson ('Bill') Clinton 1946–
American Democratic statesman, 42nd President of
the US 1993–2001; husband of Hillary Rodham
Clinton
see also **Political sayings and slogans 257:21**

1 I experimented with marijuana a time or
two. And I didn't like it, and I didn't inhale.
in *Washington Post* 30 March 1992

2 The comeback kid!
*description of himself after coming second in the
New Hampshire primary in the 1992 presidential
election (since 1952, no presidential candidate
had won the election without first winning in
New Hampshire)*
Michael Barone and Grant Ujifusa *The
Almanac of American Politics 1994*

3 I did not have sexual relations with that
woman.
in a television interview, *Daily Telegraph*
(electronic edition) 27 January 1998

4 I did have a relationship with Ms Lewinsky
that was not appropriate. In fact, it was
wrong.
*broadcast to the American people, 18 August
1998*
in *Times* 19 August 1998

5 It depends on what the meaning of 'is' is.
*videotaped evidence to the grand jury; tapes
broadcast 21 September 1998*
in *Guardian* 22 September 1998

6 The American people have spoken—but
it's going to take a little while to determine
exactly what they said.
on the US presidential election of 2000; see also
Newspaper headlines 237:3
in *Mail on Sunday* 12 November 2000

7 I tried to walk a fine line between acting
lawfully and testifying falsely but I now
recognize that I did not fully accomplish
that goal.
in *Daily Telegraph* 20 January 2001

George Clooney 1961–
American actor and director
see also **Borrowed titles 40:12**

8 Directing is really exciting. In the end, it is
more fun to be the painter than the paint.
in *Independent* 27 December 2003

9 After September 30 you won't need the
UN. You will simply need men with shovels
and bleached white linen and headstones.
*on the situation in Darfur, urging the
deployment of a UN peacekeeping force*
addressing the United Nations Security
Council, 14 September 2006; see also **Wiesel
335:5**

Vernon Coaker 1953–
British Labour politician

10 Cameron's empty idea seems to be 'let's
hug a hoodie', whatever they have done.
commenting on the text of a forthcoming
speech by David Cameron: see **Cameron
51:10, Misquotations 224:9**; in *Observer*
9 July 2006

Kurt Cobain 1967–94
American rock singer, guitarist, and songwriter
see also **Young 347:5**

11 I'd rather be dead than cool.
'Stay Away' (1991 song)

Claud Cockburn 1904–81
British writer and journalist

12 Small earthquake in Chile. Not many dead.
*said by Cockburn to have been a winning entry
for a dullest headline competition at* The Times;
*almost certainly apocryphal as the headline has
never been traced*
In Time of Trouble (1956)

Jean Cocteau 1889–1963
French dramatist and film director
on Cocteau: see **Anonymous 12:12**

13 Life is a horizontal fall.
Opium (1930)

14 Being tactful in audacity is knowing how
far one can go too far.
Le Rappel à l'ordre (1926)

15 The worst tragedy for a poet is to be
admired through being misunderstood.
Le Rappel à l'ordre (1926)

16 If it has to choose who is to be crucified, the
crowd will always save Barabbas.
Le Rappel à l'ordre (1926)

J. M. Coetzee 1940–
South African novelist

17 When we dream that we are dreaming, the
moment of awakening is at hand.
In the Heart of the Country (1977)

George M. Cohan 1878–1942
American songwriter, dramatist, and producer

1 Over there, over there,
 Send the word, send the word over there
 That the Yanks are coming, the Yanks are
  coming,
 The drums rum-tumming everywhere.
 So prepare, say a prayer,
 Send the word, send the word to beware.
 We'll be over, we're coming over
 And we won't come back till it's over, over
  there.
  'Over There' (1917 song)

Leonard Cohen 1934–
Canadian singer and writer

2 I don't consider myself a pessimist. I think
 of a pessimist as someone who is waiting
 for it to rain. And I feel soaked to the skin.
  in *Observer* 2 May 1993

Stephen Colbert 1964–
American satirist

3 Truth that comes from the gut, not books.
  *definition of 'truthiness'; the word was later
  picked by the American Dialect Society for their
  Word of the Year 2005 and voted Merriam-
  Webster's Word of the Year for 2006*
   The Colbert Report 17 October 2005

4 I don't trust books. They're all fact, no
 heart.
  The Colbert Report 17 October 2005

David Coleman 1926–
British sports commentator

5 That's the fastest time ever run—but it's
 not as fast as the world record.
  Barry Fantoni (ed.) *Private Eye's Colemanballs
  3* (1986)

Michael Coleman
and **Brian Burke** *fl.* 1978
British songwriters and musicians

6 He painted matchstalk men and
 matchstalk cats and dogs.
  on L. S. Lowry
   'Matchstalk Men and Matchstalk Cats and
   Dogs' (1977 song)

Ornette Coleman 1930–
American jazz musician

7 Jazz is the only music in which the same
 note can be played night after night but
 differently each time.
  W. H. Mellers *Music in a New Found Land*
  (1964)

Colette 1873–1954
French novelist

8 The world of the emotions that are so
 lightly called physical.
  Le Blé en herbe (1923)

R. G. Collingwood 1889–1943
English philosopher and archaeologist

9 Perfect freedom is reserved for the man
 who lives by his own work and in that
 work does what he wants to do.
  Speculum Mentis (1924)

Charles Collins *fl.* 1919
English songwriter

10 My old man said, 'Follow the van,
 Don't dilly-dally on the way!'
  'Don't Dilly-Dally on the Way' (1919 song, with
  Fred Leigh); popularized by Marie Lloyd

Joan Collins 1933–
British actress

11 Older men treat women like possessions,
 which is why I like younger men.
  in *Times* 27 October 2001

Michael Collins 1890–1922
Irish revolutionary and chairman of the provisional
government of the Irish Free State

12 Think—what I have got for Ireland?
 Something which she has wanted these
 past seven hundred years. Will anyone be
 satisfied at the bargain? Will anyone? I tell
 you this—early this morning I signed my
 death warrant.
  *on signing the treaty establishing the Irish Free
  State; he was shot from ambush in the following
  year*
   letter, 6 December 1921

on arriving at Dublin Castle for the handover by British forces on 16 January 1922, and being told that he was seven minutes late:

1 We've been waiting seven hundred years, you can have the seven minutes.
    Tim Pat Coogan *Michael Collins* (1990); attributed

Phil Collins 1951–
British rock musician

2 I thought punk was a good idea—like someone shaking an apple tree until all the bad ones fell off and you'd just got the good ones left.
    D. Bowler and D. Dray *Genesis: a biography* (1992)

John Robert Colombo 1936–
Canadian writer

3 Canada could have enjoyed:
    English government,
    French culture,
    and American know-how.

    Instead it ended up with:
    English know-how,
    French government,
    and American culture.
        'O Canada' (1965)

Betty Comden 1917–2006
and Adolph Green 1915–2002
American songwriters

4 The party's over, it's time to call it a day.
    'The Party's Over' (1956 song); see **Crosland 80:10**

Ivy Compton-Burnett 1884–1969
English novelist

5 There are different kinds of wrong. The people sinned against are not always the best.
    The Mighty and their Fall (1961)

6 There is more difference within the sexes than between them.
    Mother and Son (1955)

Gerry Conlon 1954–
Northern Irish member of the Guildford Four, the first to be released from prison

7 The life sentence goes on. It's like a runaway train that you can't just get off.
    of life after his conviction was quashed by the Court of Appeal
        in *Irish Post* 13 September 1997

Sean Connery 1930–
Scottish actor

8 It is Scotland's rightful heritage that its people should create a modern Parliament . . . This entire issue is above and beyond any political party.
    of Scottish devolution, in the Referendum campaign
        speech in Edinburgh, 7 September 1997

Billy Connolly 1942–
Scottish comedian

9 Marriage is a wonderful invention; but, then again, so is a bicycle repair kit.
    Duncan Campbell *Billy Connolly* (1976)

10 I don't want a Stormont. I don't want a wee pretendy government in Edinburgh.
    on the prospective Scottish Parliament; often quoted as 'a wee pretendy Parliament'
        interview on *Breakfast with Frost* (BBC TV), 9 February 1997

11 When I read 'Be real, don't get caught acting,' I thought, 'How the hell do you do that?'
    John Miller *Judi Dench: With a Crack in Her Voice* (1998)

12 If you want to lose a bit of weight, don't eat anything out of a bucket.
    quoted in *NPR* (online edition) 10 May 2006

13 This is my second doctorate. I read that David Attenborough has 29, but I think two will do me.
    receiving an honorary degree from the Royal Scottish Academy of Music and Drama, in *Sunday Times* (online edition) 24 December 2006

Cyril Connolly 1903–74
English writer

14 As repressed sadists are supposed to become policemen or butchers, so those

with an irrational fear of life become publishers.
Enemies of Promise (1938)

1 Whom the gods wish to destroy they first call promising.
Enemies of Promise (1938)

2 There is no more sombre enemy of good art than the pram in the hall.
Enemies of Promise (1938)

3 I have called this style the Mandarin style, since it is beloved by literary pundits, by those who would make the written word as unlike as possible to the spoken one. It is the style of those writers whose tendency is to make their language convey more than they mean or more than they feel, it is the style of most artists and all humbugs.
Enemies of Promise (1938)

4 Imprisoned in every fat man a thin one is wildly signalling to be let out.
The Unquiet Grave (1944); see **Amis 8:5, Orwell 245:5**

5 Our memories are card-indexes consulted, and then put back in disorder by authorities whom we do not control.
during the Blitz
The Unquiet Grave (1944)

6 It is closing time in the gardens of the West and from now on an artist will be judged only by the resonance of his solitude or the quality of his despair.
in *Horizon* December 1949—January 1950

7 It is the one war in which everyone changes sides.
on the generation gap
Tom Driberg, speech in House of Commons, 30 October 1959

James Connolly 1868–1916
Irish labour leader and nationalist; executed after the Easter Rising, 1916

8 The worker is the slave of capitalist society, the female worker is the slave of that slave.
The Re-conquest of Ireland (1915)

Jimmy Connors 1952–
American tennis player

9 New Yorkers love it when you spill your guts out there. Spill your guts at

Wimbledon and they make you stop and clean it up.
at Flushing Meadow
in *Guardian* 24 December 1984 'Sports Quotes of the Year'

Joseph Conrad 1857–1924
Polish-born English novelist

10 The horror! The horror!
Kurtz's dying words
Heart of Darkness (1902)

11 The terrorist and the policeman both come from the same basket.
The Secret Agent (1907)

12 Reality, as usual, beats fiction out of sight.
commenting on 'this wartime atmosphere'
letter, 11 August 1915

Shirley Conran 1932–
English writer

13 Life is too short to stuff a mushroom.
Superwoman (1975)

14 Conran's Law of Housework—it expands to fill the time available plus half an hour.
Superwoman 2 (1977); see **Parkinson 250:12**

A. J. Cook 1885–1931
English labour leader; Secretary of the Miners' Federation of Great Britain, 1924–31

15 Not a penny off the pay, not a second on the day.
often quoted with 'minute' substituted for 'second'
speech at York, 3 April 1926

Robin Cook 1946–2005
British Labour politician
see also **Epitaphs 107:16**

16 Our foreign policy must have an ethical dimension and must support the demands of other people for the democratic rights on which we insist for ourselves.
mission statement by the new Foreign Secretary, 12 May 1997, origin of the phrase 'ethical foreign policy'
in *Times* 13 May 1997

17 On Iraq, I believe the prevailing mood of the British people is sound. They do not doubt that Saddam is a brutal dictator, but they are not persuaded that he is a clear

and present danger to Britain ... from the start of the present crisis, I have insisted, as Leader of the House, on the right of this place to vote on whether Britain should go to war ... I intend to join those tomorrow night who will vote against military action now. It is for that reason, and for that reason alone, and with a heavy heart, that I resign from the Government.
resignation speech in House of Commons, 17 March 2003

Calvin Coolidge 1872–1933
American Republican statesman, 30th President of the US 1923–9
on Coolidge: see **Anonymous 12:14, Parker 250:4**

1 There is no right to strike against the public safety by anybody, anywhere, any time.
telegram to Samuel Gompers, 14 September 1919

2 The chief business of the American people is business.
speech in Washington, 17 January 1925

3 I do not choose to run for President in nineteen twenty-eight.
statement issued at Rapid City, South Dakota, 2 August 1927

4 That man has offered me unsolicited advice for six years, all of it bad.
in 1928, when asked to support the Presidential nomination of his eventual successor **Herbert Hoover**
Donald R. McCoy *Calvin Coolidge: the Quiet President* (1967)

5 The political mind is the product of men in public life who have been twice spoiled. They have been spoiled with praise and they have been spoiled with abuse. With them nothing is natural, everything is artificial.
The Autobiography of Calvin Coolidge (1929)

when asked by Mrs Coolidge what a sermon had been about:
6 'Sins,' he said. 'Well, what did he say about sin?' 'He was against it.'
John H. McKee *Coolidge: Wit and Wisdom* (1933); perhaps apocryphal

7 They hired the money, didn't they?
on war debts incurred by England and others
J. H. McKee *Coolidge: Wit and Wisdom* (1933)

8 Nothing in the world can take the place of persistence. Talent will not; nothing is more common than unsuccessful men with talent. Genius will not; unrewarded genius is almost a proverb. Education will not; the world is full of educated derelicts. Persistence and determination are omnipotent. The slogan 'press on' has solved and always will solve the problems of the human race.
attributed in the programme of a memorial service for Coolidge in 1933

9 When a great many people are unable to find work, unemployment results.
attributed

Alice Cooper 1948–
American rock singer

10 The hippies wanted peace and love. We wanted Ferraris, blondes and switchblades.
in *Independent* 5 May 2001

11 I am past writing angst songs for kids. My angst is when I can't get my Porsche roof up and when I can't get my golf handicap down.
quoted in *Times* 27 October 2001

Duff Cooper 1890–1954
British Conservative politician and writer

12 Your two stout lovers frowning at one another across the hearth rug, while your small, but perfectly formed one kept the party in a roar.
letter to Lady Diana Manners, later his wife, October 1914
Artemis Cooper *Durable Fire* (1983)

Susie Cooper 1902–95
English ceramic designer and manufacturer

13 Pottery ... is a practical and lasting form of art. Not everyone can afford original paintings, but most people can afford pottery.
in *Evening Sentinel* 16 September 1971

14 The space you leave behind is as important as the space you fill.
Ann Eatwell and Andrew Casey (eds.) *Susie Cooper: a Pioneer of Modern Design* (2002)

Wendy Cope 1945–
English poet

1 Bloody men are like bloody buses—
You wait for about a year
And as soon as one approaches your stop
Two or three others appear.
'Bloody Men' (1992)

2 Making cocoa for Kingsley Amis.
title of poem (1986)

3 I used to think all poets were Byronic—
Mad, bad and dangerous to know.
And then I met a few. Yes it's ironic—
I used to think all poets were Byronic.
They're mostly wicked as a ginless tonic
And wild as pension plans.
'Triolet' (1986); referring to Lady Caroline
Lamb (1785–1828) writing of Byron in her
journal after their first meeting at a ball in
March 1812: 'Mad, bad, and dangerous to
know'

Aaron Copland 1900–90
American composer, pianist, and conductor

4 The whole problem can be stated quite
simply by asking, 'Is there a meaning to
music?' My answer to that would be, 'Yes.'
And 'Can you state in so many words what
the meaning is?' My answer to that would
be, 'No.'
What to Listen for in Music (1939)

Ralph Cornes

5 Computers are anti-Faraday machines. He
said he couldn't understand anything until
he could count it, while computers count
everything and understand nothing.
in Guardian 28 March 1991

Bernard Cornfeld 1927–95
Turkish-born American businessman

6 Do you sincerely want to be rich?
stock question to salesmen
C. Raw et al. Do You Sincerely Want to be Rich?
(1971)

Frances Cornford 1886–1960
English poet; wife of Francis M. Cornford

7 O fat white woman whom nobody loves,
Why do you walk through the fields in
gloves,

When the grass is soft as the breast of doves
And shivering-sweet to the touch?
O why do you walk through the fields in
gloves,
Missing so much and so much?
'To a Fat Lady seen from the Train' (1910)

Francis M. Cornford 1874–1943
English academic; husband of Frances Cornford

8 Every public action, which is not
customary, either is wrong, or, if it is right,
is a dangerous precedent. It follows that
nothing should ever be done for the first
time.
Microcosmographia Academica (1908)

9 That branch of the art of lying which
consists in very nearly deceiving your
friends without quite deceiving your
enemies.
on propaganda
Microcosmographia Academica (1922 ed.)

Baron Pierre de Coubertin 1863–1937
French sportsman and educationist

10 The important thing in life is not the
victory but the contest; the essential thing
is not to have won but to have fought well.
speech in London, 24 July 1908

Émile Coué 1857–1926
French psychologist

11 Every day, in every way, I am getting
better and better.
to be said 15 to 20 times, morning and evening
De la suggestion et de ses applications (1915)

Douglas Coupland 1961–
Canadian writer

12 Generation X: tales for an accelerated
culture.
title of book (1991)

Jacques Cousteau 1910–97
French naval officer and underwater explorer
see also **Epitaphs 107:2**

13 The sea is the universal sewer.
testimony before the House Committee on
Science and Astronautics, 28 January 1971

14 Mankind has probably done more damage
to the earth in the 20th century than in all

of previous human history.
'Consumer Society is the Enemy' in *New Perspectives Quarterly* Summer 1996

Noël Coward 1899–1973
English dramatist, actor, and composer

1 Dance, dance, dance, little lady!
Leave tomorrow behind.
'Dance, Little Lady' (1928 song)

2 Don't let's be beastly to the Germans
When our Victory is ultimately won.
'Don't Let's Be Beastly to the Germans' (1943 song)

3 I believe that since my life began
The most I've had is just
A talent to amuse.
'If Love Were All' (1929 song)

4 I'll see you again,
Whenever spring breaks through again.
'I'll See You Again' (1929 song)

5 London Pride has been handed down to us.
London Pride is a flower that's free.
London Pride means our own dear town to us,
And our pride it for ever will be.
'London Pride' (1941 song)

6 Mad about the boy,
It's pretty funny but I'm mad about the boy.
He has a gay appeal
That makes me feel
There may be something sad about the boy.
'Mad about the Boy' (1932 song)

7 Mad dogs and Englishmen
Go out in the midday sun.
The Japanese don't care to,
The Chinese wouldn't dare to,
The Hindus and Argentines sleep firmly from twelve to one,
But Englishmen detest a siesta.
'Mad Dogs and Englishmen' (1931 song)

8 Don't put your daughter on the stage, Mrs Worthington,
Don't put your daughter on the stage.
'Mrs Worthington' (1935 song)

9 Poor little rich girl
You're a bewitched girl,
Better beware!
'Poor Little Rich Girl' (1925 song)

10 Someday I'll find you,
Moonlight behind you,
True to the dream I am dreaming.
'Someday I'll Find You' (1930 song)

11 The Stately Homes of England,
How beautiful they stand,
To prove the upper classes
Have still the upper hand.
'The Stately Homes of England' (1938 song); echoing Felicia Hemans (1793–1835) 'The Homes of England' (1849): 'The stately homes of England, / How beautiful they stand! / Amidst their tall ancestral trees, / O'er all the pleasant land'

12 There are bad times just around the corner,
There are dark clouds travelling through the sky
And it's no good whining
About a silver lining
For we know from experience that they won't roll by.
'There are Bad Times Just Around the Corner' (1953 song)

13 Very flat, Norfolk.
Private Lives (1930)

14 Extraordinary how potent cheap music is.
Private Lives (1930)

15 Certain women should be struck regularly, like gongs.
Private Lives (1930)

16 Dear 338171 (May I call you 338?).
letter to T. E. Lawrence, 25 August 1930

17 Just say the lines and don't trip over the furniture.
advice on acting
D. Richards *The Wit of Noël Coward* (1968)

18 Television is for appearing on, not looking at.
D. Richards *The Wit of Noël Coward* (1968)

refusing to allow his biographer to out him as gay, despite the example of the theatre critic T. C. Worsley:

19 You forget that the great British public would not care if Cuthbert Worsley had slept with mice.
in *Independent on Sunday Magazine* 12 November 1995

Hart Crane 1899–1932
American poet

1 Stars scribble on our eyes the frosty sagas,
  The gleaming cantos of unvanquished
  space.
  'Cape Hatteras' (1930)

2 Cowslip and shad-blow, flaked like tethered
  foam
  Around bared teeth of stallions, bloomed
  that spring
  When first I read thy lines, rife as the loam
  Of prairies, yet like breakers cliffward
  leaping!
  . . . My hand
  in yours,
  Walt Whitman—
  so—
  'Cape Hatteras' (1930)

3 We have seen
  The moon in lonely alleys make
  A grail of laughter of an empty ash can.
  'Chaplinesque' (1926)

4   So the 20th Century—so
  whizzed the Limited—roared by and left
  three men, still hungry on the tracks,
  ploddingly
  watching the tail lights wizen and
  converge, slipping
  gimleted and neatly out of sight.
  'The River' (1930)

5 O Sleepless as the river under thee,
  Vaulting the sea, the prairies' dreaming
  sod,
  Unto us lowliest sometime sweep, descend
  And of the curveship lend a myth to God.
  'To Brooklyn Bridge' (1930)

6 You who desired so much—in vain to
  ask—
  Yet fed your hunger like an endless task,
  Dared dignify the labor, bless the quest—
  Achieved that stillness ultimately best,

  Being, of all, least sought for: Emily, hear!
  'To Emily Dickinson' (1927)

Robert Crawford 1959–
Scottish poet

7 In Scotland we live between and across
  languages.
  Identifying Poets (1993)

Edith Cresson 1934–
French politician and European Commissioner

8 *Je ne regrette rien.*
  I have no regrets.
  *on the inquiry into fraud at the European
  Commission*
    in an interview, 16 March 1999; see **Vaucaire
    324:5**

Francis Crick 1916–2004
English biophysicist. Together with James D. **Watson**
he proposed the double helix structure of the DNA
molecule
on Crick: see **Wolpert 341:2**

9 Almost all aspects of life are engineered
  at the molecular level, and without
  understanding molecules we can only
  have a very sketchy understanding of life
  itself.
  What Mad Pursuit (1988)

10 We have discovered the secret of life!
  on the discovery of the structure of DNA, 1953
  James D. Watson *The Double Helix* (1968)

Francis Crick 1916–2004 **and James D. Watson** 1928–
English biophysicist; American biologist

11 It has not escaped our notice that the
  specific pairing we have postulated
  immediately suggests a possible copying
  mechanism for the genetic material.
  *proposing the double helix as the structure of
  DNA, and hence the chemical mechanism of
  heredity*
    in *Nature* 25 April 1953

Quentin Crisp 1908–99
English writer

12 Euphemisms are unpleasant truths
  wearing diplomatic cologne.
  Manners from Heaven (1984)

13 There was no need to do any housework at
  all. After the first four years the dirt doesn't
  get any worse.
  The Naked Civil Servant (1968)

14 An autobiography is an obituary in serial
  form with the last instalment missing.
  The Naked Civil Servant (1968)

Julian Critchley 1930–2000
British Conservative politician and journalist

1 The only safe pleasure for a
parliamentarian is a bag of boiled sweets.
in Listener 10 June 1982

2 She cannot see an institution without
hitting it with her handbag.
of Margaret **Thatcher**
in Times 21 June 1982

Richmal Crompton 1890–1969
English writer of books for children

3 I'll thcream and thcream and thcream till
I'm thick. I can.
Violet Elizabeth's habitual threat
Still—William (1925)

David Cronenberg 1943–
Canadian film director
see also **Taglines for films 309:1**

4 Canadians are very reluctant to confront
the creature from the Black Lagoon—
which is our collective unconscious, really.
But that creature wants to come out.
in Maclean's 14 February 1983; attributed

5 Everybody's a mad scientist, and life is
their lab. We're all trying to experiment to
find a way to live, to solve problems, to
fend off madness and chaos.
Chris Rodley (ed.) *Cronenberg on Cronenberg*
(1992), ch. 1

6 I don't have a moral plan. I'm a Canadian.
attributed

Walter Cronkite 1916–
American broadcaster and journalist, anchorman for
CBS television, 1962–81
see also **Catchphrases 58:4**

7 It seems now more certain than ever that
the bloody experience of Vietnam is to end
in a stalemate.
after visiting Vietnam; see **Johnson 170:2**
CBS special television report, 27 February
1968; quoted in D. Halberstam *The Powers
That Be* (1979)

Bing Crosby 1903–77
American singer and film actor
on Crosby: see also **Epitaphs 107:14**

8 Where the blue of the night

Meets the gold of the day,
Someone waits for me.
'Where the Blue of the Night' (1931 song);
with Roy Turk and Fred Ahlert

Anthony Crosland 1918–77
British Labour politician

9 If it's the last thing I do, I'm going to
destroy every fucking grammar school in
England. And Wales, and Northern
Ireland.
*c.1965, while Secretary of State for Education
and Science*
Susan Crosland *Tony Crosland* (1982)

10 The party's over.
*cutting back central government's support for
rates, as Minister of the Environment in the
1970s*
Anthony Sampson *The Changing Anatomy of
Britain* (1982); see **Comden 74:4**

Amanda Cross (Carolyn Heilbrun)
1926–2003
American crime writer and academic

11 In former days, everyone found the
assumption of innocence so easy; today we
find fatally easy the assumption of guilt.
Poetic Justice (1970)

Douglas Cross
American songwriter

12 I left my heart in San Francisco
High on a hill it calls to me.
To be where little cable cars climb half-way
to the stars,
The morning fog may chill the air—
I don't care!
'I Left My Heart in San Francisco' (1954 song)

Richard Crossman 1907–74
British Labour politician

13 While there is death there is hope.
on the death of Hugh **Gaitskell** *in 1963*
Tam Dalyell *Dick Crossman* (1989)

14 The Civil Service is profoundly
deferential—'Yes, Minister! No, Minister!
If you wish it, Minister!'
diary, 22 October 1964

Aleister Crowley 1875–1947
English diabolist

1 Do what thou wilt shall be the whole of the Law.
> *Book of the Law* (1909); used earlier by François Rabelais (c.1494–c.1553) *Gargantua* (1534): 'Do what you like'

e. e. cummings 1894–1962
American poet

2 anyone lived in a pretty how town
(with up so floating many bells down)
spring summer autumn winter
he sang his didn't he danced his did.
> *50 Poems* (1949) no. 29

3 'next to of course god america i
love you land of the pilgrims' and so
forth oh
say can you see by the dawn's early my
country 'tis of centuries come and go
and are no more what of it we should
worry.
> *is 5* (1926)

4 a politician is an arse upon
which everyone has sat except a man.
> *1 x 1* (1944) no. 10

5 plato told
him: he couldn't
believe it (jesus
told him; he
wouldn't believe
it).
> *1 x 1* (1944) no. 13

6 pity this busy monster, manunkind,
not. Progress is a comfortable disease.
> *1 x 1* (1944) no. 14

7 We doctors know
a hopeless case if—listen: there's a hell
of a good universe next door; let's go.
> *1 x 1* (1944) no. 14

8 when man determined to destroy
himself he picked the was
of shall and finding only why
smashed it into because.
> *1 x 1* (1944) no. 26

9 i like my body when it is with your
body. It is so quite new a thing.
Muscles better and nerves more.
> 'Sonnets–Actualities' no. 8 (1925)

10 the Cambridge ladies who live in furnished
souls
are unbeautiful and have comfortable
minds.
> 'Sonnets–Realities' no. 1 (1923)

William Thomas Cummings 1903–45
American priest

11 There are no atheists in the foxholes.
> C. P. Romulo *I Saw the Fall of the Philippines* (1943)

Peter Cunnah
see **Jamie Petrie and Peter Cunnah**

Mario Cuomo 1932–
American Democratic politician, Governor of New York 1983–95

12 You campaign in poetry. You govern in prose.
> in *New Republic*, Washington, DC, 8 April 1985

Don Cupitt 1934–
British theologian

13 Christmas is the Disneyfication of Christianity.
> in *Independent* 19 December 1996

John Curtin 1885–1945
Australian Labor statesman, Prime Minister 1941–5

14 Australia looks to America, free of any
pangs as to our traditional links or kinship
with the United Kingdom.
> *of the threat from Japan, and British reluctance to recall Australian troops from the Middle East*
> in *Herald* (Melbourne) 27 December 1941

15 Poor Bob. It's very sad; he would rather
make a point than make a friend.
> *of Robert* **Menzies**
> Howard Beale *This Inch of Time* (1977); attributed

Tony Curtis 1925–
American actor

16 It's like kissing Hitler.
> *when asked what it was like to kiss Marilyn* **Monroe**
> A. Hunter *Tony Curtis* (1985)

Michael Curtiz 1888–1962
Hungarian-born American film director

1 Bring on the empty horses!
while directing The Charge of the Light Brigade
(*1936 film*)
  David Niven *Bring on the Empty Horses* (1975)

Lord Curzon 1859–1925
British Conservative politician; Viceroy of India
1898–1905

2 Not even a public figure. A man of no
experience. And of the utmost
insignificance.
of Stanley **Baldwin***, appointed Prime Minister in
1923 in succession to Bonar Law*
  Harold Nicolson *Curzon: the Last Phase* (1934)

3 Dear me, I never knew that the lower
classes had such white skins.
*supposedly said by Curzon when watching
troops bathing during the First World War*
  K. Rose *Superior Person* (1969)

4 Gentlemen do not take soup at luncheon.
  E. L. Woodward *Short Journey* (1942)

d

Dalai Lama 1935–

Tibetan Buddhist, spiritual head of Tibetan Buddhism and, until the establishment of Chinese communist rule, the spiritual and temporal ruler of Tibet. The present Dalai Lama escaped to India in 1959 following the Chinese invasion of Tibet and was awarded the Nobel Peace Prize in 1989

1 Frankly speaking it is difficult to trust the Chinese. Once bitten by a snake you feel suspicious even when you see a piece of rope.
    attributed, 1981

2 We are a part of humanity, so we should take care of humanity. And if we can't do that, then we should at least do no harm.
    interview in Mcleod Ganj, India, 27 February 2004

3 If you want others to be happy, practise compassion. If you want to be happy, practise compassion.
    attributed

Richard J. Daley 1902–76

American Democratic politician, Mayor of Chicago 1955–76

4 The policeman isn't there to create disorder; the policeman is there to preserve disorder.
    to the press, on the riots during the Democratic Convention at Chicago in 1968
        Milton N. Rakove *Don't Make No Waves: Don't Back No Losers* (1975)

Tam Dalyell 1932–

Scottish-born Labour politician

5 Under the new Bill, shall I still be able to vote on many matters in relation to West Bromwich but not West Lothian, as I was under the last Bill, and will my right hon. Friend [James Callaghan, MP for Cardiff] be able to vote on many matters in relation to Carlisle but not Cardiff?
    formulation of the 'West Lothian question', identifying the constitutional anomaly that would arise if devolved assemblies were established for Scotland and for Wales but not for England
        in the House of Commons, 3 November 1977

6 I make no apology for returning yet again to the subject of the sinking of the *Belgrano*.
    on the question of whether the Argentine cruiser Belgrano *had been a legitimate target in the Falklands War*
        in the House of Commons, 13 May 1983

Joe Darion 1917–2001

American songwriter

7 Dream the impossible dream.
    'The Quest' (1965 song) from the musical *Man of La Mancha*, based on Cervantes' *Don Quixote*

Bill Darnell

Canadian environmentalist

8 Make it a *green* peace.
    at a meeting of the Don't Make a Wave Committee, which preceded the formation of Greenpeace
        in Vancouver, 1970; Robert Hunter *The Greenpeace Chronicle* (1979); see **Hunter 160:12**

Charles Brace Darrow
see **Sayings and slogans 286:16**

Clarence Darrow 1857–1938
American lawyer, noted attorney for the defence

1 I do not consider it an insult, but rather a
compliment to be called an agnostic. I do
not pretend to know where many ignorant
men are sure—that is all that agnosticism
means.
> speech at trial of John Thomas Scopes for
> teaching Darwin's theory of evolution in
> school, 15 July 1925, popularly referred to as
> the 'Monkey Trial'

2 I would like to see a time when man loves
his fellow man and forgets his colour or his
creed. We will never be civilized until that
time comes. I know the Negro race has a
long road to go. I believe that the life of the
Negro race has been a life of tragedy, of
injustice, of oppression. The law has made
him equal, but man has not.
> speech in Detroit, 19 May 1926

3 When I was a boy I was told that anybody
could become President. I'm beginning to
believe it.
> Irving Stone *Clarence Darrow for the Defence*
> (1941)

Francis Darwin 1848–1925
English botanist; son of Charles Darwin

4 In science the credit goes to the man who
convinces the world, not to the man to
whom the idea first occurs.
> in *Eugenics Review* April 1914

Elizabeth David 1913–92
British cook and writer. She played a leading role in
introducing Mediterranean cuisine to Britain in the
1950s and 1960s

5 Good food is always a trouble and its
preparation should be regarded as a labour
of love.
> *French Country Cooking* (1951) introduction

6 The cooking of the Mediterranean shores,
endowed with all the natural resources,
the colour and flavour of the South, is a
blend of tradition and brilliant

improvisation. The Latin genius flashes
from the kitchen pans.
> *Mediterranean Food* (1950) introduction

Robertson Davies 1913–95
Canadian novelist

7 I see Canada as a country torn between a
very northern, rather extraordinary,
mystical spirit which it fears and its desire
to present itself to the world as a Scotch
banker.
> *The Enthusiasms of Robertson Davies* (1990)

Ron Davies 1946–
British Labour politician

8 It was a moment of madness for which I
have subsequently paid a very, very heavy
price.
> *of the episode on Clapham Common leading to*
> *his resignation as Welsh Secretary*
> interview with BBC Wales and HTV, 30 October
> 1998

W. H. Davies 1871–1940
Welsh poet

9 A rainbow and a cuckoo's song
May never come together again;
May never come
This side the tomb.
> 'A Great Time' (1914)

10 It was the Rainbow gave thee birth,
And left thee all her lovely hues.
> 'Kingfisher' (1910)

11 What is this life if, full of care,
We have no time to stand and stare.
> 'Leisure' (1911)

Bette Davis
see **Film lines 113:3, Film lines 113:8, Film lines
116:8**

Philip J. Davis 1923–
and **Reuben Hersh** 1927–
American mathematicians

12 One began to hear it said that World War I
was the chemists' war, World War II was

the physicists' war, World War III (may it never come) will be the mathematicians' war.
The Mathematical Experience (1981)

Sammy Davis Jnr. 1925–90
American entertainer, with Dean **Martin** and Frank Sinatra (1915–98) a member of the group of actors known as 'the Rat Pack'

1 Being a star has made it possible for me to get insulted in places where the average Negro could never *hope* to go and get insulted.
Yes I Can (1965)

Richard Dawkins 1941–
English evolutionary biologist and science writer

2 [Natural selection] has no vision, no foresight, no sight at all. If it can be said to play the role of watchmaker in nature, it is the *blind* watchmaker.
in this book Dawkins discussed evolution by natural selection and suggested that the theory could answer the fundamental question of why life exists
The Blind Watchmaker (1986); referring to William Paley (1743–1805) *Natural Theology* (1802): 'Suppose I had found a *watch* upon the ground, and it should be enquired how the watch happened to be in that place . . . the inference, we think, is inevitable; that the watch must have had a maker'

3 However many ways there may be of being alive, it is certain that there are vastly more ways of being dead.
The Blind Watchmaker (1986)

4 The essence of life is statistical improbability on a colossal scale.
The Blind Watchmaker (1986); see **Fisher 112:10**

5 The selfish gene.
title of book (1976)

6 They are in you and in me; they created us, body and mind; and their preservation is the ultimate rationale for our existence . . . they go by the name of genes, and we are their survival machines.
The Selfish Gene (1976)

Christopher Dawson 1889–1970
English historian of ideas and social culture

7 As soon as men decide that all means are permitted to fight an evil, then their good becomes indistinguishable from the evil that they set out to destroy.
The Judgement of the Nations (1942)

Lord Dawson of Penn 1864–1945
English doctor; physician to King George V
on Dawson: see **Moynihan 230:4**

8 The King's life is moving peacefully towards its close.
composed on a menu card, and based on what Dawson called the 'very commonplace' final bulletin on the king's father Edward VII in 1910
bulletin, 20 January 1936; K. Rose *King George V* (1983)

Robin Day 1923–2000
British broadcaster and journalist, noted especially as a political interviewer
on Day: see **Howerd 158:12**

9 I was never a journalist. I was always an institution.
in *Independent* 29 January 2000

Cecil Day-Lewis 1904–72
Anglo-Irish poet and critic

10 Tempt me no more; for I
Have known the lightning's hour,
The poet's inward pride,
The certainty of power.
The Magnetic Mountain (1933)

11 Tell them in England, if they ask
What brought us to these wars,
To this plateau beneath the night's
Grave manifold of stars—

It was not fraud or foolishness,
Glory, revenge, or pay:
We came because our open eyes
Could see no other way.
'The Volunteer' (1938)

12 It is the logic of our times,
No subject for immortal verse—
That we who lived by honest dreams
Defend the bad against the worse.
'Where are the War Poets?' (1943)

John Dean 1938–
American lawyer, White House Counsel during the Watergate affair

1 We have a cancer within, close to the Presidency, that is growing.
   from the [Nixon] Presidential Transcripts, 21 March 1973

Simone de Beauvoir 1908–86
French novelist and feminist

2 It is not in giving life but in risking life that man is raised above the animal; that is why superiority has been accorded in humanity not to the sex that brings forth but to that which kills.
   The Second Sex (1949)

3 One is not born a woman: one becomes one.
   The Second Sex (1949)

4 Few tasks are more like the torture of Sisyphus than housework, with its endless repetition . . . The housewife wears herself out marking time: she makes nothing, simply perpetuates the present.
   The Second Sex (1949)

Louis de Bernières 1954–
British novelist and short-story writer

5 The human heart likes a little disorder in its geometry.
   Captain Corelli's Mandolin (1994) ch. 26

6 The trouble with fulfilling your ambitions is you think you will be transformed into some sort of archangel and you're not. You still have to wash your socks.
   in *Independent* 14 February 1999

Edward de Bono 1933–
British writer and physician

7 Some people are aware of another sort of thinking which . . . leads to those simple ideas that are obvious only after they have been thought of . . . the term 'lateral thinking' has been coined to describe this other sort of thinking; 'vertical thinking' is used to denote the conventional logical process.
   The Use of Lateral Thinking (1967)

8 Unhappiness is best defined as the difference between our talents and our expectations.
   in *Observer* 12 June 1977

Guy Debord 1931–94
French philosopher

9 Villages, unlike towns, have always been ruled by conformism, isolation, petty surveillance, boredom and repetitive malicious gossip about the same families. Which is a precise enough description of the global spectacle's present vulgarity.
   on the concept of the 'global village'; see **McLuhan 208:9**
   Comments on the Society of the Spectacle (1988)

Régis Debray 1940–
French Marxist theorist

10 International life is right-wing, like nature. The social contract is left-wing, like humanity.
   Charles de Gaulle (1994)

Eugene Victor Debs 1855–1926
American socialist and labor organizer, presidential candidate in the four elections between 1900 and 1912

11 When great changes occur in history, when great principles are involved, as a rule the majority are wrong. The minority are right.
   speech at his trial for sedition in Cleveland, Ohio, 11 September 1918

12 While there is a lower class, I am in it; while there is a criminal element, I am of it; while there is a soul in prison, I am not free.
   speech at his trial for sedition, in Cleveland, Ohio, 14 September 1918

Sylvia Dee 1914–
American songwriter

13 Bring me sunshine in your smile
   Bring me laughter all the while.
   'Bring Me Sunshine' (1966 song, music by Arthur Kent), theme song of Eric Morecambe and Ernie Wise

Edgar Degas 1834–1917
French artist

1 Art is vice. You don't marry it legitimately, you rape it.
  P. Lafond *Degas* (1918)

Charles de Gaulle 1890–1970
French general and statesman, head of government 1944–6, President 1959–69. A wartime organizer of the Free French movement, he is remembered particularly for his assertive foreign policy and for quelling the student uprisings and strikes of May 1968
on de Gaulle: see **Spears 299:12**

2 France has lost a battle. But France has not lost the war!
  proclamation, 18 June 1940

3 Faced by the bewilderment of my countrymen, by the disintegration of a government in thrall to the enemy, by the fact that the institutions of my country are incapable, at the moment, of functioning, I General de Gaulle, a French soldier and military leader, realize that I now speak for France.
  speech in London, 19 June 1940

4 Since they whose duty it was to wield the sword of France have let it fall shattered to the ground, I have taken up the broken blade.
  speech, 13 July 1940

5 *Je vous ai compris.*
  I have understood you.
  to French settlers in Algeria; his later move to support for self-determination for the country was regarded by many of the colonial population as a betrayal
  speech at Algiers, 4 June 1958

6 Yes, it is Europe, from the Atlantic to the Urals, it is Europe, it is the whole of Europe, that will decide the fate of the world.
  speech to the people of Strasbourg, 23 November 1959

7 Politics are too serious a matter to be left to the politicians.
  *replying to **Attlee**'s remark that 'De Gaulle is a very good soldier and a very bad politician'*
  Clement Attlee *A Prime Minister Remembers* (1961); see **Clemenceau 71:7**

8 *Europe des patries.*
  A Europe of nations.
  widely associated with De Gaulle, c.1962, and taken as encapsulating his views, although perhaps not coined by him
  J. Lacouture *De Gaulle: the Ruler* (1991)

9 How can you govern a country which has 246 varieties of cheese?
  E. Mignon *Les Mots du Général* (1962)

10 Treaties, you see, are like girls and roses: they last while they last.
  speech at Elysée Palace, 2 July 1963

11 *Vive Le Québec Libre.*
  Long Live Free Quebec.
  controversial, as it appeared to support the separatist cause
  speech in Montreal, 24 July 1967

12 The sword is the axis of the world and its power is absolute.
  Vers l'armée de métier (1934)

13 *Toute ma vie, je me suis fait une certaine idée de la France.*
  All my life I have thought of France in a certain way.
  War Memoirs (1955) vol. 1, opening line

14 And now she is like everyone else.
  on the death in 1948 of his daughter Anne, who had been born with Down's syndrome
  Jean Lacouture *De Gaulle* (1965)

15 One does not put Voltaire in the Bastille.
  *when asked to arrest **Sartre**, in the 1960s*
  in *Encounter* June 1975

16 The EEC is a horse and carriage: Germany is the horse and France is the coachman.
  attributed; Bernard Connolly *The Rotten Heart of Europe* (1995)

Jimmy de Knight 1919–2001 **and Max Freedman** 1893–1962
American songwriters

17 (We're gonna) rock around the clock.
  title of song (1953), sung by Bill Haley (1925–81); this was the first song to popularize rock-and-roll

Walter de la Mare 1873–1956
English poet and novelist

1 Oh, no man knows
Through what wild centuries
Roves back the rose.
'All That's Past' (1912)

2 He is crazed with the spell of far Arabia,
They have stolen his wits away.
'Arabia' (1912)

3 Beauty vanishes; beauty passes;
However rare—rare it be.
'Epitaph' (1912)

4 Look thy last on all things lovely,
Every hour.
'Fare Well' (1918)

5 'Is there anybody there?' said the
Traveller,
Knocking on the moonlit door.
'The Listeners' (1912)

6 'Tell them I came, and no one answered,
That I kept my word,' he said.
'The Listeners' (1912)

7 Softly along the road of evening,
In a twilight dim with rose,
Wrinkled with age, and drenched with
dew,
Old Nod, the shepherd, goes.
'Nod' (1912)

8 Slowly, silently, now the moon
Walks the night in her silver shoon.
'Silver' (1913)

Shelagh Delaney 1939–
English dramatist

9 Women never have young minds. They are
born three thousand years old.
A Taste of Honey (1959)

Don DeLillo 1936–
American novelist

10 The thing that's interesting about living in
another country is that it's difficult to
forget you're an American. The actions of
the American Government won't let you.

They make you self-conscious.
interview in New York Times 10 October 1982

11 All plots tend to move deathward.
White Noise (1985)

Frederick Delius 1862–1934
English composer, of German and Scandinavian
descent

12 It is only that which cannot be expressed
otherwise that is worth expressing in
music.
in Sackbut September 1920 'At the
Crossroads'

Jerry Della Femina 1936–
American advertising executive

13 Advertising is the most fun you can have
with your clothes on.
From Those Wonderful Folks Who Gave You
Pearl Harbor (1971)

Jacques Delors 1925–
French socialist politician

14 The clash between those who believe and
those who don't believe will be a dominant
aspect of relations between the US and
Europe in the coming years.
quoted in Guardian 14 March 2005

Agnes De Mille 1908–93
American dancer and choreographer, niece of Cecil
B. De **Mille**

15 The truest expression of a people is in its
dances and its music. Bodies never lie.
in New York Times Magazine 11 May 1975

Cecil B. De Mille 1881–1959
American film producer, famous for his spectacular
epics, uncle of Agnes **De Mille**
on De Mille: see **Leisen 195:14**

16 When anyone told me that such and such
a thing could not be done, I got someone
who could do it.
in Photoplay October 1915

Adolph Zukor, Chairman of the Board at Paramount Pictures, had protested at the escalating costs of The Ten Commandments:

1 What do you want me to do? Stop shooting now and release it as *The Five Commandments?*
   M. LeRoy *Take One* (1974)

Jack Dempsey 1895–1983
American boxer, world heavyweight champion 1919–26

2 Honey, I just forgot to duck.
   to his wife, on losing the World Heavyweight title, 23 September 1926; after a failed attempt on his life in 1981, Ronald **Reagan** *quipped 'I forgot to duck'*
   J. and B. P. Dempsey *Dempsey* (1977)

Deng Xiaoping 1904–97
Chinese Communist statesman, paramount leader of China 1977–97
on Deng: see **Anonymous 13:2**

3 It doesn't matter if a cat is black or white, as long as it catches mice.
   in the early 1960s; in Daily Telegraph 20 February 1997, obituary

Lord Denning 1899–1999
British judge

4 The keystone of the rule of law in England has been the independence of judges. It is the only respect in which we make any real separation of powers.
   The Family Story (1981)

Jacques Derrida 1930–2004
Algerian-born French philosopher and critic, the most important figure in deconstructionism

5 *Il n'y a pas de hors-texte.*
   There is nothing outside of the text.
   Of Grammatology (1967)

Buddy De Sylva 1895–1950
and **Lew Brown** 1893–1958
American and Russian-born American songwriters

6 The moon belongs to everyone,
   The best things in life are free,
   The stars belong to everyone,
   They gleam there for you and me.
   'The Best Things in Life are Free' (1927 song)

Eamonn de Valera 1882–1975
American-born Irish statesman. He was leader of Sinn Fein 1917–26 (opposing the signing of the Anglo-Irish treaty in 1921) and founder of the Fianna Fáil Party in 1926. He was Taoiseach 1937–48, 1951–4, and 1957–9, and President of the Republic of Ireland 1959–73
on de Valera: see **Lloyd George 201:12**

7 Whenever I wanted to know what the Irish people wanted, I had only to examine my own heart and it told me straight off what the Irish people wanted.
   speech in Dáil Éireann, 6 January 1922

8 Further sacrifice of life would now be in vain . . . Military victory must be allowed to rest for the moment with those who have destroyed the Republic.
   message to the Republican armed forces, 24 May 1923

9 That Ireland which we dreamed of would be the home of a people who valued material wealth only as a basis of right living, of a people who were satisfied with frugal comfort and devoted their leisure to the things of the spirit; a land whose countryside would be bright with cosy homesteads, whose fields and villages would be joyous with sounds of industry, the romping of sturdy children, the contests of athletic youths, the laughter of comely maidens; whose firesides would be the forums of the wisdom of serene old age.
   St Patrick's Day broadcast, 17 March 1943

Peter De Vries 1910–93
American novelist and humorist

10 Gluttony is an emotional escape, a sign something is eating us.
   Comfort Me With Apples (1956)

11 The value of marriage is not that adults produce children but that children produce adults.
   The Tunnel of Love (1954)

Donald Dewar 1937–2000
Scottish Labour politician; First Minister for Scotland from 1999

12 'There shall be a Scottish parliament.' Through long years, those words were first

a hope, then a belief, then a promise. Now they are a reality.
at the official opening of the Scottish Parliament speech, 1 July 1999; see **Anonymous 12:11**

Lord Dewar 1864–1930
British industrialist

1 [There are] only two classes of pedestrians in these days of reckless motor traffic—the quick, and the dead.
George Robey *Looking Back on Life* (1933)

Thomas E. Dewey 1902–71
American Republican politician and presidential candidate
see also **Newspaper headlines 237:6**

2 That's why it's time for a change!
phrase used extensively in campaigns of 1944, 1948, and 1952
campaign speech in San Francisco, 21 September 1944

Sergei Diaghilev 1872–1929
Russian ballet impresario

3 *Étonne-moi.*
Astonish me.
to Jean **Cocteau**
W. Fowlie (ed.) *Journals of Jean Cocteau* (1956)

John Diamond 1953–2001
British journalist

4 In the face of such overwhelming statistical possibilities, hypochondria has always seemed to me to be the only rational position to take on life.
C: Because Cowards Get Cancer Too (1998)

Diana, Princess of Wales 1961–97
British princess, born Lady Diana Spencer, wife of **Charles,** Prince of Wales, 1981–96
on Diana: see **Blair 35:15, Burchill 47:15, Dowd 92:11, Duffy 93:8, Elizabeth II 104:8, John 168:11, Motion 229:13, Spencer 299:14**

5 I'd like to be a queen in people's hearts but I don't see myself being Queen of this country.
interview on *Panorama*, BBC1 TV, 20 November 1995

6 There were three of us in this marriage, so it was a bit crowded.
interview on *Panorama*, BBC1 TV, 20 November 1995

Philip K. Dick 1928–82
American science fiction writer and novelist

7 Reality is that which, when you stop believing in it, doesn't go away.
I Hope I Shall Arrive Soon (1986) 'How to Build a Universe That Doesn't Fall Apart Two Days Later'

Bo Diddley 1928–
American rock musician

8 I opened the door for a lot of people, and they just ran through and left me holding the knob.
in 1971; M. Wrenn *Bitch, Bitch, Bitch* (1988)

Joan Didion 1934–
American writer

9 Was there ever in anyone's life span a point free in time, devoid of memory, a night when choice was any more than the sum of all the choices gone before?
Run River (1963)

10 We tell ourselves stories in order to live.
The White Album (1979)

Marlene Dietrich 1901–92
German-born American actress and singer

11 Glamour is what I sell in my act and it costs plenty. It's my stock-in-trade.
in *Parade* 2 August 1959

Howard Dietz
see **Sayings and slogans 286:1**

Joe DiMaggio 1914–99
American baseball player, briefly married (in 1954) to Marilyn **Monroe**

12 A ball player's got to be kept hungry to become a big leaguer. That's why no boy

from a rich family ever made the big leagues.
in *New York Times* 30 April 1961

Isak Dinesen (Karen Blixen)
1885–1962
Danish novelist and short-story writer

1 A herd of elephant . . . pacing along as if they had an appointment at the end of the world.
Out of Africa (1937)

2 What is man, when you come to think upon him, but a minutely set, ingenious machine for turning, with infinite artfulness, the red wine of Shiraz into urine?
Seven Gothic Tales (1934) 'The Dreamers'

Paul Dirac 1902–84
British theoretical physicist

3 I think it is a general rule that the originator of a new idea is not the most suitable person to develop it, because his fears of something going wrong are really too strong.
The Development of Quantum Theory (1971)

4 It is more important to have beauty in one's equations than to have them fit experiment . . . It seems that if one is working from the point of view of getting beauty in one's equations, and if one has a really sound insight, one is on a sure line of progress. If there is not complete agreement between the results of one's work and experiment, one should not allow oneself to be too discouraged, because the discrepancy may well be due to minor features that are not properly taken into account and that will get cleared up with further developments of the theory.
in *Scientific American* May 1963

5 It is nice, but in one of the chapters the author made a mistake. He describes the sun as rising twice on the same day.
on the novel Crime and Punishment
G. Gamow *Thirty Years that Shook Physics* (1966)

Everett Dirksen 1896–1969
American Republican politician

6 A billion here and a billion there, and pretty soon you're talking real money.
on federal spending
attributed, perhaps apocryphal; in *United States Senate Historical Minute Essays* (online edition, July 2006)

Walt Disney 1901–66
American animator and film producer, who made his name with the creation of such cartoon characters as Mickey Mouse

7 I don't know, fellows, I guess I'm getting too old for animation.
on seeing rushes from The Jungle Book (*1967 film*)
Richard Schickel *The Disney Version* (1986)

8 Fancy being remembered around the world for the invention of a mouse!
during his last illness
Leonard Mosley *Disney's World* (1985)

Theodosius Dobzhansky 1900–75
Russian-born American geneticist

9 Nothing in biology makes sense, except in the light of evolution.
title of paper in *American Biology Teacher* March 1973

Tommy Docherty 1928–
Scottish footballer and football manager

10 George was a fantastic player and he would have been even better if he'd been able to pass nightclubs the way he passed the ball.
on George Best's drinking
in *Metro* 25 November 2005

Ken Dodd 1931–
British comedian

11 Freud's theory was that when a joke opens a window and all those bats and bogeymen fly out, you get a marvellous feeling of relief and elation. The trouble with Freud is that he never had to play the old Glasgow Empire on a Saturday night after Rangers and Celtic had both lost.
in *Guardian* 30 April 1991; quoted in many forms since the mid-1960s

J. P. Donleavy 1926–
Irish-American novelist

1 When you don't have any money, the problem is food. When you have money, it's sex. When you have both, it's health.
The Ginger Man (1955)

Mark Doty 1953–
American poet

2 and I swear sometimes
when I put my head to his chest
I can hear the virus humming

like a refrigerator.
'Atlantis' (1996)

Keith Douglas 1920–44
English poet and soldier, killed three days after the Normandy landings in the Second World War

3 And all my endeavours are unlucky explorers
come back, abandoning the expedition.
'On Return from Egypt, 1943–4' (1946)

4 Remember me when I am dead
And simplify me when I'm dead.
'Simplify me when I'm Dead' (1941)

5 For here the lover and killer are mingled
who had one body and one heart.
And death, who had the soldier singled
has done the lover mortal hurt.
'Vergissmeinnicht, 1943'

Norman Douglas 1868–1952
Scottish-born novelist and essayist

6 To find a friend one must close one eye. To keep him—two.
Almanac (1941)

7 You can tell the ideals of a nation by its advertisements.
South Wind (1917)

O. Douglas (Anna Buchan) 1877–1948
Scottish writer, sister of John **Buchan**

8 It is wonderful how much news there is when people write every other day; if they wait for a month, there is nothing that seems worth telling.
Penny Plain (1920)

9 I know heaps of quotations, so I can always make quite a fair show of knowledge.
The Setons (1917)

William O. Douglas 1898–1980
American lawyer and Supreme Court Justice

10 Free speech is not to be regulated like diseased cattle and impure butter. The audience . . . that hissed yesterday may applaud today, even for the same performance.
dissenting opinion in *Kingsley Books, Inc. v. Brown* 1957

Maureen Dowd 1952–
American journalist

11 The Princess of Wales was the queen of surfaces, ruling over a kingdom where fame was the highest value and glamour the most cherished attribute.
in *New York Times* 3 September 1997

Arthur Conan Doyle 1859–1930
Scottish-born writer of detective fiction, creator of Sherlock Holmes
see also **Misquotations 224:6**

12 Matilda Briggs . . . was a ship which is associated with the giant rat of Sumatra, a story for which the world is not yet prepared.
The Case-Book of Sherlock Homes (1927)

13 Good old Watson! You are the one fixed point in a changing age.
His Last Bow (1917)

14 The charlatan is always the pioneer. From the astrologer came the astronomer, from the alchemist the chemist, from the mesmerist the experimental psychologist. The quack of yesterday is the professor of tomorrow.
Tales of Terror and Mystery (1922) 'The Leather Funnel'

Roddy Doyle 1958–
Irish novelist

15 I said one Hail Mary and four Our Fathers, because I preferred the Our Fathers to the Hail Mary and it was longer and better.
Paddy Clarke Ha Ha Ha (1993)

Margaret Drabble 1939–
English novelist, sister of A. S. **Byatt**
see also **Borrowed titles 41:6**

1 England's not a bad country . . . It's just a mean, cold, ugly, divided, tired, clapped-out, post-imperial, post-industrial slag-heap covered in polystyrene hamburger cartons.
A Natural Curiosity (1989)

2 Perhaps the rare and simple pleasure of being seen for what one is compensates for the misery of being it.
A Summer Bird-Cage (1963)

Richard Drew
American photojournalist

3 I didn't capture his death. I captured part of his life.
of the picture of a man falling head first from the World Trade Center, 11 September 2001, known as 'The Falling Man'; see also **Anonymous 11:16**
quoted in Peter Howe 'Richard Drew' in *Digital Journalist* 2001 (online edition)

John Drinkwater 1882–1937
English poet and dramatist

4　　　Deep is the silence, deep
On moon-washed apples of wonder.
'Moonlit Apples' (1917)

Alexander Dubček 1921–92
Czechoslovak statesman, First Secretary of the Czechoslovak Communist Party 1968–9 (he was removed from office in the wake of the Soviet invasion of August 1968)

5 In the service of the people we followed such a policy that socialism would not lose its human face.
describing the 'Prague Spring' of 1968, a brief period of liberalization initiating a programme of political, economic, and cultural reform, which was ended by the invasion of Soviet and Warsaw Pact troops in August 1968
in *Rudé Právo* 19 July 1968

W. E. B. Du Bois 1868–1963
American social reformer and political activist, a founder of the National Association for the Advancement of Coloured People (NAACP). In 1963 he became a citizen of Ghana

6 The problem of the twentieth century is the problem of the colour line—the relation of the darker to the lighter races of men in Asia and Africa, in America and the islands of the sea.
The Souls of Black Folk (1905)

7 One thing alone I charge you. As you live, believe in life! Always human beings will live and progress to greater, broader and fuller life. The only possible death is to lose belief in this truth simply because the great end comes slowly, because time is long.
last message, written 26 June, 1957, and read at his funeral, 1963

Carol Ann Duffy 1965–
English poet

8 Whatever 'in love' means,
true love is talented.
Someone vividly gifted in love has gone.
on the death of **Diana**, *Princess of Wales*
'September, 1997' (1997); see **Charles 63:15**

John Foster Dulles 1888–1959
American international lawyer and politician. He was the US adviser at the founding of the United Nations in 1945 and negotiated the peace treaty with Japan in 1951

9 The ability to get to the verge without getting into the war is the necessary art . . . We walked to the brink and we looked it in the face.
origin of the term 'brinkmanship'
in *Life* 16 January 1956; see **Stevenson 304:12**

Daphne Du Maurier 1907–89
English novelist

10 Last night I dreamt I went to Manderley again.
Rebecca (1938), opening line

Paul Lawrence Dunbar 1872–1906
American poet

1 I know why the caged bird sings!
*adopted by Maya **Angelou** as the title of her
autobiography, 1969; see **Angelou 9:3***
    'Sympathy' st. 3; referring to John Webster
    (c.1580–c.1625) *The White Devil* (1612) act 5,
    sc. 4: 'We think caged birds sing, when indeed
    they cry'

Isadora Duncan
see **Last words 190:3**

Ronald Duncan 1914–82
English dramatist

2 Where in this wide world can man find
        nobility without pride,
    Friendship without envy, or beauty
        without vanity?
    'In Praise of the Horse' (1962)

Ian Dunlop 1940–
British art historian

3 The shock of the new.
    title of 1972 book about modern art (the full
    title was *The Shock of the New: Seven Historic
    Exhibitions of Modern Art*)

Helen Dunmore 1952–
British poet and novelist

4 That killed head straining through the
        windscreen
    with its frill of bubbles in the eye-sockets
    is not trying to tell you something—
    it is telling you something.
    'Poem on the Obliteration of 100,000 Iraqi
    Soldiers' (1994)

Douglas Dunn 1942–
Scottish poet

5 In a country like this
    Our ghosts outnumber us . . .
    'At Falkland Palace' (1988)

6 My poems should be Clyde-built, crude and
        sure,
    With images of those dole-deployed
    To honour the indomitable Reds,
    Clydesiders of slant steel and angled
        cranes;
    A poetry of nuts and bolts, born, bred,

Embattled by the Clyde, tight and impure.
    'Clydesiders' (1974)

7 Look to the living, love them, and hold on.
    in 'Disenchantments' (1993)

Irina Dunn
Australian writer and politician

8 A woman needs a man like a fish needs a
    bicycle.
    graffito written 1970; attributed by Gloria
    Steinem in *Time* 9 October 2000; see **Sayings
    287:13**

Leo Durocher 1906–91
American baseball coach

9 Nice guys. Finish last.
    *casual remark at a practice ground, July 1946
    Nice Guys Finish Last (as the remark generally
    is quoted, 1975)*

Lawrence Durrell 1912–90
English novelist, poet, and travel writer

10 I love to feel events overlapping each other,
    crawling over one another like wet crabs in
    a basket.
    Balthazar (1958)

Friedrich Dürrenmatt 1921–
Swiss writer

11 What was once thought can never be
    unthought.
    The Physicists (1962)

Ian Dury 1942–2000
British rock singer and songwriter

12 Sex and drugs and rock and roll.
    title of song (1977)

Robert Duvall
see **Film lines 114:7**

Andrea Dworkin 1946–2005
American feminist and writer

13 Seduction is often difficult to distinguish
    from rape. In seduction, the rapist bothers
    to buy a bottle of wine.
    in 1976; *Letters from a War Zone* (1988)

Bob Dylan 1941–

American singer and songwriter. The leader of an
urban folk-music revival in the 1960s, he became
known for political and protest songs
on Dylan: see **Baez 20:7**

1 How many roads must a man walk down
  Before you can call him a man? . . .
  The answer, my friend, is blowin' in the
    wind,
  The answer is blowin' in the wind.
    'Blowin' in the Wind' (1962 song)

2 They're selling postcards of the hanging.
    'Desolation Row' (1965)

3 And someone says, You're in the wrong
    place, my friend
  You better leave.'
    'Desolation Row' (1965)

4 Don't think twice, it's all right.
    title of song (1963)

5 I saw ten thousand talkers whose tongues
    were all broken,
  I saw guns and sharp swords, in the hands
    of young children . . .
  And it's a hard rain's a gonna fall.
    'A Hard Rain's A Gonna Fall' (1963 song)

6 Money doesn't talk, it swears.
    'It's Alright, Ma (I'm Only Bleeding)' (1965
    song)

7 She takes just like a woman, yes, she does
  She makes love just like a woman, yes, she
    does
  And she aches just like a woman
  But she breaks like a little girl.
    'Just Like a Woman' (1966 song)

8 How does it feel
  To be on your own
  With no direction home
  Like a complete unknown
  Like a rolling stone?
    'Like a Rolling Stone' (1965 song)

9 She knows there's no success like failure
  And that failure's no success at all.
    'Love Minus Zero / No Limit' (1965 song)

10 Hey! Mr Tambourine Man, play a song for
    me.
  I'm not sleepy and there is no place I'm
    going to.
    'Mr Tambourine Man' (1965 song)

11 Ah, but I was so much older then,
  I'm younger than that now.
    'My Back Pages' (1964 song)

12 Señor, señor, do you know where we're
    headin'?
  Lincoln County Road or Armageddon?
    'Señor (Tale of Yankee Power)' (1978 song)

13 All that foreign oil controlling American
    soil.
    'Slow Train' (1979 song)

14 Come mothers and fathers,
  Throughout the land
  And don't criticize
  What you can't understand.
  Your sons and your daughters
  Are beyond your command
  Your old road is
  Rapidly agin'
  Please get out of the new one
  If you can't lend your hand
  For the times they are a-changin'!
    'The Times They Are A-Changing' (1964 song)

15 But I can't think for you
  You'll have to decide,
  Whether Judas Iscariot
  Had God on his side.
    'With God on our Side' (1963 song)

16 It was like a flying saucer landed. That's
  what the sixties were like. Everybody heard
  about it, but only a few really saw it.
    James Miller *Almost Grown: the Rise of Rock*
    (1999)

e

J. W. Eagan

1 Never judge a book by its movie.
   attributed; Michael Lent *Breakfast with Sharks* (2004)

Amelia Earhart 1898–1937
American aviator, first woman to fly the Atlantic solo; her aircraft disappeared over the Pacific Ocean during a subsequent round-the-world flight with the loss of Earhart and her navigator

2 Would you *mind* if I flew the Atlantic?
   to her husband George Putnam; George P. Putnam *Soaring Wings* (1939)

3 The best mascot is a good mechanic.
   Mary S. Lovell *The Sound of Wings* (1989)

George Eastman 1854–1932
American inventor, philanthropist, and founder of Eastman Kodak (he also created the 1888 slogan, 'You press the button, we do the rest')

4 The rich man never really gives anything, he only distributes part of the surplus. It is the person of moderate means who really gives.
   to the *Boston Post*; in *American National Biography* (online edition)

Clint Eastwood
see **Film lines 113:12**

Abba Eban 1915–2002
Israeli diplomat

5 History teaches us that men and nations behave wisely once they have exhausted all other alternatives.
   speech in London, 16 December 1970

Arthur Eddington 1882–1944
English astronomer, considered the founder of astrophysics

6 I shall use the phrase 'time's arrow' to express this one-way property of time which has no analogue in space.
   The Nature of the Physical World (1928)

7 If an army of monkeys were strumming on typewriters they *might* write all the books in the British Museum.
   The Nature of the Physical World (1928); see **Wilensky 335:17**

8 If someone points out to you that your pet theory of the universe is in disagreement with Maxwell's equations—then so much the worse for Maxwell's equations. If it is found to be contradicted by observation—well, these experimentalists do bungle things sometimes. But if your theory is found to be against the second law of thermodynamics I can give you no hope; there is nothing for it but to collapse in deepest humiliation.
   The Nature of the Physical World (1928)

9 I am standing on the threshold about to enter a room. It is a complicated business. In the first place I must shove against an atmosphere pressing with a force of fourteen pounds on every square inch of my body. I must make sure of landing on a plank travelling at twenty miles a second round the sun— a fraction of a second too early or too late, the plank would be miles away. I must do this whilst hanging from a round planet, head outward into space,

and with a wind of aether blowing at no
one knows how many miles a second
through every interstice of my body.
The Nature of the Physical World (1928)

1 I ask you to look both ways. For the road to
a knowledge of the stars leads through the
atom; and important knowledge of the
atom has been reached through the stars.
Stars and Atoms (1928)

2 Science is an edged tool, with which men
play like children, and cut their own
fingers.
attributed; R. L. Weber *More Random Walks in
Science* (1982)

Anthony Eden 1897–1977
British Conservative statesman, Prime Minister
1955–7; husband of Clarissa **Eden**. His premiership
was dominated by the Suez crisis of 1956;
widespread opposition to Britain's role in this led to
his resignation
on Eden: see **Butler 49:11**, **Churchill 67:9**,
Muggeridge 230:11

3 We are in an armed conflict; that is the
phrase I have used. There has been no
declaration of war.
on the Suez crisis
speech in the House of Commons, 1 November
1956

Clarissa Eden 1920–
British wife of Anthony **Eden**

4 For the past few weeks I have really felt as if
the Suez Canal was flowing through my
drawing room.
speech at Gateshead, 20 November 1956

Marriott Edgar 1880–1951
British actor and writer

5 There's a famous seaside place called
Blackpool,
That's noted for fresh air and fun,
And Mr and Mrs Ramsbottom
Went there with young Albert, their son.
'The Lion and Albert' (1932 monologue)

Edward VIII (Duke of Windsor)
1894–1972
British monarch, King of the United Kingdom, 1936
(from the death of his father **George V** until his own
abdication); husband of the Duchess of **Windsor**
on Edward: see **Anonymous 10:15**, **Beaverbrook
25:5**, **Blunt 37:7**, **George V 131:6**, **Farjeon 109:7**,
Mary 216:9; see also **Misquotations 225:4**

6 At long last I am able to say a few words of
my own . . . you must believe me when I
tell you that I have found it impossible to
carry the heavy burden of responsibility
and to discharge my duties as King as I
would wish to do without the help and
support of the woman I love.
following his abdication
radio broadcast, 11 December 1936

7 The thing that impresses me most about
America is the way parents obey their
children.
in *Look* 5 March 1957

Barbara Ehrenreich 1941–
American sociologist and writer

8 Exercise is the yuppie version of bulimia.
The Worst Years of Our Lives (1991) 'Food
Worship'

Paul Ralph Ehrlich 1932–
American biologist

9 The first rule of intelligent tinkering is to
save all the parts.
in *Saturday Review* 5 June 1971

John Ehrlichman 1925–99
American Presidential assistant to Richard **Nixon**; in
1976 he was jailed for his part in the Watergate
affair

10 I think we ought to let him hang there. Let
him twist slowly, slowly in the wind.
*Nixon had withdrawn his support for Patrick
Gray, nominated as director of the FBI, although
Gray himself had not been informed*
in *Washington Post* 27 July 1973

Max Ehrmann 1872–1945
American writer

1 Go placidly amid the noise and the haste,
   and remember what peace there may be
   in silence.
   often wrongly dated to 1692, the date of
   foundation of a church in Baltimore whose vicar
   circulated the poem in 1956
   'Desiderata' (1948)

Adolf Eichmann 1906–62
German Nazi administrator who was responsible for
administering the concentration camps. In 1960 he
was traced by Israeli agents and executed after trial
in Israel
on Eichmann: see **Arendt 14:5**

2 Today, 15 years after 8 May 1945, I know
   . . . that a life of obedience, led by orders,
   instructions, decrees and directives, is a
   very comfortable one in which one's
   creative thinking is diminished.
   memoirs, in *Independent* 13 August 1999

Albert Einstein 1879–1955
German-born theoretical physicist; originator of the
theory of relativity
on Einstein: see **Picasso 254:7, Squire 301:7**

3 Science without religion is lame, religion
   without science is blind.
   Science, Philosophy and Religion (1941)

4 $E = mc^2$.
   this statement of the equivalency of mass and
   energy—energy equals mass times the speed of
   light squared—derives from the special theory
   of relativity, and is the usual form of Einstein's
   original words: 'If a body releases the energy L
   in the form of radiation, its mass is decreased by
   L/V^2'
   in *Annalen der Physik* 18 (1905)

5 God is subtle but he is not malicious.
   remark made during a week at Princeton
   beginning 9 May 1921, later carved above the
   fireplace of the Common Room of Fine Hall
   (the Mathematical Institute), Princeton
   University

6 I am convinced that *He* [God] does not play
   dice.
   letter to Max Born, 4 December 1926

7 I am an absolute pacifist . . . It is an
   instinctive feeling. It is a feeling that

possesses me, because the murder of men is
disgusting.
   interview with Paul Hutchinson, in *Christian*
   Century 28 August 1929

8 If my theory of relativity is proven correct,
   Germany will claim me as a German and
   France will declare that I am a citizen of the
   world. Should my theory prove untrue,
   France will say that I am a German and
   Germany will declare that I am a Jew.
   address at the Sorbonne, Paris, possibly
   early December 1929, in *New York Times*
   16 February 1930

9 I never think of the future. It comes soon
   enough.
   in an interview, given on the *Belgenland*,
   December 1930

10 I am not only a pacifist but a militant
   pacifist. I am willing to fight for peace.
   Nothing will end war unless the people
   themselves refuse to go to war.
   interview with G. S. Viereck, January 1931

11 As a human being, one has been endowed
   with just enough intelligence to be able to
   see clearly how utterly inadequate that
   intelligence is when confronted with what
   exists.
   letter to Queen Elisabeth of Belgium,
   19 September 1932

12 The eternal mystery of the world is its
   comprehensibility . . . The fact that it is
   comprehensible is a miracle.
   usually quoted as 'The most incomprehensible
   fact about the universe is that it is
   comprehensible'
   in *Franklin Institute Journal* March 1936
   'Physics and Reality'

13 Some recent work by E. Fermi and L.
   Szilard, which has been communicated to
   me in manuscript, leads me to expect that
   the element uranium may be turned into a
   new and important source of energy in the
   immediate future. Certain aspects of the
   situation which has arisen seem to call for
   watchfulness and, if necessary, quick
   action on the part of the Administration.
   warning of the possible development of an
   atomic bomb, and leading to the setting up of
   the Manhattan Project
   letter to Franklin **Roosevelt**, 2 August 1939,
   drafted by Leo Szilard and signed by Einstein

1 The unleashed power of the atom has changed everything save our modes of thinking and we thus drift toward unparalleled catastrophe.
>   telegram to prominent Americans, 24 May 1946

2 If *A* is a success in life, then *A* equals *x* plus *y* plus *z*. Work is *x*; *y* is play; and *z* is keeping your mouth shut.
>   in *Observer* 15 January 1950

3 Common sense is nothing more than a deposit of prejudices laid down in the mind before you reach eighteen.
>   Lincoln Barnett *The Universe and Dr Einstein* (1950 ed.)

4 The grand aim of all science [is] to cover the greatest number of empirical facts by logical deduction from the smallest possible number of hypotheses or axioms.
>   Lincoln Barnett *The Universe and Dr Einstein* (1950 ed.)

5 If I would be a young man again and had to decide how to make my living, I would not try to become a scientist or scholar or teacher. I would rather choose to be a plumber or a peddler in the hope to find that modest degree of independence still available under present circumstances.
>   in *Reporter* 18 November 1954

6 The distinction between past, present and future is only an illusion, however persistent.
>   letter to Michelangelo Besso, 21 March 1955

7 One must divide one's time between politics and equations. But our equations are much more important to me.
>   C. P. Snow 'Einstein'; M. Goldsmith et al. (eds.) *Einstein* (1980)

8 Nationalism is an infantile sickness. It is the measles of the human race.
>   Helen Dukas and Banesh Hoffman *Albert Einstein, the Human Side* (1979)

9 When I was young, I found out that the big toe always ends up making a hole in a sock. So I stopped wearing socks.
>   to Philippe Halsman; A. P. French *Einstein: A Centenary Volume* (1979)

Loren Eiseley 1907–77
American anthropologist, educator, and writer

10 Every man contains within himself a ghost continent—a place circled as warily as Antarctica was circled two hundred years ago by Captain James Cook.
>   *The Unexpected Universe* (1969)

Dwight D. Eisenhower 1890–1969
American soldier and Republican statesman, Supreme Commander Allied Expeditionary Forces 1943–5, and 34th President of the US 1953–61
on Eisenhower: see **Joplin 171:5, Political sayings and slogans 257:17**

11 Humility must always be the portion of any man who receives acclaim earned in the blood of his followers and the sacrifices of his friends.
>   speech at the London Guildhall, 12 June 1945

12 Every gun that is made, every warship launched, every rocket fired signifies, in the final sense, a theft from those who hunger and are not fed, those who are cold and are not clothed. This world in arms is not spending money alone. It is spending the sweat of its labourers, the genius of its scientists, the hopes of its children.
>   speech in Washington, 16 April 1953

13 I just will not—I *refuse*—to get into the gutter with that guy.
>   *explaining why he did not try to restrain Senator* **McCarthy**
>   in 1953; in *American National Biography* (online edition) 'Joseph McCarthy'

14 You have broader considerations that might follow what you might call the 'falling domino' principle. You have a row of dominoes set up. You knock over the first one, and what will happen to the last one is that it will go over very quickly.
>   *a few weeks before the fall of the French military post at Dien Bien Phu in NW Vietnam, which was captured by the Vietminh in May 1945 after a 55-day siege*
>   speech at press conference, 7 April 1954

15 I think that people want peace so much that one of these days governments had better get out of the way and let them have it.
>   broadcast discussion, 31 August 1959

1 No easy problems ever come to the
President of the United States. If they are
easy to solve, somebody else has solved
them.
   in *Parade Magazine* 8 April 1962

2 In preparing for battle I have always found
that plans are useless, but planning is
indispensable.
   Richard Nixon *Six Crises* (1962); attributed

Alfred Eisenstaedt 1898–1995
German-born American photographer and
photojournalist

3 It's more important to click with people
than to click the shutter.
   in *Life* 24 August 1995 (electronic edition),
   obituary

T. S. Eliot 1888–1965
American-born British poet, critic, and dramatist
on Eliot: see **Elizabeth 104:4, Leavis 194:7, Lewis
199:6**

4 Because I do not hope to turn again
Because I do not hope
Because I do not hope to turn.
   Ash-Wednesday (1930) pt. 1

5 Teach us to care and not to care
Teach us to sit still.
   Ash-Wednesday (1930) pt. 1

6 Lady, three white leopards sat under a
   juniper-tree
In the cool of the day.
   Ash-Wednesday (1930) pt. 2

7 What is hell?
Hell is oneself,
Hell is alone, the other figures in it
Merely projections.
   The Cocktail Party (1950)

8 Success is relative:
It is what we can make of the mess we have
   made of things.
   The Family Reunion (1939)

9 Round and round the circle
Completing the charm
So the knot be unknotted
The cross be uncrossed
The crooked be made straight
And the curse be ended.
   The Family Reunion (1939)

10 Time present and time past

Are both perhaps present in time future,
And time future contained in time past.
   Four Quartets 'Burnt Norton' (1936) pt. 1

11 Footfalls echo in the memory
Down the passage which we did not take
Towards the door we never opened
Into the rose-garden.
   Four Quartets 'Burnt Norton' (1936) pt. 1

12   Human kind
Cannot bear very much reality.
   Four Quartets 'Burnt Norton' (1936) pt. 1.

13 At the still point of the turning world.
   Four Quartets 'Burnt Norton' (1936) pt. 2

14   Words strain,
Crack and sometimes break, under the
   burden,
Under the tension, slip, slide, perish,
Decay with imprecision, will not stay in
   place,
Will not stay still.
   Four Quartets 'Burnt Norton' (1936) pt. 5

15 In my beginning is my end.
   Four Quartets 'East Coker' (1940) pt. 1;
   compare Mary, Queen of Scots (1542–87)
   motto: 'In my end is my beginning'

16 That was a way of putting it—not very
   satisfactory:
A periphrastic study in a worn-out poetical
   fashion,
Leaving one still with the intolerable
   wrestle
With words and meanings.
   Four Quartets 'East Coker' (1940) pt. 2

17 The houses are all gone under the sea.
The dancers are all gone under the hill.
   Four Quartets 'East Coker' (1940) pt. 2

18 O dark dark dark. They all go into the dark,
The vacant interstellar spaces, the vacant
   into the vacant.
   Four Quartets 'East Coker' (1940) pt. 3

19 The wounded surgeon plies the steel
That questions the distempered part;
Beneath the bleeding hands we feel
The sharp compassion of the healer's art
Resolving the enigma of the fever chart.
   Four Quartets 'East Coker' (1940) pt. 4

20 Trying to learn to use words, and every
   attempt

Is a wholly new start, and a different kind
of failure.
Four Quartets 'East Coker' (1940) pt. 5

1 I do not know much about gods; but I
think that the river
Is a strong brown god.
Four Quartets 'The Dry Salvages' (1941) pt. 1

2 We had the experience but missed the
meaning.
Four Quartets 'The Dry Salvages' (1941) pt. 2

3 And what the dead had no speech for,
when living,
They can tell you, being dead: the
communication
Of the dead is tongued with fire beyond the
language of the living.
Four Quartets 'Little Gidding' (1942) pt. 1

4 Ash on an old man's sleeve
Is all the ash the burnt roses leave.
Four Quartets 'Little Gidding' (1942) pt. 2

5 The death of hope and despair,
This is the death of air.
Four Quartets 'Little Gidding' (1942) pt. 2

6 Since our concern was speech, and speech
impelled us
To purify the dialect of the tribe.
Four Quartets 'Little Gidding' (1942) pt. 2

7 And the end of all our exploring
Will be to arrive where we started
And know the place for the first time.
Four Quartets 'Little Gidding' (1942) pt. 5

8 What we call the beginning is often the end
And to make an end is to make a
beginning.
The end is where we start from.
Four Quartets 'Little Gidding' (1942) pt. 5

9 A people without history
Is not redeemed from time, for history is a
pattern
Of timeless moments. So, while the light
fails
On a winter's afternoon, in a secluded
chapel
History is now and England.
Four Quartets 'Little Gidding' (1942) pt. 5

10 And all shall be well and
All manner of thing shall be well
When the tongues of flame are in-folded
Into the crowned knot of fire

And the fire and the rose are one.
Four Quartets 'Little Gidding' (1942) pt. 5;
referring to Julian of Norwich (1343–after
1416) *Revelations of Divine Love*: 'Sin is
behovely [necessary], but all shall be well and
all shall be well and all manner of thing shall
be well'

11 Here I am, an old man in a dry month
Being read to by a boy, waiting for rain.
'Gerontion' (1920)

12 After such knowledge, what forgiveness?
'Gerontion' (1920)

13 Tenants of the house,
Thoughts of a dry brain in a dry season.
'Gerontion' (1920)

14 We are the hollow men
We are the stuffed men
Leaning together
Headpiece filled with straw. Alas!
'The Hollow Men' (1925)

15 Here we go round the prickly pear
Prickly pear prickly pear.
'The Hollow Men' (1925)

16 Between the idea
And the reality
Between the motion
And the act
Falls the Shadow.
'The Hollow Men' (1925)

17 This is the way the world ends
Not with a bang but a whimper.
'The Hollow Men' (1925)

18 A cold coming we had of it,
Just the worst time of the year
For a journey, and such a long journey:
The ways deep and the weather sharp,
The very dead of winter.
'Journey of the Magi' (1927); referring to
Lancelot Andrewes (1555–1626) *Of the
Nativity* (1622): 'It was no summer progress. A
cold coming they had of it, at this time of the
year; just, the worst time of the year, to take a
journey, and specially a long journey, in. The
ways deep, the weather sharp, the days short,
the sun farthest off *in solstitio brumali*, the
very dead of Winter'

19   There was a Birth, certainly,
We had evidence and no doubt. I had seen
birth and death
But had thought they were different.
'Journey of the Magi' (1927)

1 With an alien people clutching their gods.
'Journey of the Magi' (1927)

2 Let us go then, you and I,
When the evening is spread out against the sky
Like a patient etherized upon a table.
'Love Song of J. Alfred Prufrock' (1917); see
Lewis 199:6

3 In the room the women come and go
Talking of Michelangelo.
'Love Song of J. Alfred Prufrock' (1917)

4 The yellow fog that rubs its back upon the
window-panes.
'Love Song of J. Alfred Prufrock' (1917)

5 I have measured out my life with coffee
spoons.
'Love Song of J. Alfred Prufrock' (1917)

6 I should have been a pair of ragged claws
Scuttling across the floors of silent seas.
'Love Song of J. Alfred Prufrock' (1917)

7 No! I am not Prince Hamlet, nor was
meant to be;
Am an attendant lord, one that will do
To swell a progress, start a scene or two,
Advise the prince.
'Love Song of J. Alfred Prufrock' (1917)

8 I grow old . . . I grow old . . .
I shall wear the bottoms of my trousers
rolled.
Shall I part my hair behind? Do I dare to
eat a peach?
I shall wear white flannel trousers, and
walk upon the beach.
I have heard the mermaids singing, each to
each.
I do not think that they will sing to me.
'Love Song of J. Alfred Prufrock' (1917);
referring to John Donne (1572–1631) *Songs
and Sonnets* 'Song: Go and catch a falling
star': 'Teach me to hear mermaids singing'

9 Yet we have gone on living,
Living and partly living.
Murder in the Cathedral (1935)

10 The last temptation is the greatest treason:
To do the right deed for the wrong reason.
Murder in the Cathedral (1935)

11 Clear the air! clean the sky! wash the
wind!
Murder in the Cathedral (1935)

12 He always has an alibi, and one or two to
spare:
At whatever time the deed took place—
MACAVITY WASN'T THERE!
Old Possum's Book of Practical Cats (1939)
'Macavity: the Mystery Cat'

13 Where is the Life we have lost in living?
Where is the wisdom we have lost in
knowledge?
Where is the knowledge we have lost in
information?
The Rock (1934)

14 . . . Here were decent godless people:
Their only monument the asphalt road
And a thousand lost golf balls.
The Rock (1934)

15 Birth, and copulation, and death.
That's all the facts when you come to brass
tacks.
Sweeney Agonistes (1932) 'Fragment of an
Agon'

16 Any man has to, needs to, wants to
Once in a lifetime, do a girl in.
Sweeney Agonistes (1932) 'Fragment of an
Agon'

17 I gotta use words when I talk to you.
Sweeney Agonistes (1932) 'Fragment of an
Agon'

18 The nightingales are singing near
The Convent of the Sacred Heart,

And sang within the bloody wood
When Agamemnon cried aloud
And let their liquid siftings fall
To stain the stiff dishonoured shroud.
'Sweeney among the Nightingales' (1919)

19 April is the cruellest month, breeding
Lilacs out of the dead land.
The Waste Land (1922) pt. 1

20 I read, much of the night, and go south in
the winter.
The Waste Land (1922) pt. 1

21 I will show you fear in a handful of dust.
The Waste Land (1922) pt. 1

22 And still she cried, and still the world
pursues,
'Jug Jug' to dirty ears.
The Waste Land (1922) pt. 2; referring to John
Lyly (c.1554–1606) *Campaspe* (1584): 'O 'tis
the ravished nightingale. / Jug, jug, jug, jug,
tereu, she cries'

1 I think we are in rats' alley
Where the dead men lost their bones.
The Waste Land (1922) pt. 2

2 o o o o that Shakespeherian Rag—
It's so elegant
So intelligent.
The Waste Land (1922) pt. 2; see **Buck 47:9**

3 Hurry up please it's time.
The Waste Land (1922) pt. 2

4 But at my back from time to time I hear
The sound of horns and motors, which
    shall bring
Sweeney to Mrs Porter in the spring.
O the moon shone bright on Mrs Porter
And on her daughter
They wash their feet in soda water.
The Waste Land (1922) pt. 3; referring to
Andrew Marvell (1621–78) 'To His Coy
Mistress' (1681): 'But at my back I always hear
/ Time's wingèd chariot hurrying near'

5 At the violet hour, when the eyes and back
Turn upward from the desk, when the
    human engine waits
Like a taxi throbbing waiting.
The Waste Land (1922) pt. 3

6 I Tiresias, old man with wrinkled dugs.
The Waste Land (1922) pt. 3

7 When lovely woman stoops to folly and
Paces about her room again, alone,
She smoothes her hair with automatic
    hand,
And puts a record on the gramophone.
The Waste Land (1922) pt. 3; referring to
Oliver Goldsmith (1728–74) *The Vicar of
Wakefield* (1766): 'When lovely woman stoops
to folly / And finds too late that men betray'

8 Webster was much possessed by death
And saw the skull beneath the skin.
'Whispers of Immortality' (1919)

9 Culture may even be described simply as
that which makes life worth living.
Notes Towards a Definition of Culture (1948)

10 The only way of expressing emotion in the
form of art is by finding an 'objective
correlative'; in other words, a set of
objects, a situation, a chain of events
which shall be the formula of that
particular emotion; such that when the
external facts, which must terminate in
sensory experience, are given, the emotion

is immediately evoked.
The Sacred Wood (1920) 'Hamlet and his
Problems'

11 Immature poets imitate; mature poets
steal.
The Sacred Wood (1920) 'Philip Massinger'

12 Someone said: 'The dead writers are
remote from us because we *know* so much
more than they did.' Precisely, and they
are that which we know.
The Sacred Wood (1920) 'Tradition and
Individual Talent'

13 Poetry is not a turning loose of emotion,
but an escape from emotion; it is not the
expression of personality but an escape
from personality.
The Sacred Wood (1920) 'Tradition and
Individual Talent'

14 In the seventeenth century a dissociation
of sensibility set in, from which we have
never recovered; and this dissociation, as is
natural, was due to the influence of the
two most powerful poets of the century,
Milton and Dryden.
Selected Essays (1932) 'The Metaphysical
Poets' (1921)

15 [*The Waste Land*] was only the relief of a
personal and wholly insignificant grouse
against life; it is just a piece of rhythmical
grumbling.
The Waste Land (ed. Valerie Eliot, 1971)
epigraph

Queen Elisabeth of Belgium

1876–1965
German-born consort of King Albert of the Belgians

16 Between them [Germany] and me there is
now a bloody curtain which has descended
forever.
on Germany's invasion of Belgium in 1914
attributed

Elizabeth, the Queen Mother

1900–2002
British queen, Consort of **George VI**
see also **Telegrams 311:7**

17 I'm glad we've been bombed. It makes me
feel I can look the East End in the face.
to a London policeman, 13 September 1940
J. Wheeler-Bennett *King George VI* (1958)

1 The Princesses would never leave without
me and I couldn't leave without the King,
and the King will never leave.
*on the suggestion that the royal family be
evacuated to Canada during the Blitz*
Penelope Mortimer *Queen Elizabeth* (1986)

2 How small and selfish is sorrow. But it
bangs one about until one is senseless.
letter to Edith Sitwell, shortly after the death of
George VI
Victoria Glendinning *Edith Sitwell* (1983)

*after an operation to remove a fishbone stuck in
her throat:*
3 After all these years of fishing, the fish are
having their revenge.
in November 1982, attributed; Christopher
Dobson (ed.) *Queen Elizabeth the Queen
Mother: Chronicle of a Remarkable Life* (2000)

4 We had this rather lugubrious man in a
suit, and he read a poem . . . I think it was
called The Desert. And first the girls got the
giggles and then I did and then even the
King.
*of an evening at Windsor during the war, at
which T. S. **Eliot** read from 'The Waste Land' to
the King and Queen and the Princesses*
private conversation, reported in *Spectator*
30 June 1990

Elizabeth II 1926–
British monarch, Queen of the United Kingdom from
1952; daughter of **George VI** and Queen **Elizabeth**
the Queen Mother, mother of Prince **Charles**
on Elizabeth II: see **Grigg 139:5**, **Philip 253:10**

5 I declare before you all that my whole life,
whether it be long or short, shall be
devoted to your service and the service of
our great Imperial family to which we all
belong.
broadcast speech, as Princess Elizabeth, to
the Commonwealth from Cape Town, 21 April
1947

6 I think everybody really will concede that
on this, of all days, I should begin my
speech with the words 'My husband and I'.
*speech at Guildhall, London, on her 25th
wedding anniversary*
in *Times* 21 November 1972

7 In the words of one of my more
sympathetic correspondents, it has turned
out to be an 'annus horribilis'.
speech at Guildhall, London, 24 November
1992; the term 'annus horribilis' was
suggested by her former assistant private
secretary Sir Edward Ford (1910–2006)

8 I for one believe that there are lessons to be
drawn from her life and from the
extraordinary and moving reaction to her
death.
*broadcast from Buckingham Palace on the
evening before the funeral of **Diana**, Princess of
Wales, 5 September 1997*
in *Times* 6 September 1997

9 They have overcome Becher's Brook and
the Chair and all kinds of other terrible
obstacles. They have come through and
I'm very proud and wish them well. My
son is home and dry with the woman he
loves.
*in a speech to wedding guests of the Prince of
Wales and the Duchess of Cornwall*
in *Sunday Telegraph* 10 April 2005

10 I can almost feel Mrs Blair's knees
stiffening when I come into the room.
*what the Queen has joked, according to Palace
insiders, about Cherie Blair*
in *Daily Mail* 6 April 2006; attributed, perhaps
apocryphal

11 As Groucho Marx once said, 'Anyone can
get old—all you have to do is to live long
enough.'
speech at her official 80th birthday lunch, 15
June 2006, in *Independent on Sunday* 18 June
2006

Alf Ellerton
British songwriter

12 Belgium put the kibosh on the Kaiser.
title of song (1914)

Duke Ellington 1899–1974
American jazz pianist, composer, and band-leader
see also **Mills 222:15**

13 Playing 'Bop' is like scrabble with all the
vowels missing.
in *Look* 10 August 1954

Alice Thomas Ellis 1932–2005
English novelist

1 Claudia's the sort of person who goes
through life holding on to the sides.
The Other Side of the Fire (1983)

Havelock Ellis 1859–1939
English sexologist

2 What we call 'progress' is the exchange of
one nuisance for another nuisance.
Impressions and Comments (1914) 31 July
1912

3 All civilization has from time to time
become a thin crust over a volcano of
revolution.
Little Essays of Love and Virtue (1922)

Ben Elton 1959–
British writer and comedian

4 People who get through life dependent on
other people's possessions are always the
first to lecture you on how little possessions
count.
Stark (1989)

5 Uncool people never hurt anybody—all
they do is collect stamps, read science-
fiction books and stand on the end of
railway platforms staring at trains.
in *Radio Times* 18/24 April 1998

Paul Éluard 1895–1952
French poet

6 *Adieu tristesse*
Bonjour tristesse.
Farewell sadness
Good-day sadness.
'À peine défigurée' (1932)

Odysseus Elytis 1911–96
Greek poet

7 Greek the language they gave me;
poor the house on Homer's shores.
My only care my language on Homer's
shores.
There bream and perch
windbeaten verbs,
green sea currents in the blue.
'The Axion Esti' (1959)

Buchi Emecheta 1944–
Nigerian writer

8 I am a woman and a woman of Africa. I am
a daughter of Nigeria and if she is in
shame, I shall stay and mourn with her in
shame.
Destination Biafra (1982)

Tracey Emin 1963–
British artist

9 I'm not an outsider at all. I'm on every
bloody A-list there is in the art world.
in *Independent* 22 July 2000

William Empson 1906–84
English poet and literary critic

10 There is a Supreme God in the ethnological
section;
A hollow toad shape, faced with a blank
shield.
He needs his belly to include the Pantheon,
Which is inserted through a hole behind.
At the navel, at the points formally
stressed, at the organs of sense,
Lice glue themselves, dolls, local deities,
His smooth wood creeps with all the creeds
of the world.
'Homage to the British Museum' (1935)

11 Just a smack at Auden.
title of poem, 1940

12 Waiting for the end, boys, waiting for the
end.
'Just a smack at Auden' (1940)

13 You don't want madhouse and the whole
thing there.
'Let it Go' (1955)

14 Slowly the poison the whole blood stream
fills.
It is not the effort nor the failure tires.
The waste remains, the waste remains and
kills.
'Missing Dates' (1935)

15 Seven types of ambiguity.
title of book (1930)

Brian Eno 1948–
British musician and record producer

16 Hardly anyone bought the Velvets' albums
when they were originally released, but

everyone who did formed a band.
*of the American rock group Velvet Underground,
formed in 1965*
    attributed

Nora Ephron 1941–
American screenwriter and director

1 We have lived through the era when
happiness was a warm puppy, and the era
when happiness was a dry martini, and
now we have come to the era when
happiness is 'knowing what your uterus
looks like'.
    Crazy Salad (1975) 'Vaginal Politics'; see
    **Advertising slogans 3:24, Lennon 196:9,
    Schulz 288:7**

2 The anecdote is a particularly
dehumanising sort of descriptive narrative.
    Scribble, Scribble (1978)

3 I am continually fascinated at the difficulty
intelligent people have in distinguishing
what is controversial from what is merely
offensive.
    in *Esquire* January 1976

Epitaphs
see box opposite
see also **Swan 307:9**

Susan Ertz 1894–1985
American writer

4 Millions long for immortality who don't
know what to do with themselves on a
rainy Sunday afternoon.
    Anger in the Sky (1943)

Linda Evangelista 1965–
Canadian supermodel

5 We don't wake up for less than $10,000 a
day.
    *of herself and supermodel Christy Turlington;
    often quoted as, 'I don't get out of bed for less
    than $10,000 a day'*
    in *Vogue* October 1990

William Norman Ewer 1885–1976
British writer

6 I gave my life for freedom—This I know:
For those who bade me fight had told me
    so.
    'Five Souls' (1917)

7 How odd
Of God
To choose
The Jews.
    The Week-End Book (1924); see **Browne 46:6**

Winifred Ewing 1929–
Scottish Nationalist politician

8 The Scottish Parliament which adjourned
on 25 March in the year 1707 is hereby
reconvened.
    *opening speech, as oldest member of the new
    Parliament*
    in Scottish Parliament 12 May 1999

Epitaphs

1 Alan died suddenly at Saltwood on
Sunday 5th September. He said he would
like it to be stated that he regarded
himself as having gone to join Tom and
the other dogs.
*announcement of the death of Alan **Clark***
in *Times* 8 September 1999

2 Commander Jacques-Yves Cousteau has
rejoined the world of silence.
announcement by the Cousteau Foundation,
*Paris, 25 June 1997; **Cousteau** (1910–97)*
published The Silent World *in 1953*
in *Daily Telegraph* 26 June 1997

3 Even amidst fierce flames the golden lotus
can be planted.
*on the gravestone of Sylvia **Plath***
Monkey, *poem by the Chinese poet Wu*
Cheng-en (*c.*1500–82)

4 Excuse My Dust.
Dorothy **Parker**'s suggested epitaph for
herself (1925); Alexander Woollcott *While*
Rome Burns (1934) 'Our Mrs Parker'

5 Free at last, free at last
Thank God almighty
We are free at last.
*epitaph of Martin Luther **King**, Atlanta,*
Georgia
anonymous spiritual, with which he ended
his 'I have a dream' speech; see **King 180:12**

6 God damn you all: I told you so.
*H. G. **Wells'** suggestion for his own epitaph, in*
conversation with Ernest Barker, 1939
Ernest Barker *Age and Youth* (1953)

7 God give me work till my life shall end
And life till my work is done.
*epitaph of Winifred **Holtby**; see **Swan 307:9***
Vera Brittain *Testament of Friendship: the*
Story of Winifred Holtby (1940)

8 He encouraged us.
*the epitaph Tony **Benn** would like for himself*
Anthony Clare *In the Psychiatrist's Chair 111*
(1998)

9 He finally met his deadline.
Douglas **Adams**, invited to write his own
epitaph on BBC Radio 4 *Quote Unquote*

10 He helped people see God in the ordinary
things of life, and he made children
laugh.
Revd W. **Awdry**'s preferred epitaph; in
Independent 22 March 1997, obituary

11 Hereabouts died a very gallant
gentleman, Captain L. E. G. Oates of the
Inniskilling Dragoons. In March 1912,
returning from the Pole, he walked
willingly to his death in a blizzard to try
and save his comrades, beset by
hardships.
epitaph on cairn erected in the Antarctic, 15
November 1912 by E. L. Atkinson (1882–1929)
and Apsley Cherry-Garrard (1882–1959)
Apsley Cherry-Garrard *Worst Journey in the*
World (1922); see **Last words 190:6**

12 Here lies Groucho Marx—and lies and
lies and lies. P.S. He never kissed an ugly
girl.
*Groucho **Marx's** own suggestion for his*
epitaph
B. Norman *The Movie Greats* (1981)

13 Here lies W. C. Fields. I would rather be
living in Philadelphia.
suggested epitaph for himself, in *Vanity Fair*
June 1925

14 He was an average guy who could carry
a tune.
*Bing **Crosby's** suggested epitaph for himself*
in *Newsweek* 24 October 1977

15 His foe was folly and his weapon wit.
inscription for W. S. Gilbert's memorial on
the Victoria Embankment, London (1915), by
Anthony Hope (1863–1933)

16 I may not have succeeded in halting the
war, but I did secure the right of
Parliament to decide on war.
inscription on the grave of Robin **Cook**,
taken from his memoir *Point of Departure*
(2003)

17 *Duirt me leat go raibh me breoite.*
I told you I was ill.
inscription on the gravestone of Spike
Milligan

▶

▶ **Epitaphs** continued

1 I will return. And I will be millions.
  inscription on the tomb of Eva **Perón**,
  Buenos Aires

2 John Le Mesurier wishes it to be known
that he conked out on November 15th.
He sadly misses family and friends.
  obituary notice on the death of John Le
  Mesurier (1912–83), in *Times* 16 November
  1983

3 Poor G.K.C., his day is past—
Now God will know the truth at last.
  *mock epitaph for G. K. **Chesterton**, by E. V.
  Lucas (1868–1938)*
  Dudley Barker *G. K. Chesterton* (1973)

4 Rest in peace. The mistake shall not be
repeated.
  inscription on the cenotaph at Hiroshima,
  Japan

5 She did it the hard way.
  epitaph of Bette Davis, chosen by herself
  James Spada *More Than a Woman* (1993)

6 A soldier of the Great War known unto
God.
  *standard epitaph for the unidentified dead of
  World War One*
  adopted by the War Graves Commission

7 Their name liveth for evermore.
  *standard inscription on the Stone of Sacrifice
  in each military cemetery of World War One,
  proposed by Rudyard **Kipling** as a member of
  the War Graves Commission*
  Charles Carrington *Rudyard Kipling* (rev. ed.

1978); referring to the *Bible* (Apocrypha)
  Ecclesiasticus: 'Their bodies are buried in
  peace; but their name liveth for evermore'

8 Timothy has passed . . .
  *message on his Internet web page announcing
  the death of Timothy **Leary**, 31 May 1996*
  in *Guardian* 1 June 1996

9 When I was in the military, they gave me
a medal for killing two men and a
discharge for loving one.
  on the gravestone of Leonard Matlovich
  (1943–88) American Air Force Sergeant
  expelled after publicly declaring his
  homosexuality

10 When you go home, tell them of us and
say,
'For your tomorrow we gave our today.'
  Kohima memorial to the Burma campaign of
  the Second World War; in recent years used
  at Remembrance Day parades in the UK (see
  Binyon 34:10); based on John Maxwell
  Edmonds (1875–1958) *Inscriptions
  Suggested for War Memorials* (1919): 'When
  you go home, tell them of us and say, / "For
  your tomorrows these gave their today."'

11 Without you, Heaven would be too dull
to bear,
And Hell would not be Hell if you are
there.
  *epitaph for Maurice Bowra (1898–1971) by John
  Sparrow*
  in *Times Literary Supplement* 30 May 1975

f

Clifton Fadiman 1904–99
American critic

1 Milk's leap toward immortality.
of cheese
Any Number Can Play (1957)

2 The mama of dada.
of Gertrude **Stein**
Party of One (1955)

Frantz Fanon 1925–61
Martinique-born French psychoanalyst and writer, who became a supporter of the movement for Algerian independence

3 Leave this Europe where they are never done talking of Man, yet murder men everywhere they find them.
The Wretched of the Earth (1961)

4 The shape of Africa resembles a revolver, and Zaire is the trigger.
attributed

Wallace Fard c.1891–1934
American religious leader, founder of the Nation of Islam, an exclusively black Islamic sect proposing a separate black nation

5 The blue-eyed devil white man.
Malcolm X with Alex Haley *The Autobiography of Malcolm X* (1965); see **Malcolm X 212:6**

Eleanor Farjeon 1881–1965
English writer for children, sister of Herbert **Farjeon**

6 Morning has broken
Like the first morning,
Blackbird has spoken
Like the first bird.
'A Morning Song (for the First Day of Spring)' (1957)

Herbert Farjeon 1887–1945
English writer and theatre critic, brother of Eleanor **Farjeon**

7 For I've danced with a man.
I've danced with a man
Who—well, you'll never guess.
I've danced with a man who's danced with a girl
Who's danced with the Prince of Wales!
referring to the popularity of **Edward VIII** *when Prince of Wales*
'I've danced with a man who's danced with a girl'; first written for Elsa Lanchester and sung at private parties; later sung on stage (1928) by Mimi Crawford; see also **Cartoon captions 56:5**

King Farouk 1920–65
Egyptian monarch, King of Egypt, 1936–52

8 Soon there will be only five Kings left—the King of England, the King of Spades, the King of Clubs, the King of Hearts and the King of Diamonds.
he was forced to abdicate in 1952
said to Lord Boyd-Orr at a conference in Cairo, 1948; Lord Boyd-Orr *As I Recall* (1966)

Mia Farrow 1945–
American actress

9 He had polyester sheets and I wanted to get cotton sheets. He discussed it with his shrink many times before he made the switch.
of the dependence of her former partner, Woody **Allen,** *on psychotherapists*
in *Independent* 8 February 1997

William Faulkner 1897–1962
American novelist, whose stories (often set in the fictional creation of 'Yoknapatawpha County' of northern Mississippi) deal with the history and legends of the American South
on Faulkner: see **Welty 331:12**; see also **Film lines 115:11, Film titles 117:8**

1 Maybe the only thing worse than having to give gratitude constantly all the time, is having to accept it.
   Requiem for a Nun (1951)

2 He made the books and he died.
   his own 'sum and history of my life'
      letter to Malcolm Cowley, 11 February 1949

3 He [the writer] must teach himself that the basest of all things is to be afraid and, teaching himself that, forget it forever, leaving no room in his workshop for anything but the old verities and truths of the heart, the old universal truths lacking which any story is ephemeral and doomed—love and honor and pity and pride and compassion and sacrifice.
      Nobel Prize acceptance speech, Stockholm, 10 December 1950

4 The poet's voice need not merely be the record of man; it can be one of the props, the pillars, to help him endure and prevail.
      Nobel Prize acceptance speech, Stockholm, 10 December 1950

5 The writer's only responsibility is to his art. He will be completely ruthless if he is a good one. . . . If a writer has to rob his mother, he will not hesitate; the *Ode on a Grecian Urn* is worth any number of old ladies.
      in *Paris Review* Spring 1956

6 A man shouldn't fool with booze until he's fifty; then he's a damn fool if he doesn't.
      James M. Webb and A. Wigfall Green *William Faulkner of Oxford* (1965)

Dianne Feinstein 1933–
American Democratic politician, Mayor of San Francisco 1978–88

7 Toughness doesn't have to come in a pinstripe suit.
      in *Time* 4 June 1984

James Fenton 1949–
English poet

8 It is not what they built. It is what they knocked down.
   It is not the houses. It is the spaces between the houses.
   It is not the streets that exist. It is the streets that no longer exist.
      German Requiem (1981)

9 'I didn't exist at Creation
   I didn't exist at the Flood,
   And I won't be around for Salvation
   To sort out the sheep from the cud—

   'Or whatever the phrase is. The fact is
   In soteriological terms
   I'm a crude existential malpractice
   And you are a diet of worms.'
      'God, A Poem' (1983)

Edna Ferber 1887–1968
American writer

10 Being an old maid is like death by drowning, a really delightful sensation after you cease to struggle.
      R. E. Drennan *Wit's End* (1973)

Enrico Fermi 1901–54
Italian-born American atomic physicist, who directed the first controlled nuclear chain reaction in 1942
on Fermi: see **Segrè 290:3**

11 But where is everybody?
   the 'Fermi paradox', suggested by a question asked by Fermi: if extraterrestrial civilizations exist throughout the galaxy, then they would have developed the technology to contact others, and evidence of such contact should be apparent on earth. But no such evidence has been observed
      attributed, *c.*1950

12 If I could remember the names of all these particles I'd be a botanist.
      R. L. Weber *More Random Walks in Science* (1973)

13 Whatever Nature has in store for mankind, unpleasant as it may be, men must accept, for ignorance is never better than knowledge.
      Laura Fermi *Atoms in the Family* (1955)

Kathleen Ferrier
see **Last words 191:4**

Paul Feyerabend 1924–94
Austrian philosopher, who taught for many years at the University of Berkeley, California

1 The only principle that does not inhibit progress is: *anything goes.*
   Against Method (1975)

2 The time is overdue for adding the separation of state and science to the by now customary separation of state and church. Science is only *one* of the many instruments man has invented to cope with his surroundings. It is not the only one, it is not infallible, and it has become too powerful, too pushy, and too dangerous to be left on its own.
   Against Method (1975)

Richard Phillips Feynman 1918–88
American theoretical physicist

3 The world looks so different after learning science. For example, trees are made of air, primarily. When they are burned, they go back to air, and in the flaming heat is released the flaming heat of the sun which was bound in to convert the air into tree.
   speech to the 15th annual meeting of the National Science Teachers Association, New York City, 1966

4 For a successful technology, reality must take precedence over public relations, for nature cannot be fooled.
   Appendix to the *Rogers Commission Report on the Space Shuttle Challenger Accident* 6 June 1986

5 What I cannot create, I do not understand.
   attributed

Frank Field 1942–
British Labour politician

6 The archbishop is usually to be found nailing his colours to the fence.
   of Archbishop **Runcie***; a similar comment has been recorded on A. J.* **Balfour***, c.1904*
   attributed in *Crockfords 1987/88* (1987)

Helen Fielding 1958–
British writer

7 Head is full of moony fantasies about . . . being trendy Smug Married instead of sheepish Singleton.
   Bridget Jones's Diary (1996)

Dorothy Fields 1905–74
American songwriter

8 The minute you walked in the joint,
   I could see you were a man of distinction,
   A real big spender . . .
   Hey! big spender, spend a little time with me.
   'Big Spender' (1966 song)

9 A fine romance with no kisses.
   A fine romance, my friend, this is.
   'A Fine Romance' (1936 song)

10 Grab your coat, and get your hat,
   Leave your worry on the doorstep,
   Just direct your feet
   To the sunny side of the street.
   'On the Sunny Side of the Street' (1930 song)

11 Pick yourself up,
   Dust yourself off,
   Start all over again.
   'Pick Yourself Up' (1936 song)

W. C. Fields 1880–1946
American humorist and actor
on Fields: see **Rosten 275:13**; see also **Epitaphs 107:13, Film lines 114:13**

12 Some weasel took the cork out of my lunch.
   You Can't Cheat an Honest Man (1939 film)

13 Never give a sucker an even break.
   title of a W. C. Fields film (1941); the catchphrase (Fields's own) is said to have originated in the musical comedy *Poppy* (1923)

14 It ain't a fit night out for man or beast.
   adopted by Fields but claimed by him not to be original; letter, 8 February 1944

15 Hell, I never vote *for* anybody. I always vote *against.*
   R. L. Taylor *W. C. Fields* (1950); see **Adams 2:6**

16 The funniest thing about comedy is that you never know why people laugh. I know

what makes them laugh but trying to get your hands on the *why* of it is like trying to pick an eel out of a tub of water.
R. J. Anobile *A Flask of Fields* (1972)

1 If at first you don't succeed, try, try again. Then quit. No use being a damn fool about it.
attributed

2 Last week, I went to Philadelphia, but it was closed.
R. J. Anobile *Godfrey Daniels* (1975)

Zlata Filipovic 1980–
Bosnian child writer

3 Why is politics making us unhappy, separating us, when we ourselves know who is good and who isn't? We mix with the good, not with the bad. And among the good there are Serbs and Croats and Muslims, just as there are among the bad. I simply don't understand it.
Zlata's Diary: A Child's Life in Sarajevo (1993) 19 November 1992

Film lines
see box opposite
see also **Woody Allen, W. C. Fields, Stan Laurel, Puzo, Taglines for films 309:1, Mae West**

Film titles
see box overleaf

Michael Fish 1944–
British weather forecaster

4 A woman rang to say she heard there was a hurricane on the way. Well don't worry, there isn't.
weather forecast on the night before serious and destructive gales in southern England
BBC TV, 15 October 1987

Carrie Fisher 1956–
American actress and writer

5 Here's how men think. Sex, work—and those are reversible, depending on age— sex, work, food, sports and lastly, begrudgingly, relationships. And here's how women think. Relationships, relationships, relationships, work, sex, shopping, weight, food.
Surrender the Pink (1990)

H. A. L. Fisher 1856–1940
English historian

6 Purity of race does not exist. Europe is a continent of energetic mongrels.
A History of Europe (1935)

Lord Fisher 1841–1920
British admiral, responsible for the introduction of dreadnought battleships to the Royal Navy

7 Sack the lot!
on government overmanning and overspending, specifically in regard to the Navy
letter to *Times*, 2 September 1919

8 Never contradict. Never explain. Never apologize.
recommendation for a happy life
letter to *Times*, 5 September 1919

Marve Fisher
American songwriter

9 I want an old-fashioned house
With an old-fashioned fence
And an old-fashioned millionaire.
'An Old-Fashioned Girl' (1954 song)

R. A. Fisher 1890–1962
English statistician and geneticist

10 It was Darwin's chief contribution, not only to Biology but to the whole of natural science, to have brought to light a process by which contingencies *a priori* improbable are given, in the process of time, an increasing probability, until it is their non-occurrence, rather than their occurrence, which becomes highly probable.
sometimes quoted as 'Natural selection is a mechanism for generating an exceedingly high degree of improbability'
'Retrospect of the criticisms of the Theory of Natural Selection' in Julian Huxley *Evolution as a Process* (1954)

Gerry Fitt 1926–2005
Northern Irish politician

11 People [in Northern Ireland] don't march as an alternative to jogging. They do it to assert their supremacy. It is pure tribalism, the cause of troubles all over the world.
referring to the 'marching season' in Northern Ireland, leading up to the anniversary of the Battle of the Boyne on 12 July, when parades by Orange communities traditionally take place
in *Times* 5 August 1994

Film lines

1 Anyway, Ma, I made it . . . Top of the world!
White Heat (1949 film) written by Ivan Goff (1910–) and Ben Roberts (1916–84); last lines—spoken by James Cagney

2 Cancel the kitchen scraps for lepers and orphans. No more merciful beheadings. And call off Christmas!
Robin Hood, Prince of Thieves (1991 film), written by Pen Densham and John Watson; spoken by Alan Rickman

3 Don't let's ask for the moon! We have the stars!
Now, Voyager (1942 film), from the novel (1941) by Olive Higgins Prouty (1882–1974); spoken by Bette Davis

4 Dark and difficult times lie ahead, Harry. Soon we must all face the choice between what is right . . . and what is easy.
spoken by Professor Dumbledore
Harry Potter and the Goblet of Fire (2005 film) written by Steven Kloves from the novel by J. K. **Rowling**, spoken by Michael Gambon; see also **Taglines for films 309:3**

5 Either he's dead, or my watch has stopped.
A Day at the Races (1937 film) written by Robert Pirosh, George Seaton, and George Oppenheimer; spoken by Groucho **Marx**

6 E.T. phone home.
E.T. (1982 film) written by Melissa Mathison (1950–)

7 Even the smallest person can change the course of the future.
Galadriel's parting words to Frodo
The Lord of the Rings: The Fellowship of the Ring (2001 film) written by Fran Walsh, Philippa Boyens, and Peter **Jackson**, based on the book by J. R. R. **Tolkien**, spoken by Cate Blanchett

8 Fasten your seat-belts, it's going to be a bumpy night.
All About Eve (1950 film) written by Joseph L. Mankiewicz (1909–); spoken by Bette Davis

9 Figures you wouldn't know how to work it, if it's got a computer.
Strange Brew (1983 film), directed and written by Dave **Thomas** and Rick Moranis (1953–); spoken by Dave Thomas as Doug McKenzie to his brother Bob (Rick Moranis)

10 Follow the money.
All the President's Men (1976 film), written by William Goldman; spoken by Hal Holbrook as Deep Throat to Bob Woodward; see **Bernstein and Woodward 31:9**

11 Frankly, my dear, I don't give a damn!
Gone with the Wind (1939 film) written by Sidney Howard; spoken by Clark Gable as Rhett Butler to Scarlett O'Hara; see **Mitchell 226:2**

12 Go ahead, make my day.
Sudden Impact (1983 film) written by Joseph C. Stinson (1947–); spoken by Clint Eastwood

13 Greed—for lack of a better word—is good. Greed is right. Greed works.
Wall Street (1987 film) written by Stanley Weiser and Oliver Stone (1946–); see **Boesky 38:1**

14 Here's looking at you, kid.
Casablanca (1942 film) written by Julius J. Epstein (1909–2001), Philip G. Epstein (1909–52), and Howard Koch (1902–); spoken by Humphrey Bogart to Ingrid Bergman; see **Film lines 114:3**, **Film lines 115:8**, **Film lines 115:16**

15 I ate his liver with some fava beans and a nice chianti.
The Silence of the Lambs (1991 film, based on the novel by Thomas Harris), written by Thomas Harris (1940–) and Ted Tally (1952–); spoken by Anthony **Hopkins** as Hannibal Lecter

16 I could have had class. I could have been a contender.
On the Waterfront (1954 film) written by Budd Schulberg (1914–); spoken by Marlon Brando

▶

► **Film lines** continued

1 I do wish we could chat longer, but I'm having an old friend for dinner.
The Silence of the Lambs (1991 film, based on the novel by Thomas Harris), written by Thomas Harris (1940–) and Ted Tally (1952–); spoken by Anthony **Hopkins** as Hannibal Lecter

2 I fear all we have done is awaken a sleeping giant and fill him with a terrible resolve.
Tora! Tora! Tora! (1970 film about the Japanese attack on Pearl Harbor, written by Larry Forrester, Hideo Oguni, and Ryuzo Kikushima); see **Yamamoto 344:1**

3 If she can stand it, I can. Play it!
usually quoted as 'Play it again, Sam'
Casablanca (1942 film) written by Julius J. Epstein (1909–2001), Philip G. Epstein (1909–52), and Howard Koch (1902–); spoken by Humphrey Bogart; see **Film lines 113:14**, **Film lines 115:8**, **Film lines 115:16**, **Misquotations 224:15**

4 If you can't leave in a taxi you can leave in a huff. If that's too soon, you can leave in a minute and a huff.
Duck Soup (1933 film) written by Bert Kalmar (1884–1947), Harry Ruby (1895–1974), Arthur Sheekman (1891–1978), and Nat Perrin; spoken by Groucho **Marx**; see **Film lines 116:2**, **Film lines 116:11**

5 If you carry a oo number it means you're licensed to kill, not get killed.
Dr No (1962 film, written by Richard Maibaum, Johanna Harwood, and Berkely Mather, and based on the novel by Ian **Fleming**), spoken by Bernard Lee as 'M'; see **Fleming 118:15**

6 I'll be back.
The Terminator (1984 film) written by James Cameron (1954–) and Gale Anne Hurd; spoken by Arnold Schwarzenegger; see **Taglines for films 309:5**

7 I love the smell of napalm in the morning. It smells like victory.
Apocalypse Now (1979 film) written by John Milius and Francis Ford Coppola (1939–); spoken by Robert Duvall

8 I love the smell of commerce in the morning.
Mallrats (1995 film) written by Kevin Smith (1970–), spoken by Jason Lee as Brodie

9 I'm mad as hell, and I'm not going to take this anymore!
Network (1976 film) written by Paddy Chayevsky (1923–1981), spoken by Peter Finch as Howard Beale

Julius Caesar of his assassins:
10 Infamy, infamy, they've all got it in for me!
Carry on, Cleo (1964 film) written by Talbot Rothwell (1916–74); according to Frank Muir's letter to the *Guardian*, 22 July 1995, the line had actually been written by him and Denis Norden for a radio sketch for 'Take It From Here', and was later used by Rothwell with their permission

11 In Italy for thirty years under the Borgias they had warfare, terror, murder, bloodshed—they produced Michelangelo, Leonardo da Vinci and the Renaissance. In Switzerland they had brotherly love, five hundred years of democracy and peace and what did that produce . . . ? The cuckoo clock.
The Third Man (1949 film); words added by Orson **Welles** to Graham **Greene**'s screenplay

12 I see dead people.
The Sixth Sense (1999 film) written by Manoj Night Shyamalan: spoken by Haley Joel Osment

13 It's a funny old world—a man's lucky if he gets out of it alive.
You're Telling Me (1934 film) written by Walter de Leon and Paul M. Jones; spoken by W. C. **Fields**; see **Thatcher 313:13**

14 DRIFTWOOD (Groucho Marx): It's all right. That's—that's in every contract. That's—that's what they call a sanity clause.
FIORELLO (Chico Marx): You can't fool me. There ain't no Sanity Claus.
Night at the Opera (1935 film) written by George S. **Kaufman** and Morrie Ryskind (1895–1985)

►

▶ Film lines continued

1 It's not a lie, it's a gift for fiction.
State and Main (2000 film), written by David
Mamet; spoken by William H. Macy

2 I want to be alone.
Grand Hotel (1932 film) written by Vicki
Baum and William A. Drake; spoken by Greta
Garbo. It was earlier part of a subtitle in her
silent film *The Single Standard* (1929)

3 Let's get out of these wet clothes and into
a dry Martini.
line coined in the 1920s by Robert
Benchley's press agent and adopted by Mae
West in *Every Day's a Holiday* (1937 film)

4 Let's go to work.
Reservoir Dogs (1992 film) written and
directed by Quentin Tarantino; spoken by
Lawrence Tierney

5 Luca Brasi sleeps with the fishes.
The Godfather (1972 film), written by Mario
Puzo; spoken by Richard S. Castellano as
Peter Clemenza

6 Lunch is for wimps.
Wall Street (1987 film) written by Stanley
Weiser and Oliver Stone (1946–); spoken
by Michael Douglas as Gordon Gecko

7 Madness! Madness!
The Bridge on the River Kwai (1957 film of
the novel by Pierre Boulle) written by Carl
Foreman (1914–), closing line

8 Major Strasser has been shot. Round up
the usual suspects.
Casablanca (1942 film) written by Julius J.
Epstein (1909–2001), Philip G. Epstein
(1909–52), and Howard Koch (1902–);
spoken by Claude Rains; see **Film lines
113:14, Film lines 114:3, Film lines 115:16**

9 Man your ships, and may the force be
with you.
Star Wars (1977 film) written by George
Lucas (1944–)

10 Marriage isn't a word . . . it's a *sentence*!
The Crowd (1928 film) written by King Vidor
(1895–1982)

11 Maybe just whistle. You know how to
whistle, don't you, Steve? You just put
your lips together and blow.
To Have and Have Not (1944 film) written by
Jules Furthman (1888–1960) and William
Faulkner; spoken by Lauren **Bacall** to
Humphrey Bogart

12 EUNICE GRAYSON: Mr— ?
SEAN CONNERY: Bond. James Bond.
Dr No (1962 film, written by Richard
Maibaum, Johanna Harwood, and Berkely
Mather, and based on the novel by Ian
Fleming)

13 Mr Kane was a man who got everything
he wanted, and then lost it. Maybe
Rosebud was something he couldn't get
or something he lost. Anyway, it
wouldn't have explained anything. I
don't think any word can explain a
man's life. No, I guess Rosebud is just a
piece in a jigsaw puzzle, a missing piece.
Citizen Kane (1941 film) written by Herman J.
Mankiewicz (1897–1953) and Orson **Welles**

14 My momma always said life was like a
box of chocolates . . . you never know
what you're gonna get.
Forrest Gump (1994 film), written by Eric
Ross, based on the novel (1986) by Winston
Groom; spoken by Tom Hanks

15 Nature, Mr Allnutt, is what we are put
into this world to rise above.
The African Queen (1951 film) written by
James Agee 1909–55; not in the novel by
C. S. Forester

16 Of all the gin joints in all the towns in all
the world, she walks into mine.
Casablanca (1942 film) written by Julius J.
Epstein (1909–2001), Philip G. Epstein
(1909–52), and Howard Koch (1902–);
spoken by Humphrey Bogart; see **Film lines
113:14, Film lines 114:3, Film lines 115:8**

17 Oh no, it wasn't the aeroplanes. It was
Beauty killed the Beast.
King Kong (1933 film) written by James
Creelman (1901–41) and Ruth Rose

▶

▶ **Film lines** continued

1 The pellet with the poison's in the vessel with the pestle. The chalice from the palace has the brew that is true.
   The Court Jester (1955 film) written by Norman Panama (1914–) and Melvin Frank (1913–88); spoken by Danny Kaye

2 Remember, you're fighting for this woman's honour . . . which is probably more than she ever did.
   Duck Soup (1933 film) written by Bert Kalmar (1884–1947), Harry Ruby (1895–1974), Arthur Sheekman (1891–1978), and Nat Perrin; spoken by Groucho **Marx**; see **Film lines 114:4**, **Film lines 116:11**

3 Show me the money!
   Jerry Maguire (1996 film), written by Cameron Crowe (1957–), motto given to Tom Cruise as Jerry Maguire by Cuba Golding Jr. as Rod Tidwell

4 The son of a bitch stole my watch!
   The Front Page (1931 film), from the play (1928) by Charles MacArthur (1895–1956) and Ben Hecht (1894–1964)

5 This movie was shot in 3B, three beers and it looks good, eh?
   Strange Brew (1983 film), directed and written by Dave **Thomas** and Rick Moranis (1953–); spoken by Rick Moranis as Bob McKenzie

6 Toto, I've a feeling we're not in Kansas any more.
   The Wizard of Oz (1939 film), written by Noel Langley (1911–80) from the novel *The Wonderful Wizard of Oz* (1900) by L. Frank Baum (1856–1919), and spoken by Judy Garland (1922–69) as Dorothy

7 GERRY: We can't get married at all....I'm a man.
   OSGOOD: Well, nobody's perfect.
   Some Like It Hot (1959 film) written by Billy **Wilder** and I. A. L. Diamond; closing words spoken by Jack Lemmon and Joe E. Brown

8 What a dump!
   Beyond the Forest (1949 film) written by Lenore Coffee (?1897–1984); line spoken by Bette Davis, entering a room

9 We've gotta protect our phoney-baloney jobs!
   Blazing Saddles (1974 film), written by Mel Brooks (1927–), spoken by Mel Brooks as Governor William J. Le Petomaine

10 What have the Romans ever done for us?
   Monty Python's Life of Brian (1983 film) written by John Cleese, Graham Chapman, Eric Idle, Michael Palin, Terry Gilliam, and Terry Jones

11 Why, a four-year-old child could understand this report. Run out and find me a four-year-old child. I can't make head or tail of it.
   Duck Soup (1933 film) written by Bert Kalmar (1884–1947), Harry Ruby (1895–1974), Arthur Sheekman (1891–1978), and Nat Perrin; spoken by Groucho **Marx**; see **Film lines 114:4**, **Film lines 116:2**

12 You can't handle the truth!
   A Few Good Men (1996 film), written by Aaron Sorkin, spoken by Jack Nicholson as Colonel Nathan R. Jessep

13 You finally, really did it—you maniacs! You blew it up! Damn you! Damn you all to hell!
   Planet of the Apes (1968 film, written by Michael Wilson and Rod Serling); spoken by Charlton **Heston**

14 You're going out a youngster but you've *got* to come back a star.
   42nd Street (1933 film) written by James Seymour and Rian James

15 You talkin' to me?
   Taxi Driver (1976 film), written by Paul Schrader, spoken by Robert De Niro as Travis Bickle

16 JOE GILLIS: You used to be in pictures. You used to be big.
   NORMA DESMOND: I am big. It's the pictures that got small.
   Sunset Boulevard (1950 film) written by Charles Brackett (1892–1969), Billy **Wilder**, and D. M. Marshman Jr.

Film titles

1 Back to the future.
written by Robert Zemeckis and Bob Gale, 1985

2 Bend it like Beckham.
written by Gurinder Chadha, Guljit Bindra, and Paul Mayeda Berges, 1985

3 Close encounters of the third kind.
written by Steven Spielberg (1947–), 1977

4 The discreet charm of the bourgeoisie.
written by Luis **Buñuel**, 1972

5 The Empire strikes back.
written by George Lucas (1944–), 1980; the sequel to *Star Wars*

6 Every which way but loose.
written by Jeremy Joe Kronsberg, 1978; starring Clint Eastwood

7 The good, the bad, and the ugly.
written by Age Scarpelli, Luciano Vincenzoni (1926–), and Sergio Leone (1921–), 1966

8 The long hot summer.
written by Irving Ravetch and Harriet Frank, 1958; based on stories by William **Faulkner**

9 Never on Sunday.
written by Jules Dassin (1911–), 1959

10 Rebel without a cause.
written by R. M. Lindner (1914–56), 1959, based on his book (1944); starring James Dean

11 Sunday, bloody Sunday.
written by Penelope Gilliatt, 1971

12 Sweet smell of success.
written by Ernest Lehman, 1957

13 Take the money and run.
written by Mickey Rose and Woody **Allen**, 1969

F. Scott Fitzgerald 1896–1940
American novelist

14 Let me tell you about the very rich. They are different from you and me.
*to which Ernest **Hemingway** replied, 'Yes, they have more money'*
All the Sad Young Men (1926) 'Rich Boy'

15 The beautiful and damned.
title of novel (1922)

16 At eighteen our convictions are hills from which we look; at forty-five they are caves in which we hide.
'Bernice Bobs her Hair' (1920)

17 Her voice is full of money.
of Daisy
The Great Gatsby (1925)

18 They were careless people, Tom and Daisy—they smashed up things and creatures and then retreated back into their money or their vast carelessness, or whatever it was that kept them together, and let other people clean up the mess they had made.
The Great Gatsby (1925)

19 See that little stream—we could walk to it in two minutes. It took the British a month to walk it—a whole empire walking very slowly, dying in front and pushing forward behind. And another empire walked very slowly backward a few inches a day, leaving the dead like a million bloody rugs.
Tender is the Night (1934)

20 The test of a first-rate intelligence is the ability to hold two opposed ideas in the mind at the same time, and still retain the ability to function.
in *Esquire* February 1936 'The Crack-Up'

21 In a real dark night of the soul it is always three o'clock in the morning.
'dark night of the soul' being a translation of the Spanish title of a work (1578–80) by St John of the Cross
'Handle with Care' in *Esquire* March 1936

22 No grand idea was ever born in a conference, but a lot of foolish ideas have died there.
Edmund Wilson (ed.) *The Crack-Up* (1945) 'Note-Books E'

1 Show me a hero and I will write you a
tragedy.
   Edmund Wilson (ed.) *The Crack-Up* (1945)
   'Note-Books E'

2 There are no second acts in American lives.
   Edmund Wilson (ed.) *The Last Tycoon* (1941)
   'Hollywood, etc.'

Penelope Fitzgerald 1916–2000
English novelist and biographer

3 Why read when you can pick up a spade
and find out for yourself?
   of archaeology
   The Golden Child (1977)

4 Duty is what no-one else will do at the
moment.
   Offshore (1979)

Bud Flanagan 1896–1968
British comedian, singer, and songwriter; with his
partner Chesney Allen (1894?–1982), a leading
member of the 'Crazy Gang'
see also **Perry 253:2**

5 Underneath the Arches,
I dream my dreams away,
Underneath the Arches,
On cobble-stones I lay.
   'Underneath the Arches' (1932 song)

Michael Flanders 1922–75 and Donald Swann 1923–94
English songwriters and performers

6 Have some Madeira, m'dear.
   title of song (*c.*1956)

7 Mud! Mud! Glorious mud!
Nothing quite like it for cooling the blood.
   'The Hippopotamus' (1952 song)

8 Eating people is wrong!
   'The Reluctant Cannibal' (1956 song)

9 That monarch of the road,
Observer of the Highway Code,
That big six-wheeler
Scarlet-painted
London Transport
Diesel-engined
Ninety-seven horse power

Omnibus!
   'A Transport of Delight' (*c.*1956 song)

James Elroy Flecker 1884–1915
English poet

10 West of these out to seas colder than the
Hebrides
I must go
Where the fleet of stars is anchored and the
young
Star captains glow.
   'The Dying Patriot' (1913)

11 The dragon-green, the luminous, the dark,
the serpent-haunted sea.
   'The Gates of Damascus' (1913)

12 We are the Pilgrims, master: we shall go
Always a little further: it may be
Beyond that last blue mountain barred
with snow,
Across that angry or that glimmering sea.
   The Golden Journey to Samarkand (1913) pt. 1,
   'Epilogue'

13 For lust of knowing what should not be
known,
We take the Golden Road to Samarkand.
   The Golden Journey to Samarkand (1913) pt. 1,
   'Epilogue'

14 I have seen old ships sail like swans asleep
Beyond the village which men still call
Tyre,
With leaden age o'ercargoed, dipping deep
For Famagusta and the hidden sun
That rings black Cyprus with a lake of fire.
   'Old Ships' (1915)

Ian Fleming 1908–64
English thriller writer, creator of James Bond
see also **Film lines 114:5**

15 The licence to kill for the Secret Service, the
double-o prefix, was a great honour.
   Dr No (1958); see **Film lines 114:5**

16 A medium Vodka dry Martini—with a slice
of lemon peel. Shaken and not stirred.
   Dr No (1958)

17 From Russia with love.
   title of novel (1957)

18 Live and let die.
   title of novel (1954)

Peter Fleming 1907–71
English journalist and travel writer

1 São Paulo is like Reading, only much farther away.
Brazilian Adventure (1933)

Dario Fo 1926–
Italian dramatist

2 *Non si paga, non si paga.*
We won't pay, we won't pay.
title of play (1975; translated by Lino Pertile in 1978 as 'We Can't Pay? We Won't Pay!' and performed in London in 1981 as *'Can't Pay? Won't Pay!'*); see **Political sayings and slogans 257:10**

Ferdinand Foch 1851–1929
French soldier and marshal, who was made Supreme Commander of Allied Forces on the Western Front early in 1918

3 My centre is giving way, my right is retreating, situation excellent, I am attacking.
message during the first Battle of the Marne, September 1914; as a strategist before the First World War, Foch had supported the policy of offensive à l'outrance [all-out offensive]
R. Recouly *Foch* (1919)

4 This is not a peace treaty, it is an armistice for twenty years.
at the signing of the Treaty of Versailles, 1919; Foch was the senior French representative at the Armistice negotiations
P. Reynaud *Mémoires* (1963)

J. Foley 1906–70
British songwriter

5 Old soldiers never die,
They simply fade away.
'Old Soldiers Never Die' (1920 song); copyrighted by Foley but possibly a folk-song from the First World War; see **MacArthur 205:5**

Jane Fonda 1937–
American actress and radical, nicknamed 'Hanoi Jane' after her 1972 trip to Hanoi to denounce US bombing of North Vietnam

6 A man has every season, while a woman has only the right to spring.
in *Daily Mail* 13 September 1989

Michael Foot 1913–
British Labour politician; Leader of the Labour Party 1980–83

7 A speech from Ernest Bevin on a major occasion had all the horrific fascination of a public execution. If the mind was left immune, eyes and ears and emotions were riveted.
Aneurin Bevan (1962)

8 Think of it! A second Chamber selected by the Whips. A seraglio of eunuchs.
speech in the House of Commons, 3 February 1969

9 It is not necessary that every time he rises he should give his famous imitation of a semi-house-trained polecat.
*of Norman **Tebbit***
speech in the House of Commons, 2 March 1978

Anna Ford 1943–
English journalist and broadcaster, who in 1978 became the first female newscaster for Independent Television News

10 Let's face it, there are no plain women on television.
in *Observer* 23 September 1979

Gerald Ford 1909–2006
American Republican statesman, 38th President of the US 1974–7. He replaced Spiro T. **Agnew** as Vice-President, and succeeded to the presidency on the resignation of Richard **Nixon**
on Ford: see **Abzug 1:3, Johnson 170:5**

11 I am a Ford, not a Lincoln.
on taking the vice-presidential oath, 6 December 1973

12 Our long national nightmare is over. Our Constitution works; our great Republic is a Government of laws and not of men.
on being sworn in as President, 9 August 1974; quoting John Adams (1735–1826) in *Boston Gazette* (1774): 'A government of laws, and not of men'

13 If the Government is big enough to give you everything you want, it is big enough to take away everything you have.
J. F. Parker *If Elected* (1960)

Henry Ford 1863–1947

American car manufacturer and businessman, pioneer of large-scale mass production

1 Any customer can have a car painted any colour that he wants so long as it is black.
on the Model T Ford, 1909 (black paint dried more quickly than other colours)
My Life and Work (with Samuel Crowther, 1922)

2 History is more or less bunk.
in *Chicago Tribune* 25 May 1916

3 What we call evil is simply ignorance bumping its head in the dark.
in *Observer* 16 March 1930

Lena Guilbert Ford 1870–1916

American poet, killed in an air raid

4 Keep the Home-fires burning,
While your hearts are yearning,
Though your lads are far away
They dream of Home.
There's a silver lining
Through the dark cloud shining;
Turn the dark cloud inside out,
Till the boys come Home.
'Till the Boys Come Home!' (1914 song); music by Ivor Novello

Howell Forgy 1908–83

American naval chaplain

5 Praise the Lord and pass the ammunition.
at Pearl Harbor, 7 December 1941, while sailors passed ammunition by hand to the deck
in *New York Times* 1 November 1942 and H. Forgy *And Pass the Ammunition* (1944) (also title of song by Frank Loesser, 1942). In *Life* 2 November 1942 the words were wrongly attributed to William A. Maguire

E. M. Forster 1879–1970

English novelist

6 Yes—oh dear yes—the novel tells a story.
Aspects of the Novel (1927)

7 How can I tell what I think till I see what I say?
Aspects of the Novel (1927); see **Wallas 327:5**

8 It is a period between two wars—the long week-end it has been called.
The Development of English Prose between 1918 and 1939 (1945)

9 Railway termini. They are our gates to the glorious and the unknown. Through them we pass out into adventure and sunshine, to them, alas! we return.
Howards End (1910)

10 It will be generally admitted that Beethoven's Fifth Symphony is the most sublime noise that has ever penetrated into the ear of man.
Howards End (1910)

11 To trust people is a luxury in which only the wealthy can indulge; the poor cannot afford it.
Howards End (1910)

12 She felt that those who prepared for all the emergencies of life beforehand may equip themselves at the expense of joy.
Howards End (1910)

13 Personal relations are the important thing for ever and ever, and not this outer life of telegrams and anger.
Howards End (1910)

14 Only connect! . . . Only connect the prose and the passion, and both will be exalted, and human love will be seen at its height.
Howards End (1910)

15 Death destroys a man: the idea of death saves him.
Howards End (1910)

16 The sick had no rights . . . one could lie to them remorselessly.
Howards End (1910)

17 There is much good luck in the world, but it is luck. We are none of us safe. We are children, playing or quarrelling on the line.
The Longest Journey (1907)

18 The so-called white races are really pinko-grey.
A Passage to India (1924)

19 Nothing in India is identifiable, the mere asking of a question causes it to disappear or to merge in something else.
A Passage to India (1924)

1 Pathos, piety, courage—they exist, but are identical, and so is filth. Everything exists, nothing has value.
   A Passage to India (1924)

2 Where there is officialism every human relationship suffers.
   A Passage to India (1924)

3 God si [is] Love. Is this the final message of India?
   A Passage to India (1924)

4 Think before you speak is criticism's motto; speak before you think creation's.
   Two Cheers for Democracy (1951) 'Raison d'être of Criticism'

5 If I had to choose between betraying my country and betraying my friend, I hope I should have the guts to betray my country.
   Two Cheers for Democracy (1951) 'What I Believe'

6 So Two cheers for Democracy: one because it admits variety and two because it permits criticism. Two cheers are quite enough: there is no occasion to give three. Only Love the Beloved Republic deserves that.
   Two Cheers for Democracy (1951) 'What I Believe'; referring to Algernon Charles Swinburne (1837–1909) 'Hertha' (1871): 'Even love, the beloved Republic, that feeds upon freedom lives'

Frederick Forsyth 1938–
English novelist

7 Everyone seems to remember with great clarity what they were doing on November 22nd, 1963, at the precise moment they heard President Kennedy was dead.
   The Odessa File (1972)

Harry Emerson Fosdick 1878–1969
American Baptist minister and religious broadcaster

8 I renounce war for its consequences, for the lies it lives on and propagates, for the undying hatred it arouses, for the dictatorships it puts in the place of democracy, for the starvation that stalks after it.
   Armistice Day Sermon in New York, 1933

Gene Fowler 1890–1960
American writer

9 Will Hays is my shepherd, I shall not want, He maketh me to lie down in clean postures.
   on the establishment of the 'Hays Office' in 1922 to monitor the Hollywood film industry
   Clive Marsh and Gaye Ortiz (eds.) *Explorations in Theology and Film* (1997); referring to the *Bible* Psalm 23 (Scottish Metrical Psalms, 1650): 'The Lord's my shepherd, I'll not want. / He makes me down to lie / In pastures green'

H. W. Fowler 1858–1933
English lexicographer and grammarian

10 The English speaking world may be divided into (1) those who neither know nor care what a split infinitive is; (2) those who do not know, but care very much; (3) those who know and condemn; (4) those who know and approve; and (5) those who know and distinguish. Those who neither know nor care are the vast majority and are a happy folk, to be envied by most of the minority classes.
   Modern English Usage (1926)

Norman Fowler 1938–
British Conservative politician

11 I have a young family and for the next few years I should like to devote more time to them.
   often quoted as 'spend more time with my family'
   resignation letter to the Prime Minister, in *Guardian* 4 January 1990; see **Thatcher 313:10**

Michael J. Fox 1961–
Canadian actor

12 It's all about losing your brain without losing your mind.
   on his fight against Parkinson's disease
   in *Times Weekend* 16 September 2000

Terry Fox 1958–81
Canadian runner, whose right leg was amputated because of cancer

1 I'm not a dreamer . . . but I believe in miracles. I have to.
   planning a fund-raising run across Canada; he completed two thirds of his 'Marathon of Hope'
   letter to the Canadian Cancer Society, 15 October 1979

Theodore Fox 1899–1989
English doctor; editor of *The Lancet*, 1948–64

2 We shall have to learn to refrain from doing things merely because we know how to do them.
   speech to Royal College of Physicians, 18 October 1965

Janet Frame 1924–2004
New Zealand writer

3 For your own good is a persuasive argument that will eventually make a man agree to his own destruction.
   Faces in the Water (1961), ch. 4

Anatole France 1844–1924
French novelist and man of letters

4 Without lies humanity would perish of despair and boredom.
   La Vie en fleur (1922)

5 You think you are dying for your country; you die for the industrialists.
   in *L'Humanité* 18 July 1922

Anne Frank 1929–45
German-born Jewish diarist, who recorded the experiences of her family living for two years in hiding from the Nazis in occupied Amsterdam. They were eventually betrayed and sent to concentration camps; Anne died in Belsen

6 I want to go on living even after death!
   diary, 4 April 1944

7 I still believe that people are really good at heart.
   diary, 15 July 1944

Felix Frankfurter 1882–1965
American judge and US Supreme Court Justice

8 It is a fair summary of history to say that the safeguards of liberty have been forged in controversies involving not very nice people.
   dissenting opinion in *United States v. Rabinowitz* 1950

Lord Franks 1905–92
British philosopher and administrator

9 A secret in the Oxford sense: you may tell it to only one person at a time.
   in *Sunday Telegraph* 30 January 1977

Tommy Franks 1945–
American general

10 This will be a campaign unlike any other in history. A campaign characterized by shock, by surprise, by flexibility, by the employment of precise munitions on a scale never before seen, and by the application of overwhelming force.
   encapsulated in the phrase 'shock and awe', originally deriving from a Pentagon briefing document by Harlan Ullman and James P. Wade; see **Ullman 321:1**
   briefing in Qatar, 22 March 2003

Dawn Fraser 1937–
Australian swimmer

11 I hated the easy assumption that girls had to be slower than boys.
   attributed; Colin Jarman *Guinness Dictionary of Sports Quotations* (1990)

Malcolm Fraser 1930–
Australian Liberal statesman, Prime Minister 1975–83
on Fraser: see **Keating 175:11**

12 Life is not meant to be easy.
   5th Alfred Deakin Lecture, 20 July 1971; see **Shaw 291:13**

Arthur Freed 1894–1973
American songwriter and film producer

13 Singin' in the rain.
   title of song (1929, with Nacio Herb Brown), later the title of a musical (1952) starring Gene Kelly (1912–96)

Cathy Freeman 1973–
Australian athlete

14 I was so angry because they were denying they had done anything wrong, denying

that a whole generation was stolen.
of official response to concerns about the 'stolen generation' of Aboriginal children forcibly removed from their families
interview in *Daily Telegraph* 16 July 2000

Dawn French 1957–
British comedy actress

1 If I were alive in Rubens's time, I'd be celebrated as a model. Kate Moss would be used as a paint brush.
in *Sunday Times* 13 August 2006

Marilyn French 1929–
American writer

2 Whatever they may be in public life, whatever their relations with men, in their relations with women, all men are rapists, and that's all they are. They rape us with their eyes, their laws, and their codes.
The Women's Room (1977)

3 'I hate discussions of feminism that end up with who does the dishes,' she said. So do I. But at the end, there are always the damned dishes.
The Women's Room (1977)

Lucian Freud 1922–
German-born British painter, whose subjects, typically portraits and nudes, are painted in a powerful naturalistic style

4 I would wish my portraits to be *of* the people, not *like* them. Not having a look of the sitter, *being* them.
Lawrence Gowing *Lucian Freud* (1982)

Sigmund Freud 1856–1939
Austrian psychiatrist; originator of psychoanalysis
on Freud: see **Auden 17:8, Dodd 91:11**

5 We are so made, that we can only derive intense enjoyment from a contrast, and only very little from a state of things.
Civilization and its Discontents (1930)

6 Anatomy is destiny.
Collected Writings (1924) vol. 5

7 The interpretation of dreams is the royal road to a knowledge of the unconscious activities of the mind.
The Interpretation of Dreams (2nd ed., 1909); see **Misquotations 224:5**

8 Intolerance of groups is often, strangely enough, exhibited more strongly against small differences than against fundamental ones.
Moses and Monotheism (1938)

9 Analogies decide nothing, that is true, but they can make one feel more at home.
New Introductory Lectures on Psychoanalysis (1933)

10 Why do we, you and I and many another, protest so vehemently against war, instead of just accepting it as another of life's odious importunities? For it seems a natural enough thing, biologically sound and practically unavoidable.
letter in 1931 to Albert Einstein, who had invited him to be one of 'an association of intellectuals' actively opposed to war; Otto Nathan and Heinz Norden (eds.) *Einstein on Peace* (1960)

11 The great question that has never been answered and which I have not yet been able to answer, despite my thirty years of research into the feminine soul, is 'What does a woman want?'
letter to Marie Bonaparte, in E. Jones *Sigmund Freud* (1955)

12 All that matters is love and work.
attributed

13 Frozen anger.
his definition of depression
attributed

14 Yes, America is gigantic, but a gigantic mistake.
Peter Gay *Freud: A Life for Our Time* (1988)

Betty Friedan 1921–2006
American feminist

15 The problem that has no name.
the prevention of American women from growing to their full human capacities
The Feminine Mystique (1963); see **Friedan 123:17**

16 It is easier to live through someone else than to become complete yourself.
The Feminine Mystique (1963)

17 Today the problem that has no name is how to juggle work, love, home and children.
The Second Stage (1987); see **Friedan 123:15**

Kinky Friedman 1944–

American singer, writer, and politician, candidate for the Texas governorship

1 I support gay marriage because I believe they have a right to be just as miserable as the rest of us.
   quoted on CBS News, 21 August 2005

Milton Friedman 1912–2006

American economist and exponent of monetarism; policy adviser to President **Reagan** 1981–9
see also **Sayings 287:6**

2 There is an invisible hand in politics that operates in the opposite direction to the invisible hand in the market. In politics, individuals who seek to promote only the public good are led by an invisible hand to promote special interests that it was no part of their intention to promote.
   Bright Promises, Dismal Performance: An Economist's Protest (1983)

3 History suggests that capitalism is a necessary condition for political freedom. Clearly it is not a sufficient condition for it.
   Capitalism and Freedom (1962)

4 A society that puts equality—in the sense of equality of outcome—ahead of freedom will end up with neither equality nor freedom.
   Free to Choose (1980)

5 Inflation is the one form of taxation that can be imposed without legislation.
   in *Observer* 22 September 1974

6 Thank heavens we do not get all of the government that we are made to pay for.
   attributed; quoted in the House of Lords, 24 November 1994

Brian Friel 1929–

Irish dramatist

7 Do you want the whole countryside to be laughing at us?—women of our years?— mature women, *dancing*?
   Dancing at Lughnasa (1990 play)

Max Frisch 1911–91

Swiss novelist and dramatist

8 Technology . . . the knack of so arranging the world that we need not experience it.
   Homo Faber (1957)

Charles Frohman

see **Last words 191:10**

Erich Fromm 1900–80

American philosopher and psychologist

9 Man's main task in life is to give birth to himself, to become what he potentially is. The most important product of his effort is his own personality.
   Man for Himself (1947)

10 In the nineteenth century the problem was that *God is dead*; in the twentieth century the problem is that *man is dead*. In the nineteenth century inhumanity meant cruelty; in the twentieth century it means schizoid self-alienation. The danger of the past was that men became slaves. The danger of the future is that men may become robots.
   The Sane Society (1955)

David Frost 1939–

English broadcaster and writer
on Frost: see **Muggeridge 230:8**; see also
Catchphrases 59:9, Catchphrases 60:24

11 Having one child makes you a parent; having two you are a referee.
   in *Independent* 16 September 1989

Robert Frost 1874–1963

American poet

12 I'd like to get away from earth awhile
   And then come back to it and begin over.
   May no fate wilfully misunderstand me
   And half grant what I wish and snatch me away
   Not to return. Earth's the right place for love:
   I don't know where it's likely to go better.
   'Birches' (1916)

13 Most of the change we think we see in life
   Is due to truths being in and out of favour.
   'The Black Cottage' (1914)

14 Forgive, O Lord, my little jokes on Thee
   And I'll forgive Thy great big one on me.
   'Cluster of Faith' (1962)

15 And nothing to look backward to with pride,
   And nothing to look forward to with hope.
   'The Death of the Hired Man' (1914)

1 'Home is the place where, when you have
    to go there,
  They have to take you in.'
  'I should have called it
  Something you somehow haven't to
    deserve.'
    'The Death of the Hired Man' (1914)

2 They cannot scare me with their empty
    spaces
  Between stars—on stars where no human
    race is.
  I have it in me so much nearer home
  To scare myself with my own desert places.
    'Desert Places' (1936)

3 Some say the world will end in fire,
  Some say in ice.
  From what I've tasted of desire
  I hold with those who favour fire.
  But if it had to perish twice,
  I think I know enough of hate
  To say that for destruction ice
  Is also great
  And would suffice.
    'Fire and Ice' (1923)

4 The land was ours before we were the
    land's.
    'The Gift Outright' (1942)

5 Happiness makes up in height for what it
  lacks in length.
    title of poem (1942)

6 Never ask of money spent
  Where the spender thinks it went.
  Nobody was ever meant
  To remember or invent
  What he did with every cent.
    'The Hardship of Accounting' (1936)

7 How hard it is to keep from being king
  when it's in you and in the situation.
    title of poem, 1962

8 And were an epitaph to be my story
  I'd have a short one ready for my own.
  I would have written of me on my stone:
  I had a lover's quarrel with the world.
    'The Lesson for Today' (1942)

9 Something there is that doesn't love a wall,
  That sends the frozen-ground-swell under
    it.
    'Mending Wall' (1914)

10 My apple trees will never get across
  And eat the cones under his pines, I tell
    him.

He only says, 'Good fences make good
  neighbours.'
    'Mending Wall' (1914)

11 Before I built a wall I'd ask to know
  What I was walling in or walling out,
  And to whom I was like to give offence.
    'Mending Wall' (1914)

12 Nothing gold can stay.
    title of poem, 1923

13 I never dared be radical when young
  For fear it would make me conservative
    when old.
    'Precaution' (1936)

14 No memory of having starred
  Atones for later disregard,
  Or keeps the end from being hard.
    'Provide Provide' (1936)

15 Two roads diverged in a wood, and I—
  I took the one less travelled by,
  And that has made all the difference.
    'The Road Not Taken' (1916)

16 We dance round in a ring and suppose,
  But the Secret sits in the middle and
    knows.
    'The Secret Sits' (1942)

17 I've broken Anne of gathering bouquets.
  It's not fair to the child. It can't be helped
    though:
  Pressed into service means pressed out of
    shape.
    'The Self-Seeker' (1914)

18 The best way out is always through.
    'A Servant to Servants' (1914)

19 Whose woods these are I think I know.
  His house is in the village though;
  He will not see me stopping here
  To watch his woods fill up with snow.
    'Stopping by Woods on a Snowy Evening'
    (1923); see **O'Rourke 244:7**

20 The woods are lovely, dark and deep.
  But I have promises to keep,
  And miles to go before I sleep.
    'Stopping by Woods on a Snowy Evening'
    (1923)

21 It should be of the pleasure of a poem itself
  to tell how it can. The figure a poem makes.
  It begins in delight and ends in wisdom.
  The figure is the same as for love.
    Collected Poems (1939) 'The Figure a Poem
    Makes'

1 Like a piece of ice on a hot stove the poem must ride on its own melting. A poem may be worked over once it is in being, but may not be worried into being.
   Collected Poems (1939) 'The Figure a Poem Makes'

2 Poetry is a way of taking life by the throat.
   E. S. Sergeant *Robert Frost* (1960)

3 I'd as soon write free verse as play tennis with the net down.
   E. Lathem *Interviews with Robert Frost* (1966)

4 Poetry is what is lost in translation. It is also what is lost in interpretation.
   L. Untermeyer *Robert Frost* (1964)

Barbara Frum 1937–92
Canadian journalist

5 I don't care if I'm understood. I just don't want to be misunderstood.
   her view of journalism
   interview in Paul McLaughlin *Asking Questions: the Art of the Media Interview* (1986)

Christopher Fry 1907–2005
English dramatist

6 The dark is light enough.
   title of play (1954)

7 The lady's not for burning.
   title of play (1949); see **Thatcher 312:10**

8   What after all
   Is a halo? It's only one more thing to keep clean.
   The Lady's not for Burning (1949)

9 Where in this small-talking world can I find
   A longitude with no platitude?
   The Lady's not for Burning (1949)

10   The best
   Thing we can do is to make wherever we're lost in
   Look as much like home as we can.
   The Lady's not for Burning (1949)

Roger Fry 1866–1934
English art historian, critic, and painter, member of the Bloomsbury Group

11 Art is significant deformity.
   Virginia Woolf *Roger Fry* (1940)

12 Bach almost persuades me to be a Christian.
   Virginia Woolf *Roger Fry* (1940)

Stephen Fry 1957–
English actor and writer

13 The email of the species is deadlier than the mail.
   in *Sunday Telegraph* 23 December 2001

Mary E. Frye 1905–2004
American housewife and poet

14 Do not stand at my grave and weep:
   I am not there. I do not sleep.
   I am a thousand winds that blow.
   I am the diamond glints on snow.
   I am the sunlight on ripened grain.
   I am the gentle autumn's rain.
   When you awaken in the morning's hush,
   I am the swift uplifting rush
   Of quiet birds in circled flight.
   I am the soft stars that shine at night.
   Do not stand at my grave and cry;
   I am not there, I did not die.
   quoted in letter left by British soldier Stephen Cummins when killed by the IRA, March 1989
   originally circulated privately from 1932 on

Carlos Fuentes 1928–
Mexican novelist and writer

15 To be a gringo in Mexico . . . ah, that is euthanasia.
   The Old Gringo (1985)

16 High on the agenda for the 21st century will be the need to restore some kind of tragic consciousness.
   Rushworth M. Kidder *An Agenda for the 21st Century* (1987)

Athol Fugard 1932–
South African dramatist

17 Caring. Not the most exciting of words, is it? Almost as humble as a tool. But that is the Alchemist's Stone of human endeavour.
   Dimetos (1975)

Francis Fukuyama 1952–
American historian

18 What we may be witnessing is not just the end of the Cold War but the end of history

as such: that is, the end point of man's ideological evolution and the universalism of Western liberal democracy.

in *Independent* 20 September 1989

J. William Fulbright 1905–95
American politician; the Fulbright Act of 1946, which authorized funds from the sale of surplus war materials to be used to finance exchange programmes of students and teachers between the US and other countries, is named after him

1 The Soviet Union has indeed been our greatest menace, not so much because of what it has done, but because of the excuses it has provided us for our failures.

in *Observer* 21 December 1958

R. Buckminster Fuller 1895–1983
American designer and architect, noted for his ideals of using the world's resources with maximum purpose and least waste

2 God, to me, it seems,
is a verb
not a noun,
proper or improper.

untitled poem written in 1940, in *No More Secondhand God* (1963)

3 Now there is one outstandingly important fact regarding Spaceship Earth, and that is that no instruction book came with it.

Operating Manual for Spaceship Earth (1969)

4 Spaceship Earth was so extraordinarily well invented and designed that to our knowledge humans have been on board it for two million years not even knowing that they were on board a ship.

Operating Manual for Spaceship Earth (1969)

5 Either war is obsolete or men are.

in *New Yorker* 8 January 1966

Alfred Funke 1869–1941
German writer

6 *Gott strafe England!*

God punish England!

Schwert und Myrte (1914); see **Squire 301:8**; see also **Political sayings and slogans 257:15**

Will Fyffe 1885–1947
Scottish comedian

7 I belong to Glasgow

Dear Old Glasgow town!
But what's the matter wi' Glasgow?
For it's going round and round.
I'm only a common old working chap,
As anyone can see,
But when I get a couple of drinks on a
Saturday,
Glasgow belongs to me.

'I Belong to Glasgow' (1920 song)

Rose Fyleman 1877–1957
English writer for children

8 There are fairies at the bottom of our garden!

'The Fairies' (1918)

g

Clark Gable
see **Film lines 113:11**

Zsa Zsa Gabor 1919–
Hungarian-born film actress

1 I never hated a man enough to give him diamonds back.
in *Observer* 25 August 1957

2 A man in love is incomplete until he has married. Then he's finished.
in *Newsweek* 28 March 1960

3 You mean apart from my own?
when asked how many husbands she had had
K. Edwards *I Wish I'd Said That* (1976)

Hugh Gaitskell 1906–63
British Labour politician; leader of the Opposition 1955–63
on Gaitskell: see **Bevan 33:10, Crossman 80:13**

4 There are some of us . . . who will fight and fight and fight again to save the Party we love.
rejecting proposals for a policy of unilateral nuclear disarmament
speech at Labour Party Conference, 5 October 1960

5 It means the end of a thousand years of history.
on a European federation
speech at Labour Party Conference, 3 October 1962

J. K. Galbraith 1908–2006
Canadian-born American economist; presidential adviser to John F. **Kennedy** and Lyndon B. **Johnson**

6 The affluent society.
title of book (1958)

7 The conventional wisdom.
ironic term for 'the beliefs that are at any time assiduously, solemnly and mindlessly traded between the conventionally wise'
The Affluent Society (1958)

8 In a community where public services have failed to keep abreast of private consumption things are very different. Here, in an atmosphere of private opulence and public squalor, the private goods have full sway.
The Affluent Society (1958); quoting Sallust (86–35 BC) *Catiline*: 'We have public poverty and private opulence'

9 It is not necessary to advertise food to hungry people, fuel to cold people, or houses to the homeless.
American Capitalism (1952)

10 The salary of the chief executive of the large corporation is not a market reward for achievement. It is frequently in the nature of a warm personal gesture by the individual to himself.
Annals of an Abiding Liberal (1979)

11 Trickle-down theory—the less than elegant metaphor that if one feeds the horse enough oats, some will pass through to the road for the sparrows.
The Culture of Contentment (1992)

12 Politics is not the art of the possible. It consists in choosing between the disastrous and the unpalatable.
letter to President Kennedy, 2 March 1962; referring to Bismarck (1815–98), in conversation with Meyer von Waldeck, 11 August 1867: 'Politics is the art of the possible'; see also **Butler 49:12**

1 If all else fails, immortality can always be assured by a spectacular error.
   attributed

John Galsworthy 1867–1933
English novelist, creator of the Forsyte Saga

2 He was afflicted by the thought that where Beauty was, nothing ever ran quite straight, which, no doubt, was why so many people looked on it as immoral.
   In Chancery (1920)

3 A man of action forced into a state of thought is unhappy until he can get out of it.
   Maid in Waiting (1931)

4 I know nothing—nobody tells me anything.
   A Man of Property (1906)

Ray Galton 1930–
and Alan Simpson 1929–
English scriptwriters

5 I came in here in all good faith to help my country. I don't mind giving a reasonable amount [of blood], but a pint . . . why that's very nearly an armful.
   Hancock's Half Hour 'The Blood Donor' (1961 television programme); words spoken by Tony Hancock

George Gamow 1904–68
Russian-born American physicist

6 We do not know why they [elementary particles] have the masses they do; we do not know why they transform into another the way they do; we do not know anything! The one concept that stands like the Rock of Gibraltar in our sea of confusion is the Pauli [exclusion] principle.
   in *Scientific American* July 1959

Indira Gandhi 1917–84
Indian stateswoman, Prime Minister 1966–77 and 1980–4, assassinated by her Sikh bodyguard following prolonged religious disturbances. She was the daughter of Jawaharlal **Nehru** and mother-in-law of Sonia **Gandhi**

7 We do not tilt on either side . . . we walk upright.
   when asked by a reporter why India 'always tilted towards the Soviet Union'
   in Washington, 1982; Inder Malhotra *Indira Gandhi* (1989)

Mahatma Gandhi 1869–1948
Indian nationalist and spiritual leader, who became prominent in opposition to British rule of India, pursuing a policy of non-violent civil disobedience
on Gandhi: see **Naidu 233:7, Nehru 235:7**

8 What difference does it make to the dead, the orphans and the homeless, whether the mad destruction is wrought under the name of totalitarianism or the holy name of liberty or democracy?
   Non-Violence in Peace and War (1942) vol. 1

9 The moment the slave resolves that he will no longer be a slave, his fetters fall. He frees himself and shows the way to others. Freedom and slavery are mental states.
   Non-Violence in Peace and War (1949) vol. 2

10 Non-violence is the first article of my faith. It is also the last article of my creed.
   speech on a charge of sedition
   at Shahi Bag, 18 March 1922

11 In my humble opinion, non-cooperation with evil is as much a duty as is cooperation with good.
   speech in Ahmadabad, 23 March 1922

   on being asked what he thought of modern civilization:
12 That would be a good idea.
   while visiting England in 1930
   E. F. Schumacher *Good Work* (1979)

Sonia Gandhi 1946–
Italian-born Indian politician; widow of Rajiv Gandhi (assassinated in 1991) and daughter-in-law of Indira **Gandhi**

13 There is no question. It is my inner voice, it is my conscience.
   on turning down the post of Prime Minister of India
   in *Independent* 19 May 2004

Greta Garbo 1905–90
Swedish film actress
on Garbo: see **Taglines for films 309:4**; see also **Film lines 115:2**

14 I tank I go home.
   on being refused a pay rise by Louis B. Mayer
   Norman Zierold *Moguls* (1969)

Federico García Lorca
see **Federico García Lorca**

Gabriel García Márquez 1928–
Colombian novelist

1 One hundred years of solitude.
  title of novel, 1967

2 The world must be all fucked up when men travel first class and literature goes as freight.
  One Hundred Years of Solitude (1967)

3 A famous writer who wants to continue writing has to be constantly defending himself against fame.
  in *Writers at Work* (6th series, 1984)

Ed Gardner 1901–63
American radio comedian

4 Opera is when a guy gets stabbed in the back and, instead of bleeding, he sings.
  Duffy's Tavern (US radio programme, 1940s)

John Nance Garner 1868–1967
American Democratic politician; vice-president 1933–41

5 The vice-presidency isn't worth a pitcher of warm piss.
  O. C. Fisher *Cactus Jack* (1978)

Bill Gates 1955–
American computer entrepreneur

6 If they want we will give them a sleeping bag, but there is something romantic about sleeping under the desk. They want to do it.
  on his young software programmers
  in *Independent* 18 November 1995 'Quote Unquote'

7 The world has had a tendency to focus a disproportionate amount of attention on me.
  announcing that he will move to concentrate on his charity work, in *Washington Post* (online edition) 16 June 2006

Noel Gay 1898–1954
British songwriter

8 I'm leaning on a lamp-post at the corner of the street,
  In case a certain little lady comes by.
  'Leaning on a Lamp-Post' (1937); sung by George Formby

Eric Geddes 1875–1937
British politician and administrator

9 The Germans . . . are going to be squeezed as a lemon is squeezed—until the pips squeak.
  speech at Cambridge, 10 December 1918

Frank Gehry 1929–
Canadian-born American architect

10 People ask me if I'm an artist or an architect. But I think they're the same.
  in *Toronto Star* 4 September 1987

Bob Geldof 1954–
Irish rock musician

11 Most people get into bands for three very simple rock and roll reasons: to get laid, to get fame, and to get rich.
  in *Melody Maker* 27 August 1977

Bob Geldof 1954–
and Midge Ure 1953–
Irish rock musician; Scottish rock musician

12 Feed the world
  Feed the world.
  Feed the world
  Let them know it's Christmas time again.
  'Do They Know it's Christmas?' (1984 song)

Martha Gellhorn 1908–98
American journalist and war reporter, married to Ernest **Hemingway** 1940–45

  of the defeat of the Spanish Republic:
13 I daresay we all became more competent press tourists because of it, since we never again cared so much. You can only love one war; afterward, I suppose, you do your duty.
  The Honeyed Peace (1953)

14 Never believe governments, not any of them, not a word they say; keep an untrusting eye on all they do.
  in obituary, *Daily Telegraph* 17 February 1998

Jean Genet 1910–86
French novelist, poet, and dramatist

15 What we need is hatred. From it our ideas are born.
  The Blacks (1959); epigraph

16 Are you there . . . Africa of the millions of royal slaves, deported Africa, drifting continent, are you there? Slowly you

vanish, you withdraw into the past, into the tales of castaways, colonial museums, the works of scholars.
The Blacks (1959)

1 Anyone who hasn't experienced the ecstasy of betrayal knows nothing about ecstasy at all.
Prisoner of Love (1986)

Daniel George (Daniel George Bunting) 1890–1967
English writer

2 O Freedom, what liberties are taken in thy name!
referring to the words of the revolutionary Mme Roland (1754–93) before being guillotined: 'O liberty! what crimes are committed in thy name!'
The Perpetual Pessimist (1963, with Sagittarius)

George V 1865–1936
British monarch, King of Great Britain and Ireland from 1910; father of **Edward VIII** and **George VI**
on George V: see **Nicolson 236:10**; see also **Last words 190:1, Last words 190:5**

3 Wake up, England.
title of 1911 reprint of his speech at Guildhall, 5 December 1901: 'I venture to allude to the impression which seemed generally to prevail among their brethren across the seas, that the Old Country must wake up if she intends to maintain her old position of pre-eminence in her Colonial trade against foreign competitors'

4 I pray that my coming to Ireland today may prove to be the first step towards an end of strife among her people, whatever their race or creed. In that hope I appeal to all Irishmen to pause, to stretch out the hand of forbearance and conciliation, to forgive and forget, and to join with me in making for the land they love a new era of peace, contentment and goodwill.
speech to the new Ulster Parliament at Stormont, 22 June 1921

5 I have many times asked myself whether there can be more potent advocates of peace upon earth through the years to come than this massed multitude of silent witnesses to the desolation of war.
message read at Terlincthun Cemetery, Boulogne, 13 May 1922

6 After I am dead, the boy will ruin himself in twelve months.
*of his son, the future **Edward VIII***
K. Middlemas and J. Barnes *Baldwin* (1969)

*on H. G. **Wells**'s comment on 'an alien and uninspiring court':*
7 I may be uninspiring, but I'll be damned if I'm an alien!
Sarah Bradford *George VI* (1989); attributed

8 My father was frightened of his mother; I was frightened of my father, and I am damned well going to see to it that my children are frightened of me.
attributed in Randolph S. Churchill *Lord Derby* (1959), but said by Kenneth Rose in *George V* (1983) to be almost certainly apocryphal; see **Morshead 229:5**

George VI 1895–1952
British monarch, son of **George V**, King of Great Britain and Northern Ireland from 1936 following the abdication of his brother **Edward VIII**
see also **Haskins 147:5**

9 I feel happier now that we have no allies to be polite to and to pamper.
*to his mother Queen **Mary**, 27 June 1940*
J. Wheeler-Bennett *King George VI* (1958)

10 Abroad is bloody.
W. H. Auden *A Certain World* (1970) 'Royalty'; see **Mitford 226:5**

11 The family firm.
description of the British monarchy
attributed

Ira Gershwin 1896–1983
American songwriter, frequently for the music of his brother, the composer George Gershwin (1898–1937)
see also **Heyward and Gershwin**

12 I got rhythm,
I got music,
I got my man
Who could ask for anything more?
'I Got Rhythm' (1930 song)

13 Lady, be good!
title of musical (1924)

14 You like potato and I like po-tah-to,
You like tomato and I like to-mah-to;
Potato, po-tah-to, tomato, to-mah-to—
Let's call the whole thing off!
'Let's Call the Whole Thing Off' (1937 song)

1 In time the Rockies may crumble,
Gibraltar may tumble,
They're only made of clay,
But our love is here to stay.
'Love is Here to Stay' (1938 song)

2 Holding hands at midnight
'Neath a starry sky,
Nice work if you can get it,
And you can get it if you try.
'Nice Work If You Can Get It' (1937 song)

3 The way you wear your hat,
The way you sip your tea,
The mem'ry of all that—
No, no! They can't take that away from
me!
'They Can't Take That Away from Me' (1937 song)

J. Paul Getty 1892–1976
American industrialist who made a large fortune in the oil industry and was a noted art collector

4 If you can actually count your money,
then you are not really a rich man.
in *Observer* 3 November 1957

5 The best form of charity I know is the art of meeting a payroll.
Russell Miller *The House of Getty* (1985)

Stella Gibbons 1902–89
English novelist, known particular for her first novel, Cold Comfort Farm, a parody of the rural novels of Mary Webb (1881–1927)

6 Something nasty in the woodshed.
*Aunt Ada Doom's dominance over her family,
the Starkadders, is maintained by constant
references to her having 'seen something nasty
in the woodshed' in her youth; the details of this
experience remain unexplained*
Cold Comfort Farm (1932)

Wolcott Gibbs 1902–58
American critic and editor; theatre critic of the *New Yorker* for 18 years

7 Backward ran sentences until reeled the mind.
satirizing the style of Time *magazine*
in *New Yorker* 28 November 1936 'Time . . .
Fortune . . . Life . . . Luce'

Kahlil Gibran 1883–1931
Lebanese-born American writer and painter

8 Are you a politician who says to himself: 'I will use my country for my own benefit'?
. . . Or are you a devoted patriot, who whispers in the ear of his inner self: 'I love to serve my country as a faithful servant.'
The New Frontier (1931); see **Kennedy 177:9**

9 Your children are not your children.
They are the sons and daughters of Life's longing for itself.
They came through you but not from you
And though they are with you yet they belong not to you.
The Prophet (1923) 'On Children'

10 Work is love made visible. And if you cannot work with love but only with distaste, it is better that you should leave your work and sit at the gate of the temple and take alms of those who work with joy.
The Prophet (1923) 'On Work'

11 An exaggeration is a truth that has lost its temper.
Sand and Foam (1926)

André Gide 1869–1951
French novelist and critic

12 One must allow others to be right, it consoles them for not being anything else.
The Immoralist (1930), tr. D. Bussy, spoken by Ménalque

Eric Gill 1882–1940
English sculptor, engraver, and typographer

13 That state is a state of slavery in which a man does what he likes to do in his spare time and in his working time that which is required of him.
Art-nonsense and Other Essays (1929) 'Slavery and Freedom'

Penelope Gilliatt
see **Film titles 117:11**

Andrew Gilligan 1968–
British journalist

14 I have spoken to a British official who was involved in the preparation of the dossier, and he told me that until the week before it was published, the draft dossier produced by the intelligence services added little to what was already publicly known. He said: [Voiceover]: 'It was transformed in the week before it was published, to make it sexier'.

BBC Radio 4 *Today* programme, 29 May 2003; in *Guardian* 27 June 2003

Hermione Gingold 1897–1987
English actress

1 Contrary to popular belief, English women do not wear tweed nightgowns.

in *Saturday Review* 16 April 1955

Allen Ginsberg 1926–97
American poet and novelist, a leading poet of the beat generation, and later influential in the hippy movement of the 1960s
see also **Last words 190:9**

2 What if someone gave a war & Nobody came?

'Graffiti' (1972); see **Sandburg 283:8**

3 I saw the best minds of my generation destroyed by madness, starving hysterical naked.
dragging themselves through the negro streets at dawn looking for an angry fix,
angelheaded hipsters burning for the ancient heavenly connection to the starry dynamo in the machinery of the night.

Howl (1956)

4 What thoughts I have of you tonight, Walt Whitman, for I walked
down the sidestreets under the trees with a headache self-
conscious looking at the full moon.

'A Supermarket in California' (1956)

5 What peaches and what penumbras! Whole families shopping at night! Aisles full of husbands! Wives in the avocados, babies in the tomatoes!—and you, Garcia Lorca what were you doing down by the watermelons?

'A Supermarket in California' (1956)

6 Ah, dear father, graybeard, lonely old courage-teacher, what
America did you have when Charon quit poling his ferry and you
got out on a smoking bank and stood watching the boat

disappear on the black waters of Lethe?

'A Supermarket in California' (1956)

Nikki Giovanni 1943–
American poet

7 Mistakes are a fact of life
It is the response to error that counts.

'Of Liberation' (1970)

George Gipp 1895–1920
American college footballer, star player 1918–20 for the Notre Dame team

8 Win just one for the Gipper.

according to the Notre Dame coach Knute Rockne (1888–1931), Gipp, when dying of pneumonia, had urged the coach to use his death as an inspiration to his team
attributed; the catchphrase later became associated with Ronald **Reagan**, who uttered the immortal words in the 1940 film *Knute Rockne, All American*

Jean Giraudoux 1882–1944
French dramatist

9 No poet ever interpreted nature as freely as a lawyer interprets the truth.

La Guerre de Troie n'aura pas lieu (1935)

Rudolph Giuliani 1944–
American Republican politician, Mayor of New York 1993–2001
on Giuliani: see **Letterman 198:1**

10 The number of casualties will be more than any of us can bear.

in the aftermath of the terrorist attacks which destroyed the World Trade Center in New York, and damaged the Pentagon, 11 September 2001
in *Times* 12 September 2001

Edna Gladney
American philanthropist

11 There are no illegitimate children, only illegitimate parents.

during her successful lobbying of the Texas legislature to expunge the word 'illegitimate' from birth certificates; MGM paid her a large sum for the line for the 1941 film based on her life, 'Blossoms in the Dust'
A. Loos *Kiss Hollywood Good-Bye* (1978)

George Glass 1910–84
American film producer

1 An actor is a kind of a guy who if you ain't talking about him ain't listening.
> Bob Thomas *Brando* (1973); said to be often quoted by Marlon Brando, as in *Observer* 1 January 1956

Victoria Glendinning 1937–
English biographer and novelist

2 There's no greater bliss in life than when the plumber eventually comes to unblock your drains. No writer can give that sort of pleasure.
> in *Observer* 3 January 1993

Jean-Luc Godard 1930–
French film director

3 Photography is truth. The cinema is truth 24 times per second.
> *Le Petit Soldat* (1960 film)

4 *Ce n'est pas une image juste, c'est juste une image.*
This is not a just image, it is just an image.
> Colin MacCabe *Godard: Images, Sounds, Politics* (1980)

5 GEORGES FRANJU: Movies should have a beginning, a middle and an end.
JEAN-LUC GODARD: Certainly, but not necessarily in that order.
> in *Time* 14 September 1981

A. D. Godley 1856–1925
English classicist

6 What is this that roareth thus?
Can it be a Motor Bus?
Yes, the smell and hideous hum
Indicat Motorem Bum!
> letter, 10 January 1914, in *Reliquiae* (1926)

Joseph Goebbels 1897–1945
German Nazi leader, who from 1933 was Hitler's Minister of Propaganda, with control of press, radio, and all aspects of culture

7 We can manage without butter but not, for example, without guns. If we are attacked we can only defend ourselves with guns not with butter.
> speech in Berlin, 17 January 1936; see **Goering 134:9**

8 Making noise is an effective means of opposition.
> Ernest K. Bramsted *Goebbels and National Socialist Propaganda 1925–45* (1965)

Hermann Goering 1893–1946
German Nazi leader, responsible for the German rearmament programme (a former World War One fighter pilot, in 1935 he was made Supreme Commander of the air force)
see also **Johst 170:10**

9 Would you rather have butter or guns? . . . preparedness makes us powerful. Butter merely makes us fat.
> speech at Hamburg, 1936, in W. Frischauer *Goering* (1951); see **Goebbels 134:7**

10 I herewith commission you to carry out all preparations with regard to . . . a *total solution* of the Jewish question in those territories of Europe which are under German influence.
> instructions to Reinhard **Heydrich**, 31 July 1941; W. L. Shirer *Rise and Fall of the Third Reich* (1962); see **Heydrich 153:1**

William Golding 1911–93
English novelist

11 Nothing is so impenetrable as laughter in a language you don't understand.
> *An Egyptian Journal* (1985)

12 Anyone who moved through those years without understanding that man produces evil as a bee produces honey, must have been blind or wrong in the head.
> *of the Second World War*
> *The Hot Gates* (1965) 'Fable'

13 Sleep is when all the unsorted stuff comes flying out as from a dustbin upset in a high wind.
> *Pincher Martin* (1956)

James Goldsmith 1933–97
British financier and politician, founder of the Referendum Party

14 When you marry your mistress you create a job vacancy.
> *marrying Lady Annabel Birley in 1978*
> G. Wansell *Tycoon* (1987)

Barry Goldwater 1909–98
American Republican politician; presidential candidate in the 1964 election

1 I would remind you that extremism in the defence of liberty is no vice! And let me remind you also that moderation in the pursuit of justice is no virtue!
  accepting the presidential nomination, 16 July 1964; see **Johnson 170:1**

Sam Goldwyn 1882–1974
American film producer, famous for his 'Goldwynisms' (many of which are in fact apocryphal)
on Goldwyn: see **Hand 143:16**, **Hecht 149:14**; see also **Shaw 293:14**

2 Gentlemen, include me out.
  resigning from the Motion Picture Producers and Distributors of America, October 1933
  M. Freedland *The Goldwyn Touch* (1986)

3 A verbal contract isn't worth the paper it is written on.
  Alva Johnston *The Great Goldwyn* (1937)

4 'I can answer you in two words, "im-possible"' is almost the cornerstone of the Goldwyn legend, but Sam did not say it. It was printed late in 1925 in a humorous magazine and credited to an anonymous Potash or Perlmutter.
  Alva Johnston *The Great Goldwyn* (1937)

5 That's the way with these directors, they're always biting the hand that lays the golden egg.
  Alva Johnston *The Great Goldwyn* (1937)

6 Why should people go out and pay to see bad movies when they can stay at home and see bad television for nothing?
  in *Observer* 9 September 1956

7 I'll give you a definite maybe.
  attributed

8 Let's have some new clichés.
  attributed, perhaps apocryphal

9 Pictures are for entertainment, messages should be delivered by Western Union.
  A. Marx *Goldwyn* (1976); see **Behan 26:19**

10 What we need is a story that starts with an earthquake and works its way up to a climax.
  attributed, perhaps apocryphal

Amy Goodman 1957–
American journalist

11 Go to where the silence is and say something.
  accepting an award from Columbia University for her coverage of the 1991 massacre in East Timor by Indonesian troops
  in *Columbia Journalism Review* March/April 1994

Mikhail Sergeevich Gorbachev 1931–
Soviet statesman, General Secretary of the Communist Party of the USSR 1985–91 and President 1988–91, noted for a foreign policy which brought about an end to the cold war, as well as the liberalizing domestic reforms known as glasnost and perestroika
on Gorbachev: see **Gromyko 139:11, Thatcher 313:4**

12 The guilt of Stalin and his immediate entourage before the Party and the people for the mass repressions and lawlessness they committed is enormous and unforgivable.
  speech on the seventieth anniversary of the Russian Revolution, 2 November 1987

13 The idea of restructuring [perestroika] . . . combines continuity and innovation, the historical experience of Bolshevism and the contemporaneity of socialism.
  speech on the seventieth anniversary of the Russian Revolution, 2 November 1987

14 After leaving the Kremlin . . . my conscience was clear. The promise I gave to the people when I started the process of perestroika was kept: I gave them freedom.
  Memoirs (1995)

Nadine Gordimer 1923–
South African novelist and short-story writer

15 Censorship is never over for those who have experienced it.
  'Censorship and its Aftermath', keynote address to International Writers' Day, P.E.N. International, 2 June 1990, in *Index on Censorship* August 1990

Mack Gordon 1904–59
American songwriter

16 Pardon me boy is that the Chattanooga Choo-choo,
  Track twenty nine,

Boy you can gimme a shine.
'Chattanooga Choo-choo' (1941 song)

Albert Gore Jr. 1948–
American Democratic politician, Vice-President
1993–2001; presidential candidate in 2000

1 I am Al Gore, and I used to be the next
president of the United States of America.
addressing Bocconi University in Milan
in *Newsweek* 19 March 2001; see **Carter 55:1**

Maxim Gorky 1868–1936
Russian writer and revolutionary

2 The proletarian state must bring up
thousands of excellent 'mechanics of
culture', 'engineers of the soul'.
speech at the Writers' Congress 1934; see
Kennedy 177:16, Stalin 301:10

Stuart Gorrell 1902–63
American songwriter

3 Georgia, Georgia, no peace I find,
Just an old sweet song keeps Georgia on my
mind.
'Georgia on my Mind' (1930 song)

Stephen Jay Gould 1941–2002
American palaeontologist and noted popularizer of
science, who studied modifications of Darwinian
evolutionary theory and proposed the concept of
punctuated equilibrium—the concept that
evolutionary development is marked by isolated
episodes of rapid speciation between long periods
of little or no change

4 A man does not attain the status of Galileo
merely because he is persecuted; he must
also be right.
Ever since Darwin (1977)

5 Science is an integral part of culture. It's
not this foreign thing, done by an arcane
priesthood. It's one of the glories of human
intellectual tradition.
in *Independent* 24 January 1990

Lew Grade 1906–98
British television producer and executive

6 All my shows are great. Some of them are
bad. But they are all great.
in *Observer* 14 September 1975

D. M. Graham 1911–99
British broadcaster

7 That this House will in no circumstances
fight for its King and Country.
motion worded by Graham, when an
undergraduate, for a debate at the Oxford
Union, 9 February 1933; the proposition was
carried by 275 votes to 153

Katherine Graham 1917–2001
American newspaper proprietor, publisher of the
Washington Post at the time of Watergate
on Graham: see **Bradlee 42:8, Mitchell 223:14**

8 A miracle of sorts had taken place—this
country was about to change presidents
in an utterly democratic way, with the
processes that had been put into place
two centuries before working in this
unprecedented situation.
of the resignation of Richard Nixon
Personal History (1997)

Antonio Gramsci 1891–1937
Italian political theorist and activist

9 Our motto is still alive and to the point:
Pessimism of the intellect, optimism of the
will.
the motto of the periodical L'Ordine Nuovo *was*
borrowed from the French writer Romain Rolland
(1866–1944)
in *L'Ordine Nuovo* 4 March 1921

Bernie Grant 1944–2000
British Labour politician, born in British Guiana; he
became the first black council leader in Britain when
in 1985 Labour won control of Haringey Council

10 The police were to blame for what
happened on Sunday night and what they
got was a bloody good hiding.
after the Broadwater Farm riot in which a
policeman was killed
speech as leader of Haringey Council,
8 October 1985

11 White students were sent on scholarships
to South Africa. But the black students had

to go into the mines in Dunfermline and work as coal miners.
explaining why he had dropped out of a degree course in mining engineering at Heriot-Watt University in the 1960s
> quoted in *Oxford Dictionary of National Biography* (online edition), 'Bernard Alexander Montgomery Grant'

Robert Graves 1895–1985
English poet and novelist

1 There's a cool web of language winds us in,
  Retreat from too much joy or too much fear.
  'The Cool Web' (1927)

2 Truth-loving Persians do not dwell upon
  The trivial skirmish fought near Marathon.
  'The Persian Version' (1945)

3 Love is a universal migraine.
  A bright stain on the vision
  Blotting out reason.
  'Symptoms of Love'

4 Goodbye to all that.
  title of autobiography (1929)

5 If there's no money in poetry, neither is there poetry in money.
  speech at London School of Economics, 6 December 1963

6 LSD reminds me of the minks that escape from mink-farms and breed in the forest and become dangerous and destructive. It has escaped from the drug factory and gets made in college laboratories.
  George Plimpton (ed.) *The Writer's Chapbook* (1989)

Muriel Gray 1959–
Scottish writer and broadcaster

7 Of course I want political autonomy but not cultural autonomy. You just have to watch the Scottish Baftas to want to kill yourself.
  explaining her preference for devolution rather than full independence
  in *Scotland on Sunday* 14 January 1996

Jimmy Greaves 1940–
English footballer

8 The thing about sport, any sport, is that swearing is very much part of it.
  attributed, 1989

Graham Greene 1904–91
English novelist, much of whose work reflects the moral paradoxes he saw in his Roman Catholic faith
see also **Film lines 114:11**

9 Catholics and Communists have committed great crimes, but at least they have not stood aside, like an established society, and been indifferent. I would rather have blood on my hands than water like Pilate.
  The Comedians (1966)

10 They had been corrupted by money, and he had been corrupted by sentiment. Sentiment was the more dangerous, because you couldn't name its price. A man open to bribes was to be relied upon below a certain figure, but sentiment might uncoil in the heart at a name, a photograph, even a smell remembered.
  The Heart of the Matter (1948)

11 Here you could love human beings nearly as God loved them, knowing the worst; you didn't love a pose, a pretty dress, a sentiment artfully assumed.
  The Heart of the Matter (1948)

12 He felt the loyalty we all feel to unhappiness—the sense that that is where we really belong.
  The Heart of the Matter (1948)

13 Any victim demands allegiance.
  The Heart of the Matter (1948)

14 His hilarity was like a scream from a crevasse.
  The Heart of the Matter (1948)

15 Goodness has only once found a perfect incarnation in a human body and never will again, but evil can always find a home there. Human nature is not black and white but black and grey.
  The Lost Childhood and Other Essays (1951)
  title essay

16 There is always one moment in childhood when the door opens and lets the future in.
  The Power and the Glory (1940)

17 Innocence always calls mutely for protection, when we would be so much wiser to guard ourselves against it: innocence is like a dumb leper who has lost

his bell, wandering the world meaning no harm.
The Quiet American (1955)

1 There is a splinter of ice in the heart of a writer.
A Sort of Life (1971)

Alan Greenspan 1926–
American economist, chairman of the Federal Reserve 1987–2006

2 How do we know when irrational exuberance has unduly escalated asset values?
speech in Washington, 5 December 1996

3 History suggests that they [valuations] also reflect waves of optimism and pessimism that can be set off by small exogenous events.
remarks to a symposium at Jackson Hole, Wyoming, 27 August 1999

4 What the chief accountant creates is a work of art.
describing financial reporting as less of a historical record and more of a forecast
speech, Boston, 9 November 2006

Germaine Greer 1939–
Australian feminist

5 Women have very little idea of how much men hate them.
The Female Eunuch (1971)

6 You can now see the Female Eunuch the world over . . . spreading herself wherever blue jeans and Coca-Cola may go. Wherever you see nail varnish, lipstick, brassieres, and high heels, the Eunuch has set up her camp.
The Female Eunuch (20th anniversary ed., 1991) foreword

7 I didn't fight to get women out from behind the vacuum cleaner to get them onto the board of Hoover.
in *Guardian* 27 October 1986

Hubert Gregg 1914–2004
English songwriter, broadcaster, and actor

8 Maybe it's because I'm a Londoner

That I love London so.
'Maybe It's Because I'm a Londoner' (1947 song)

9 I'm blessed with total recall, except about where I left my umbrella.
on his knowledge of popular music
quoted in *Daily Telegraph* (online edition) 31 March 2004

Dick Gregory 1932–
American comedian and civil rights activist

10 You gotta say this for the white race—its self-confidence knows no bounds. Who else could go to a small island in the South Pacific where there's no poverty, no crime, no unemployment, no war and no worry—and call it a 'primitive society'?
From the Back of the Bus (1962)

11 Wouldn't it be a hell of a thing if all this was burnt cork and you people were being tolerant for nothing?
Nigger (1965)

12 Baseball is very big with my people. It figures. It's the only way we can get to shake a bat at a white man without starting a riot.
D. H. Nathan (ed.) *Baseball Quotations* (1991)

Joyce Grenfell 1910–79
English comedy actress and writer

13 George—don't do that.
recurring line in monologues about a nursery school
from the 1950s; *George—Don't Do That* (1977)

14 So gay the band,
So giddy the sight,
Full evening dress is a must,
But the zest goes out of a beautiful waltz
When you dance it bust to bust.
'Stately as a Galleon' (1978 song)

Julian Grenfell 1888–1915
English soldier and poet, killed in action in the First World War

15 And Life is Colour and Warmth and Light
And a striving evermore for these;
And he is dead, who will not fight;
And who dies fighting has increase.
written during the second battle of Ypres
'Into Battle' in *Times* 28 May 1915

Wayne Gretzky 1961–
Canadian ice-hockey player

1 I skate to where the puck is going to be, not where it's been.
attributed, 1985; John Robert Colombo
Colombo's New Canadian Quotations (1987)

Clifford Grey 1887–1941
English songwriter

2 If you were the only girl in the world
And I were the only boy.
'If You Were the Only Girl in the World' (1916 song)

Lord Grey of Fallodon 1862–1933
British Liberal politician, Foreign Secretary 1905–16

3 The lamps are going out all over Europe; we shall not see them lit again in our lifetime.
on the eve of the First World War
25 Years (1925)

Mervyn Griffith-Jones 1909–79
British lawyer, member of the British prosecuting team at the Nuremberg war trials

4 Is it a book you would even wish your wife or your servants to read?
*appearing for the prosecution against Penguin Books for publishing the unexpurgated text of D. H. **Lawrence**'s novel* Lady Chatterley's Lover; *in his opening address to the jury, it was suggested that asking themselves this question was one of the ways in which they could assess the book*
in *Times* 21 October 1960

John Grigg 1924–2001
British writer and journalist, who as Lord Altrincham disclaimed his hereditary title in 1963

5 The personality conveyed by the utterances which are put into her mouth is that of a priggish schoolgirl, captain of the hockey team, a prefect, and a recent candidate for confirmation. It is not thus that she will be able to come into her own as an independent and distinctive character.
*of Queen **Elizabeth II**; at the time, this criticism of the Queen caused a storm of protest, and Lord Altrincham was hit in the face by a member of the League of Empire Loyalists on the steps of*

Television House after an interview
in *National and English Review* August 1957

6 Autobiography is now as common as adultery and hardly less reprehensible.
in *Sunday Times* 28 February 1962

Joseph ('Jo') Grimond 1913–93
British Liberal politician, Leader of the Liberal Party 1956–67

7 In bygone days, commanders were taught that when in doubt, they should march their troops towards the sound of gunfire. I intend to march my troops towards the sound of gunfire.
speech to the Liberal Party Assembly, 14 September 1963; although the subsequent election in October 1964 showed the Liberals gaining ground, the incoming Labour Prime Minister Harold **Wilson** was not interested in establishing closer relations between the two parties

Matt Groening 1954–
American humorist and satirist
see also **Catchphrases 58:18, Catchphrases 60:1**

8 Kids, you tried your best, and you failed miserably. The lesson is, never try.
Homer Simpson
The Simpsons 'Burns' Heir' (1994), written by Jack Richdale

9 Bonjourr, you cheese-eating surrender monkeys.
Groundskeeper Willie as French teacher
The Simpsons 'Round Springfield' (1995), written by Jeffrey Ventimilia and Joshua Sternin

10 Kids are the best, Apu. You can teach them to hate the things you hate. And they practically raise themselves, what with the internet and all.
Homer Simpson
The Simpsons 'Eight Misbehavin'' (1999), written by Matt Selman

Andrei Gromyko 1909–89
Soviet statesman, President of the USSR 1985–8

11 Comrades, this man has a nice smile, but he's got iron teeth.
*of Mikhail **Gorbachev***
speech to Soviet Communist Party Central Committee, 11 March 1985

Andrew Grove 1936–
Hungarian-born American businessman

1 Only the paranoid survive.
dictum on which he has long run his company,
the Intel Corporation
   in *New York Times* 18 December 1994

Philip Guedalla 1889–1944
British historian and biographer

2 The little ships, the unforgotten Homeric
catalogue of *Mary Jane* and *Peggy IV*, of
Folkestone Belle, *Boy Billy*, and *Ethel Maud*,
of *Lady Haig* and *Skylark* . . . the little ships
of England brought the Army home.
on the evacuation of Dunkirk
   Mr Churchill (1941)

3 The work of Henry James has always
seemed divisible by a simple dynastic
arrangement into three reigns: James I,
James II, and the Old Pretender.
   Supers and Supermen (1920) 'Some Critics'

Ernesto ('Che') Guevara 1928–67
Argentinian revolutionary and guerrilla leader

4 The Revolution is made by man, but man
must forge his revolutionary spirit from
day to day.
   Socialism and Man in Cuba (1968)

Alec Guinness 1914–2000
English actor
on Guinness: see **le Carré 195:2**

5 I just couldn't go on speaking those bloody
awful, banal lines. I'd had enough of the
mumbo-jumbo.
of his refusal to play Obi-Wan Kenobi in Star
Wars *sequels*
   attributed, September 1998

Nubar Gulbenkian 1896–1972
British industrialist and philanthropist

6 The best number for a dinner party is
two—myself and a dam' good head waiter.
   in *Daily Telegraph* 14 January 1965

Thom Gunn 1929–2004
English poet

7 My thoughts are crowded with death
and it draws so oddly on the sexual
that I am confused

confused to be attracted
by, in effect, my own annihilation.
   'In Time of Plague' (1992)

Alan Guth 1947–
American physicist

8 It is often said that there is no such thing as
a free lunch. The Universe, however, is a
free lunch.
   in *Harpers* November 1994; see **Sayings
   287:6**

Woody Guthrie 1912–67
American folksinger and songwriter, many of whose
songs were inspired by the hardships of the
Depression

9 This land is your land, this land is my land,
From California to the New York Island.
From the redwood forest to the Gulf Stream
   waters
This land was made for you and me.
   'This Land is Your Land' (1956 song)

10 I ain't a communist necessarily, but I been
in the red all my life.
   Joe Klein *Woody Guthrie* (1988)

Ferenc Gyurcsany 1961–
Hungarian statesman, Prime Minister since 2004

11 We lied morning, noon and night.
comments on a leaked tape recorded after a
general election in April 2006 that sparked riots
in Budapest in September 2006
   quoted on news.bbc.co.uk 19 September
   2006

William Hague 1961–
British Conservative politician; Leader of the
Conservative Party 1997–2001

1 Feather-bedding, pocket-lining, money-
grabbing cronies.
*during the debate on lobbyists' influence and
'cronyism'*
in the House of Commons, 8 July 1998

2 There was so little English in that answer
that President Chirac would have been
happy with it.
confronting John Prescott at Prime Minister's
questions in the House of Commons,
29 March 2006

Lord Haig 1861–1928
British soldier, Commander-in-Chief of British
armies in France, 1915–18. The strategy of attrition
maintained throughout his command is associated
with heavy losses.

3 A very weak-minded fellow I am afraid,
and, like the feather pillow, bears the
marks of the last person who has sat on
him!
*describing the 17th Earl of Derby, Secretary of
State for War, 1916–18, and one of Haig's
supporters*
letter to Lady Haig, 14 January 1918

4 Every position must be held to the last
man: there must be no retirement. With
our backs to the wall, and believing in the
justice of our cause, each one of us must
fight on to the end.
*at the time of the German spring offensive,
following the collapse of Russia*
order to British troops, 12 April 1918; A. Duff
Cooper *Haig* (1936)

Lord Hailsham (Quintin Hogg)
1907–2001
British Conservative politician

5 Conservatives do not believe that the
political struggle is the most important
thing in life . . . The simplest of them prefer
fox-hunting—the wisest religion.
The Case for Conservatism (1947)

6 A great party is not to be brought down
because of a scandal by a woman of easy
virtue and a proved liar.
*John Profumo (1915–2006), then Secretary of
State for War, initially denied 'any impropriety'
with Christine Keeler, but later admitted that he
had lied to the House of Commons, and resigned
from the Government*
BBC television interview on the Profumo
affair; in *Times* 14 June 1963; see also
Macmillan 209:6

7 The English and, more latterly, the British,
have the habit of acquiring their
institutions by chance or inadvertence,
and shedding them in a fit of absent-
mindedness.
'The Granada Guildhall Lecture 1987' 10
November 1987; quoting John Seeley
(1834–95) *The Expansion of England* (1883):
'We seem . . . to have conquered and peopled
half the world in a fit of absence of mind'; see
also **Harlech 146:1**

8 The elective dictatorship.
*meaning that the capacity of the government
to make laws depends on its parliamentary
majority, rather than on countrywide support.*
title of the Dimbleby Lecture, 19 October 1976

J. B. S. Haldane 1892–1964
Scottish mathematical biologist

1 Now, my own suspicion is that the universe is not only queerer than we suppose, but queerer than we *can* suppose.
  Possible Worlds (1927)

2 If my mental processes are determined wholly by the motions of atoms in my brain, I have no reason for supposing that my beliefs are true. They may be sound chemically, but that does not make them sound logically. And hence I have no reason for supposing my brain to be composed of atoms.
  Possible Worlds (1927) 'When I am Dead'

3 I wish I had the voice of Homer
  To sing of rectal carcinoma,
  Which kills a lot more chaps, in fact,
  Than were bumped off when Troy was
    sacked.
  'Cancer's a Funny Thing'; Ronald Clark *J. B. S.*
  (1968)

4 The Creator, if He exists, has a special preference for beetles.
  on observing that there are 400,000 species of beetles on this planet, but only 8,000 species of mammals
  in *Journal of the British Interplanetary Society* (1951)

5 I'd lay down my life for two brothers or eight cousins.
  on the evolutionary theory of altruistic behaviour
  attributed; in *New Scientist* 8 August 1974

H. R. Haldeman 1929–93
American Presidential assistant to Richard **Nixon**; White House Chief of Staff 1969–73, indicted for his role in the Watergate cover-up and imprisoned 1975–8

6 Once the toothpaste is out of the tube, it is awfully hard to get it back in.
  *on the emergence of information about the Watergate affair, when revelations of an attempt to bug the national headquarters of the Democratic Party led ultimately to the resignation of President **Nixon***
  to John **Dean**, 8 April 1973, in *Hearings Before the Select Committee on Presidential Campaign Activities of US Senate: Watergate and Related Activities* (1973)

Bill Haley
see **Jimmy de Knight and Max Freedman 87:17**

Radclyffe Hall 1883–1943
English novelist

7 The well of loneliness.
  title of novel (1928), an exploration of a lesbian relationship, which caused outrage and was banned in Britain for many years

8 You're neither unnatural, nor abominable, nor mad; you're as much a part of what people call nature as anyone else; only you're unexplained as yet— you've not got your niche in creation.
  The Well of Loneliness (1928)

Margaret Halsey 1910–
American writer

9 Englishwomen's shoes look as if they had been made by someone who had often heard shoes described but had never seen any.
  With Malice Toward Some (1938)

10 The English never smash in a face. They merely refrain from asking it to dinner.
  With Malice Toward Some (1938)

W. F. ('Bull') Halsey 1882–1959
American admiral, Commander of Allied naval forces in the South Pacific 1942–44, and of the US Third Fleet 1944–45

11 The Third Fleet's sunken and damaged ships have been salvaged and are retiring at high speed toward the enemy.
  on hearing claims that the Japanese had virtually annihilated the US fleet in the Second Battle of the Philippines
  report, 14 October 1944; E. B. Potter *Bull Halsey* (1985)

Oscar Hammerstein II 1895–1960
American songwriter

12 Fish got to swim and birds got to fly
  I got to love one man till I die,
  Can't help lovin' dat man of mine.
  'Can't Help Lovin' Dat Man of Mine' (1927 song), from *Showboat*

13 Climb ev'ry mountain, ford ev'ry stream

Follow ev'ry rainbow, till you find your
   dream!
   'Climb Ev'ry Mountain' (1959 song), from *The
   Sound of Music*

1 I'm gonna wash that man right outa my
  hair.
   title of song (1949), from *South Pacific*

2 June is bustin' out all over.
   title of song (1945), from *Carousel*

3 The last time I saw Paris
  Her heart was warm and gay,
  I heard the laughter of her heart in ev'ry
    street café.
   'The Last Time I saw Paris' (1941 song), from
   Lady be Good

4 The corn is as high as an elephant's eye.
   'Oh, What a Beautiful Mornin' ' (1943 song).
   from *Oklahoma!*

5 Oh, what a beautiful mornin',
  Oh, what a beautiful day!
  I got a beautiful feelin'
  Ev'rything's goin' my way.
   'Oh, What a Beautiful Mornin' ' (1943 song),
   from *Oklahoma!*

6 Ol' man river, dat ol' man river,
  He must know sumpin', but don't say
   nothin',
  He jus' keeps rollin',
  He jus' keeps rollin' along.
   'Ol' Man River' (1927 song), from *Showboat*

7 Some enchanted evening,
  You may see a stranger,
  You may see a stranger,
  Across a crowded room.
   'Some Enchanted Evening' (1949 song), from
   South Pacific

8 The hills are alive with the sound of music,
  With songs they have sung for a thousand
   years.
  The hills fill my heart with the sound of
   music,
  My heart wants to sing ev'ry song it hears.
   'The Sound of Music' (1959 song), from *The
   Sound of Music*

9 There is nothin' like a dame.
   title of song (1949), from *South Pacific*

10 I'm as corny as Kansas in August,

High as a flag on the Fourth of July!
   'A Wonderful Guy' (1949 song), from *South
   Pacific*

11 You'll never walk alone.
   title of song (1945), from *Carousel*; in Britain,
   it has become the club anthem of Liverpool
   Football Club

Katharine Hamnett
see **Sayings and slogans 286:14**

Christopher Hampton 1946–
English dramatist

12 Masturbation is the thinking man's
  television.
   Philanthropist (1970)

13 A definition of capitalism . . . the process
  whereby American girls turn into
  American women.
   Savages (1974)

Tony Hancock
see **Ray Galton 129:5**

Learned Hand 1872–1961
American federal judge; a saying on the American
circuit relating to him and his cousin Augustus Hand
ran, 'Always quote Learned and follow Gus'
on Hand: see **Cardozo 53:9**

14 No plagiarist can excuse the wrong by
  showing how much of his work he did not
  pirate.
   in *Sheldon v. Metro-Goldwyn Pictures Corp.*
   1936

15 Right conclusions are more likely to be
  gathered out of a multitude of tongues,
  than through any kind of authoritative
  selection. To many this is, and will always
  be, folly; but we have staked upon it our
  all.
   in *United States v. Associated Press* 1943; see
   Brennan 44:1

16 A self-made man may prefer a self-made
  name.
   on Samuel Goldfish's changing his name to
   Samuel **Goldwyn**
   Bosley Crowther *Lion's Share* (1957)

Carol Hanisch
see **Political sayings and slogans 258:5**

Brian Hanrahan 1949–
British journalist

1 I counted them all out and I counted them all back.
on the number of British aeroplanes joining the raid on Port Stanley in the Falklands War
BBC broadcast report, 1 May 1982

Lorraine Hansberry 1930–65
American dramatist

2 Though it be a thrilling and marvellous thing to be merely young and gifted in such times, it is doubly so, doubly dynamic—to be young, gifted and *black*.
To be young, gifted and black: Lorraine Hansberry in her own words (1969) adapted by Robert Nemiroff; see **Irvine 163:4**

Rick Hansen 1957–
Canadian wheelchair athlete

3 You have to be the best with what you have.
in *Globe and Mail* 3 November 1986

Otto Harbach 1873–1963
American songwriter

4 Now laughing friends deride tears I cannot hide,
So I smile and say 'When a lovely flame dies,
Smoke gets in your eyes.'
'Smoke Gets in your Eyes' (1933 song)

E. Y. ('Yip') Harburg 1898–1981
American songwriter

5 Brother can you spare a dime?
title of song (1932)

6 Say, it's only a paper moon,
Sailing over a cardboard sea.
'It's Only a Paper Moon' (1933 song, with Billy Rose)

7 Wanna cry, wanna croon.
Wanna laugh like a loon.
It's that Old Devil Moon in your eyes.
'Old Devil Moon' (1946 song)

8 Somewhere over the rainbow
Way up high,

There's a land that I heard of
Once in a lullaby.
'Over the Rainbow' (1939 song), from *The Wizard of Oz*

9 Follow the yellow brick road.
'We're Off to See the Wizard' (1939 song), from *The Wizard of Oz*; referring to L. Frank Baum (1856–1919) *The Wonderful Wizard of Oz* (1900): 'The road to the City of Emeralds is paved with yellow brick'; see **John 169:1**

D. W. Harding 1906–
British psychologist and critic

10 Regulated hatred.
title of an article on the novels of Jane Austen
in *Scrutiny* March 1940

Warren G. Harding 1865–1923
American Republican statesman, 29th President of the US 1921–3

11 I must utter my belief in the divine inspiration of the founding fathers.
inaugural address, 4 March 1921

Godfrey Harold Hardy 1877–1947
English mathematician

12 Beauty is the first test: there is no permanent place in the world for ugly mathematics.
A Mathematician's Apology (1940)

Oliver Hardy
see **Stan Laurel**

Thomas Hardy 1840–1928
English novelist and poet (after publication of his last novels *Tess of the Durbervilles* (1891) and *Jude the Obscure* (1896), Hardy returned to poetry)

13 'Peace upon earth!' was said. We sing it,
And pay a million priests to bring it.
After two thousand years of mass
We've got as far as poison-gas.
'Christmas: 1924' (1928)

14 In a solitude of the sea
Deep from human vanity
And the Pride of Life that planned her,
stilly couches she.
on the loss of the Titanic
'Convergence of the Twain' (1914)

1 The Immanent Will that stirs and urges
   everything.
   'Convergence of the Twain' (1914)

2 And as the smart ship grew
   In stature, grace, and hue,
   In shadowy silent distance grew the
      Iceberg too . . .
   Till the Spinner of the Years
   Said 'Now!' And each one hears,
   And consummation comes, and jars two
      hemispheres.
   'Convergence of the Twain' (1914)

3 An aged thrush, frail, gaunt, and small,
   In blast-beruffled plume.
   'The Darkling Thrush' (1902)

4 So little cause for carollings
   Of such ecstatic sound
   Was written on terrestrial things
   Afar or nigh around,
   That I could think there trembled through
   His happy good-night air
   Some blessed Hope, whereof he knew
   And I was unaware.
   'The Darkling Thrush' (1902)

5 If way to the Better there be, it exacts a full
   look at the worst.
   'De Profundis' (1902)

6 I am the family face;
   Flesh perishes, I live on,
   Projecting trait and trace
   Through time to times anon,
   And leaping from place to place
   Over oblivion.
   'Heredity' (1917)

7 Yes; quaint and curious war is!
   You shoot a fellow down
   You'd treat if met where any bar is,
   Or help to half-a-crown.
   'The Man he Killed' (1909)

8 What of the faith and fire within us
   Men who march away
   Ere the barn-cocks say
   Night is growing grey,
   To hazards whence no tears can win us;
   What of the faith and fire within us
   Men who march away?
   'Men Who March Away' (1914)

9 In the third-class seat sat the journeying
      boy
   And the roof-lamp's oily flame

Played down on his listless form and face,
Bewrapt past knowing to what he was
   going,
Or whence he came.
   'Midnight on the Great Western' (1917)

10 Woman much missed, how you call to me,
   call to me.
   'The Voice' (1914)

11 When I set out for Lyonnesse,
   A hundred miles away,
   The rime was on the spray,
   And starlight lit my lonesomeness.
   'When I set out for Lyonnesse' (1914)

12 War makes rattling good history; but
   Peace is poor reading.
   The Dynasts (1904)

David Hare 1947–
English actor and dramatist

13 Being taken no notice of in 10 million
   homes.
   of appearing on television
   Amy's View (1997)

14 To portray only what you would like to be
   true is the beginning of censorship.
   The History Plays (1984)

15 If Christ were to return today, the Church
   of England would ask him to set out his
   ideas on a single sheet of A4.
   Racing Demon (1990)

W. F. Hargreaves 1846–1919
British songwriter

16 I'm Burlington Bertie
   I rise at ten thirty and saunter along like a
      toff,
   I walk down the Strand with my gloves on
      my hand,
   Then I walk down again with them off.
   'Burlington Bertie from Bow' (1915 song)

17 I acted so tragic the house rose like magic,
   The audience yelled 'You're sublime.'
   They made me a present of Mornington
      Crescent
   They threw it a brick at a time.
   'The Night I Appeared as Macbeth' (1922
   song)

Lord Harlech 1918–85
British diplomat

1 Britain will be honoured by historians more for the way she disposed of an empire than for the way in which she acquired it.
   in *New York Times* 28 October 1962; see also **Acheson 1:8, Hailsham 141:7**

Charles Eustace Harman 1894–1970
British judge

2 Accountants are the witch-doctors of the modern world and willing to turn their hands to any kind of magic.
   speech, February 1964, in A. Sampson *The New Anatomy of Britain* (1971)

3 You cannot pick out one bit—pick out the plums and leave the duff behind.
   Post Office v. Norwich Union Fire Insurance Society Ltd (1967)

Jimmy Harper, Will E. Haines, and Tommie Connor *fl.* 1938
British songwriters

4 The biggest aspidistra in the world.
   title of song (1938); popularized by Gracie Fields

Stephen Harper 1959–
Canadian Conservative statesman, Prime Minister since 2006

5 I'm basically a cautious person . . . I believe that it is better to light one candle than promise a million light bulbs.
   announcing his party's full platform on 13 January 2006
   in *New York Times* 24 January 2006; see also **Stevenson 304:13**

Michael Harrington 1928–89
American writer and sociologist

6 For the urban poor the police are those who arrest you. In almost any slum there is a vast conspiracy against the forces of law and order.
   The Other America: Poverty in the United States (1962)

Arthur Harris 1892–1984
British Air Force Marshal

7 I would not regard the whole of the remaining cities of Germany as worth the bones of one British Grenadier.
   supporting the continued strategic bombing of German cities (Dresden was bombed 13–14 February 1945); see also **Bell 27:3**
   letter to Norman Bottomley, deputy Chief of Air Staff, 29 March 1945; Max Hastings *Bomber Command* (1979); referring to Bismarck (1815–98): 'Not worth the healthy bones of a single Pomeranian grenadier'

Paul Harrison 1936–
American dramatist and director

8 The poor tread lightest upon the earth. The higher our income, the more resources we control and the more havoc we wreak.
   in *Guardian* 1 May 1992

Basil Liddell Hart 1895–1970
British military thinker and historian

9 Self-exhaustion in war has killed more states than any foreign assailant.
   Strategy: the indirect approach (1954)

Josephine Hart 1942–
Irish novelist

10 Damaged people are dangerous. They know they can survive.
   Damage (1991); see **Starkie 302:1**

Lorenz Hart 1895–1943
American songwriter

11 Bewitched, bothered, and bewildered am I.
   'Bewitched' (1941 song), from *Pal Joey*

12 When love congeals
   It soon reveals
   The faint aroma of performing seals.
   'I Wish I Were in Love Again' (1937 song), from *Babes in Arms*

13 I get too hungry for dinner at eight.
   I like the theatre, but never come late.
   I never bother with people I hate.
   That's why the lady is a tramp.
   'The Lady is a Tramp' (1937 song), from *Babes in Arms*

14 In a mountain greenery
   Where God paints the scenery—

Just two crazy people together.
'Mountain Greenery' (1926 song)

1 Thou swell! Thou witty!
Thou sweet! Thou grand!
Wouldst kiss me pretty?
Wouldst hold my hand?
'Thou Swell' (1927 song)

Moss Hart 1904–61
and George S. Kaufman 1889–1961
American songwriter; American dramatist

2 You can't take it with you.
title of play (1936)

L. P. Hartley 1895–1972
English novelist

3 The past is a foreign country: they do
things differently there.
The Go-Between (1953), opening line

F. W. Harvey 1888–1957
English poet and soldier

4 From troubles of the world
I turn to ducks
Beautiful comical things.
'Ducks' (1919), written while a prisoner of war
in Germany

Minnie Louise Haskins 1875–1957
English teacher and writer

5 And I said to the man who stood at the gate
of the year: 'Give me a light that I may
tread safely into the unknown.'
And he replied:
'Go out into the darkness and put your
hand into the Hand of God. That shall be to
you better than light and safer than a
known way.'
*quoted by George VI in his Christmas broadcast,
1939*
Desert (1908) 'God Knows'

Václav Havel 1936–
Czech dramatist and statesman, President of
Czechoslovakia 1989–92 and of the Czech Republic
1993–2003

6 Hope is definitely not the same thing as
optimism. It is not the conviction that
something will turn out well, but the
certainty that something makes sense,

regardless of how it turns out.
Disturbing the Peace (1986)

7 Let us teach ourselves and others that
politics can be not only the art of the
possible, especially if this means the art of
speculation, calculation, intrigue, secret
deals, and pragmatic manoeuvring, but
that it can even be the art of the impossible,
namely, the art of improving ourselves and
the world.
speech, Prague, 1 January 1990; see **Butler
49:12**

8 Even a purely moral act that has no hope of
any immediate and visible political effect
can gradually and indirectly, over time,
gain in political significance.
letter to Alexander **Dubček**, August 1969,
following Dubček's removal from office after
the Soviet invasion of Czechoslovakia (see
also **Dubček 93:5**)

9 The Gypsies are a litmus test not of
democracy but of civil society.
attributed

Jacquetta Hawkes 1910–96
English archaeologist and writer, wife of J. B.
Priestley

10 I was conscious of this vanished woman
and myself as part of an unbroken stream
of consciousness . . . With an imaginative
effort it is possible to see the eternal present
in which all days, all the seasons of the
plain stand in enduring unity.
discovering a Neanderthal skeleton
Man on Earth (1954)

Stephen Hawking 1942–
English theoretical physicist. His main work has
been on space–time, quantum mechanics, and black
holes

11 Someone told me that each equation I
included in the book would halve the sales.
A Brief History of Time (1988)

12 In effect, we have redefined the task of
science to be the discovery of laws that will
enable us to predict events up to the limits
set by the uncertainty principle.
A Brief History of Time (1988)

13 What is it that breathes fire into the
equations and makes a universe for them
to describe . . . Why does the universe go to

all the bother of existing?
A Brief History of Time (1988)

1 If we find the answer to that [why it is that we and the universe exist], it would be the ultimate triumph of human reason—for then we would know the mind of God.
A Brief History of Time (1988)

2 By 2600, the world population would be standing shoulder to shoulder and the electricity consumed would make the earth glow red-hot.
on what will happen if the population continues to increase at the present rate
in *Times* 17 February 2001

3 We won't find anywhere as nice as Earth unless we go to another star system.
on colonizing space
in *Mail on Sunday* 18 June 2006

Ian Hay 1876–1952
Scottish novelist and dramatist

4 War is hell, and all that, but it has a good deal to recommend it. It wipes out all the small nuisances of peace-time.
The First Hundred Thousand (1915)

5 What do you mean, funny? Funny-peculiar or funny ha-ha?
The Housemaster (1938)

Bill Hayden 1933–
Australian Labor politician

6 I am not convinced the Labor Party could not win under my leadership. I believe a drover's dog could lead the Labor Party to victory the way the country is.
*Hayden had resigned as Opposition leader in 1983 as Malcolm **Fraser** was in the process of calling the election*
John Stubbs *Hayden* (1989)

Alfred Hayes 1911–85
American songwriter

7 I dreamed I saw Joe Hill last night
Alive as you and me.
Says I, 'But Joe, you're ten years dead.'
'I never died,' says he.
'I Dreamed I Saw Joe Hill Last Night' (1936 song); see **Hill 154:2**

Lee Hazlewood 1929–
American singer and songwriter

8 These boots are made for walkin'.
title of song (1966)

Bessie Head 1937–86
South African-born writer

9 Love is mutually feeding each other, not one living on another like a ghoul.
A Question of Power (1973)

Denis Healey 1917–
British Labour politician, Chancellor of the Exchequer 1974–79, husband of Edna **Healey**
see also **Phillips 254:1**

10 I warn you there are going to be howls of anguish from the 80,000 people who are rich enough to pay over 75% [tax] on the last slice of their income.
speech at Labour Party Conference, 1 October 1973

11 Like being savaged by a dead sheep.
*on being criticized by Geoffrey **Howe** in the House of Commons*
in the House of Commons, 14 June 1978

Edna Healey 1918–
British writer, wife of Denis **Healey**

12 She has no hinterland; in particular she has no sense of history.
*of Margaret **Thatcher***
Denis Healey *The Time of My Life* (1989)

Seamus Heaney 1939–
Irish poet, winner of the Nobel Prize for Literature in 1995

13 And found myself thinking: if it were nowadays,
This is how Death would summon Everyman.
'A Call' (1996)

14 How culpable was he
That last night when he broke
Our tribe's complicity?
'Now you're supposed to be
An educated man,'
I hear him say. 'Puzzle me
The right answer to that one.'
'Casualty' (1979)

15 History says, *Don't hope*

On this side of the grave.
But then, once in a lifetime
The longed-for tidal wave
Of justice can rise up
And hope and history rhyme.
    The Cure at Troy (version of Sophocles'
    Philoctetes, 1990)

1 Between my finger and my thumb
The squat pen rests.
I'll dig with it.
    'Digging' (1966)

2 Me waiting until I was nearly fifty
To credit marvels.
    'Fosterling' (1991)

3 The annals say: when the monks of
    Clonmacnoise
Were all at prayers inside the oratory
A ship appeared above them in the air.
    'Lightenings viii' (1991)

4 Don't be surprised
If I demur, for, be advised
My passport's green.
No glass of ours was ever raised
To toast *The Queen.*
    rebuking the editors of The Penguin Book of
    Contemporary British Poetry *for including him
    among its authors*
    Open Letter (1983)

5 Who would connive
in civilised outrage
yet understand the exact
and tribal, intimate revenge.
    'Punishment' (1975)

6 My heart besieged by anger, my mind a
    gap of danger,
I walked among their old haunts, the home
    ground where they bled;
And in the dirt lay justice like an acorn in
    the winter
Till its oak would sprout in Derry where
    the thirteen men lay dead.
    of Bloody Sunday, Londonderry, 30 January 1972
    'The Road to Derry'

7   HERE IS THE NEWS,
Said the absolute speaker. Between him
    and us
A great gulf was fixed where
    pronunciation
Reigned tyrannically.
    'A Sofa in the Forties' (1996)

8   The famous
Northern reticence, the tight gag of place
And times: yes, yes. Of the 'wee six' I sing
Where to be saved you only must save face
And whatever you say, you say nothing.
    'Whatever You Say Say Nothing' (1975)

9 No death outside my immediate family has
left me more bereft. No death in my lifetime
has hurt poets more.
    funeral oration for Ted **Hughes**, 3 November
    1998

Edward Heath 1916–2005
British Conservative statesman, Prime Minister
1970–4

10 This would, at a stroke, reduce the rise in
prices, increase production and reduce
unemployment.
    press release from Conservative Central
    Office, 16 June 1970, never actually spoken by
    Heath

11 The unpleasant and unacceptable face of
capitalism.
    *after the revelation of the covert financial
    arrangements by which the chairman of Lonrho
    had been given a large tax-free payment in the
    Cayman Isles, at a time of wage freezes and
    national austerity*
    in the House of Commons, 15 May 1973

12 Rejoice, rejoice, rejoice.
    *telephone call to his office on hearing of
    Margaret **Thatcher**'s fall from power in 1990; see*
    Thatcher 312:11
    attributed; in *Daily Telegraph* 24 September
    1998 (online edition)

Fred Heatherton *fl.* 1944
British songwriter

13 I've got a loverly bunch of coconuts,
There they are a-standing in a row.
    'I've Got a Lovely Bunch of Coconuts' (1944
    song; revised version 1948)

Ben Hecht 1894–1964
American screenwriter
see also **Film lines 116:4**

14 [Goldwyn] filled the room with wonderful
panic and beat at your mind like a man in
front of a slot machine, shaking it for a
jackpot.
    A. Scott Berg *Goldwyn* (1989)

Tippi Hedren 1935–
American actress

1 [Alfred Hitchcock] thought of himself as looking like Cary Grant. That's tough, to think of yourself one way and look another.
   interview in California, 1982; P. F. Boller and R. L. Davis *Hollywood Anecdotes* (1988)

Robert Heinlein 1907–88
American science fiction writer
see also **Sayings and slogans 287:6**

2 More than three can't agree on when to have dinner, much less when to strike.
   of revolutionaries (*the Professor speaking*)
   The Moon is a Harsh Mistress (1966) ch. 5

3 More than six people cannot decide on anything.
   of committees (*the Professor speaking*)
   The Moon is a Harsh Mistress (1966) ch. 14

Werner Heisenberg 1901–76
German mathematical physicist, who developed a system of quantum mechanics based on matrix algebra in which he stated his famous uncertainty principle (1927)

4 An expert is someone who knows some of the worst mistakes that can be made in his subject and who manages to avoid them.
   Der Teil und das Ganze (1969); tr. A. J. Pomerans as *Physics and Beyond*, 1971

   on Felix Bloch's stating that space was the field of linear operations:
5 Nonsense. Space is blue and birds fly through it.
   Felix Bloch 'Heisenberg and the early days of quantum mechanics' in *Physics Today* December 1976

Joseph Heller 1923–99
American novelist

6 There was only one catch and that was Catch-22, which specified that a concern for one's own safety in the face of dangers that were real and immediate was the process of a rational mind ... Orr would be crazy to fly more missions and sane if he didn't, but if he was sane he had to fly them. If he flew them he was crazy and

didn't have to; but if he didn't want to he was sane and had to.
   Catch-22 (1961)

7 Some men are born mediocre, some men achieve mediocrity, and some men have mediocrity thrust upon them. With Major Major it had been all three.
   Catch-22 (1961); referring to William Shakespeare (1564–1616) *Twelfth Night* (1601): 'Some men are born great, some achieve greatness, and some have greatness thrust upon them'

8 When I read something saying I've not done anything as good as *Catch-22* I'm tempted to reply, 'Who has?'
   in *Times* 9 June 1993

Lillian Hellman 1905–84
American dramatist, whose leftwing sympathies led to her being blacklisted in the 1950s
on Hellman: see **McCarthy 206:3**

9 Cynicism is an unpleasant way of saying the truth.
   The Little Foxes (1939)

10 I cannot and will not cut my conscience to fit this year's fashions.
   letter to John S. Wood, Chairman of the House Committee on Un-American Activities (HUAC), 19 May 1952

Leona Helmsley c.1920–
American hotelier

11 Only the little people pay taxes.
   comment made to her housekeeper in 1983, and reported at her trial for tax evasion
   in *New York Times* 12 July 1989

Ernest Hemingway 1899–1961
American novelist and journalist, noted for his terse prose style and tough masculine image
on Hemingway: see **Vidal 325:3**; see also **Borrowed titles 40:1, Borrowed titles 40:10, Fitzgerald 117:14, Stein 302:12**

12 Where do the noses go? I always wondered where the noses would go.
   For Whom the Bell Tolls (1940)

13 But did thee feel the earth move?
   For Whom the Bell Tolls (1940)

1 Cowardice, as distinguished from panic, is almost always simply a lack of ability to suspend the functioning of the imagination.
Men at War (1942)

2 Paris is a movable feast.
A Movable Feast (1964) epigraph

3 A man can be destroyed but not defeated.
The Old Man and the Sea (1952)

4 The sun also rises.
title of novel (1926)

5 Grace under pressure.
*when asked what he meant by 'guts' in an interview with Dorothy **Parker***
in *New Yorker* 30 November 1929

6 The most essential gift for a good writer is a built-in, shock-proof shit detector. This is the writer's radar and all great writers have had it.
in *Paris Review* Spring 1958

Jimi Hendrix 1942–70
American rock guitarist, noted for the flamboyance and originality of his improvisations

7 Purple haze is in my brain
Lately things don't seem the same.
'Purple Haze' (1967 song)

8 A musician, if he's a messenger, is like a child who hasn't been handled too many times by man, hasn't had too many fingerprints across his brain.
in *Life Magazine* (1969)

Arthur W. D. Henley *fl.* 1934
British songwriter

9 Nobody loves a fairy when she's forty.
title of song (1934)

Thierry Henry 1977–
French football player, striker for the English club Arsenal since 1999

10 We need a player who will be a fox in the box and on the pitch. We need a player like Owen is for Liverpool.
reflecting on an unsuccessful season for Arsenal in *Guardian* (online edition) 14 May 2001

Barbara Hepworth 1903–75
English sculptor. A pioneer of abstraction in British sculpture, she worked in wood, stone, and bronze and is noted for her simple monumental works in landscape and architectural settings

11 I rarely draw what I see—I draw what I feel in my body.
Drawings from a Sculptor's Landscape (1966)

A. P. Herbert 1890–1971
English writer and humorist

12 Don't let's go to the dogs tonight,
For mother will be there.
'Don't Let's Go to the Dogs Tonight' (1926)

13 The Farmer will never be happy again;
He carries his heart in his boots;
For either the rain is destroying his grain
Or the drought is destroying his roots.
'The Farmer' (1922)

14 Let's find out what everyone is doing,
And then stop everyone from doing it.
'Let's Stop Somebody from Doing Something!' (1930)

15 As my poor father used to say
In 1863,
Once people start on all this Art
Goodbye, moralitee!
'Lines for a Worthy Person' (1930)

16 This high official, all allow,
Is grossly overpaid;
There wasn't any Board, and now
There isn't any Trade.
'The President of the Board of Trade' (1922)

17 Nothing is wasted, nothing is in vain:
The seas roll over but the rocks remain.
Tough at the Top (operetta *c.*1949)

18 Holy deadlock.
title of novel (1934)

19 People must not do things for fun. We are not here for fun. There is no reference to fun in any Act of Parliament.
Uncommon Law (1935) 'Is it a Free Country?'

John Richard Hersey 1914–93
American journalist and novelist

20 There is one sacred rule of journalism. The writer must not invent. The legend on the licence must read: *None* of this was made up.

'The Legend on the Licence' in *Yale Review* vol. 70, 1980

Maurice Herzog 1919–
French mountaineer, who in 1950 became the first person to climb Annapurna

1 For us the mountains had been a natural field of activity where, playing on the frontiers of life and death, we had found the freedom for which we were blindly groping and which was as necessary to us as bread.
Annapurna (1952)

2 There are other Annapurnas in the lives of men.
Annapurna (1952), closing line

Michael Heseltine 1933–
British Conservative politician, who resigned from Margaret **Thatcher**'s government over the Westland affair in 1986, and challenged her for the party leadership in 1990; despite Heseltine's early lead, the succession contest was eventually won by John **Major**

3 I knew that, 'He who wields the knife never wears the crown.'
in *New Society* 14 February 1986

4 The market has no morality.
on *Panorama*, BBC1 TV, 27 June 1988

5 Polluted rivers, filthy streets, bodies bedded down in doorways are no advertisement for a prosperous or caring society.
speech at Conservative Party Conference 10 October 1989

6 If I have to intervene to help British companies . . . I'll intervene—before breakfast, before lunch, before tea and before dinner. And I'll get up the next morning and I'll start all over again.
of his role as President of the Board of Trade, a title revived for him
to the Conservative Party Conference, 7 October 1992

7 The fundamental question is is the Conservative Party leadable?
in the aftermath of disastrous electoral defeat in *Daily Telegraph* 9 June 2001 (electronic edition)

Hermann Hesse 1877–1962
German-born Swiss novelist and poet

8 If you hate a person, you hate something in him that is part of yourself. What isn't part of ourselves doesn't disturb us.
Demian (1919)

9 The bourgeois prefers comfort to pleasure, convenience to liberty, and a pleasant temperature to the deathly inner consuming fire.
Der Steppenwolf (1927) 'Tractat vom Steppenwolf'

Charlton Heston 1924–
American actor
see also **Film lines 116:13**

10 It's not the guns that kill, it's the maladjusted kids.
in *Independent* on 22 April 2000

Lord Hewart 1870–1943
British lawyer and politician

11 Justice should not only be done, but should manifestly and undoubtedly be seen to be done.
Rex v. *Sussex Justices*, 9 November 1923

Dorothy Hewett 1923–2002
Australian poet, dramatist, and radical

12 Clancy and Dooley and Don McLeod
Walked by the wurlies when the wind was loud,
And their voice was new as the fresh sap running,
And we keep on fighting and we keep on coming.
'Clancy and Dooley and Don McLeod'

13 I had a tremendous world in my head and more than three-quarters of it will be buried with me.
The Chapel Perilous (1973)

John Hewitt 1907–87
Northern Irish poet

14 We would be strangers in the Capitol;
this is our country also, no-where else;
and we shall not be outcast on the world.
'The Colony' (1950)

15 I'm an Ulsterman, of planter stock. I was born in the island of Ireland, so secondarily

I'm an Irishman. I was born in the British archipelago and English is my native tongue, so I am British. The British archipelago consists of offshore islands to the continent of Europe, so I'm European. This is my hierarchy of values and so far as I am concerned, anyone who omits one step in that sequence of values is falsifying the situation.
in *Irish Times* 4 July 1974

Reinhard Heydrich 1904–42
German Nazi leader. He was assassinated by Czech nationalists and in retaliation the Czech village of Lidice was destroyed by the SS and Gestapo

1 Now the rough work has been done we begin the period of finer work. We need to work in harmony with the civil administration. We count on you gentlemen as far as the final solution is concerned.
on the planned mass murder of eleven million European Jews
speech in Wannsee, 20 January 1942; see **Goering 134:10**

Du Bose Heyward 1885–1940 and Ira Gershwin 1896–1983
American songwriters

2 It ain't necessarily so,
De t'ings dat yo' li'ble
To read in de Bible
It ain't necessarily so.
'It ain't necessarily so' (1935 song), from *Porgy and Bess*

3 Summer time an' the livin' is easy,
Fish are jumpin' an' the cotton is high.
'Summertime' (1935 song), from *Porgy and Bess*

4 A woman is a sometime thing.
title of song (1935), from *Porgy and Bess*

J. R. Hicks 1904–89
British economist

5 The best of all monopoly profits is a quiet life.
Econometrica (1935) 'The Theory of Monopoly'

Seymour Hicks 1871–1949
English actor-manager and writer

6 You will recognize, my boy, the first sign of old age: it is when you go out into the streets of London and realize for the first time how young the policemen look.
C. R. D. Pulling *They Were Singing* (1952)

David Hilbert 1862–1943
German mathematician

7 The importance of a scientific work can be measured by the number of previous publications it makes it superfluous to read.
attributed; Lewis Wolpert *The Unnatural Nature of Science* (1993)

Christopher Hill 1912–2003
British Marxist historian

8 Only very slowly and late have men come to realize that unless freedom is universal it is only extended privilege.
Century of Revolution (1961)

Damon Hill 1960–
English motor-racing driver, winner of the Formula One world championship in 1996

9 Winning is everything. The only ones who remember you when you come second are your wife and your dog.
in *Sunday Times* 18 December 1994

Geoffrey Hill 1932–
English poet

10 She kept the siege. And every day
We watched her brooding over death
Like a strong bird above its prey.
The room filled with the kettle's breath.

Damp curtains glued against the pane
Sealed time away. Her body froze
As if to freeze us all, and chain
Creation to a stunned repose.
'In Memory of Jane Fraser' (1959)

11 I love my work and my children. God
Is distant, difficult. Things happen.
Too near the ancient troughs of blood
Innocence is no earthly weapon.
'Ovid in the Third Reich' (1968)

Joe Hill 1879–1915

Swedish-born American labour leader and songwriter. He was executed for robbery and murder but his guilt or innocence has been a subject of debate
on Hill: see **Hayes 148:7**

1 Work and pray, live on hay,
   You'll get pie in the sky when you die.
   'Preacher and the Slave' (1911 song)

2 I will die like a true-blue rebel. Don't waste any time in mourning—organize.
   before his death by firing squad
   farewell telegram to Bill Haywood, 18 November 1915

Pattie S. Hill 1868–1946

American educationist

3 Happy birthday to you.
   title of song (1935)

Edmund Hillary 1919–

New Zealand mountaineer

4 Well, we knocked the bastard off!
   on conquering Mount Everest, 1953
   Nothing Venture, Nothing Win (1975)

Richard Hillary

see **Borrowed titles 40:16**

Fred Hillebrand 1893–1963

American songwriter

5 Home James, and don't spare the horses.
   title of song (1934)

James Hilton 1900–54

English novelist

6 Nothing really wrong with him—only anno domini, but that's the most fatal complaint of all, in the end.
   Goodbye, Mr Chips (1934)

Emperor Hirohito 1901–89

Japanese monarch, Emperor from 1926

7 The war situation has developed not necessarily to Japan's advantage.
   announcing Japan's surrender, in a broadcast to his people after atom bombs had destroyed Hiroshima and Nagasaki
   on 15 August 1945

Damien Hirst 1965–

English artist

8 It's amazing what you can do with an E in A-level art, twisted imagination and a chainsaw.
   after winning the 1995 Turner Prize
   in *Observer* 3 December 1995

Ian Hislop 1960–

English satirical journalist, editor of *Private Eye*

9 If this is justice, I am a banana.
   on the libel damages awarded against Private Eye *to Sonia Sutcliffe, wife of the Yorkshire Ripper*
   comment, 24 May 1989

Alfred Hitchcock 1899–1980

British-born film director, whose thrillers were noted for their suspense and technical ingenuity
on Hitchcock: see **Hedren 150:1**

10 Actors are cattle.
   quoted in *Saturday Evening Post* 22 May 1943; Hitchcock later explained that he had said that actors should be treated like cattle

11 Television has brought back murder into the home—where it belongs.
   in *Observer* 19 December 1965

12 There is no terror in a bang, only in the anticipation of it.
   Leslie Halliwell (ed.) *Halliwell's Filmgoer's Companion* (1984); attributed

Adolf Hitler 1889–1945

Austrian-born Nazi leader, Chancellor of Germany 1933–45. His expansionist foreign policy precipitated the Second World War, while his fanatical anti-Semitism led to the Holocaust; he committed suicide in 1945
on Hitler: see **Buchman 47:8**, **Chamberlain 62:10**

13 The night of the long knives.
   *referring to the massacre of Ernst Roehm and the 'Brownshirts' by Hitler on 29–30 June 1934 (subsequently associated with Harold **Macmillan**'s Cabinet dismissals of 13 July 1962)*
   S. H. Roberts *The House Hitler Built* (1937)

14 I go the way that Providence dictates with the assurance of a sleepwalker.
   speech in Munich, 15 March 1936

1 It is the last territorial claim which I have
to make in Europe.
*on the Sudetenland, which had been allocated
to Czechoslovakia after the First World War, and
which became an object of Nazi expansionist
policies; it was ceded to Germany as a result of
the Munich Agreement of September 1938 (but
in 1945 was returned to Czechoslovakia)*
speech in Berlin, 26 September 1938

2 Is Paris burning?
on 5 August 1944, as the occupying German
troops withdrew; L. Collins and D. Lapierre *Is
Paris Burning?* (1965)

3 The broad mass of a nation . . . will more
easily fall victim to a big lie than to a small
one.
Mein Kampf [My Struggle] (1925)

Eric Hobsbawm 1917–
British Marxist historian

4 This was the kind of war which existed in
order to produce victory parades.
of the Falklands War
in *Marxism Today* January 1983

David Hockney 1937–
British artist

5 All you can do with most ordinary
photographs is stare at them—they stare
back, blankly—and presently your
concentration begins to fade. They stare
you down. I mean, photography is all right
if you don't mind looking at the world from
the point of view of a paralysed cyclops—
for a split second.
as told to Lawrence Weschler, *Cameraworks*
(1984)

6 All painting, no matter what you're
painting, is abstract in that it's got to be
organized.
David Hockney (1976)

7 The thing with high-tech is that you
always end up using scissors.
in *Observer* 10 July 1994

8 The reason you start painting yourself . . .
is that you are a model; a cheap model. I
mean you've always got yourself!
interview with *British Satellite News*
11 October 2006

Dorothy Hodgkin 1910–94
British chemist

9 Nobody who lived through the first year or
two of the trials of penicillin in Oxford
could possibly not care about what it was.
But also it's difficult not to enjoy just
growing the crystals.
Lewis Wolpert and Alison Richards *A Passion
for Science* (1988)

Ralph Hodgson 1871–1962
English poet

10 'Twould ring the bells of Heaven
The wildest peal for years,
If Parson lost his senses
And people came to theirs,
And he and they together
Knelt down with angry prayers
For tamed and shabby tigers
And dancing dogs and bears,
And wretched, blind, pit ponies,
And little hunted hares.
'Bells of Heaven' (1917)

Eric Hoffer 1902–83
American philosopher

11 When people are free to do as they please,
they usually imitate each other. Originality
is deliberate and forced, and partakes of the
nature of a protest.
Passionate State of Mind (1955)

Al Hoffman 1902–60
and **Dick Manning** 1912–91
American songwriters

12 Takes two to tango.
title of song (1952)

Gerard Hoffnung 1925–59
English humorist

13 Standing among savage scenery, the hotel
offers stupendous revelations. There is a
French widow in every bedroom, affording
delightful prospects.
*supposedly quoting a letter from a Tyrolean
landlord*
in speech at the Oxford Union, 4 December
1958

Lancelot Hogben 1895–1975
English scientist

1 This is not the age of pamphleteers. It is the age of the engineers. The spark-gap is mightier than the pen.
   Science for the Citizen (1938) epilogue

Billie Holiday 1915–59
American singer
see also **Allen 7:4**

2 Mama may have, papa may have,
   But God bless the child that's got his own!
   'God Bless the Child' (1941 song, with Arthur Herzog Jnr)

3 Mom and Pop were just a couple of kids when they got married. He was eighteen, she was sixteen, and I was three.
   Lady Sings the Blues (1956), opening line

4 You can be up to your boobies in white satin, with gardenias in your hair and no sugar cane for miles, but you can still be working on a plantation.
   Lady Sings the Blues (1956, with William Duffy)

5 In this country, don't forget, a habit is no damn private hell. There's no solitary confinement outside of jail. A habit is hell for those you love.
   of a drug habit
   Lady Sings the Blues (1956, with William Duffy)

John H. Holmes 1879–1964
American Unitarian minister

6 This, now, is the judgement of our scientific age—the third reaction of man upon the universe! This universe is not hostile, nor yet is it friendly. It is simply indifferent.
   The Sensible Man's View of Religion (1932)

Oliver Wendell Holmes Jr. 1841–1935
American lawyer and Supreme Court Justice
see also **Misquotations 225:2**

7 I have long thought that if you knew a column of advertisements by heart, you could achieve unexpected felicities with them. You can get a happy quotation anywhere if you have the eye.
   letter to Harold Laski, 31 May 1923

Winifred Holtby 1898–1935
English novelist
see also **Epitaphs 107:7**

8 The crown of life is neither happiness nor annihilation; it is understanding.
   Vera Brittain *Testament of Friendship: the Story of Winifred Holtby* (1940)

Miroslav Holub 1923–98
Czech poet

9 But above all
   we have
   the ability
   to sort peas,
   to cup water in our hands,
   to seek
   the right screw
   under the sofa
   for hours.
   'Wings' (1967)

Alec Douglas-Home, Lord Home
1903–95
British Conservative statesman, who as Earl of Home became Prime Minister in 1963 on the resignation of Harold **Macmillan** (see **Macleod 208:7**); he subsequently disclaimed his hereditary title

10 When I have to read economic documents I have to have a box of matches and start moving them into position to simplify and illustrate the points to myself.
   in *Observer* 16 September 1962

11 As far as the fourteenth earl is concerned, I suppose Mr Wilson, when you come to think of it, is the fourteenth Mr Wilson.
   *replying to Harold **Wilson**'s remark (on Home's becoming leader of the Conservative party) that 'the whole* [democratic] *process has ground to a halt with a fourteenth Earl'*
   in *Daily Telegraph* 22 October 1963

John Lee Hooker 1917–2001
American blues singer and guitarist

12 When Adam and Eve first saw each other, that's when the blues started. No matter what anybody says, it all comes down to the same thing: a man and a woman, a

broken heart and a broken home.
> in *The Healer* (1989 album); in *Independent* 23 June 2001, obituary

1 When I die they'll bury the blues with me. But the blues will never die.
> in conversation, *c.*1991; Charles Shaar Murray 'The death of the Boogie Man: an Appreciation' (online obituary, salon.com, 2001)

Herbert Hoover 1874–1964
American Republican statesman, 31st President of the US 1929–33
on Hoover: see **Coolidge 76:4**

2 Our country has deliberately undertaken a great social and economic experiment, noble in motive and far-reaching in purpose.
> *on the Eighteenth Amendment enacting Prohibition*
> letter to Senator W. H. Borah, 23 February 1928

3 The American system of rugged individualism.
> speech, 22 October 1928

4 The slogan of progress is changing from the full dinner pail to the full garage.
> *sometimes paraphrased as, 'a car in every garage and a chicken in every pot'*
> speech, 22 October 1928; referring to Henri IV, King of France (1553–1610) in Hardouin de Péréfixe *Histoire de Henry le Grand* (1681): 'I want there to be no peasant in my kingdom so poor that he is unable to have a chicken in his pot every Sunday'

5 The grass will grow in the streets of a hundred cities, a thousand towns.
> *on proposals 'to reduce the protective tariff to a competitive tariff for revenue'*
> speech, 31 October 1932

6 Older men declare war. But it is youth who must fight and die.
> speech at the Republican National Convention, Chicago, 27 June 1944

A. D. Hope 1907–2000
Australian poet

7 And her five cities, like teeming sores,

Each drains her: a vast parasite robber-state
Where second-hand Europeans pullulate
Timidly on the edge of alien shores.
> 'Australia' (1939)

Anthony Hope 1863–1933
English novelist, author of *The Prisoner of Zenda* and creator of Ruritania
see also **Epitaphs 107:15**

8 Oh, for an hour of Herod!
> *at the first night of* Peter Pan *in* 1904
> D. Mackail *Story of JMB* (1941)

Bob Hope 1903–2003
American comedian

9 A bank is a place that will lend you money if you can prove that you don't need it.
> Alan Harrington *Life in the Crystal Palace* (1959) 'The Tyranny of Farms'

Philip Hope-Wallace 1911–79
British critic

10 Never work for a liberal employer, dear boy, they'll sack you on Christmas Eve.
> *learned at his father's knee*
> in *Spectator* 7 August 1999; attributed

Harry Lloyd Hopkins 1890–1946
American government official and presidential adviser

11 We really believed in our hearts that this was the dawn of the new day we had all been praying for and talking about for so many years. We were absolutely certain that we had won the first great victory of the peace.
> *after the Yalta Conference, 1945*
> Robert E. Sherwood *Roosevelt and Hopkins* (1948)

Edward Hopper 1882–1967
American artist

12 Maybe I'm not very human. What I wanted to do was to paint sunlight on the side of the house.
> interview with Lloyd Goodrich, 20 April 1946; S. Wagstaff (ed.) *Edward Hopper* (2004)

Nick Hornby 1957–
British writer

1 The natural state of the football fan is bitter
disappointment, no matter what the score.
Fever Pitch (1992)

A. E. Housman 1859–1936
English poet and classical scholar, author of *A
Shropshire Lad* (1896), a series of nostalgic verses
based on ballad forms
on Housman: see **Kingsmill 181:4, Kingsmill 181:5**;
see also **Last words 191:6**

2 The Grizzly Bear is huge and wild;
He has devoured the infant child.
The infant child is not aware
He has been eaten by the bear.
'Infant Innocence' (1938)

3 And how am I to face the odds
Of man's bedevilment and God's?
I, a stranger and afraid
In a world I never made.
Last Poems (1922) no. 12

4 Their shoulders held the sky suspended;
They stood, and earth's foundations stay;
What God abandoned, these defended,
And saved the sum of things for pay.
Last Poems (1922) no. 37 'Epitaph on an Army
of Mercenaries'

5 For nature, heartless, witless nature,
Will neither care nor know
What stranger's feet may find the meadow
And trespass there and go,
Nor ask amid the dews of morning
If they are mine or no.
Last Poems (1922) no. 40

6 Life, to be sure, is nothing much to lose;
But young men think it is, and we were
young.
More Poems (1936) no. 36

7 A year or two ago . . . I received from
America a request that I would define
poetry. I replied that I could no more define
poetry than a terrier can define a rat, but
that I thought we both recognized the
object by the symptoms which it provokes
in us.
The Name and Nature of Poetry (1933)

8 Experience has taught me, when I am
shaving of a morning, to keep watch over
my thoughts, because, if a line of poetry

strays into my memory, my skin bristles so
that the razor ceases to act . . . The seat of
this sensation is the pit of the stomach.
The Name and Nature of Poetry (1933)

John Howard 1939–
Australian Liberal statesman, Prime Minister since
1996

9 The times will suit me.
as Leader of the Opposition
at a dinner in Washington, July 1986; David
Barnett with Pru Goward *John Howard: Prime
Minister* (1997)

Geoffrey Howe 1926–
British Conservative politician, Foreign Secretary
1983–9; his resignation from Margaret **Thatcher**'s
government in 1990 precipitated her downfall
on Howe: see **Healey 148:11**

10 It is rather like sending your opening
batsmen to the crease only for them to find
the moment that the first balls are bowled
that their bats have been broken before the
game by the team captain.
*on the difficulties caused him as Foreign
Secretary by Margaret Thatcher's anti-European
views*
resignation speech as Deputy Prime Minister,
in the House of Commons, 13 November 1990

11 The time has come for others to consider
their own response to the tragic conflict of
loyalties with which I have myself wrestled
for perhaps too long.
in the House of Commons, 13 November 1990

Frankie Howerd 1922–92
British comedian
see also **Catchphrases 60:18**

12 Such cruel glasses.
*of Robin **Day***
That Was The Week That Was (BBC television
series, from 1963)

Fred Hoyle 1915–2001
English astrophysicist

13 Space isn't remote at all. It's only an hour's
drive away if your car could go straight
upwards.
in *Observer* 9 September 1979

Elbert Hubbard 1859–1915
American writer

1 Life is just one damned thing after another.
in *Philistine* December 1909; often attributed
to Frank Ward O'Malley; see **Millay 221:16**

Frank McKinney ('Kin') Hubbard
1868–1930
American humorist

2 When a feller says, 'It hain't the money,
but th' principle o' th' thing,', it's the
money.
Hoss Sense and Nonsense (1926)

Howard Hughes Jr. 1905–76
American industrialist, aviator, and film producer

3 That man's ears make him look like a taxi-
cab with both doors open.
of Clark Gable
Charles Higham and Joel Greenberg *Celluloid
Muse* (1969)

Jimmy Hughes *fl.* 1940
and **Frank Lake** *fl.* 1940
British writers

4 Bless 'em all! Bless 'em all! The long and
the short and the tall.
'Bless 'Em All' (1940 song)

Langston Hughes 1902–67
American writer and poet

5 I, too, sing America.
I am the darker brother.
They send me to eat in the kitchen
When company comes.
'I, Too' (1925)

6 That Justice is a blind goddess
Is a thing to which we black are wise.
Her bandage hides two festering sores
That once perhaps were eyes.
'Justice'

7 Sometimes a crumb falls
From the tables of joy,
Sometimes a bone
Is flung.
To some people
Love is given,
To others
Only heaven.
'Luck'

8 I've known rivers:
I've known rivers ancient as the world and
older than the flow of human blood in
human veins.
'The Negro Speaks of Rivers' (1921)

9 I bathed in the Euphrates when dawns
were young.
I built my hut near the Congo and it lulled
me to sleep.
I looked upon the Nile and raised the
pyramids above it.
I heard the singing of the Mississippi when
Abe Lincoln went down to New Orleans,
and I've seen its muddy bosom turn all
golden in the sunset.
'The Negro Speaks of Rivers' (1921)

10 'It's powerful,' he said.
'What?'
'That one drop of Negro blood—because
just *one* drop of black blood makes a man
coloured. *One* drop—you are a Negro!'
Simple Takes a Wife (1953)

11 I got the Weary Blues
And I can't be satisfied.
'Weary Blues' (1926)

Robert Hughes 1938–
Australian writer

12 What the convict system bequeathed to
later Australian generations was not the
sturdy, skeptical independence . . . but an
intense concern with social and political
respectability. The idea of the 'convict
stain', a moral blot soaked into our fabric,
dominated all argument about Australian
selfhood by the 1840s.
The Fatal Shore (1987), introduction

Ted Hughes 1930–98
English poet, husband of Sylvia **Plath**
on Hughes: see **Heaney 149:9**

13   At that time
I had not understood
How the death hurtling to and fro
Inside your head, had to alight somewhere
And again somewhere, and had to be kept
moving.
And had to be rested
Temporarily somewhere.
Birthday Letters (1998) 'The 59th Bear' (1998)

14 It took the whole of Creation

To produce my foot, my each feather:
Now I hold Creation in my foot.
'Hawk Roosting' (1960)

1   I saw the horses:
Huge in the dense grey—ten together—
Megalith-still.
'The Horses' (1957)

2 Adam ate the apple.
Eve ate Adam.
The serpent ate Eve.
This is the dark intestine.
'Theology' (1967)

3 . . . With a sudden sharp hot stink of fox,
It enters the dark hole of the head.
'The Thought-Fox' (1957)

4 Ten years after your death
I meet on a page of your journal, as never
before,
The shock of your joy.
'Visit' (1998)

William Morris 'Billy' Hughes
1862–1952
British-born Australian statesman, Prime Minister of
Australia (as leader of the newly-formed Nationalist
Party) 1917–23

5 Oh well, I suppose it's right that the
members of these old families should stick
together nowadays. After all, their
ancestors in those days were probably
chained together.
*of support for a political rival in North Sydney,
1931*
John Thompson *On the Lips of Living Men*
(1962)

6 I don't want justice, I want mercy.
on having his portrait painted
John Thompson *On the Lips of Living Men*
(1962)

7 He couldn't lead a flock of homing pigeons.
of Robert **Menzies**
Howard Beale *This Inch of Time . . .* (1977)

Basil Hume 1923–99
English cardinal

8 I have received two wonderful graces.
First, I have been given time to prepare for
a new future. Secondly, I find myself—

uncharacteristically—calm and at peace.
*breaking the news of his imminent death from
cancer*
letter to priests of Westminster diocese, 16
April 1999

9 It is harder for some people to believe that
God loves them than to believe that he
exists.
in *Guardian* 18 June 1999

Hubert Humphrey 1911–78
American Democratic politician, Vice President
1965–69

10 There are not enough jails, not enough
policemen, not enough courts to enforce a
law not supported by the people.
speech at Williamsburg, 1 May 1965

11 Here we are the way politics ought to be in
America, the politics of happiness, the
politics of purpose and the politics of joy.
speech in Washington, 27 April 1968

Robert Hunter 1941–2005
Canadian writer

12 The word *Greenpeace* had a ring to it—it
conjured images of Eden; it said ecology
and antiwar in two syllables; it fit easily
into even a one-column headline.
Warriors of the Rainbow (1979); see **Darnell
83:8**

Samuel Huntington 1927–
American political scientist

13 The clash of civilizations and the remaking
of world order.
title of book, 1996, expanding a theory
originally introduced in an article 'The Clash of
Civilizations?' in *Foreign Affairs* Summer 1993

Herman Hupfeld 1894–1951
American songwriter

14 You must remember this, a kiss is still a
kiss,
A sigh is just a sigh;
The fundamental things apply,
As time goes by.
'As Time Goes By' (1931 song); see
Misquotations 224:15

Douglas Hurd 1930–
British Conservative politician; Foreign Secretary 1989–95

1 One of the principal props which have allowed Britain to punch above its weight in the world.
   of American support for Nato
      speech at Chatham House; in *Financial Times* 4 February 1993

Saddam Hussein 1937–2006
Iraqi statesman, President 1979–2003; following the Allied intervention in Iraq in 2003 he was tried for crimes against humanity and executed

2 The mother of battles.
   popular interpretation of his description of the approaching Gulf War; in The Times *7 January 1991 it was reported that he was ready for the 'mother of all wars'*
      speech in Baghdad, 6 January 1991

Aldous Huxley 1894–1963
English novelist
see also **Borrowed titles 40:5**

3 The greatest triumphs of propaganda have been accomplished, not by doing something, but by refraining from doing. 'Great is the truth', but still greater . . . is silence about truth.
   Brave New World (1946) foreword

4 That men do not learn very much from the lessons of history is the most important of all the lessons that history has to teach.
   Collected Essays (1959) 'Case of Voluntary Ignorance'

5 The proper study of mankind is books.
   Crome Yellow (1921); referring to Alexander Pope (1688–1744) *An Essay on Man* (1733): 'The proper study of mankind is man'

6 The end cannot justify the means, for the simple and obvious reason that the means employed determine the nature of the ends produced.
   Ends and Means (1937)

7 So long as men worship the Caesars and Napoleons, Caesars and Napoleons will duly arise and make them miserable.
   Ends and Means (1937)

8 Revolution's delightful in the preliminary stages. So long as it's a question of getting rid of people at the top.
   Eyeless in Gaza (1936), said by Mark Staithes

9 There is no substitute for talent. Industry and all the virtues are of no avail.
   Point Counter Point (1928)

10 Those who believe that they are exclusively in the right are generally those who achieve something.
   Proper Studies (1927) 'Note on Dogma'

11 Facts do not cease to exist because they are ignored.
   Proper Studies (1927) 'Note on Dogma'

12 Most human beings have an almost infinite capacity for taking things for granted.
   Themes and Variations (1950) 'Variations on a Philosopher'

13 A million million spermatozoa,
   All of them alive:
   Out of their cataclysm but one poor Noah
   Dare hope to survive.
   And among that billion minus one
   Might have chanced to be
   Shakespeare, another Newton, a new Donne—
   But the One was Me.
   'Fifth Philosopher's Song' (1920)

14 Beauty for some provides escape,
   Who gain a happiness in eyeing
   The gorgeous buttocks of the ape
   Or Autumn sunsets exquisitely dying.
   'Ninth Philosopher's Song' (1920)

15 Even if I could be Shakespeare, I think I should still choose to be Faraday.
   in 1925, attributed; Walter M. Elsasser *Memoirs of a Physicist in the Atomic Age* (1978)

Julian Huxley 1887–1975
English biologist

16 Operationally, God is beginning to resemble not a ruler but the last fading smile of a cosmic Cheshire cat.
   Religion without Revelation (1957 ed.)

i

Dolores Ibarruri ('La Pasionaria') 1895–1989
Spanish Communist leader

1 *No pasarán.*
 They shall not pass.
 the Nationalist military revolts which marked the start of the Spanish Civil War had begun the previous day
   radio broadcast, Madrid, 19 July 1936; see **Military sayings 221:7**

2 It is better to die on your feet than to live on your knees.
   speech in Paris, 3 September 1936; also attributed to Emiliano **Zapata**

Ice Cube (O'Shea Jackson) 1970–
American rap musician

3 If I'm more of an influence to your son as a rapper than you are as a father . . . you got to look at yourself as a parent.
   to Mike Sager in *Rolling Stone* 4 October 1990

Francis Iles 1893–1970
English crime writer

4 It was not until several weeks after he had decided to murder his wife that Dr Bickleigh took any active steps in the matter. Murder is a serious business.
   Malice Aforethought (1931), opening line

Ivan Illich 1926–
American sociologist

5 In a consumer society there are inevitably two kinds of slaves: the prisoners of addiction and the prisoners of envy.
   Tools for Conviviality (1973)

Dean Inge 1860–1954
English clergyman, writer, and essayist; Dean of St. Paul's, 1911–34

6 The enemies of Freedom do not argue; they shout and they shoot.
   End of an Age (1948)

7 It takes in reality only one to make a quarrel. It is useless for the sheep to pass resolutions in favour of vegetarianism, while the wolf remains of a different opinion.
   Outspoken Essays: First Series (1919) 'Patriotism'

8 The nations which have put mankind and posterity most in their debt have been small states—Israel, Athens, Florence, Elizabethan England.
   Outspoken Essays: Second Series (1922) 'State, visible and invisible'

9 A man may build himself a throne of bayonets, but he cannot sit on it.
   Philosophy of Plotinus (1923); see **Yeltsin 346:12**

Bernard Ingham 1932–
British journalist and public relations specialist, Press Secretary to Margaret **Thatcher**

10 Blood sport is brought to its ultimate refinement in the gossip columns.
   speech, 5 February 1986

Richard Ingrams 1937–
English satirical journalist, editor of *Private Eye* 1963–86

11 My motto is publish and be sued.
   on BBC Radio 4, 4 May 1977

Eugène Ionesco 1912–94
Romanian-born French dramatist, a leading exponent of the Theatre of the Absurd

1 A civil servant doesn't make jokes.
The Killer (1958)

2 Living is abnormal.
The Rhinoceros (1959)

3 You can only predict things after they have happened.
The Rhinoceros (1959)

Weldon J. Irvine 1942–2002
American songwriter

4 Young, gifted and black.
title of song (1969), music by Nina Simone;
see **Hansberry 144:2**

Steve Irwin
see **Catchphrases 58:13**

Christopher Isherwood 1904–86
British-born American novelist; his novel *Goodbye to Berlin* (1939) was filmed as *Cabaret* in 1972
see also **Auden 17:3**

5 The common cormorant (or shag)
Lays eggs inside a paper bag,
You follow the idea, no doubt?
It's to keep the lightning out.

But what these unobservant birds
Have never thought of, is that herds
Of wandering bears might come with buns
And steal the bags to hold the crumbs.
'The Common Cormorant' (written *c.*1925)

6 I am a camera with its shutter open, quite passive, recording, not thinking.
Goodbye to Berlin (1939) 'Berlin Diary'
Autumn 1930

Hastings Lionel ('Pug') Ismay
1887–1965
British general and Secretary to the Committee of Imperial Defence; first Secretary-General of Nato

7 NATO exists for three reasons—to keep the Russians out, the Americans in and the Germans down.
to a group of British Conservative backbenchers in 1949
Peter Hennessy *Never Again* (1992); oral tradition

Alec Issigonis 1906–88
Turkish-born British car designer; his most famous designs were the Morris Minor (1948) and the Mini (1959)
see also **Nuffield 240:6**

8 A camel is a horse designed by a committee.
on his dislike of working in teams
in *Guardian* 14 January 1991 'Notes and Queries'; attributed

Charles Ives 1874–1954
American composer

9 If he [a composer] has a nice wife and some nice children, how can he let the children starve on his dissonances?
Memos (1972)

10 Beauty in music is too often confused with something that lets the ears lie back in an easy chair.
Joseph Machlis *Introduction to Contemporary Music* (1963)

11 Music is life.
quoted in *American National Biography* (online edition)

Molly Ivins 1944–2007
and Lou Dubose
American journalists

12 Young political reporters are always told there are three ways to judge a politician. The first is to look at the record. The second is to look at the record. And third, look at the record.
Molly Ivins and Lou Dubose *Shrub* (2000)

13 If you think his daddy had trouble with 'the vision thing', wait till you meet this one.
*of presidential candidate George W. **Bush**; see* **Bush 48:14**
Molly Ivins and Lou Dubose *Shrub* (2000)

Alija Izetbegović 1925–2003
Bosnian statesman, President of Bosnia and Herzegovina 1990–2003

14 And to my people I say, this may not be a just peace, but it is more just than a continuation of war.
after signing the Dayton accord with representatives of Serbia and Croatia
in Dayton, Ohio, 21 November 1995

Eddie Izzard 1962–
British comedian

1 'Cake or death?' 'Cake, please.'
*imagining how a Church of England Inquisition
might have worked*
   Dress to Kill (stage show, San Francisco, 1998)

j

Jesse Jackson 1941–
American Democratic politician and clergyman

1 When I look out at this convention, I see the face of America, red, yellow, brown, black, and white. We are all precious in God's sight—the real rainbow coalition.
   speech at Democratic National Convention, Atlanta, 19 July 1988; see **Mandela 213:9**

2 She sat down in order that we all might stand up—and the walls of segregation came down.
   of the civil rights activist Rosa **Parks**
   in *BBC News* (online edition) 25 October 2005

Michael Jackson 1958–
American pop singer and songwriter. Having started singing with his four brothers, as the Jackson Five, he became the most commercially successful American star of the 1980s

3 Before you judge me, try hard to love me, look within your heart
   Then ask,—have you seen my childhood?
   'Childhood' (1995 song)

Peter Jackson 1961–
New Zealand film director, producer, and screenwriter, director of *The Lord of the Rings*
see also **Film lines 113:7**

4 We got to go there—but not back again.
   email to theonering.net, on being informed that he would not be involved in filming The Hobbit
   in *Daily Telegraph* 21 November 2006 (online ed.); see **Tolkien 316:10**

Robert H. Jackson 1892–1954
American lawyer and judge, Supreme Court Justice and chief American prosecutor at the Nuremberg trials

5 That four great nations, flushed with victory and stung with injury, stay the hands of vengeance and voluntarily submit their captive enemies to the judgement of the law, is one of the most significant tributes that Power has ever paid to Reason.
   opening statement for the prosecution at Nuremberg
   before the International Military Tribunal in Nuremberg, 21 November 1945

6 We are not final because we are infallible, but we are infallible only because we are final.
   Brown v. Allen (1953)

Joe Jacobs 1896–1940
American boxing manager

7 We was robbed!
   after Jack Sharkey beat Max Schmeling (of whom Jacobs was manager) in the heavyweight title fight, 21 June 1932 by a split decision
   P. Heller *In This Corner* (1975)

8 I should of stood in bed.
   after leaving his sick-bed to attend the World Baseball Series in Detroit, 1935, and betting on the losers
   J. Lardner *Strong Cigars* (1951)

Mick Jagger 1943–
English rock musician, co-founder, with Keith Richards, of the Rolling Stones, *c.*1962
on Jagger: see **Newspaper headlines 238:7**

9 We don't look like a bunch of schoolmasters, I admit, but at least we try

to educate people in American blues music.
*Pete Goodman In: Our Own Story by the
Rolling Stones (1964)*

Mick Jagger 1943– **and Keith Richards**
1943–
English rock musicians

1 Get off of my cloud.
title of song (1966)

2 And though she's not really ill,
There's a little yellow pill:
She goes running for the shelter
Of a mother's little helper.
'Mother's Little Helper' (1966 song)

3 I can't get no satisfaction
I can't get no girl reaction.
'(I Can't Get No) Satisfaction' (1965 song)

4 Ev'rywhere I hear the sound of marching,
charging feet, boy,
'Cause summer's here and the time is right
for fighting in the street, boy.
'Street Fighting Man' (1968 song)

5 There's just no place for a street fighting
man!
'Street Fighting Man' (1968 song)

Carwyn James 1929–83
Welsh rugby player and coach

6 Get your retaliation in first.
to the British Lions team in 1971; quoted in
David Pickering (ed.) *Cassell's Sports
Quotations* (2002)

Clive James 1939–
Australian-born critic and writer

7 Television is simultaneously blamed, often
by the same people, for worsening the
world and for being powerless to change it.
Glued to the Box (1981)

Cyril Lionel Robert James 1901–89
Trinidadian historian and writer

8 Bodyline was not an incident, it was not
an accident, it was not a temporary
aberration. It was the violence and ferocity
of our age expressing itself in cricket.
*of the 'bodyline' bowling tactics employed by
England in the Ashes series in Australia in
1932–3*
Beyond a Boundary (1963)

Henry James 1843–1916
American novelist and critic. His early novels,
notably *The Portrait of a Lady* (1881), deal with the
relationship between European civilization and
American life, while later works such as *What Maisie
Knew* (1897) depict English life
on James: see **Guedalla 140:3**

9 The deep well of unconscious cerebration.
The American (1909 ed.) preface

10 The house of fiction has in short not one
window, but a million . . . but they are,
singly or together, as nothing without the
posted presence of the watcher.
The Portrait of a Lady (1908 ed.) preface

11 Life being all inclusion and confusion, and
art being all discrimination and selection.
The Spoils of Poynton (1909 ed.) preface

12 The war has used up words.
in *New York Times* 21 March 1915

13 So here it is at last, the distinguished thing!
on experiencing his first stroke
Edith Wharton *A Backward Glance* (1934)

14 Summer afternoon—summer afternoon
. . . the two most beautiful words in the
English language.
Edith Wharton *A Backward Glance* (1934)

P. D. James 1920–
English writer of detective stories

15 What the detective story is about is not
murder but the restoration of order.
in *Face* December 1986

16 I believe that political correctness can be a
form of linguistic fascism, and it sends
shivers down the spine of my generation
who went to war against fascism.
in *Paris Review* 1995

Randall Jarrell 1914–65
American poet and literary critic

17 From my mother's sleep I fell into the State,
And I hunched in its belly till my wet fur
froze.
Six miles from earth, loosed from its dream
of life,
I woke to black flak and the nightmare
fighters.

When I died they washed me out of the
turret with a hose.
'The Death of the Ball Turret Gunner' (1945)

1 In bombers named for girls, we burned
The cities we had learned about in
school—
Till our lives wore out; our bodies lay
among
The people we had killed and never seen.
When we lasted long enough they gave us
medals;
When we died they said, 'Our casualties
were low.'
'Losses' (1963)

2 To Americans, English manners are far
more frightening than none at all.
Pictures from an Institution (1954)

3 It is better to entertain an idea than to take
it home to live with you for the rest of your
life.
Pictures from an Institution (1954)

4 One of the most obvious facts about grown-
ups, to a child, is that they have forgotten
what it is like to be a child.
introduction to Christina Stead *The Man Who
Loved Children* (1965)

Antony Jay
see **Jonathan Lynn and Antony Jay**

Douglas Jay 1907–96
British Labour politician
see also **Political sayings and slogans 257:13**

5 In the case of nutrition and health, just as
in the case of education, the gentleman in
Whitehall really does know better what is
good for people than the people know
themselves.
The Socialist Case (1939)

Margaret Jay 1939–
British Labour politician, daughter of James
Callaghan, formerly married to Peter **Jay**

6 We're simply saying that what may have
been right 800 or even 200 years ago is
not right now.
*on the abolition of the hereditary right to sit in
the House of Lords*
in *Guardian* 12 November 1999

Peter Jay 1931–
British and economist and diplomat, former
husband of Margaret **Jay**

*claiming to have been the first person to explain
monetarism to Margaret **Thatcher**:*
7 It makes one feel like the geography
teacher who showed a map of the world to
Genghis Khan.
in *Tory !Tory! Tory!* (BBC Four television
documentary) 8 March 2006

James Jeans 1877–1946
English astronomer, physicist, and mathematician

8 If we assume that the last breath of, say,
Julius Caesar has by now become
thoroughly scattered through the
atmosphere, then the chances are that
each of us inhales one molecule of it with
every breath we take.
An Introduction to the Kinetic Theory of Gases
(1940)

9 Life exists in the universe only because the
carbon atom possesses certain exceptional
properties.
The Mysterious Universe (1930)

10 From the intrinsic evidence of his creation,
the Great Architect of the Universe now
begins to appear as a pure mathematician.
The Mysterious Universe (1930)

David Jenkins 1925–
English Anglican clergyman and theologian; Bishop
of Durham 1984–94

11 I am not clear that God manoeuvres
physical things . . . After all, a conjuring
trick with bones only proves that it is as
clever as a conjuring trick with bones.
on the Resurrection
in 'Poles Apart' (BBC radio, 4 October 1984)

Roy Jenkins 1920–2003
British politician; co-founder of the Social
Democratic Party, 1981

12 The politics of the left and centre of this
country are frozen in an out-of-date mould
which is bad for the political and economic
health of Britain and increasingly

inhibiting for those who live within the mould. Can it be broken?
> speech to Parliamentary Press Gallery, 9 June 1980

Elizabeth Jennings 1926–2001
English poet

1 Do they know they're old,
These two who are my father and my
    mother
Whose fire from which I came, has now
    grown cold?
> 'One Flesh' in *Collected Poems* (1967)

C. E. M. Joad
see **Catchphrases 60:4**

Steve Jobs 1955–
American computer executive

2 It's kind of like being in the ocean. We're on the bottom, so it doesn't matter what the weather is like up top.
> *on Apple's small market share*
> Apple shareholder meeting, 27 April 2006

John XXIII 1881–1963
Italian cleric, Pope from 1958. He convened the Second Vatican Council (1962–65) and made energetic efforts to liberalize Roman Catholic policy, especially on social questions, such as the need to help the poor and the need for international peace

3 If civil authorities legislate for or allow anything that is contrary to that order and therefore contrary to the will of God, neither the laws made or the authorizations granted can be binding on the consciences of the citizens, since God has more right to be obeyed than man.
> *Pacem in Terris* (1963)

4 The social progress, order, security and peace of each country are necessarily connected with the social progress, order, security and peace of all other countries.
> *Pacem in Terris* (1963)

5 I want to throw open the windows of the Church so that we can see out and the people can see in.
> attributed

Elton John 1947–
English pop singer and songwriter

6 It's the only song I've ever written where I get goose bumps every time I play it.
> *of 'Candle in the Wind', written of Marilyn* ***Monroe****, and revived for* ***Diana****, Princess of Wales; see* **John 168:9, John 168:11**
> in *Daily Telegraph* 9 September 1997

7 I'm not a nest-egg person.
> *giving evidence in court on his average monthly expenditure*
> in *Sunday Times* 19 November 2000

8 An overview of my career is usually glasses, homosexuality, Watford Football Club, tantrums, flowers. But the music was pretty phenomenal.
> quoted in www.metro.co.uk 29 December 2006 'Quotes of the Year'

Elton John 1947–
and Bernie Taupin 1950–
English pop singer and songwriter; songwriter

9 Goodbye Norma Jean . . .
It seems to me you lived your life
Like a candle in the wind.
Never knowing who to cling to
When the rain set in.
And I would have liked to have known you
But I was just a kid
The candle burned out long before
Your legend ever did.
> *of Marilyn* ***Monroe***
> 'Candle in the Wind' (song, 1973)

10 Even when you died
Oh the press still hounded you.
> 'Candle in the Wind' (song, 1973)

11 Goodbye England's rose;
May you ever grow in our hearts.
> *rewritten for and sung at the funeral of* ***Diana****, Princess of Wales, 7 September 1997*
> 'Candle in the Wind' (song, revised version, 1997)

12 And it seems to me you lived your life
Like a candle in the wind:
Never fading with the sunset
When the rain set in.
And your footsteps will always fall here
On England's greenest hills;

Your candle's burned out long before
Your legend ever will.
'Candle in the Wind' (song, revised version, 1997)

1 Goodbye yellow brick road.
title of song (1973); see **Harburg 144:9**

John Paul II 1920–2005
Polish cleric, Pope from 1978
see also **Last words 190:13**

2 It would be simplistic to say that Divine Providence caused the fall of communism. It fell by itself as a consequence of its own mistakes and abuses. It fell by itself because of its own inherent weaknesses.
when asked by the Italian writer Vittorio Missori if the fall of the USSR could be ascribed to God
Carl Bernstein and Marco Politi *His Holiness: John Paul II and the Hidden History of our Time* (1996)

3 The tree was already rotten. I just gave it a good shake and the rotten apples fell.
of the Soviet Union
Carl Bernstein and Marco Politi *His Holiness: John Paul II and the Hidden History of our Time* (1996)

4 This liberation [of the whole human race] cannot be reduced to its social and political aspects, but rather reaches its fullness in the exercise of freedom of conscience—the basis and foundation of all other human rights.
homily in Havana, Cuba, 25 January 1998

Amryl Johnson 1944–2001
Trinidadian poet

5 for ... I am
Black
And I am
Angry
My name is
Midnight
Without
Pity.
'Midnight Without Pity' (1982)

Lyndon Baines Johnson 1908–73
American Democratic statesman, 36th President of the US 1963–9 (as Vice-President, he succeeded to the Presidency on the assassination of John F. **Kennedy**)
on Johnson: see **Political sayings and slogans 257:2, Political sayings and slogans 257:16**

*to a reporter who had queried his embracing Richard **Nixon** on the vice-president's return from a controversial tour of South America in 1958:*
6 Son, in politics you've got to learn that overnight chicken shit can turn to chicken salad.
Fawn Brodie *Richard Nixon* (1983)

7 I am a free man, an American, a United States Senator, and a Democrat, in that order.
in *Texas Quarterly* Winter 1958

8 All I have I would have given gladly not to be standing here today.
*following the assassination of J. F. **Kennedy***
first speech to Congress as President, 27 November 1963

9 We have talked long enough in this country about equal rights. We have talked for a hundred years or more. It is time now to write the next chapter, and to write it in the books of law.
speech to Congress, 27 November 1963

10 This administration today, here and now declares unconditional war on poverty in America.
State of the Union address to Congress, 8 January 1964

11 In your time we have the opportunity to move not only toward the rich society and the powerful society, but upward to the Great Society.
speech at University of Michigan, 22 May 1964

12 We still seek no wider war.
after the incident in the Tonkin Gulf, in which North Vietnam patrol boats were said to have attacked a US ship
speech on radio and television, 4 August 1964; see also **Morse 229:4**

13 We are not about to send American boys 9 or 10,000 miles away from home to do

what Asian boys ought to be doing for themselves.
> speech at Akron University, 21 October 1964; see **Roosevelt 274:1**

1 Extremism in the pursuit of the Presidency is an unpardonable vice. Moderation in the affairs of the nation is the highest virtue.
> speech in New York, 31 October 1964; see **Goldwater 135:1**

2 If I've lost Walter Cronkite I've lost Mr Average Citizen.
> *in 1968, after hearing Walter **Cronkite**'s comment on the position in Vietnam (now often quoted as '. . . I've lost the country'); see **Cronkite 80:7***
> to his press secretary George Christian; reported in D. Halberstam *The Powers That Be* (1979)

3 Better to have him inside the tent pissing out, than outside pissing in.
> *of J. Edgar Hoover, Director of the FBI 1924–72*
> D. Halberstam *The Best and the Brightest* (1972)

4 I don't want loyalty. I want *loyalty*. I want him to kiss my ass in Macy's window at high noon and tell me it smells like roses. I want his pecker in my pocket.
> *discussing a prospective assistant*
> D. Halberstam *The Best and the Brightest* (1972)

5 So dumb he can't fart and chew gum at the same time.
> *of Gerald **Ford***
> R. Reeves *A Ford, not a Lincoln* (1975)

Philander Chase Johnson 1866–1939
American journalist

6 Cheer up! the worst is yet to come!
> in *Everybody's Magazine* May 1920

Philip Johnson 1906–2005
American architect known for his use of glass

7 Merely that a building works is not sufficient.
> *Perspectives III* (1955)

8 Architecture is the art of how to waste space.
> in *New York Times* 27 December 1964

9 I would rather sleep in Chartres Cathedral with the nearest toilet two blocks away

than in a Harvard house with back to back bathrooms.
> quoted in *New York Times* 27 January 2005; obituary

Hanns Johst 1890–1978
German dramatist

10 Whenever I hear the word culture . . . I release the safety-catch of my Browning!
> *often attributed to Hermann **Goering**, and quoted 'Whenever I hear the word culture, I reach for my pistol!'*
> *Schlageter* (1933); Albert Leo Schlageter had been court-martialled and executed by French occupying troops in the Rhineland in 1924, and this play about him was favoured by the Nazi leadership

Al Jolson 1886–1950
American singer

11 You think that's noise—you ain't heard nuttin' yet!
> *first said in a café, competing with the din from a neighbouring building site, in 1906; subsequently an aside in the 1927 film* The Jazz Singer
> M. Abramson *Real Story of Al Jolson* (1950); also the title of a Jolson song, 1919, 'You Ain't Heard Nothing Yet'

Barry Owen Jones 1932–
Australian Labor politician

12 The sheer incompetence of Australia's current management is for the time being an asset in maintaining high employment levels. But we cannot count on that incompetence for ever.
> *Sleepers, Wake!* (1982) preface

13 Academic economists have about the status and reliability of astrologers or the readers of Tarot cards. If the medical profession was as lacking in resources . . . we would not have advanced very far beyond the provision of splints for broken arms.
> John Wilkes (ed.) *The Future of Work* (1981)

LeRoi Jones
see **Imamu Amiri Baraka**

Steve Jones 1944–
English biologist and geneticist

1 The Admiralty sent the *Beagle* to South America with Darwin on board not because they were interested in evolution but because they knew that the first step to understanding (and, with luck, controlling) the world was to make a map of it. The same is true of the genes.
The Language of the Genes (1993)

2 Sex and taxes are in many ways the same. Tax does to cash what males do to genes. It dispenses assets among the population as a whole. Sex, not death, is the great leveller.
speech to the Royal Society; in *Independent* 25 January 1997

Erica Jong 1942–
American novelist

3 The zipless fuck is the purest thing there is. And it is rarer than the unicorn. And I have never had one.
Fear of Flying (1973)

Janis Joplin 1943–70
American rock singer. She died from a heroin overdose just before her most successful album, *Pearl*, and her number-one single 'Me and Bobby McGee' were released
see also **Kristofferson 185:7**

4 Oh, Lord, won't you buy me a Mercedes Benz
My friends all drive Porsches,
I must make amends.
'Mercedes Benz' (1970 song)

5 Fourteen heart attacks and he had to die in my week. In MY week.
when ex-President **Eisenhower**'s death prevented her photograph appearing on the cover of Newsweek
in *New Musical Express* 12 April 1969

6 Onstage I make love to twenty-five thousand people, then I go home alone.
quoted in *New Yorker* 14 August 1971

Jenny Joseph 1932–
English poet

7 When I am an old woman I shall wear purple
With a red hat which doesn't go, and doesn't suit me.
And I shall spend my pension on brandy and summer gloves
And satin sandals, and say we've got no money for butter.
'Warning' (1974)

James Joyce 1882–1941
Irish novelist, whose novel *Ulysses* (1922) revolutionized the structure of the modern novel and developed the stream-of-consciousness technique
on Joyce: see **Lawrence 193:1, Woolf 342:4**

8 His soul swooned slowly as he heard the snow falling faintly through the universe and faintly falling, like the descent of their last end, upon all the living and the dead.
Dubliners (1914) 'The Dead'

9 riverrun, past Eve and Adam's, from swerve of shore to bend of bay, brings us by a commodious vicus of recirculation back to Howth Castle and Environs.
Finnegans Wake (1939), opening line

10 That ideal reader suffering from an ideal insomnia.
Finnegans Wake (1939)

11 All moanday, tearsday, wailsday, thumpsday, frightday, shatterday till the fear of the Law.
Finnegans Wake (1939)

12 Three quarks for Muster Mark!
the name quark, *originally* quork, *for various subatomic particles was changed by association with this line*
Finnegans Wake (1939)

13 A portrait of the artist as a young man.
title of novel, 1916

14 Once upon a time and a very good time it was there was a moocow coming down along the road and this moocow that was down along the road met a nicens little boy named baby tuckoo.
A Portrait of the Artist as a Young Man (1916), opening line

1 When the soul of a man is born in this country, there are nets flung at it to hold it back from flight. You talk to me of nationality, language, religion. I shall try to fly by those nets.
A Portrait of the Artist as a Young Man (1916)

2 Ireland is the old sow that eats her farrow.
A Portrait of the Artist as a Young Man (1916)

3 Pity is the feeling which arrests the mind in the presence of whatsoever is grave and constant in human sufferings and unites it with the human sufferer. Terror is the feeling which arrests the mind in the presence of whatsoever is grave and constant in human sufferings and unites it with the secret cause.
A Portrait of the Artist as a Young Man (1916)

4 The artist, like the God of the creation, remains within or behind or beyond or above his handiwork, invisible, refined out of existence, indifferent, paring his fingernails.
A Portrait of the Artist as a Young Man (1916)

5 I will not serve that in which I no longer believe whether it call itself my home, my fatherland or my church: and I will try to express myself in some mode of life or art as freely as I can and as wholly as I can, using for my defence the only arms I allow myself to use, silence, exile, and cunning.
A Portrait of the Artist as a Young Man (1916)

6 Stately, plump Buck Mulligan came from the stairhead, bearing a bowl of lather on which a mirror and a razor lay crossed.
Ulysses (1922), opening line

7 The snotgreen sea. The scrotumtightening sea.
Ulysses (1922)

8 It is a symbol of Irish art. The cracked lookingglass of a servant.
Ulysses (1922)

9 I fear those big words, Stephen said, which make us so unhappy.
Ulysses (1922)

10 History, Stephen said, is a nightmare from which I am trying to awake.
Ulysses (1922)

11 A man of genius makes no mistakes. His errors are volitional and are the portals of discovery.
Ulysses (1922)

12 Greater love than this, he said, no man hath that a man lay down his wife for his friend.
Ulysses (1922); referring to the *Bible* St John: 'Greater love hath no man than this, that a man lay down his life for his friends'; see **Thorpe 315:12**

13 The heaventree of stars hung with humid nightblue fruit.
Ulysses (1922)

14 When a young man came up to him in Zurich and said, 'May I kiss the hand that wrote *Ulysses?*' Joyce replied, somewhat like King Lear, 'No, it did lots of other things too.'
Richard Ellmann *James Joyce* (1959); referring to William Shakespeare (1564–1616) *King Lear* (1605–6): 'GLOUCESTER: O! let me kiss that hand! LEAR: Let me wipe it first; it smells of mortality.'

William Joyce (Lord Haw-Haw)

1906–46
American-born British wartime broadcaster from Nazi Germany, executed for treason

15 Germany calling! Germany calling!
habitual introduction to propaganda broadcasts to Britain during the Second World War

Juan Carlos I 1938–

Spanish monarch, King from 1975

16 The Crown, the symbol of the permanence and unity of Spain, cannot tolerate any actions by people attempting to disrupt by force the democratic process.
on the occasion of an attempted right-wing coup in 1981
television broadcast at 1.15 a.m., 24 February 1981

17 I will neither abdicate the Crown nor leave Spain. Whoever rebels will provoke a new civil war and will be responsible.
television broadcast, 24 February 1981

Jack Judge 1878–1938
and Harry Williams 1874–1924
British songwriters

1 It's a long way to Tipperary,
It's a long way to go;
It's a long way to Tipperary,
To the sweetest girl I know!
   'It's a Long Way to Tipperary' (1912 song),
   associated with the First World War

Carl Gustav Jung 1875–1961
Swiss psychologist

2 A man who has not passed through the inferno of his passions has never overcome them.
   Memories, Dreams, Reflections (1962)

3 As far as we can discern, the sole purpose of human existence is to kindle a light in the darkness of mere being.
   Memories, Dreams, Reflections (1962)

4 Every form of addiction is bad, no matter whether the narcotic be alcohol or morphine or idealism.
   Memories, Dreams, Reflections (1962)

5 The meeting of two personalities is like the contact of two chemical substances: if there is any reaction, both are transformed.
   Modern Man in Search of a Soul (1933)

6 The afternoon of human life must also have a significance of its own and cannot be merely a pitiful appendage to life's morning.
   The Stages of Life (1930)

7 Where love rules, there is no will to power, and where power predominates, love is lacking. The one is the shadow of the other.
   'Über die Psychologie des Unbewussten' (1917)

8 I do not believe . . . I know.
   L. van der Post *Jung and the Story of our Time* (1976)

Jung Chang 1952–
Chinese writer

9 At the age of fifteen my grandmother became the concubine of a warlord general.
   Wild Swans (1991), opening line

John Junor 1919–97
British journalist, Editor of the *Sunday Express* 1954–86
see also **Catchphrases 59:14, Catchphrases 60:22, Newspaper headlines 238:5**

10 Such a graceful exit. And then he had to go and do this on the doorstep.
   *on Harold **Wilson**'s 'Lavender List' (the honours list he drew up on resigning the British premiership in 1976)*
      in *Observer* 23 January 1990

11 No first-class journalist ever has a beard.
   often quoted as: 'Never trust a man with a beard'
      quoted in *Oxford Dictionary of National Biography* (online edition, 2004–) 'John Junor'

Donald Justice 1925–2004
American poet

12 Men at forty
Learn to close softly
The doors to rooms they will not be
Coming back to.
   'Men at Forty' (1967)

k

Pauline Kael 1919–2001
American film critic

1 The words 'Kiss Kiss Bang Bang' which I saw on an Italian movie poster, are perhaps the briefest statement imaginable of the basic appeal of movies.
   Kiss Kiss Bang Bang (1968) 'Note on the Title'

2 Being able to talk about movies with someone—to share the giddy high excitement you feel—is enough for a friendship.
   Movie Love (1991)

3 A good movie can take you out of your dull funk and the hopelessness that so often goes with slipping into a theatre; a good movie can make you feel alive again, in contact, not just lost in another city.
   Going Steady: Film Writing 1968–1969 (1994) 'Trash, Art, and the Movies'

Franz Kafka 1883–1924
Czech novelist, who wrote in German. His work is characterized by its portrayal of an enigmatic and nightmarish reality where the individual is perceived as lonely, perplexed, and threatened

4 When Gregor Samsa awoke one morning from uneasy dreams he found himself transformed in his bed into a gigantic insect.
   The Metamorphosis (1915), opening line

5 Someone must have traduced Joseph K., for without having done anything wrong he was arrested one fine morning.
   The Trial (1925), opening line

6 You may object that it is not a trial at all; you are quite right, for it is only a trial if I recognize it as such.
   The Trial (1925)

7 It's often better to be in chains than to be free.
   The Trial (1925)

Gus Kahn 1886–1941
and Raymond B. Egan 1890–1952
American songwriters

8 There's nothing surer,
   The rich get rich and the poor get children.
   In the meantime, in between time,
   Ain't we got fun.
   'Ain't We Got Fun' (1921 song)

Beatrice Kaufman 1895–1945
American writer, wife of George S. **Kaufman**

9 I've been rich and I've been poor: rich is better.
   in *Washington Post* 12 May 1937; often associated with Sophie **Tucker**

George S. Kaufman 1889–1961
American dramatist and director, member of the Alquonquin Circle, husband of Beatrice **Kaufman**
see also **Film lines 114:14, Hart 147:2**

10 Beware of flu. Avoid crowds. See *Someone in the House.*
   advertisement for his unsuccessful revision of the Broadway play, staged during the influenza epidemic of 1918
      Howard Teichmann *George S. Kaufman: an intimate portrait* (1972)

11 Satire is what closes Saturday night.
      Scott Meredith *George S. Kaufman and his Friends* (1974)

George S. Kaufman 1889–1961 **and** Howard Teichmann 1916–87
American dramatists

1 Shakespeare is so tiring. You never get a chance to sit down unless you're a king.
The Solid Gold Cadillac (1953); spoken by Josephine Hull

Gerald Kaufman 1930–
British Labour politician

2 The longest suicide note in history.
on the Labour Party manifesto New Hope for Britain (*1983*). *The subsequent general election was a disaster for the Labour party*
Denis Healey *The Time of My Life* (1989)

Paul Kaufman and **Mike Anthony**
American songwriters

3 Poetry in motion.
title of song (1960)

Kenneth Kaunda 1924–
Zambian statesman, President 1964–91

4 Westerners have aggressive problem-solving minds; Africans experience people.
attributed, 1990

Patrick Kavanagh 1904–67
Irish poet

5 Cassiopeia was over
Cassidy's hanging hill,
I looked and three whin bushes rode across
The horizon—the Three Wise Kings.
'A Christmas Childhood' (1947)

6 Clay is the word and clay is the flesh
Where the potato-gatherers like
mechanized scarecrows move
Along the side-fall of the hill—Maguire and
his men.
'The Great Hunger' (1947)

7 I hate what every poet hates in spite
Of all the solemn talk of contemplation.
Oh, Alexander Selkirk knew the plight
Of being king and government and nation.
A road, a mile of kingdom, I am king

Of banks and stones and every blooming
thing.
'Inniskeen Road: July Evening' (1936);
referring to William Cowper (1731–1800)
'Verses Supposed to be Written by Alexander
Selkirk' (1782): 'I am monarch of all I survey
. . . / Better dwell in the midst of alarms, /
Than reign in this horrible place'

David Kay
American official, weapons inspector in Iraq 1991–2 and 2003–4

8 We have not yet found shiny, pointy things that I would call a weapon.
interview, CNN *Late Edition* 5 October 2003;
transcript quoted on CNN.com

Peter Kay 1973–
British comedian

9 Garlic bread—it's the future, I've tasted it.
Brian Potter envisages a reborn Phoenix Club
Phoenix Nights 'Brian Gets Everyone Back
Together' (Series 2, 2002)

10 All castles had one major weakness. The enemy used to get in through the gift shop.
attributed; in *Nuts* May 2005 (second in
competition for funniest one-liner ever)

Danny Kaye
see **Film lines 116:1**

Paul Keating 1944–
Australian Labor statesman, Prime Minister 1991–6

11 You look like an Easter Island statue with an arse full of razor blades.
in the Australian Parliament to Malcolm **Fraser***,*
1983
Michael Gordon *A Question of Leadership*
(1993)

12 This is a recession that Australia had to have.
speaking as Federal Treasurer, 29 November
1990

13 Even as it [Great Britain] walked out on you and joined the Common Market, you were still looking for your MBEs and your knighthoods, and all the rest of the regalia that comes with it. You would take Australia right back down the time tunnel to the cultural cringe where you have always come from.

addressing Australian Conservative supporters of Great Britain

speech, House of Representatives (Australia) 27 February 1992; see **Phillips 253:12**

1 Leadership is not about being nice. It's about being right and being strong.

in *Time* 9 January 1995

John Keats 1920–
American journalist
see also **Nader 233:6**

2 The automobile changed our dress, manners, social customs, vacation habits, the shape of our cities, consumer purchasing patterns, common tastes and positions in intercourse.

The Insolent Chariots (1958)

Garrison Keillor 1942–
American humorous writer and broadcaster

3 Years ago, manhood was an opportunity for achievement, and now it is a problem to be overcome.

The Book of Guys (1994)

4 Ronald Reagan, the President who never told bad news to the American people.

We Are Still Married (1989)

Helen Keller 1880–1968
American writer and social reformer, blind and deaf from the age of 19 months

5 Science may have found a cure for most evils; but it has found no remedy for the worst of them all—the apathy of human beings.

My Religion (1927)

6 The mystery of language was revealed to me. I knew then that 'w-a-t-e-r' meant the wonderful cool something that was flowing over my hand. That living word awakened my soul, gave it light, joy, set it free!

The Story of My Life (1902)

7 For some inexplicable reason the sense of smell does not hold the high position it deserves among its sisters. There is something of the fallen angel about it.

The World I Live In (1908)

Walt Kelly
see **Cartoons 56:12**

Jaan Kenbrovin
and **William Kellette** *fl.* 1919
American songwriters

8 I'm forever blowing bubbles.

title of song (1919)

Charles Kennedy 1959–
British Liberal Democrat politician, Party Leader 1999–2006

9 War is not the word; nor is crusade. Resolve is.

of the appropriate response to the danger of world terrorism

speech to the Liberal Democrat Party Conference, 24 September 2001; see **Bush 49:5**

Florynce Kennedy 1916–2000
American lawyer

10 If men could get pregnant, abortion would be a sacrament.

in *Ms.* March 1973

11 When you want to get to the suites, start in the streets.

her rule for political activism

attributed; in *Los Angeles Times* 28 December 2000 (obituary)

12 Freedom is like taking a bath: You got to keep doing it every day.

attributed; in *Madison Capital Times* 28 December 2000 (obituary)

Jacqueline Kennedy
see **Jacqueline Kennedy Onassis**

James B. Kennedy
and **John W. Bratton** *fl.* 1932
British songwriters

13 If you go down in the woods today
You're sure of a big surprise
If you go down in the woods today
You'd better go in disguise
For every Bear that ever there was
Will gather there for certain because,
Today's the day the Teddy Bears have their
    Picnic.

'Teddy Bear's Picnic' (1932 song)

Jimmy Kennedy *fl.* 1939 and **Michael Carr** 1904–68
British songwriters

1 We're gonna hang out the washing on the Siegfried Line.
>   title of song (1939); the Siegfried Line was the line of defence constructed by the Germans along the western frontier of Germany before the Second World War

John Fitzgerald Kennedy 1917–63
American Democratic statesman, 35th President of the US, 1961–3, who in 1962 successfully demanded the withdrawal of Soviet missiles from Cuba; he was assassinated while riding in a motorcade through Dallas, Texas. He was the son of Joseph and Rose **Kennedy**, brother of Robert **Kennedy**, and first husband of Jacqueline Kennedy **Onassis**
on Kennedy: see **Bentsen 30:2**, **Kennedy 178:1**; see also **Forsyth 121:7**

2 Don't buy a single vote more than necessary. I'll be damned if I'm going to pay for a landslide.
>   telegraphed message from his father, read at a Gridiron dinner in Washington, 15 March 1958, and almost certainly JFK's invention

3 We stand today on the edge of a new frontier.
>   speech accepting the Democratic nomination, 15 July 1960

4 The torch has been passed to a new generation of Americans—born in this century, tempered by war, disciplined by a hard and bitter peace.
>   inaugural address, 20 January 1961

5 We shall pay any price, bear any burden, meet any hardship, support any friend, oppose any foe to assure the survival and the success of liberty.
>   inaugural address, 20 January 1961

6 If a free society cannot help the many who are poor, it cannot save the few who are rich.
>   inaugural address, 20 January 1961

7 Let us never negotiate out of fear. But let us never fear to negotiate.
>   inaugural address, 20 January 1961

8 All this will not be finished in the first 100 days. Nor will it be finished in the first 1,000 days, nor in the life of this Administration, nor even perhaps in our lifetime on this planet. But let us begin.
>   inaugural address, 20 January 1961

9 And so, my fellow Americans: ask not what your country can do for you—ask what you can do for your country.
>   inaugural address, 20 January 1961; see **Gibran 132:8**

10 I believe that this Nation should commit itself to achieving the goal, before this decade is out, of landing a man on the Moon and returning him safely to earth.
>   Supplementary State of the Union message to Congress, 25 May 1961

11 Mankind must put an end to war or war will put an end to mankind.
>   speech to United Nations General Assembly, 25 September 1961

12 Those who make peaceful revolution impossible will make violent revolution inevitable.
>   speech at the White House, 13 March 1962

13 Probably the greatest concentration of talent and genius in this house except for perhaps those times when Thomas Jefferson ate alone.
>   *of a dinner for Nobel Prizewinners at the White House*
>   in *New York Times* 30 April 1962

14 There are no 'white' or 'coloured' signs on the foxholes or graveyards of battle.
>   *on proposed Civil Rights Bill*
>   message to Congress, 19 June 1963

15 All free men, wherever they may be, are citizens of Berlin. And, therefore, as a free man, I take pride in the words *Ich bin ein Berliner* [I am a Berliner].
>   speech in West Berlin, 26 June 1963, after visiting the Berlin Wall

16 In free society art is not a weapon . . . Artists are not engineers of the soul.
>   speech at Amherst College, Mass., 26 October 1963; see **Gorky 136:2**

17 It was involuntary. They sank my boat.
>   *on being asked how he became a war hero*
>   A. M. Schlesinger Jr. *A Thousand Days* (1965)

Joseph P. Kennedy 1888–1969

American financier and diplomat; father of John F. **Kennedy** and Robert **Kennedy**
see also **Sayings and slogans 287:12**

1 We're going to sell Jack like soapflakes.
   when his son John made his bid for the Presidency
      John H. Davis *The Kennedy Clan* (1984)

Robert Kennedy 1925–68

American Democratic politician, assassinated while campaigning for the presidential nomination; son of Joseph **Kennedy** and Rose **Kennedy**, brother of John Fitzgerald **Kennedy**

2 One-fifth of the people are against everything all the time.
      speech, University of Pennsylvania, 6 May 1964

3 Each time a man stands up for an ideal, or acts to improve the lot of others, or strikes out against injustice, he sends forth a tiny ripple of hope, and crossing each other from a million different centres of energy and daring those ripples build a current which can sweep down the mightiest walls of oppression and resistance.
      speech, Cape Town, 6 June 1966

Rose Kennedy 1890–1995

American wife of Joseph **Kennedy**, mother of John F. **Kennedy** and Robert **Kennedy**

4 Now Teddy must run.
   to her daughter, on hearing of the assassination of Robert Kennedy
      in *Times* 24 January 1995 (obituary); attributed, perhaps apocryphal

Jomo Kenyatta 1891–1978

Kenyan statesman, Prime Minister of Kenya 1963 and President 1964–78

5 The African is conditioned, by the cultural and social institutions of centuries, to a freedom of which Europe has little conception, and it is not in his nature to accept serfdom forever. He realizes that he must fight unceasingly for his own emancipation; for without this he is doomed to remain the prey of rival imperialisms.
      Facing Mount Kenya (1938); conclusion

Jack Kerouac 1922–69

American novelist and poet, a leading member of the beat generation, known particularly for his semi-autobiographical novel *On the Road*
on Kerouac: see **Burroughs 48:8**

6 The beat generation.
      phrase coined in the course of a conversation; in *Playboy* June 1959

7 It is not my fault that certain so-called bohemian elements have found in my writings something to hang their peculiar beatnik theories on.
      in *New York Journal-American* 8 December 1960

Jean Kerr 1923–2003

American writer

8 I feel about airplanes the way I feel about diets. It seems to me that they are wonderful things for other people to go on.
      The Snake Has All the Lines (1958)

John Kerry 1943–

American Democratic politician, presidential candidate in 2004

9 How do you ask a man to be the last man to die in Vietnam? How do you ask a man to be the last man to die for a mistake?
      speech to Senate Committee, 23 April 1971

John Maynard Keynes 1883–1946

English economist. He laid the foundations of modern macroeconomics with *The General Theory of Employment, Interest and Money* (1936), in which he argued that full employment is determined by effective demand and requires government spending on public works to stimulate this

10 I work for a Government I despise for ends I think criminal.
   he had strong reservations on war policy and conscription
      letter to Duncan Grant, 15 December 1917

11 Lenin was right. There is no subtler, no surer means of overturning the existing basis of society than to debauch the currency.
      Economic Consequences of the Peace (1919)

12 I do not know which makes a man more conservative—to know nothing but the present, or nothing but the past.
      The End of Laissez-Faire (1926)

1 The important thing for Government is not to do things which individuals are doing already, and to do them a little better or a little worse; but to do those things which at present are not done at all.
The End of Laissez-Faire (1926)

2 This extraordinary figure of our time, this syren, this goat-footed bard, this half-human visitor to our age from the hag-ridden magic and enchanted woods of Celtic antiquity.
Essays in Biography (1933) 'Mr Lloyd George'

3 If the Treasury were to fill old bottles with banknotes, bury them at suitable depths in disused coalmines which are then filled up to the surface with town rubbish, and leave it to private enterprise on well-tried principles of *laissez-faire* to dig the notes up again . . . there need be no more unemployment and, with the help of the repercussions, the real income of the community, and its capital wealth also, would probably become a good deal greater than it actually is.
General Theory (1936)

4 Practical men, who believe themselves to be quite exempt from any intellectual influences, are usually the slaves of some defunct economist. Madmen in authority, who hear voices in the air, are distilling their frenzy from some academic scribbler of a few years back.
General Theory (1947 ed.)

5 *In the long run* we are all dead.
A Tract on Monetary Reform (1923)

6 Words ought to be a little wild, for they are the assault of thoughts upon the unthinking.
in *New Statesman and Nation* 15 July 1933

7 I evidently knew more about economics than my examiners.
explaining why he performed badly in the Civil Service examinations
Roy Harrod *Life of John Maynard Keynes* (1951)

8 We threw good housekeeping to the winds. But we saved ourselves and helped save the world.
of Britain in the Second World War
A. J. P. Taylor *English History, 1914–1945* (1965)

9 LADY VIOLET BONHAM-CARTER: What do you think happens to Mr Lloyd George when he is alone in the room?
KEYNES: When he is alone in the room there is nobody there.
Lady Violet Bonham-Carter *Impact of Personality in Politics* (Romanes Lecture, 1963)

Ruhollah Khomeini (Ayatollah Khomeini) 1900–89
Iranian Shiite Muslim leader, who in 1979 returned from exile to lead an Islamic revolution which established Iran as a fundamentalist Islamic republic

10 If laws are needed, Islam has established them all. There is no need . . . after establishing a government, to sit down and draw up laws.
Islam and Revolution: Writings and Declarations of Imam Khomeini (1981) 'Islamic Government'

11 I would like to inform all the intrepid Muslims in the world that the author of the book entitled *The Satanic Verses*, which has been compiled, printed and published in opposition to Islam, the Prophet and the Qur'an, as well as those publishers who were aware of its contents, have been declared *madhur el dam* [those whose blood must be shed]. I call on all zealous Muslims to execute them quickly, wherever they find them, so that no-one will dare to insult Islam again. Whoever is killed in this path will be regarded as a martyr.
fatwa against Salman **Rushdie**, issued 14 February 1989; see **Wesker 331:15**

Nikita Khrushchev 1894–1971
Soviet statesman, Premier 1958–64; he denounced **Stalin** in 1956, and came close to war with the US over the Cuban Missile Crisis in 1962

12 If anyone believes that our smiles involve abandonment of the teaching of Marx, Engels and Lenin he deceives himself. Those who wait for that must wait until a shrimp learns to whistle.
speech in Moscow, 17 September 1955

13 Comrades! We must abolish the cult of the individual decisively, once and for all.
speech to secret session of 20th Congress of the Communist Party, 25 February 1956

1 If you don't like us, don't accept our invitations and don't invite us to come to see you. Whether you like it or not, history is on our side. We will bury you.
   speech to Western diplomats in Moscow, 18 November 1956

2 If one cannot catch the bird of paradise, better take a wet hen.
   in *Time* 6 January 1958

3 If you start throwing hedgehogs under me, I shall throw a couple of porcupines under you.
   in *New York Times* 7 November 1963

Joyce Kilmer 1886–1918
American poet

4 I think that I shall never see
  A poem lovely as a tree.
  'Trees' (1914)

5 Poems are made by fools like me,
  But only God can make a tree.
  'Trees' (1914)

Lord Kilmuir (David Maxwell Fyfe)
1900–67
British Conservative politician and lawyer

6 Loyalty is the Tory's secret weapon.
   Anthony Sampson *Anatomy of Britain* (1962)

David King 1939–
British scientist

7 In my view, climate change is the most severe problem we are facing today—more serious even than the threat of terrorism.
   in *Science* 9 January 2004

Martin Luther King 1929–68
American civil rights leader who organized non-violent resistance and peaceful mass demonstrations and was a notable orator; he was assassinated in Memphis
see also: **Epitaphs 107:5**

8 I want to be the white man's brother, not his brother-in-law.
   in *New York Journal-American* 10 September 1962

9 Judicial decrees may not change the heart; but they can restrain the heartless.
   speech in Nashville, Tennessee, 27 December 1962

10 The Negro's great stumbling block in the stride toward freedom is not the White Citizens Councillor or the Ku Klux Klanner but the white moderate who is more devoted to order than to justice; who prefers a negative peace which is the absence of tension to a positive peace which is the presence of justice.
   letter from Birmingham Jail, Alabama, 16 April 1963

11 If a man hasn't discovered something he will die for, he isn't fit to live.
   speech in Detroit, 23 June 1963

12 I have a dream that one day on the red hills of Georgia the sons of former slaves and the sons of former slave owners will be able to sit down together at the table of brotherhood.
   speech at Civil Rights March in Washington, 28 August 1963

13 I have a dream that my four little children will one day live in a nation where they will not be judged by the colour of their skin but by the content of their character.
   speech at Civil Rights March in Washington, 28 August 1963

14 We must learn to live together as brothers or perish together as fools.
   speech at St Louis, 22 March 1964

15 I just want to do God's will. And he's allowed me to go up to the mountain. And I've looked over, and I've seen the promised land . . . So I'm happy tonight. I'm not worried about anything. I'm not fearing any man.
   on the day before his assassination
   speech in Memphis, 3 April 1968

16 Nothing in all the world is more dangerous than sincere ignorance and conscientious stupidity.
   Strength to Love (1963)

17 The means by which we live have outdistanced the ends for which we live. Our scientific power has outrun our spiritual power. We have guided missiles and misguided men.
   Strength to Love (1963)

18 A riot is at bottom the language of the unheard.
   Where Do We Go From Here? (1967)

Stephen King 1947–
American writer, known for his novels of horror and
suspense

1 Terror . . . often arises from a pervasive
sense of disestablishment; that things are
in the unmaking.
Danse Macabre (1981)

William Lyon Mackenzie King
1874–1950
Canadian Liberal statesman, Prime Minister 1921–6,
1926–30, and 1935–48

2 If some countries have too much history,
we have too much geography.
speech, Canadian House of Commons, 18 June
1936

3 Not necessarily conscription, but
conscription if necessary.
speech, Canadian House of Commons, 7 July
1942

Hugh Kingsmill 1889–1949
English man of letters

4 What still alive at twenty-two,
A clean upstanding chap like you?
Sure, if your throat 'tis hard to slit,
Slit your girl's, and swing for it.
'Two Poems, after A. E. Housman' (1933) no. 1

5 But bacon's not the only thing
That's cured by hanging from a string.
'Two Poems, after A. E. Housman' (1933) no. 1

Neil Kinnock 1942–
British Labour politician, Party Leader 1983–92

*to a heckler who said that Mrs **Thatcher** 'showed
guts' during the Falklands War*
6 It's a pity others had to leave theirs on the
ground at Goose Green to prove it.
television interview, 6 June 1983

7 If Margaret Thatcher wins on Thursday, I
warn you not to be ordinary, I warn you
not to be young, I warn you not to fall ill,
and I warn you not to grow old.
on the prospect of a Conservative re-election
speech at Bridgend, 7 June 1983

8 The grotesque chaos of a Labour council
hiring taxis to scuttle round the city

handing out redundancy notices to its own
workers.
of the actions of the city council in Liverpool
speech at the Labour Party Conference,
1 October 1985

9 I would die for my country but I could
never let my country die for me.
speech at Labour Party Conference,
30 September 1986

10 Why am I the first Kinnock in a thousand
generations to be able to get to a
university?
*later plagiarized by the American politician Joe
Biden*
speech in party political broadcast, 21 May
1987

11 Politics without compromise is like a car
without a gear box: it can look quite
elegant but you won't get anything out of
it.
to BBC breakfast television, quoted in
Guardian (online edition) 20 January 2006;
see also **Blair 36:5**

Alfred Kinsey 1894–1956
American zoologist and sex researcher. He carried
out pioneering studies into sexual behaviour by
interviewing large numbers of people. His best-
known work, *Sexual Behaviour in the Human Male*
(1948, also known as the *Kinsey Report*), was
controversial but highly influential

12 The only unnatural sex act is that which
you cannot perform.
in *Time* 21 January 1966

Rudyard Kipling 1865–1936
English writer and poet
see also **Epitaphs 108:7**

13 Foot—foot—foot—foot—sloggin' over
Africa—
(Boots—boots—boots—boots—movin' up
and down again!)
'Boots' (1903)

14 If any question why we died,
Tell them, because our fathers lied.
'Epitaphs of the War: Common Form' (1919)

15 I could not dig: I dared not rob:
Therefore I lied to please the mob.
Now all my lies are proved untrue
And I must face the men I slew.
What tale shall serve me here among

Mine angry and defrauded young?
'Epitaphs of the War: A Dead Statesman'
(1919)

1 My son was killed while laughing at some
   jest. I would I knew
What it was, and it might serve me in a
   time when jests are few.
'Epitaphs of the War: A Son' (1919)

2 The female of the species is more deadly
   than the male.
'The Female of the Species' (1919)

3 For all we have and are,
   For all our children's fate,
   Stand up and take the war.
   The Hun is at the gate!
For All We Have and Are (1914)

4 The Garden called Gethsemane
   In Picardy it was.
'Gethsemane' (1918)

5 And all the time we halted there
   I prayed my cup might pass.
   It didn't pass—it didn't pass—
   It didn't pass from me.
   I drank it when we met the gas
   Beyond Gethsemane!
'Gethsemane' (1918); referring to the *Bible* St
Matthew: 'If it be possible, let this cup pass
from me'

6 Our England is a garden, and such gardens
   are not made
By singing:—'Oh, how beautiful!' and
   sitting in the shade,
While better men than we go out and start
   their working lives
At grubbing weeds from gravel paths with
   broken dinner-knives.
'The Glory of the Garden' (1911)

7 If you can keep your head when all about
   you
Are losing theirs and blaming it on you.
'If—' (1910)

8 If you can meet with Triumph and Disaster
And treat those two impostors just the
   same.
'If—' (1910)

9 If you can talk with crowds and keep your
   virtue,
Or walk with Kings—nor lose the common
   touch . . .
If you can fill the unforgiving minute

With sixty seconds' worth of distance run,
Yours is the Earth and everything that's in
   it,
And—which is more—you'll be a Man, my
   son!
'If—' (1910)

10 Then ye returned to your trinkets; then ye
   contented your souls
With the flannelled fools at the wicket or
   the muddied oafs at the goals.
'The Islanders' (1903)

11 They shall not return to us, the resolute,
   the young,
The eager and whole-hearted whom we
   gave:
But the men who left them thriftily to die in
   their own dung,
Shall they come with years and honour to
   the grave?
'Mesopotamia' (1917)

12 Dawn off the Foreland—the young flood
   making
Jumbled and short and steep—
Black in the hollows and bright where it's
   breaking—
Awkward water to sweep.
'Mines reported in the fairway,
'Warn all traffic and detain.
' 'Sent up *Unity, Claribel, Assyrian,
   Stormcock,* and *Golden Gain.*'
'Mine Sweepers' (1915)

13 'Have you news of my boy Jack?'
Not this tide.
'When d'you think that he'll come back?
Not with this wind blowing, and this tide.
'My Boy Jack' (1916)

14 Brothers and Sisters, I bid you beware
Of giving your heart to a dog to tear.
'The Power of the Dog' (1909)

15 Five and twenty ponies,
   Trotting through the dark—
   Brandy for the Parson,
   'Baccy for the Clerk;
   Laces for a lady, letters for a spy,
   Watch the wall, my darling, while the
      Gentlemen go by!
'A Smuggler's Song' (1906)

16 Of all the trees that grow so fair,
   Old England to adorn,
   Greater are none beneath the Sun,

Than Oak, and Ash, and Thorn.
'A Tree Song' (1906)

1 What answer from the North?
One Law, one Land, one Throne.
'Ulster' (1912)

2 They shut the road through the woods
Seventy years ago.
Weather and rain have undone it again,
And now you would never know
There was once a road through the woods.
'The Way through the Woods' (1910)

3 And that is called paying the Dane-geld;
But we've proved it again and again,
That if once you have paid him the Dane-
geld
You never get rid of the Dane.
'What Dane-geld means' (1911)

4 But the wildest of all the wild animals was
the Cat. He walked by himself, and all
places were alike to him.
Just So Stories (1902) 'The Cat that Walked by
Himself'

5 An Elephant's Child—who was full of
'satiable curtiosity.
Just So Stories (1902) 'The Elephant's Child'

6 Go to the banks of the great grey-green,
greasy Limpopo River, all set about with
fever-trees, and find out.
Just So Stories (1902) 'The Elephant's Child'

7 Little Friend of all the World.
Kim's nickname
Kim (1901)

8 'Tisn't beauty, so to speak, nor good talk
necessarily. It's just It. Some women'll stay
in a man's memory if they once walked
down a street.
Traffics and Discoveries (1904) 'Mrs Bathurst'

9 Words are, of course, the most powerful
drug used by mankind.
speech, 14 February 1923; see **Lowell 203:8**

10 Power without responsibility: the
prerogative of the harlot throughout the
ages.
*summing up Lord **Beaverbrook**'s political
standpoint vis-à-vis the Daily Express, and
quoted by Kipling's cousin Stanley **Baldwin**,
18 March 1931*
in *Kipling Journal* December 1971

Henry Kissinger 1923–
American politician, Secretary of State to Richard
Nixon

11 The management of a balance of power is a
permanent undertaking, not an exertion
that has a foreseeable end.
White House Years (1979)

12 The conventional army loses if it does not
win. The guerrilla wins if he does not lose.
in *Foreign Affairs* January 1969

13 There cannot be a crisis next week. My
schedule is already full.
in *New York Times Magazine* 1 June 1969

14 Withdrawal of US troops will become like
salted peanuts to the American public: the
more US troops come home, the more will
be demanded.
memo to President **Nixon**, 10 September
1969, produced by Kissinger at a meeting with
George W. **Bush**'s speechwriter Michael
Gerson in 2005; Bob Woodward *State of
Denial* (2006)

15 Power is the great aphrodisiac.
in *New York Times* 19 January 1971

16 We are the President's men.
M. and B. Kalb *Kissinger* (1974)

17 Africa tugs at the American conscience.
Does America Need a Foreign Policy? (2001)

18 For other nations, Utopia is a blessed past
never to be recovered; for Americans it is
just beyond the horizon.
attributed

Lord Kitchener 1850–1916
British soldier and statesman, Secretary of State for
War from 1914; he was drowned when the HMS
Hampshire was torpedoed
on Kitchener: see **Asquith 15:5**; see also **Military
sayings 221:11**

19 Do your duty bravely. Fear God. Honour
the King.
*message to soldiers of the British Expeditionary
Force (1914)*
in *Times* 19 August 1914

20 I don't mind your being killed, but I object
to your being taken prisoner.
to the Prince of Wales during the First World War
Journals and Letters of Viscount Esher (1938)
vol. 3, 18 December 1914

Paul Klee 1879–1940

Swiss painter, resident in Germany from 1906; his work is characterized by his sense of colour and moves freely between abstraction and figuration

1 Art does not reproduce the visible; rather, it makes visible.
Inward Vision (1958) 'Creative Credo' (1920)

2 An active line on a walk, moving freely without a goal. A walk for walk's sake. The agent is a point which moves around.
Pedagogical Sketchbook (1925)

3 Colour has taken hold of me; no longer do I have to chase after it. I know that it has hold of me for ever. That is the significance of this blessed moment.
on a visit to Tunis in 1914
Herbert Read *A Concise History of Modern Painting* (1968)

Charles Knight
and Kenneth Lyle *fl.* 1914

British songwriters

4 When there's trouble brewing,
When there's something doing,
Are we downhearted?
No! Let 'em all come!
'Here we are! Here we are again!!' (1914 song)

Frank H. Knight 1885–1972

American economist and philosopher, who developed an influential theory of profit

5 Costs merely register competing attractions.
Risk, Uncertainty and Profit (1921)

Ronald Knox 1888–1957

English writer and Roman Catholic priest

6 When suave politeness, tempering bigot zeal,
Corrected *I believe* to *One does feel.*
'Absolute and Abitofhell' (1913)

7 There once was a man who said, 'God
Must think it exceedingly odd
If he finds that this tree
Continues to be
When there's no one about in the Quad.'
L. Reed *Complete Limerick Book* (1924), to which came the anonymous reply: 'Dear Sir, / Your astonishment's odd: / *I* am always about

in the Quad. / And that's why the tree / Will continue to be, / Since observed by / Yours faithfully, / God'

8 It is stupid of modern civilization to have given up believing in the devil, when he is the only explanation of it.
Let Dons Delight (1939)

9 The baby doesn't understand English and the Devil knows Latin.
on being asked to perform a baptism in English
Evelyn Waugh *Ronald Knox* (1959)

10 A loud noise at one end and no sense of responsibility at the other.
definition of a baby
attributed

Ted Koehler 1894–1973

American songwriter

11 Stormy weather,
Since my man and I ain't together.
'Stormy Weather' (1933 song)

Arthur Koestler 1905–83

Hungarian-born British novelist and essayist

12 One may not regard the world as a sort of metaphysical brothel for emotions.
Darkness at Noon (1940) 'The Second Hearing'

13 Behaviourism is indeed a kind of flat-earth view of the mind . . . it has substituted for the erstwhile anthropomorphic view of the rat, a ratomorphic view of man.
The Ghost in the Machine (1967)

14 God seems to have left the receiver off the hook, and time is running out.
The Ghost in the Machine (1967)

15 The most persistent sound which reverberates through man's history is the beating of war drums.
Janus (1978)

16 Man can leave the earth and land on the moon, but cannot cross from East to West Berlin. Prometheus reaches for the stars with an insane grin on his face and a totem-symbol in his hand.
Janus (1978)

Helmut Kohl 1930–
German statesman, Chancellor of West Germany (1982–90) and first postwar Chancellor of united Germany (1990–8)

1 We Germans now have the historic chance to realize the unity of our fatherland.
on the reunification of Germany
in *Guardian* 15 February 1990

2 The policy of European integration is in reality a question of war and peace in the 21st century.
speech at Louvain University, 2 February 1996

Karl Kraus 1874–1936
Austrian satirist

3 How is the world ruled and how do wars start? Diplomats tell lies to journalists and then believe what they read.
Aphorisms and More Aphorisms (1909)

Jiddu Krishnamurti 1895–1986
Indian spiritual philosopher and religious teacher

4 Religion is the frozen thought of men out of which they build temples.
in *Observer* 22 April 1928

5 Truth is a pathless land, and you cannot approach it by any path whatsoever, by any religion, by any sect.
speech in Holland, 3 August 1929

6 Happiness is a state of which you are unconscious, of which you are not aware. The moment you are aware that you are happy, you cease to be happy ... You want to be consciously happy; the moment you are consciously happy, happiness is gone.
Penguin Krishnamurti Reader (1970)
'Questions and Answers'

Kris Kristofferson 1936–
American actor

7 Freedom's just another word for nothin' left to lose,
Nothin' ain't worth nothin', but it's free.
'Me and Bobby McGee' (1969 song, with Fred Foster), sung by Janis **Joplin**

Joseph Wood Krutch 1893–1970
American critic and naturalist

8 The most serious charge which can be brought against New England is not

Puritanism but February.
The Twelve Seasons (1949)

9 Cats seem to go on the principle that it never does any harm to ask for what you want.
The Twelve Seasons (1949)

Stanley Kubrick 1928–99
American film director

10 The great nations have always acted like gangsters, and the small nations like prostitutes.
in *Guardian* 5 June 1963

Satish Kumar 1937–
Indian writer

11 Lead me from death to life, from falsehood to truth.
Lead me from despair to hope, from fear to trust.
Lead me from hate to love, from war to peace.
Let peace fill our heart, our world, our universe.
'Prayer for Peace' (1981); adapted from the Upanishads

Milan Kundera 1929–
Czech novelist, emigrated to France in 1975

12 *I think, therefore I am* is the statement of an intellectual who underrates toothaches.
Immortality (1991); referring to René Descartes (1596–1650) *Le Discours de la méthode* (1637): 'I think, therefore I am'

13 The unbearable lightness of being.
title of novel (1984)

14 Mankind's true moral test, its fundamental test (which lies deeply buried from view) consists of its attitudes towards those who are at its mercy: animals.
The Unbearable Lightness of Being (1984)

15 A man able to think isn't defeated—even when he is defeated.
in *Sunday Times* 20 May 1984

Hari Kunzru 1969–
British novelist

16 This is what Big Brother is for. It holds up a mirror to national attitudes. If we don't like

what we see, we ought to change.
on reported racist abuse of the Indian
Bollywood star Shilpa Shetty on the Channel 4
television programme Celebrity Big Brother
    in *Guardian* (online edition) 17 January 2007

l

Christian Lacroix 1951–
French couturier

1 Haute Couture should be fun, foolish and
almost unwearable.
in *Observer* 27 December 1987

Fiorello La Guardia 1882–1947
American Republican politician, Mayor of New York
1934–45; he took office when the city was on the
verge of bankruptcy

2 When I make a mistake, it's a beaut!
*on the appointment of Herbert O'Brien as a
judge in 1936*
William Manners *Patience and Fortitude*
(1976)

3 I am a captain of a broken ship who must
patch and repair and struggle continually
to keep it afloat.
in *American National Biography* (online
edition) 'Fiorello La Guardia'

John Lahr 1941–
American critic

4 Society drives people crazy with lust and
calls it advertising.
in *Guardian* 2 August 1989

5 I know in an existential sense that life can
change on a dime . . . something has
instantly and inexorably changed in
American life.
*in the aftermath of the terrorist attacks which
destroyed the World Trade Center in New York,
and damaged the Pentagon*
'Forever Changed', online correspondence
with August Wilson in *Slate*, posted 11
September 2001

R. D. Laing 1927–89
Scottish psychiatrist. He became famous for his
controversial views on madness and in particular on
schizophrenia, linking what society calls insanity
with politics and family structure

6 The divided self.
title of book on schizophrenia, 1960

7 The brotherhood of man is evoked by
particular men according to their
circumstances. But it seldom extends to all
men. In the name of our freedom and our
brotherhood we are prepared to blow up
the other half of mankind and to be blown
up in turn.
The Politics of Experience (1967)

8 The experience and behaviour that gets
labelled schizophrenic is a special strategy
that a person invents in order to live in an
unlivable situation.
The Politics of Experience (1967)

9 Madness need not be all breakdown. It may
also be break-through.
The Politics of Experience (1967)

Constant Lambert 1905–51
English composer and conductor, musical director of
Sadler's Wells

10 The whole trouble with a folk song is that
once you have played it through there is
nothing much you can do except play it
over again and play it rather louder.
Music Ho! (1934)

George Lamming 1927–
Barbados-born novelist and poet

11 In the castle of my skin.
title of novel (1953)

1 The architecture of our future is not only unfinished; the scaffolding has hardly gone up.

'The West Indian People' (1966) in Andrew Salkey (ed.) *Caribbean Essays* (1973); quoted by Owen Arthur, Prime Minister of Barbados, symposium 28–30 June 2006

Norman Lamont 1942–
British Conservative politician, Chancellor of the Exchequer 1990–93
see also **Misquotations 224:8**

2 Rising unemployment and the recession have been the price that we've had to pay to get inflation down. [Labour shouts] That is a price well worth paying.

speech in the House of Commons, 16 May 1991

3 We give the impression of being in office but not in power.

as a backbencher, having left the government in the previous month
speech in the House of Commons, 9 June 1993

Giuseppe di Lampedusa 1896–1957
Italian novelist. His only novel *The Leopard* was originally rejected by publishers but won worldwide acclaim on its posthumous publication

4 If we want things to stay as they are, things will have to change.

The Leopard (1957)

5 Love. Of course, love. Flames for a year, ashes for thirty.

The Leopard (1957)

Osbert Lancaster 1908–86
English writer and cartoonist

6 For self-revelation, whether it be a Tudor villa on the by-pass or a bomb-proof chalet at Berchtesgaden, there's no place like home.

Homes Sweet Homes (1939)

Lev Landau 1908–68
Russian physicist

7 Cosmologists are often in error, but never in doubt.

attributed in Simon Singh *Big Bang* (2004)

Ann Landers (Esther Pauline Friedman Lederer) 1918–2002
American advice columnist

8 At every party there are two kinds of people—those who want to go home and those who don't. The trouble is, they are usually married to each other.

in *International Herald Tribune* 19 June 1991

Julia Lang
see **Catchphrases 58:7**

Susanne Langer 1895–1985
American philosopher

9 Art is the objectification of feeling, and the subjectification of nature.

Mind (1967) vol. 1

Dominique Lapierre 1931–
French writer and journalist

10 I discovered on the battlefield that one cannot at the same time be Hemingway and Mother Teresa.

in *Guardian* 15 April 2000

Ring Lardner Jr. 1915–2000
American screenwriter, one of the Hollywood Ten who in 1947 were indicted for refusing to testify before Congress's House Un-American Activities Committee

of the question, 'Are you now, or have you ever been . . . ':

11 HUAC CHAIRMAN: It is a very simple question. Any real American would be proud to answer it.
RING LARDNER JR.: I could answer the question exactly the way you want, but if I did, I would hate myself in the morning.

refusing to testify before HUAC, 30 October 1947 (see **Political sayings and slogans 257:3**); Lardner was subsequently imprisoned for contempt of Congress, and blacklisted by film studios

Philip Larkin 1922–85
English poet and librarian, whose poetry is characterized by an air of melancholy and bitterness, and by stoic wit

12 Sexual intercourse began
In nineteen sixty-three
(Which was rather late for me)—

Between the end of the *Chatterley* ban
And the Beatles' first LP.
'Annus Mirabilis' (1974)

1 Time has transfigured them into
Untruth. The stone fidelity
They hardly meant has come to be
Their final blazon, and to prove
Our almost-instinct almost true:
What will survive of us is love.
'An Arundel Tomb' (1964)

2 Life is first boredom, then fear.
Whether or not we use it, it goes,
And leaves what something hidden from
us chose,
And age, and then the only end of age.
'Dockery & Son' (1964)

3 And that will be England gone,
The shadows, the meadows, the lanes,
The guildhalls, the carved choirs.
There'll be books; it will linger on
In galleries; but all that remains
For us will be concrete and tyres.
'Going, Going' (1974)

4 Nothing, like something, happens
anywhere.
'I Remember, I Remember' (1955)

5 Perhaps being old is having lighted rooms
Inside your head, and people in them,
acting.
People you know, yet can't quite name.
'The Old Fools' (1974)

6 They fuck you up, your mum and dad.
They may not mean to, but they do.
They fill you with the faults they had
And add some extra, just for you.
'This Be The Verse' (1974)

7 Man hands on misery to man.
It deepens like a coastal shelf.
Get out as early as you can,
And don't have any kids yourself.
'This Be The Verse' (1974)

8 Why should I let the toad *work*
Squat on my life?
Can't I use my wit as a pitchfork
And drive the brute off?
'Toads' (1955)

9 Give me your arm, old toad;
Help me down Cemetery Road.
'Toads Revisited' (1964)

10 I thought of London spread out in the sun,

Its postal districts packed like squares of
wheat.
'The Whitsun Weddings' (1964)

11 I listen to money singing. It's like looking
down
From long french windows at a provincial
town,
The slums, the canal, the churches ornate
and mad
In the evening sun. It is intensely sad.
'Money' (1974)

12 That nice little Shetland pony of a job you
so confidently bestrode in the beginning
suddenly grows to a frightful Grand
National winner.
on his work as Librarian of Hull University
in *Times Educational Supplement* 19 May 1972

13 Deprivation is for me what daffodils were
for Wordsworth.
Required Writing (1983)

14 The notion of expressing sentiments in
short lines having similar sounds at their
ends seems as remote as mangoes on the
moon.
letter to Barbara Pym, 22 January 1975

Harold Laski 1893–1950
British Labour political theorist and academic
on Laski: see **Attlee 16:5**

15 It was like watching someone organize her
own immortality. Every phrase and
gesture was studied. Now and again, when
she said something a little out of the
ordinary, she wrote it down herself in a
notebook.
of Virginia **Woolf**
letter to Oliver Wendell **Holmes** Jr., 30
November 1930

Last words
see box overleaf

Harry Lauder 1870–1950
Scottish music-hall entertainer

16 Keep right on to the end of the road,
Keep right on to the end.
Tho' the way be long, let your heart be
strong,
Keep right on round the bend.
'The End of the Road' (1924 song)

Last words

1 Bugger Bognor.
*King **George V** (1865–1936) on his deathbed in
1936, when someone remarked 'Cheer up, your
Majesty, you will soon be at Bognor again';
alternatively, a comment made in 1929, when it
was proposed that the town be named Bognor
Regis on account of the king's convalescence
there after a serious illness*
   K. Rose *King George V* (1983); see **Last
   words 190:5**

2 Come closer, boys. It will be easier for
you.
*Erskine **Childers** (1870–1922) to the firing
squad at his execution*
   Burke Wilkinson *The Zeal of the Convert*
   (1976)

3 Farewell, my friends. I go to glory.
*last words of Isadora Duncan (1878–1927)
before her scarf caught in a car wheel,
breaking her neck*
   Mary Desti *Isadora Duncan's End* (1929)

4 For God's sake look after our people.
*Robert Falcon **Scott** (1868–1912)*
   last diary entry, 29 March 1912

5 How's the Empire?
*said by King **George** V (1865–1936) to his
private secretary on the morning of his death*
   K. Rose *King George V* (1983); see **Last
   words 190:1**

6 I am just going outside and may be some
time.
*last words of Captain Lawrence Oates
(1880–1912)*
   Robert Falcon **Scott** diary entry, 16–17 March
   1912; see **Epitaphs 107:11, Mahon 211:5**

7 If this is dying, then I don't think much of
it.
*Lytton **Strachey** (1880–1932) on his deathbed*
   M. Holroyd *Lytton Strachey* (1968) vol. 2

8 I'm stuck in this building . . . I just
wanted you to know that I love you. Bye
bye.
*final recorded message for her husband from
Melissa Hughes in the World Trade Center, 11
September 2001; 'I love you' was the final
telephone message from many of those
trapped in the buildings and planes involved*

in the day's terrorist attacks
   in *Guardian* 14 September 2001; see also
   Last words 191:8, McEwan 207:7

9 I'm tired, and I have to go to sleep.
*Allen **Ginsberg** (1912–97), before lapsing into
a final coma*
   in *Athens News* 9 April 1997

10 In this life there's nothing new in dying,
But nor, of course, is living any newer.
*the final poem of Sergei **Yesenin** (1895–1925),
written in his own blood the day before he
hanged himself in his Leningrad hotel room*
   'Goodbye, my Friend, Goodbye' (1925)

11 It is dark for writing but I will try to by
touch. It looks as though there is no
chance.
*final written message from Dmitry Kolesnikov,
one of those lost in the Russian nuclear
submarine Kursk*
   in *Daily Telegraph* 3 November 2000

12 I've got the bows up . . . I'm going . . . I'm
on my back . . . I've gone. Oh.
*last recorded words of Donald Campbell
(1921-67), killed while trying to break his own
water speed record; the wreckage of his boat
Bluebird, with Campbell's body, was found and
raised in March 2001*
   in *Times* 9 March 2001

13 Let me go to the house of the Father.
*last words, spoken in Polish, of Pope **John
Paul II** (1920–2005)*
   in *Independent* 19 September 2005

14 Let's do it!
*Gary Gilmore (1941–77) to the firing squad at
his execution; after his conviction for murder,
Gilmore had refused to appeal, and petitioned
the Supreme Court that the execution should
be carried out*
   Norman Mailer *The Executioner's Song*
   (1979)

15 Let's roll.
Todd Beamer, 11 September 2001
   heard by telephone operator as Beamer and
   other passengers were planning to storm
   the cockpit of the hijacked United Airlines
   Flight 93; the plane crashed in Pennsylvania
   minutes later; in *Washington Post* 17
   September 2001; see **Burnett 48:7**

▶

▶ **Last words** continued

1 Lord take my soul, but the struggle continues.
Ken Saro-Wiwa (1941–95), just before he was hanged
in *Daily Telegraph* 13 November 1995

2 The love boat has crashed against the everyday. You and I, we are quits, and there is no point in listing mutual pains, sorrows, and hurts.
*from an unfinished poem found among Vladimir **Mayakovsky**'s papers, a variant of which he quoted in his suicide letter*
letter, 12 April 1930

3 Love? What is it? Most natural painkiller. What there is . . . LOVE.
*final entry in the journal of William S. **Burroughs**, 1 August 1997, the day before he died*
in *New Yorker* 18 August 1997

4 Now I'll have eine kleine Pause.
last words of Kathleen Ferrier (1912–53)
Gerald Moore *Am I Too Loud?* (1962)

5 Tell them I've had a wonderful life.
*Ludwig **Wittgenstein** (1889–1951) to his doctor's wife, before losing consciousness, 28 April 1951*
Ray Monk *Ludwig Wittgenstein* (1990)

6 That is indeed very good. I shall have to repeat that on the Golden Floor!
*said by A. E. **Housman** (1859–1936) to his physician who had told him a risqué story*
attributed

7 We are putting passengers off in small boats . . . Engine room getting flooded . . . CQ.
CQD was the original SOS call for shipping
last signals sent from the *Titanic*, 15 April 1912

8 What do I tell the pilot to do?
American lawyer Barbara Olson (1955–2001), in a final telephone conversation to her husband, the US Solicitor-General, from the hijacked plane which crashed into the Pentagon, 11 September 2001
in *Daily Telegraph* 14 September 2001, obituary; see also **Last words190:8**

9 'What *is* the answer?' No answer came. She laughed and said, 'In that case what is the question?'
*Gertrude **Stein** (1874–1946)*
Donald Sutherland *Gertrude Stein, A Biography of her Work* (1951)

10 Why fear death? It is the most beautiful adventure in life.
the American theatrical manager Charles Frohman (1860–1915) before drowning in the Lusitania, 7 May 1915
I. F. Marcosson and D. Frohman *Charles Frohman* (1916); see **Barrie 24:2**

11 Why not? Why not? Why not? Yeah.
*Timothy **Leary** (1920–96)*
in *Independent* 1 June 1996

12 Yes, I believe in God.
reply to gunman
attributed to the American schoolgirl Cassie Bernall (1981–99), Columbine High School, Littleton, Colorado, 20 April 1999; the words have also been attributed to a survivor

Harry Lauder continued

13 I love a lassie, a bonnie, bonnie lassie,
She's as pure as the lily in the dell.
She's as sweet as the heather, the bonnie bloomin' heather—
Mary, ma Scotch Bluebell.
'I Love a Lassie' (1905 song)

14 Roamin' in the gloamin'.
title of song (1911)

Stan Laurel 1890–1965
British-born American film comedian and screenwriter. He played the scatterbrained and often tearful innocent, Oliver Hardy his pompous, overbearing, and frequently exasperated friend

15 Another nice mess you've gotten me into.
often 'another fine mess'
Another Fine Mess (1930 film) and many other Laurel and Hardy films; spoken by Oliver Hardy

1 Why don't you do something to *help* me?
   Drivers' Licence Sketch (1947); spoken by
   Oliver Hardy

William L. Laurence 1888–1977
Lithuanian-born American journalist and science
writer, who became the official historian of the
Manhattan Project, and flew in the plane which
dropped an atomic bomb on Nagasaki

2 At first it was a giant column that soon
   took the shape of a supramundane
   mushroom.
   *on the first atomic explosion in New Mexico, 16
   July 1945*
      in *New York Times* 26 September 1945

D. H. Lawrence 1885–1930
English novelist and poet. His work is characterized
by its condemnation of industrial society and by its
frank exploration of sexual relationships
on Lawrence: see **Griffith-Jones 139:4, Robinson
271:14**

3 To the Puritan all things are impure, as
   somebody says.
   Etruscan Places (1932) 'Cerveteri'; referring to
   the *Bible* Titus: 'Unto the pure all things are
   pure'

4 It was in 1915 the old world ended.
   Kangaroo (1923)

5 John Thomas says good-night to Lady
   Jane, a little droopingly, but with a hopeful
   heart.
   Lady Chatterley's Lover (1928)

6 Pornography is the attempt to insult sex, to
   do dirt on it.
   Phoenix (1936) 'Pornography and Obscenity'

7 The novel is the one bright book of life.
   Phoenix (1936) 'Why the novel matters'

8 The bridge to the future is the phallus.
   Sex, Literature and Censorship (1955)

9 Never trust the artist. Trust the tale. The
   proper function of a critic is to save the tale
   from the artist who created it.
   Studies in Classic American Literature (1923)

10 Be a good animal, true to your instincts.
   The White Peacock (1911)

11 Don't you find it a beautiful clean thought,
   a world empty of people, just uninterrupted
   grass, and a hare sitting up?
   Women in Love (1920)

12 How beastly the bourgeois is
   Especially the male of the species.
   'How Beastly the Bourgeois Is' (1929)

13 While we have sex in the mind, we truly
   have none in the body.
   'Leave Sex Alone' (1929)

14 Men! The only animal in the world to fear!
   'Mountain Lion' (1923)

15 I never saw a wild thing
   Sorry for itself.
   'Self-Pity' (1929)

16 A snake came to my water-trough
   On a hot, hot day, and I in pyjamas for the
   heat,
   To drink there.
   'Snake' (1923)

17 And so, I missed my chance with one of the
   lords
   Of life.
   And I have something to expiate:
   A pettiness.
   'Snake' (1923)

18 Not I, not I, but the wind that blows
   through me!
   'Song of a Man who has Come Through' (1917)

19 When I read Shakespeare I am struck with
   wonder
   That such trivial people should muse and
   thunder
   In such lovely language.
   'When I Read Shakespeare' (1929)

20 Curse the blasted, jelly-boned swines, the
   slimy, the belly-wriggling invertebrates,
   the miserable sodding rotters, the flaming
   sods, the snivelling, dribbling, dithering,
   palsied, pulse-less lot that make up
   England today. They've got white of egg in
   their veins, and their spunk is that watery
   it's a marvel they can breed. They *can*
   nothing but frog-spawn—the gibberers!
   God, how I hate them!
   letter to Edward Garnett, 3 July 1912

21 The dead don't die. They look on and help.
   letter to J. Middleton Murry, 2 February 1923

22 I want to go south, where there is no
   autumn, where the cold doesn't crouch
   over one like a snow-leopard waiting to
   pounce. The heart of the North is dead, and

the fingers of cold are corpse fingers.
   letter to J. Middleton Murry, 3 October 1924

1 My God, what a clumsy *olla putrida* James
   Joyce is! Nothing but old fags and cabbage-
   stumps of quotations from the Bible and
   the rest, stewed in the juice of deliberate,
   journalistic dirty-mindedness.
      letter to Aldous and Maria Huxley, 15 August
      1928

T. E. Lawrence 1888–1935
English soldier and writer, known as Lawrence of
Arabia. From 1916 onwards he helped to organize
the Arab revolt against the Turks in the Middle East,
contributing to General Allenby's eventual victory in
Palestine in 1918
on Lawrence: see **Berners 31:7, Shaw 293:13**; see
also **Borrowed titles 41:3**

2 Many men would take the death-sentence
   without a whimper to escape the life-
   sentence which fate carries in her other
   hand.
      The Mint (1955)

3 I loved you, so I drew these tides of men
   into my hands and wrote my will across
   the sky in stars.
   To earn you freedom, the seven pillared
      worthy house, that your eyes might be
      shining for me
   When we came.
      Seven Pillars of Wisdom (1926) dedication

4 The people of England have been led in
   Mesopotamia into a trap from which it will
   be hard to escape with dignity and honour
   . . . Things have been far worse than we
   have been told, our administration more
   bloody and inefficient than the public
   knows.
      *of insurgency in the British mandatory area of
      Mesopotamia (now Iraq)*
         in *Sunday Times* 22 August 1920; see also
         Newspaper headlines and leaders 237:12

5 The trouble with Communism is that it
   accepts too much of today's furniture. I
   hate furniture.
      letter to Cecil Day Lewis, 20 December 1934

6 Surely the sex business isn't worth all this
   damned fuss? I've met only a handful of
   people who cared a biscuit for it.
      on reading Lady Chatterley's Lover
         Christopher Hassall *Edward Marsh* (1959)

Nigel Lawson 1932–
British Conservative politician, Chancellor of the
Exchequer 1983–89

7 It represented the tip of a singularly ill-
   concealed iceberg, with all the destructive
   potential that icebergs possess.
      *of an article by Alan Walters, Margaret
      Thatcher's economic adviser, criticizing the
      Exchange Rate Mechanism*
         in the House of Commons following his
         resignation as Chancellor, 31 October 1989

Nigella Lawson 1960–
British journalist and cookery writer

8 Diets are like boyfriends—it never really
   works to go back to them.
      in *Sunday Times* 5 March 2006

Irving Layton 1912–2006
Romanian-born Canadian poet

9 We love in another's soul
   whatever of ourselves
   we can deposit in it;
   the greater the deposit,
   the greater the love.
      The Whole Bloody Bird (1969) 'Aphs'

Edmund Leach 1910–89
English social anthropologist

10 Far from being the basis of the good
   society, the family, with its narrow privacy
   and tawdry secrets, is the source of all our
   discontents.
      BBC Reith Lectures, 1967, in *Listener* 30
      November 1967

Stephen Leacock 1869–1944
Canadian humorist

11 The parent who could see his boy as he
   really is, would shake his head and say:
   'Willie, is no good; I'll sell him.'
      Essays and Literary Studies (1916) 'Lot of a
      Schoolmaster'

12 Advertising may be described as the
   science of arresting human intelligence
   long enough to get money from it.
      Garden of Folly (1924) 'The Perfect Salesman'

13 A sportsman is a man who, every now and
   then, simply has to get out and kill
   something. Not that he's cruel. He

wouldn't hurt a fly. It's not big enough.
My Remarkable Uncle (1942)

Timothy Leary 1920–96
American psychologist and drug pioneer. After
experimenting with consciousness-altering drugs
including LSD, he was dismissed from his teaching
post at Harvard University in 1963 and became a
figurehead for the hippy drug culture
on Leary: see **Epitaphs 108:8**; see also **Last words
191:11**

1 If you take the game of life seriously, if you
take your nervous system seriously, if you
take your sense organs seriously, if you
take the energy process seriously, you
must turn on, tune in and drop out.
The Politics of Ecstasy (1968)

2 The PC is the LSD of the '90s.
remark made in the early 1990s; in *Guardian*
1 June 1996

*on abandoning his plan to have his head
preserved by the cryonics movement:*
3 They have no sense of humour. I was
worried I would wake up in 50 years
surrounded by people with clipboards.
in *Daily Telegraph* 10 May 1996

F. R. Leavis 1895–1978
English literary critic. Founder and editor of the
quarterly *Scrutiny* (1932–53), he emphasized the
value of critical study of English literature to
preserving cultural continuity

4 The common pursuit.
title of book (1952)

5 The great tradition.
title of book (1948)

6 It is well to start by distinguishing the few
really great—the major novelists who
count in the same way as the major poets,
in the sense that they not only change the
possibilities of the art for practitioners and
readers, but that they are significant in
terms of the human awareness they
promote; awareness of the possibilities of
life.
The Great Tradition (1948)

7 Self-contempt, well-grounded.
on the foundation of T. S. ***Eliot****'s work*
in *Times Literary Supplement* 21 October 1988

Fran Lebowitz 1946–
American humorous writer

8 If people don't want to listen to *you*, what
makes you think they want to hear from
your sweater?
of slogans on clothing
Metropolitan Life (1978)

9 The opposite of talking isn't listening. The
opposite of talking is waiting.
Social Studies (1981)

10 Remember that as a teenager you are at
the last stage in your life when you will be
happy to hear that the phone is for you.
Social Studies (1981)

11 The best fame is a writer's fame: it's
enough to get a table at a good restaurant,
but not enough that you get interrupted
when you eat.
in *Observer* 30 May 1993

Stanislaw Lec 1909–66
Polish writer

12 One has to multiply thoughts to the point
where there aren't enough policemen to
control them.
Unkempt Thoughts (1962)

13 When smashing monuments, save the
pedestals—they always come in handy.
Unkempt Thoughts (1962)

14 Is it progress if a cannibal uses knife and
fork?
Unkempt Thoughts (1962)

John le Carré 1931–
English thriller writer. He is known for his
unromanticized and thoughtful spy novels, which
often feature the British agent George Smiley

15 A desk is a dangerous place from which to
watch the world.
The Honourable Schoolboy (1977)

16 Do you know what love is? I'll tell you: it is
whatever you can still betray.
The Looking Glass War (1965), spoken by
Haldane

1 The spy who came in from the cold.
   title of novel (1963) set in the Cold War

2 He gives his trust slowly and with the greatest care. And he is ready at any time to take it back.
   of Alec **Guinness**, *who played George Smiley* in *Daily Telegraph* 7 August 2000

Le Corbusier 1887–1965
Swiss-born French architect and town planner, who developed theories on functionalism and the use of new materials and industrial techniques

3 A house is a machine for living in.
   Vers une architecture (1923)

David Lee 1926–
and Herbert Kretzmer 1925–
British songwriters

4 Goodness gracious me.
   title of song (1960), sung by Peter Sellers and Sophia Loren, which later inspired the BBC radio and television comedy show *Goodness Gracious Me* (1996–2001)

Gypsy Rose Lee 1914–70
American striptease artiste

5 God is love, but get it in writing.
   attributed

Harper Lee 1926–
American novelist

6 Shoot all the bluejays you want, if you can hit 'em, but remember it's a sin to kill a mockingbird.
   To Kill a Mockingbird (1960)

Laurie Lee 1914–97
English writer

7 I was set down from the carrier's cart at the age of three; and there with a sense of bewilderment and terror my life in the village began.
   Cider with Rosie (1959)

Ursula K. Le Guin 1929–
American science fiction and fantasy writer

8 He had grown up in a country run by politicians who sent the pilots to man the bombers to kill the babies to make the world safer for children to grow up in.
   The Lathe of Heaven (1971) ch. 6

9 Love doesn't just sit there, like a stone, it has to be made, like bread; remade all the time, made new.
   The Lathe of Heaven (1971) ch. 10

10 We like to think we live in daylight, but half the world is always dark; and fantasy, like poetry, speaks the language of the night.
   in *World Magazine* 21 November 1979

Tom Lehrer 1928–
American humorist

11 Plagiarize! Let no one else's work evade your eyes,
   Remember why the good Lord made your eyes.
   'Lobachevski' (1953 song)

12 Poisoning pigeons in the park.
   song title, 1953

13 When the air becomes uranious, we will all go simultaneous.
   'We Will All Go Together When We Go' (1959 song)

Mitchell Leisen 1898–1972
American film director, who worked with Cecil B. **De Mille** 1919–32

14 Everything was in neon lights six feet tall: LUST, REVENGE, SEX.
   of the films of Cecil B. **De Mille**
      quoted in *American National Biography* (online edition) 'Cecil B. De Mille'

Curtis E. LeMay 1906–90
American air-force officer

15 We're going to bomb them back into the Stone Age.
   on the North Vietnamese
      Mission with LeMay (1965)

John Le Mesurier
see **Epitaphs 108:2**

Lenin (Vladimir Ilich Ulyanov)
1870–1924
Russian revolutionary, the principal figure in the
Russian Revolution and first Premier of the Soviet
Union 1918–24

1 Imperialism is the monopoly stage of
capitalism.
Imperialism as the Last Stage of Capitalism
(1916)

2 No, Democracy is *not* identical with
majority rule. Democracy is a *State* which
recognizes the subjection of the minority to
the majority, that is, an organization for
the systematic use of *force* by one class
against the other, by one part of the
population against another.
State and Revolution (1919)

3 While the State exists, there can be no
freedom. When there is freedom there will
be no State.
State and Revolution (1919)

4 What is to be done?
title of pamphlet (1902); originally the title of
a novel (1863) by N. G. Chernyshevsky

5 A good man fallen among Fabians.
of George Bernard Shaw
A. Ransome *Six Weeks in Russia in 1919* (1919)
'Notes of Conversations with Lenin'

6 Communism is Soviet power plus the
electrification of the whole country.
report to 8th Congress, 1920

7 Who? Whom?
*definition of political science, meaning 'Who will
outstrip whom?'*
in *Polnoe Sobranie Sochinenii* vol. 44 (1970)
17 October 1921 and elsewhere

8 Liberty is precious—so precious that it
must be rationed.
Sidney and Beatrice Webb *Soviet Communism*
(1936)

John Lennon 1940–80
English pop singer and songwriter, who as a founder
member of the Beatles also wrote most of their
songs in collaboration with Paul **McCartney**; he was
assassinated outside his home in New York
see also **Lennon and McCartney, Ono 243:14**

9 Happiness is a warm gun.
title of song (1968); see **Advertising slogans
3:24, Ephron 106:1, Schulz 288:7**

10 Imagine there's no heaven
It's easy if you try.
'Imagine' (1971 song)

11 Will the people in the cheaper seats clap
your hands? All the rest of you, if you'll
just rattle your jewellery.
at the Royal Variety Performance, 4 November
1963

12 We're more popular than Jesus now; I
don't know which will go first—rock 'n'
roll or Christianity.
of The Beatles
interview in *Evening Standard* 4 March 1966

John Lennon 1940–80 **and Paul McCartney** 1942–
English pop singers and songwriters
see also **Lennon, Macartney**

13 All you need is love.
title of song (1967)

14 For I don't care too much for money,
For money can't buy me love.
'Can't Buy Me Love' (1964 song)

15 All the lonely people, where do they all
come from?
'Eleanor Rigby' (1966 song)

16 Give peace a chance.
title of song (1969)

17 It's been a hard day's night,
And I've been working like a dog.
'A Hard Day's Night' (1964 song)

18 Strawberry fields forever.
title of song (1967)

19 She's got a ticket to ride, but she don't
care.
'Ticket to Ride' (1965 song)

20 Will you still need me, will you still feed
me,
When I'm sixty four?
'When I'm Sixty Four' (1967 song)

1 Oh I get by with a little help from my
  friends,
  Mm, I get high with a little help from my
  friends.
    'With a Little Help From My Friends' (1967
    song)

2 We all live in a yellow submarine.
    'Yellow Submarine' (1966 song)

3 Yesterday, all my troubles seemed so far
  away,
  Now it looks as though they're here to
  stay.
  Oh I believe in yesterday.
    'Yesterday' (1965 song)

Jay Leno 1950–
American comedian

4 The US finally came up with an exit
  strategy. Unfortunately it's for the World
  Cup.
    after the United States were knocked out in the
    early stages of the football World Cup
    in *Independent* 28 December 2006

Alan Jay Lerner 1918–86
American songwriter

5 Don't let it be forgot
  That once there was a spot
  For one brief shining moment that was
    known
  As Camelot.
    now particularly associated with the White
    House of John Fitzgerald **Kennedy** (*see* **Onassis**
    243:6)
    'Camelot' (1960 song), from *Camelot*

6 I'm getting married in the morning,
  Ding! dong! the bells are gonna chime.
  Pull out the stopper;
  Let's have a whopper;
  But get me to the church on time!
    'Get Me to the Church on Time' (1956 song),
    from *My Fair Lady*

7 Why can't a woman be more like a man?
  Men are so honest, so thoroughly square;
  Eternally noble, historically fair.
    'A Hymn to Him' (1956), from *My Fair Lady*

8 We met at nine.
  We met at eight.
  I was on time.
  No, you were late.

Ah yes! I remember it well.
    'I Remember it Well' (1958 song), from *Gigi*

9 I've grown accustomed to the trace
  Of something in the air;
  Accustomed to her face.
    'I've Grown Accustomed to her Face' (1956
    song), from *My Fair Lady*

10 On a clear day (you can see forever).
    title of song (1965), from *On a Clear Day You*
    Can See Forever

11 The rain in Spain stays mainly in the plain.
    'The Rain in Spain' (1956), from *My Fair Lady*

12 Thank heaven for little girls!
  For little girls get bigger every day.
    'Thank Heaven for Little Girls' (1958 song),
    from *Gigi*

13 All I want is a room somewhere,
  Far away from the cold night air,
  With one enormous chair;
  Oh, wouldn't it be loverly?
    'Wouldn't it be Lovely' (1956 song), from *My*
    Fair Lady

14 Oozing charm from every pore,
  He oiled his way around the floor.
    'You Did It' (1956 song), from *My Fair Lady*

15 The French never care what they do,
  actually,
  As long as they pronounce it properly.
    'Why Can't the English' (1956 song), from *My*
    Fair Lady

Doris Lessing 1919–
British novelist and short-story writer, brought up in
Rhodesia

16 There's only one real sin, and that is to
  persuade oneself that the second-best is
  anything but the second-best.
    Golden Notebook (1962)

17 When old settlers say 'One has to
  understand the country,' what they mean
  is, 'You have to get used to our ideas about
  the native.'
    The Grass is Singing (1950)

18 What of October, that ambiguous month,
  the month of tension, the unendurable
  month?
    Martha Quest (1952)

David Letterman 1947–
American broadcaster

1 If you didn't know how to behave, all you had to do at any moment was watch the mayor.
*of Rudolph **Giuliani**'s leadership after the terrorist destruction of the World Trade Center, 11 September 2001*
on *The Late Show* (CBS), 17 September 2001

Winifred Mary Letts 1882–1972
English writer

2 I saw the spires of Oxford
As I was passing by,
The grey spires of Oxford
Against a pearl-grey sky;
My heart was with the Oxford men
Who went abroad to die.
'The Spires of Oxford' (1916)

Oscar Levant 1906–72
American pianist, actor, and composer
see also **Marx 216:7**

3 Underneath this flabby exterior is an enormous lack of character.
Memoirs of an Amnesiac (1965)

4 Self-pity? It's the only pity that counts.
quoted in *American National Biography* (online edition)

Lord Leverhulme 1851–1925
English industrialist and philanthropist

5 Half the money I spend on advertising is wasted, and the trouble is I don't know which half.
also attributed to American businessman John Wanamaker (1838–1922)
David Ogilvy *Confessions of an Advertising Man* (1963)

Denise Levertov 1923–
English-born American poet

6 Images
split the truth
in fractions.
'A Sequence' (1961)

7 two by two in the ark of
the ache of it.
'The Ache of Marriage' (1964)

René Lévesque 1922–87
Canadian politician, founder of the separatist Parti Québecois

8 A nation is judged by how it treats its minorities.
attributed, 1978; John Robert Colombo *Colombo's New Canadian Quotations* (1987)

Primo Levi 1919–87
Italian novelist and poet, of Jewish descent, whose first book *If This is a Man* concerned his experiences as a survivor of Auschwitz; he committed suicide in 1987

9 Our language lacks words to express this offence, the demolition of a man.
of a year spent in Auschwitz
If This is a Man (1958)

Bernard Levin 1928–2004
British journalist

10 I have heard tell of a Professor of Economics who has a sign on the wall of his study, reading 'the future is not what it was'. The sentiment was admirable; unfortunately, the past is not getting any better either.
in *Sunday Times* 22 May 1977; see **Berra 31:11**

11 Whom the mad would destroy, they first make gods.
*of **Mao** Zedong in 1967*
Levin quoting himself in *Times* 21 September 1987; referring to the scholiastic annotation to Sophocles's *Antigone* translated by James Duport (1606–79) *Homeri Gnomologia* (1660) as 'Whom God would destroy He first sends mad'

Claude Lévi-Strauss 1908–
French social anthropologist

12 Language is a form of human reason, and has its reasons which are unknown to man.
The Savage Mind (1962) ch. 9

13 The purpose of myth is to provide a logical model capable of overcoming a contradiction (an impossible achievement if, as it happens, the contradiction is real).
Structural Anthropology (1968) ch. 11

Andrea Levy 1956–
British novelist

1 Most of all I would like to thank all those people in Britain who work hard to make sure the rivers in this country never run with blood, only with water.
speech on winning the Whitbread Book of the Year prize, 25 January 2005
in *Guardian* 26 January 2005; see **Powell 261:1**

C. S. Lewis 1898–1963
English novelist, religious writer, and literary scholar. He broadcast and wrote on religious and moral issues, and created the imaginary land of Narnia for a series of children's books

2 No one ever told me that grief felt so like fear.
A Grief Observed (1961)

3 Grown-ups are always thinking of uninteresting explanations.
Digory's view
The Magician's Nephew (1955)

4 She's the sort of woman who lives for others—you can always tell the others by their hunted expression.
The Screwtape Letters (1942)

5 A young man who wishes to remain a sound atheist cannot be too careful of his reading.
Surprised by Joy (1955)

6 For twenty years I've stared my level best
To see if evening—any evening—would suggest
A patient etherized upon a table;
In vain. I simply wasn't able.
on contemporary poetry
'A Confession' (1964); see **Eliot 102:2**

7 Often when I pray I wonder if I am not posting letters to a non-existent address.
letter to Arthur Greeves, 24 December 1930

8 Courage is not simply *one* of the virtues but the form of every virtue at the testing point.
Cyril Connolly *The Unquiet Grave* (1944); see **Barrie 24:6**

9 He that but looketh on a plate of ham and eggs to lust after it, hath already committed breakfast with it in his heart.
letter, 10 March 1954

Jerry Lee Lewis 1935–
American rock-and-roll singer

10 Elvis was the greatest, but I'm the best.
in *Face* May 1989

Sam M. Lewis 1885–1959 and Joe Young 1889–1939
American songwriters

11 How 'ya gonna keep 'em down on the farm (after they've seen Paree)?
title of song (1919)

Sinclair Lewis 1885–1951
American novelist, known for satirical works such as *Main Street* and *Babbitt*

12 Our American professors like their literature clear and cold and pure and very dead.
The American Fear of Literature (Nobel Prize Address, 12 December 1930)

13 To George F. Babbitt, as to most prosperous citizens of Zenith, his motor car was poetry and tragedy, love and heroism. The office was his pirate ship but the car his perilous excursion ashore.
Babbitt (1922)

14 She did her work with the thoroughness of a mind which reveres details and never quite understands them.
Babbitt (1922)

Willmott Lewis 1877–1950
British journalist, Washington correspondent of *The Times* 1920–1948

15 I think it well to remember that, when writing for the newspapers, we are writing for an elderly lady in Hastings who has two cats of which she is passionately fond. Unless our stuff can successfully compete for her interest with those cats, it is no good.
Claud Cockburn *In Time of Trouble* (1957)

Wyndham Lewis 1882–1957
English novelist, painter, and critic

16 Gertrude Stein's prose-song is a cold, black suet-pudding . . . Cut it at any point, it is the same thing . . . all fat, without nerve.
of Three Lives (*1909*)
Time and Western Man (1927)

1 Angels in jumpers.
*describing the figures in Stanley **Spencer**'s*
paintings
   attributed

Liberace 1919–87
American entertainer

2 I cry all the way to the bank.
on bad reviews (from the mid-1950s)
   Autobiography (1973)

A. J. Liebling 1904–63
American journalist

3 Freedom of the press is guaranteed only to
those who own one.
   'The Wayward Press: Do you belong in
   Journalism?' (1960)

Vachel Lindsay 1879–1931
American poet

4 Then I saw the Congo, creeping through
the black,
Cutting through the forest with a golden
track.
   'The Congo' pt. 1 (1914)

5 Booth led boldly with his big bass drum—
(Are you washed in the blood of the
Lamb?)
   'General William Booth Enters into Heaven'
   (1913); referring to the *Bible* Revelation: ' . . .
   Have washed their robes, and made them
   white in the blood of the Lamb'

6 Booth died blind and still by faith he trod,
Eyes still dazzled by the ways of God.
   'General William Booth Enters into Heaven'
   (1913)

Gary Lineker 1960–
English footballer

7 Coaching a football team is not rocket
science and most of the advice is blindingly
obvious.
   in *Independent* 21 October 2000

8 Football is a simple game; 22 men chase a
ball for 90 minutes and at the end, the
Germans win.
   attributed

Eric Linklater 1899–1974
Scottish novelist

9 'There won't be any revolution in
America,' said Isadore. Nikitin agreed.
'The people are all too clean. They spend
all their time changing their shirts and
washing themselves. You can't feel fierce
and revolutionary in a bathroom.'
   Juan in America (1931)

Walter Lippmann 1889–1974
American journalist and political columnist

10 The final test of a leader is that he leaves
behind him in other men the conviction
and the will to carry on.
   *after the death of Franklin D. **Roosevelt***
   in *New York Herald Tribune* 14 April 1945
   'Roosevelt is Gone'

Joan Littlewood 1914–2002
and Charles Chilton 1914–
British theatre director; British writer

11 Oh what a lovely war.
   title of stage show (1963), a satire on the First
   World War

Maxim Litvinov 1876–1951
Soviet diplomat

12 Peace is indivisible.
   note to the Allies, 25 February 1920; A. U.
   Pope *Maxim Litvinoff* (1943)

Penelope Lively 1933–
English novelist

13 Language tethers us to the world; without
it we spin like atoms.
   Moon Tiger (1987)

14 We are walking lexicons. In a single
sentence of idle chatter we preserve
Latin, Anglo-Saxon, Norse; we carry a
museum inside our heads, each day we
commemorate peoples of whom we have
never heard.
   Moon Tiger (1987)

Ken Livingstone 1945–
British Labour politician, Mayor of London from
2000

15 This was not a terrorist attack against the
mighty and the powerful. It was not aimed

at Presidents or Prime Ministers. It was aimed at ordinary, working-class Londoners, black and white, Muslim and Christian, Hindu and Jew, young and old. It was an indiscriminate attempt to slaughter, irrespective of any considerations for age, for class, for religion.

on the suicide bombings in London, 7 July 2005
speech, Singapore, 7 July 2005; in *Observer* 10 July 2005

Richard Llewellyn 1907–83
Welsh novelist and dramatist

1 How green was my valley.
title of book (1939)

David Lloyd George 1863–1945
British Liberal statesman, Prime Minister 1916–22
on Lloyd George: see **Anonymous 11:14**,
Clemenceau 71:4, Keynes 179:2, Keynes 179:9

2 A mastiff? It is the Right Hon. Gentleman's poodle.
*on the House of Lords and A. J. **Balfour** respectively*
in the House of Commons, 26 June 1907

3 A fully-equipped duke costs as much to keep up as two Dreadnoughts; and dukes are just as great a terror and they last longer.
speech at Newcastle, 9 October 1909

4 The great peaks of honour we had forgotten—Duty, Patriotism, and—clad in glittering white—the great pinnacle of Sacrifice, pointing like a rugged finger to Heaven.
speech at Queen's Hall, London, 19 September 1914

5 At eleven o'clock this morning came to an end the cruellest and most terrible war that has ever scourged mankind. I hope we may say that thus, this fateful morning, came to an end all wars.
speech in the House of Commons, 11 November 1918; see also **Wells 331:8**

6 What is our task? To make Britain a fit country for heroes to live in.
speech at Wolverhampton, 23 November 1918

7 Unless I am mistaken, by the steps we have taken [in Ireland] we have murder by the throat.
speech at the Mansion House, 9 November 1920

*on being asked what place Arthur **Balfour** would have in history:*
8 He will be just like the scent on a pocket handkerchief.
Thomas Jones diary, 9 June 1922

9 Death is the most convenient time to tax rich people.
Lord Riddell diary, 23 April 1919

10 The world is becoming like a lunatic asylum run by lunatics.
in *Observer* 8 January 1933; see **Rowland 276:8**

11 A politician was a person with whose politics you did not agree. When you did agree, he was a statesman.
speech at Central Hall, Westminster, 2 July 1935

12 Negotiating with de Valera . . . is like trying to pick up mercury with a fork.
*to which **de Valera** replied, 'Why doesn't he use a spoon?'*
M. J. MacManus *Eamon de Valera* (1944)

13 Sufficient conscience to bother him, but not sufficient to keep him straight.
*of Ramsay **MacDonald***
A. J. Sylvester *Life with Lloyd George* (1975)

David Lodge 1935–
English novelist

14 Literature is mostly about having sex and not much about having children. Life is the other way round.
The British Museum is Falling Down (1965)

15 Four times, under our educational rules, the human pack is shuffled and cut—at eleven-plus, sixteen-plus, eighteen-plus and twenty-plus—and happy is he who comes top of the deck on each occasion, but especially the last. This is called Finals, the very name of which implies that nothing of importance can happen after it.
Changing Places (1975)

Frank Loesser 1910–69
American songwriter

1 See what the boys in the back room will
have
And tell them I'm having the same.
'Boys in the Back Room' (1939 song), from
Destry Rides Again; see **Beaverbrook 25:6**

Frederick Loewe 1904–88
American composer

2 I don't like my music, but what is my
opinion against that of millions of others.
Nat Shapiro (ed.) *An Encyclopedia of
Quotations about Music* (1978)

Christopher Logue 1926–
English poet

3 Come to the edge.
We might fall.
Come to the edge.
It's too high!
COME TO THE EDGE!
And they came
and he pushed
and they flew . . .
on **Apollinaire**
'Come to the edge' (1969)

4 I, Christopher Logue, was baptized the year
Many thousands of Englishmen,
Fists clenched, their bellies empty,
Walked day and night on the capital city.
'The Song of Autobiography' (1996)

Vince Lombardi 1913–70
American football coach

5 Show me a good loser and I'll show you a
loser.
attributed

Huey Long 1893–1935
American Democratic politician, successively
Governor of Louisiana and US Senator, noted for his
demagogic prowess and radical populism; he was
assassinated

6 For the present you can just call me the
Kingfish.
*accepting a nickname reflecting his political
persona*
Every Man a King (1933)

Michael Longley 1939–
Irish poet

7 I am travelling from one April to another.
It is the same train between the same
embankments.
Gorse fires are smoking, but primroses
burn
And celandines and white may and gorse
flowers.
'Gorse Fires' (1991)

Alice Roosevelt Longworth 1884–1980
American daughter of Theodore **Roosevelt**
see also **Anonymous 12:14**

8 If you haven't got anything good to say
about anyone come and sit by me.
maxim embroidered on a cushion in her home
Michael Teague *Mrs L: Conversations with
Alice Roosevelt Longworth* (1981)

Anita Loos 1893–1981
American writer and child actress

9 Gentlemen prefer blondes.
title of book (1925)

10 So I really think that American gentlemen
are the best after all, because kissing your
hand may make you feel very very good
but a diamond and safire bracelet lasts
forever.
Gentlemen Prefer Blondes (1925); see
Advertising slogans 3:13, Robin 271:9

11 Fun is fun but no girl wants to laugh all of
the time.
Gentlemen Prefer Blondes (1925)

12 In my youth I never kept a diary, feeling
that a girl who could sell her words for
money had other fish to fry.
Kiss Hollywood Goodbye (1974)

13 I'm furious about the women's
liberationists. They keep getting up on soap
boxes and proclaiming that women are
brighter than men. That's true, but it
should be kept very quiet or it ruins the
whole racket.
attributed

Federico García Lorca 1899–1936
Spanish poet and dramatist

14 *A las cinco de la tarde.*
Eran las cinco en punto de la tarde.
Un niño trajo la blanca sábana

a las cinco de la tarde.
At five in the afternoon.
It was exactly five in the afternoon.
A boy brought the white sheet
at five in the afternoon.
> *Llanto por Ignacio Sánchez Mejías* (1935) 'La Cogida y la muerte'

1 *Verde que te quiero verde.*
Verde viento. Verdes ramas.
El barco sobre la mar
y el caballo en la montaña.
Green how I love you green.
Green wind.
Green boughs.
The ship on the sea
and the horse on the mountain.
> *Romance sonámbulo* (1924–7)

Edward N. Lorenz 1917–
American meteorologist

2 Predictability: Does the flap of a butterfly's wings in Brazil set off a tornado in Texas?
> title of paper given to the American Association for the Advancement of Science, Washington, 29 December 1979; James Gleick *Chaos* (1988)

Konrad Lorenz 1903–89
Austrian zoologist, who pioneered the science of ethology, emphasizing innate rather than learned behaviour or conditioned reflexes

3 It is a good morning exercise for a research scientist to discard a pet hypothesis every day before breakfast.
> *On Aggression* (1966)

Joe Louis 1914–81
American boxer; known as the Brown Bomber. He was heavyweight champion of the world 1937–49

4 He can run. But he can't hide.
> *of Billy Conn, his opponent, before a heavyweight title fight, 19 June 1946*
> Louis: *My Life Story* (1947)

James Lovell 1928–
American astronaut

5 Houston, we've had a problem.
> *during the Apollo 13 space mission, 14 April 1970; the damaged spacecraft was eventually brought safely back to earth*
> in *Times* 15 April 1970

James Lovelock 1919–
English scientist, originator of the Gaia hypothesis: that living matter on the earth collectively defines and regulates the material conditions necessary for the continuance of life

6 I always think it grossly unfair that people accept the selfish gene as a metaphor—and I think it's a lovely metaphor—but they won't accept Gaia or the living Earth.
> *of the response to his Gaia hypothesis*
> in *New Scientist* 9 September 2000; see
> **Dawkins 85:5**

David Low 1891–1963
British political cartoonist, creator of Colonel Blimp

7 I have never met anyone who wasn't against war. Even Hitler and Mussolini were, according to themselves.
> in *New York Times Magazine* 10 February 1946

Amy Lowell 1874–1925
American poet

8 All books are either dreams or swords,
You can cut, or you can drug, with words.
> 'Sword Blades and Poppy Seed' (1914); see
> **Kipling 183:9**

Robert Lowell 1917–77
American poet

9 The aquarium is gone. Everywhere,
giant finned cars nose forward like fish;
a savage servility
slides by on grease.
> 'For the Union Dead' (1964)

10 Their monument sticks like a fishbone
in the city's throat.
> 'For the Union Dead' (1964)

11 These are the tranquillized *Fifties*,
and I am forty. Ought I to regret my seed-
time?
> 'Memories of West Street and Lepke' (1956)

12 At forty-five,
What next, what next?
At every corner,
I meet my Father,
my age, still alive.
> 'Middle Age' (1964)

13   This is death.
To die and know it. This is the Black
Widow, death.
> 'Mr Edwards and the Spider' (1950)

1 The Lord survives the rainbow of His will.
  'The Quaker Graveyard in Nantucket' (1950)

2 We feel the machine slipping from our
  hands
  As if someone else were steering;
  If we see light at the end of the tunnel,
  It's the light of the oncoming train.
  'Since 1939' (1977)

L. S. Lowry 1887–1976
English painter, who characteristically depicted
small matchstick figures set against the iron and
brick expanse of urban and industrial landscapes
on Lowry: see **Coleman 73:6**

3 I'm a simple man, and I use simple
  materials.
  Mervyn Levy *Paintings of L. S. Lowry* (1975)

Malcolm Lowry 1909–57
English novelist

4 How alike are the groans of love to those of
  the dying.
  Under the Volcano (1947)

Clare Booth Luce 1903–87
American diplomat, politician, and writer

5 Much of . . . his global thinking is, no
  matter how you slice it, still globaloney.
  on the post-war theories of Henry Wallace (*US
  Vice-President, 1941–5*)
    speech to the House of Representatives,
    February 1943

6 But if God had wanted us to think just with
  our wombs, why did He give us a brain?
  in *Life* 16 October 1970

Salvador Luria 1912–91
Italian-born American microbiologist

7 Each human being is the actualization of
  an extremely improbable chance—in fact,
  a series of improbable chances, extending
  all the way back to the unique event that
  more than 3 billion years ago started life on
  the earth on its chancy course.
  Life: the Unfinished Experiment (1973)

Alison Lurie 1926–
American novelist

8 Clothes which make a woman's life
  difficult and handicap her in competition

with men are always felt to be sexually
attractive
  The Language of Clothes (1981)

9 There's a rule, I think. You get what you
  want in life, but not your second choice
  too.
  Real People (1969)

Rosa Luxemburg 1871–1919
Polish-born German revolutionary leader. Together
with the German socialist Karl Liebknecht she
founded the revolutionary group known as the
Spartacus League in 1916 and the German
Communist Party in 1918. The following year she and
Liebknecht were assassinated after organizing an
abortive communist uprising in Berlin

10 Freedom is always and exclusively freedom
   for the one who thinks differently.
   Die Russische Revolution (1918)

11 The revolution will 'raise itself again
   clashing', and to your horror it will
   proclaim to the sound of trumpets, *I was, I
   am, I shall be*!
   *quoting lines from 19th-century German poet
   and radical Ferdinand Freiligrath (1810–76)*
     'Order Reigns in Berlin' in *Die Rote Fahne* [The
     Red Flag] 14 January 1919

Jonathan Lynn 1943–
and **Antony Jay** 1930–
English writers

12 'We went in,' he said, 'to screw the French
   by splitting them off from the Germans.
   The French went in to protect their
   inefficient farmers from commercial
   competition. The Germans went in to
   cleanse themselves of genocide and apply
   for readmission to the human race.'
   *Sir Humphrey Appleby explains the European
   Community to Jim Hacker*
     Yes Minister (1982) vol. 2

13 I think it will be a clash between the
   political will and the administrative won't.
   Yes Prime Minister (1987) vol. 2

Mary McAleese 1951–
Irish stateswoman; President from 1997

1 People ask me what does the Celtic Tiger
look like; it looks like this place.
visiting Clonaslee in Co. Laois
in *Irish Times* 13 April 1998

2 Those whom we commemorate . . . fell
victim to a war against oppression in
Europe. Their memory, too, fell victim to a
war for independence at home in Ireland
. . . Respect for the memory of one set of
heroes was often at the expense of respect
for the memory of another.
*at the Armistice Day commemorations in
Belgium*
in *Irish Times* 14 November 1998

Douglas MacArthur 1880–1964
American general. Commander of US (later Allied)
forces in the SW Pacific during the Second World
War, he accepted Japan's surrender in 1945, and
administered the ensuing Allied occupation
on MacArthur: see **Truman 319:2**

3 I came through and I shall return.
*on reaching Australia, having broken through
Japanese lines en route from Corregidor*
statement in Adelaide, 20 March 1942

4 In war, indeed, there can be no substitute
for victory.
address to a Joint Meeting of Congress, 19
April 1951

5 I still remember the refrain of one of the
most popular barracks ballads of that day,
which proclaimed most proudly that old
soldiers never die; they just fade away. I
now close my military career and just fade
away.
address to a Joint Meeting of Congress, 19
April 1951; see **Foley 119:5**

Rose Macaulay 1881–1958
English novelist

6 'Take my camel, dear,' said my aunt Dot,
as she climbed down from this animal on
her return from High Mass.
Rose Macaulay *The Towers of Trebizond*
(1956)

Anthony McAuliffe 1898–1975
American general

7 Nuts!
replying to the German demand for surrender
at Bastogne, Belgium, 22 December 1944; this
would have been a key point for a German
breakthrough in the Battle of the Bulge

Joseph McCarthy 1908–57
American politician and anti-Communist agitator
on McCarthy: see **Cartoons 57:3, Eisenhower 99:13,
Murrow 232:3, Welch 330:10**

8 I have here in my hand a list of two
hundred and five [people] that were known
to the Secretary of State as being members
of the Communist Party and who
nevertheless are still working and shaping
the policy of the State Department.
speech at Wheeling, West Virginia, 9 February
1950

9 McCarthyism is Americanism with its
sleeves rolled.
speech in Wisconsin, 1952; Richard Rovere
Senator Joe McCarthy (1973)

Mary McCarthy 1912–89
American novelist

10 The immense popularity of American
movies abroad demonstrates that Europe is

the unfinished negative of which America is the proof.
On the Contrary (1961) 'America the Beautiful'

1 If someone tells you he is going to make a 'realistic decision', you immediately understand that he has resolved to do something bad.
On the Contrary (1961) 'American Realist Playwrights'

2 Bureaucracy, the rule of no one, has become the modern form of despotism.
On the Contrary (1961) 'The *Vita Activa*'

3 Every word she writes is a lie, including 'and' and 'the'.
on Lillian **Hellman**
quoting herself, on Hellman's autobiographical publications, in *New York Times* 16 February 1980

Linda McCartney 1941–98
American photographer, wife of Paul **McCartney**

4 I don't eat anything with a face.
quoted in *BBC News* (online edition) 19 April 1998; obituary

Paul McCartney 1942–
English pop singer and songwriter, who as a founder member of the Beatles also wrote most of their songs in collaboration with John **Lennon**
see also **Lennon and McCartney**

5 Ballads and babies. That's what happened to me.
on reaching the age of fifty
in *Time* 8 June 1992

Ewan MacColl (Jimmy Miller) 1915–89
English folksinger and songwriter

6 I found my love by the gasworks crofts
Dreamed a dream by the old canal
Kissed my girl by the factory wall
Dirty old town, dirty old town.
'Dirty Old Town' (1950 song)

7 And I used to sleep standing on my feet
As we hunted for the shoals of herring.
'The Shoals of Herring' (1960 song, from the BBC Radio broadcast *Singing the Fishing*)

David McCord 1897–1997
American poet

8 By and by

God caught his eye.
'Remainders' (1935); epitaph for a waiter

Horace McCoy 1897–1955
American novelist

9 They shoot horses don't they.
title of novel (1935)

John McCrae 1872–1918
Canadian poet and military physician

10 In Flanders fields the poppies blow
Between the crosses, row on row.
'In Flanders Fields' (1915)

Carson McCullers
see **Borrowed titles 40:14**

Derek McCulloch
see **Catchphrases 59:7**

Hugh MacDiarmid (Christopher Murray Grieve) 1892–1978
Scottish poet and nationalist

11 I'll ha'e nae hauf-way hoose, but aye be whaur
Extremes meet—it's the only way I ken
To dodge the curst conceit o' bein' richt
That damns the vast majority o' men.
A Drunk Man Looks at the Thistle (1926)

12 The rose of all the world is not for me.
I want for my part
Only the little white rose of Scotland
That smells sharp and sweet—and breaks the heart.
'The Little White Rose' (1934)

13 ⠀⠀⠀⠀I must be a Bolshevik
Before the Revolution, but I'll cease to be one quick
When Communism comes to rule the roost,
For real literature can exist only when it's produced
By madmen, hermits, heretics,
Dreamers, rebels, sceptics,
—And such a door of utterance has been given to me
As none may close whosoever they be.
'Talking with Five Thousand People in Edinburgh' (1972)

1 Scotland small? Our multiform, our infinite
   Scotland *small*?
   Only as a patch of hillside may be a cliché
   corner
   To a fool who cries 'Nothing but heather!'
   . . .
   Direadh 1 (1974)

Dwight Macdonald 1906–82
American writer and film critic

2 Götterdämmerung without the gods.
   of the use of atomic bombs against the Japanese
   in *Politics* September 1945 'The Bomb'

Ramsay MacDonald 1866–1937
British Labour statesman, Prime Minister 1924,
1929–31, and 1931–5. He was Britain's first Labour
Prime Minister, but his agreement in 1931 to lead a
National Government was bitterly resented by many
of his party
on MacDonald: see **Churchill 66:15, Lloyd George
201:13**

3 We hear war called murder. It is not: it is
   suicide.
   in *Observer* 4 May 1930

4 Tomorrow every Duchess in London will
   be wanting to kiss me!
   *after forming the National Government, 25
   August 1931*
   Viscount Snowden *An Autobiography* (1934)

John McEnroe 1959–
American tennis player

5 You cannot be serious!
   said to tennis umpire at Wimbledon, early
   1980s

Ian McEwan 1948–
English novelist

6 Mostly, we are good when it makes sense.
   A good society is one that makes sense of
   being good.
   Enduring Love (1998)

7 I love you . . . That is what they were all
   saying down their phones, from the
   hijacked planes and the burning towers.
   There is only love, and then oblivion. Love

was all they had to set against the hatred of
their murderers.
*of the last messages received from those
trapped by terrorist attack in buildings and
planes, 11 September 2001*
   in *Guardian* 15 September 2001; see **Last
   words 190:8**

Phyllis McGinley 1905–78
American poet

8 A poet with a poem in mind is like a robin
   with a worm. Let go the worm (or the idea)
   for an instant, and both have slithered
   inevitably away.
   The Province of the Heart (1959)

Roger McGough 1937–
English poet

9 You will put on a dress of guilt
   and shoes with broken high ideals.
   'Comeclose and Sleepnow' (1967)

10 I wanna be the leader
   I wanna be the leader
   Can I be the leader?
   Can I? Can I?
   Promise? Promise?
   Yippee, I'm the leader
   I'm the leader.
   Ok what shall we do now?
   'I Wanna be the Leader'

11 Let me die a youngman's death
   Not a clean & in-between-
   The-sheets, holy-water death.
   'Let Me Die a Youngman's Death' (1967)

George McGovern 1922–
American Democratic politician, presidential
candidate in 1972

12 Sometimes, when they say you're ahead of
   your time, it's just a polite way of saying
   you have a real bad sense of timing.
   in *Observer* 18 March 1990

Jimmie McGregor 1932–
Scottish singer and songwriter

13 Oh, he's football crazy, he's football mad
   And the football it has robbed him o' the
   wee bit sense he had.
   And it would take a dozen skivvies, his
   clothes to wash and scrub,

Since our Jock became a member of that
  terrible football club.
  'Football Crazy' (1960 song)

Lord McGregor 1921––
British sociologist

1 An odious exhibition of journalists
dabbling their fingers in the stuff of other
people's souls.
*on Press coverage of the marital difficulties of
the Prince and Princess of Wales, speaking as
Chairman of the Press Complaints Commission
in* Times *9 June 1992*

Compton Mackenzie 1883–1972
English novelist

2 Love makes the world go round? Not at all.
Whisky makes it go round twice as fast.
Whisky Galore (1947)

Alistair Maclean 1922–87
Scottish thriller writer

3 Where eagles dare.
title of novel (1967)

Don McLean 1945–
American songwriter

4 Something touched me deep inside
The day the music died.
on the death of Buddy Holly
'American Pie' (1972 song)

5 So, bye, bye, Miss American Pie,
Drove my Chevy to the levee
But the levee was dry.
Them good old boys was drinkin' whiskey
  and rye
Singin' 'This'll be the day that I die.'
'American Pie' (1972 song)

Archibald MacLeish 1892–1982
American poet and public official

6 A poem should not mean
But be.
'Ars Poetica' (1926)

Hugh MacLennan
see **Borrowed titles 41:7**

Iain Macleod 1913–70
British Conservative politician
on Macleod: see **Salisbury 282:9**

7 It is some measure of the tightness of the
magic circle on this occasion that neither
the Chancellor of the Exchequer nor the
Leader of the House of Commons had any
inkling of what was happening.
*of the 'evolvement' of Alec Douglas-**Home** as
Conservative leader after the resignation of
Harold **Macmillan**
in* Spectator *17 January 1964*

8 The Conservative Party always in time
forgives those who were wrong. Indeed
often, in time, they forgive those who were
right.
in Spectator *21 February 1964*

Marshall McLuhan 1911–80
Canadian communications scholar

9 The new electronic interdependence
recreates the world in the image of a global
village.
The Gutenberg Galaxy (1962); see **Debord
86:9**

10 When this circuit learns your job, what are
you going to do?
The Medium is the Massage (1967)

11 The medium is the message.
Understanding Media (1964)

12 The car has become the carapace, the
protective and aggressive shell, of urban
and suburban man.
Understanding Media (1964)

13 Television brought the brutality of war into
the comfort of the living room. Vietnam
was lost in the living rooms of America—
not the battlefields of Vietnam.
in Montreal Gazette *16 May 1975*

14 Gutenberg made everybody a reader.
Xerox makes everybody a publisher.
in Guardian Weekly *12 June 1977*

Harold Macmillan 1894–1986
British Conservative statesman, Prime Minister 1957–63
on Macmillan: see **Thorpe 315:12**; see also **Hitler 154:13, Misquotations 225:1, Stockton 305:4**

1 We . . . are Greeks in this American empire . . . We must run the Allied Forces HQ as the Greeks ran the operations of the Emperor Claudius.
*to Richard **Crossman** in 1944*
   in *Sunday Telegraph* 9 February 1964

2 There ain't gonna be no war.
following the Geneva summit
   at a London press conference, 24 July 1955

3 Let us be frank about it: most of our people have never had it so good.
'You Never Had It So Good' was the Democratic Party slogan during the 1952 US election campaign
   speech at Bedford, 20 July 1957

4 I thought the best thing to do was to settle up these little local difficulties, and then turn to the wider vision of the Commonwealth.
*on leaving for a Commonwealth tour, following the resignations of Peter Thorneycroft, Chancellor of the Exchequer, and Treasury Ministers Enoch **Powell** and Nigel **Birch***
   statement at London airport 7 January 1958

5 The wind of change is blowing through this continent, and, whether we like it or not, this growth of [African] national consciousness is a political fact.
   speech at Cape Town, 3 February 1960; *Pointing the Way* (1972)

6 I was determined that no British government should be brought down by the action of two tarts.
comment on the Profumo affair, July 1963
   A. Sampson *Macmillan* (1967); see also **Hailsham 141:6**

7 Power? It's like a Dead Sea fruit. When you achieve it, there is nothing there.
   Anthony Sampson *The New Anatomy of Britain* (1971)

8 There are three bodies no sensible man directly challenges: the Roman Catholic Church, the Brigade of Guards and the National Union of Mineworkers.
   in *Observer* 22 February 1981; see **Baldwin 22:1**

9 The opposition of events.
on his biggest problem; popularly quoted as, 'Events, dear boy. Events'
   David Dilks *The Office of Prime Minister in Twentieth Century Britain* (1993)

on the appointment of Michael Ramsey to succeed Geoffrey Fisher as Archbishop of Canterbury:
10 We have had enough of Martha and it is time for some Mary.
   attributed

Robert McNamara 1916–
American Democratic politician, Secretary of Defense during the Vietnam War

11 I don't object to it's being called 'McNamara's War' . . . It is a very important war and I am pleased to be identified with it and do whatever I can to win it.
   in *New York Times* 25 April 1964

12 We . . . acted according to what we thought were the principles and traditions of this nation. We were wrong. We were terribly wrong.
*of the conduct of the Vietnam War by the **Kennedy** and **Johnson** administrations*
   in *Daily Telegraph* (electronic edition) 10 April 1995

Scott McNealy 1954–
American businessman, co-founder of Sun Microsystems

13 You have zero privacy anyway. Get over it.
   on the introduction of Jini networking technology; quoted in *Wired News* (online edition), 26 January 1999

14 I'm thrilled not to have to be CEO anymore. That was a temporary thing I took on about 22 years ago.
   comment on stepping down as CEO of Sun Microsystems, San Francisco, 19 May 2006

Louis MacNeice 1907–63
Northern Irish poet

15 Better authentic mammon than a bogus god.
   Autumn Journal (1939)

16 It's no go the merrygoround, it's no go the rickshaw,

All we want is a limousine and a ticket for
the peepshow.
'Bagpipe Music' (1938)

1 It's no go the picture palace, it's no go the
stadium,
It's no go the country cot with a pot of pink
geraniums,
It's no go the Government grants, it's no
go the elections,
Sit on your arse for fifty years and hang
your hat on a pension.
'Bagpipe Music' (1938)

2 The glass is falling hour by hour, the glass
will fall for ever,
But if you break the bloody glass you won't
hold up the weather.
'Bagpipe Music' (1938)

3 So they were married—to be the more
together—
And found they were never again so much
together,
Divided by the morning tea,
By the evening paper,
By children and tradesmen's bills.
'Les Sylphides' (1941)

4 Time was away and somewhere else,
There were two glasses and two chairs
And two people with the one pulse.
'Meeting Point' (1941)

5 I am not yet born; O fill me
With strength against those who would
freeze my
humanity.
'Prayer Before Birth' (1944)

6 Let them not make me a stone and let them
not spill me,
Otherwise kill me.
'Prayer Before Birth' (1944)

7 The sunlight on the garden
Hardens and grows cold,
We cannot cage the minute
Within its net of gold.
'Sunlight on the Garden' (1938)

8 By a high star our course is set,
Our end is Life. Put out to sea.
'Thalassa' (1964)

Robert McNeil 1931–
Canadian journalist and writer

9 Canadians feel that any people can live
where the climate is gentle. It takes a
special people to prosper where nature
makes it so hard.
in *Travel and Leisure* June 1978 'Notes of a
Native Son'

William Macpherson of Cluny 1926–
Scottish lawyer

10 For the purposes of our Inquiry the concept
of institutional racism which we apply
consists of:
The collective failure of an organisation
to provide an appropriate and professional
service to people because of their colour,
culture, or ethnic origin. It can be seen or
detected in processes, attitudes and
behaviour which amount to
discrimination through unwitting
prejudice, ignorance, thoughtlessness and
racist stereotyping which disadvantage
minority ethnic people.
The Stephen Lawrence Inquiry: Report
(February 1999)

Denis MacShane 1948–
British Labour politician

11 I liken the French/British relationship to a
very old married couple who often think of
killing each other but would never dream
of divorce.
*on the revelation that in 1956 the French Prime
Minister Guy Mollet suggested to Anthony **Eden**
a union between the United Kingdom and France*
in *Times* (online edition) 15 January 2007

Candia McWilliam 1955–
English novelist

12 With the birth of each child, you lose two
novels.
in *Guardian* 5 May 1993

Salvador de Madariaga 1886–1978
Spanish writer and diplomat

13 Since, in the main, it is not armaments
that cause wars but wars (or the fears
thereof) that cause armaments, it follows
that every nation will at every moment
strive to keep its armament in an efficient
state as required by its fear, otherwise
styled security.
Morning Without Noon (1974)

Madonna 1958–
American pop singer and actress
on Madonna: see **Boy George 42:5**

1 Being blonde is definitely a different state of mind. I can't really put my finger on it, but the artifice of being blonde has some incredible sort of sexual connotation.
   in *Rolling Stone* 23 March 1989

John Gillespie Magee 1922–41
American airman, member of the Royal Canadian Airforce

2 Oh! I have slipped the surly bonds of earth
   And danced the skies on laughter-silvered wings.
   *quoted by Ronald **Reagan** following the explosion of the space shuttle* Challenger, *January 1986*
   'High Flight' (1943); see **Reagan 268:7**

3 And, while with silent lifting mind I've trod
   The high, untrespassed sanctity of space,
   Put out my hand and touched the face of God.
   'High Flight' (1943); see **Reagan 268:7**

Bill Maher 1956–
American comedian

4 Suicide is our way of saying to God: 'You can't fire me. I quit'.
   Politically Incorrect (American TV show, 1993–2002)

Derek Mahon 1941–
Northern Irish poet

5 'I am just going outside and may be some time.'
   The others nod, pretending not to know.
   At the heart of the ridiculous, the sublime.
   'Antarctica' (1985); see **Last words 190:6**

6 Even now there are places where a thought might grow—
   Peruvian mines, worked out and abandoned
   To a slow clock of condensation,
   An echo trapped for ever, and a flutter
   Of wildflowers in the lift-shaft . . .
   And in a disused shed in Co. Wexford.
   'A Disused Shed in Co. Wexford' (1978)

Norman Mailer 1923–
American novelist and essayist

7 So we think of Marilyn who was every man's love affair with America, Marilyn Monroe who was blonde and beautiful and had a sweet little rinky-dink of a voice and all the cleanliness of all the clean American backyards.
   Marilyn (1973)

8 Society is built on many people hurting many people, it is just who does the hurting, which is forever in dispute.
   Miami and the Siege of Chicago (1968)

9 The world stood like a playing card on edge . . . One looked at the buildings one passed and wondered if one was to see them again.
   looking back at the week of the Cuban Missile Crisis
   The Presidential Papers (1964)

10 Hip is the sophistication of the wise primitive in a giant jungle.
   Voices of Dissent (1959) 'The White Negro'

11 Once a newspaper touches a story, the facts are lost forever, even to the protagonists.
   in *Esquire* June 1960

12 All the security around the American president is just to make sure the man who shoots him gets caught.
   in *Sunday Telegraph* 4 March 1990

John Major 1943–
British Conservative statesman, Prime Minister 1990–7

13 If the policy isn't hurting, it isn't working.
   on controlling inflation
   speech in Northampton, 27 October 1989; see **Political sayings and slogans 258:13**

14 Society needs to condemn a little more and understand a little less.
   interview with *Mail on Sunday* 21 February 1993

15 Fifty years on from now, Britain will still be the country of long shadows on county [cricket] grounds, warm beer, invincible green suburbs, dog lovers, and—as George Orwell said—old maids bicycling to Holy

Communion through the morning mist.
speech to the Conservative Group for Europe,
22 April 1993; see **Orwell 245:13**

1 It is time to get back to basics: to self-discipline and respect for the law, to consideration for others, to accepting responsibility for yourself and your family, and not shuffling it off on the state.
speech to the Conservative Party Conference,
8 October 1993

Bernard Malamud 1914–86
American novelist and short-story writer

2 The past exudes legend: one can't make pure clay of time's mud. There is no life that can be recaptured wholly; as it was. Which is to say that all biography is ultimately fiction.
Dubin's Lives (1979)

3 There comes a time in a man's life when to get where he has to go—if there are no doors or windows—he walks through a wall.
Rembrandt's Hat (1972)

Malcolm X 1925–65
American civil rights campaigner. He joined the Nation of Islam in 1946 and became a vigorous campaigner for black rights, initially advocating the use of violence. In 1964 he converted to orthodox Islam and moderated his views on black separatism; he was assassinated the following year

4 If you're born in America with a black skin, you're born in prison.
in an interview, June 1963

5 You can't separate peace from freedom because no one can be at peace unless he has his freedom.
speech in New York, 7 January 1965

6 The white man was *created* a devil, to bring chaos upon this earth.
speech, *c.*1953; Malcolm X with Alex Haley *The Autobiography of Malcolm X* (1965); see **Fard 109:5**

7 We are not speaking of any *individual* white man. We are speaking of the *collective* white man's *historical* record.We are speaking of the collective white man's cruelties, and evils, and greeds, that have

seen him *act* like a devil toward the non-white man.
Malcolm X with Alex Haley *The Autobiography of Malcolm X* (1965)

George Leigh Mallory 1886–1924
British mountaineer

8 Because it's there.
on being asked why he wanted to climb Mount Everest (Mallory disappeared on Everest in the following year; his body was discovered in May 1999)
in *New York Times* 18 March 1923

Ruth Mallory *fl.* 1924
British wife of George Leigh **Mallory**

9 Whether he got to the top of the mountain or not, whether he lived or died, makes no difference to my admiration for him.
letter written shortly after her husband was lost on Everest
David Robertson *George Mallory* (1969)

David Malouf 1934–
Australian writer

10 I am a B-b-british object!
Remembering Babylon (1993), spoken by Gemmy Fairly; using the words of James Morrill (1824–65) who used these words on meeting white settlers after living with Aboriginals for 17 years

André Malraux 1901–76
French novelist, essayist, and art critic

11 There are not fifty ways of fighting, there's only one, and that's to win. Neither revolution nor war consists in doing what one pleases.
L'Espoir (1937)

12 *L'art est un anti-destin.*
Art is a revolt against fate.
Les Voix du silence (1951)

Lord Mancroft 1914–87
British Conservative politician

13 Cricket—a game which the English, not being a spiritual people, have invented in order to give themselves some conception of eternity.
Bees in Some Bonnets (1979)

Nelson Mandela 1918–

South African statesman, President 1994–9. He was sentenced to life imprisonment in 1964 as an activist for the African National Congress (ANC). Released in 1990, as leader of the ANC he engaged in talks on the introduction of majority rule with President F. W. de Klerk, and became the country's first democratically elected President in 1994

1 I have dedicated my life to this struggle of the African people. I have fought against white domination, and I have fought against black domination. I have cherished the ideal of a democratic and free society in which all persons live together in harmony with equal opportunities. It is an ideal which I hope to live for, and to see realized. But my lord, if needs be, it is an ideal for which I am prepared to die.
   speech in Pretoria, 20 April 1964, which he quoted on his release in Cape Town, 11 February 1990

2 I stand here before you not as a prophet but as a humble servant of you, the people. Your tireless and heroic sacrifices have made it possible for me to be here today. I therefore place the remaining years of my life in your hands.
   speech in Cape Town, 11 February 1990

3 No one is born hating another person because of the colour of his skin, or his background, or his religion. People must learn to hate, and if they can learn to hate, they can be taught to love, for love comes more naturally to the human heart than its opposite.
   Long Walk to Freedom (1994)

4 True reconciliation does not consist in merely forgetting the past.
   speech, 7 January 1996

5 We close the century with most people still languishing in poverty, subjected to hunger, preventable disease, illiteracy and insufficient shelter.
   speaking at a ceremony at his former prison cell on Robben Island
   in *Observer* on 2 January 2000

6 One of the things I learnt when I was negotiating was that until I changed myself I could not change others.
   in *Sunday Times* 16 April 2000

7 Overcoming poverty is not a gesture of charity. It is an act of justice.
   speech in Trafalgar Square, London, 3 February 2005

Winnie Madikizela-Mandela 1934–

South African political activist; former wife of Nelson **Mandela**

8 With that stick of matches, with our necklace, we shall liberate this country.
   speech in black townships, 14 April 1986

9 Maybe there is no rainbow nation after all because it does not have the colour black.
   at the funeral of a black child reportedly shot dead by a white farmer; see **Jackson 165:1**
   in *Irish Times* 25 April 1998

Peter Mandelson 1953–

British Labour politician

10 Before this campaign started, it was said that I was facing political oblivion, my career in tatters . . . They underestimated me, because I am a fighter and not a quitter.
   on winning back his Hartlepool seat in the General Election
   speech, 8 June 2001

Osip Mandelstam 1892–1938

Russian poet. Sent into internal exile in 1934, he died in a prison camp

11 Perhaps my whisper was already born before my lips.
   'Poems Published Posthumously' (written 1934)

Herbie Mann 1930–

American jazz musician

12 If you're in jazz and more than ten people like you, you're labelled commercial.
   Henry Pleasants *Serious Music and all that Jazz!* (1969)

Thomas Mann 1875–1955

German novelist and essayist. The role and character of the artist in relation to society is a constant theme in his works

13 Death in Venice.
   title of novella (1912)

14 Time has no divisions to mark its passage, there is never a thunderstorm or blare of

trumpets to announce the beginning of a new month or year. Even when a new century begins it is only we mortals who ring bells and fire off pistols.
The Magic Mountain (1924)

1 We come out of the dark and go into the dark again, and in between lie the experiences of our life.
The Magic Mountain (1924)

2 A man's dying is more the survivors' affair than his own.
The Magic Mountain (1924)

3 Speech is civilization itself. The word, even the most contradictory word, preserves contact—it is silence which isolates.
The Magic Mountain (1924)

Mao Zedong 1893–1976
Chinese statesman, chairman of the Communist Party of the Chinese People's Republic 1949–76 and head of state 1949–59; he was effectively leader of the Chinese Communist Party from the time of the Long March (1934–5). Despite having resigned as head of state Mao instigated the Cultural Revolution (1966–8)
on Mao: see **Levin 198:11**

4 Politics is war without bloodshed while war is politics with bloodshed.
lecture, 1938; *Selected Works* (1965) vol. 2

5 Every Communist must grasp the truth, 'Political power grows out of the barrel of a gun'.
speech, 6 November 1938

6 The atom bomb is a paper tiger which the United States reactionaries use to scare people. It looks terrible, but in fact it isn't . . . All reactionaries are paper tigers.
interview, 1946; *Selected Works* (1961) vol. 4

7 Letting a hundred flowers blossom and a hundred schools of thought contend is the policy for promoting progress in the arts and the sciences and a flourishing socialist culture in our land.
speech in Peking, 27 February 1957

Diego Maradona 1960–
Argentine football player

8 The goal was scored a little bit by the hand of God, another bit by head of Maradona.
on his controversial goal against England in the 1986 World Cup
in *Guardian* 1 July 1986

John Marchi 1921–
American Republican politician

9 We ought not to permit a cottage industry in the God business.
on hearing that British scientists had successfully cloned a lamb (Dolly)
in *Guardian* 28 February 1997

Princess Margaret 1930–2002
British princess, sister of **Elizabeth II**

10 Mindful of the Church's teaching that Christian marriage is indissoluble, and conscious of my duty to the Commonwealth, I have resolved to put these considerations before any others.
announcing her decision not to marry a divorced man, Group Captain Peter Townsend
statement from Clarence House, 31 October 1955

11 My children are not royal, they just happen to have the Queen as their aunt.
Elizabeth Longford (ed.) *The Oxford Book of Royal Anecdotes* (1989)

Lynn Margulis 1938–
American biologist

12 Gaia is a tough bitch. People think the earth is going to die and they have to save it, that's ridiculous . . . There's no doubt that Gaia can compensate for our output of greenhouse gases, but the environment that's left will not be happy for any people.
in *New York Times Biographical Service* January 1996

Johnny Marks 1909–85
American songwriter

13 Rudolph, the Red-Nosed Reindeer
Had a very shiny nose,
And if you ever saw it,
You would even say it glows.
'Rudolph, the Red-Nosed Reindeer' (1949 song)

Bob Marley 1945–81
Jamaican reggae musician and songwriter

1 Get up, stand up
Stand up for your rights
Get up, stand up
Never give up the fight.
'Get up, Stand up' (1973 song)

2 I shot the sheriff
But I swear it was in self-defence
I shot the sheriff
And they say it is a capital offence.
'I Shot the Sheriff' (1974 song)

Don Marquis 1878–1937
American poet and journalist

3 procrastination is the
art of keeping
up with yesterday.
archy and mehitabel (1927) 'certain maxims of
archy'

4 an optimist is a guy
that has never had
much experience.
archy and mehitabel (1927) 'certain maxims of
archy'

5 it s cheerio
my deario that
pulls a lady through.
archy and mehitabel (1927) 'cheerio, my
deario'

6 I have got you out here
in the great open spaces
where cats are cats.
archy and mehitabel (1927) 'mehitabel has an
adventure'

7 but wotthehell archy wotthehell
jamais triste archy jamais triste
that is my motto.
archy and mehitabel (1927) 'mehitabel sees
paris'

8 boss there is always
a comforting thought
in time of trouble when
it is not our trouble.
archy does his part (1935) 'comforting
thoughts'

9 did you ever
notice that when
a politician
does get an idea

he usually
gets it all wrong.
archys life of mehitabel (1933) 'archygrams'

10 now and then
there is a person born
who is so unlucky
that he runs into accidents
which started to happen
to somebody else.
archys life of mehitabel (1933) 'archy says'

11 Prohibition makes you want to cry into
your beer and denies you the beer to cry
into.
Sun Dial Time (1936)

12 The art of newspaper paragraphing is to
stroke a platitude until it purrs like an
epigram.
E. Anthony *O Rare Don Marquis* (1962)

13 Writing a book of poetry is like dropping a
rose petal down the Grand Canyon and
waiting for the echo.
E. Anthony *O Rare Don Marquis* (1962)

Anthony Marriott 1931–
and **Alistair Foot**
British writers

14 No sex please—we're British.
title of play (1971)

Arthur Marshall 1910–89
British humorous writer and former schoolmaster

15 What, knocked a tooth out? Never mind,
dear, laugh it off, laugh it off; it's all part of
life's rich pageant.
The Games Mistress (recorded monologue,
1937)

Thomas R. Marshall 1854–1925
American Democratic politician, Vice-President
1913–21

16 What this country needs is a really good
5-cent cigar.
in *New York Tribune* 4 January 1920

Thurgood Marshall 1908–93
American civil rights lawyer, the first African-
American Supreme Court justice

17 We must never forget that the only real
source of power that we as judges can tap

is the respect of the people.
in *Chicago Tribune* 15 August 1981

Dean Martin 1917–95
American singer and actor

1 You're not drunk if you can lie on the floor without holding on.
Paul Dickson *Official Rules* (1978)

Holt Marvell
English songwriter

2 These foolish things remind me of you.
title of song (1935)

3 A cigarette that bears a lipstick's traces,
An airline ticket to romantic places.
'These Foolish Things Remind Me of You'
(1935 song)

Chico Marx 1891–1961
American film comedian

4 I wasn't kissing her, I was just whispering in her mouth.
on being discovered by his wife with a chorus girl
Groucho Marx and Richard J. Anobile *Marx Brothers Scrapbook* (1973)

Groucho Marx 1890–1977
American film comedian
see also **Elizabeth 104:11, Epitaphs 107:12, Film lines 113:5, Film lines 114:4, Film lines 114:14, Film lines 116:2, Film lines 116:11**

5 PLEASE ACCEPT MY RESIGNATION. I DON'T WANT TO BELONG TO ANY CLUB THAT WILL ACCEPT ME AS A MEMBER.
Groucho and Me (1959)

6 I never forget a face, but in your case I'll be glad to make an exception.
Leo Rosten *People I have Loved, Known or Admired* (1970) 'Groucho'

7 I've been around so long, I knew Doris Day before she was a virgin.
Max Wilk *The Wit and Wisdom of Hollywood* (1972); also attributed to Oscar **Levant**

Queen Mary 1867–1953
British princess, Queen Consort of **George V**

8 Well, Mr Baldwin! *this* is a pretty kettle of fish!
*to the Prime Minister, Stanley **Baldwin**, after **Edward VIII** had told her he was prepared to give up the throne to marry Mrs Simpson*
said on 17 November 1936; James Pope-Hennessy *Life of Queen Mary* (1959)

9 I do not think you have ever realised the shock, which the attitude you took up caused your family and the whole nation. It seemed inconceivable to those who had made such sacrifices during the war that you, as their King, refused a lesser sacrifice.
letter to the Duke of Windsor (formerly **Edward VIII**), July 1938; James Pope-Hennessy *Queen Mary* (1959)

Eric Maschwitz 1901–69
British writer

10 A nightingale sang in Berkeley Square.
title of song (1940)

Donald Mason 1913–
American naval officer

11 Sighted sub, sank same.
on sinking a Japanese submarine in the Atlantic region (the first US naval success in the war)
radio message, 28 January 1942; in *New York Times* 27 February 1942

Nick Mason 1944–
English drummer and percussionist, member of **Pink Floyd**
see also **Pink Floyd 254:12**

12 In the 1960s, the record companies seemed to sign anything with long hair; if it was a sheepdog, so what.
N. Shaffner *A Saucerful of Secrets: the Pink Floyd Odyssey*

Leonard Matlovich
see **Epitaphs 108:9**

W. Somerset Maugham 1874–1965
English novelist

13 You can't learn too soon that the most useful thing about a principle is that it can always be sacrificed to expediency.
The Circle (1921)

1 It is not true that suffering ennobles the character; happiness does that sometimes, but suffering, for the most part, makes men petty and vindictive.
  The Moon and Sixpence (1919)

2 A woman can forgive a man for the harm he does her, but she can never forgive him for the sacrifices he makes on her account.
  The Moon and Sixpence (1919)

3 Money is like a sixth sense without which you cannot make a complete use of the other five.
  Of Human Bondage (1915)

4 I [Death] was astonished to see him in Baghdad, for I had an appointment with him tonight in Samarra.
  Sheppey (1933)

5 I am told that today rather more than 60 per cent of the men who go to the universities go on a Government grant. This is a new class that has entered upon the scene . . . They are scum.
  in *Sunday Times* 25 December 1955

to a friend who had said that he hated English food:
6 All you have to do is eat breakfast three times a day.
  Ted Morgan *Somerset Maugham* (1980)

7 Dying is a very dull, dreary affair. And my advice to you is to have nothing whatever to do with it.
  to his nephew Robin, in 1965
  Robin Maugham *Conversations with Willie* (1978)

Bill Mauldin
American cartoonist
see **Cartoons 56:4**

André Maurois 1885–1967
French writer

8 Growing old is no more than a bad habit which a busy man has no time to form.
  The Art of Living (1940)

James Maxton 1885–1946
British Labour politician

9 All I say is, if you cannot ride two horses you have no right in the circus.
  opposing disaffiliation of the Scottish Independent Labour Party from the Labour Party; usually quoted as, '. . . no right in the bloody circus'
  in *Daily Herald* 12 January 1931

Theresa May 1956–
British Conservative politician

10 You know what some people call us: the nasty party.
  speech to the Conservative Conference, 7 October 2002

Vladimir Mayakovsky 1893–1930
Russian poet
see also **Last words 191:2**

11 If you wish—
  . . . I'll be irreproachably tender;
  not a man, but—a cloud in trousers!
  'The Cloud in Trousers' (1915)

12 Not a sound. The universe sleeps, resting a huge ear on its paw with mites of stars.
  'The Cloud in Trousers' (1915)

Louis B. Mayer 1885–1957
Russian-born American film executive, head of MGM

13 We've got more stars than there are in the heavens, all of them except for that damned Mouse over at Disney.
  Sheridan Morley and Ruth Leon *Gene Kelly* (1996)

Percy Mayfield 1920–84
American songwriter

14 Hit the road, Jack.
  title of song (1961)

Charles H. Mayo 1865–1939
American doctor, co-founder of the Mayo Clinic

15 The definition of a specialist as one who 'knows more and more about less and less' is good and true.
  in *Modern Hospital* September 1938; see **Butler 49:10**

Margaret Mead 1901–78
American anthropologist

1 The knowledge that the personalities of the two sexes are socially produced is congenial to every programme that looks forward towards a planned order of society. It is a two-edged sword.
   Sex and Temperament in Three Primitive Societies (1935)

2 Never doubt that a small group of thoughtful committed citizens can change the world. In fact, it's the only thing that ever has.
   attributed; Mary Bowman-Kruhm *Margaret Mead: a biography* (2003)

Shepherd Mead 1914–
American advertising executive

3 How to succeed in business without really trying.
   title of book (1952)

Hughes Mearns 1875–1965
American writer

4 As I was walking up the stair
   I met a man who wasn't there.
   He wasn't there again today.
   I wish, I wish he'd stay away.
   lines written for an amateur play *The Psychoed* (1910) and set to music in 1939 as 'The Little Man Who Wasn't There'

Peter Medawar 1915–87
English immunologist and writer

5 A bishop wrote gravely to the *Times* inviting all nations to destroy 'the formula' of the atomic bomb. There is no simple remedy for ignorance so abysmal.
   The Hope of Progress (1972)

6 If politics is the art of the possible, research is surely the art of the soluble. Both are immensely practical-minded affairs.
   in *New Statesman* 19 June 1964; see **Butler 49:12, Galbraith 128:12**

7 During the 1950s, the first great age of molecular biology, the English Schools of Oxford and particularly of Cambridge produced more than a score of graduates of quite outstanding ability—much more brilliant, inventive, articulate and dialectically skilful than most young

scientists; right up in the Watson class. But Watson had one towering advantage over all of them: in addition to being extremely clever he had something important to be clever *about*.
   review of James D. **Watson**'s *The Double Helix* in *New York Review of Books* 28 March 1968

Bertie Mee 1918–2001
English football player and manager

8 When you've done it all, what do you do for an encore?
   of Arsenal's League and FA cup double in 1971 in *Times* 23 October 2001, obituary

Golda Meir 1898–1978
Israeli stateswoman, Prime Minister 1969–74

9 Those that perished in Hitler's gas chambers were the last Jews to die without standing up to defend themselves.
   speech to United Jewish Appeal Rally, New York, 11 June 1967

10 Women's Liberation is just a lot of foolishness. It's the men who are discriminated against. They can't bear children. And no-one's likely to do anything about that.
   in *Newsweek* 23 October 1972

David Mellor 1949–
British Conservative politician and broadcaster

11 I do believe the popular press is drinking in the last chance saloon.
   interview on *Hard News* (Channel 4), 21 December 1989

H. L. Mencken 1880–1956
American journalist and literary critic

12 Love is the delusion that one woman differs from another.
   Chrestomathy (1949)

13 Puritanism. The haunting fear that someone, somewhere, may be happy.
   Chrestomathy (1949)

14 Democracy is the theory that the common people know what they want, and deserve to get it good and hard.
   A Little Book in C major (1916)

1 Conscience: the inner voice which warns us that someone may be looking.
  A Little Book in C major (1916)

2 It is now quite lawful for a Catholic woman to avoid pregnancy by a resort to mathematics, though she is still forbidden to resort to physics and chemistry.
  Notebooks (1956) 'Minority Report'

3 No one in this world, so far as I know—and I have searched the records for years, and employed agents to help me—has ever lost money by underestimating the intelligence of the great masses of the plain people.
  in *Chicago Tribune* 19 September 1926

4 If there had been any formidable body of cannibals in the country he would have promised to provide them with free missionaries fattened at the taxpayer's expense.
  *of Harry **Truman** in the 1948 presidential campaign*
  in *Baltimore Sun* 7 November 1948

Elsie Mendl 1865–1950
American socialite and fashionable decorator

  explaining her dislike of soup:
5 I do not believe in building a meal on a lake.
  Elsie de Wolfe *After All* (1935)

6 It's just my colour: it's *beige*!
  her first view of the Parthenon
  Osbert Sitwell *Rat Week: An Essay on the Abdication* (1986)

Robert Gordon Menzies 1894–1978
Australian Liberal statesman, Prime Minister 1939–41 and 1949–66
on Menzies: see **Curtin 81:15, Hughes 160:7**

7 What Great Britain calls the Far East is to us the near north.
  in *Sydney Morning Herald* 27 April 1939

David Mercer 1928–80
English dramatist

8 A suitable case for treatment.
  title of television play (1962); later filmed as *Morgan—A Suitable Case for Treatment* (1966)

Johnny Mercer 1909–76
American songwriter

9 You've got to ac-cent-tchu-ate the positive
  Elim-my-nate the negative
  Latch on to the affirmative
  Don't mess with Mister In-between.
  'Ac-cent-tchu-ate the Positive' (1944 song)

10 Jeepers Creepers—where you get them peepers?
  'Jeepers Creepers' (1938 song)

11 We're drinking my friend,
  To the end of a brief episode,
  Make it one for my baby
  And one more for the road.
  'One For My Baby' (1943 song)

12 That old black magic.
  title of song (1942)

Rick Mercer 1969–
Canadian comedian

13 America is our neighbour, our ally, our trading partner, and our friend. Still, sometimes you'd like to give them such a smack.
  This Hour Has 22 Minutes (CBC television, 11 November 1996)

William Meredith 1919–
American poet

14 Look hard at the world, they said—
  generously, if you can
  manage that, but hard.
  'What I Remember the Writers Telling Me When I Was Young' (1987)

Bob Merrill 1921–98
American songwriter and composer

15 How much is that doggie in the window?
  title of song (1953)

16 People who need people are the luckiest people in the world.
  'People who Need People' (1964 song)

James Merrill 1926–95
American poet

17 Always that same old story—
  Father Time and Mother Earth,

a marriage on the rocks.
    'The Broken Home' (1966)

Thomas Merton 1915–68
American Trappist monk and writer

1 Our culture is one which is geared in many
    ways to help us evade any need to face this
    inner, silent self. We live in a state of
    constant semi-attention.
        'Creative Silence' in *Baptist Student* February
        1969

W. S. Merwin 1927–
American poet

2 The sea curling
    Star-climbed, wind-combed, cumbered
        with itself still
    As at first it was, is the hand not yet
        contented
    Of the Creator. And he waits for the world
        to begin.
        'Leviathan' (1956)

Duane Michals 1932–
American photographer

3 I am a reflection photographing other
    reflections within a reflection.
        'A Failed Attempt to Photograph Reality'
        (photographic print, *c.*1975), in M. Livingstone
        The Essential Duane Michals (1997)

4 Photography deals exquisitely with
    appearances, but nothing is what it
    appears to be.
        attributed

Kate Middleton 1982–
British girlfriend of Prince William

5 I love the uniform. It's so so sexy.
    *interpretation by an ITN lipreader of a remark
    made at Prince William's passing out ceremony
    at Sandhurst*
        in *Guardian* (online edition) 16 December
        2006

Bette Midler 1945–
American actress

6 When it's three o'clock in New York, it's
    still 1938 in London.
        attributed

Ludwig Mies van der Rohe 1886–1969
German-born architect and designer

7 Less is more.
    P. Johnson *Mies van der Rohe* (1947); see
    Venturi 324:9

8 God is in the details.
    in *New York Times* 19 August 1969

George Mikes 1912–87
Hungarian-born British writer

9 An Englishman, even if he is alone, forms
    an orderly queue of one.
        How to be an Alien (1946)

Military sayings and slogans
see box opposite

Edna St Vincent Millay 1892–1950
American poet

10 Childhood is the kingdom where nobody
        dies.
    Nobody that matters, that is.
        'Childhood is the Kingdom where Nobody
        dies' (1934)

11 Down, down, down into the darkness of
        the grave
    Gently they go, the beautiful, the tender,
        the kind;
    Quietly they go, the intelligent, the witty,
        the brave.
    I know. But I do not approve. And I am not
        resigned.
        'Dirge Without Music' (1928)

12 My candle burns at both ends;
    It will not last the night;
    But ah, my foes, and oh, my friends—
    It gives a lovely light.
        A Few Figs From Thistles (1920) 'First Fig'

13 Euclid alone
    Has looked on Beauty bare. Fortunate they
    Who, though once only and then but far
        away,
    Have heard her massive sandal set on
        stone.
        The Harp-Weaver and Other Poems (1923)
        sonnet 22

14 Justice denied in Massachusetts.
    *relating to the trial of Sacco and **Vanzetti** and
    their execution on 22 August 1927*
        title of poem (1928)

Military sayings and slogans

1 Action this day.
   annotation as used by Winston Churchill at
   the Admiralty in 1940

2 Are we downhearted? No!
   expression much taken up by British
   soldiers during the First World War

3 Daddy, what did you do in the Great
   War?
   daughter to father in First World War
   recruiting poster

4 The difficult we do immediately, the
   impossible takes a little longer.
   US Armed Forces slogan

5 Fifty million Frenchmen can't be wrong.
   saying popular with American servicemen
   during the First World War; later associated
   with Mae **West** and Texas Guinan
   (1884–1933), it was also the title of a 1927
   song by Billy Rose and Willie Raskin

6 If it moves, salute it; if it doesn't move,
   pick it up; and if you can't pick it up,
   paint it.
   1940s saying; P. Dickson *The Official Rules*
   (1978)

7 *Ils ne passeront pas.*
   They shall not pass.
   slogan of the French army at the defence of
   Verdun 1916; variously attributed to Marshal
   Pétain and to General Robert Nivelle, and
   taken up by the Republicans in the Spanish
   Civil War; see **Ibarruri 162:1**

8 Lions led by donkeys.
   *associated with British soldiers during the First
   World War*
   attributed to Max Hoffman (1869–1927) in
   Alan Clark *The Donkeys* (1961); this
   attribution has not been traced elsewhere,
   and the phrase was well-known by the
   1870s

9 Loose lips sink ships.
   American Second World war security slogan

10 Who dares wins.
   motto of the British Special Air Service
   regiment, from 1942

11 Your country needs you.
   slogan on First World War recruitment
   poster, 1914, showing Lord **Kitchener**
   pointing, designed by Alfred Leete
   (1882–1933); see **Asquith 15:5**, **Military
   sayings 221:12**

12 Your King and Country need you.
   recruitment slogan for First World War,
   coined by Eric Field, July 1914; *Advertising*
   (1959); see **Military sayings 221:11**, **Rubens
   276:14**

Edna St Vincent Millay continued

13 The sun that warmed our stooping backs
   and withered the weeds uprooted—
   We shall not feel it again.
   We shall die in darkness, and be buried in
   the rain.
   'Justice Denied in Massachusetts' (1928)

14 Death devours all lovely things;
   Lesbia with her sparrow
   Shares the darkness—presently
   Every bed is narrow.
   'Passer Mortuus Est' (1921)

15 After all, my erstwhile dear,
   My no longer cherished,
   Need we say it was not love,
   Now that love is perished?
   'Passer Mortuus Est' (1921)

16 It's not true that life is one damn thing
   after another—it's one damn thing over
   and over.
   letter to Arthur Davison Ficke, 24 October
   1930; see **Hubbard 159:1**

Alice Duer Miller 1874–1942
American writer

17 I am American bred,
   I have seen much to hate here—much to
   forgive,
   But in a world where England is finished
   and dead,
   I do not wish to live.
   The White Cliffs (1940)

Arthur Miller 1915–2005

American dramatist. He established his reputation with *Death of a Salesman* (1949). *The Crucible* (1953) used the Salem witch trials of 1692 as an allegory for McCarthyism in America in the 1950s. Miller was married to Marilyn **Monroe** between 1956 and 1961

on Miller: see **Newspaper headlines 237:8**

1 A suicide kills two people, Maggie, that's what it's for!
   After the Fall (1964)

2 All organization is and must be grounded on the idea of exclusion and prohibition just as two objects cannot occupy the same space.
   The Crucible (1953)

3 Death of a salesman
   title of play (1949)

4 The world is an oyster, but you don't crack it open on a mattress.
   Death of a Salesman (1949)

5 Willy Loman never made a lot of money. His name was never in the paper. He's not the finest character that ever lived. But he's a human being, and a terrible thing is happening to him. So attention must be paid.
   Death of a Salesman (1949)

6 For a salesman, there is no rock bottom to the life. He don't put a bolt to a nut, he don't tell you the law or give you medicine. He's a man way out there in the blue, riding on a smile and a shoeshine. And when they start not smiling back—that's an earthquake . . . A salesman is got to dream, boy. It comes with the territory.
   Death of a Salesman (1949) 'Requiem'

7 The car, the furniture, the wife, the children—everything has to be disposable. Because you see the main thing today is—shopping.
   The Price (1968)

8 The ultimate human mystery may not be anything more than the claims on us of clan and race, which may yet turn out to have the power, because they defy the rational mind, to kill the world.
   Timebends (1987)

9 A good newspaper, I suppose, is a nation talking to itself.
   in *Observer* 26 November 1961

Henry Miller 1891–1980

American novelist. His autobiographical novels *Tropic of Cancer* (1934) and *Tropic of Capricorn* (1939) were banned in the US until the 1960s due to their frank depiction of sex and use of obscenities

10 Even before the music begins there is that bored look on people's faces. A polite form of self-imposed torture, the concert.
   Tropic of Cancer (1934)

11 Every man with a bellyful of the classics is an enemy to the human race.
   Tropic of Cancer (1934)

Jonathan Miller 1934–

English writer and director

12 I'm not really a *Jew*. Just Jew-*ish*. Not the whole hog, you know.
   Beyond the Fringe (1960 revue) 'Real Class'

Spike Milligan 1918–2002

Irish comedian
see also **Catchphrases 59:15, Catchphrases 61:21, Catchphrases 62:1, Epitaphs 107:17**

13 Money couldn't buy friends but you got a better class of enemy.
   Puckoon (1963)

A. J. Mills, Fred Godfrey, and Bennett Scott

British songwriters

14 Take me back to dear old Blighty.
   title of song (1916)

Irving Mills 1894–1985

American songwriter

15 It don't mean a thing
   If it ain't got that swing.
   'It Don't Mean a Thing' (1932 song; music by Duke **Ellington**)

A. A. Milne 1882–1956

English writer for children
on Milne: see **Parker 249:15**

16 The more he looked inside the more Piglet wasn't there.
   The House at Pooh Corner (1928)

17 '*The more it snows, tiddely pom*—'
   'Tiddely what?' said Piglet.

'Pom,' said Pooh. 'I put that in to make it more hummy.'
The House at Pooh Corner (1928); see **Parker 249:15**

1 I am a Bear of Very Little Brain, and long words Bother me.
Winnie-the-Pooh (1926)

2 Time for a little something.
Winnie-the-Pooh (1926)

3 My spelling is Wobbly. It's good spelling but it Wobbles, and the letters get in the wrong places.
Winnie-the-Pooh (1926)

4 Owl hasn't exactly got Brain, but he Knows Things.
Winnie-the-Pooh (1926)

5 They're changing guard at Buckingham Palace—
Christopher Robin went down with Alice.
Alice is marrying one of the guard.
'A soldier's life is terrible hard,'
Says Alice.
'Buckingham Palace' (1924)

6 James James
Morrison Morrison
Weatherby George Dupree
Took great
Care of his Mother,
Though he was only three.
James James
Said to his Mother,
'Mother,' he said, said he;
'You must never go down to the end of the town, if you don't go down with me.'
'Disobedience' (1924)

7 King John was not a good man—
He had his little ways.
And sometimes no one spoke to him
For days and days and days.
'King John's Christmas' (1927)

8 The King asked
The Queen, and
The Queen asked
The Dairymaid:
'Could we have some butter for
The Royal slice of bread?'
'The King's Breakfast' (1924)

9 *What* is the matter with Mary Jane?
She's perfectly well and she hasn't a pain,
And it's lovely rice pudding for dinner again!

What *is* the matter with Mary Jane?
'Rice Pudding' (1924)

10 Hush! Hush! Whisper who dares!
Christopher Robin is saying his prayers.
'Vespers' (1924); see **Morton 229:7**

Misquotations
see box overleaf

Adrian Mitchell 1932–
English poet, novelist, and dramatist

11 Most people ignore most poetry because
most poetry ignores most people.
Poems (1964) p. 8

George Mitchell 1933–
American politician, chairman of the Northern Ireland peace talks 1996–99

12 Although he is regularly asked to do so, God does not take sides in American politics.
comment during the hearing of the Senate Select Committee on the Iran-Contra affair, July 1987

13 Peace, political stability and reconciliation are not too much to ask for. They are the minimum that a decent society provides.
in *Irish Post* 18 April 1998

John Mitchell 1913–88
American lawyer and US Attorney-General to the Nixon administration

14 Katie Graham's gonna get her tit caught in a big fat wringer if that's published.
on hearing that Katherine **Graham**'s *Washington Post was to reveal the connection between Watergate and the campaign funding for the Committee to Re-Elect the President*
in 1973; Katherine Graham *Personal History* (1997)

Joni Mitchell 1945–
Canadian singer and songwriter

15 You don't know what you've got
Till it's gone.
'Big Yellow Taxi' (1970 song)

16 They paved paradise
And put up a parking lot.
'Big Yellow Taxi' (1970 song)

Misquotations

1 Beam me up, Scotty.
   supposedly the form in which Captain Kirk
   habitually requested to be returned from a
   planet to the Starship *Enterprise*; in fact the
   nearest equivalent found is 'Beam us up, Mr
   Scott' in Gene **Roddenberry** *Star Trek* (1966
   onwards) 'Gamesters of Triskelion'

2 Come with me to the Casbah.
   often attributed to Charles Boyer (1898–1978)
   in the film Algiers (*1938*), *but the line does not*
   in fact occur
   L. Swindell *Charles Boyer* (1983)

3 Crisis? What crisis?
   in *Sun* headline, 11 January 1979;
   summarizing James **Callaghan**'s remark 'I
   don't think other people in the world would
   share the view there is mounting chaos',
   interview at London Airport, 10 January 1979

4 Dark forces at work.
   popular summary of comment attributed to
   Queen **Elizabeth II** by former royal butler
   Paul Burrell, reported in the *Daily Mirror* as,
   'There are powers at work in this country
   about which we have no knowledge'

5 Dreams are the royal road to the
   unconscious.
   summary of **Freud**'s view; see **Freud 123:7**

6 Elementary, my dear Watson,
   elementary.
   remark attributed to Sherlock Holmes, but not
   found in this form in any book by Arthur Conan
   Doyle, first found in P.G. Wodehouse Psmith
   Journalist (*1915*)
   attributed

7 A good day to bury bad news.
   popular misquotation of Jo **Moore**'s email of
   11 September 2001; see **Moore 227:12**

8 The green shoots of recovery.
   popular misquotation of the Chancellor
   Norman **Lamont**'s upbeat assessment of the
   economic situation: 'The green shoots of
   economic spring are appearing once again',
   speech at Conservative Party Conference,
   9 October 1991

9 Hug a hoodie.
   Vernon Coaker's summary of a speech by
   David Cameron calling for more
   understanding of apparently threatening
   young people (see **Cameron 51:10, Coaker
   72:10**)

10 I paint with my prick.
    attributed to Pierre Auguste Renoir
    (1841–1919); possibly an inversion of his 'It's
    with my brush I make love', A. André *Renoir*
    (1919)

11 It's life, Jim, but not as we know it.
    saying associated with the television series
    Star Trek (1966–), created by Gene
    Roddenberry; the saying does not occur in
    the series but derives from the 1987 song
    'Star Trekkin'' sung by The Firm. The nearest
    equivalent found in the series is 'No life as
    we know it', said by Mr Spock in 'The Devil
    in the Dark' (1967)

when asked what jazz is:
12 Man, if you gotta ask you'll never know.
    frequently quoted version of Louis
    Armstrong's response 'If you still have to
    ask . . . shame on you', quoted in Max Jones
    et al. *Salute to Satchmo* (1970)

13 Me Tarzan, you Jane.
    Johnny Weissmuller summing up his role in
    Tarzan, the Ape Man (*1932 film*); *the words*
    occur neither in the film nor the original, by
    Edgar Rice Burroughs
    in *Photoplay Magazine* June 1932

14 My lips are sealed.
    misquotation from Stanley **Baldwin**'s
    speech on the Abyssinian crisis: 'I shall be
    but a short time tonight. I have seldom
    spoken with greater regret, for my lips are
    not yet unsealed. Were these troubles over I
    would make a case, and I guarantee that not
    a man would go into the lobby against us',
    speech in the House of Commons, 10
    December 1935

15 Play it again, Sam.
    in the film Casablanca, *written by Julius J.*
    Epstein et al., Humphrey Bogart says, 'If she
    can stand it, I can. Play it!'; earlier in the film
    Ingrid Bergman says, 'Play it, Sam. Play As
    Time Goes By.*'*
    Casablanca (1942 film); see **Film lines 114:3,
    Hupfeld 160:14**

▶

▶ Misquotations continued

1 Selling off the family silver.
summary of Harold **Macmillan**'s attack on privatization: 'First of all the Georgian silver goes, and then all that nice furniture that used to be in the saloon. Then the Canalettos go', speech to the Tory Reform Group, 8 November 1985

2 Shouting fire in a crowded theatre.
popular summary of Oliver Wendell **Holmes** Jr.'s definition of the limits of free speech: 'The most stringent protection of free speech would not protect a man falsely shouting fire in a theatre and causing a panic', in *Schenck v. United States* (1919)

3 The soft under-belly of Europe.
popular version of Winston **Churchill**'s phrase: 'We make this wide encircling movement in the Mediterranean, having for its primary object the recovery of the command of that vital sea, but also having for its object the exposure of the under-belly of the Axis, especially Italy, to heavy attack', speech in the House of Commons, 11 November 1942

4 Something must be done.
popular summary of King **Edward VIII**'s words at the derelict Dowlais Iron and Steel Works, 18 November 1936: 'These works brought all these people here. Something should be done to get them at work again', in *Western Mail* 19 November 1936

5 We are the masters now.
from Hartley **Shawcross**'s assertion of Labour's strength after winning the 1945 election, '"But," said Alice, "the question is whether you can make a word mean different things." "Not so," said Humpty-Dumpty, "the question is which is to be master. That's all." We are the masters at the moment, and not only at the moment, but for a very long time to come.'
in the House of Commons, 2 April 1946, quoting Lewis Carroll (1832–98) *Through the Looking-Glass* (1872): '"When *I* use a word," Humpty Dumpty said in a rather scornful tone, "it means just what I choose it to mean—neither more nor less" ... "The question is," said Humpty Dumpty, "which is to be master—that's all."'; see **Blair 35:14**

6 Well, that's a lie.
comment allegedly made by Cherie Blair (and subsequently strongly denied by her and by Downing Street) on hearing Gordon **Brown** assert in his speech to the Labour Party Conference that it had been a privilege for him to work with Tony Blair
quoted in *Guardian* 26 September 2006

7 The white heat of technology.
phrase deriving from Harold **Wilson**'s speech at the Labour Party Conference, 1 October 1963: 'The Britain that is going to be forged in the white heat of this revolution will be no place for restrictive practices or for outdated methods on either side of industry'

8 Why don't you come up and see me sometime?
alteration of Mae **West**'s invitation: 'Why don't you come up sometime, and see me?', *She Done Him Wrong* (1933 film)

9 You dirty rat!
associated with James Cagney (1899–1986), but not used by him in any film; in a speech at the American Film Institute banquet, 13 March 1974, Cagney said, 'I never said "Mmm, you dirty rat!"'
Cagney by Cagney (1976)

Joni Mitchell continued

10 I've looked at life from both sides now,
From win and lose and still somehow
It's life's illusions I recall;
I really don't know life at all.
'Both Sides Now' (1967 song)

11 We are stardust,
We are golden,
And we got to get ourselves
Back to the garden.
'Woodstock' (1969 song)

Margaret Mitchell 1900–49
American novelist

12 Providing you have enough courage—or money—you can do without a reputation.
said by Rhett Butler
Gone with the Wind (1936)

1 Death and taxes and childbirth! There's never any convenient time for any of them.
Gone with the Wind (1936)

2 I wish I could care what you do or where you go but I can't . . . My dear, I don't give a damn.
Gone with the Wind (1936), spoken by Rhett Butler; see **Film lines 113:11**

3 After all, tomorrow is another day.
Gone with the Wind (1936); closing words, spoken by Scarlett O'Hara

Warren Mitchell 1926–
British actor
see also **Catchphrases 61:2**

4 You don't retire in this business. You just notice the phone has not rung for 10 years.
in *Guardian* 30 December 2000

Nancy Mitford 1904–73
English writer

5 Abroad is unutterably bloody and foreigners are fiends.
Uncle Matthew's view
The Pursuit of Love (1945); see **George VI 131:10**

François Mitterrand 1916–96
French socialist statesman, President of France 1981–95

6 She has the eyes of Caligula, but the mouth of Marilyn Monroe.
*of Margaret **Thatcher**, briefing his new European Minister Roland Dumas*
in *Observer* 25 November 1990

Wilson Mizner 1876–1933
American dramatist

7 Be nice to people on your way up because you'll meet 'em on your way down.
A. Johnston *The Legendary Mizners* (1953)

8 If you steal from one author, it's plagiarism; if you steal from many, it's research.
A. Johnston *The Legendary Mizners* (1953)

9 A trip through a sewer in a glass-bottomed boat.
of Hollywood
A. Johnston *The Legendary Mizners* (1953)

Ariane Mnouchkine 1934–
French theatre director

10 A cultural Chernobyl.
of Euro Disney
in *Harper's Magazine* July 1992; see **Ballard 22:6**

Emilio Mola 1887–1937
Spanish nationalist general

11 Fifth column.
an extra body of supporters claimed by General Mola in a broadcast as being within Madrid when he besieged the city with four columns of Nationalist forces
in *New York Times* 16 and 17 October 1936

Walter Mondale 1928–
American Democratic politician, Vice President 1977–81

12 When I hear your new ideas I'm reminded of that ad, 'Where's the beef?'
in a televised debate with Gary Hart, 11 March 1984; see **Advertising slogans 5:12**

Piet Mondrian 1872–1944
Dutch painter

13 The essence of painting has actually always been to make it [the universal] plastically perceptible through colour and line.
'Natural Reality and Abstract Reality' (written 1919)

Jean Monnet 1888–1979
French economist and diplomat; founder of the European Community

14 Europe has never existed. It is not the addition of national sovereignties in a conclave which creates an entity. One must genuinely *create* Europe.
Anthony Sampson *The New Europeans* (1968)

15 We should not create a nation Europe instead of a nation France.
François Duchêne *Jean Monnet* (1994)

Marilyn Monroe 1926–62
American actress, married to Joe **DiMaggio** (in 1954) and Arthur **Miller** (from 1956 to 1961)
on Monroe: see **Curtis 81:16, John 168:9, Mailer 211:7, Newspaper headlines 237:8, Wilder 335:13**; see also **Mitterrand 226:6**

when asked if she really had nothing on in a calendar photograph:
1 I had the radio on.
in *Time* 11 August 1952

on being asked what she wore in bed:
2 Chanel No. 5.
Pete Martin *Marilyn Monroe* (1956)

John Montague 1929–
Irish poet and writer

3   To grow
a second tongue, as
harsh a humiliation
as twice to be born.
'A Grafted Tongue' (1972)

4 Like dolmens round my childhood, the old people.
'Like Dolmens Round my Childhood' (1972)

Lord Montgomery of Alamein
1887–1976
British field marshal, who in August 1942 replaced Auchinleck as commander of the Eighth Army
on Montgomery: see **Churchill 68:18**

5 *Here* we will stand and fight; there will be no further withdrawal. I have ordered that all plans and instructions dealing with further withdrawal are to be burnt, and at once. We will stand and fight *here*. If we can't stay here alive, then let us stay here dead.
speech in Cairo, 13 August 1942; the battle of Alam Halfa, sometimes called the first battle of Alamein, began 30 August 1942

6 Rule 1, on page 1 of the book of war, is: 'Do not march on Moscow' . . . [Rule 2] is: 'Do not go fighting with your land armies in China.'
speech in the House of Lords, 30 May 1962

7 I have heard some say . . . [homosexual] practices are allowed in France and in other NATO countries. We are not French, and we are not other nationals. We are British, thank God!
on the 2nd reading of the Sexual Offences Bill
speech in the House of Lords, 24 May 1965

Monty Python's Flying Circus 1969–74
British BBC TV programme, written by Graham Chapman (1941–89), John Cleese (1939–), Terry Gilliam (1940–), Eric Idle (1943–), Terry Jones (1942–), and Michael Palin (1943–)
see also **Catchphrases 58:3**

8 Your wife interested in . . . *photographs?* Eh? Know what I mean—*photographs?* He asked him knowingly . . . nudge nudge, snap snap, grin grin, wink wink, say no more.
Monty Python's Flying Circus (1969)

9 It's *not* pining—it's passed on! This parrot is no more! It has ceased to be! It's expired and gone to meet its maker! This is a late parrot! It's a stiff! Bereft of life it rests in peace—if you hadn't nailed it to the perch it would be pushing up the daisies! It's rung down the curtain and joined the choir invisible! THIS IS AN EX-PARROT!
Monty Python's Flying Circus (1969)

10 Nobody expects the Spanish Inquisition!
Monty Python's Flying Circus (1970)

Henry Moore 1898–1986
English sculptor and draughtsman

11 The first hole made through a piece of stone is a revelation.
in *Listener* 18 August 1937

Jo Moore
British government adviser

12 It is now a very good day to get out anything we want to bury.
email sent in the aftermath of the terrorist action in America, 11 September 2001
in *Daily Telegraph* 10 October 2001; see **Misquotations 224:7**

Marianne Moore 1887–1972
American poet

13   O to be a dragon,
a symbol of the power of Heaven—of silkworm
size or immense; at times invisible.

Felicitous phenomenon!
'O To Be a Dragon' (1959)

1 I, too, dislike it: there are things that are
important beyond all this fiddle.
Reading it, however, with a perfect
contempt for it, one discovers in it, after
all, a place for the genuine.
'Poetry' (1935)

2 Nor till the poets among us can be
'literalists of
the imagination'—above
insolence and triviality and can present
for inspection, imaginary gardens with real
toads in them, shall we have
it.
'Poetry' (1935)

3 My father used to say,
'Superior people never make long visits,
have to be shown Longfellow's grave
or the glass flowers at Harvard.'
'Silence' (1935)

Eric Morecambe
see **Catchphrases 61:12, Dee 86:13**

Larry Morey 1905–71

4 Heigh-ho, heigh-ho,
It's off to work we go.
'Heigh-Ho' (1937 song), from the film *Snow
White and the Seven Dwarfs*

5 Whistle while you work.
title of song (1937), from the film *Snow White
and the Seven Dwarfs*

Robin Morgan 1941–
American feminist

6 Sisterhood is powerful.
title of book (1970)

Christopher Morley 1890–1957
American writer

7 Life is a foreign language: all men
mispronounce it.
Thunder on the Left (1925)

Desmond Morris 1928–
English anthropologist

8 The city is not a concrete jungle, it is a
human zoo.
The Human Zoo (1969) introduction

9 There are one hundred and ninety-three
living species of monkeys and apes. One
hundred and ninety-two of them are
covered with hair. The exception is a naked
ape self-named *Homo sapiens*.
The Naked Ape (1967) introduction

Herbert Morrison 1888–1965
British Labour politician, grandfather of Peter
Mandelson

10 Work is the call. Work at war speed. Goodnight—and go to it.
broadcast as Minister of Supply, 22 May 1940

11 Socialism is what the Labour Government
does.
attributed

Herbert 'Herb' Morrison d. 1989
American radio announcer

12 It's bursting into flames . . . Oh, the
humanity, and all the passengers!
*eyewitness account of the Hindenburg airship
bursting into flames*
recorded broadcast, 6 May 1937

13 Listen folks, I'm going to have to stop for a
minute, because I've lost my voice—This is
the worst thing I've ever witnessed.
eyewitness account of the Hindenburg disaster
recorded broadcast, 6 May 1937

Jim Morrison 1943–71
American rock singer and songwriter, lead singer of
The Doors

14 C'mon, baby, light my fire.
'Light My Fire' (1967 song, with Robby Krieger)

15 We want the world and we want it now!
'When the Music's Over' (1967 song)

16 I'm interested in anything about revolt,
disorder, chaos, especially activity that
appears to have no meaning. It seems to
me to be the road toward freedom.
in *Time* 24 January 1968

17 When you make your peace with
authority, you become an authority.
Andrew Doe and John Tobler *In Their Own
Words: The Doors* (1988)

Toni Morrison 1931–
American novelist

1 At some point in life the world's beauty becomes enough. You don't need to photograph, paint or even remember it. It is enough.
Tar Baby (1981)

Van Morrison 1945–
Irish singer, songwriter, and musician

2 Music is spiritual. The music business is not.
in *Times* 6 July 1990

Morrissey 1959–
English singer and songwriter

3 I was looking for a job, and then I found a job
And heaven knows I'm miserable now.
'Heaven Knows I'm Miserable Now' (1984 song)

Wayne Lyman Morse 1900–74
American Democratic politician

4 I believe that history will record that we have made a great mistake.
in the Senate debate on the Tonkin Gulf Resolution, which committed the United States to intervention in Vietnam; Morse was the only Senator to vote against the resolution
in *Congressional Record* 6–7 August 1964; see also **Johnson 169:12**

Owen Morshead 1893–1977
English librarian, in charge of the Royal Library at Windsor Castle, 1926–58

5 The House of Hanover, like ducks, produce bad parents—they trample on their young.
as Royal Librarian, in conversation with Harold Nicolson, biographer of George V
Harold Nicolson, letter to Vita Sackville-West, 7 January 1949

John Mortimer 1923–
English novelist, barrister, and dramatist

6 The worst fault of the working classes is telling their children they're not going to succeed, saying: 'There is life, but it's not for you.'
in *Daily Mail* 31 May 1988

J. B. Morton ('Beachcomber')
1893–1975
British journalist

7 Hush, hush,
Nobody cares!
Christopher Robin
Has
Fallen
Down-
Stairs.
By the Way (1931); see **Milne 223:10**

8 Dr Strabismus (Whom God Preserve) of Utrecht has patented a new invention. It is an illuminated trouser-clip for bicyclists who are using main roads at night.
Morton's Folly (1933)

Jelly Roll Morton 1885–1941
American jazz pianist, composer, and bandleader

9 Jazz music is to be played sweet, soft, plenty rhythm.
Mister Jelly Roll (1950)

Rogers Morton 1914–79
American public relations officer

10 I'm not going to rearrange the furniture on the deck of the Titanic.
having lost five of the previous six primaries as President Ford's campaign manager
in *Washington Post* 16 May 1976

Edwin Moses 1955–
American athlete and Olympic gold medallist

11 I don't really see the hurdles. I sense them like a memory.
attributed

Oswald Mosley 1896–1980
British politician and Fascist leader

12 I am not, and never have been, a man of the right. My position was on the left and is now in the centre of politics.
letter to *Times* 26 April 1968

Andrew Motion 1952–
English poet

13 Beside the river, swerving under ground.
your future tracked you, snapping at your heels:

Diana, breathless, hunted by your own
    quick hounds.
    'Mythology' (1997)

Earl Mountbatten of Burma 1900–79
British sailor, soldier, and statesman

1 Right, now I understand people think
  you're the Forgotten Army on the
  Forgotten Front. I've come here to tell you
  you're quite wrong. You're not the
  Forgotten Army on the Forgotten Front.
  No, make no mistake about it. Nobody's
  ever *heard* of you.
    encouragement to troops when taking over as
    Supreme Allied Commander South-East Asia in
    late 1943
      R. Hough *Mountbatten* (1980)

Marjorie ('Mo') Mowlam 1949–2005
British Labour politician

2 It takes courage to push things forward.
    on her decision to visit Loyalist prisoners in The
    Maze while Secretary of State for Northern
    Ireland
      in *Guardian* 8 January 1998

Daniel P. Moynihan 1927–
American Democratic politician

3 Welfare became a term of opprobrium—a
  contentious, often vindictive area of
  political conflict in which liberals and
  conservatives clashed and children were
  lost sight of.
    in *Washington Post* 25 November 1994

Lord Moynihan 1865–1936
British surgeon

4 Lord Dawson of Penn
  Has killed lots of men.
  So that's why we sing
  God save the King.
    *on Lord **Dawson** as royal physician*
      Kenneth Rose *King George V* (1983)

Robert Mugabe 1924–
African statesman, Prime Minister of Zimbabwe
1980–7, President 1987–

5 Cricket civilizes people and creates good
  gentlemen. I want everyone to play cricket
  in Zimbabwe; I want ours to be a nation of
  gentlemen.
    in *Sunday Times* 26 February 1984

6 Our present state of mind is that you are
  now our enemies.
    to white farmers in Zimbabwe, against the
    background of Mugabe's land reforms
      television broadcast, 18 April 2000

7 Blair, keep your England and let me keep
  my Zimbabwe.
    at the Earth Summit in Johannesburg,
    2 September 2002

Kitty Muggeridge
British wife of Malcolm **Muggeridge**

8 David Frost has risen without trace.
    said *c.*1965 to Malcolm Muggeridge

Malcolm Muggeridge 1903–90
British journalist

9 Something beautiful for God.
    title of book (1971); see **Teresa 311:15**

10 The orgasm has replaced the Cross as the
  focus of longing and the image of
  fulfilment.
    Tread Softly (1966)

11 He was not only a bore; he bored for
  England.
    *of Anthony **Eden***
      Tread Softly (1966)

Edwin Muir 1887–1959
Scottish poet

12 And without fear the lawless roads
  Ran wrong through all the land.
    'Hölderlin's Journey' (1937)

13 Barely a twelvemonth after
  The seven days war that put the world to
    sleep,
  Late in the evening the strange horses
    came.
    'The Horses' (1956)

Frank Muir 1920–98
English writer and broadcaster

14 The thinking man's crumpet.
    of Joan Bakewell
      attributed

Jean Muir 1928–95
English fashion designer

1 Engineering with fabric.
her definition of dressmaking
in *Times* 30 May 1995, obituary

2 The clothes in themselves do not make a
statement. The woman makes the
statement and the dress helps.
in *Vogue* August 1995

Paul Muldoon 1951–
Northern Irish poet

3 The Volkswagen parked in the gap,
But gently ticking over.
You wonder if it's lovers
And not men hurrying back
Across two fields and a river.
'Ireland' (1980)

Herbert J. Muller 1905–80
American historian

4 Few have heard of Fra Luca Pacioli, the
inventor of double-entry book-keeping; but
he has probably had much more influence
on human life than has Dante or
Michelangelo.
Uses of the Past (1957)

H. J. Muller 1890–1967
American geneticist

5 To say, for example, that a man is made
up of certain chemical elements is a
satisfactory description only for those
who intend to use him as a fertilizer.
Science and Criticism (1943)

Lewis Mumford 1895–1990
American sociologist

6 Every generation revolts against its fathers
and makes friends with its grandfathers.
The Brown Decades (1931)

7 Our national flower is the concrete
cloverleaf.
in *Quote Magazine* 8 October 1961

Alice Munro 1931–
Canadian writer

8 Any woman who tells the truth about
herself is a feminist.
in *Toronto Star* 6 May 1979; attributed

Iris Murdoch 1919–99
English novelist and philosopher. She is primarily
known for her novels, many of which explore
complex sexual relationships and spiritual life

9 Dora Greenfield left her husband because
she was afraid of him. She decided six
months later to return to him for the same
reason.
The Bell (1958)

10 All our failures are ultimately failures in
love.
The Bell (1958)

11 The chief requirement of the good life, is to
live without any image of oneself.
The Bell (1958)

12 Only in our virtues are we original,
because virtue is difficult . . . Vices are
general, virtues are particular.
Nuns and Soldiers (1980)

13 One doesn't have to get anywhere in a
marriage. It's not a public conveyance.
A Severed Head (1961)

Rupert Murdoch 1931–
Australian-born American publisher and media
entrepreneur

asked why he had allowed Page 3 to develop:
14 I don't know. The editor did it when I was
away.
in *Guardian* 25 February 1994

Les Murray 1938–
Australian poet

15 In a place where 'please' is pronounced 'I
s'pose you couldn't'
it is rare to meet with any belief in help.
The Boys Who Stole the Funeral (1989)

16 Nothing's said till it's dreamed out in
words
And nothing's true that figures in words
only.
The Daylight Moon (1987) 'Poetry and
Religion'

17 Men must have legends, else they will die
of strangeness.
The Ilex Tree (1965) 'The Noonday Axeman'

1 Waiting for the Australian republic is like waiting for the other shoe to drop. We all know it is coming; according to one's convictions, the waiting is therefore either a sour and uncreative delaying operation or a sort of null interregnum in which all energies are frustrated.
> 'The Coming Republic' in *Quadrant* April 1976

Edward R. Murrow 1908–65
American broadcaster and journalist, who came to prominence through his radio broadcasts from London during the Second World War; as a television presenter and interviewer, his noted series included *See It Now* (1951–8)
See also: **Borrowed titles 40:12, Catchphrases 59:6**

2 When you report the invasion of Holland . . . understate the situation. Don't say the streets are rivers of blood. Say that the little policeman I usually say hello to every morning is not there today.
> *to the reporter Mary Marvin Breckinridge*
> quoted in *American National Biography* (online edition) 'Edward R. Murrow'

3 No one can terrorize a whole nation, unless we are all his accomplices.
> *of Joseph McCarthy*
> 'See It Now', broadcast, 9 March 1954

4 The timing was right and the instrument powerful.
> *of the 'See It Now' programme which attacked Joseph McCarthy*
> quoted in *American National Biography* (online edition) 'Edward R. Murrow'

5 He mobilized the English language and sent it into battle to steady his fellow countrymen and hearten those Europeans upon whom the long dark night of tyranny had descended.
> *of Winston Churchill*
> broadcast, 30 November 1954; *In Search of Light* (1967)

6 Anyone who isn't confused doesn't really understand the situation.
> *on the Vietnam War*
> Walter Bryan *The Improbable Irish* (1969)

Benito Mussolini 1883–1945
Italian Fascist statesman, Prime Minister 1922–43, known as '*Il Duce*'. Forced to resign after the Allied invasion of Sicily, he was rescued from imprisonment by German paratroopers, but was captured and executed by Italian communist partisans
on Mussolini: see **Taylor 310:10**

7 We must leave exactly on time . . . From now on everything must function to perfection.
> *to a station-master*
> Giorgio Pini *Mussolini* (1939); see Infanta Eulalia of Spain *Courts and Countries after the War* (1925): 'The first benefit of Benito Mussolini's direction in Italy begins to be felt when one crosses the Italian Frontier and hears "*Il treno arriva all'orario* [the train is arriving on time]" '

A. J. Muste 1885–1967
American pacifist and labour organizer

8 If I can't love Hitler, I can't love at all.
> at a Quaker meeting 1940; in *New York Times* 12 February 1967

9 There is no way to peace. Peace is the way.
> in *New York Times* 16 November 1967

Vladimir Nabokov 1899–1977
Russian-born American novelist and poet

1 Lolita, light of my life, fire of my loins. My sin, my soul. Lo-lee-ta: the tip of the tongue taking a trip of three steps down the palate to tap, at three, on the teeth. Lo. Lee. Ta.
Lolita (1955), opening line

2 You can always count on a murderer for a fancy prose style.
Lolita (1955)

3 Life is a great surprise. I do not see why death should not be an even greater one.
Pale Fire (1962)

4 The cradle rocks above an abyss, and common sense tells us that our existence is but a brief crack of light between two eternities of darkness.
Speak, Memory (1951)

5 I never imagined that I should be able to live by my writing, but now I am kept by a little girl named Lolita.
quoted in *American National Biography* (online edition)

Ralph Nader 1934–
American lawyer and reformer, noted for campaigns on behalf of public safety which prompted legislation concerning car design, radiation hazards, food packaging, and insecticides

6 Unsafe at any speed.
title of book (1965); the phrase was used earlier by John **Keats** in *The Insolent Chariots* (1958)

Sarojini Naidu 1879–1949
Indian politician and poet

7 If only Bapu knew the cost of setting him up in poverty!
of ***Gandhi***
A. Campbell-Johnson *Mission with Mountbatten* (1951)

Shiva Naipaul 1945–85
Trinidadian writer

8 The Third World is an artificial construction of the West—an ideological empire on which the sun is always setting.
An Unfinished Journey (1986)

V. S. Naipaul 1932–
Trinidadian writer of Indian descent, resident in Britain since 1950, noted especially for his satirical novels
see also **Walcott 326:4**

9 The world is what it is; men who are nothing, who allow themselves to become nothing, have no place in it.
A Bend in the River (1979 novel), opening sentence

10 How terrible it would have been . . . to have lived without even attempting to lay claim to one's portion of the earth; to have lived as one had been born, unnecessary and unaccommodated.
A House for Mr Biswas (1961 novel)

11 History is built around creation and achievement, and nothing was created in the West Indies.
The Middle Passage (1962); see **Walcott 326:4**

12 We pretended to be real, to be learning, to be preparing ourselves for life, we mimic

men of the New World.
'Ralph Singh''s words
 The Mimic Men (1967 novel)

Fridtjof Nansen 1861–1930
Norwegian Arctic explorer. In 1888 he led the first
expedition to cross the Greenland ice fields, and five
years later he sailed from Siberia for the North Pole,
which he failed to reach, on board the *Fram*

1 Never stop because you are afraid—you
are never so likely to be wrong. Never keep
a line of retreat: it is a wretched invention.
The difficult is what takes a little time; the
impossible is what takes a little longer.
in *Listener* 14 December 1939; see **Military
sayings 221:4**

Ogden Nash 1902–71
American humorist

2 The turtle lives 'twixt plated decks
Which practically conceal its sex.
I think it clever of the turtle
In such a fix to be so fertile.
'Autres Bêtes, Autres Moeurs' (1931)

3 A bit of talcum
Is always walcum.
'The Baby' (1931)

4 The cow is of the bovine ilk;
One end is moo, the other, milk.
'The Cow' (1931)

5 A door is what a dog is perpetually on the
wrong side of.
'A Dog's Best Friend is his Illiteracy' (1953)

6 Let us pause to consider the English,
Who when they pause to consider
themselves they get all reticently thrilled
and tinglish,
Because every Englishman is convinced of
one thing, viz.:
That to be an Englishman is to belong to
the most exclusive club there is.
'England Expects' (1938)

7 One would be in less danger
From the wiles of the stranger
If one's own kin and kith
Were more fun to be with.
'Family Court' (1931)

8 Parsley

Is gharsley.
'Further Reflections on Parsley' (1942)

9 I believe a little incompatibility is the spice
of life, particularly if he has income and she
is pattable.
'I Do, I Will, I Have' (1949)

10 The trouble with a kitten is
THAT
Eventually it becomes a
CAT.
'The Kitten' (1940)

11 Beneath this slab
John Brown is stowed.
He watched the ads,
And not the road.
'Lather as You Go' (1942)

12 Do you think my mind is maturing late,
Or simply rotted early?
'Lines on Facing Forty' (1942)

13 Good wine needs no bush,
And perhaps products that people really
want need no hard-sell or soft-sell TV
push.
Why not?
Look at pot.
'Most Doctors Recommend or Yours For Fast,
Fast, Fast Relief' (1972)

14 Children aren't happy with nothing to
ignore,
And that's what parents were created for.
'The Parent' (1933)

15 He tells you when you've got on too much
lipstick,
And helps you with your girdle when your
hips stick.
'The Perfect Husband' (1949)

16 Any kiddie in school can love like a fool,
But hating, my boy, is an art.
'Plea for Less Malice Toward None' (1933)

17 Candy
Is dandy
But liquor
Is quicker.
'Reflections on Ice-breaking' (1931)

18 I test my bath before I sit,
And I'm always moved to wonderment

That what chills the finger not a bit
Is so frigid upon the fundament.
'Samson Agonistes' (1942)

1 I think that I shall never see
A billboard lovely as a tree.
Perhaps, unless the billboards fall,
I'll never see a tree at all.
'Song of the Open Road' (1933); see **Kilmer 180:4**

2 Sure, deck your lower limbs in pants;
Yours are the limbs, my sweeting.
You look divine as you advance—
Have you seen yourself retreating?
'What's the Use?' (1940)

3 Life is not having been told that the man
has just waxed the floor.
'You and Me and P. B. Shelley' (1942)

Terry Nation
see **Catchphrases 59:1**

James Ball Naylor 1860–1945
American writer and physician

4 King David and King Solomon
Led merry, merry lives,
With many, many lady friends,
And many, many wives;
But when old age crept over them—
With many, many qualms!—
King Solomon wrote the Proverbs
And King David wrote the Psalms.
'King David and King Solomon' (1935)

Jawaharlal Nehru 1889–1964
Indian statesman, Prime Minister 1947–64; father of
Indira **Gandhi**

5 There is no easy walk-over to freedom
anywhere, and many of us will have to
pass through the valley of the shadow
again and again before we reach the
mountain-tops of our desire.
'From Lucknow to Tripuri' (1939)

6 At the stroke of the midnight hour, while
the world sleeps, India will awake to life
and freedom.
immediately prior to Independence
speech to the Indian Constituent Assembly, 14
August 1947

7 The light has gone out of our lives and
there is darkness everywhere.
following **Gandhi**'s *assassination*
broadcast, 30 January 1948

A. S. Neill 1883–1973
Scottish teacher and educationist, founder of the
progressive Summerhill School

8 Let us think of a bad school. I mean a
school where children sit at desks and
speak when they are spoken to.
attributed; in *Oxford Dictionary of National
Biography* (2004)

Howard Nemerov 1920–91
American poet and novelist, poet laureate 1988–91

9 praise without end the go-ahead zeal
of whoever it was invented the wheel;
but never a word for the poor soul's sake
that thought ahead, and invented the
brake.
'To the Congress of the United States,
Entering Its Third Century' 26 February 1989

Pablo Neruda 1904–73
Chilean poet and diplomat, born Ricardo Eliezer
Neftalí Reyes, who took his pseudonym from the
Czech poet Jan Neruda

10 Forgive me.
If you are not living,
If you, beloved, my love,
If you have died
All the leaves will fall on my breast
It will rain on my soul, all night, all day
My feet will want to march to where you
are sleeping
But I shall go on living.
'The Dead Woman'

11 Night, snow, and sand make up the form
of my thin country,
all silence lies in its long line,
all foam flows from its marine beard,
all coal covers it with mysterious kisses.
'Discoverers of Chile' (1950)

12 I have gone marking the blank atlas of
your body
with crosses of fire.
My mouth went across: a spider, trying to
hide.
In you, behind you, timid, driven by thirst.
'I Have Gone Marking' (1924), translated 1969
by W. S. Merwin

1 Look around—there's only one thing of
danger to you here—poetry.
*watching from his deathbed as a military raid
searched his garden, September 1973*
   Adam Feinstein *Pablo Neruda: A Passion for
   Life* (2004)

Edith Nesbit 1858–1924
English novelist. She is best known for her children's
books, including *Five Children and It* (1902) and *The
Railway Children* (1906)

2 The affection you get back from children is
sixpence given as change for a sovereign.
   Julia Briggs *A Woman of Passion* (1987)

John von Neumann 1903–57
Hungarian-born American mathematician and
computer pioneer

3 In mathematics you don't understand
things. You just get used to them.
   Gary Zukav *The Dancing Wu Li Masters* (1979)

Anthony Newley 1931–99
English singer, songwriter, and actor
and **Leslie Bricusse** 1931–
English songwriter and composer

4 Stop the world, I want to get off.
   title of musical (1961)

Newspaper headlines and leaders
see box opposite
see also **Cockburn 72:12**

Huey Newton 1942–89
American political activist, leader of the Black
Panther Party

5 I suggested [in 1966] that we use the
panther as our symbol and call our
political vehicle the Black Panther Party.
The panther is a fierce animal, but he will
not attack until he is backed into a corner;
then he will strike out.
   Revolutionary Suicide (1973)

Chester Nez *c.*1924–
American Navajo Indian

6 Back in the '20s and '30s, we were told
'Don't speak Navajo.' . . . Then Uncle Sam
came along and told us to use our

language in World War II.
*one of the 29 'Navajo Code Talkers', who
constructed an unbreakable code from the
Navajo language to use against the Japanese in
the Pacific*
   in *Los Angeles Times* 26 July 2001

Nancy Nicholson *d.* 77
English daughter of artist William Nicholson

7 God is a man, so it must be all rot.
*reading the marriage service for the first time,
on the morning of her wedding to Robert **Graves***
   R. Graves *Goodbye to All That* (1929)

Vivian Nicholson 1936–
British pools winner

8 I want to spend, and spend, and spend.
*said to reporters on arriving to collect her
husband's football pools winnings of £152,000*
   in *Daily Herald* 28 September 1961

Harold Nicolson 1886–1968
English diplomat, politician, and writer; husband of
Vita **Sackville-West**

9 To be a good diarist one must have a little
snouty, sneaky mind.
   diary, 9 November 1947

10 For seventeen years he did nothing at all
but kill animals and stick in stamps.
*of King **George V***
   diary, 17 August 1949

Reinhold Niebuhr 1892–1971
American theologian and political journalist

11 Man's capacity for justice makes
democracy possible, but man's inclination
to injustice makes democracy necessary.
   Children of Light and Children of Darkness
   (1944)

12 Our gadget-filled paradise suspended in a
hell of international insecurity.
   Pious and Secular America (1957)

Newspaper headlines and leaders

1 Believe it or not.
   title of syndicated newspaper feature (from 1918), written by Robert L. Ripley (1893–1949)

2 British Rail, which last week predicted that it was ready for the worst the weather could do, now blames the near-total dislocation of its services on 'the wrong sort of snow'.
   leader in *Evening Standard* 12 February 1991; see **Worrall 342:10**

3 Bush wins it.
   original headline in the Miami Herald *for 8 November 2000; changed in final edition to 'It's not over yet'*
   in *Daily Telegraph* 9 November 2000

4 By appointment: teddy bear to the nation.
   heading to profile of John **Betjeman**
   Alan Bell 'Times Profile: Sir John Betjeman' in *Times* 20 September 1982

5 Crisis? What crisis?
   summarizing an interview with James **Callaghan**
   headline in *Sun* 11 January 1979; see **Misquotations 224:3**

6 Dewey defeats Truman.
   anticipating the result of the Presidential election, which **Truman** *won against expectation*
   in *Chicago Tribune* 3 November 1948

7 Downing Street's dodgy dossier of 'intelligence' about Iraq.
   referring to a briefing document on Iraqi weaponry which was later withdrawn
   leading article, *Observer* 9 February 2003

8 Egghead weds hourglass.
   on the marriage of Arthur **Miller** *and Marilyn* **Monroe**
   headline in *Variety* 1956; attributed

9 The filth and the fury.
   following a notorious interview with the Sex Pistols broadcast live on Thames Television
   headline in *Daily Mirror* 2 December 1976

10 Freddie Starr ate my hamster.
   headline in *Sun* 13 March 1986

11 GOTCHA!
   on the sinking of the General Belgrano
   headline in *Sun* 4 May 1982

12 How much longer are valuable lives to be sacrificed in the vain endeavour to impose upon the Arab population an elaborate and expensive administration which they never asked for and do not want?
   of the British mandatory area of Mesopotamia (now Iraq)
   leader in *Times* 7 August 1920; see also **Lawrence 193:4**

13 If Kinnock wins today will the last person to leave Britain please turn out the lights.
   on election day, showing Neil Kinnock's head inside a light bulb
   headline in *Sun* 9 April 1992

14 It *is* a moral issue.
   leader following the resignation of Profumo
   in *Times* 11 June 1963; see also **Hailsham 141:6, Macmillan 209:6**

15 It's that man again ... ! At the head of a cavalcade of seven black motor cars Hitler swept out of his Berlin Chancellery last night on a mystery journey.
   the acronym ITMA became the title of a BBC radio show, from September 1939 (see individual entries at **Catchphrases**)
   headline in *Daily Express* 2 May 1939

16 It's The Sun Wot Won It.
   following the 1992 general election
   headline in *Sun* 11 April 1992

17 King's Moll Reno'd in Wolsey's Home Town.
   on Wallis Simpson's divorce proceedings in Ipswich
   US newspaper headline; F. Donaldson *Edward VIII* (1974)

18 Named Shamed.
   headline announcing a campaign to publish names and addresses said to identify convicted paedophiles
   in *News of the World* 23 July 2000

▶

▶ Newspaper headlines and leaders continued

1 Outside the G.O.P.'s big tent, hoping he's let back in.
of the former Republican Robert C. Smith, whose independent campaign for the presidential nomination had failed; G.O.P. = 'Grand Old Party'
   headline in *New York Times* 1 November 1999; see **Political sayings and slogans 257:7**

2 Sawdust Caesars: Mods v. Rockers battles flare again.
   Daily Express 19 May 1964

3 Sticks nix hick pix.
on the lack of enthusiasm for farm dramas among rural populations
   headline in *Variety* 17 July 1935

4 The Sun backs Blair.
the day after the announcement of the general election
   headline in *Sun* 18 March 1997

5 Tomorrow a time of hardship starts for everyone. For everyone? Include the politicians out of that . . . the tanks of the politicians will be brimming over.
under the government's petrol rationing

scheme, constituency parties were to receive a generous allocation
   leader in *Sunday Express* 16 December 1956, written by John **Junor**

6 Wall St. lays an egg.
on the Wall St. crash
   headline in *Variety* 30 October 1929

7 Who breaks a butterfly on a wheel?
*defending Mick **Jagger** after his arrest for cannabis possession*
   leader in *Times* 1 June 1967, written by William Rees-Mogg, referring to Alexander Pope (1688–1744) 'An Epistle to Dr Arbuthnot' (1735): 'Who breaks a butterfly upon a wheel?'

8 Whose finger do you want on the trigger?
referring to the atom bomb
   in *Daily Mirror* 21 September 1951

9 Winter of discontent.
   headline in *Sun* 30 April 1979, referring to William Shakespeare (1564–1616) *Richard III* (1591): 'Now is the winter of our discontent / Made glorious summer by this sun of York'; see **Callaghan 51:2**

Reinhold Niebuhr continued

10 God, give us the serenity to accept what cannot be changed;
Give us the courage to change what should be changed;
Give us the wisdom to distinguish one from the other.
in circulation since the 1940s; the 'Serenity Prayer' is known in varying versions, and has been used by Alcoholics Anonymous
   Richard Wightman Fox *Reinhold Niebuhr* (1985)

for the trade unionists, and I didn't speak up because I wasn't a trade unionist; and then they came for the Jews, and I didn't speak up because I wasn't a Jew; and then . . . they came for me . . . and by that time there was no-one left to speak up.
   quoted in many versions since the Second World War; this version was approved by Niemöller as the original (in *'Quote Unquote' Newsletter* April 2001)

Martin Niemöller 1892–1984
German Lutheran pastor. An outspoken opponent of Nazism, he was imprisoned in Sachsenhausen and Dachau concentration camps (1937–45)

11 In Germany they came first for the Communists, and I didn't speak up because I wasn't a Communist; and then they came

Richard Nixon 1913–94

American Republican statesman, 37th President of the US, 1969–74. His period of office was overshadowed by the Vietnam War. Re-elected in 1972, he became the first President to resign from office, owing to his involvement in the Watergate scandal.

on Nixon: see **Abzug 1:3, Political sayings and slogans 258:12, Stevenson 304:11, Stevenson 304:14, Ziegler 348:10**

1 She's pink right down to her underwear.
in 1950, accusing Helen Gahagan Douglas, his opponent for a Senate seat, of Communist sympathies
   Stephen E. Ambrose *Nixon: The Education of a Politician* (1987); see **Roosevelt 273:8**

2 You won't have Nixon to kick around any more because, gentlemen, this is my last press conference.
after losing the election for Governor of California
   to the press, 5 November 1962

3 This is the greatest week in the history of the world since the Creation.
welcoming the return of the first men to land on the moon
   speech 24 July 1969

4 The great silent majority.
   broadcast, 3 November 1969

5 There can be no whitewash at the White House.
on Watergate
   television speech 30 April 1973

6 People have got to know whether or not their President is a crook. Well, I'm not a crook.
   speech, 17 November 1973

7 I brought myself down. I gave them a sword. And they stuck it in.
   television interview, 19 May 1977; David Frost *I Gave Them a Sword* (1978)

8 When the President does it, that means that it is not illegal.
   David Frost *I Gave Them a Sword* (1978)

Louis Nizer 1902–94

British-born American lawyer

9 When a man points a finger at someone else, he should remember that four of his fingers are pointing to himself.
   My Life in Court (1963)

Kwame Nkrumah 1900–72

Ghanaian statesman, Prime Minister 1957–60, President 1960–6

10 Freedom is not something that one people can bestow on another as a gift. They claim it as their own and none can keep it from them.
   speech in Accra, 10 July 1953

11 We face neither East nor West: we face forward.
   conference speech, Accra, 7 April 1960; *Axioms of Kwame Nkrumah* (1967)

Christopher Nolan 1965–

Irish writer

12 My real motive is to describe how my brain-damaged life is as normal for me as my friends' able-bodied life is to them. My mind is just like a spin-dryer at full speed; my thoughts fly around my skull while millions of beautiful words cascade down into my lap. Images gunfire across my consciousness and while trying to discipline them I jump in awe at the soulfilled bounty of my mind's expanse. Try then to imagine how frustrating it is to give expression to that avalanche in efforts of one great nod after the other.
   of his reasons for writing The Eye of the Clock
   in *Observer* 8 November 1987

Peggy Noonan 1950–

American writer, speechwriter for Ronald **Reagan**

13 If you woke most Americans up at 3:00 in the morning and said, 'Tell me, looking back, what would you have liked in an American president after 9/11?' most of them would answer, 'I was just hoping for a good man who did moderately good things.' . . . Not this historical drama queen, this good witch or bad.
   of George W. Bush
   in *Wall Street Journal* (online edition) 15 September 2006

Oodgeroo Noonuccal (Kath Walker)
1920–93
Australian poet

1 But I'll tell instead of brave and fine
   When lives of black and white entwine.
   And men in brotherhood combine,
   This would I tell you, son of mine.
   'Son of Mine (To Denis)' (1964)

2 The scrubs are gone, the hunting and the
   laughter.
   The eagle is gone, the emu and the
   kangaroo are gone from this place.
   The bora ring is gone.
   The corroboree is gone.
   And we are going.
   'We are Going' (1964)

Grover Norquist 1956–
American lobbyist, founder of Americans for Tax Reform

3 I don't want to abolish government. I
   simply want to reduce it to the size where I
   can drag it into the bathroom and drown it
   in the bathtub.
   interview on National Public Radio, Morning
   Edition, 25 May 2001

Lord Northcliffe 1865–1922
British newspaper proprietor

4 The power of the press is very great, but
   not so great as the power of suppress.
   office message, *Daily Mail* 1918; R. Rose and
   G. Harmsworth *Northcliffe* (1959)

5 When I want a peerage, I shall buy it like
   an honest man.
   Tom Driberg *Swaff* (1974)

Lord Nuffield 1877–1963
British motor manufacturer and philanthropist

on seeing the Morris Minor prototype in 1945:
6 It looks like a poached egg—we can't make
   that.
   attributed (the Morris Minor, designed by Alec
   Issigonis, went into production in October
   1948)

Sam Nunn 1938–
American Democratic politician

7 Don't ask, don't tell.
   *summary of the **Clinton** administration's
   compromise policy on homosexuals serving in
   the armed forces*
   in *New York Times* 12 May 1993

Simon Nye 1958–
British writer

8 Twenty years ago when we had no respect
   for women they just used to say, 'You're
   chucked.' And now we do respect them we
   have to lie to them sensitively.
   Men Behaving Badly (ITV, series 1, 1992)
   'Intruders'

9 GARY: She put me right on a few technical
   details, yes.
   DERMOT: She said it was like sleeping with a
   badly-informed labrador.
   Men Behaving Badly (ITV, series 1, 1992)
   'Intruders'

Julius Nyerere 1922–99
Tanzanian statesman, President of Tanganyika
1962–4 and of Tanzania 1964–85

10 Should we really let our people starve so
   we can pay our debts?
   in *Guardian* 21 March 1985

O

Lawrence Oates
see **Last words 190:6**

Conor Cruise O'Brien 1917–
Irish politician, writer, and journalist

1 If I saw Mr Haughey buried at midnight at
a crossroads, with a stake driven through
his heart—politically speaking—I should
continue to wear a clove of garlic round
my neck, just in case.
in *Observer* 10 October 1982

Edna O'Brien 1932–
Irish novelist and short-story writer

2 August is a wicked month.
title of novel (1965)

Flann O'Brien 1911–66
Irish novelist and journalist

3 A pint of plain is your only man.
At Swim-Two-Birds (1939)

4 Waiting for the German verb is surely the
ultimate thrill.
The Hair of the Dogma (1977)

Sean O'Casey 1880–1964
Irish dramatist

5 I killin' meself workin', an' he sthruttin'
about from mornin' till night like a
paycock!
Juno and the Paycock (1925)

6 He's an oul' butty o' mine—oh, he's a
darlin' man, a daarlin' man.
Juno and the Paycock (1925)

7 The whole worl's in a state o' chassis!
Juno and the Paycock (1925)

8 It's my rule never to lose me temper till it
would be dethrimental to keep it.
The Plough and the Stars (1926)

9 English literature's performing flea.
of P. G. **Wodehouse**
P. G. Wodehouse *Performing Flea* (1953)

Bernard O'Donoghue 1945–
Irish poet and academic

10 We were terribly lucky to catch
The Ceauşescus' execution, being
By sheer chance that Christmas Day
In the only house for twenty miles
With satellite TV. We sat,
Cradling brandies, by the fire
Watching those two small, cranky
autocrats
Lying in snow against a blood-spattered
wall,
Hardly able to believe our good fortune.
'Carolling' (1995)

11 The reporter told us how
The cross woman's peasant origins
Came out at the last, shouting
At her executioners 'I have been
A mother to you and this is how
You thank me for it.'
'Carolling' (1995)

Official advice
see box overleaf

David Ogilvy 1911–99
British-born advertising executive

12 The consumer isn't a moron; she is your
wife.
Confessions of an Advertising Man (1963)

Official advice

1 Careless talk costs lives.
   wartime security slogan, 1940s

2 Charley says . . .
   a series of films for children including 'Don't
   Play with Matches' and 'Don't Go with
   Strangers', featuring the voice of Kenny
   Everett (1944–95) as the cat Charley, first
   screened in 1973

3 Clunk, click, every trip.
   road safety campaign promoting the use of
   seat-belts, 1971

4 Coughs and sneezes spread diseases. Trap
   the germs in your handkerchief.
   Second World War health slogan, 1942

5 Dig for victory.
   radio broadcast by Reginald Dorman-Smith
   (1899–1977), Minister for Agriculture,
   3 October 1939

6 Don't ask a man to drink and drive.
   UK road safety slogan, from 1964

7 Don't die of ignorance.
   Aids publicity campaign, 1987

8 Duck and cover.
   US advice in the event of a missile attack,
   *c.*1950; associated particularly with
   children's cartoon character 'Bert the Turtle'

9 Is your journey *really* necessary?
   slogan coined to discourage Civil Servants
   from going home for Christmas, 1939

10 Just say no.
   motto of the Nancy Reagan Drug Abuse
   Fund, founded 1985

11 Keep Britain tidy.
   issued by the Central Office of Information,
   1950s

12 Kids and water. They love it!
   'Youngsters Learn To Swim' campaign
   featuring Rolf Harris, from 1973

13 Make do and mend.
   wartime slogan, 1940s

14 Slip, slop, slap.
   sun protection slogan, meaning slip *on a
   T-shirt,* slop *on some suncream,* slap *on a hat*
   Australian health education programme,
   1980s

15 Smoking can seriously damage your
   health.
   *government health warning now required by
   British law to be printed on cigarette packets*
   from early 1970s, in form 'Smoking can
   damage your health'

16 Stop-look-and-listen.
   road safety slogan, current in the US from
   1912

17 *Taisez-vous! Méfiez-vous! Les oreilles
   ennemies vous écoutent.*
   Keep your mouth shut! Be on your
   guard! Enemy ears are listening to you.
   official notice in France, 1915

18 Whenever possible, remember that you
   are still free and that there is still beauty
   in the world. It's OK to smile.
   flier distributed by the American Red Cross
   to survivors in the week following the
   destruction of the World Trade Center,
   11 September 2001

John O'Hara 1905–70
American novelist and short-story writer
see also **Borrowed titles 40:4**

19 George [Gershwin] died on July 11, 1937,
   but I don't have to believe that if I don't
   want to.
   in *Newsweek* 15 July 1940

20 An artist is his own fault.
   The Portable F. Scott Fitzgerald (1945)
   introduction

Georgia O'Keefe 1887–1986
American painter

21 Filling a space in a beautiful way. That's
   what art means to me.
   in *Art News* December 1977

Abraham Okpik d. 1997
Canadian Inuit spokesman

22 There are very few Eskimos, but millions
   of Whites, just like mosquitoes. It is
   something very special and wonderful to

be an Eskimo—they are like the snow geese. If an Eskimo forgets his language and Eskimo ways, he will be nothing but just another mosquito.

attributed, 1966

Bruce Oldfield 1950–
English fashion designer

1 Fashion is more usually a gentle progression of revisited ideas.

in *Independent* 9 September 1989

Laurence Olivier 1907–89
English actor and director. He performed all the major Shakespearean roles; he was also director of the National Theatre (1963–73)

2 The tragedy of a man who could not make up his mind.

introduction to his 1948 screen adaptation of *Hamlet*

3 Shakespeare—the nearest thing in incarnation to the eye of God.

in *Kenneth Harris Talking To* (1971) 'Sir Laurence Olivier'

4 Acting is a masochistic form of exhibitionism. It is not quite the occupation of an adult.

in *Time* 3 July 1978

Aristotle Onassis 1906–75
Greek shipping magnate and international businessman, husband of Jacqueline Kennedy **Onassis**
on Onassis: see **Vidal 325:8**

5 After a certain point money is meaningless. It ceases to be the goal. The game is what counts.

attributed, perhaps apocryphal

Jacqueline Kennedy Onassis 1929–94
American wife of John F. **Kennedy** and Aristotle **Onassis**, First Lady of the US 1961–3

6 There'll be great Presidents again—and the Johnsons are wonderful, they've been wonderful to me—but there'll never be another Camelot again.

in *Life* 6 December 1963; see **Lerner 197:5**

Michael Ondaatje 1943–
Sri Lankan-born Canadian writer

7 The heart is an organ of fire.

The English Patient (1992)

8 We die containing a richness of lovers and tribes, tastes we have swallowed, bodies we have plunged into and swum up as if rivers of wisdom, characters we have climbed into as if trees, fears we have hidden as if in caves.

The English Patient (1992)

Eugene O'Neill 1888–1953
American dramatist

9 For de little stealin' dey gits you in jail soon or late. For de big stealin' dey makes you Emperor and puts you in de Hall o' Fame when you croaks.

The Emperor Jones (1921)

10 The iceman cometh.

title of play (1946)

11 A long day's journey into night.

title of play (written 1940–1)

12 Mourning becomes Electra

title of play (1931)

13 The sea hates a coward!

Mourning becomes Electra (1931)

Yoko Ono 1933–
Japanese poet and songwriter

14 Woman is the nigger of the world.

interview for *Nova* magazine (1968); adopted by her husband John **Lennon** as song title (1972)

Oodgeroo Noonuccal
see **Oodgeroo Noonuccal**

J. Robert Oppenheimer 1904–67
American theoretical physicist; he was director of the laboratory at Los Alamos during the development of the first atom bomb, but opposed the post-war development of the hydrogen bomb. His security clearance was withdrawn following investigation for alleged un-American activities, but with the passing of the McCarthy era his public standing was restored

15 I remembered the line from the Hindu scripture, the *Bhagavad Gita* . . . 'I am

become death, the destroyer of worlds.'
*on the explosion of the first atomic bomb near
Alamogordo, New Mexico, 16 July 1945*
   Len Giovannitti and Fred Freed *The Decision to
   Drop the Bomb* (1965)

1 The physicists have known sin; and this is
a knowledge which they cannot lose.
   lecture at Massachusetts Institute of
   Technology, 25 November 1947

2 When you see something that is
technically sweet, you go ahead and do it
and you argue about what to do about it
only after you have had your technical
success. That is the way it was with the
atomic bomb.
   in *In the Matter of J. Robert Oppenheimer,
   USAEC Transcript of Hearing Before Personnel
   Security Board* (1954)

Susie Orbach 1946–
American psychotherapist

3 Fat is a feminist issue.
   title of book (1978)

Roy Orbison 1936–88
and Joe Melson
American singer and songwriter

4 Only the lonely (know the way I feel).
   title of song (1960)

P. J. O'Rourke 1947–
American humorous writer

5 You can't shame or humiliate modern
celebrities. What used to be called shame
and humiliation is now called publicity.
   Give War a Chance (1992)

6 Every government is a parliament of
whores. The trouble is, in a democracy the
whores are us.
   Parliament of Whores (1991)

7 Whose woods are whose everybody knows
exactly, and everybody knows who got
them rezoned for a shopping mall and
who couldn't get the financing to begin
construction and why it was he couldn't
get it.
   on a traditional New England community
   Parliament of Whores (1991); see **Frost 125:19**

8 Anybody can have one kid. But going from
one kid to two is like going from owning a
dog to running a zoo.
   in *Observer* 9 September 2001

José Ortega y Gasset 1883–1955
Spanish writer and philosopher

9 I am I plus my surroundings, and if I do not
preserve the latter I do not preserve myself.
   Meditaciones del Quijote (1914)

10 Civilization is nothing more than the effort
to reduce the use of force to the last resort.
   La Rebelión de las Masas (1930)

Joe Orton 1933–67
English dramatist, author of a number of
unconventional black comedies, examining
corruption, sexuality, and violence

11 I'd the upbringing a nun would envy and
that's the truth. Until I was fifteen I was
more familiar with Africa than my own
body.
   Entertaining Mr Sloane (1964)

12 KATH: Can he be present at the birth of his
child? . . .
   ED: It's all any reasonable child can expect
if the dad is present at the conception.
   Entertaining Mr Sloane (1964)

13 Reading isn't an occupation we encourage
among police officers. We try to keep the
paper work down to a minimum.
   Loot (1967)

14 You were born with your legs apart.
They'll send you to the grave in a Y-shaped
coffin.
   What the Butler Saw (1969)

George Orwell (Eric Arthur Blair)
1903–50
English novelist, whose work is characterized by his
concern for social injustice; his most famous works
are *Animal Farm* (1945), a satire on Communism as it
developed under Stalin, and *Nineteen Eighty-four*
(1949), a dystopian account of a future state in
which every aspect of life is controlled by 'Big
Brother'

15 Man is the only creature that consumes
without producing.
   Animal Farm (1945)

1 Four legs good, two legs bad.
slogan adopted by the animals
Animal Farm (1945)

2 All animals are equal but some animals are more equal than others.
Animal Farm (1945)

3 The creatures outside looked from pig to man, and from man to pig, and from pig to man again, but already it was impossible to say which was which.
Animal Farm (1945); closing words

4 Good prose is like a window-pane.
Collected Essays (1968) vol. 1 'Why I Write'

5 I'm fat, but I'm thin inside. Has it ever struck you that there's a thin man inside every fat man, just as they say there's a statue inside every block of stone?
Coming up For Air (1939); see **Connolly 75:4**

6 Roast beef and Yorkshire, or roast pork and apple sauce, followed up by suet pudding and driven home, as it were, by a cup of mahogany-brown tea, have put you in just the right mood . . . In these blissful circumstances, what is it that you want to read about?
Naturally, about a murder.
Decline of the English Murder and other essays (1965) title essay, written 1946

7 Down and out in Paris and London
title of book (1933)

8 There was much in it that I did not understand, in some ways I did not even like it, but I recognized it immediately as a state of affairs worth fighting for.
Homage to Catalonia (1938)

9 Down here it was still the England I had known in my childhood: the railway cuttings smothered in wild flowers . . . the red buses, the blue policemen—all sleeping the deep, deep sleep of England, from which I sometimes fear that we shall never wake till we are jerked out of it by the roar of bombs.
Homage to Catalonia (1938)

10 Keep the aspidistra flying.
title of novel (1936)

11 Advertising is the rattling of a stick inside a swill bucket.
Keep the Aspidistra Flying (1936)

12 England is not the jewelled isle of Shakespeare's much-quoted passage, nor is it the inferno depicted by Dr Goebbels. More than either it resembles a family, a rather stuffy Victorian family, with not many black sheep in it but with all its cupboards bursting with skeletons . . . A family with the wrong members in control.
The Lion and the Unicorn (1941) pt. 1 'England Your England'

13 Old maids biking to Holy Communion through the mists of the autumn mornings . . . these are not only fragments, but *characteristic* fragments, of the English scene.
The Lion and the Unicorn (1941) pt. 1 'England Your England'; see **Major 211:15**

14 Probably the battle of Waterloo *was* won on the playing-fields of Eton, but the opening battles of all subsequent wars have been lost there.
The Lion and the Unicorn (1941) pt. 1 'England Your England'; referring to the words traditionally attributed to the Duke of Wellington (1769–1852): 'The battle of Waterloo was won on the playing fields of Eton'

15 It was a bright cold day in April, and the clocks were striking thirteen.
Nineteen Eighty-Four (1949), opening line

16 BIG BROTHER IS WATCHING YOU.
Nineteen Eighty-Four (1949)

17 Who controls the past controls the future: who controls the present controls the past.
Nineteen Eighty-Four (1949)

18 Freedom is the freedom to say that two plus two make four. If that is granted, all else follows.
Nineteen Eighty-Four (1949)

19 The Lottery, with its weekly pay-out of enormous prizes, was the one public event to which the proles paid serious attention . . . It was their delight, their folly, their anodyne, their intellectual stimulant . . . the prizes were largely imaginary. Only small sums were actually paid out, the winners of the big prizes being non-existent persons.
Nineteen Eighty-Four (1949)

20 *Doublethink* means the power of holding two contradictory beliefs in one's mind

simultaneously, and accepting both of them.

Nineteen Eighty-Four (1949)

1 Power is not a means, it is an end. One does not establish a dictatorship in order to safeguard a revolution; one makes the revolution in order to establish the dictatorship.

Nineteen Eighty-Four (1949)

2 If you want a picture of the future, imagine a boot stamping on a human face—for ever.

Nineteen Eighty-Four (1949)

3 The road to Wigan Pier.

title of book (1937)

4 To the ordinary working man, the sort you would meet in any pub on Saturday night, Socialism does not mean much more than better wages and shorter hours and nobody bossing you about.

The Road to Wigan Pier (1937)

5 Political language . . . is designed to make lies sound truthful and murder respectable, and to give an appearance of solidity to pure wind.

Shooting an Elephant (1950) 'Politics and the English Language'

6 [Serious sport] is war minus the shooting.

Shooting an Elephant (1950) 'The Sporting Spirit'

7 Whatever is funny is subversive, every joke is ultimately a custard pie . . . A dirty joke is a sort of mental rebellion.

in *Horizon* September 1941 'The Art of Donald McGill'

8 The Catholic and the Communist are alike in assuming that an opponent cannot be both honest and intelligent.

in *Polemic* January 1946 'The Prevention of Literature'

9 The quickest way of ending a war is to lose it.

in *Polemic* May 1946 'Second Thoughts on James Burnham'

10 I have always thought that there might be a lot of cash in starting a new religion.

letter, 16 February 1938; in *Collected Essays, Journalism and Letters* (1968); see also
Anonymous 11:4

11 At 50, everyone has the face he deserves.

last words in his notebook, 17 April 1949;
Collected Essays, Journalism and Letters . . . (1968)

George Osborne 1971–
British Conservative politician, Shadow Chancellor from 2005

12 Sound money is the oldest Conservative principle of all.

speech to Conservative Party Conference, 3 October 2006

John Osborne 1929–94
English dramatist. His first play, *Look Back in Anger* (1956), ushered in a new era of kitchen-sink drama; its hero Jimmy Porter personified contemporary disillusioned youth, the so-called 'angry young man'

13 Don't clap too hard—it's a very old building.

The Entertainer (1957)

14 But I have a go, lady, don't I? I 'ave a go. I do.

The Entertainer (1957)

15 Look back in anger.

title of play (1956)

16 I don't think one 'comes down' from Jimmy's university. According to him, it's not even red brick, but white tile.

Look Back in Anger (1956)

17 There aren't any good, brave causes left. If the big bang does come, and we all get killed off, it won't be in aid of the old-fashioned, grand design. It'll just be for the Brave New-nothing-very-much-thank-you. About as pointless and inglorious as stepping in front of a bus.

Look Back in Anger (1956)

18 Royalty is the gold filling in a mouthful of decay.

'They call it cricket' in T. Maschler (ed.)
Declaration (1957)

19 This is a letter of hate. It is for you my countrymen, I mean those men of my country who have defiled it. The men with manic fingers leading the sightless, feeble, betrayed body of my country to its death . . . damn you England.

in *Tribune* 18 August 1961

David Owen 1938–

British Social Democratic politician. He was one of a group of four Labour MPs who broke away from the Labour Party in 1981 to form the Social Democratic Party

1 We are fed up with fudging and mudging, with mush and slush. We need courage, conviction, and hard work.
> speech to his supporters at Labour Party Conference in Blackpool, 2 October 1980

Wilfred Owen 1893–1918

English poet, killed in action in the closing days of the First World War

2 My subject is War, and the pity of War. The Poetry is in the pity.
> *Poems* (1963) preface (written 1918)

3 All a poet can do today is warn.
> *Poems* (1963) preface (written 1918)

4 What passing-bells for these who die as cattle?
Only the monstrous anger of the guns.
> 'Anthem for Doomed Youth' (written 1917)

5 The shrill, demented choirs of wailing shells;
And bugles calling for them from sad shires.
> 'Anthem for Doomed Youth' (written 1917)

6 The pallor of girls' brows shall be their pall;
Their flowers the tenderness of patient minds,
And each slow dusk a drawing-down of blinds.
> 'Anthem for Doomed Youth' (written 1917)

7 If you could hear, at every jolt, the blood
Come gargling from the froth-corrupted lungs,
Obscene as cancer, bitter as the cud
Of vile, incurable sores on innocent tongues,—
My friend, you would not tell with such high zest
To children ardent for some desperate glory,
The old Lie: Dulce et decorum est
Pro patria mori.
> 'Dulce et Decorum Est' (1963 ed.); referring to Horace (65–8 BC) *Odes*: '*Dulce et decorum est pro patria mori* [Lovely and honourable it is to die for one's country]'; see also **Pound 259:14**

8 Was it for this the clay grew tall?
> 'Futility' (written 1918)

9 'Strange friend,' I said, 'here is no cause to mourn.'
'None,' said that other, 'save the undone years,
The hopelessness. Whatever hope is yours,
Was my life also.'
> 'Strange Meeting' (written 1918)

10 Courage was mine, and I had mystery,
Wisdom was mine, and I had mastery.
> 'Strange Meeting' (written 1918)

11 I am the enemy you killed, my friend.
I knew you in this dark.
> 'Strange Meeting' (written 1918)

12 Let us sleep now.
> 'Strange Meeting' (written 1918)

p

Vance Packard 1914–97
American journalist and social critic

1 The hidden persuaders.
   title of a study of the advertising industry
   (1957)

Ignacy Jan Paderewski 1860–1941
Polish pianist, composer, and statesman, first Prime
Minister (for 10 months in 1919) of independent
Poland

2 What a terrible revenge by the culture of
   the Negroes on that of the whites!
   of jazz
   Nat Shapiro (ed.) *An Encyclopedia of
   Quotations about Music* (1978)

Camille Paglia 1947–
American writer and critic

3 Modern body building is ritual, religion,
   sport, art, and science, awash in Western
   chemistry and mathematics. Defying
   nature, it surpasses it.
   Sex, Art, and American Culture (1992)

4 Television is actually closer to reality than
   anything in books. The madness of TV is
   the madness of human life.
   in *Harper's Magazine* March 1991

5 There is no female Mozart because there is
   no female Jack the Ripper.
   in *International Herald Tribune* 26 April 1991

Leroy ('Satchel') Paige 1906–82
American baseball player

6 Don't look back. Something may be
   gaining on you.
   in *Collier's* 13 June 1953; recorded as one of
   his 'Six Rules' for longevity

Ian Paisley 1926–
Northern Irish politician and Presbyterian minister

7 I would rather be British than just.
   remark to Bernadette Devlin, October 1969,
   reported by *Sunday Times* Insight Team in
   Ulster (1972)

8 The mother of all treachery.
   on the Good Friday agreement
   in *Times* 16 April 1998

Christabel Pankhurst 1880–1958
English suffragette; daughter of Emmeline
Pankhurst
see also **Political sayings and slogans 258:10**

9 Never lose your temper with the Press or
   the public is a major rule of political life.
   Unshackled (1959)

10 We are here to claim our right as women,
   not only to be free, but to fight for freedom.
   That it is our right as well as our duty.
   speech in London, 23 March 1911

Emmeline Pankhurst 1858–1928
English suffragette leader; founder of the Women's
Social and Political Union, 1903
see also **Political sayings and slogans 258:10**

11 There is something that Governments care
   far more for than human life, and that is
   the security of property, and so it is
   through property that we shall strike the
   enemy . . . I say to the Government: You
   have not dared to take the leaders of Ulster
   for their incitement to rebellion. Take me if
   you dare.
   speech at Albert Hall, 17 October 1912

1 The argument of the broken window pane is the most valuable argument in modern politics.

> G. Dangerfield *The Strange Death of Liberal England* (1936)

Mitchell Parish 1900–93
American songwriter

2 When the deep purple falls over sleepy garden walls.

> 'Deep Purple' (1939 song)

3 Writing song lyrics was my deliverance from deprivation . . . I sometimes think that all the lyrics I wrote about the moon and stars expressed a longing for what I couldn't see back then.

> attributed; in *American National Biography* (1999)

Nick Park 1958–
British film director and animator

4 I never thought that playing with Plasticine would lead to such a glamorous life.

> *the creator of Wallace and Gromit, on arriving at the Cannes Film Festival*
> in *Independent* 13 May 2005

Charlie Parker 1920–55
American jazz saxophonist

5 Music is your own experience, your thoughts, your wisdom. If you don't live it, it won't come out of your horn.

> Nat Shapiro and Nat Hentoff *Hear Me Talkin' to Ya* (1955)

Dorothy Parker 1893–1967
American critic and humorist
on Parker: see **Benchley 28:9**, **Woollcott 342:8**; see also **Epitaphs 107:4**, **Telegrams 311:3**

6 Oh, life is a glorious cycle of song,
A medley of extemporanea;
And love is a thing that can never go wrong;
And I am Marie of Roumania.

> 'Comment' (1937)

7 Four be the things I'd been better without:
Love, curiosity, freckles, and doubt.

> 'Inventory' (1937)

8 Men seldom make passes

At girls who wear glasses.

> 'News Item' (1937)

9 Why is it no one ever sent me yet
One perfect limousine, do you suppose?
Ah no, it's always just my luck to get
One perfect rose.

> 'One Perfect Rose' (1937)

10 Whose love is given over-well
Shall look on Helen's face in hell
Whilst they whose love is thin and wise
Shall see John Knox in Paradise.

> 'Partial Comfort' (1937)

11 If, with the literate, I am
Impelled to try an epigram,
I never seek to take the credit;
We all assume that Oscar said it.

> 'A Pig's-Eye View of Literature' (1937)

12 Guns aren't lawful;
Nooses give;
Gas smells awful;
You might as well live.

> 'Résumé' (1937)

13 Where's the man could ease a heart like a satin gown?

> 'The Satin Dress' (1937)

14 By the time you say you're his,
Shivering and sighing
And he vows his passion is
Infinite, undying—
Lady, make a note of this:
One of you is lying.

> 'Unfortunate Coincidence' (1937)

15 And it is that word 'hummy', my darlings, that marks the first place in 'The House at Pooh Corner' at which Tonstant Weader fwowed up.

> in *New Yorker* 20 October 1928 (review by Dorothy Parker as 'Constant Reader'); see **Milne 222:17**

16 *House Beautiful* is play lousy.

> *New Yorker* review (1933); P. Hartnoll *Plays and Players* (1984)

17 She ran the whole gamut of the emotions from A to B.

> *of Katharine Hepburn at a Broadway first night, 1933*
> attributed

1 That woman speaks eighteen languages, and can't say No in any of them.
Alexander Woollcott *While Rome Burns* (1934)
'Our Mrs Parker'

2 And there was that wholesale libel on a Yale prom. If all the girls attending it were laid end to end, Mrs Parker said, she wouldn't be at all surprised.
Alexander Woollcott *While Rome Burns* (1934)
'Our Mrs Parker'

3 There's a hell of a distance between wise-cracking and wit. Wit has truth in it; wise-cracking is simply callisthenics with words.
in *Paris Review* Summer 1956

4 How do they know?
*on being told that Calvin **Coolidge** had died*
M. Cowley *Writers at Work* 1st Series (1958)

5 Hollywood money isn't money. It's congealed snow, melts in your hand, and there you are.
Malcolm Cowley *Writers at Work* 1st Series (1958)

6 It serves me right for putting all my eggs in one bastard.
on her abortion
J. Keats *You Might as well Live* (1970)

7 One more drink and I'd have been under the host.
Howard Teichmann *George S. Kaufman* (1972)

8 You can lead a horticulture, but you can't make her think.
J. Keats *You Might as well Live* (1970)

Ross Parker 1914–74 **and Hugh Charles** 1907–
British songwriters

9 There'll always be an England
While there's a country lane,
Wherever there's a cottage small
Beside a field of grain.
'There'll always be an England' (1939 song)

10 We'll meet again, don't know where,
Don't know when,
But I know we'll meet again some sunny day.
'We'll Meet Again' (1939 song)

C. Northcote Parkinson 1909–93
English writer and historian

11 Expenditure rises to meet income.
The Law and the Profits (1960)

12 Work expands so as to fill the time available for its completion.
Parkinson's Law (1958)

13 Perfection of planned layout is achieved only by institutions on the point of collapse.
Parkinson's Law (1958)

14 The man who is denied the opportunity of taking decisions of importance begins to regard as important the decisions he is allowed to take.
Parkinson's Law (1958)

Rosa Parks 1913–2005
American civil rights activist
on Parks: see **Jackson 165:2**

15 Our mistreatment was just not right, and I was tired of it.
of her refusal, in December 1955, to surrender her seat on a segregated bus in Alabama to a white man
Quiet Strength (1994)

Matthew Parris 1949–
British journalist and former Conservative politician

16 Being an MP feeds your vanity and starves your self-respect.
in *Times* 9 February 1994

Dolly Parton 1946–
American singer and actress

17 It costs a lot of money to look this cheap.
attributed, perhaps apocryphal

Boris Pasternak 1890–1960
Russian novelist and poet. His best-known novel, *Doctor Zhivago* (1957), describes the experience of the Russian intelligentsia during the Revolution; it was banned in the Soviet Union

18 Man is born to live, not to prepare for life.
Doctor Zhivago (1958)

19 Most people experience love, without noticing that there is anything remarkable about it.
Doctor Zhivago (1958)

1 I don't like people who have never fallen or stumbled. Their virtue is lifeless and it isn't of much value. Life hasn't revealed its beauty to them.
Doctor Zhivago (1958)

2 The whole human way of life has been destroyed and ruined. All that's left is the bare, shivering human soul, stripped to the last shred, the naked force of the human psyche for which nothing has changed because it was always cold and shivering and reaching out to its nearest neighbour, as cold and lonely as itself.
Doctor Zhivago (1958)

Alan Paton 1903–88
South African writer, educationist, and politician, founder of the South African Liberal Party

3 Cry, the beloved country.
title of novel (1948)

4 When a deep injury is done to us, we never recover until we forgive.
Too Late the Phalarope (1953)

Leslie Paul 1905–85
Irish writer and college teacher, founder of the Woodcraft Folk

5 Angry young man.
title of autobiography (1951); the phrase subsequently associated with John **Osborne**'s play *Look Back in Anger* (1956)

Wolfgang Pauli 1900–58
Austrian-born American physicist, who made a major contribution to quantum theory with the Pauli exclusion principle; in 1931 he postulated the existence of the neutrino, later discovered by Enrico **Fermi**
on Pauli: see **Weisskopf 330:8**

6 I don't mind your thinking slowly: I mind your publishing faster than you think.
attributed

shown a paper by a young theoretician:
7 That is not even wrong.
attributed in *Oxford Dictionary of Scientific Quotations* (2005)

Tom Paulin 1949–
English-born Northern Irish poet and critic

8 That stretch of water, it's always

There for you to cross over
To the other shore, observing
The light of cities on blackness.
'States' (1977)

Jeremy Paxman 1950–
British journalist and broadcaster

9 No government in history has been as obsessed with public relations as this one . . . Speaking for myself, if there is a message I want to be off it.
*after criticism from Alastair **Campbell** of his interviewing tactics*
in *Daily Telegraph* 3 July 1998

Octavio Paz 1914–98
Mexican poet and essayist. His poems reflect a preoccupation with Aztec mythology. He is also noted for his essays written in response to the brutal suppression of student demonstrations in 1968

10 Surrealism has been the drunken flame that guides the steps of the sleepwalker who tiptoes along the edge of the shadow that the blade of the guillotine casts on the neck of the condemned.
'This and This and This' (1988)

11 Love is one of the answers humankind invented to stare death in the face: time ceases to be a measure, and we can briefly know paradise.
The Double Flame (1995)

Mervyn Peake 1911–68
British novelist, poet, and artist

12 To live at all is miracle enough.
The Glassblower (1950)

Norman Vincent Peale 1898–1993
American religious broadcaster and writer

13 The power of positive thinking.
title of book (1952)

Patrick Pearse 1879–1916
Irish nationalist leader; executed after the Easter Rising

14 The fools, the fools, the fools, they have left us our Fenian dead, and while Ireland

holds these graves Ireland unfree shall
never be at peace.
    oration over the grave of the Fenian Jeremiah
    O'Donovan Rossa, 1 August 1915

Hesketh Pearson 1887–1964
English actor and biographer

1 Misquotation is, in fact, the pride and
privilege of the learned. A widely-read man
never quotes accurately, for the rather
obvious reason that he has read too widely.
    Common Misquotations (1934)

Lester Pearson 1897–1972
Canadian diplomat and Liberal statesman, Prime
Minister 1963–8

2 The grim fact is that we prepare for war
like precocious giants and for peace like
retarded pygmies.
    speech in Toronto, 14 March 1955

Pelé 1940–
Brazilian footballer. Regarded as one of the greatest
footballers of all time, he appeared 111 times for
Brazil and is credited with over 1,200 goals in first-
class soccer

3 Football? It's the beautiful game.
    attributed

Nancy Pelosi 1940–
American Democratic politician, since 2007 first
woman Speaker of the House of Representatives

4 Am I going to have to use my 'Mother of
Five Voice' to be heard?
    to an inattentive audience while campaigning
    quoted in a profile in *Newsweek* 23 October
    2006 (online edition)

Roger Penrose 1931–
British mathematician and theoretical physicist

5 Consciousness . . . is the phenomenon
whereby the universe's very existence is
made known.
    The Emperor's New Mind (1989)

S. J. Perelman 1904–79
American humorist

6 Crazy like a fox.
    title of book (1944)

Shimon Peres 1923–
Polish-born Israeli statesman, Prime Minister
1984–6 and 1995–6; as Foreign Minister under
Yitzhak Rabin played a major part in negotiating the
PLO–Israeli peace accord of 1993

7 Television has made dictatorship
impossible, but democracy unbearable.
    at a Davos meeting, in *Financial Times* 31
    January 1995

Anthony Perkins 1932–92
American actor

8 I have learned more about love, selflessness
and human understanding in this great
adventure in the world of Aids than I ever
did in the cut-throat, competitive world in
which I spent my life.
    posthumous statement, in *Independent on
    Sunday* 20 September 1992

Eva Perón 1919–52
Argentinian politician, wife of Juan **Perón**; known as
Evita. A former actress, after her marriage in 1945
she became de facto Minister of Health and of
Labour until her death from cancer; her social
reforms earned her great popularity with the poor
on Perón: see **Epitaphs 108:1, Rice 270:5**

9 Keeping books on charity is capitalist
nonsense! I just use the money for the
poor. I can't stop to count it.
    Fleur Cowles *Bloody Precedent: the Peron
    Story* (1952)

Juan Perón 1895–1974
Argentine soldier and statesman, President 1946–55
and 1973–4; husband of Eva **Perón**. As President, he
won popular support with his social reforms, but the
faltering economy and conflict with the Church led
to his removal and exile

10 If I had not been born Perón, I would have
liked to be Perón.
    in *Observer* 21 February 1960

H. Ross Perot 1930–
American businessman; independent presidential candidate in the 1992 election

1 An activist is the guy who cleans the river, not the guy who concludes it's dirty.
a favourite saying; Ken Gross *Ross Perot* (1992)

Jimmy Perry 1923–
British writer and actor

2 Who do you think you are kidding, Mister Hitler?
theme song of *Dad's Army*, BBC television comedy (1968–77) about the Home Guard, sung by Bud **Flanagan**

Ted Persons *fl.* 1941
songwriter

3 Things ain't what they used to be.
title of song (1941)

Marshal Pétain 1856–1951
French general and statesman, head of state 1940–2. He concluded an armistice with Nazi Germany in 1940 and established the French government at Vichy (effectively a puppet regime for the Third Reich) until 1944
see also **Military sayings 221:7**

4 To write one's memoirs is to speak ill of everybody except oneself.
in *Observer* 26 May 1946

Laurence J. Peter 1919–90
Canadian writer

5 My analysis . . . led me to formulate *The Peter Principle*: In a Hierarchy Every Employee Tends to Rise to His Level of Incompetence.
The Peter Principle (1969)

Jamie Petrie
and **Peter Cunnah** 1963–
British singers and songwriters

6 Things can only get better.
title of song (1994); see **Political sayings and slogans 258:8**

Kim Philby 1912–88
British intelligence officer and Soviet spy. After the defection of Guy Burgess and Donald Maclean in 1951, Philby was asked to resign on suspicion of being a Soviet agent, although there was no firm evidence to this effect. He defected to the USSR in 1963 and was officially revealed to have spied for the Soviets from 1933

7 To betray, you must first belong.
in *Sunday Times* 17 December 1967

Prince Philip, Duke of Edinburgh 1921–
British prince, husband of **Elizabeth II**. The son of Prince Andrew of Greece and Denmark, he served in the Royal Navy until Elizabeth's accession in 1952

8 Gentlemen, I think it is about time we 'pulled our fingers out' . . . If we want to be more prosperous we've simply got to get down to it and work for it. The rest of the world does not owe us a living.
speech in London, 17 October 1961

9 If you stay here much longer you'll all be slitty-eyed.
remark to Edinburgh University students in Peking, 16 October 1986

10 Tolerance is the one essential ingredient . . . You can take it from me that the Queen has the quality of tolerance in abundance.
his recipe for a successful marriage, during celebrations for their golden wedding anniversary
in *Times* 20 November 1997

11 I can only assume that it is largely due to the accumulation of toasts to my health over the years that I am still enjoying a fairly satisfactory state of health and have reached such an unexpectedly great age.
speech to the Corporation of the City of London, 6 June 2001

Arthur Angell Phillips 1900–85
Australian critic and editor

12 Above our writers—and other artists— looms the intimidating mass of Anglo-Saxon culture. Such a situation almost inevitably produces the characteristic Australian Cultural Cringe—appearing either as the Cringe Direct, or as the Cringe Inverted, in the attitude of the Blatant Blatherskite, the God's-Own-Country and

I'm-a-better-man-than-you-are Australian bore.
Meanjin (1950) 'The Cultural Cringe'; see **Keating 175:13**

Morgan Phillips 1902–63
British Labour politician

1 The Labour Party owes more to Methodism than to Marxism.
James Callaghan *Time and Chance* (1987); coined by Denis **Healey** as speechwriter for Phillips at the Socialist International Conference, Copenhagen, 1953

Edith Piaf
see **Michel Vaucaire 324:5**

Pablo Picasso 1881–1973
Spanish painter, sculptor, and graphic artist. His prolific inventiveness and technical versatility made him the dominant figure in avant-garde art in the first half of the 20th century

2 The fact that for a long time Cubism has not been understood and that even today there are people who cannot see anything in it, means nothing. I do not read English, an English book is a blank book to me. This does not mean that the English language does not exist.
interview with Marius de Zayas, 1923; Herschel B. Chipp *Theories of Modern Art* (1968)

3 No, painting is not made to decorate apartments. It's an offensive and defensive weapon against the enemy.
interview with Simone Téry, 24 March 1945

4 When I was the age of these children I could draw like Raphael: it took me many years to learn how to draw like these children.
*to Herbert **Read**, when visiting an exhibition of children's drawings*
quoted in letter from Read to *Times* 27 October 1956

5 I paint objects as I think them, not as I see them.
John Golding *Cubism* (1959)

6 God is really only another artist. He invented the giraffe, the elephant, and the cat. He has no real style. He just goes on trying other things.
F. Gilot and C. Lake *Life With Picasso* (1964)

7 Every positive value has its price in negative terms . . . The genius of Einstein leads to Hiroshima.
F. Gilot and C. Lake *Life With Picasso* (1964)

8 We all know that Art is not truth. Art is a lie that makes us realize truth.
Dore Ashton *Picasso on Art* (1972) 'Two statements by Picasso'

Frank Pick 1878–1941
British transport administrator, who encouraged excellence of design in London Transport

9 Good design is intelligence made visible.
attributed; Paul Clark and Julian Freeman *Design: a Crash Course* (2000)

John Pilger 1939–
Australian journalist

10 It was all too easy for journalists to see Vietnam as a war, rather than a country.
comment, *c.*1995

Ben Pimlott 1945–2004
English historian and royal biographer

11 If you have a Royal Family you have to make the best of whatever personalities the genetic lottery comes up with.
in *Independent* 13 September 1997

Pink Floyd
British rock group formed in 1964 by Syd Barrett, Roger Waters, Nick **Mason**, and Rick Wright

12 Dark side of the moon.
title of album, 1973

Harold Pinter 1930–
English dramatist, actor, and director. His plays are associated with the Theatre of the Absurd and are typically marked by a sense of menace

13 If only I could get down to Sidcup! I've been waiting for the weather to break. He's got my papers, this man I left them with, it's got it all down there, I could prove everything.
The Caretaker (1960)

14 Apart from the known and the unknown, what else is there?
The Homecoming (1965)

1 The weasel under the cocktail cabinet.
on being asked what his plays were about
J. Russell Taylor *Anger and After* (1962)

Luigi Pirandello 1867–1936
Italian dramatist and novelist. His plays, including *Six Characters in Search of an Author* (1921) and *Henry IV* (1922), challenged the conventions of naturalism

2 Six characters in search of an author.
title of play (1921)

Armand J. Piron 1888–1943
American jazz musician

3 I wish I could shimmy like my sister Kate,
She shivers like the jelly on a plate.
'Shimmy like Kate' (1919 song)

Robert M. Pirsig 1928–
American writer

4 Zen and the art of motorcycle maintenance.
title of book (1974)

5 That's the classical mind at work, runs fine inside but looks dingy on the surface.
Zen and the Art of Motorcycle Maintenance (1974)

Walter B. Pitkin 1878–1953
American writer

6 Life begins at forty.
title of book (1932)

Pius XII 1876–1958
Italian cleric; Pope from 1939

7 One Galileo in two thousand years is enough.
on being asked to proscribe the works of **Teilhard de Chardin**
attributed; Stafford Beer *Platform for Change* (1975)

Max Planck 1858–1947
German theoretical physicist who founded quantum theory, announcing the radiation law named after him in 1900

8 A new scientific truth does not triumph by convincing its opponents and making them see the light, but rather because its opponents eventually die, and a new

generation grows up that is familiar with it.
A Scientific Autobiography (1949)

Sylvia Plath 1932–63
American poet, wife of Ted **Hughes**. Her work is notable for its treatment of extreme and painful states of mind. In 1963 she committed suicide
see also **Epitaphs 107:3**

9 Is there no way out of the mind?
'Apprehensions' (1971)

10 Every woman adores a Fascist,
The boot in the face, the brute
Brute heart of a brute like you.
'Daddy' (1963)

11 I am the ghost of an infamous suicide,
My own blue razor rusting in my throat.
O pardon the one who knocks for pardon at Your gate, father—your hound-bitch, daughter, friend.
It was my love that did us both to death.
'Electra on Azalea Path' (1959)

12 The blood jet is poetry,
There is no stopping it.
'Kindness' (1965)

13 Dying,
Is an art, like everything else.
'Lady Lazarus' (1963)

14 Out of the ash
I rise with my red hair
And I eat men like air.
'Lady Lazarus' (1963)

15 Love set you going like a fat gold watch.
'Morning Song' (1965)

16 Widow. The word consumes itself.
'Widow' (1971)

William Plomer 1903–73
South African-born British poet and novelist

17 Out of that bungled, unwise war
An alp of unforgiveness grew.
'The Boer War' (1960)

18 On a sofa upholstered in panther skin
Mona did researches in original sin.
'Mews Flat Mona' (1960)

John C. Polanyi 1929–
German-born Canadian scientist

19 When . . . we fear science, we really fear ourselves. Human dignity is better served

by embracing knowledge.
> accepting the Nobel Prize for Chemistry, 10 December 1986

Political sayings and slogans
see box opposite

Harry Pollitt 1890–1960
British political organizer, leader of the Communist Party of Great Britain

*on being asked by Stephen **Spender** in the 1930s how best a poet could serve the Communist cause:*
1 Go to Spain and get killed. The movement needs a Byron.
> attributed, perhaps apocryphal

Jackson Pollock 1912–56
American painter. He was a leading figure in the abstract expressionist movement and from 1947 became the chief exponent of the style known as action painting, whereby he poured, splashed, or dripped paint on to the canvas

2 There was a reviewer a while back who wrote that my pictures didn't have any beginning or any end. He didn't mean it as a compliment, but it was. It was a fine compliment.
> Francis V. O'Connor *Jackson Pollock* (1967)

John Pope-Hennessy 1913–94
British art historian

3 I still recall, with something of a shock the moment, at the end of the first sitting, when I looked at what had been a lump of clay, and found that a third person was in the room.
> *on sitting to Elizabeth Frink*
> *Learning to Look* (1991)

Karl Popper 1902–94
Austrian-born British philosopher

4 I shall certainly admit a system as empirical or scientific only if it is capable of being *tested* by experience. These considerations suggest that not the *verifiability* but the *falsifiability* of a system is to be taken as a criterion of demarcation . . . *It must be possible for an empirical scientific system to be refuted by experience.*
> *The Logic of Scientific Discovery* (1934)

5 We may become the makers of our fate when we have ceased to pose as its prophets.
> *The Open Society and its Enemies* (1945)

6 We should therefore claim, in the name of tolerance, the right not to tolerate the intolerant.
> *The Open Society and Its Enemies* (1945)

7 There is no history of mankind, there are only many histories of all kinds of aspects of human life. And one of these is the history of political power. This is elevated into the history of the world.
> *The Open Society and its Enemies* (1945)

8 Science must begin with myths, and with the criticism of myths.
> 'The Philosophy of Science' in C. A. Mace (ed.) *British Philosophy in the Mid-Century* (1957)

9 For this, indeed, is the true source of our ignorance—the fact that our knowledge can only be finite, while our ignorance must necessarily be infinite.
> lecture to British Academy, 20 January 1960

Cole Porter 1891–1964
American songwriter

10 But I'm always true to you, darlin', in my fashion.
Yes I'm always true to you, darlin', in my way.
> 'Always True to You in my Fashion' (1949 song), from *Kiss Me, Kate*

11 In olden days a glimpse of stocking
Was looked on as something shocking
Now, heaven knows,
Anything goes.
> 'Anything Goes' song (1934), from *Anything Goes*

12 When they begin the Beguine
It brings back the sound of music so tender,
It brings back a night of tropical splendour,
It brings back a memory ever green.
> 'Begin the Beguine' (1935 song)

13 Oh, give me land, lots of land
Under starry skies above
DON'T FENCE ME IN.
> 'Don't Fence Me In' (1934 song), from *Hollywood Canteen*

Political sayings and slogans

1 All power to the Soviets.
   workers in Petrograd, 1917

2 All the way with LBJ.
   US Democratic Party campaign slogan, 1960

3 Are you now, or have you ever been, a
   member of the Communist Party?
   from 1947, the question habitually put by
   the House Un-American Activities
   Committee (HUAC) to those appearing
   before it, now particularly associated with
   the McCarthy period of the 1950s; see
   Lardner 188:11

4 Ban the bomb.
   US anti-nuclear slogan, adopted by the
   Campaign for Nuclear Disarmament, 1953
   onwards

5 A bayonet is a weapon with a worker at
   each end.
   British pacifist slogan, 1940

6 Better red than dead.
   slogan of nuclear disarmament
   campaigners, late 1950s

7 The big tent.
   *slogan used by the Republican Party to denote
   a policy of inclusiveness*
   recorded from 1990; see also **Newspaper
   headlines 238:1**

8 Black is beautiful.
   slogan of American civil rights campaigners,
   mid-1960s

9 Burn, baby, burn.
   black extremist slogan, Los Angeles riots,
   August 1965

10 Can't pay, won't pay.
   anti-Poll Tax slogan, *c.*1990; see **Fo 119:2**

11 Dr. Spock is worried.
   Committee for a Sane Nuclear Policy (SANE),
   1962; slogan devised by the Doyle Dane
   Bernbach agency co-founded by Bill
   Bernbach

12 *Ein Reich, ein Volk, ein Führer.*
   One realm, one people, one leader.
   Nazi Party slogan, early 1930s

13 Fair shares for all, is Labour's call.
   *slogan for the North Battersea by-election,
   1946, coined by Douglas Jay*
   Douglas Jay *Change and Fortune* (1980)

14 Free by '93.
   Scottish National Party, general election
   campaign, 1992

15 *Gott strafe England!*
   God punish England!
   a common salutation in Germany in 1914
   and the following years, often wrongly
   attributed to the poem *Hassgesang gegen
   England* (1914) by Ernst Lissauer
   (1882–1937), known as the 'Hymn of Hate';
   see **Squire 301:8**; see also **Funke 127:6**

16 Hey, hey, LBJ, how many kids did you kill
   today?
   anti-Vietnam marching slogan, 1960s

17 I like Ike.
   *used when General **Eisenhower** was first seen
   as a potential presidential nominee*
   US button badge, 1947; coined by Henry D.
   Spalding (d. 1990)

18 It'll play in Peoria.
   catchphrase of the **Nixon** administration
   (early 1970s) meaning 'it will be acceptable
   to middle America', but originating in a
   standard music hall joke of the 1930s

19 It's morning again in America.
   Ronald **Reagan**'s 1984 election campaign
   slogan; coined by Hal Riney (1932–)

20 It's Scotland's oil.
   Scottish National Party, 1972

21 It's the economy, stupid.
   on a sign put up at the 1992 **Clinton**
   presidential campaign headquarters by
   campaign manager James Carville

22 Keep the bastards honest.
   coined by the Australian politician Don
   Chipp (1925–), on leaving the Liberal Party
   to form the Australian Democrats

23 *Kraft durch Freude.*
   Strength through joy.
   German Labour Front slogan, from 1933;
   coined by Robert Ley (1890–1945)

▶

> ▶ **Political sayings and slogans** continued

1 Labour isn't working.
on poster showing a long queue outside an unemployment office
    Conservative Party slogan 1978–9

2 Labour's double whammy.
    Conservative Party election slogan 1992

3 Life's better with the Conservatives. Don't let Labour ruin it.
    Conservative Party election slogan, 1959

4 New Labour, new danger.
    Conservative slogan, 1996

5 The personal is political.
    1970s feminist slogan, attributed to Carol Hanisch (1945–)

6 Power to the people.
    slogan of the Black Panther movement, from *c.*1968; see **Newton 236:5**

7 Save the pound.
    slogan for those opposed to the single currency, used particularly in the Conservative campaign for the 2001 British General Election

8 Things can only get better.
    Labour campaign slogan, 1997; see **Petrie 253:6**

9 Thirteen years of Tory misrule.
    unofficial Labour party election slogan, also in the form 'Thirteen wasted years', 1964

10 Votes for women.
    *adopted when it proved impossible to use a banner with the longer slogan 'Will the Liberal Party Give Votes for Women?' made by Emmeline **Pankhurst** (1858–1928), Christabel **Pankhurst** (1880–1958), and Annie Kenney (1879–1953)*
    slogan of the women's suffrage movement, from 13 October 1905; Emmeline Pankhurst *My Own Story* (1914)

11 War will cease when men refuse to fight.
    pacifist slogan, often quoted 'Wars will cease . . .', from *c.*1936

12 Would you buy a used car from this man?
    campaign slogan directed against Richard **Nixon**, 1968

13 Yes it hurt, yes it worked.
    Conservative Party slogan, 1996; see **Major 211:13**

14 Yesterday's men (they failed before!).
    Labour Party slogan, referring to the Conservatives, 1970; coined by David Kingsley, Dennis Lyons, and Peter Lovell-Davis

Cole Porter continued

15 There's no love song finer,
    But how strange the change from major to minor
    Every time we say goodbye.
    'Every Time We Say Goodbye' (1944 song)

16 I get no kick from champagne,
    Mere alcohol doesn't thrill me at all.
    'I Get a Kick Out of You' song (1934), from *Anything Goes*

17 I've got you under my skin.
    title of song (1936), from *Born to Dance*

18 Night and day, you are the one,
    Only you beneath the moon and under the sun.
    'Night and Day' (1932 song), from *Gay Divorce*

19 So goodbye dear, and Amen,

Here's hoping we meet now and then,
    It was great fun,
    But it was just one of those things.
    'Just One of Those Things' (1935 song)

20 Birds do it, bees do it,
    Even educated fleas do it.
    Let's do it, let's fall in love.
    'Let's Do It' (1954 song; words added to the 1928 original)

21 Miss Otis regrets (she's unable to lunch today).
    title of song (1934)

22 My heart belongs to Daddy.
    title of song (1938)

23 SHE: Have you heard it's in the stars,
    Next July we collide with Mars?

HE: WELL, DID YOU EVAH! What a swell party this is.
'Well, Did You Evah?' (1940 song)

1 Who wants to be a millionaire?
title of song (1956), from *High Society*

Michael Portillo 1953–
British Conservative politician and broadcaster

2 A truly terrible night for the Conservatives.
after losing Enfield South to Labour in the General Election of 1997
comment, 2 May 1997; Brian Cathcart *Were You Still Up for Portillo?* (1997)

Dennis Potter 1935–94
English television dramatist

3 Below my window . . . the blossom is out in full now . . . I *see* it is the whitest, frothiest, blossomiest blossom that there ever could be, and I can see it. . . . The nowness of everything is absolutely wondrous.
on his heightened awareness of things, in the face of his imminent death
interview with Melvyn Bragg on Channel 4, March 1994

4 Religion to me has always been the wound, not the bandage.
interview with Melvyn Bragg on Channel 4, March 1994

Stephen Potter 1900–69
British writer and radio producer

5 A good general rule is to state that the bouquet is better than the taste, and vice versa.
on wine-tasting
One-Upmanship (1952)

6 *How to be one up*—how to make the other man feel that something has gone wrong, however slightly.
Lifemanship (1950)

7 'Yes, but not in the South', with slight adjustments, will do for any argument about any place, if not about any person.
Lifemanship (1950)

8 The theory and practice of gamesmanship or The art of winning games without actually cheating.
title of book (1947)

Ezra Pound 1885–1972
American poet whose modernist poetry drew on a vast range of classical and other references. In 1945 he was charged with treason following his pro-Fascist radio broadcasts from Italy during the Second World War; he was committed to a mental institution until 1958

9 Winter is icummen in,
Lhude sing Goddamm,
Raineth drop and staineth slop,
And how the wind doth ramm!
Sing: Goddamm.
'Ancient Music' (1917); referring to an anonymous 'Cuckoo Song' (*c.*1250): 'Sumer is icumen in, / Lhude sing cuccu! / Groweth sed, and bloweth med, / And springeth the wude nu'

10 With usura hath no man a house of good stone
each block cut smooth and well fitting.
Cantos (1954) no. 45

11 Tching prayed on the mountain and
wrote MAKE IT NEW
on his bath tub.
Cantos (1954) no. 53

12 And even I can remember
A day when the historians left blanks in their writings,
I mean for things they didn't know.
Draft of XXX Cantos (1930) no. 13

13 Christ follows Dionysus,
Phallic and ambrosial
Made way for macerations;
Caliban casts out Ariel.
Hugh Selwyn Mauberley (1920) 'E. P. *Ode* . . .' pt. 3

14 Died some, pro patria,
non 'dulce' non 'et decor' . . .
walked eye-deep in hell
believing in old men's lies, the unbelieving came home, home to a lie.
Hugh Selwyn Mauberley (1920) 'E. P. *Ode* . . .' pt. 4; referring to Horace (65–8 BC) *Odes*: '*Dulce et decorum est pro patria mori* [Lovely and honourable it is to die for one's country]'; see also **Owen 247:7**

15 There died a myriad,
And of the best, among them,
For an old bitch gone in the teeth,

For a botched civilization.
Hugh Selwyn Mauberley (1920) 'E. P. *Ode* . . .'
pt. 5

1 The tip's a good one, as for literature
It gives no man a sinecure.

And no one knows, at sight, a masterpiece.
And give up verse, my boy,
There's nothing in it.
Hugh Selwyn Mauberley (1920) 'Mr Nixon'

2 The ant's a centaur in his dragon world.
Pisan Cantos (1948) no. 81

3 Music begins to atrophy when it departs
too far from the dance . . . poetry begins to
atrophy when it gets too far from music.
The ABC of Reading (1934) 'Warning'

4 One of the pleasures of middle age is to *find
out* that one was right, and that one was
much righter than one knew at say 17 or
23.
The ABC of Reading (1934)

5 Literature is news that stays news.
The ABC of Reading (1934)

6 Great literature is simply language charged
with meaning to the utmost possible
degree.
How To Read (1931)

Anthony Powell 1905–2000
English novelist, best known for his sequence of
twelve novels *A Dance to the Music of Time*
(1951–75), a satirical portrayal of the English upper
middle classes between the two World Wars
see also **Borrowed titles 40:8**

7 He fell in love with himself at first sight and
it is a passion to which he has always
remained faithful.
The Acceptance World (1955)

8 Dinner at the Huntercombes' possessed
'only two dramatic features—the wine was
a farce and the food a tragedy'.
The Acceptance World (1955)

9 Books do furnish a room.
title of novel (1971)

10 Parents—especially step-parents—are
sometimes a bit of a disappointment to
their children. They don't fufil the promise
of their early years.
A Buyer's Market (1952)

11 He's so wet you could shoot snipe off him.
A Question of Upbringing (1951)

12 Growing old is like being increasingly
penalized for a crime you haven't
committed.
Temporary Kings (1973)

13 She was the sort of woman who, if she had
been taken in adultery, would have caught
the first stone and thrown it back.
A Writer's Notebook (2001)

Colin Powell 1937–
American general and Republican politician;
Secretary of State 2001–3

14 First, we are going to cut it off, and then,
we are going to kill it.
*strategy for dealing with the Iraqi Army in the
Gulf War*
at a press conference, 23 January 1991

15 Some in our party miss no opportunity to
roundly and loudly condemn affirmative
action that helped a few thousand black
kids get an education, but hardly a
whimper is heard from them over
affirmative action for lobbyists who load
our federal tax codes with preferences for
special interest.
speech at the Republican Convention, 31
August 2000

16 A great tragedy has struck our country. It
will not affect the nature of our society.
*after the terrorist attacks on the World Trade
Center and the Pentagon, 11 September 2001*
in *Times* 12 September 2001

Enoch Powell 1912–98
British Conservative politician
on Powell: see **Macmillan 209:4**

17 History is littered with the wars which
everybody knew would never happen.
speech to Conservative Party Conference, 19
October 1967

18 Those whom the gods wish to destroy, they
first make mad. We must be mad, literally
mad, as a nation to be permitting the
annual inflow of some 50,000 dependents,
who are for the most part the material of
the future growth of the immigrant
descended population. It is like watching a

nation busily engaged in heaping up its own funeral pyre.
speech at Annual Meeting of West Midlands Area Conservative Political Centre, Birmingham, 20 April 1968

1 As I look ahead, I am filled with foreboding. Like the Roman, I seem to see 'the River Tiber foaming with much blood'.
speech at Birmingham, 20 April 1968, referring to Virgil (70–19 BC) *Aeneid*: 'I see wars, horrible wars, and the Tiber foaming with much blood'; see also **Levy 199:1**

2 To write a diary every day is like returning to one's own vomit.
interview in *Sunday Times* 6 November 1977

3 For a politician to complain about the press is like a ship's captain complaining about the sea.
in *Guardian* 3 December 1984

4 ANNE BROWN: How would you like to be remembered?
ENOCH POWELL: I should like to have been killed in the war.
in a radio interview, 13 April 1986

5 To be and to remain a member of the House of Commons was the overriding and undiscussable motivation of my life as a politician.
'Theory and Practice' 1990

6 All political lives, unless they are cut off in midstream at a happy juncture, end in failure, because that is the nature of politics and of human affairs.
Joseph Chamberlain (1977)

Vince Powell *fl.* 1960s **and Harry Driver** 1931–73
British writers

7 Never mind the quality, feel the width.
title of ITV comedy series set in an East London tailoring firm, 1967–9

Terry Pratchett 1948–
English fantasy writer, creator of the Discworld

8 Personal isn't the same as important.
Men at Arms (1993)

9 Most modern fantasy just rearranges the furniture in Tolkien's attic.
Stan Nicholls (ed.) *Wordsmiths of Wonder* (1993)

Keith Preston 1884–1927
American poet

10 Of all the literary scenes
Saddest this sight to me:
The graves of little magazines
Who died to make verse free.
'The Liberators'

Jacques Prévert 1900–77
French poet and screenwriter

11 *C'est tellement simple, l'amour.*
It's so simple, love.
Les Enfants du Paradis (1945) film)

Anthony Price 1928–
English thriller writer and editor

12 The Devil himself had probably redesigned Hell in the light of information he had gained from observing airport layouts.
The Memory Trap (1989)

Gerald Priestland 1927–91
English writer and journalist

13 Journalists belong in the gutter because that is where the ruling classes throw their guilty secrets.
on Radio London 19 May 1988

J. B. Priestley 1894–1984
English novelist, dramatist, and critic, husband of Jacquetta **Hawkes**

14 I never read the life of any important person without discovering that he knew more and could do more than I could ever hope to know or to do in half a dozen lifetimes.
Apes and Angels (1928)

15 The first fall of snow is not only an event, but it is a magical event. You go to bed in one kind of world and wake up to find yourself in another quite different, and if this is not enchantment, then where is it to be found?
Apes and Angels (1928) 'First Snow'

16 To say that these men paid their shillings to watch twenty-two hirelings kick a ball is merely to say that a violin is wood and catgut, that *Hamlet* is so much paper and ink. For a shilling the Bruddersford United

AFC offered you Conflict and Art.
Good Companions (1929)

1 First you take their faces from 'em by calling 'em the masses and then you accuse 'em of not having any faces.
Saturn Over the Water (1961)

2 Our great-grand-children, when they learn how we began this war by snatching glory out of defeat, and then swept on to victory, may also learn how the little holiday steamers made an excursion to hell and came back glorious.
on the evacuation of Dunkirk
radio broadcast, 5 June 1940

3 The weakness of American civilization, and perhaps the chief reason why it creates so much discontent, is that it is so curiously abstract. It is a bloodless extrapolation of a satisfying life . . . You dine off the advertiser's 'sizzling' and not the meat of the steak.
in *New Statesman* 10 December 1971

Matthew Pritchett
see **Cartoons 56:5**

V. S. Pritchett 1900–97
English writer and critic

4 The principle of procrastinated rape is said to be the ruling one in all the great best-sellers.
The Living Novel (1946) 'Clarissa'

5 The detective novel is the art-for-art's-sake of our yawning Philistinism, the classic example of a specialized form of art removed from contact with the life it pretends to build on.
in *New Statesman* 16 June 1951 'Books in General'

Romano Prodi 1939–
Italian statesman, Prime Minister 1996–98, 2006– , President of the European Commission 1999–2004

6 The pillars of the nation state are the sword and the currency, and we changed that. The euro-decision changed the concept of the nation state.
in *Daily Telegraph* 7 April 1999

Marcel Proust 1871–1922
French novelist, essayist, and critic. He devoted much of his life to writing his novel *À la recherche du temps perdu* (published in seven sections between 1913 and 1927). Its central theme is the recovery of the lost past and the releasing of its creative energies through the stimulation of unconscious memory

7 *À la recherche du temps perdu.*
In search of lost time.
translated by C. K. Scott-Moncrieff and S. Hudson, 1922–31, as Remembrance of things past: *see* **Borrowed titles 41:1**
title of novel (1913–27)

8 I have a horror of sunsets, they're so romantic, so operatic.
Cities of the Plain (1922)

9 Everything we think of as great has come to us from neurotics. It is they and they alone who found religions and create great works of art. The world will never realise how much it owes to them and what they have suffered in order to bestow their gifts on it.
Guermantes Way (1921)

10 And suddenly the memory revealed itself. The taste was that of the little piece of madeleine which . . . my aunt Léonie used to give me, dipping it first in her own cup of tea or tisane.
Swann's Way (1913)

11 The true paradises are the paradises that we have lost.
Time Regained (1926)

John Pudney 1909–77
English poet and journalist

12 Do not despair
For Johnny-head-in-air;
He sleeps as sound
As Johnny underground.
'For Johnny' (1942)

13 And keep your tears
For him in after years.
Better by far
For Johnny-the-bright-star,
To keep your head,
And see his children fed.
'For Johnny' (1942)

Philip Pullman 1946–
British writer for children
see also **Borrowed titles 40:15**

1 I thought physics could be done to the
   glory of God, till I saw there wasn't any
   God at all and that physics was more
   interesting anyway.
   Amber Spyglass (2000), Mary Malone
   speaking

Al Purdy 1918–2000
Canadian poet and writer

2 Look here
   You've never seen this country
   it's not the way you thought it was
   Look again.
   of Canada
   'The Country of the Young' (1976)

3 Looking into his eyes
   it is possible to see the first hunters
   (if you have your own vision)
   after the last ice age.
   'Inuit' (1967)

Mario Puzo 1920–99
American novelist
see also **Film lines 115:5**

4 I'll make him an offer he can't refuse.
   The Godfather (1969)

5 A lawyer with his briefcase can steal more
   than a hundred men with guns.
   The Godfather (1969)

Barbara Pym 1913–80
English novelist. She wrote a number of novels
dealing satirically with English middle-class village
life

6 She experienced all the cosiness and
   irritation which can come from living with
   thoroughly nice people with whom one
   has nothing in common.
   Less than Angels (1955)

q

Mary Quant 1934–

English fashion designer, a principal creator of the '1960s look', launching the miniskirt in 1966 and promoting bold colours and geometric designs

1 It was she who established the fact that this latter half of the twentieth century belongs to Youth.
of her invention, the Chelsea Girl
Quant by Quant (1966)

2 Being young is greatly overestimated . . . Any failure seems so total. Later on you realize you can have another go.
interview in *Observer* 5 May 1996

Dan Quayle 1947–

American Republican politician, Vice President 1989–93
on Quayle: see **Bentsen 30:2**

3 Space is almost infinite. As a matter of fact, we think it is infinite.
in *Daily Telegraph* 8 March 1989

4 What a waste it is to lose one's mind, or not to have a mind. How true that is.
speech to the United Negro College Fund, whose slogan is 'a mind is a terrible thing to waste'; in *Times* 26 May 1989

Arthur Quiller-Couch 1863–1944

English writer and critic

5 All the old statues of Victory have wings: but Grief has no wings. She is the unwelcome lodger that squats on the hearthstone between us and the fire and will not move or be dislodged.
Armistice Day anniversary sermon, Cambridge, November 1923

W. V. O. Quine 1908–2000

American philosopher and logician, a radical critic of modern empiricism

6 On the doctrinal side, I do not see that we are farther along today than where [David] Hume left us. The Humean predicament is the human predicament.
Ontological Relativity and Other Essays (1969)

7 Language is conceived in sin and science is its redemption.
The Roots of Reference (1973)

8 Different persons growing up in the same language are like different bushes trimmed and trained to take the shape of identical elephants. The anatomical details of twigs and branches will fulfill the elephantine shape differently from bush to bush, but the overall outward results are alike.
Word and Object (1960)

r

Yitzhak Rabin 1922–95

Israeli statesman and military leader, Prime Minister 1974–7 and 1992–5, who in 1993 negotiated a PLO–Israeli peace accord with Yasser **Arafat**, for which he shared the 1994 Nobel Peace Prize with Arafat and Shimon **Peres**; he was assassinated in the following year

1 You don't make peace with friends. You make it with very unsavoury enemies.
in *New York Times* 10 September 1993

2 We say to you today in a loud and a clear voice: enough of blood and tears. Enough.
to the Palestinians, at the signing of the Israel–Palestine Declaration
in Washington, 13 September 1993

Paula Radcliffe 1973–

British long-distance runner

3 All you need to run is good shoes.
in *Observer* 6 November 2005

James Rado 1939–
and Gerome Ragni 1942–

American songwriters

4 When the moon is in the seventh house,
And Jupiter aligns with Mars,
Then peace will guide the planets,
And love will steer the stars;
This is the dawning of the age of Aquarius.
'Aquarius' (1967 song)

John Rae 1931–2006

English writer and educationist

5 War is, after all, the universal perversion. We are all tainted: if we cannot experience our perversion at first hand we spend our time reading war stories, the pornography of war; or seeing war films, the blue films of war; or titillating our senses with the imagination of great deeds, the masturbation of war.
The Custard Boys (1960)

Craig Raine 1944–

English poet

6 In homes, a haunted apparatus sleeps, that snores when you pick it up.
If the ghost cries, they carry it to their lips and soothe it to sleep
with sounds. And yet, they wake it up deliberately, but tickling it with a finger.
'A Martian sends a Postcard Home' (1979)

Claude Rains

see **Film lines 115:8**

Walter Raleigh 1861–1922

English lecturer and critic

7 In examinations those who do not wish to know ask questions of those who cannot tell.
Laughter from a Cloud (1923) 'Some Thoughts on Examinations'

8 I wish I loved the Human Race;
I wish I loved its silly face;
I wish I liked the way it walks;
I wish I liked the way it talks;
And when I'm introduced to one
I wish I thought *What Jolly Fun!*
'Wishes of an Elderly Man' (1923)

9 An anthology is like all the plums and orange peel picked out of a cake.
letter to Mrs Robert Bridges, 15 January 1915

Srinivasa Ramanujan 1887–1920
Indian mathematician

replying to G. H. Hardy's suggestion that the number of a taxi-cab (1729) was 'dull':

1 No, it is a very interesting number; it is the smallest number expressible as a sum of two cubes in two different ways.
the two ways being 1^3+12^3 and 9^3+10^3
in *Proceedings of the London Mathematical Society* 26 May 1921

Michael Ramsey 1904–88
British clergyman, Archbishop of York (1956–61) and Canterbury (1961–74)

2 I should love to think of a black Archbishop of York holding a mission to the University of Oxford, and telling a future generation of the scandal and glory of the Church.
address at the Sheldonian Theatre, Oxford, February 1960, in *Introducing the Christian Faith* (1961); see also **Sentamu 290:10**

on being asked if he was in good heart about being Archbishop:

3 The phrase 'in good heart' gives me pause . . . We are here as a church to represent Christ crucified and the compassion of Christ crucified before the world. And, because that is so, it may be the will of God that our church should have its heart broken and perhaps the heart of its Archbishop broken with it.
in *Church Times* 9 June 1961

Ayn Rand 1905–82
Russian-born American writer and philosopher

4 Civilization is the progress toward a society of privacy. The savage's noble existence is public, ruled by the laws of his tribe. Civilization is the process of setting man free from men.
The Fountainhead (1947)

John Crowe Ransom 1888–1974
American poet and critic

5 Two evils, monstrous either one apart,
Possessed me, and were long and loath at going:
A cry of Absence, Absence, in the heart,

And in the wood the furious winter blowing.
'Winter Remembered' (1945)

Arthur Ransome
see **Telegrams 311:2**

Frederic Raphael 1931–
British novelist and screenwriter
see also **Borrowed titles 40:11**

6 'So this is the city of dreaming spires,' Sheila said. 'Theoretically speaking that's Oxford,' Adam said. 'This is the city of perspiring dreams.'
of Cambridge
The Glittering Prizes (1976), referring to Matthew Arnold (1822–88) 'Thyrsis' (1866): 'And that sweet City with her dreaming spires'

Joe Raposo 1937–89
American songwriter

7 It's not that easy being green.
sung by the Kermit the frog
'Bein' Green', song from Jim Henson's *Sesame Street* (TV show, 1969–)

Gerald Ratner 1949–
English businessman

8 We even sell a pair of earrings for under £1, which is cheaper than a prawn sandwich from Marks & Spencers. But I have to say the earrings probably won't last as long.
speech to the Institute of Directors, Albert Hall, 23 April 1991; publicity surrounding the reports of his speech had an immediate and disastrous effect on the share price of the company

Terence Rattigan 1911–77
English dramatist

9 Let us invent a character, a nice respectable, middle-class, middle-aged, maiden lady, with time on her hands and the money to help her pass it. She enjoys pictures, books, music, and the theatre and though to none of these arts (or rather, for consistency's sake, to none of these three arts and the one craft) does she bring much knowledge or discernment, at least, as she

is apt to tell her cronies, she 'does know what she likes'. Let us call her Aunt Edna ... Aunt Edna is universal, and to those who may feel that all the problems of the modern theatre might be solved by her liquidation, let me add that I have no doubt at all that she is also immortal.
Collected Plays (1953) vol. 2, preface

1 French without tears.
title of play (1937)

2 Do you know what 'le vice Anglais'—the English vice—really is? Not flagellation, not pederasty—whatever the French believe it to be. It's our refusal to admit our emotions. We think they demean us, I suppose.
In Praise of Love (1973)

Irina Ratushinskaya 1954–
Russian poet; confined in a Soviet labour camp 1982–6

3 Russian literature saved my soul. When I was a young girl in school and I asked what is good and what is evil, no one in that corrupt system could show me.
in *Observer* 15 October 1989

Maurice Ravel 1875–1937
French composer

4 I don't have ideas. To begin with, nothing forces itself on me.
when asked how he composed
in Roger Nichols (ed.) *Ravel Remembered* (1987)

Derek Raymond 1931–94
English thriller writer

5 The psychopath is the furnace that gives no heat.
The Hidden Files (1992)

Claire Rayner 1931–
English journalist

6 I always say I don't think everyone has the right to happiness or to be loved. Even the Americans have written into their constitution that you have the right to the 'pursuit of happiness'. You have the right to try but that is all.
G. Kinnock and F. Miller (eds.) *By Faith and Daring* (1993)

Herbert Read 1893–1968
English art historian

7 Do not judge this movement kindly. It is not just another amusing stunt. It is defiant—the desperate act of men too profoundly convinced of the rottenness of our civilization to want to save a shred of its respectability.
International Surrealist Exhibition Catalogue, New Burlington Galleries, London, 11 June–4 July 1936, introduction

8 Art is . . . pattern informed by sensibility.
The Meaning of Art (1955)

9 Lorca was killed, singing,
and Fox who was my friend.
The rhythm returns: the song
which has no end.
'The Heart Conscripted' (1938)

10 I saw him stab
And stab again
A well-killed Boche.
This is the happy warrior,
This is he . . .
Naked Warriors (1919) 'The Scene of War, 4. The Happy Warrior', referring to William Wordsworth (1770–1850) 'Character of the Happy Warrior' (1807): 'Who is the happy Warrior?'

Piers Paul Read 1941–
English novelist

11 Sins become more subtle as you grow older. You commit sins of despair rather than lust.
in *Daily Telegraph* 3 October 1990

Nancy Reagan 1923–
American actress and wife of Ronald **Reagan**, First Lady of the US, 1981–9
see also **Official advice 242:10**

12 A woman is like a teabag—only in hot water do you realize how strong she is.
in *Observer* 29 March 1981

13 If the President has a bully pulpit, then the First Lady has a white glove pulpit . . . more

refined, restricted, ceremonial, but it's a pulpit all the same.
> in *New York Times* 10 March 1988; see **Roosevelt 274:11**

Ronald Reagan 1911–2004
American Republican statesman, 40th President of the US 1981–9
on Reagan: see **Keillor 176:4**, **Schroeder 288:5**, **Vidal 325:7**, **Warner 328:1**; see also **Dempsey 89:2**, **Gipp 133:8**

1 I paid for this microphone.
> *in 1980, debating for the Republican nomination against George **Bush**; the moderator had ordered Reagan's microphone turned off when he asked for the participation of other candidates, and the refusal to allow this was held to be very damaging to Bush*
>> Lou Cannon *Ronald Reagan* (1982)

President Carter had described a proposal for a national health insurance plan
2 JIMMY CARTER: Governor Reagan, again, typically is against such a proposal.
RONALD REAGAN: There you go again!
> as Republican challenger debating with President Carter in the 1980 presidential campaign; in *Times* 30 October 1980

3 Politics is supposed to be the second oldest profession. I have come to realize that it bears a very close resemblance to the first.
> at a conference in Los Angeles, 2 March 1977

4 You can tell a lot about a fellow's character by his way of eating jellybeans.
> in *New York Times* 15 January 1981

5 My fellow Americans, I am pleased to tell you I just signed legislation which outlaws Russia forever. The bombing begins in five minutes.
> *inadvertently recorded, and subsequently widely reported and criticized, especially in the Western European press*
>> said during radio microphone test, 11 August 1984

6 We are especially not going to tolerate these attacks from outlaw states run by the strangest collection of misfits, Looney Tunes, and squalid criminals since the advent of the Third Reich.
> *following the release in Lebanon of a hijacked US plane; the reference was to Iran, Libya, North Korea, Cuba, and Nicaragua, characterized by*

the President as 'a confederation of terrorist states'
> speech, 8 July 1985

7 We will never forget them, nor the last time we saw them this morning, as they prepared for the journey and waved goodbye and 'slipped the surly bonds of earth' to 'touch the face of God.'
> *after the loss of the space shuttle Challenger with all its crew*
>> broadcast from the Oval Office, 28 January 1986; see **Magee 211:2**, **Magee 211:3**

8 I now begin the journey that will lead me into the sunset of my life.
> *statement to the American people revealing that he had Alzheimer's disease*
>> in *Daily Telegraph* 5 January 1995

Louis Reard d. 84
French designer, inventor of the bikini

9 A bikini is not a bikini unless it can be pulled through a wedding ring.
> attributed

Henry Reed 1914–86
English poet and dramatist

10 Today we have naming of parts. Yesterday,
We had daily cleaning. And tomorrow morning,
We shall have what to do after firing. But today,
Today we have naming of parts.
> 'Lessons of the War: 1, Naming of Parts' (1946)

11 They call it easing the Spring: it is perfectly easy
If you have any strength in your thumb: like the bolt,
And the breech, and the cocking-piece, and the point of balance,
Which in our case we have not got.
> 'Lessons of the War: 1, Naming of Parts' (1946)

John Reed 1887–1920
American journalist and revolutionary

12 Ten days that shook the world.
> title of book (1919), on the seizure of power by the Bolsheviks in the Russian Revolution (known as the 'October Revolution')

John Reid 1947–
British Labour politician

1 Our system is not fit for purpose.
on the Home Office Immigration and Nationality Directorate (IND)
speaking to the Commons Home Affairs Committee, 23 May 2006, in *Times* (online edition) 23 May 2006

Keith Reid 1946–
English pop singer and songwriter

2 Her face, at first . . . just ghostly
Turned a whiter shade of pale.
'A Whiter Shade of Pale' (1967 song)

Lord Reith 1889–1971
British administrator and politician, first general manager (1922–7) and first director-general (1927–38) of the BBC

3 By the time the civil service has finished drafting a document to give effect to a principle, there may be little of the principle left.
Into the Wind (1949)

4 When people feel deeply, impartiality is bias.
Into the Wind (1949)

Erich Maria Remarque 1898–1970
German novelist

5 All quiet on the western front.
English title of *Im Westen nichts Neues* (1929 novel)

David Remnick 1958–
American journalist and writer, Editor of the New Yorker since 1998

6 Generalship is not about fighting the battle; it's about inspiring the enlisted.
*in a profile of Ben **Bradlee**, Editor of the Washington Post*
The Devil Problem (1996)

Montague John Rendall 1862–1950
British educationist, member of the first BBC Board of Governors 1927–32

7 Nation shall speak peace unto nation.
motto of the BBC (1927), from the *Bible*
Isaiah: 'Nation shall not lift up sword against nation'

Jean Renoir 1894–1979
French film director, son of the painter Pierre Auguste Renoir

8 Is it possible to succeed without any act of betrayal?
My Life and My Films (1974) 'Nana'

Pierre Auguste Renoir
see **Misquotations 224:10**

David Reuben 1933–
American psychiatrist

9 Everything you always wanted to know about sex, but were afraid to ask.
title of book (1969)

Charles Revson 1906–75
American businessman, co-founder of Revlon cosmetics company

10 In the factory we make cosmetics; in the store we sell hope.
A. Tobias *Fire and Ice* (1976)

11 Theme is my religion.
quoted in *American National Biography* (online edition)

Malvina Reynolds 1900–78
American songwriter

12 Little boxes on the hillside,
Little boxes made of ticky-tacky,
Little boxes on the hillside,
Little boxes all the same.
on the tract houses in the hills to the south of San Francisco
'Little Boxes' (1962 song)

Jean Rhys *c.*1890–1979
British novelist and short-story writer

13 We can't all be happy, we can't all be rich, we can't all be lucky—and it would be so much less fun if we were . . . Some must cry so that others may be able to laugh the more heartily.
Good Morning, Midnight (1939)

14 The perpetual hunger to be beautiful and that thirst to be loved which is the real curse of Eve.
The Left Bank (1927) 'Illusion'

1 A doormat in a world of boots.
describing herself
in *Guardian* 6 December 1990

Grantland Rice 1880–1954
American sports journalist

2 For when the One Great Scorer comes to
   mark against your name,
He writes—not that you won or lost—but
   how you played the Game.
'Alumnus Football' (1941)

3 All wars are planned by old men
In council rooms apart.
'The Two Sides of War' (1955)

4 Outlined against a blue-grey October sky,
the Four Horsemen rode again. In
dramatic lore they were known as Famine,
Pestilence, Destruction, and Death. These
are only aliases. Their real names are
Stuhldreher, Miller, Crowley, and Layden.
They formed the crest of the South Bend
cyclone before which another fighting
Army football team was swept over the
precipice.
   report of football match between US Military
   Academy at West Point NY and University of
   Notre Dame, in *New York Tribune* 19 October
   1924

Tim Rice 1944–
English songwriter

5 Don't cry for me Argentina.
   title of song (1976) from the musical *Evita*,
   based on the life of Eva **Perón**

6 Prove to me that you're no fool
Walk across my swimming pool.
   Jesus Christ Superstar (1970) 'Herod's Song'

Mandy Rice-Davies 1944–
English model and showgirl

7 He would, wouldn't he?
   *on hearing that Lord Astor denied her
   allegations, concerning himself and his house
   parties at Cliveden*
   at the trial of Stephen Ward, 29 June 1963

Adrienne Rich 1923–
American poet and critic

8 The thing I came for:
the wreck and not the story of the wreck

the thing itself and not the myth.
   'Diving into the Wreck' (1973)'

9 Memory says: Want to do right? Don't
   count on me.
   'Eastern War Time' (1991)

10 I'm accused of child-death of drinking
   blood . . .
there is spit on my sleeve there are
   phonecalls in the night . . .
   'Eastern War Time' (1991)

11 If I could have one wish for my own sons, it
is that they should have the courage of
women.
   Of Woman Born (1976)

Ann Richards 1933–2006
American Democratic politician

12 Poor George, he can't help it—he was born
with a silver foot in his mouth.
   of George **Bush**
      keynote speech at the Democratic convention,
      1988; in *Independent* 20 July 1988

I. A. Richards 1893–1979
English literary critic and poet. He emphasized the
importance of close textual study, and praised irony,
ambiguity, and allusiveness

13 It [poetry] is capable of saving us; it is a
perfectly possible means of overcoming
chaos.
   Science and Poetry (1926)

Justin Richardson 1900–75
British poet

14 People who have three daughters try once
   more
And then it's fifty-fifty they'll have four.
Those with a son or sons will let things be.
Hence all these surplus women. Q.E.D.
   'Note for the Scientist' (1959)

15 For years a secret shame destroyed my
   peace—
I'd not read Eliot, Auden or MacNeice.
But then I had a thought that brought me
   hope—
Neither had Chaucer, Shakespeare, Milton,
Pope.
   'Take Heart, Illiterates' (1966)

Ralph Richardson 1902–83
English actor

1 Acting is merely the art of keeping a large
   group of people from coughing.
   in New York Herald Tribune 19 May 1946

Mordecai Richler 1931–2001
Canadian writer

2 I'm world famous, Dr Parks said, all over
   Canada.
   The Incomparable Atuk (1963)

Laura Riding 1901–91
American poet and novelist

3 Without dressmakers to connect
   The good-will of the body
   With the purpose of the head,
   We should be two worlds
   Instead of a world and its shadow
   The flesh.
   'Because of Clothes' (1938)

Rainer Maria Rilke 1875–1926
German poet, born in Bohemia

4 We live our lives, for ever taking leave.
   Duineser Elegien [Duino Elegies] (1948) no. 8

5 Love consists in this, that two solitudes
   protect and touch and greet each other.
   Letters to a Young Poet (1929) 14 May 1904
   (translated by Hugh MacLennan); see also
   Borrowed titles 41:7

César Ritz 1850–1918
Swiss hotel proprietor, founder of the Paris Ritz
(1890) and other Ritz hotels

6 *Le client n'a jamais tort.*
   The customer is never wrong.
   R. Nevill and C. E. Jerningham *Piccadilly to Pall
   Mall* (1908)

Joan Riviere 1883–1962
British psychoanalyst

7 Civilization and its discontents.
   title given to her translation of Sigmund
   Freud's *Das Unbehagen in der Kultur* (1930)

Lord Robbins 1898–1984
British economist

8 Economics is the science which studies
   human behaviour as a relationship
   between ends and scarce means which
   have alternative uses.
   *Essay on the Nature and Significance of
   Economic Science* (1932)

Leo Robin 1900–84
American songwriter

9 A kiss on the hand may be quite
      continental,
   But diamonds are a girl's best friend.
   'Diamonds are a Girl's Best Friend' (1949
   song); from the film *Gentlemen Prefer
   Blondes*; see **Loos 202:10**

10 Thanks for the memory.
   title of song (with Ralph Rainger, 1937)

Edwin Arlington Robinson 1869–1935
American poet

11 I shall have more to say when I am dead.
   'John Brown' (1920)

12 So on we worked, and waited for the light,
   And went without meat, and cursed the
      bread;
   And Richard Cory, one calm summer
      night,
   Went home and put a bullet through his
      head.
   'Richard Cory' (1897)

John Robinson 1919–83
English theologian and clergyman, Bishop of
Woolwich, 1959–69

13 Honest to God.
      title of book (1963), which argued that the
      imagery in which God was presented must
      change for the modern world; it became a
      bestseller

14 I think Lawrence tried to portray this [sex]
   relation as in a real sense an act of holy
   communion. For him flesh was
   sacramental of the spirit.
   *as defence witness in the case against Penguin
   Books for publishing* Lady Chatterley's Lover
      comment, 27 October 1960; see also **Griffith-
      Jones 139:4**

Mary Robinson 1944–
Irish Labour stateswoman; President 1990–97

1 Instead of rocking the cradle, they rocked the system.
in her victory speech, paying tribute to the women of Ireland
in *Times* 10 November 1990

Sugar Ray Robinson 1920–89
American boxer

when asked by the coroner if he had intended to 'get Doyle in trouble':
2 Mister, it's my *business* to get him in trouble.
following the death of Jimmy Doyle from his injuries after fighting Robinson, 24 June 1947
Sugar Ray Robinson with Dave Anderson *Sugar Ray* (1970)

Gene Roddenberry 1921–91
American film producer
see also **Misquotations 224:1, Misquotations 224:11**

3 These are the voyages of the starship *Enterprise*. Its five-year mission . . . to boldly go where no man has gone before.
Star Trek (television series, from 1966)

Andy Roddick 1982–
American tennis player

4 Maybe I'll just punch him or something.
on attempting to beat Roger Federer
quoted on news.bbc.co.uk, 3 July 2006

Anita Roddick 1942–
English businesswoman, who in 1976 opened a shop selling cosmetics sourced and produced with minimal harm to the environment; this developed into the Body Shop chain

5 I think that business practices would improve immeasurably if they were guided by 'feminine' principles—qualities like love and care and intuition.
Body and Soul (1991)

6 I watch where the cosmetics industry is going and then walk in the opposite direction.
quoted in *Harvard Business Review* 1 July 1996

7 Running a company on market research is like driving while looking in the rear view mirror.
in *Independent* 22 August 1997

Almiro Rodrigues 1932–
Portuguese judge, presiding at the War Crimes Tribunal in The Hague

8 Individually you agreed to evil.
sentencing the Bosnian Serb General Radislav Krstic for his part in the massacre of Bosnian Muslims at Srebenica in July 1995
at The Hague, 2 August 2001

Sue Rodriguez 1951–94
Canadian activist for the legalization of assisted suicide

9 If I cannot give consent to my own death, then whose body is this? Who owns my life?
appealing to a subcommittee of the Canadian Commons, November 1992, as the victim of a terminal illness
in *Globe and Mail* 5 December 1992

Theodore Roethke 1908–63
American poet

10 I have known the inexorable sadness of pencils,
Neat in their boxes, dolour of pad and paper-weight,
All the misery of manilla folders and mucilage,
Desolation in immaculate public places.
'Dolour' (1948)

11 The body and the soul know how to play
In that dark world where gods have lost their way.
'Four for Sir John Davies' (1953) no. 2

12 I wake to sleep, and take my waking slow.
I feel my fate in what I cannot fear.
I learn by going where I have to go.
The Waking (1953)

Will Rogers 1879–1935
American actor and humorist

13 There is only one thing that can kill the movies, and that is education.
Autobiography of Will Rogers (1949)

1 Income Tax has made more Liars out of the American people than Golf.
> *The Illiterate Digest* (1924) 'Helping the Girls with their Income Taxes'

2 Well, all I know is what I read in the papers.
> in *New York Times* 30 September 1923

3 Heroing is one of the shortest-lived professions there is.
> newspaper article, 15 February 1925, in Paula McSpadden Grove *The Will Rogers Book* (1961)

4 Communism is like prohibition, it's a good idea but it won't work.
> *Weekly Articles* (1981); first published 1927

5 You can't say civilization don't advance, however, for in every war they kill you in a new way.
> in *New York Times* 23 December 1929

6 Half our life is spent trying to find something to do with the time we have rushed through life trying to save.
> letter in *New York Times* 29 April 1930

Eleanor Roosevelt 1884–1962
American humanitarian and diplomat. She was the niece of Theodore **Roosevelt**, and married Franklin D. **Roosevelt** in 1905
on Roosevelt: see **Stevenson 304:13**

7 I cannot believe that war is the best solution. No one won the last war, and no one will win the next war.
> letter to Harry Truman, 22 March 1948

8 I have always felt that anyone who wanted an election so much that they would use those methods did not have the character that I really admired in public life.
> *on the tactics used by Richard **Nixon** in his 1950 Senatorial campaign against the actress and politician Helen Gahagan Douglas (see **Nixon 239:1**)*
> on 'Meet the Press' (NBC TV), 16 September 1956

9 No one can make you feel inferior without your consent.
> in *Catholic Digest* August 1960

Franklin D. Roosevelt 1882–1945
American Democratic statesman, 32nd President of the US 1933–45, cousin of Theodore **Roosevelt** and husband of Eleanor **Roosevelt**. His New Deal of 1933 helped to lift the US out of the Great Depression, and he played an important part in Allied policy during the Second World War; he died suddenly while still in office, and was succeeded by Harry **Truman**
on Roosevelt: see **Lippmann 200:10**

10 These unhappy times call for the building of plans that . . . build from the bottom up and not from the top down, that put their faith once more in the forgotten man at the bottom of the economic pyramid.
> radio address, 7 April 1932

11 I pledge you, I pledge myself, to a new deal for the American people.
> speech to the Democratic Convention in Chicago, 2 July 1932, accepting the presidential nomination

12 The only thing we have to fear is fear itself.
> inaugural address, 4 March 1933

13 In the field of world policy I would dedicate this Nation to the policy of the good neighbour.
> inaugural address, 4 March 1933

14 We face the arduous days that lie before us in the warm courage of national unity.
> inaugural address, 4 March 1933; see **Bush 49:4**

15 I have seen war. I have seen war on land and sea. I have seen blood running from the wounded. I have seen men coughing out their gassed lungs. I have seen the dead in the mud. I have seen cities destroyed. I have seen 200 limping, exhausted men come out of line—the survivors of a regiment of 1,000 that went forward 48 hours before. I have seen children starving. I have seen the agony of mothers and wives. I hate war.
> speech at Chautauqua, NY, 14 August 1936

16 I see one-third of a nation ill-housed, ill-clad, ill-nourished.
> second inaugural address, 20 January 1937

17 I am reminded of four definitions: A Radical is a man with both feet firmly planted—in the air. A Conservative is a man with two perfectly good legs who, however, has never learned to walk

forward. A Reactionary is a somnambulist walking backwards. A Liberal is a man who uses his legs and his hands at the behest—at the command—of his head.
radio address to New York Herald Tribune Forum, 26 October 1939

1 I have said this before, but I shall say it again and again and again: Your boys are not going to be sent into any foreign wars.
speech in Boston, 30 October 1940; see **Johnson 169:13**

2 We must be the great arsenal of democracy.
broadcast, 29 December 1940

3 We look forward to a world founded upon four essential human freedoms. The first is freedom of speech and expression— everywhere in the world. The second is freedom of every person to worship God in his own way—everywhere in the world. The third is freedom from want . . . The fourth is freedom from fear.
message to Congress, 6 January 1941

4 Yesterday, December 7, 1941—a date which will live in infamy—the United States of America was suddenly and deliberately attacked by naval and air forces of the Empire of Japan.
address to Congress, 8 December 1941

5 Books can not be killed by fire. People die, but books never die. No man and no force can abolish memory. No man and no force can put thought in a concentration camp forever. No man and no force can take from the world the books that embody man's eternal fight against tyranny of every kind. In this war, we know, books are weapons. And it is a part of your dedication always to make them weapons for man's freedom.
'Message to the Booksellers of America' 6 May 1942

6 It is fun to be in the same decade with you.
acknowledging congratulations on his 60th birthday
  cabled reply to Winston **Churchill**, *in W. S. Churchill The Hinge of Fate (1950)*

7 The work, my friend, is peace. More than an end of this war—an end to the

beginnings of all wars.
undelivered address for Jefferson Day, 13 April 1945 (the day after Roosevelt died)

Theodore Roosevelt 1858–1919
American Republican statesman, 26th President of the US 1901–9, cousin of Franklin **Roosevelt**; as Vice-President he had succeeded to office on the assassination of President McKinley

8 Speak softly and carry a big stick; you will go far.
quoting an 'old adage'
  speech in Chicago, 3 April 1903

9 A man who is good enough to shed his blood for the country is good enough to be given a square deal afterwards.
speech at the Lincoln Monument, Springfield, Illinois, 4 June 1903

10 The men with the muck-rakes are often indispensable to the well-being of society; but only if they know when to stop raking the muck.
speech in Washington, 14 April 1906

11 I have got such a bully pulpit!
his personal view of the presidency
  in Outlook (New York) 27 February 1909; see **Reagan 267:13**

12 It is not the critic who counts; not the man who points out how the strong man stumbles, or where the doer of deeds could have done better. The credit belongs to the man who is actually in the arena.
speech at the Sorbonne, Paris, 23 April 1910

13 We stand at Armageddon, and we battle for the Lord.
speech at the Republican National Convention, 18 June 1912

14 There is no room in this country for hyphenated Americanism.
rejecting the concept of dual nationality as expressed in terms such as 'German-American' and 'Irish-American'
  speech in New York, 12 October 1915

15 One of our defects as a nation is a tendency to use what have been called 'weasel words'. When a weasel sucks eggs the meat is sucked out of the egg. If you use a 'weasel word' after another, there is

nothing left of the other.
speech in St Louis, 31 May 1916

1 Foolish fanatics . . . the men who form the lunatic fringe in all reform movements.
Autobiography (1913)

Lord Rootes 1894–1964
English motor-car manufacturer

2 No other man-made device since the shields and lances of ancient knights fulfils a man's ego like an automobile.
attributed, 1958

Billy Rose 1899–1966
and **Marty Bloom**
American songwriters

3 Does the spearmint lose its flavour on the bedpost overnight?
revived in 1959 by Lonnie Donegan with the title 'Does your chewing-gum lose its flavour on the bedpost overnight?'
title of song (1924)

Charles Rosen 1927–
American pianist and writer

4 The music that survives is the music that musicians want to play. They perform it until it finds an audience.
Critical Entertainments: Music Old and New (2000)

Ethel Rosenberg 1916–53
and **Julius Rosenberg** 1918–53
American husband and wife; convicted of spying for the Russians and executed

5 We are innocent, as we have proclaimed and maintained from the time of our arrest. This is the whole truth. To forsake this truth is to pay too high a price even for the priceless gift of life—for life thus purchased we could not live out in dignity and self-respect.
petition for executive clemency, filed 9 January 1953

6 Ethel wants it made known that we are the first victims of American Fascism.
letter from Julius to his lawyer Emanuel Bloch before the execution, 19 June 1953

Joe Rosenthal 1911–2006
American photographer, noted for his award-winning picture of US Marines raising the flag at Iwo Jima

7 I took the photo. The Marines took Iwo Jima.
attributed in *New York Post* (online edition) 22 August 2006, obituary; see also **Anonymous 10:13**

Harold Ross 1892–1951
American journalist and editor of the *New Yorker*, 1925–51

8 The *New Yorker* will be the magazine which is not edited for the old lady in Dubuque.
James Thurber *The Years with Ross* (1959)

9 Who he?
frequent comment on manuscripts and proofs
Dale Kramer *Ross and The New Yorker* (1952)

Jean Rostand 1894–1977
French biologist

10 The biologist passes, the frog remains.
sometimes quoted as 'Theories pass. The frog remains', meaning that while theories may be discarded, the facts do not alter
Inquiétudes d'un Biologiste (1967)

11 To be adult is to be alone.
Pensées d'un biologiste (1954)

12 Kill a man, and you are an assassin. Kill millions of men, and you are a conqueror. Kill everyone, and you are a god.
Pensées d'un biologiste (1939)

Leo Rosten 1908–97
American writer and social scientist

13 Any man who hates dogs and babies can't be all bad.
*of W. C. **Fields**, and often attributed to him*
speech at Masquers' Club dinner, 16 February 1939; letter in *Times Literary Supplement* 24 January 1975

Philip Roth 1933–
American novelist

14 A Jewish man with parents alive is a fifteen-year-old boy, and will remain a fifteen-year-old boy until *they die*!
Portnoy's Complaint (1967)

1 Doctor, my doctor, what do you say, LET'S
PUT THE ID BACK IN YID!
Portnoy's Complaint (1967)

Johnny Rotten (John Lydon) 1956–
English singer and songwriter, member of the Sex
Pistols
on Rotten: see **Newspaper headlines 237:9**

2 I am an Anti-Christ
I am an anarchist.
'Anarchy in the UK' (1976 song)

3 We're so pretty, oh so pretty
We're vacant.
'Pretty Vacant' (1977 song)

4 If you accept the forms that be, then you're
doomed to your own ultimate blandness.
R. Palmer *Dancing in the Street; a rock and roll
history* (1996)

Matthew Rowbottom, Richard Stannard, and The Spice Girls
English songwriters and English pop singers

5 Yo I'll tell you what I want, what I really
really want
so tell me what you want, what you really
really want.
'Wannabe' (1996 song)

Helen Rowland 1875–1950
American writer

6 A husband is what is left of a lover, after
the nerve has been extracted.
A Guide to Men (1922)

7 The follies which a man regrets most, in his
life, are those which he didn't commit
when he had the opportunity.
A Guide to Men (1922)

Richard Rowland c.1881–1947
American film producer

8 The lunatics have taken charge of the
asylum.
*on the take-over of United Artists by Charles
Chaplin and others*
T. Ramsaye *A Million and One Nights* (1926)

J. K. Rowling 1965–
English novelist
on Rowling: see **Snicket 297:15**; see also **Film lines
113:4**

9 DUMBLEDORE: It is our choices, Harry, that
show what we truly are, far more than our
abilities.
Harry Potter and the Chamber of Secrets
(1998)

10 We are dealing with pure evil here. They
don't target extras, do they? They go for
the main characters. Well, I do.
interview, Channel 4 *Richard and Judy* 25 June
2006

Maude Royden 1876–1956
English religious writer

11 The Church [of England] should go
forward along the path of progress and be
no longer satisfied only to represent the
Conservative Party at prayer.
in *Times* 17 July 1917

Mike Royko 1932–97
American journalist

12 No self-respecting fish would be wrapped in
a Murdoch newspaper.
resigning from the Chicago Sun-Times *in 1984
when the paper was sold to Rupert **Murdoch***
Karl E. Meyer (ed.) *Pundits, Poets, and Wits*
(1990)

13 My only reaction to the Mona Lisa is the
thought that if she went into a singles bar,
she'd spend the entire evening buying her
own drinks.
quoted in *American National Biography*
(online edition, 2006)

Paul Alfred Rubens 1875–1917
English songwriter

14 Oh! we don't want to lose you but we think
you ought to go
For your King and your Country both need
you so.
'Your King and Country Want You' (1914 song);
see also **Military sayings 221:12**

Helena Rubinstein 1882–1965
Polish-born American beautician and businesswoman

> *on hearing that her rival Elizabeth **Arden** had had the tip of her index finger bitten off by a horse:*

1 What happened to the horse?
> quoted in *American National Biography* (online edition) 'Elizabeth Arden'

2 With my product and her packaging we could have ruled the world.
> *of Elizabeth **Arden***
> Lindy Woodhead *War Paint* (2003) ch. 6

Donald Rumsfeld 1932–
American Republican politician and businessman, US Defense Secretary 2001–6

3 Reports that say that something hasn't happened are always interesting to me, because as we know, there are known knowns; there are things we know we know. We also know there are known unknowns; that is to say we know there are some things we do not know. But there are also unknown unknowns—the ones we don't know we don't know.
> news briefing, February 2002; the statement won the Plain English Campaign's Foot in Mouth award

4 You're thinking of Europe as Germany and France. I don't. I think that's old Europe. If you look at the entire Nato Europe today, the centre of gravity is shifting to the east.
> *to journalists who asked him about European hostility to a possible war, 22 January 2003*
> in *Independent* 21 February 2003

5 Stuff happens.
> *on looting in Iraq*
> press conference, 11 April 2003

6 You go to war with the Army you have. They're not the Army you might want or wish to have at a later time.
> briefing to troops at a Town Hall Meeting in Kuwait, 8 December 2004

Robert Runcie 1921–2000
English Protestant clergyman; Archbishop of Canterbury 1980–91
on Runcie: see **Field 111:6**

7 People are mourning on both sides of this conflict. In our prayers we shall quite rightly remember those who are bereaved in our own country and the relations of the young Argentinian soldiers who were killed. Common sorrow could do something to reunite those who were engaged in this struggle. A shared anguish can be a bridge of reconciliation. Our neighbours are indeed like us.
> service of thanksgiving at the end of the Falklands war, St. Paul's Cathedral, London, 26 July 1982

8 In the middle ages people were tourists because of their religion, whereas now they are tourists because tourism is their religion.
> speech in London, 6 December 1988

9 It is part of an archbishop's task to prevent the Church trying to sting itself to death like a demented scorpion.
> quoted in *Tablet* 15 July 2000

Damon Runyon 1884–1946
American writer

10 'My boy,' he says, 'always try to rub up against money, for if you rub up against money long enough, some of it may rub off on you.'
> in *Cosmopolitan* August 1929, 'A Very Honourable Guy'

11 I do see her in tough joints more than somewhat.
> in *Collier's* 22 May 1930, 'Social Error'

12 I long ago come to the conclusion that all life is 6 to 5 against.
> in *Collier's* 8 September 1934, 'A Nice Price'

Salman Rushdie 1947–
Indian-born British novelist. His work, chiefly associated with magic realism, includes *Midnight's Children* (1981) and *The Satanic Verses* (1988). The latter, regarded by Muslims as blasphemous, caused Ayatollah **Khomeini** to issue a fatwa in 1989 condemning Rushdie to death (in 1998 the Iranian government dissociated itself from the fatwa)
on Rushdie: see **Khomeini 179:11**; see also **Advertising slogans 4:17**

13 Most of what matters in your life takes place in your absence.
> *Midnight's Children* (1981)

14 Family history, of course, has its proper dietary laws. One is supposed to swallow

and digest only the permitted parts of it, the halal portions of the past, drained of their redness, their blood.
Midnight's Children (1981)

1 What is freedom of expression? Without the freedom to offend, it ceases to exist.
in *Weekend Guardian* 10 February 1990

2 One of the things a writer is for is to say the unsayable, speak the unspeakable and ask difficult questions.
in *Independent on Sunday* 10 September 1995

Dean Rusk 1909–94
American politician; Secretary of State, 1961–9

3 We're eyeball to eyeball, and I think the other fellow just blinked.
on the Cuban missile crisis; on 28 October the Soviet Union agreed to dismantle and remove its missiles from Cuba
24 October 1962; in *Saturday Evening Post* 8 December 1962

4 Scratch any American and underneath you'll find an isolationist.
Tony Benn, diary, 12 January 1968

Bertrand Russell 1872–1970
British philosopher and mathematician

5 Three passions, simple but overwhelmingly strong, have governed my life: the longing for love, the search for knowledge, and unbearable pity for the suffering of mankind.
Autobiography (1967)

6 I was told that the Chinese said they would bury me by the Western Lake and build a shrine to my memory. I have some slight regret that this did not happen as I might have become a god, which would have been very *chic* for an atheist.
Autobiography (1968)

7 One of the symptoms of approaching nervous breakdown is the belief that one's work is terribly important, and that to take a holiday would bring all kinds of disaster.
The Conquest of Happiness (1930)

8 One should as a rule respect public opinion in so far as is necessary to avoid starvation and to keep out of prison, but anything that goes beyond this is voluntary submission to an unnecessary tyranny.
The Conquest of Happiness (1930)

9 A sense of duty is useful in work, but offensive in personal relations. People wish to be liked, not to be endured with patient resignation.
The Conquest of Happiness (1930)

10 Of all forms of caution, caution in love is perhaps the most fatal to true happiness.
The Conquest of Happiness (1930)

11 To be able to fill leisure intelligently is the last product of civilization.
The Conquest of Happiness (1930)

12 Aristotle maintained that women have fewer teeth than men; although he was twice married, it never occurred to him to verify this statement by examining his wives' mouths.
Impact of Science on Society (1952)

13 Work is of two kinds: first, altering the position of matter at or near the earth's surface relatively to other such matter; second, telling other people to do so. The first kind is unpleasant and ill paid; the second is pleasant and highly paid.
In Praise of Idleness and Other Essays (1986) title essay (1932)

14 The method of 'postulating' what we want has many advantages; they are the same as the advantages of theft over honest toil.
Introduction to Mathematical Philosophy (1919)

15 The fact that an opinion has been widely held is no evidence whatever that it is not utterly absurd; indeed in view of the silliness of the majority of mankind, a widespread belief is more likely to be foolish than sensible.
Marriage and Morals (1929)

16 Mathematics may be defined as the subject in which we never know what we are talking about, nor whether what we are saying is true.
Mysticism and Logic (1918)

17 Mathematics, rightly viewed, possesses not only truth, but supreme beauty—a beauty cold and austere, like that of sculpture.
Philosophical Essays (1910)

18 The man who has fed the chicken every day throughout its life at last wrings its neck instead, showing that a more refined view as to the uniformity of nature would

have been useful to the chicken.
The Problems of Philosophy (1912)

1 Every man, wherever he goes, is
encompassed by a cloud of comforting
convictions, which move with him like flies
on a summer day.
Sceptical Essays (1928) 'Dreams and Facts'

2 We have, in fact, two kinds of morality side
by side: one which we preach but do not
practise, and another which we practise
but seldom preach.
Sceptical Essays (1928) 'Eastern and Western
Ideals of Happiness'

3 The fundamental defect of fathers, in our
competitive society, is that they want their
children to be a credit to them.
Sceptical Essays (1928) 'Freedom versus
Authority in Education'

4 Machines are worshipped because they are
beautiful, and valued because they confer
power; they are hated because they are
hideous, and loathed because they impose
slavery.
Sceptical Essays (1928) 'Machines and
Emotions'

5 The infliction of cruelty with a good
conscience is a delight to moralists. That is
why they invented Hell.
Sceptical Essays (1928) 'On the Value of
Scepticism'

6 It is obvious that 'obscenity' is not a term
capable of exact legal definition; in the
practice of the Courts, it means 'anything
that shocks the magistrate'.
Sceptical Essays (1928) 'The Recrudescence of
Puritanism'

7 Man is a credulous animal, and must
believe *something*; in the absence of good
grounds for belief, he will be satisfied with
bad ones.
Unpopular Essays (1950) 'An Outline of
Intellectual Rubbish'

8 Fear is the main source of superstition, and
one of the main sources of cruelty.
Unpopular Essays (1950) 'An Outline of
Intellectual Rubbish'

9 'Change' is scientific, 'progress' is ethical;
change is indubitable, whereas progress is
a matter of controversy.
Unpopular Essays (1950) 'Philosophy and
Politics'

10 If I were to suggest that between the Earth
and Mars there is a china teapot revolving
about the sun in an elliptical orbit, nobody
would be able to disprove my assertion
provided I were careful to add that the
teapot is too small to be revealed even by
our most powerful telescopes. But if I were
to go on to say that, since my assertion
cannot be disproved, it is intolerable
presumption on the part of human reason
to doubt it, I should rightly be thought to
be talking nonsense.
'Is There a God?', commissioned (but not
published) by *The Illustrated Magazine*, 1952;
first published in *Collected Papers* vol. 11
(1997)

11 The linguistic philosophy, which cares
only about language, and not about the
world, is like the boy who preferred the
clock without the pendulum because,
although it no longer told the time, it went
more easily than before and at a more
exhilarating pace.
foreword to Ernest Gellner *Words and Things*
(1959)

12 All intellectuals should suffer a certain
amount of persecution as early in life as
possible. Not too much. That is bad for
them. But a certain amount.
Kenneth Harris *Kenneth Harris Talking To*
(1971) 'Bertrand Russell'

Dora Russell 1894–1986
English feminist, wife of Bertrand **Russell**

13 We want better reasons for having
children than not knowing how to prevent
them.
Hypatia (1925)

Ernest Rutherford 1871–1937
New Zealand physicist, regarded as the founder of
nuclear physics

14 All science is either physics or stamp
collecting.
J. B. Birks *Rutherford at Manchester* (1962)

15 If your experiment needs statistics, you
ought to have done a better experiment.
Norman T. J. Bailey *The Mathematical
Approach to Biology and Medicine* (1967)

16 It was quite the most incredible event that
has ever happened to me in my life. It was

almost as incredible as if you fired a
15-inch shell at a piece of tissue paper and
it came back and hit you.
*on the back-scattering effect of metal foil on
alpha-particles*
E. N. da C. Andrade *Rutherford and the Nature
of the Atom* (1964)

1 We haven't got the money, so we've got to
think!
in *Bulletin of the Institute of Physics* (1962)
vol. 13

Sue Ryder 1923–2000
British philanthropist. She co-founded an
organization to care for former inmates of
concentration camps, which expanded to provide
homes for the mentally and physically disabled

2 I don't look for reward. Surely, according
to God's judgement, our reward is when
we die. We are all pilgrims on this earth.
after her peerage was awarded in 1979
in *Daily Telegraph* 3 November 2000; obituary

3 Each place had its own individuality,
atmosphere and tradition—all foul, of
course.
of Nazi concentration camps
in *Daily Telegraph* 3 November 2000; obituary

Gilbert Ryle 1900–76
English philosopher

4 A myth is, of course, not a fairy story. It is
the presentation of facts belonging to one
category in the idioms appropriate to
another. To explode a myth is accordingly
not to deny the facts but to re-allocate
them.
The Concept of Mind (1949)

5 The dogma of the Ghost in the Machine.
the mind viewed as distinct from the body
The Concept of Mind (1949)

Martin Ryle 1918–84
English radio astronomer

6 I always multiply deadlines by pi.
*response to the reminder that the deadline for
the* Cambridge Encyclopedia of Astronomy *was
only two months away*
Derek Birdsall *Notes on Book Design* (2004)

S

Jonathan Sacks 1948–
British Chief Rabbi

1 Modernity is the transition from fate to choice.

'The Persistence of Faith' (Reith Lecture, 1990)

Vita Sackville-West 1892–1962
English writer and gardener; wife of Harold **Nicolson**

2 The greater cats with golden eyes
Stare out between the bars.

The King's Daughter (1929)

Anwar al-Sadat 1918–81
Egyptian statesman, President 1970–81, who visited Israel in 1977 and attended talks with Menachim Begin at Camp David in 1978, the year they shared the Nobel Peace Prize; he was assassinated by members of the Islamic Jihad

3 Peace is much more precious than a piece of land.

speech in Cairo, 8 March 1978

Carl Sagan 1934–96
American astronomer

4 If you wish to make an apple pie from scratch, you must first invent the universe.

Cosmos (1980)

5 The Universe is not obliged to conform to what we consider comfortable or plausible.

Pale Blue Dot (1995)

6 The visions we offer our children shape the future. It *matters* what those visions are. Often they become self-fulfilling prophecies. Dreams are maps.

Pale Blue Dot (1995)

7 Extraordinary claims require extraordinary evidence.

interview in *Nova* 1996

on an image of the earth seen from deep space:

8 This distant image . . . underscores our responsibility to deal more kindly and compassionately with one another and to preserve and cherish that pale blue dot, the only home we've ever known.

commencement address, 11 May 1996

Françoise Sagan 1935–2004
French novelist

9 To jealousy, nothing is more frightful than laughter.

La Chamade (1965)

Antoine de Saint-Exupéry 1900–44
French novelist and aviator, killed on active service

10 Grown-ups never understand anything for themselves, and it is tiresome for children to be always and forever explaining things to them.

The Little Prince (1943)

11 The thing that is important is the thing that is not seen.

The Little Prince (1943), spoken by the Little Prince

12 Experience shows us that love does not consist in gazing at each other but in looking together in the same direction.

Wind, Sand and Stars (1939)

Yves Saint Laurent 1936–
French couturier. Trained by Dior, he opened his own fashion house in 1962

13 I don't really like knees.

in *Observer* 3 August 1958

14 I have often said that I wish I had invented blue jeans: the most spectacular, the most practical, the most relaxed and

nonchalant. They have expression,
modesty, sex appeal, simplicity—all I hope
for in my clothes.
in *Ritz* no. 85 (1984)

Andrei Sakharov 1921–89
Russian nuclear physicist and civil rights
campaigner who helped to develop the Soviet
hydrogen bomb but campaigned against nuclear
proliferation; he was awarded the Nobel Peace Prize
in 1975 but was also sentenced to internal exile
1980–6

1 Every day I saw the huge material,
intellectual and nervous resources of
thousands of people being poured into the
creation of a means of total destruction,
something capable of annihilating all
human civilization. I noticed that the
control levers were in the hands of people
who, though talented in their own ways,
were cynical.
Sakharov Speaks (1974)

Saki (Hector Hugh Munro) 1870–1916
British short-story writer

2 'I must be going,' said Mrs Eggelby, in a
tone which had been thoroughly sterilised
of even perfunctory regret.
Beasts and Super-Beasts (1914) 'Clovis on
Parental Responsibilities'

3 Waldo is one of those people who would be
enormously improved by death.
Beasts and Super-Beasts (1914) 'The Feast of
Nemesis'

4 The people of Crete unfortunately make
more history than they can consume
locally.
Chronicles of Clovis (1911) 'The Jesting of
Arlington Stringham'

5 The cook was a good cook, as cooks go;
and as cooks go, she went.
Reginald (1904) 'Reginald on Besetting Sins'

J. D. Salinger 1919–
American novelist and short-story writer. He is best
known for his colloquial novel of adolescence *The
Catcher in the Rye* (1951)
see **Borrowed titles 40:7**

6 What really knocks me out is a book that,
when you're all done reading it, you wish
the author that wrote it was a terrific friend
of yours and you could call him up on the
phone whenever you felt like it.
The Catcher in the Rye (1951)

7 Sex is something I really don't understand
too hot. You never know *where* the hell you
are. I keep making up these sex rules for
myself, and then I break them right away.
The Catcher in the Rye (1951)

8 'You know that song "If a body catch a
body comin' through the rye"? I'd like—'
'It's "If a body *meet* a body coming
through the rye"!' old Phoebe said . . .
'I thought it was "If a body catch a
body",' I said.
The Catcher in the Rye (1951); see **Borrowed
titles 40:7**

Lord Salisbury 1893–1972
British Conservative politician

9 Too clever by half.
of Iain **Macleod**, *Colonial Secretary; the term
'too clever by half' had been applied by an
earlier Lord Salisbury (1830–1903) to Disraeli's
amendment on Disestablishment, 30 March
1868*
in the House of Lords, 7 March 1961

Alex Salmond 1954–
Scottish Nationalist politician

10 I do not want to be separate from anything.
I want for my country to be joined in
co-operation and mutual respect—on a
footing of equality—with all the nations of
Europe.
in *Scotsman* 27 November 1998

Anthony Sampson 1926–2004
British writer and journalist

11 A secret tome of *The Great and the Good* is
kept, listing everyone who has the right,
safe qualifications of worthiness,
soundness and discretion; and from this
tome came the stage army of committee
people.
Anatomy of Britain Today (1965)

12 Of all the legacies of empire, the most
dangerous is surely an immobile
bureaucracy which can perpetuate its own
interests and values, like those ancient
hierarchies which presided over declining
civilizations . . . As the British mandarins

reinforce their defences, awarding each other old imperial honours, do they hear any echoes from Castile or Byzantium?
The Changing Anatomy of Britain (1982)

Lord Samuel 1870–1963
British Liberal politician

1 A library is thought in cold storage.
A Book of Quotations (1947)

Paul A. Samuelson 1915–
American economist

2 The consumer, so it is said, is the king ... each is a voter who uses his money as votes to get the things done that he wants done.
Economics (8th ed., 1970)

Carl Sandburg 1878–1967
American poet

3 Hog Butcher for the World,
Tool Maker, Stacker of Wheat,
Player with Railroads and the Nation's
  Freight Handler;
Stormy, husky, brawling,
City of the Big Shoulders.
'Chicago' (1916)

4 When Abraham Lincoln was shovelled
  into the tombs,
he forgot the copperheads and the assassin
  ...
in the dust, in the cool tombs.
'Cool Tombs' (1918)

5 The fog comes
on little cat feet.
It sits looking
over harbour and city
on silent haunches
and then moves on.
'Fog' (1916)

6 Pile the bodies high at Austerlitz and
  Waterloo.
Shovel them under and let me work—
I am the grass; I cover all.
'Grass' (1918)

7 I tell you the past is a bucket of ashes.
'Prairie' (1918)

8 Little girl ... Sometime they'll give a war and nobody will come.
The People, Yes (1936); 'Suppose They Gave a War and No One Came?' was the title of a piece by Charlotte Keyes in *McCall's* October

1966; 'Suppose They Gave a War and Nobody Came?' was the title of a 1970 film; see **Ginsberg 133:2**

9 Poetry is the achievement of the synthesis of hyacinths and biscuits.
in *Atlantic Monthly* March 1923 'Poetry Considered'

10 Slang is a language that rolls up its sleeves, spits on its hands and goes to work.
in *New York Times* 13 February 1959

Henry 'Red' Sanders 1905–58
American football coach

11 Sure, winning isn't everything. It's the only thing.
in *Sports Illustrated* 26 December 1955; often attributed to the coach Vince **Lombardi**

George Santayana 1863–1952
Spanish-born philosopher and critic

12 Fanaticism consists in redoubling your effort when you have forgotten your aim.
The Life of Reason (1905)

13 Those who cannot remember the past are condemned to repeat it.
The Life of Reason (1905)

John Singer Sargent 1856–1925
American painter, best known for his portraiture in a style noted for its bold brushwork

14 Every time I paint a portrait I lose a friend.
N. Bentley and E. Esar *Treasury of Humorous Quotations* (1951)

Nicolas Sarkozy 1955–
French politician

15 I speak with real words. When someone shouts at a policeman, he's not just a youth, he's a lout, full stop.
on rioters
quoted in *Guardian* 11 November 2005

Leslie Sarony 1897–1985
British songwriter

16 Ain't it grand to be blooming well dead?
title of song (1932)

Ken Saro-Wiwa
see **Last words 191:1**

Nathalie Sarraute 1902–99
French novelist

1 Radio and television, to which we devote so many of the leisure hours once spent listening to parlour chatter and parlour music, have succeeded in lifting the manufacture of banality out of the sphere of handicraft and placed it in that of a major industry.
   in *Times Literary Supplement* 10 June 1960

Jean-Paul Sartre 1905–80
French philosopher, novelist, dramatist, and critic. A leading existentialist, he dealt in his work with the nature of human life and the structures of consciousness
on Sartre: see **de Gaulle 87:15**

2 When the rich wage war it's the poor who die.
   Le Diable et le bon Dieu (The Devil and the Good Lord, 1951)

3 Nothingness haunts being.
   L'Être et le néant (Being and Nothingness, 1943)

4 I am condemned to be free.
   L'Être et le néant (Being and Nothingness, 1943)

5 Hell is other people.
   Huis Clos (1944)

6 Like all dreamers, I mistook disenchantment for truth.
   Les Mots (The Words, 1964) 'Écrire'

7 I confused things with their names: that is belief.
   Les Mots (The Words, 1964) 'Écrire'

8 The poor don't know that their function in life is to exercise our generosity.
   Les Mots (The Words, 1964) 'Lire'

9 She believed in nothing; only her scepticism kept her from being an atheist.
   Les Mots (The Words, 1964) 'Lire'

10 Human life begins on the far side of despair.
   Les Mouches (1943)

11 Three o'clock is always too late or too early for anything you want to do.
   La Nausée (Nausea, 1938) 'Vendredi'

12 I hate victims who respect their executioners.
   Les Séquestrés d'Altona (The Condemned of Altona, 1960)

13 A writer must refuse, therefore, to allow himself to be transformed into an institution.
   refusing the Nobel Prize
   declaration read at Stockholm, 22 October 1964

14 The whole question boils down to knowing whether one is interested in talking about the flight of butterflies or the condition of the Jews.
   attributed

Siegfried Sassoon 1886–1967
English poet and novelist. He is known for his starkly realistic poems written while serving in the First World War, expressing his contempt for war leaders as well as compassion for his comrades

15 If I were fierce, and bald, and short of breath,
   I'd live with scarlet Majors at the Base,
   And speed glum heroes up the line to death.
   'Base Details' (1918)

16 Does it matter?—losing your sight? . . .
   There's such splendid work for the blind;
   And people will always be kind,
   As you sit on the terrace remembering
   And turning your face to the light.
   'Does it Matter?' (1918)

17 You are too young to fall asleep for ever;
   And when you sleep you remind me of the dead.
   'The Dug-Out' (1919)

18 Everyone suddenly burst out singing;
   And I was filled with such delight
   As prisoned birds must find in freedom.
   'Everyone Sang' (1919)

19 The song was wordless; the singing will never be done.
   'Everyone Sang' (1919)

20 'He's a cheery old card,' grunted Harry to Jack
   As they slogged up to Arras with rifle and pack.
   But he did for them both by his plan of attack.
   'The General' (1918)

1 Here was the world's worst wound. And
   here with pride
   'Their name liveth for ever' the Gateway
   claims.
   Was ever an immolation so belied
   As these intolerably nameless names?
   'On Passing the New Menin Gate' (1928); see
   Epitaphs 108:7

2 You smug-faced crowds with kindling eye
   Who cheer when soldier lads march by,
   Sneak home and pray you'll never know
   The hell where youth and laughter go.
   'Suicide in the Trenches' (1918)

3 I am making this statement as an act of
   wilful defiance of military authority,
   because I believe that the War is being
   deliberately prolonged by those who have
   the power to end it.
   'A Soldier's Declaration' addressed to his
   commanding officer and sent to the *Bradford
   Pioneer* July 1917; Stanley Jackson *The
   Sassoons* (1968)

Cicely Saunders 1916–2005
English doctor, founder of the modern hospice
movement

4 Deception is not as creative as truth. We do
   best in life if we look at it with clear eyes,
   and I think that applies to coming up to
   death as well.
   of the hospice movement
   in *Time* 5 September 1988

5 You matter because you are you, and you
   matter to the last moment of your life. We
   will do all that we can not only to help you
   die peacefully, but also to live until you die.
   quoted in Robert Twycross 'A Tribute to Dame
   Cicely Saunders', Memorial Service, 8 March
   2006

Dorothy L. Sayers 1893–1957
English novelist and dramatist. She is chiefly known
for her detective fiction featuring the amateur
detective Lord Peter Wimsey

6 I admit it is better fun to punt than to be
   punted, and that a desire to have all the
   fun is nine-tenths of the law of chivalry.
   Gaudy Night (1935)

7 I always have a quotation for everything—
   it saves original thinking.
   Have His Carcase (1932)

8 Perhaps it is no wonder that women were
   first at the Cradle and the Cross. They had
   never known a man like this man—there
   has never been such another . . . who
   never made jokes about them, never
   treated them either as 'The women, God
   help us', or 'The ladies, God bless them!'
   Unpopular Opinions (1946) 'The Human-Not-
   Quite-Human'

9 As I grow older and older,
   And totter towards the tomb,
   I find that I care less and less
   Who goes to bed with whom.
   'That's Why I Never Read Modern Novels', in
   Janet Hitchman *Such a Strange Lady* (1975)

10 Those who prefer their English sloppy
   have only themselves to thank if the
   advertisement writer uses his mastery of
   vocabulary and syntax to mislead their
   weak minds . . . The moral of all this . . . is
   that we have the kind of advertising we
   deserve.
   in *Spectator* 19 November 1937 'The
   Psychology of Advertising'

Sayings and slogans
see box overleaf

Gerald Scarfe 1936–
English caricaturist

11 I find a particular delight in taking the
   caricature as far as I can. It satisfies me to
   stretch the human frame about and
   recreate it and yet keep a likeness.
   Scarfe by Scarfe (1986)

Arthur Scargill 1938–
British trades-union leader

12 Parliament itself would not exist in its
   present form had people not defied the law.
   evidence to House of Commons Select
   Committee on Employment, 2 April 1980

Lord Scarman 1911–2004
British judge

13 A government above the law is a menace
   to be defeated.
   Why Britain Needs a Written Constitution
   (1992)

Sayings and slogans

1 *Ars gratia artis.*

Art for art's sake.
motto of Metro-Goldwyn-Mayer film studios,
apparently intended to say 'Art is beholden to
the artists'
> coined by American songwriter Howard
> Dietz (1896–1983), Bosley Crowthier *The*
> *Lion's Share* (1957); compare Benjamin
> Constant (1767–1834) *Journal intime* 11
> February 1804: '*L'art pour l'art* [Art for art's
> sake]'

2 Been there, done that, got the T-shirt.
> 'been there, done that' recorded from 1980s,
> expanded form from 1990s

3 Burn your bra.
> feminist slogan, 1970s

4 Business is like a car: it will not run by
itself except downhill.
> American saying

5 Children: one is one, two is fun, three is a
houseful.
> American saying

6 A committee is a group of the unwilling,
chosen from the unfit, to do the
unnecessary.
> various attributions (origin unknown)

7 A conservative is a liberal who's been
mugged.
> American saying, 1980s; see **Wolfe 340:16**

8 Crime doesn't pay.
> a slogan of the FBI and the cartoon detective
> Dick Tracy

9 [Death is] nature's way of telling you to
slow down.
> life insurance proverb; in *Newsweek* 25 April
> 1960

10 A dog is for life, not just for Christmas.
> slogan of the National Canine Defence
> League, now the Dogs Trust

11 Do not fold, spindle or mutilate.
> instruction on punched cards (1950s, and in
> differing forms from the 1930s)

12 Don't be evil.
> informal corporate motto of the search
> engine Google

13 The family that prays together stays
together.
> motto devised by Al Scalpone for the Roman
> Catholic Family Rosary Crusade, 1947

14 58% Don't Want Pershing.
> anti-nuclear weapons slogan on T-shirt worn
> by British fashion designer Katharine
> Hamnett (1952–) when she attended a
> drinks party at 10 Downing Street in 1984

15 Garbage in, garbage out.
> in computing, incorrect or faulty input will
> always cause poor output; origin of the
> acronym GIGO

16 Go to jail. Go directly to jail. Do not pass
go. Do not collect £200.
> instructions on 'Community Chest' card in
> the game 'Monopoly'; invented by Charles
> Brace Darrow (1889–1967) in 1931

17 If it ain't broke, don't fix it.
> Bert Lance (1931–), in *Nation's Business*
> May 1977

18 If you pay peanuts, you get monkeys.
> recorded from the mid 1960s, and most
> commonly associated with pay negotiations

19 I'm backing Britain.
> slogan coined by workers at the Colt factory,
> Surbiton, Surrey and subsequently used in a
> national campaign, in *Times* 1 January 1968

20 It takes 40 dumb animals to make a fur
coat, but only one to wear it.
> slogan of an anti-fur campaign poster,
> 1980s; sometimes attributed to David
> **Bailey**

21 Lousy but loyal.
> London East End slogan at **George V**'s
> Jubilee (1935)

22 Make love not war.
> student slogan, 1960s

23 Make poverty history.
> slogan of a campaign launched in 2005 by a
> coalition of charities and other groups to
> pressure governments to take action to
> reduce poverty

▶

> ▶ **Sayings and slogans** continued

1 Not in my name.
protesters against the war in Iraq, 2003

2 The opera ain't over 'til the fat lady sings.
Dan Cook, in *Washington Post* 3 June 1978

3 Pile it high, sell it cheap.
slogan coined by John Cohen (1898–1979), founder of Tesco

4 Save the whale.
environmental slogan associated with alarm over the rapidly declining whale population which led in 1985 to a moratorium on commercial whaling

5 There is one thing stronger than all the armies in the world; and that is an idea whose time has come.
in flyer for *Nation* 15 April 1943

6 There's no such thing as a free lunch.
colloquial axiom in US economics, from the 1960s, much associated with Milton **Friedman**; recorded in form 'there ain't no such thing as a free lunch' from 1938, which gave rise to the acronym TANSTAAFL in Robert **Heinlein**'s *The Moon is a Harsh Mistress* (1966)

7 Think globally, act locally.
Friends of the Earth slogan, *c.*1985

8 To err is human but to really foul things up requires a computer.
Farmers' Almanac for 1978 'Capsules of Wisdom'; referring to Alexander Pope (1688–1744) *An Essay on Criticism* (1711): 'To err is human; to forgive, divine'

9 We shall not be moved.
title of labour and civil rights song (1931) adapted from an earlier gospel hymn

10 We shall overcome.
title of song, originating from before the American Civil War, adapted as a Baptist hymn ('I'll Overcome Some Day', 1901) by C. A. Tindley; revived in 1946 as a protest song by black tobacco workers, and in 1963 during the black Civil Rights Campaign

11 What you see is what you get.
often shortened to the acronym *wysiwyg*, especially in computing

12 When the going gets tough, the tough get going.
attributed to Joseph P. **Kennedy**, and also to Knute Rockne (1888–1931)

13 A woman without a man is like a fish without a bicycle.
often attributed to Gloria **Steinem**, who was reported to have planned to wear a T-shirt with the slogan in *People* 26 July 1976. The slogan was adapted from Irina **Dunn**: see **Dunn 94:8**

Elsa Schiaparelli 1896–1973
Italian-born French fashion designer

14 The daring is gone. No one can dream any more.
on fashions after her last collection in 1954
Palmer White *Elsa Schiaparelli: Empress of Paris Fashion* (1986) ch. 22

Arthur M. Schlesinger Jr. 1917–2007
American historian

15 The answer to the runaway Presidency is not the messenger-boy Presidency. The American democracy must discover a middle way between making the President a czar and making him a puppet.
The Imperial Presidency (1973) preface

Moritz Schlick 1882–1936
German philosopher

16 The meaning of a proposition is the method of its verification.
in *Philosophical Review* (1936) vol. 45

Artur Schnabel 1882–1951
Austrian-born American pianist

17 I know two kinds of audiences only—one coughing, and one not coughing.
My Life and Music (1961)

18 Applause is a receipt, not a note of demand.
in *Saturday Review of Literature* 29 September 1951

1 The notes I handle no better than many pianists. But the pauses between the notes—ah, that is where the art resides!
  in *Chicago Daily News* 11 June 1958

Arnold Schoenberg 1874–1951
Austrian-born American composer and musical theorist

2 If it is art, it is not for the masses. 'If it is for the masses it is not art' is a topic which is rather similar to a word of yourself.
  letter to W. S. Schlamm, 1 July 1945

3 I am delighted to add another unplayable work to the repertoire. I want the Concerto to be difficult and I want the little finger to become longer. I can wait.
  of his Violin Concerto
    Joseph Machlis *Introduction to Contemporary Music* (1963)

4 There is nothing I long for more intensely than to be taken for a better sort of Tchaikovsky—for heaven's sake: a bit better, but really that's all. Or if anything more, that people should know my tunes and whistle them.
  H. H. Stuckenschmidt *Schoenberg: His Life, World, and Work* (1977, tr. H. Searle)

Patricia Schroeder 1940–
American Democratic politician

5 Ronald Reagan . . . is attempting a great breakthrough in political technology—he has been perfecting the Teflon-coated Presidency. He sees to it that nothing sticks to him.
  speech in the US House of Representatives, 2 August 1983

Budd Schulberg 1914–
American screenwriter and novelist
see also **Film lines 113:16**

6 What makes Sammy run?
  title of book (1941)

Charles Monroe Schulz 1922–2000
American cartoonist. He is remembered as the creator of the 'Peanuts' comic strip

7 Happiness is a warm puppy.
  title of book (1962); see **Advertising slogans 3:24, Ephron 106:1, Lennon 196:9**

E. F. Schumacher 1911–77
German-born British economist

8 Small is beautiful. A study of economics as if people mattered.
  title of book (1973)

9 Call a thing immoral or ugly, soul-destroying or a degradation of man, a peril to the peace of the world or to the well-being of future generations: as long as you have not shown it to be 'uneconomic' you have not really questioned its right to exist, grow, and prosper.
  Small is Beautiful (1973)

J. A. Schumpeter 1883–1950
Austrian-born American economist

10 The cold metal of economic theory is in Marx's pages immersed in such a wealth of steaming phrases as to acquire a temperature not naturally its own.
  Capitalism, Socialism and Democracy (1942)

11 Early in life I had three ambitions: to be the greatest economist in the world, the greatest horseman in Austria, and the best lover in Vienna. Well, in one of those goals I have failed.
  Richard Swedberg *Schumpeter: a Biography* (1991)

Delmore Schwartz 1913–66
American poet

12 Dogs are Shakespearean, children are strangers.
  Let Freud and Wordsworth discuss the child,
  Angels and Platonists shall judge the dog.
  'Dogs are Shakespearean, Children are Strangers' (1938)

13 The heavy bear who goes with me,
  A manifold honey to smear his face,
  Clumsy and lumbering here and there,
  The central ton of every place,
  The hungry beating brutish one
  In love with candy, anger, and sleep,
  Crazy factotum, dishevelling all,
  Climbs the building, kicks the football,
  Boxes his brother in the hate-ridden city.
  'The Heavy Bear Who Goes With Me' (1958)

H. Norman Schwarzkopf 1934–
American general, Commander-in-chief of Allied forces in the Gulf War, 1990–91

1 Seven months ago I could give a single command and 541,000 people would immediately obey it. Today I can't get a plumber to come to my house.
in *Newsweek* 11 November 1991; see **Truman 319:1**

Albert Schweitzer 1875–1965
German theologian, musician, and medical missionary, born in Alsace. In 1913 he qualified as a doctor and went as a missionary to Gabon, where he established a hospital

2 'Hullo! friend,' I call out, 'Won't you lend us a hand?' 'I am an intellectual and don't drag wood about,' came the answer. 'You're lucky,' I reply. 'I too wanted to become an intellectual, but I didn't succeed.'
More from the Primeval Forest (1931)

3 Late on the third day, at the very moment when, at sunset, we were making our way through a herd of hippopotamuses, there flashed upon my mind, unforeseen and unsought, the phrase, 'Reverence for Life'.
My Life and Thought (1933)

Kurt Schwitters 1887–1948
German-born artist and painter

4 I am a painter and I nail my pictures together.
R. Hausmann *Am Anfang war Dada* (1972)

5 A perambulator wheel, wire netting, string and cotton wool are factors having equal rights with paint. The artist creates through choice, distribution, and disassociation of the materials.
in *Der Sturm* November 1919

Felipe Scolari 1948–
Brazilian football coach, manager of Portugal

6 Now there is so much professionalism, we have to revert to urging players to like the game, love it, do it with joy.
on football
in *Times* 17 June 2006

C. P. Scott 1846–1932
British newspaper editor and proprietor; editor of the *Manchester Guardian*, 1872–1929

7 Comment is free, but facts are sacred.
in *Manchester Guardian* 5 May 1921; see **Stoppard 305:13**

8 *Television?* The word is half Greek, half Latin. No good can come of it.
Asa Briggs *The BBC: the First Fifty Years* (1985)

9 I have a useful knack of falling without hurting myself.
of continuing to cycle to the Manchester Guardian *offices into his eighties*
attributed; in *Oxford Dictionary of National Biography* (2004)

Robert Falcon Scott 1868–1912
English explorer. In 1910–12 Scott and four companions made a journey to the South Pole by sledge, arriving there in January 1912 to discover that Roald Amundsen had beaten them by a month. Scott and his companions died on the journey back to base
see also **Last words 190:4**

10 Great God! this is an awful place.
of the South Pole
diary, 17 January 1912

11 We took risks, we knew we took them; things have come out against us, and therefore we have no cause for complaint.
'The Last Message' in *Scott's Last Expedition* (1913)

George Seddon 1927–
Australian environmental scientist

12 The most important fact in the environmental history of Australia is that it had a radically new technology imposed upon it, suddenly, twice.
attributed; quoted in G. Davison, J. Hirst, and S. Macintyre (eds.) *Oxford Companion to Australian History* (2001)

Alan Seeger 1888–1916
American poet and soldier, killed in the First World War while fighting with the French Foreign Legion

13 I have a rendezvous with Death At some disputed barricade.
'I Have a Rendezvous with Death' (1916)

1 This experience will teach me the
sweetness and worth of the common
things of life.
> letter to his mother from the Western Front,
> quoted in *American National Biography*
> (online edition)

Pete Seeger 1919–
American folk singer and songwriter

2 Where have all the flowers gone?
> title of song (1961)

Erich Segal
see **Taglines for films 309:9**

Emilio Segrè 1905–89
Italian-born American physicist

3 Fermi was a steamroller that moved
slowly, but knew no obstacles.
> *of the physicist Enrico* **Fermi**
> quoted in in *American National Biography*
> (online edition) 'Enrico Fermi'

Arthur Seldon 1916–2005
British economist, co-founder of the Institute for
Economic Affairs

4 Government of the busy by the bossy for
the bully.
> *on over-government*
> *Capitalism* (1990)

W. C. Sellar 1898–1951
and R. J. Yeatman 1898–1968
British writers

5 1066 and all that.
> title of book (1930)

6 History is not what you thought. *It is what
you can remember.*
> *1066 and All That* (1930) 'Compulsory Preface'

7 The Cavaliers (Wrong but Wromantic) and
the Roundheads (Right but Repulsive).
> *1066 and All That* (1930)

8 The National Debt is a very Good Thing
and it would be dangerous to pay it off, for
fear of Political Economy.
> *1066 and All That* (1930)

9 AMERICA was thus clearly top nation, and
History came to a .
> *1066 and All That* (1930)

John Sentamu 1949–
Uganda-born Anglican cleric, Archbishop of York
from 2005

> *referring to Archbishop Michael* **Ramsey**'s *words*
> '*I should love to think of a black Archbishop of
> York holding a mission here*':
10 Well here I am, and you have already
acknowledged that fact!
> sermon preached at his Inauguration as
> Archbishop of York, 30 November 2005; see
> also **Ramsey 266:2**

Gitta Sereny 1923–
Hungarian-born British writer and journalist

> *to the German architect and Nazi government
> official Albert Speer, who having always denied
> knowledge of the Holocaust had said that he
> was at fault in having 'looked away':*
11 You cannot look away from something
you don't know. If you looked away, then
you knew.
> recalled on BBC2 *Reputations*, 2 May 1996

Nicholas Serota 1946–
British art expert, Director of the Tate Gallery

12 This is a plea for patience. Your scepticism
will gradually diminish and your fear will
turn to love . . . All art was modern once.
> *to critics of modern art*
> in *Independent* 26 November 2000

Robert W. Service 1874–1958
British-born Canadian poet and novelist, known as
the 'Poet of the Yukon'

13 A promise made is a debt unpaid, and the
trail has its own stern code.
> 'The Cremation of Sam McGee' (1907)

14 Ah! the clock is always slow;
It is later than you think.
> 'It Is Later Than You Think' (1921)

15 This is the law of the Yukon, that only the
Strong shall thrive;
That surely the Weak shall perish, and
only the Fit survive.
> 'The Law of the Yukon' (1907)

16 Back of the bar, in a solo game, sat
Dangerous Dan McGrew,
And watching his luck was his light-
o'-love, the lady that's known as Lou.
> 'The Shooting of Dan McGrew' (1907)

Vikram Seth 1952–
Indian writer

1 I do need your help. Getting you married is not easy.
   A Suitable Boy (1993)

Anne Sexton 1928–74
American poet; she committed suicide

2 I was tired of being a woman,
   tired of the spoons and the pots,
   tired of my mouth and my breasts
   tired of the cosmetics and silks . . .
   I was tired of the gender of things.
   'Consorting with angels' (1967)

3 God owns heaven
   but He craves the earth.
   'The Earth' (1975)

4 My sleeping pill is white.
   It is a splendid pearl;
   it floats me out of myself,
   my stung skin as alien
   as a loose bolt of cloth.
   'Lullaby' (1960)

5 In a dream you are never eighty.
   'Old' (1962)

6 But suicides have a special language.
   Like carpenters they want to know *which
   tools*.
   They never ask *why build*.
   'Wanting to Die' (1966)

Peter Shaffer 1926–
English dramatist

7 The Normal is the good smile in a child's
   eyes—all right. It is also the dead stare in a
   million adults. It both sustains and kills—
   like a God. It is the Ordinary made
   beautiful; it is also the Average made
   lethal.
   Equus (1983 ed.)

Bill Shankly 1914–81
Scottish footballer and football manager, manager
of Liverpool 1960–74

8 Some people think football is a matter of life
   and death . . . I can assure them it is much
   more serious than that.
   in *Guardian* 24 December 1973

Ariel Sharon 1928–
Israeli general and Likud statesman, Prime Minister
2001–6

9 I'm not going to make any compromise
   whatsoever.
   on relations with the Palestinians
      in *Sunday Times* 12 August 2001

William Shatner 1931–
American actor, 'Captain Kirk' in *Star Trek*

10 Get a life!
   to Star Trek fans on Saturday Night Live, *1986*
   William Shatner *Get a Life!* (1999)

George Bernard Shaw 1856–1950
Irish dramatist and writer, whose plays such as *Man
and Superman* (1903), *Pygmalion* (1913), and *St
Joan* (1923) combine comedy with a questioning of
conventional morality and thought; a socialist, he
became an active member of the Fabian Society
on Shaw: see **Agate 5:17, Lenin 196:5, Taylor 310:9**;
see also **Catchphrases 58:5**

11 You see things; and you say 'Why?' But I
   dream things that never were; and I say
   'Why not?'
   Back to Methuselah (1921)

12 I enjoy convalescence. It is the part that
   makes illness worth while.
   Back to Methuselah (1921)

13 Life is not meant to be easy, my child; but
   take courage: it can be delightful.
   Back to Methuselah (rev. ed., 1930); see also
   Fraser 122:12

14 The British soldier can stand up to
   anything except the British War Office.
   The Devil's Disciple (1901)

15 There is at bottom only one genuinely
   scientific treatment for all diseases, and
   that is to stimulate the phagocytes.
   The Doctor's Dilemma (1911)

16 All professions are conspiracies against the
   laity.
   The Doctor's Dilemma (1911)

17 Parentage is a very important profession,
   but no test of fitness for it is ever imposed in
   the interest of the children.
   Everybody's Political What's What? (1944)

1 A government which robs Peter to pay Paul can always depend on the support of Paul.
Everybody's Political What's What? (1944)

2 The captain is in his bunk, drinking bottled ditch-water; and the crew is gambling in the forecastle. She will strike and sink and split. Do you think the laws of God will be suspended in favour of England because you were born in it?
Heartbreak House (1919)

3 The greatest of evils and the worst of crimes is poverty.
Major Barbara (1907) preface

4 I am a Millionaire. That is my religion.
Major Barbara (1907)

5 I can't talk religion to a man with bodily hunger in his eyes.
Major Barbara (1907)

6 Wot prawce Selvytion nah?
Major Barbara (1907)

7 Alcohol is a very necessary article . . . It enables Parliament to do things at eleven at night that no sane person would do at eleven in the morning.
Major Barbara (1907)

8 Nothing is ever done in this world until men are prepared to kill one another if it is not done.
Major Barbara (1907)

9 But a lifetime of happiness! No man alive could bear it: it would be hell on earth.
Man and Superman (1903)

10 Of all human struggles there is none so treacherous and remorseless as the struggle between the artist man and the mother woman.
Man and Superman (1903)

11 Hell is full of musical amateurs: music is the brandy of the damned.
Man and Superman (1903)

12 Englishmen never will be slaves: they are free to do whatever the Government and public opinion allow them to do.
Man and Superman (1903)

13 In the arts of peace Man is a bungler.
Man and Superman (1903)

14 When the military man approaches, the world locks up its spoons and packs off its womankind.
Man and Superman (1903)

15 There are two tragedies in life. One is not to get your heart's desire. The other is to get it.
Man and Superman (1903)

16 The golden rule is that there are no golden rules.
Man and Superman (1903) 'Maxims for Revolutionists: The Golden Rule'

17 Democracy substitutes election by the incompetent many for appointment by the corrupt few.
Man and Superman (1903) 'Maxims: Democracy'

18 Liberty means responsibility. That is why most men dread it.
Man and Superman (1903) 'Maxims: Liberty and Equality'

19 He who can, does. He who cannot, teaches.
Man and Superman (1903) 'Maxims: Education'

20 Marriage is popular because it combines the maximum of temptation with the maximum of opportunity.
Man and Superman (1903) 'Maxims: Marriage'

21 If you strike a child take care that you strike it in anger, even at the risk of maiming it for life. A blow in cold blood neither can nor should be forgiven.
Man and Superman (1903) 'Maxims: How to Beat Children'

22 Youth, which is forgiven everything, forgives itself nothing: age, which forgives itself everything, is forgiven nothing.
Man and Superman (1903) 'Maxims: Stray Sayings'

23 Take care to get what you like or you will be forced to like what you get.
Man and Superman (1903) 'Maxims: Stray Sayings'

24 Anarchism is a game at which the police can beat you.
Misalliance (1914)

1 You'll never have a quiet world till you knock the patriotism out of the human race.
O'Flaherty V.C. (1919)

2 A perpetual holiday is a good working definition of hell.
Parents and Children (1914) 'Children's Happiness'

3 It is impossible for an Englishman to open his mouth without making some other Englishman hate or despise him.
Pygmalion (1916) preface

4 Remember that you are a human being with a soul and the divine gift of articulate speech: that your native language is the language of Shakespeare and Milton and The Bible; and don't sit there crooning like a bilious pigeon.
Pygmalion (1916)

5 I don't want to talk grammar, I want to talk like a lady.
Pygmalion (1916)

6 I'm one of the undeserving poor . . . up agen middle-class morality all the time . . . What is middle-class morality? Just an excuse for never giving me anything.
Pygmalion (1916)

7 Gin was mother's milk to her.
Pygmalion (1916)

8 Walk! Not bloody likely.
Pygmalion (1916)

9 No Englishman is ever fairly beaten.
Saint Joan (1924)

10 Must then a Christ perish in torment in every age to save those that have no imagination?
Saint Joan (1924)

11 Assassination is the extreme form of censorship.
The Showing-Up of Blanco Posnet (1911) 'Limits to Toleration'

12 The photographer is like the cod which produces a million eggs in order that one may reach maturity.
introduction to the catalogue for Alvin Langdon Coburn's exhibition at the Royal Photographic Society, 1906; Bill Jay and Margaret Moore *Bernard Shaw and Photography* (1989)

13 You always hide just in the middle of the limelight.
to T. E. **Lawrence**, who had complained of Press attention
reported in Count Harry Kessler diary 14 November 1929, in *Diaries of a Cosmopolitan 1918–1937* (1971); see also **Berners 31:7**

14 The trouble, Mr Goldwyn, is that you are only interested in art and I am only interested in money.
telegraphed version of the outcome of a conversation between Shaw and Sam **Goldwyn**
A. Johnson *The Great Goldwyn* (1937)

replying to a lady's proposal 'You have the greatest brain in the world, and I have the most beautiful body; so we ought to produce the most perfect child':
15 What if the child inherits my body and your brains?
Hesketh Pearson *Bernard Shaw* (1942)

16 [Dancing is] a perpendicular expression of a horizontal desire.
in *New Statesman* 23 March 1962; attributed

17 England and America are two countries divided by a common language.
attributed in this and other forms, but not found in Shaw's published writings

Hartley Shawcross 1902–2003
British lawyer and Labour politician, Attorney General 1945–51
see also **Misquotations 225:5**

18 I don't think it was right. It was victors' justice.
of the Nuremberg trials, at which he appeared for the prosecution
interviewed on his 95th birthday, in *Daily Telegraph* 10 February 1997

Patrick Shaw-Stewart 1888–1917
English poet, killed in action

19 I saw a man this morning
Who did not wish to die;
I ask and cannot answer
If otherwise wish I.
written 1916; M. Baring *Have You Anything to Declare?* (1936)

20 Stand in the trench, Achilles,
Flame-capped, and shout for me.
written 1916; M. Baring *Have You Anything to Declare?* (1936)

Burt Shevelove 1915–82
and **Larry Gelbart** ?1928–
American writers

1 A funny thing happened on the way to the
Forum.
title of musical (1962)

Carol Shields 1935–2003
American-born Canadian novelist and poet

2 To be like everyone else. Isn't that what we
all want in the end?
Larry's Party (1997)

3 Canada is . . . a country always dressed in
its Sunday go-to-meeting clothes. A
country you wouldn't ask to dance a
second waltz. Clean. Christian. Dull.
Quiescent. But growing.
The Stone Diaries (1993)

4 When we say a thing or an event is real,
never mind how suspect it sounds, we
honour it. But when a thing is made
up—regardless of how true and just it
seems—we turn up our noses.
The Stone Diaries (1995)

Mikhail Sholokhov 1905–84
Russian novelist

5 And quiet flows the Don.
title of novel (1934), describing the impact of
the First World War, revolution, and civil war
on Cossack life

Clare Short 1946–
British Labour politician

6 It will be golden elephants next.
*suggesting that the government of Montserrat
was 'talking mad money' in claiming assistance
for evacuating the island after a volcanic
eruption*
in *Observer* 24 August 1997

7 Reckless with our government; reckless
with his own future, position and place in
history. It's extraordinarily reckless.
*when asked if she thought that Tony **Blair** was
acting recklessly on Iraq*
in an interview on *Westminster Hour* (BBC
Radio 4), 9 March 2003

Alexandra Shulman 1957–
British journalist

8 I long for the day when a new generation
of Anita Roddicks can address the AGM in
a bright pink dress and strappy sandals.
in *Sunday Times* 23 May 1999

Jean Sibelius 1865–1957
Finnish composer

9 Remember, a statue has never been set up
in honour of a critic!
Bengt de Törne *Sibelius: A Close-Up* (1937)

Maurice Sigler 1901–61
and **Al Hoffman** 1902–60
American songwriters

10 Little man, you've had a busy day.
title of song (1934)

Jim Sillars 1937–
Scottish Nationalist politician

11 I think the greatest problem we have is that
we will sing Flower of Scotland at
Hampden or Murrayfield, and that we
have too many 90-minute patriots.
*Roy **Williamson**'s 'O Flower of Scotland' is
regarded as an unofficial Scottish Nationalist
anthem*
interview on Scottish Television, 23 April 1992

Alan Sillitoe 1928–
English writer, noted for his novels about working-
class provincial life

12 The loneliness of the long-distance runner.
title of novel (1959)

Frank Silver 1892–1960
and **Irving Cohn** 1898–1961
American songwriters

13 Yes! we have no bananas,
We have no bananas today.
'Yes! We Have No Bananas' (1923 song)

Georges Simenon 1903–89
Belgian-born French novelist, best known for his
series of detective novels featuring Commissaire
Maigret

14 Writing is not a profession but a vocation
of unhappiness.
interview in *Paris Review* Summer 1955

Neil Simon 1927–
American dramatist

1 I *love* living. I have some problems with my *life*, but living is the best thing they've come up with so far.
   Last of the Red Hot Lovers (1970)

Paul Simon 1942–
American singer and songwriter

2 Like a bridge over troubled water
   I will lay me down.
   'Bridge over Troubled Water' (1970 song)

3 And here's to you, Mrs Robinson
   Jesus loves you more than you will know.
   'Mrs Robinson' (1967 song, from the film *The Graduate*)

4 People talking without speaking
   People hearing without listening . . .
   'Fools,' said I, 'You do not know
   Silence like a cancer grows.'
   'Sound of Silence' (1964 song)

5 Still crazy after all these years.
   title of song (1975)

6 Improvisation is too good to leave to chance.
   in *International Herald Tribune* 12 October 1990

Kirke Simpson 1881–1972
American journalist

7 [Warren] Harding of Ohio was chosen by a group of men in a smoke-filled room early today as Republican candidate for President.
   often attributed to Harry Daugherty, one of Harding's supporters, who appears merely to have concurred with this version of events, when pressed for comment by Simpson
   news report, filed 12 June 1920; W. Safire *New Language of Politics* (1968)

O. J. Simpson 1947–
American football player and actor

8 Fame vaporizes, money goes with the wind, and all that's left is character.
   Juice: O. J. Simpson's Life (1977)

Frank Sinatra
see **Paul Anka 9:9**

Upton Sinclair 1878–1968
American novelist and social reformer

9 It is difficult to get a man to understand something when his salary depends on his not understanding it.
   I, Candidate for Governor (1935)

Manmohan Singh 1932–
Indian statesman, Prime Minister since 2004

10 No one can make India kneel.
   after the bombings in Mumbai
   in *Hindu* 12 July 2006

C. H. Sisson 1914–2003
English poet

11 Here lies a civil servant. He was civil
   To everyone, and servant to the devil.
   The London Zoo (1961)

Edith Sitwell 1887–1964
English poet and critic, sister of Osbert **Sitwell**
on Sitwell: see **Bowen 41:15**

12 Jane, Jane,
   Tall as a crane,
   The morning light creaks down again.
   Façade (1923) 'Aubade'

13 Still falls the Rain—
   Dark as the world of man, black as our loss—
   Blind as the nineteen hundred and forty nails
   Upon the Cross.
   'Still Falls the Rain' (1942)

14 I enjoyed talking to her, but thought *nothing* of her writing. I considered her 'a beautiful little knitter'.
   of Virginia **Woolf**
   letter to Geoffrey Singleton, 11 July 1955

Osbert Sitwell 1892–1969
English writer, brother of Edith **Sitwell**

15 On the coast of Coromandel
   Dance they to the tunes of Handel.
   'On the Coast of Coromandel' (1943)

1 *Educ*: during the holidays from Eton.
   entry in *Who's Who* (1929)

'Red' Skelton 1913–97
American actor and comedian

2 Well, it only proves what they always
   say—give the public something they want
   to see, and they'll come out for it.
   on crowds attending the funeral of Harry Cohn
   comment, on 2 March 1958; Bob Thomas *King
   Cohn* (1967)

B. F. Skinner 1904–90
American psychologist

3 The real question is not whether machines
   think but whether men do.
   Contingencies of Reinforcement (1969)

4 Education is what survives when what has
   been learned has been forgotten.
   in *New Scientist* 21 May 1964

Gillian Slovo 1952–
South African writer

5 In most families it is the children who leave
   home. In mine it was the parents.
   *of her anti-apartheid activist parents, Joe Slovo
   and Ruth First*
   Every Secret Thing (1997)

Alfred Emanuel Smith 1873–1944
American Democratic politician, presidential
candidate in 1928, defeated by Herbert **Hoover**

6 All the ills of democracy can be cured by
   more democracy.
   speech in Albany, 27 June 1933

7 No sane local official who has hung up
   an empty stocking over the municipal
   fireplace, is going to shoot Santa Claus
   just before a hard Christmas.
   on the New Deal
   in *New Outlook* December 1933

Delia Smith
English cookery expert

8 A hen's egg is, simply, a work of art, a
   masterpiece of design, construction, and
   brilliant packaging.
   Delia Smith's How to Cook (1998)

Dodie Smith 1896–1990
English novelist and dramatist

9 The family—that dear octopus from whose
   tentacles we never quite escape.
   Dear Octopus (1938)

F. E. Smith, Lord Birkenhead
1872–1930
British lawyer and Conservative politician
on Smith: see **Chesterton 64:5**

10 The world continues to offer glittering
   prizes to those who have stout hearts and
   sharp swords.
   Rectorial Address, Glasgow University, 7
   November 1923

11 JUDGE: You are extremely offensive, young
   man.
   SMITH: As a matter of fact, we both are, and
   the only difference between us is that I am
   trying to be, and you can't help it.
   2nd Earl of Birkenhead *Earl of Birkenhead*
   (1933)

Godfrey Smith 1926–
English journalist and columnist

12 In a world full of audio visual marvels, may
   words matter to you and be full of magic.
   letter to a new grandchild, in *Sunday Times*
   5 July 1987

Iain Duncan Smith 1954–
British Conservative politician, Leader of the
Conservative Party 2001–3

13 Do not underestimate the determination of
   a quiet man.
   speech to the Conservative Party Conference,
   10 October 2002

Ian Smith 1919–
Rhodesian statesman, Prime Minister of Rhodesia
(now Zimbabwe) 1964–79

14 I don't believe in black majority rule in
   Rhodesia—not in a thousand years.
   broadcast speech, 20 March 1976

Linda Smith 1958–2006
British comedian

15 I'm a dyslexic Satanist; I worship the
   drivel.
   in *Daily Telegraph* (obituary), 1 March 2006

1 I play all my country and western music backwards. Your lover returns, your dog comes back to life and you cease to be an alcoholic.
   in *Daily Telegraph* (obituary), 1 March 2006

Logan Pearsall Smith 1865–1946
American-born man of letters

2 What music is more enchanting than the voices of young people, when you can't hear what they say?
   Afterthoughts (1931) 'Age and Death'

3 A best-seller is the gilded tomb of a mediocre talent.
   Afterthoughts (1931) 'Art and Letters'

4 People say that life is the thing, but I prefer reading.
   Afterthoughts (1931) 'Myself'

Stevie Smith 1902–71
English poet and novelist

5 Oh I am a cat that likes to
   Gallop about doing good.
   'The Galloping Cat' (1972)

6 Why does my Muse only speak when she is
      unhappy?
   She does not, I only listen when I am
      unhappy
   When I am happy I live and despise writing
   For my Muse this cannot but be dispiriting.
   'My Muse' (1964)

7 I was much too far out all my life
   And not waving but drowning.
   'Not Waving but Drowning' (1957)

8 People who are always praising the past
   And especially the times of faith as best
   Ought to go and live in the Middle Ages
   And be burnt at the stake as witches and
      sages.
   'The Past' (1957)

9 This Englishwoman is so refined
   She has no bosom and no behind.
   'This Englishwoman' (1937)

10 I long for the Person from Porlock
   To bring my thoughts to an end,
   I am growing impatient to see him
   I think of him as a friend.
   'Thoughts about the "Person from Porlock" '
   (1962); referring to Samuel Taylor Coleridge
   (1772–1834) 'Kubla Khan' (1816) preliminary

note: 'At this moment he was unfortunately called out by a person on business from Porlock'

11 A good time was had by all.
   title of book (1937)

12 If there wasn't death, I think you couldn't go on.
   in *Observer* 9 November 1969

Jan Christiaan Smuts 1870–1950
South African soldier and statesman, Prime Minister 1919–24 and 1939–48. He led Boer forces during the Second Boer War, but afterwards supported the policy of Anglo-Boer cooperation

13 Mankind is once more on the move. The very foundations have been shaken and loosened, and things are again fluid. The tents have been struck, and the great caravan of humanity is once more on the march.
   on the setting up of the League of Nations, in the wake of the First World War
   W. K. Hancock *Smuts* (1968)

John Snagge 1904–96
English sports commentator

14 I can't see who's in the lead but it's either Oxford or Cambridge.
   commentary on the 1949 Boat Race
   C. Dodd *Oxford and Cambridge Boat Race* (1983)

Lemony Snicket (Daniel Handler)
1970–
American writer

15 I wouldn't stoop to giving advice to anyone who lives in a castle in Scotland. I think the last people to give someone like that advice were the witches in Macbeth and they didn't come out so well.
   declining an offer to advise J. K. **Rowling** *on how best to end her Harry Potter series*
   quoted in *Ottawa Citizen* 26 December 2006

C. P. Snow 1905–80
English novelist and scientist, best known for his sequence of eleven novels *Strangers and Brothers*, which deals with moral dilemmas in the academic world

16 The official world, the corridors of power.
   Homecomings (1956)

1 The two cultures and the scientific revolution.
  title of The Rede Lecture (1959)

2 The great edifice of modern physics goes up, and the majority of the cleverest people in the western world have about as much insight into it as their neolithic ancestors would have had.
  The Two Cultures (1959)

Alexander Solzhenitsyn 1918–

Russian novelist. He spent eight years in a labour camp for criticizing Stalin and began writing on his release. From 1963 his books were banned in the Soviet Union, and he was exiled in 1974, eventually returning to Russia in 1994

3 If decade after decade the truth cannot be told, each person's mind begins to roam irretrievably. One's fellow countrymen become harder to understand than Martians.
  Cancer Ward (1968)

4 You only have power over people as long as you don't take *everything* away from them. But when you've robbed a man of *everything* he's no longer in your power— he's free again.
  The First Circle (1968)

5 The Gulag archipelago.
  title of book (1973–5)

6 Work was like a stick. It had two ends. When you worked for the knowing you gave them quality; when you worked for a fool you simply gave him eyewash.
  One Day in the Life of Ivan Denisovich (1962)

7 How can you expect a man who's warm to understand one who's cold?
  One Day in the Life of Ivan Denisovich (1962)

8 After the suffering of decades of violence and oppression, the human soul longs for higher things, warmer and purer than those offered by today's mass living habits, introduced as by a calling card by the revolting invasion of commercial advertising, by TV stupor and by intolerable music.
  speech in Cambridge, Massachusetts, 8 June 1978

9 The Iron Curtain did not reach the ground and under it flowed liquid manure from the West.
  speaking at Far Eastern Technical University, Vladivostok, 30 May 1994; see **Churchill 68:8**

Anastasio Somoza 1925–80

Nicaraguan statesman, President 1967–79. His dictatorial regime was overthrown by the Sandinistas and he was assassinated while in exile in Paraguay

10 You won the elections, but I won the count.
  replying to an accusation of ballot-rigging
  in *Guardian* 17 June 1977

Stephen Sondheim 1930–

American songwriter

11 I like to be in America!
  OK by me in America!
  Ev'rything free in America
  For a small fee in America!
  'America' (1957 song), from *West Side Story*

12 Everything's coming up roses.
  title of song (1959), from *Gypsy*

13 A toast to that invincible bunch
  The dinosaurs surviving the crunch
  Let's hear it for the ladies who lunch.
  'The Ladies who Lunch' (1970), from *Company*

14 Send in the clowns.
  title of song (1973), from *A Little Night Music*

Susan Sontag 1933–2004

American writer and critic

15 What pornography is really about, ultimately, isn't sex but death.
  in *Partisan Review* Spring 1967

16 The white race *is* the cancer of human history, it is the white race, and it alone— its ideologies and inventions—which eradicates autonomous civilizations wherever it spreads, which has upset the ecological balance of the planet, which now threatens the very existence of life itself.
  in *Partisan Review* Winter 1967

17 The camera makes everyone a tourist in other people's reality, and eventually in one's own.
  in *New York Review of Books* 18 April 1974

1 Illness is the night-side of life, a more
onerous citizenship. Everyone who is born
holds dual citizenship, in the kingdom of
the well and in the kingdom of the sick.
in *New York Review of Books* 26 January 1978

Charles Hamilton Sorley 1895–1915
English poet, killed in action

2 I do wish people would not deceive
themselves by talk of a just war. There is no
such thing as a just war. What we are
doing is casting out Satan by Satan.
letter to his mother from Aldershot, March
1915

John Philip Sousa 1854–1932
American composer and conductor

3 Jazz will endure, just as long as people hear
it through their feet instead of their brains.
Nat Shapiro (ed.) *An Encyclopedia of
Quotations about Music* (1978)

Wole Soyinka 1934–
Nigerian dramatist, novelist, and critic. In 1986 he
became the first African to receive the Nobel Prize
for Literature

4 Books and all forms of writing have always
been objects of terror to those who seek to
suppress truth.
The Man Died (1972)

5 The man dies in all who keep silent in the
face of tyranny.
The Man Died (1972)

6 Justice is the first condition of humanity.
The Man Died (1972)

Muriel Spark 1918–2006
British novelist

7 Long ago in 1945 all the nice people in
England were poor, allowing for
exceptions.
The Girls of Slender Means (1963), opening
line

8 I am putting old heads on your young
shoulders . . . all my pupils are the crème de
la crème.
The Prime of Miss Jean Brodie (1961)

9 Give me a girl at an impressionable age,
and she is mine for life.
The Prime of Miss Jean Brodie (1961)

10 One's prime is elusive. You little girls,
when you grow up, must be on the alert to
recognise your prime at whatever time of
your life it may occur.
The Prime of Miss Jean Brodie (1961)

John Sparrow 1906–92
English academic, Warden of All Souls College,
Oxford, 1952–77
see also **Epitaphs 108:11**

11 That indefatigable and unsavoury engine
of pollution, the dog.
letter to *Times* 30 September 1975

Edward Spears 1886–1974
British soldier and diplomat

12 Of all the crosses I have had to bear during
this war, the heaviest has been the Cross of
Lorraine.
*in the Second World War the Cross of Lorraine
was the symbol of the Free French forces, led by
General **de Gaulle***
attributed in *Times* 1 June 2006, and often
attributed to Winston **Churchill** who
subsequently used it; Martin Gilbert *Churchill:
A Life* (1991)

Lord Spencer 1964–
English peer, brother of **Diana**, Princess of Wales

13 I always believed the press would kill her in
the end. But not even I could believe they
would take such a direct hand in her death
as seems to be the case . . . Every proprietor
and editor of every publication that has
paid for intrusive and exploitative
photographs of her . . . has blood on their
hands today.
*on the death of **Diana**, Princess of Wales, in a car
crash while being pursued by photographers, 31
August 1997*
in *Daily Telegraph* 1 September 1997

14 She needed no royal title to continue to
generate her particular brand of magic.
*tribute at the funeral of **Diana**, Princess of Wales,
7 September 1997*
in *Guardian* 8 September 1997

15 We, your blood family, will do all we can to
continue the imaginative way in which
you were steering these two exceptional
young men so that their souls are not
simply immersed by duty and tradition but

can sing openly as you planned.
of his nephews, Prince William and Prince Harry;
in *Guardian* 8 September 1997

Raine, Countess Spencer 1929–
English peeress, daughter of Barbara **Cartland**,
stepmother of **Diana**, Princess of Wales

1 Alas, for our towns and cities. Monstrous
carbuncles of concrete have erupted in
gentle Georgian Squares.
The Spencers on Spas (1983); see also
Charles 63:16

Stanley Spencer 1891–1959
English painter. He is best known for his religious
and visionary works in the modern setting of his
native village of Cookham in Berkshire
on Spencer: see **Lewis 200:1**

2 Painting is saying 'Ta' to God.
letter from Spencer's daughter Shirin, in
Observer 7 February 1988

Stephen Spender 1909–95
English poet and critic, member of the 'Pylon
School' of poetry
on Spender: see **Waugh 329:11**; see also **Pollitt
256:1**

3 After the first powerful plain manifesto
The black statement of pistons, without
more fuss
But gliding like a queen, she leaves the
station.
'The Express' (1933)

4 I think continually of those who were truly
great.
'I think continually of those who were truly
great' (1933)

5 Born of the sun they travelled a short while
towards the sun,
And left the vivid air signed with their
honour.
'I think continually of those who were truly
great' (1933)

6 My parents kept me from children who
were rough
And who threw words like stones and who
wore torn clothes.
'My parents kept me from children who were
rough' (1933)

7 Pylons, those pillars

Bare like nude, giant girls that have no
secret.
'The Pylons' (1933)

8 What I had not foreseen
Was the gradual day
Weakening the will
Leaking the brightness away.
'What I expected, was' (1933)

9 Who live under the shadow of a war,
What can I do that matters?
'Who live under the shadow of a war' (1933)

Oswald Spengler 1880–1936
German philosopher. In his book *The Decline of the
West* (1918–22) he argues that civilizations undergo
a seasonal cycle of a thousand years and are subject
to growth and decay analogous to biological species

10 Socialism is nothing but the capitalism of
the lower classes.
The Hour of Decision (1933)

Spice Girls
see **Matthew Rowbottom**

Benjamin Spock 1903–98
American paediatrician and writer. His influential
manual *The Common Sense Book of Baby and Child
Care* (1946) challenged traditional ideas in child-
rearing in favour of a psychological approach

11 You know more than you think you do.
Common Sense Book of Baby and Child Care
(1946) [later *Baby and Child Care*], opening
words

12 To win in Vietnam, we will have to
exterminate a nation.
Dr Spock on Vietnam (1968)

William Archibald Spooner 1844–1930
English clergyman and Warden of New College,
Oxford, 1903–24, famous for his 'Spoonerisms'

13 Her late husband, you know, a very sad
death—eaten by missionaries—poor soul!
William Hayter *Spooner* (1977)

14 You have tasted your worm, you have
hissed my mystery lectures, and you must
leave by the first town drain.
to an undergraduate
Oxford University What's What (1948); William
Hayter in *Spooner* (1977) maintains this
saying is apocryphal

Cecil Spring-Rice 1859–1918
British diplomat; Ambassador to Washington from 1912

1 I vow to thee, my country—all earthly
  things above—
  Entire and whole and perfect, the service of
    my love,
  The love that asks no question: the love
    that stands the test,
  That lays upon the altar the dearest and
    the best:
  The love that never falters, the love that
    pays the price,
  The love that makes undaunted the final
    sacrifice.
  'I Vow to Thee, My Country' (written on the eve
  of his departure from Washington, 12 January
  1918)

Bruce Springsteen 1949–
American rock singer and songwriter

2 Born in the USA.
  title of song (1984)

3 Born down in a dead man's town
  The first kick I took was when I hit the
    ground.
  'Born in the USA' (1984 song)

4 We gotta get out while we're young,
  'Cause tramps like us, baby, we were born
    to run.
  'Born to Run' (1974 song)

5 57 channels (and nothin' on).
  title of song, 1992

J. C. Squire 1884–1958
English man of letters

6 I'm not so think as you drunk I am.
  'Ballade of Soporific Absorption' (1931)

7 It did not last: the Devil howling 'Ho!
  Let Einstein be!' restored the status quo.
  'In continuation of Pope on Newton' (1926),
  referring to Alexander Pope (1688–1744)
  'Epitaph: Intended for Sir Isaac Newton'
  (1730): 'Nature, and Nature's laws lay hid in
  night. / God said, *Let Newton be!* and all was
  light'

8 God heard the embattled nations sing and
    shout
  'Gott strafe England!' and 'God save the
    King!'

God this, God that, and God the other
  thing—
'Good God!' said God, 'I've got my work
  cut out.'
  'The Dilemma' (1916); see **Funke 127:6**

Joseph Stalin 1879–1953
Soviet statesman, General Secretary of the
Communist Party of the USSR 1922–53. The
succession of five-year plans for rapid
industrialization and collectivization of agriculture
launched by him in 1928 are thought to have
resulted in the death of some 10 million peasants,
and his large-scale purges of the intelligentsia in the
1930s were equally ruthless

9 The State is an instrument in the hands of
  the ruling class, used to break the
  resistance of the adversaries of that class.
  Foundations of Leninism (1924)

10 There are various forms of production:
  artillery, automobiles, lorries. You also
  produce 'commodities', 'works',
  'products'. Such things are highly
  necessary. Engineering things. For people's
  souls. 'Products' are highly necessary too.
  'Products' are very important for people's
  souls. You are engineers of human souls.
  speech to writers at **Gorky's** house, 26
  October 1932; A. Kemp-Welch *Stalin and the
  Literary Intelligentsia, 1928–39* (1991); see
  Gorky 136:2

11 The Pope! How many divisions has *he* got?
  *on being asked to encourage Catholicism in
  Russia by way of conciliating the Pope, 13 May
  1935*
  W. S. Churchill *The Gathering Storm* (1948)

12 One death is a tragedy, a million deaths a
  statistic.
  attributed

Charles E. Stanton 1859–1933
American soldier

13 *Lafayette, nous voilà!*
  Lafayette, we are here.
  at the tomb of Lafayette in Paris, 4 July 1917

Freya Stark 1893–1993
English writer and traveller

14 The great and almost only comfort about
  being a woman is that one can always

pretend to be more stupid than one is and no one is surprised.

The Valleys of the Assassins (1934)

Enid Starkie 1897–1970
English academic

1 Unhurt people are not much good in the world.

letter, 18 June 1943; Joanna Richardson *Enid Starkie* (1973); see **Hart 146:10**

Joseph Starnes 1895–1962
American Republican politician

2 CONGRESSMAN STARNES: You are quoting from this Marlowe. Is he a Communist?
HALLIE FLANAGAN: I am very sorry. I was quoting from Christopher Marlowe . . . the greatest dramatist in the period immediately preceding Shakespeare.

at the hearing on the Federal Theatre Project by the House Un-American Activities Committee, 6 December 1938

Christina Stead 1902–83
Australian novelist

3 If all the rich people in the world divided up their money among themselves there wouldn't be enough to go round.

House of All Nations (1938)

4 A self-made man is one who believes in luck and sends his son to Oxford.

House of All Nations (1938)

David Steel 1938–
British Liberal politician; Leader of the Liberal Party 1976–88

5 I have the good fortune to be the first Liberal leader for over half a century who is able to say to you at the end of our annual assembly: go back to your constituencies and prepare for government.

speech to the Liberal Party Assembly, 18 September 1981

6 It is the settled will of the majority of people in Scotland that they want not just the symbol, but the substance of the return of democratic control over internal affairs.

on the announcement that the Stone of Scone, on which medieval Scottish kings were crowned, and which had been taken to England by Edward I and preserved in the coronation chair at

Westminster, would be returned to Scotland in *Scotsman* 4 July 1996

Lincoln Steffens 1866–1936
American journalist

7 I have seen the future; and it works.

following a visit to the Soviet Union in 1919 letter to Marie Howe, 3 April 1919

Gertrude Stein 1874–1946
American writer who developed an esoteric stream-of-consciousness style, notably in *The Autobiography of Alice B. Toklas* (1933); her home in Paris became a focus for the avant-garde during the 1920s and 1930s

on Stein: see **Fadiman 109:2, Lewis 199:16**; see also **Last words 191:9**

8 Remarks are not literature.

Autobiography of Alice B. Toklas (1933)

9 'Native' always means people who belong somewhere else, because they had once belonged somewhere. That shows us the white race does not really belong anywhere, because they think of everybody else as native.

Everybody's Autobiography (1937)

10 In the United States there is more space where nobody is than where anybody is. That is what makes America what it is.

The Geographical History of America (1936)

11 Rose is a rose is a rose is a rose, is a rose.

Sacred Emily (1913)

12 You are all a lost generation.

of the young who served in the First World War subsequently taken by Ernest **Hemingway** as epigraph to *The Sun Also Rises* (1926)

John Steinbeck 1902–68
American novelist. His work, for example *Of Mice and Men* (1937) and *The Grapes of Wrath* (1939), is noted for its sympathetic and realistic portrayal of the migrant agricultural workers of California

see also **Borrowed titles 40:11**

13 All the world's great have been little boys who wanted the moon.

Cup of Gold (1953)

14 Man, unlike any other thing organic or inorganic in the universe, grows beyond his work, walks up the stairs of his

concepts, emerges ahead of his accomplishments.
The Grapes of Wrath (1939)

1 I know this—a man got to do what he got to do.
The Grapes of Wrath (1939)

2 Okie use' ta mean you was from Oklahoma. Now it means you're a dirty son-of-a-bitch. Okie means you're scum. Don't mean nothing itself, it's the way they say it.
The Grapes of Wrath (1939)

3 How can you frighten a man whose hunger is not only in his own cramped stomach but in the wretched bellies of his children? You can't scare him—he has known a fear beyond every other.
The Grapes of Wrath (1939)

4 I guess—what may happen is what keeps us alive. We want to see tomorrow.
letter to Carlton Sheffield, 16 October 1952

Gloria Steinem 1934–
American journalist
see also **Dunn 94:8, Sayings 287:13**

5 We are becoming the men we wanted to marry.
in *Ms* July/August 1982

Casey Stengel 1891–1975
American baseball player and manager

6 All you have to do is keep the five players who hate your guts away from the five who are undecided.
John Samuel (ed.) *The Guardian Book of Sports Quotes* (1985)

James Stephens 1880–1950
Irish poet and nationalist

7 Finality is death. Perfection is finality. Nothing is perfect. There are lumps in it.
The Crock of Gold (1912)

8 I hear a sudden cry of pain!
There is a rabbit in a snare:
Now I hear the cry again,
But I cannot tell from where . . .
Little one! Oh, little one!
I am searching everywhere.
'The Snare' (1915)

9 People say: 'Of course, they will be beaten.' The statement is almost a query, and they continue, 'but they are putting up a decent fight.' For being beaten does not matter greatly in Ireland, but not fighting does matter.
The Insurrection in Dublin (1916)

10 In my definition they were good men— men, that is, who willed no evil. No person living is the worse off for having known Thomas MacDonagh.
of the leaders of the Easter Rising
The Insurrection in Dublin (1916)

Brooks Stevens 1911–95
American industrial designer

11 Our whole economy is based on planned obsolescence.
V. Packard *The Waste Makers* (1960)

Wallace Stevens 1879–1955
American poet

12 The poet is the priest of the invisible.
'Adagia' (1957)

13 Chieftain Iffucan of Azcan in caftan
Of tan with henna hackles, halt!
'Bantams in Pine Woods' (1923)

14 Call the roller of big cigars,
The muscular one, and bid him whip
In kitchen cups concupiscent curds.
'The Emperor of Ice-Cream' (1923)

15 Let be be finale of seem.
The only emperor is the emperor of ice-cream.
'The Emperor of Ice-Cream' (1923)

16 Frogs eat butterflies. Snakes eat frogs. Hogs eat snakes. Men eat hogs.
title of poem (1923)

17 Poetry is the supreme fiction, madame.
'A High-Toned old Christian Woman' (1923)

18 They said, 'You have a blue guitar,
You do not play things as they are.'
The man replied, 'Things as they are
Are changed upon the blue guitar.'
'The Man with the Blue Guitar' (1937)

19 The inconceivable idea of the sun.
You must become an ignorant man again
And see the sun again with an ignorant eye

And see it clearly in the idea of it.
Notes Toward a Supreme Fiction (1947) 'It Must Be Abstract' no. 1

1 They will get it straight one day at the Sorbonne.
We shall return at twilight from the lecture
Pleased that the irrational is rational.
Notes Toward a Supreme Fiction (1947) 'It Must Give Pleasure' no. 10

2 Music is feeling, then, not sound.
'Peter Quince at the Clavier' (1923)

3 Beauty is momentary in the mind—
The fitful tracing of a portal;
But in the flesh it is immortal.
The body dies; the body's beauty lives.
'Peter Quince at the Clavier' (1923)

4 I do not know which to prefer,
The beauty of inflections
Or the beauty of innuendoes,
The blackbird whistling
Or just after.
'Thirteen Ways of Looking at a Blackbird' (1923)

Adlai Stevenson 1900–65
American Democratic politician, unsuccessful presidential candidate in 1952 and 1956
see also **Adler 2:11**

5 I suppose flattery hurts no one, that is, if he doesn't inhale.
television broadcast, 30 March 1952

6 If they [the Republicans] will stop telling lies about the Democrats, we will stop telling the truth about them.
speech during 1952 Presidential campaign; J. B. Martin *Adlai Stevenson and Illinois* (1976)

7 Let's talk sense to the American people. Let's tell them the truth, that there are no gains without pains.
speech of acceptance at the Democratic National Convention, 26 July 1952

8 There is no evil in the atom; only in men's souls.
speech at Hartford, Connecticut, 18 September 1952

9 In America any boy may become President and I suppose it's just one of the risks he takes!
speech in Indianapolis, 26 September 1952

10 A free society is a society where it is safe to be unpopular.
speech in Detroit, 7 October 1952

11 The young man [Richard Nixon] who asks you to set him one heart-beat from the Presidency of the United States.
commonly quoted as 'just a heart-beat away . . . '
speech at Cleveland, Ohio, 23 October 1952

12 We hear the Secretary of State boasting of his brinkmanship—the art of bringing us to the edge of the abyss.
speech in Hartford, Connecticut, 25 February 1956; see **Dulles 93:9**

13 She would rather light a candle than curse the darkness, and her glow has warmed the world.
on learning of Eleanor **Roosevelt**'s *death*
in *New York Times* 8 November 1962; see also **Harper 146:5**

14 The kind of politician who would cut down a redwood tree, and then mount the stump and make a speech on conservation.
of Richard **Nixon**
Fawn M. Brodie *Richard Nixon* (1983)

Anne Stevenson 1933–
English poet

15 Blackbirds are the cellos of the deep farms.
'Green Mountain, Black Mountain' (1982)

Ian Stewart 1945–
British mathematician

16 Genes are not like engineering blueprints; they are more like recipes in a cookbook. They tell us what ingredients to use, in what quantities, and in what order—but they do not provide a complete, accurate plan of the final result.
Life's Other Secret (1998) preface

Potter Stewart 1915–85
American judge, US Supreme Court justice

17 Newspapers, television networks, and magazines have sometimes been outrageously abusive, untruthful, arrogant, and hypocritical. But it hardly follows that elimination of a strong and independent press is the way to eliminate abusiveness, untruth, arrogance, or

hypocrisy from government itself.
address to Yale Law School, 2 November 1974, in *Hastings Law Journal* January 1975

Rod Stewart 1945–
British pop singer and songwriter

1 They could do with a pub here, a nice pint of lager would be nice.
at a Buckingham Palace garden party
quoted in www.metro.co.uk 29 December 2006 'Quotes of the Year'

Sting 1951–
English rock singer, songwriter, and actor

2 If I were a Brazilian without land or money or the means to feed my children, I would be burning the rain forest too.
in *International Herald Tribune* 14 April 1989

Michael Stipe 1960–
American singer and songwriter

3 On the ladder of important things in this world, being in a rock band is probably on a lower rung, but then again, being Secretary of State is probably way down there too.
T. Fletcher *Remarks: the story of REM* (1993)

Lord Stockton 1943–
British peer, grandson of Harold **Macmillan**

4 As an old man he only had nightmares about two things: the trenches in the Great War and what would have happened if the Cuban Missile Crisis had gone wrong.
of Harold **Macmillan**
in 1998; Peter Hennessy *The Prime Minister: the Office and its Holders since 1945* (2000)

Mervyn Stockwood 1913–95
English Anglican clergyman, Bishop of Southwark 1959–80

5 A psychiatrist is a man who goes to the Folies-Bergère and looks at the audience.
in *Observer* 15 October 1961

I. F. Stone 1907–89
American journalist

6 The difference between burlesque and the newspapers is that the former never

pretended to be performing a public service by exposure.
I. F. Stone's Weekly 7 September 1952

on why the Washington Post *was an exciting paper to read:*
7 You never know on what page you will find a page-one story.
attributed; David Halberstam *The Powers That Be* (1979)

Marie Stopes 1880–1958
Scottish pioneer of birth-control clinics

8 An impersonal and scientific knowledge of the structure of our bodies is the surest safeguard against prurient curiosity and lascivious gloating.
Married Love (1918)

Tom Stoppard 1937–
British dramatist, born in Czechoslovakia

9 It's not the voting that's democracy, it's the counting.
Jumpers (1972)

10 The House of Lords, an illusion to which I have never been able to subscribe— responsibility without power, the prerogative of the eunuch throughout the ages.
Lord Malquist and Mr Moon (1966); see **Kipling 183:10**

11 The media. It sounds like a convention of spiritualists.
Night and Day (1978)

12 I'm with you on the free press. It's the newspapers I can't stand.
Night and Day (1978)

13 Comment is free but facts are on expenses.
Night and Day (1978); see **Scott 289:7**

14 Save the gerund and screw the whale.
The Real Thing (1982); see **Sayings and slogans 287:4**

15 I can do you blood and love without the rhetoric, and I can do you blood and rhetoric without the love, and I can do you all three concurrent or consecutive, but I can't do you love and rhetoric without the blood. Blood is compulsory—they're all blood, you see.
Rosencrantz and Guildenstern are Dead (1967)

1 We're *actors*—we're the opposite of people!
   . . . Think, in your head, *now*, think of the
   most . . . *private* . . . *secret* . . . *intimate* thing
   you have ever done secure in the
   knowledge of its privacy . . . Are you
   thinking of it? . . . *Well, I saw you do it!*
   Rosencrantz and Guildenstern Are Dead
   (1967)

2 Eternity's a terrible thought. I mean,
   where's it all going to end?
   Rosencrantz and Guildenstern are Dead
   (1967)

3 The bad end unhappily, the good
   unluckily. That is what tragedy means.
   Rosencrantz and Guildenstern are Dead
   (1967)

4 Life is a gamble at terrible odds—if it was a
   bet, you wouldn't take it.
   Rosencrantz and Guildenstern are Dead
   (1967)

Lytton Strachey 1880–1932
English biographer, a prominent member of the
Bloomsbury Group
see also **Last words 190:7**

5 CHAIRMAN OF MILITARY TRIBUNAL: What
   would you do if you saw a German soldier
   trying to violate your sister?
   STRACHEY: I would try to get between them.
   *otherwise rendered as, 'I should interpose my
   body'*
   Robert Graves *Good-bye to All That* (1929)

6 Discretion is not the better part of
   biography.
   M. Holroyd *Lytton Strachey* (1967) vol. 1

William L. Strauss 1900–81 and A. J. E. Cave 1900–2001
American anatomist; British anatomist

7 Notwithstanding, if he could be
   reincarnated and placed in a New York
   subway—provided that he were bathed,
   shaved, and dressed in modern clothing—
   it is doubtful whether he would attract any
   more attention than some of its other
   denizens.
   of Neanderthal man
   in *Quarterly Review of Biology* Winter 1957

Igor Stravinsky 1882–1971
Russian-born composer, resident in the US from
1939. He made his name with the ballets *The
Firebird* (1910) and *The Rite of Spring* (1913); both
shocked Paris audiences with their irregular
rhythms and frequent dissonances

8 My music is best understood by children
   and animals.
   in *Observer* 8 October 1961

9 Music is, by its very nature, essentially
   powerless to *express* anything at all . . .
   music expresses itself.
   in *Esquire* December 1972

John Whitaker ('Jack') Straw 1946–
British Labour politician

10 What you have within the UK is three
   small nations who've been under the cosh
   of the English.
   in *Sunday Times* 6 January 2000

Janet Street-Porter 1946–
English broadcaster and programme-maker

11 A terminal blight has hit the TV industry
   nipping fun in the bud and stunting our
   growth. This blight is management—the
   dreaded Four M's: male, middle class,
   middle-aged and mediocre.
   MacTaggart Lecture, Edinburgh Television
   Festival, 25 August 1995

Simeon Strunsky 1879–1948
Russian-born American journalist and writer

12 People who want to understand
   democracy should spend less time in the
   library with Aristotle and more time on the
   buses and in the subway.
   No Mean City (1944)

13 Famous remarks are very seldom quoted
   correctly.
   No Mean City (1944)

Jan Struther 1901–53
English-born novelist and poet

14 Lord of all hopefulness, Lord of all joy,
   Whose trust, ever childlike, no cares could
      destroy,
   Be there at our waking, and give us, we
      pray,

Your bliss in our hearts, Lord, at the break
of the day.
'All Day Hymn' (1931)

G. A. Studdert Kennedy 1883–1929
British poet

1 When Jesus came to Birmingham they
simply passed Him by,
They never hurt a hair of Him, they only
let Him die.
'Indifference' (1921)

2 Waste of Blood, and waste of Tears,
Waste of youth's most precious years,
Waste of ways the saints have trod,
Waste of Glory, waste of God,
War!
'Waste' (1919)

J. W. N. Sullivan 1886–1937
British journalist and science writer

3 It is much easier to make measurements
than to know exactly what you are
measuring.
comment, 1928; R. L. Weber *More Random
Walks in Science* (1982)

Louis Henri Sullivan 1856–1924
American architect

4 Form follows function.
relating to his theory of skyscraper design
The Tall Office Building Artistically Considered
(1896)

Arthur Hays Sulzberger 1891–1968
American newspaper proprietor

5 We tell the public which way the cat is
jumping. The public will take care of the
cat.
on journalism
in *Time* 8 May 1950

Edith Summerskill 1901–80
British Labour politician

6 Nagging is the repetition of unpalatable
truths.
speech to the Married Women's Association,
14 July 1960

Jacqueline Susann 1921–74
American novelist

7 Valley of the dolls.
title of novel (1966)

Hannen Swaffer 1879–1962
British journalist

8 Freedom of the press in Britain means
freedom to print such of the proprietor's
prejudices as the advertisers don't object
to.
Tom Driberg *Swaff* (1974)

Annie S. Swan 1859–1943
Scottish-born popular novelist

9 O God, give me work till the end of my life
And life till the end of my work.
'A Worker's Prayer' in *We Travel Home* (1935);
chosen by Winifred **Holtby**'s mother as her
daughter's epitaph: see **Epitaphs 107:7**

Herbert Bayard Swope 1882–1958
American journalist and editor
see also **Baruch 24:13**

10 The First Duty of a newspaper is to be
Accurate. If it is Accurate, it follows that it
is Fair.
letter to *New York Herald Tribune* 16 March
1958

11 He [Swope] enunciated no rules for
success, but offered a sure formula for
failure: *Just try to please everyone.*
E. J. Kahn Jr. *World of Swope* (1965)

Thomas Szasz 1920–
Hungarian-born psychiatrist

12 A child becomes an adult when he realizes
that he has a right not only to be right but
also to be wrong.
The Second Sin (1973) 'Childhood'

13 Happiness is an imaginary condition,
formerly often attributed by the living to
the dead, now usually attributed by adults
to children, and by children to adults.
The Second Sin (1973) 'Emotions'

14 The stupid neither forgive nor forget; the
naive forgive and forget; the wise forgive
but do not forget.
The Second Sin (1973) 'Personal Conduct'

1 If you talk to God, you are praying; if God talks to you, you have schizophrenia. If the dead talk to you, you are a spiritualist; if God talks to you, you are a schizophrenic.
The Second Sin (1973) 'Schizophrenia'

2 Formerly, when religion was strong and science weak, men mistook magic for medicine; now, when science is strong and religion weak, men mistake medicine for magic.
The Second Sin (1973) 'Science and Scientism'

3 Traditionally, sex has been a very private, secretive activity. Herein perhaps lies its powerful force for uniting people in a strong bond. As we make sex less secretive, we may rob it of its power to hold men and women together.
The Second Sin (1973) 'Sex'

4 Two wrongs don't make a right, but they make a good excuse.
The Second Sin (1973) 'Social Relations'

George Szell 1897–1970
American conductor

5 Conductors must give unmistakable and suggestive signals to the orchestra—not choreography to the audience.
in *Newsweek* 28 January 1963

6 I wanted to combine American purity and beauty of sound and the virtuosity of execution with the European sense of tradition, warmth of expression, and sense of style.
Harold Schonberg *The Great Conductors* (1967)

Albert von Szent-Györgyi 1893–1986
Hungarian-born American biochemist

7 Discovery consists of seeing what everybody has seen and thinking what nobody has thought.
I. Good (ed.) *The Scientist Speculates* (1962)

8 Water is life's *mater* and *matrix*, mother and medium. There is no life without water.
in *Perspectives in Biology and Medicine* Winter 1971

Wislawa Szymborska 1923–
Polish poet and critic

9 When the piranha strikes, it feels no shame.
If snakes had hands, they'd claim their hands were clean.
A jackal doesn't understand remorse.
Lions and lice don't waver in their course.
Why should they, when they know they're right?
'In Praise of Feeling Bad about Yourself' (1976)

10 There's no life
that couldn't be immortal
if only for a moment.
'On Death, without Exaggeration' (1995)

t

Taglines for films

1 Be afraid. Be very afraid.
   The Fly (1986 film), written by David
   Cronenberg

2 Being the adventures of a young man
   whose principal interests are rape, ultra-
   violence and Beethoven.
   A Clockwork Orange (1972 film)

3 Difficult times lie ahead, Harry.
   Harry Potter and the Goblet of Fire (2005
   film); see **Film lines 113:4**

4 Garbo talks.
   Anna Christie (1930 film), her first talkie

5 He said 'I'll be back!' . . . and he meant it!
   Terminator 2: Judgment Day (1991 film); see
   Film lines 114:6

6 In space no one can hear you scream.
   Alien (1979 film)

7 Just when you thought it was safe to go
   back in the water.
   publicity for *Jaws 2* (1978 film)

8 A long time ago in a galaxy far, far away
   . . .
   Star Wars (1977)

9 Love means never having to say you're
   sorry.
   Love Story (1970 film); from the novel (1970)
   by Erich Segal (1937–)

10 The man you love to hate.
   anonymous billing for Erich von Stroheim in
   the film *The Heart of Humanity* (1918)

11 Mean, Moody and Magnificent!
   The Outlaw (1946 film) starring Jane Russell

12 Please don't tell the ending. It's the only
   one we have.
   Psycho (1960 film)

13 Somewhere in the universe, there must
   be something better than Man.
   Planet of the Apes (1968 film)

14 They're young . . . they're in love . . . and
   they kill people.
   Bonnie and Clyde (1967 film)

15 We are not alone.
   Close Encounters of the Third Kind (1977
   film)

16 Where were you in '62?
   American Graffiti (1973 film)

Rabindranath Tagore 1861–1941
Bengali poet and philosopher

17 Bigotry tries to keep truth safe in its hand
   With a grip that kills it.
   Fireflies (1928)

18 Man goes into the noisy crowd to drown
   his own clamour of silence.
   'Stray Birds' (1916)

Nellie Talbot *fl.* 1921
American hymn-writer

19 Jesus wants me for a sunbeam.
   title of hymn (1921)

Sony Labou Tansi 1947–95
African writer

20 What good is an ounce of justice in an
   ocean of shit?
   The Antipeople (1983)

1 The most important revolution the first
one: the soldier exchanged for the heart
and the intellect.
The Antipeople (1983)

Catherine Tate
see **Catchphrases 58:2**

Bernie Taupin
see **Elton John and Bernie Taupin**

R. H. Tawney 1880–1962
British economic historian and political thinker

2 Private property is a necessary institution,
at least in a fallen world; men work more
and dispute less when goods are private
than when they are common. But it is to be
tolerated as a concession to human frailty,
not applauded as desirable in itself.
Religion and the Rise of Capitalism (1926)

3 To take usury is contrary to Scripture; it is
contrary to Aristotle; it is contrary to
nature, for it is to live without labour; it is
to sell time, which belongs to God, for the
advantage of wicked men.
Religion and the Rise of Capitalism (1926)

4 What harm have I ever done to the Labour
Party?
declining the offer of a peerage
in *Evening Standard* 18 January 1962

A. J. P. Taylor 1906–90
British historian

5 History gets thicker as it approaches recent
times.
English History 1914–45 (1965) bibliography

6 The First World War had begun—imposed
on the statesmen of Europe by railway
timetables.
The First World War (1963)

7 A racing tipster who only reached Hitler's
level of accuracy would not do well for his
clients.
Origins of the Second World War (1962)

8 The glories of his revolutionary triumph
pale before the nobility of his later defeats.
on Trotsky
in *New Statesman and Nation* 20 February
1954

9 The magic of Shaw's words may still
bewitch posterity . . . but it will find that he
has nothing to say.
in *Observer* 22 July 1956

10 A great showman whose technique
improved as the real situation deteriorated.
of Mussolini
in *Observer* 28 February 1982

Ronald Taylor *fl*. 1996
Scottish headteacher

11 Evil visited us yesterday. We don't know
why.
*following the murder of sixteen children and
their teacher at Dunblane primary school*
in *Daily Telegraph* 15 March 1996

Norman Tebbit 1931–
British Conservative politician
on Tebbit: see **Foot 119:9**

12 I grew up in the Thirties with our
unemployed father. He did not riot, he got
on his bike and looked for work.
speech, 15 October 1981

13 The cricket test—which side do they cheer
for? . . . Are you still looking back to where
you came from or where you are?
*on the loyalties of Britain's immigrant
population*
interview in *Los Angeles Times*, reported in
Daily Telegraph 20 April 1990

Pierre Teilhard de Chardin 1881–1955
French Jesuit philosopher and palaeontologist. He is
best known for his theory, blending science and
Christianity, that man is evolving mentally and
socially towards a perfect spiritual state. The Roman
Catholic Church declared his views were unorthodox
and his major works were published posthumously
on Teilhard de Chardin: see **Pius XII 255:7**

14 The history of the living world can be
summarized as the elaboration of ever
more perfect eyes within a cosmos in
which there is always something more to
be seen.
The Phenomenon of Man (1959)

Telegrams

1 AM IN MARKET HARBOROUGH. WHERE OUGHT I TO BE?
   *sent by G. K. **Chesterton** to his wife in London*
   G. K. Chesterton *Autobiography* (1936)

2 BETTER DROWNED THAN DUFFERS IF NOT DUFFERS WONT DROWN.
   Arthur Ransome *Swallows and Amazons* (1930)

3 GOOD WORK, MARY. WE ALL KNEW YOU HAD IT IN YOU.
   *from Dorothy **Parker** to Mrs Sherwood on the arrival of her baby*
   Alexander Woollcott *While Rome Burns* (1934) 'Our Mrs Parker'

4 HOW DARE YOU BECOME PRIME MINISTER WHEN I'M AWAY GREAT LOVE CONSTANT THOUGHT VIOLET.
   *from Violet Bonham Carter (1887–1969) to her father, H. H. **Asquith**, 7 April 1908*
   Mark Bonham Carter and Mark Pottle (eds.) *Lantern Slides* (1996)

5 NURSE UNUPBLOWN.
   *Evelyn **Waugh**'s terse response to the cable request 'Require earliest name life story photograph American nurse upblown Adowa.'*
   Waugh in Abyssinia (1936)

in response to a telegraphic enquiry, HOW OLD CARY GRANT?:
6 OLD CARY GRANT FINE. HOW YOU?
   from Cary Grant (1904–86)
   R. Schickel *Cary Grant* (1983)

7 ON YOUR 100TH BIRTHDAY, ALL THE FAMILY JOIN WITH ME IN SENDING YOU OUR LOVE AND BEST WISHES FOR THIS SPECIAL DAY. LILIBET.
   *Queen **Elizabeth II** to the Queen Mother*
   in *Daily Telegraph* 5 August 2000

8 STREETS FLOODED. PLEASE ADVISE.
   *message sent by Robert **Benchley** on arriving in Venice*
   R. E. Drennan (ed.) *Wits End* (1973)

9 UNABLE OBTAIN BIDET. SUGGEST HANDSTAND IN SHOWER.
   *from Billy **Wilder** to his wife, who had asked him to send her a bidet from Paris*
   Leslie Halliwell *Filmgoer's Book of Quotes* (1973)

10 WELCOME STORIES EX-CHICAGO NOT UNDULY EMPHASISING CRIME.
   authorizing the young Times *correspondent in America, Claud Cockburn, to report a murder in Al Capone's Chicago*
   Claud Cockburn *In Time of Trouble* (1956)

William Temple 1881–1944
English theologian; Archbishop of Canterbury from 1942

11 In place of the conception of the power-state we are led to that of the welfare-state.
   Citizen and Churchman (1941)

12 Christianity is the most materialistic of all great religions.
   Readings in St John's Gospel (1939) vol. 1

13 Personally, I have always looked on cricket as organized loafing.
   attributed

Mother Teresa 1910–97
Roman Catholic nun and missionary, born in what is now Macedonia of Albanian parentage. She became an Indian citizen in 1948. She founded the Order of Missionaries of Charity, which became noted for its work among the poor in Calcutta and now operates in many parts of the world

14 We ourselves feel that what we are doing is just a drop in the ocean. But if that drop was not in the ocean, I think the ocean would be less because of that missing drop. I do not agree with the big way of doing things.
   A Gift for God (1975)

15 Now let us do something beautiful for God.
   letter to Malcolm Muggeridge before making a BBC TV programme about the Missionaries of Charity, 1971; see **Muggeridge 230:9**

16 The biggest disease today is not leprosy or tuberculosis, but rather the feeling of being unwanted, uncared for and deserted by everybody.
   in *Observer* 3 October 1971

17 By blood and origin I am Albanian. My citizenship is Indian. I am a Catholic nun.

As to my calling, I belong to the whole world. As to my heart, I belong entirely to the heart of Jesus.
in *Independent* 6 September 1997; obituary

A. S. J. Tessimond 1902–62
British poet

1 Cats, no less liquid than their shadows, Offer no angles to the wind.
Cats (1934)

Margaret Thatcher 1925–
British Conservative stateswoman; Prime Minister, 1979–90, first woman Premier of the United Kingdom. Her period in office was marked by monetarist policies, privatization of nationalized industries, and trade union legislation, and for an emphasis on individual responsibility and enterprise
on Thatcher: see **Anonymous 11:5**, **Callaghan 51:4**, **Carrington 54:5**, **Critchley 80:2**, **Healey 148:12**, **Kinnock 181:6**, **Mitterrand 226:6**, **West 332:22**

2 No woman in my time will be Prime Minister or Chancellor or Foreign Secretary—not the top jobs. Anyway I wouldn't want to be Prime Minister. You have to give yourself 100%.
on her appointment as Shadow Education Spokesman
in *Sunday Telegraph* 26 October 1969

3 In politics if you want anything said, ask a man. If you want anything done, ask a woman.
in *People* (New York) 15 September 1975

4 I stand before you tonight in my red chiffon evening gown, my face softly made up, my fair hair gently waved . . . the Iron Lady of the Western World! Me? A cold war warrior? Well, yes—if that is how they wish to interpret my defence of values and freedoms fundamental to our way of life.
speech at Finchley, 31 January 1976; see **Anonymous 11:5**

5 Where there is discord may we bring harmony.
Where there is error may we bring truth.
Where there is doubt may we bring faith.
Where there is despair may we bring hope.
Downing Street, London, 4 May 1979, referring to St Francis of Assisi (1181–1226) 'Prayer of St Francis' (attributed): 'Lord, make me an instrument of Your peace! / Where

there is hatred let me sow love; / Where there is injury, pardon; / Where there is doubt, faith; / Where there is despair, hope'

6 Pennies don't fall from heaven. They have to be earned on earth.
in *Observer* 18 November 1979; see **Burke 48:5**

7 No one would remember the Good Samaritan if he'd only had good intentions. He had money as well.
television interview, 6 January 1980

8 I don't mind how much my Ministers talk, as long as they do what I say.
in *Observer* 27 January 1980

9 We have to get our production and our earnings in balance. There's no easy popularity in what we are proposing, but it is fundamentally sound. Yet I believe people accept there is no real alternative.
popularly encapsulated in the acronym TINA
speech at Conservative Women's Conference, 21 May 1980

10 To those waiting with bated breath for that favourite media catchphrase, the U-turn, I have only this to say. 'You turn if you want; the lady's not for turning.'
speech at Conservative Party Conference in Brighton, 10 October 1980; see **Fry 126:7**

11 Just rejoice at that news and congratulate our armed forces and the Marines. Rejoice!
on the recapture of South Georgia, usually quoted as, 'Rejoice, rejoice!'; see also **Heath 149:12**
to newsmen outside 10 Downing Street, 25 April 1982

12 It is exciting to have a real crisis on your hands, when you have spent half your political life dealing with humdrum issues like the environment.
on the Falklands campaign, 1982
speech to Scottish Conservative Party conference, 14 May 1982; Hugo Young *One of Us* (1990)

13 We have to see that the spirit of the South Atlantic—the real spirit of Britain—is kindled not only by war but can now be fired by peace. We have the first prerequisite. We know that we can do

it—we haven't lost the ability. That is the Falklands Factor.
　speech in Cheltenham, 3 July 1982

1 Let me make one thing absolutely clear. The National Health Service is safe with us.
　speech at Conservative Party Conference, 8 October 1982

2 I was asked whether I was trying to restore Victorian values. I said straight out I was. And I am.
　speech to the British Jewish Community, 21 July 1983, referring to an interview with Brian Walden on 17 January 1983

3 Now it must be business as usual.
　on the steps of Brighton police station a few hours after the bombing of the Grand Hotel, Brighton; often quoted as 'We shall carry on as usual'
　in *Times* 13 October 1984

4 We can do business together.
　of Mikhail **Gorbachev**
　in *Times* 18 December 1984

5 We must try to find ways to starve the terrorist and the hijacker of the oxygen of publicity on which they depend.
　speech, 15 July 1985

6 There is no such thing as society. There are individual men and women, and there are families.
　in *Woman's Own* 31 October 1987

7 We have not successfully rolled back the frontiers of the State in Britain only to see them reimposed at European level, with a European super-State exercising a new dominance from Brussels.
　speech in Bruges, 20 September 1988

8 We have become a grandmother.
　in *Times* 4 March 1989

9 Advisers advise and ministers decide.
　on the respective roles of her personal economic adviser, Alan Walters, and her Chancellor, Nigel **Lawson** *(who resigned the following day)*
　in the House of Commons, 26 October 1989

10 I am naturally very sorry to see you go, but understand . . . your wish to be able to spend more time with your family.
　reply to Norman **Fowler**'s *resignation letter*
　in *Guardian* 4 January 1990; see **Fowler 121:11**

11 No! No! No!
　making clear her opposition to a single European currency, and more centralized controls from Brussels
　in the House of Commons, 30 October 1990

12 I fight on, I fight to win.
　having failed to win outright in the first ballot for party leader
　comment, 21 November 1990

13 It's a funny old world.
　on withdrawing from the contest for leadership of the Conservative party
　comment, 22 November 1990; see **Film lines 114:13**

14 I shan't be pulling the levers there but I shall be a very good back-seat driver.
　after leaving office as Prime Minister
　in *Independent* 27 November 1990

15 Home is where you come to when you have nothing better to do.
　in *Vanity Fair* May 1991

　of the poll tax:
16 Given time, it would have been seen as one of the most far-reaching and beneficial reforms ever made in the working of local government.
　The Downing Street Years (1993)

17 In my lifetime all our problems have come from mainland Europe and all the solutions have come from the English-speaking nations of the world.
　in *Times* 6 October 1999

Charlize Theron 1975–
South African actress

18 That little gold statue doesn't clean your house.
　on her Oscar
　in *Mail on Sunday* 19 February 2006

Dave Thomas 1949–
Canadian comic writer and actor
see also **Film lines 113:9, Film lines 116:5**

19 We thought, 'Well, they get what they deserve. This is their Canadian content. I hope they like it.'
　of the creation of the 'Mckenzie Brothers' to fulfil the requirements of Canadian broadcasting law for the SCTV comedy show
　interview on *Film Force* (online ed.), 10 February 2000

Dylan Thomas 1914–53
Welsh poet

1 Though lovers be lost love shall not;
And death shall have no dominion.
    'And death shall have no dominion' (1936);
    referring to the *Bible* Romans: 'Christ being
    raised from the dead dieth no more; death
    hath no more dominion over him'

2 Do not go gentle into that good night,
Old age should burn and rave at close of
day;
Rage, rage against the dying of the light.
    'Do Not Go Gentle into that Good Night' (1952)

3 The force that through the green fuse
drives the flower
Drives my green age.
    'The force that through the green fuse' (1934)

4 The hand that signed the paper felled a
city;
Five sovereign fingers taxed the breath,
Doubled the globe of dead and halved a
country;
These five kings did a king to death.
    'The hand that signed the paper felled a city'
    (1936)

5 Light breaks where no sun shines;
Where no sea runs, the waters of the heart
Push in their tides.
    'Light breaks where no sun shines' (1934)

6 It was my thirtieth year to heaven.
    'Poem in October' (1946)

7 There could I marvel
My birthday
Away but the weather turned around.
    'Poem in October' (1946)

8 After the first death, there is no other.
    'A Refusal to Mourn the Death, by Fire, of a
    Child in London' (1946)

9 I can never remember whether it snowed
for six days and six nights when I was
twelve or whether it snowed for twelve
days and twelve nights when I was six.
    A Child's Christmas in Wales (1954)

10 Books that told me everything about the
wasp, except why.
    A Child's Christmas in Wales (1954)

11 To begin at the beginning: It is spring,
moonless night in the small town, starless
and bible-black.
    Under Milk Wood (1954), opening line

12 Chasing the naughty couples down the
grassgreen gooseberried double bed of the
wood.
    Under Milk Wood (1954)

13 Oh, isn't life a terrible thing, thank God?
    Under Milk Wood (1954)

14 I want, above all, to work like a fiend, a
good fiend.
    letter to Edith **Sitwell**, 11 April 1947; *Collected
    Letters* (1987)

15 The land of my fathers. My fathers can
have it.
    of Wales
    in *Adam* December 1953

16 A man you don't like who drinks as much
as you do.
    definition of an alcoholic
    Constantine Fitzgibbon *Life of Dylan Thomas*
    (1965)

17 Poetry is not the most important thing in
life . . . I'd much rather lie in a hot bath
reading Agatha Christie and sucking
sweets.
    Joan Wyndham *Love is Blue* (1986) 6 July 1943

Edward Thomas 1878–1917
English poet

18 Yes; I remember Adlestrop—
The name, because one afternoon
Of heat the express-train drew up there
Unwontedly. It was late June.
    'Adlestrop' (1917)

19 The past is the only dead thing that smells
sweet.
    'Early one morning in May I set out' (1917)

20 If I should ever by chance grow rich
I'll buy Codham, Cockridden, and
Childerditch,
Roses, Pyrgo, and Lapwater,
And let them all to my elder daughter.
    'Household Poems: Bronwen' (1917)

21   I see and hear nothing;
Yet seem, too, to be listening, lying in wait
For what I should, yet never can,
remember.
    'Old Man' (1917)

22 Out in the dark over the snow
The fallow fawns invisible go.
    'Out in the dark' (1917)

23 As well as any bloom upon a flower

I like the dust on the nettles, never lost
Except to prove the sweetness of a shower.
'Tall Nettles' (1917)

Gwyn Thomas 1913–81
Welsh novelist and dramatist

1 I wanted a play that would paint the full
face of sensuality, rebellion and revivalism.
In South Wales these three phenomena
have played second fiddle only to Rugby
Union which is a distillation of all three.
introduction to *Jackie the Jumper* (1962)

2 There are still parts of Wales where the
only concession to gaiety is a striped
shroud.
in *Punch* 18 June 1958

Irene Thomas 1919–2001
British writer and broadcaster

3 Protestant women may take the pill.
Roman Catholic women must keep taking
The Tablet.
in *Guardian* 28 December 1990

R. S. Thomas 1913–2000
Welsh poet and clergyman

4 There is no love
For such, only a willed
gentleness.
'They' (1968)

5 There is no present in Wales,
And no future;
There is only the past,
Brittle with relics . . .
And an impotent people,
Sick with inbreeding,
Worrying the carcase of an old song.
'Welsh Landscape' (1955)

Emma Thompson 1959–
English actress and screenwriter

6 [The gym is] really depressing—so I just
trot in an elderly fashion around the
cricket pitch for 20 minutes.
in *Daily Mail* (online edition) 2 December 2006

E. P. Thompson 1924–
British social historian

7 This 'going into Europe' will not turn out
to be the thrilling mutual exchange

supposed. It is more like nine middle-aged
couples with failing marriages meeting in a
darkened bedroom in a Brussels hotel for a
Group Grope.
in *Sunday Times* 27 April 1975

Hunter S. Thompson 1939–2005
American writer and journalist

8 Fear and loathing in Las Vegas.
title of two articles in *Rolling Stone* 11 and 25
November 1971 (under the pseudonym 'Raoul
Duke')

Julian Thompson 1934–
British soldier, second-in-command of the land
forces during the Falklands campaign.

9 You don't mind dying for Queen and
country, but you certainly don't want to
die for politicians.
'The Falklands War— the Untold Story'
(Yorkshire Television) 1 April 1987; see **France
122:5, Graham 136:7**

David Thomson 1941–
British film critic

10 Fiction is the great virus waiting to do
away with fact—that is one of the most
ominous meanings of the film.
of Citizen Kane (*1941 film*)
Rosebud: the Story of Orson Welles (1996)

Roy Thomson 1894–1976
Canadian-born British newspaper proprietor

11 It's just like having a licence to print your
own money.
*on the profitability of commercial television in
Britain*
R. Braddon *Roy Thomson* (1965)

Jeremy Thorpe 1929–
British Liberal politician, Leader of the Liberal Party
1967–76

12 Greater love hath no man than this, that
he lay down his friends for his life.
on Harold ***Macmillan****'s sacking seven of his
Cabinet on 13 July 1962*
D. E. Butler and A. King *General Election of
1964* (1965); referring to the *Bible* St John:
'Greater love hath no man than this, that a
man lay down his life for his friends'

James Thurber 1894–1961
American humorist
see also **Cartoons 56:1, Cartoons 56:6, Cartoons 57:1**

1 I suppose that the high-water mark of my youth in Columbus, Ohio, was the night the bed fell on my father.
My Life and Hard Times (1933)

2 Her own mother lived the latter years of her life in the horrible suspicion that electricity was dripping invisibly all over the house.
My Life and Hard Times (1933)

3 The war between men and women.
cartoon series title in *New Yorker* 20 January–28 April 1934

4 Then, with that faint fleeting smile playing about his lips, he faced the firing squad; erect and motionless, proud and disdainful, Walter Mitty, the undefeated, inscrutable to the last.
in *New Yorker* 18 March 1939 'The Secret Life of Walter Mitty'

5 Humour is emotional chaos remembered in tranquillity.
in *New York Post* 29 February 1960, referring to William Wordsworth (1770–1850) *Lyrical Ballads* (2nd ed., 1802): 'Poetry . . . takes its origin from emotion recollected in tranquillity'

Anthony Thwaite 1930–
English writer

6 The name is history.
      The thick Miljacka flows
Under its bridges through a canyon's breadth
Fretted with minarets and plump with domes,
Cupped in its mountains, caught on a drawn breath.
'Sarajevo: I' (1973)

Lionel Tiger 1937–
American anthropologist

7 Male bonding.
Men in Groups (1969)

Paul Tillich 1886–1965
German-born American theologian and philosopher. He proposed a form of Christian existentialism

8 Neurosis is the way of avoiding non-being by avoiding being.
The Courage To Be (1952)

Alvin Toffler 1928–
American writer

9 Future shock.
in Horizon *Summer 1965* Toffler had written of 'the dizzying disorientation brought on by the premature arrival of the future'
title of book (1970)

J. R. R. Tolkien 1892–1973
British philologist and writer
on Tolkien: see **Pratchett 261:9**; see also **Film lines 113:7**

10 There and back again.
subtitle of *The Hobbit* (1937); see **Jackson 165:4**

11 In a hole in the ground there lived a hobbit.
The Hobbit (1937), opening line

12 One Ring to rule them all, One Ring to find them
One Ring to bring them all and in the darkness bind them.
The Lord of the Rings pt. 1 *The Fellowship of the Ring* (1954) epigraph

Arturo Toscanini 1867–1957
Italian conductor, resident in the US from the late 1930s

13 I smoked my first cigarette and kissed my first woman on the same day. I have never had time for tobacco since.
in *Observer* 30 June 1946

Sue Townsend 1946–
English humorous writer

14 The secret diary of Adrian Mole aged 13¾.
title of book (1982)

Pete Townshend 1945–
British rock musician and songwriter

15 Hope I die before I get old.
'My Generation' (1965 song)

Arnold Toynbee 1889–1975
English historian

1 The twentieth century will be remembered chiefly, not as an age of political conflicts and technical inventions, but as an age in which human society dared to think of the health of the whole human race as a practical objective.
  attributed

Polly Toynbee 1946–
English journalist

2 Feminism is the most revolutionary idea there has ever been. Equality for women demands a change in the human psyche more profound than anything Marx dreamed of. It means valuing parenthood as much as we value banking.
  in *Guardian* 19 January 1987

Merle Travis 1917–83
American country singer

3 Sixteen tons, what do you get?
  Another day older and deeper in debt.
  Say brother, don't you call me 'cause I can't go
  I owe my soul to the company store.
  'Sixteen Tons' (1947 song)

Herbert Beerbohm Tree 1852–1917
English actor-manager

4 Ladies, just a little more virginity, if you don't mind.
  to a motley collection of females, assembled to play ladies-in-waiting to a queen
  Alexander Woollcott *Shouts and Murmurs* (1923)

G. M. Trevelyan 1876–1962
English historian

5 Disinterested intellectual curiosity is the life-blood of real civilization.
  English Social History (1942)

6 If the French noblesse had been capable of playing cricket with their peasants, their chateaux would never have been burnt.
  English Social History (1942)

7 [Education] has produced a vast population able to read but unable to distinguish what is worth reading, an easy prey to sensations and cheap appeals.
  English Social History (1942)

John Trevelyan 1903–86
British film censor

8 We are paid to have dirty minds.
  in *Observer* 15 November 1959

William Trevor 1928–
Irish novelist and short story writer

9 A disease in the family that is never mentioned.
  of the troubles in Northern Ireland
  in *Observer* 18 November 1990

Calvin Trillin 1935–
American journalist and writer

10 The shelf life of the modern hardback writer is somewhere between the milk and the yoghurt.
  in *Sunday Times* 9 June 1991; attributed

David Trimble 1944–
Northern Irish politician, leader of the Ulster Unionists 1995–2005

11 The fundamental Act of Union is there, intact.
  of the Northern Ireland settlement
  in *Daily Telegraph* 11 April 1998

Tommy Trinder 1909–89
British comedian

12 Overpaid, overfed, oversexed, and over here.
  of American troops in Britain during the Second World War
    associated with Trinder, but probably not original

Leon Trotsky 1879–1940
Russian revolutionary. He helped to organize the October Revolution with Lenin, and built up the Red Army. He was expelled from the Communist Party by Stalin in 1927 and exiled in 1929. He settled in Mexico in 1937, where he was later murdered by a Stalinist assassin
on Trotsky: see **Taylor 310:8**

13 You [the Mensheviks] are pitiful isolated individuals; you are bankrupts; your role is played out. Go where you belong from

now on—into the dustbin of history!
History of the Russian Revolution (1933)

1 Where force is necessary, there it must be
applied boldly, decisively and completely.
But one must know the limitations of force;
one must know when to blend force with a
manoeuvre, a blow with an agreement.
What Next? (1932)

2 It was the supreme expression of the
mediocrity of the apparatus that Stalin
himself rose to his position.
My Life (1930)

3 Old age is the most unexpected of all things
that happen to a man.
diary, 8 May 1935

Pierre Trudeau 1919–2000
Canadian Liberal statesman, Prime Minister
1968–79 and 1980–4

4 The state has no place in the nation's
bedrooms.
interview, Ottawa, 22 December 1967

5 The twentieth century really belongs to
those who will build it. The future can be
promised to no one.
in 1968, referring to Wilfrid Laurier
(1841–1919) speech, Ottawa, 18 January 1904:
'The nineteenth century was the century of
the United States. I think we can claim that it
is Canada that shall fill the twentieth century'

6 Living next to you is in some ways like
sleeping with an elephant. No matter how
friendly and even-tempered the beast, one
is affected by every twitch and grunt.
on relations between Canada and the US
speech at National Press Club, Washington
D.C., 25 March 1969

Fred Trueman 1931–2006
British cricketer

*asked if he thought anyone would surpass his
achievement in taking 300 Test wickets:*
7 If anyone beats it, they'll be bloody tired.
in 1964; quoted in obituary, *BBC Sport* (online
edition) 1 July 2006

Harry S. Truman 1884–1972
American Democratic statesman, 33rd President of
the US 1945–53; as Vice-President he succeeded to
office on the death of Franklin **Roosevelt**
on Truman: see **Mencken 219:4**; see also
Newspaper headlines 237:6

*to reporters the day after his accession to the
Presidency on the death of Franklin **Roosevelt**:*
8 When they told me yesterday what had
happened, I felt like the moon, the stars
and all the planets had fallen on me.
on 13 April 1945

9 Sixteen hours ago an American airplane
dropped one bomb on Hiroshima . . . The
force from which the sun draws its power
has been loosed against those who brought
war to the Far East.
*first announcement of the dropping of the
atomic bomb*
on 6 August 1945

10 Effective, reciprocal, and enforceable
safeguards acceptable to all nations.
*Declaration on Atomic Energy by President
Truman, Clement **Attlee**, and W. L. Mackenzie
King*
on 15 November 1945

11 What we are doing in Korea is this: we are
trying to prevent a third world war.
*after the recall of **MacArthur***
address to the nation, 16 April 1951

12 I never give them [the public] hell. I just tell
the truth, and they think it is hell.
in *Look* 3 April 1956

13 A statesman is a politician who's been
dead 10 or 15 years.
in *New York World Telegram and Sun* 12 April
1958

14 It's a recession when your neighbour loses
his job; it's a depression when you lose
yours.
in *Observer* 13 April 1958

15 Wherever you have an efficient
government you have a dictatorship.
lecture at Columbia University, 28 April 1959

16 Always be sincere, even if you don't mean
it.
attributed

17 The buck stops here.
unattributed motto on Truman's desk

1 He'll sit right here and he'll say do this, do that! And nothing will happen. Poor Ike— it won't be a bit like the Army.
*of his successor **Eisenhower***
Harry S. Truman (1973) vol. 2; see **Schwarzkopf 289:1**

2 I didn't fire him [General MacArthur] because he was a dumb son of a bitch, although he was, but that's not against the law for generals. If it was, half to three-quarters of them would be in jail.
Merle Miller *Plain Speaking* (1974)

3 If you can't stand the heat, get out of the kitchen.
attributed by Truman himself to his White House aide Harry Vaughan (1893–1981), his 'military jester'
in *Time* 28 April 1952

Donald Trump 1946–
American businessman

4 Deals are my art form. Other people paint beautifully on canvas or write wonderful poetry. I like making deals, preferably big deals. That's how I get my kicks.
Donald Trump and Tony Schwartz *The Art of the Deal* (1987)

Lynne Truss 1955–
British writer and journalist

5 Abuse is the currency of all reality shows.
Talk to the Hand (2005)

Morton Tsvangirai 1952–
Zimbabwean politician, founder and leader of the Movement for Democratic Change

6 This country is for blacks. But we need the knowledge of the whites to train people and create jobs.
in *Times* 15 April 2000

Marina Tsvetaeva 1892–1941
Russian poet

7 In this
most Christian of worlds all poets are Jews.
'Poem of the End' (1924)

Sophie Tucker 1884–1966
Russian-born American vaudeville artiste
see also **Kaufman 174:9**

8 From birth to 18 a girl needs good parents. From 18 to 35, she needs good looks. From 35 to 55, good personality. From 55 on, she needs good cash.
M. Freedland *Sophie* (1978)

Alan Turing 1912–54
English mathematician. He developed the concept of a theoretical computing machine, a key step in the development of the first computer, and carried out important code-breaking work in the Second World War. He also investigated artificial intelligence

9 We are not interested in the fact that the brain has the consistency of cold porridge.
A. P. Hodges *Alan Turing: the Enigma* (1983)

Sherry Turkle 1948–
American sociologist

10 Like the anthropologist returning home from a foreign culture, the voyager in virtuality can return home to a real world better equipped to understand its artifices.
Life on the Screen: Identity in the Age of the Internet (1995)

Walter James Redfern Turner 1889–1946
British writer and critic

11 When I was but thirteen or so
I went into a golden land,
Chimborazo, Cotopaxi
Took me by the hand.
'Romance' (1916)

John Tusa 1936–
British broadcaster and radio journalist

12 Management that wants to change an institution must first show it loves that institution.
in *Observer* 27 February 1994

Desmond Tutu 1931–
South African Anglican clergyman, Archbishop of
Cape Town 1986–96

1 I have struggled against tyranny. I didn't
do that in order to substitute one tyranny
with another.
*on the ANC's attempt to prevent publication of
the Truth Commission report*
in *Irish Times* 31 October 1998

2 We may be surprised at the people we find
in heaven. God has a soft spot for sinners.
His standards are quite low.
in *Sunday Times* 15 April 2001

Jill Tweedie 1936–93
British journalist

3 I blame the women's movement for ten
years in a boiler suit.
attributed, 1989

Kenneth Tynan 1927–80
English theatre critic

4 Oh, I think so, certainly. I doubt if there are
very many rational people in this world to
whom the word 'fuck' is particularly
diabolical or revolting or totally forbidden.
*on 13 November 1965 on a late-night
programme called* BBC-3; *the comment caused
considerable outrage*
Kathleen Tynan (ed.) *Kenneth Tynan: Letters*
(1994)

5 A critic is a man who knows the way but
can't drive the car.
in *New York Times Magazine* 9 January 1966

6 'Sergeant Pepper'—a decisive moment in
the history of Western Civilization.
in 1967; Howard Elson *McCartney* (1986)

7 A neurosis is a secret you don't know
you're keeping.
Kathleen Tynan *Life of Kenneth Tynan* (1987)

Mike Tyson 1966–
American boxer, world heavyweight champion
1987–90

8 I'm in the hurt business.
in *Independent on Sunday* 24 December 2000

Harlan K. Ullman and James P. Wade
American strategic analysts

1 The basis for rapid dominance rests in the ability to affect the will, perception, and understanding of the adversary through imposing sufficient Shock and Awe to achieve the necessary political, strategic, and operational goals of the conflict or crisis that led to the use of force.
> *Shock and Awe: Achieving Rapid Dominance* (1996) ch. 2; see also **Anonymous 12:5**

Tracey Ullman 1959–
British actress

2 The most remarkable thing about my mother is that for 30 years she served nothing but leftovers. The original meal was never found.
> in *Observer* 23 May 1999

Miguel de Unamuno 1864–1937
Spanish philosopher and writer

3 *La vida es duda,*
y la fe sin la duda es sólo muerte.

Life is doubt,
And faith without doubt is nothing but death.
> 'Salmo II' (1907)

John Updike 1932–
American novelist and short-story writer

4 A healthy male adult bore consumes *each year* one and a half times his own weight in other people's patience.
> *Assorted Prose* (1965) 'Confessions of a Wild Bore'

5 A soggy little island huffing and puffing to keep up with Western Europe.
> *of England*
> *Picked Up Pieces* (1976) 'London Life' (written 1969)

6 America is a vast conspiracy to make you happy.
> *Problems* (1980) 'How to love America and Leave it at the Same Time'

7 You shouldn't sit in judgment of your parents. We did the best we could while being people too.
> *Rabbit at Rest* (1990)

8 Without the cold war, what's the point of being an American?
> *Rabbit at Rest* (1990)

9 Rain is grace; rain is the sky condescending to the earth; without rain, there would be no life.
> *Self-Consciousness: Memoirs* (1989)

10 Celebrity is a mask that eats into the face.
> *Self-Consciousness: Memoirs* (1989)

11 A mistress knows the man to be a liar, where the wife only guesses.
> *Terrorist* (2006)

12 Neutrinos, they are very small
They have no charge and have no mass
And do not interact at all.
> 'Cosmic Gall ' (1964)

13 I've never much enjoyed going to plays . . . The unreality of painted people standing on a platform saying things they've said to each other for months is more than I can overlook.
> George Plimpton (ed.) *Writers at Work* 4th Series (1977)

Peter Ustinov 1921–2004
British actor, director, and writer

1 Laughter . . . the most civilized music in the world.
   Dear Me (1977)

2 I do not believe that friends are necessarily the people you like best, they are merely the people who got there first.
   Dear Me (1977)

3 At the age of four with paper hats and wooden swords we're all Generals. Only some of us never grow out of it.
   Romanoff and Juliet (1956)

4 Laughter would be bereaved if snobbery died.
   in *Observer* 13 March 1955

5 Toronto is a kind of New York operated by the Swiss.
   in *Globe & Mail* 1 August 1987; attributed

V

Paul Valéry 1871–1945
French poet, critic, and man of letters

1 A poem is never finished; it's always an accident that puts a stop to it—that is to say, gives it to the public.
Littérature (1930)

2 Science means simply the aggregate of all the recipes that are always successful. The rest is literature.
Moralités (1932)

3 God created man and, finding him not sufficiently alone, gave him a companion to make him feel his solitude more keenly.
Tel Quel 1 (1941) 'Moralités'

4 Politics is the art of preventing people from taking part in affairs which properly concern them.
Tel Quel 2 (1943) 'Rhumbs'

5 For direct feeling, [erudition] substitutes theories, for the marvellous actuality an encyclopedic memory; and the immense museum is further saddled with a limitless library. Venus becomes a document.
'The Problem of Museums' in *Les Introuvables* (1925)

Paul Vance
and Lee Pockriss *fl.* 1960
American singer and American songwriter

6 Itsy bitsy teenie weenie, yellow polkadot bikini.
title of song (1960)

Vivian van Damm *c.*1889–1960
British theatre manager

7 We never closed.
of the Windmill Theatre, London, during the Second World War
Tonight and Every Night (1952)

Laurens van der Post 1906–96
South African explorer and writer

8 Human beings are perhaps never more frightening than when they are convinced beyond doubt that they are right.
Lost World of the Kalahari (1958)

9 I don't think a man who has watched the sun going down could walk away and commit a murder.
in *Daily Telegraph* 17 December 1996; obituary

Henry Van Dyke 1852–1933
American Presbyterian minister and writer

10 Time is
Too slow for those who wait,
Too swift for those who fear,
Too long for those who grieve,
Too short for those who rejoice;
But for those who love,
Time is eternity.
'Time is too slow for those who wait' (1905), read at the funeral of **Diana**, Princess of Wales; Nigel Rees in 'Quote . . . Unquote' October 1997 notes that the original form of the last line is 'Time is not'

Raoul Vaneigem 1934–
Belgian philosopher

11 Never before has a civilization reached such a degree of a contempt for life; never before has a generation, drowned in

mortification, felt such a rage to live.
of the 1960s
   The Revolution of Everyday Life (1967)

1 The same people who are murdered slowly
in the mechanized slaughterhouses of
work are also arguing, singing, drinking,
dancing, making love, holding the streets,
picking up weapons and inventing a new
poetry.
   The Revolution of Everyday Life (1967)

2 Work to survive, survive by consuming,
survive to consume: the hellish cycle is
complete.
   The Revolution of Everyday Life (1967)

Bartolomeo Vanzetti 1888–1927
American anarchist, born in Italy, who with Nicolo
Sacco was executed for murder and robbery after a
sensational and controversial trial
see also **Millay 220:14**, **Millay 221:13**

3 Sacco's name will live in the hearts of the
people and in their gratitude when
Katzmann's and yours bones will be
dispersed by time, when your name, his
name, your laws, institutions, and your
false god are but a deem rememoring of a
cursed past in which man was wolf to the
man.
   statement disallowed at his trial, referring to
   Plautus (*c.*250–184 BC) *Asinaria*: 'A man is a
   wolf rather than a man to another man, when
   he hasn't yet found out what he's like'; M. D.
   Frankfurter and G. Jackson *Letters of Sacco
   and Vanzetti* (1928)

4 If it had not been for these thing, I might
have live out my life talking at street
corners to scorning men. I might have die,
unmarked, unknown, a failure. Now we
are not a failure. This is our career and our
triumph. Never in our full life could we
hope to do such work for tolerance, for
joostice, for man's ondersanding of man
as now we do by accident.
   statement after being sentenced to death,
   9 April 1927

Michel Vaucaire
French songwriter

5 *Non! rien de rien,*
   Non! je ne regrette rien,
   Ni le bien, qu'on m'a fait,

Ni le mal—tout ça m'est bien égal!
No, no regrets,
No, we will have no regrets,
As you leave, I can say—
Love was king, tho' for only a day.
   '*Non, je ne regrette rien*' (1960 song); sung by
   Edith Piaf (1915–63)

Janet-Maria Vaughan 1899–1993
English scientist

6 I am here—trying to do science in hell.
   *working as a doctor in Belsen at the end of the
   war*
   letter to a friend, 12 May 1945; P. A. Adams
   (ed.) *Janet-Maria Vaughan* (1993)

Ralph Vaughan Williams 1872–1958
English composer. His strongly melodic music
frequently reflects his interest in Tudor composers
and English folk songs

7 I don't know whether I like it, but it's what
I meant.
   on his 4th symphony
   Christopher Headington *Bodley Head History
   of Western Music* (1974)

   *on being asked by a reporter, 'What do you think
   about music?':*
8 It's a Rum Go!
   Leslie Ayr *The Wit of Music* (1966)

Robert Venturi 1925–
American architect, pioneer of postmodernist
architecture

9 Less is a bore.
   Complexity and Contradiction in Architecture
   (1966); see **Mies van der Rohe 220:7**

Gianni Versace 1949–97
Italian designer, known for his extravagant designs
for both men and women

10 I like to dress egos. If you haven't got an
ego today, you can forget it.
   in *Guardian* 16 July 1997; obituary

Hendrik Frensch Verwoerd 1901–66
South African statesman, Prime Minister 1958–66,
when he was assassinated; as Minister of Bantu
Affairs (1950–8) he had developed the segregation
policy of apartheid

11 Up till now he [the Bantu] has been
subjected to a school system which drew

him away from his own community and
practically misled him by showing him the
green pastures of the European but still did
not allow him to graze there . . . It is
abundantly clear that unplanned
education creates many problems, disrupts
the communal life of the Bantu and
endangers the communal life of the
European.
  speech in South African Senate, 7 June 1954

Sid Vicious 1957–79
British rock musician, member of the Sex Pistols
on Vicious: see **Newspaper headlines 237:9**

1 You just pick a chord, go twang, and
  you've got music.
    attributed

Vicky (Victor Weisz) 1913–66
German-born British cartoonist, creator of the
'Supermac' image of Harold **Macmillan**

2 I don't make fun of a face. I make fun of
  what is behind that face.
    quoted in *Oxford Dictionary of National
    Biography* (2004–)

Gore Vidal 1925–
American novelist and critic

3 What other culture could have produced
  someone like Hemingway and *not* seen the
  joke?
    Pink Triangle and Yellow Star (1982)

4 I'm all for bringing back the birch, but only
  between consenting adults.
    in *Sunday Times Magazine* 16 September
    1973

5 Whenever a friend succeeds, a little
  something in me dies.
    in *Sunday Times Magazine* 16 September
    1973

6 It is not enough to succeed. Others must
  fail.
    G. Irvine *Antipanegyric for Tom Driberg*
    8 December 1976

7 A triumph of the embalmer's art.
    of Ronald **Reagan**
    in *Observer* 26 April 1981

*on being asked what would have happened in
1963, had* **Khrushchev** *and not* **Kennedy** *been
assassinated:*
8 With history one can never be certain, but
  I think I can safely say that Aristotle
  Onassis would not have married Mrs
  Khrushchev.
    in *Sunday Times* 4 June 1989

9 A genius with the IQ of a moron.
    of Andy **Warhol**
    in *Observer* 18 June 1989

of Truman **Capote***'s death:*
10 Good career move.
    attributed

11 He will lie even when it is inconvenient:
   the sign of the true artist.
    attributed

José Antonio Viera Gallo 1943–
Chilean politician

12 Socialism can only arrive by bicycle.
    Ivan Illich *Energy and Equity* (1974) epigraph

Gilles Vigneault 1928–
Canadian singer, songwriter and poet

13 *Mon pays ce n'est pas un pays, c'est l'hiver.*
   My country is not a country, it is winter.
    'Mon Pays' (1964)

Diana Vreeland 1903–89
American fashion editor

14 [The bikini] revealed everything about a
   girl except her mother's maiden name.
    attributed; Lena Lencek *The Beach* (1998)

John Wain 1925–94
English poet and novelist

1 Poetry is to prose as dancing is to walking.
   BBC radio broadcast, 13 January 1976

Derek Walcott 1930–
West Indian poet and dramatist

2 You spit on your people,
   your people applaud,
   your former oppressors
   laurel you.
   The thorns biting your forehead
   are contempt
   disguised as concern,
   still, you can come home, now.
   to exiled novelists
      'At Last' (1976)

3 I who have cursed
   The drunken officer of British rule, how
      choose
   Between this Africa and the English tongue
      I love?
      'A Far Cry From Africa' (1962)

4 Nothing will always be created in the West
   Indies for quite long time, because what
   will come out of there is like nothing one
   has ever seen before.
   *in response to V. S. **Naipaul**'s comment: see*
   Naipaul 233:11
      'The Caribbean: Culture or Mimicry?' in
      *Journal of Interamerican Studies and World
      Affairs* February 1974

5 The English language is nobody's special
   property. It is the property of the
   imagination: it is the property of the
   language itself.
      Edward Hirsch 'The Art of Poetry' (1986) in R.
      Hanmer (ed.) *Critical Perspectives on Derek
      Walcott* (1993)

6 I come from a backward place: your duty is
   supplied by life around you. One guy plants
   bananas; another plants cocoa; I'm a
   writer, I plant lines. There's the same
   clarity of occupation, and the sense of
   devotion.
      in *Guardian* 12 July 1997

Lech Wałęsa 1943–
Polish trade unionist and statesman, President
1990–5. The founder of Solidarity (1980), he was
imprisoned 1981–2 after the movement was banned.
After Solidarity's landslide victory in the 1989
elections he became President

7 You have riches and freedom here but I feel
   no sense of faith or direction. You have so
   many computers, why don't you use them
   in the search for love?
      in Paris, on his first journey outside the Soviet
      area, in *Daily Telegraph* 14 December 1988

Alice Walker 1944–
American poet

8 Did this happen to your mother? Did your
   sister throw up a lot?
      title of poem, 1979

9 Expect nothing. Live frugally
   on surprise.
      'Expect nothing' (1973)

10 The quietly pacifist peaceful
   always die
   to make room for men
   who shout.
      'The QPP' (1973)

11 We have a beautiful
   mother
   Her green lap
   immense
   Her brown embrace

eternal
Her blue body
everything
we know.
'We Have a Beautiful Mother' (1991)

1 I think it pisses God off if you walk by the colour purple in a field somewhere and don't notice it.
The Colour Purple (1982)

2 Womanist is to feminist as purple to lavender.
In Search of Our Mother's Gardens (1983), epigraph

George Wallace 1919–98
American Democratic politician, who attempted unsuccessfully to block federal efforts to end racial segregation in Alabama state schools

3 Segregation now, segregation tomorrow and segregation forever!
inaugural speech as Governor of Alabama, January 1963

Henry Wallace 1888–1965
American Democratic politician

4 The century on which we are entering— the century which will come out of this war—can be and must be the century of the common man.
speech, 8 May 1942

Graham Wallas 1858–1932
British politician scientist

5 The little girl had the making of a poet in her who, being told to be sure of her meaning before she spoke, said, 'How can I know what I think till I see what I say?'
The Art of Thought (1926)

Julie Walters 1950–
British actress

6 I have a rare intolerance to herbs which means I can only drink fermented liquids, such as gin.
in *Observer* 14 March 1999

Barbara Ward 1914–81
British writer and educator

7 We cannot cheat on DNA. We cannot get round photosynthesis. We cannot say I am

not going to give a damn about phytoplankton. All these tiny mechanisms provide the preconditions of our planetary life. To say we do not care is to say in the most literal sense that 'we choose death'.
Only One Earth (1972)

Andy Warhol 1927–87
American painter, graphic artist, and film-maker. A major exponent of pop art, he achieved fame for a series of silk-screen prints and acrylic paintings of familiar objects (such as Campbell's soup tins) and famous people (such as Marilyn Monroe), treated with objectivity and precision
on Warhol: see **Vidal 325:9**

8 In the future everybody will be world famous for fifteen minutes.
Andy Warhol (1968)

9 My idea of a good picture is one that's in focus and of a famous person doing something unfamous. It's being in the right place at the wrong time.
Andy Warhol's Exposures (1979)

10 Being good in business is the most fascinating kind of art.
Philosophy of Andy Warhol (From A to B and Back Again) (1975)

11 An artist is someone who produces things that people don't need to have but that he—for *some reason*—thinks it would be a good idea to give them.
Philosophy of Andy Warhol (From A to B and Back Again) (1975)

12 Isn't life a series of images that change as they repeat themselves?
Victor Bokris *Andy Warhol* (1989)

13 The things I want to show are mechanical. Machines have less problems.
Mike Wrenn *Andy Warhol: In His Own Words* (1991)

Shane Warne 1969–
Australian cricketer

14 I have learnt to think of three words all the time—what, when and why. That means always knowing what I am going to bowl, when I am going to bowl it and to be clear why I have chosen that option.
My Autobiography (2001)

Jack Warner 1892–1978
American film producer, co-founder (in 1923) of the production company Warner Brothers

> *on hearing that Ronald **Reagan** was seeking nomination as Governor of California:*

1 No, *no. Jimmy Stewart* for governor—Reagan for his best friend.
> Max Wilk *The Wit and Wisdom of Hollywood* (1972)

Sylvia Townsend Warner 1893–1978
English writer

2 One need not write in a diary what one is to remember for ever.
> diary, 22 October 1930

3 One cannot overestimate the power of a good rancorous hatred on the part of the *stupid*. The stupid have so much more industry and energy to expend on hating. They build it up like coral insects.
> diary, 26 September 1954

Earl Warren 1891–1974
American judge, chief justice of the US Supreme Court

4 The freedom to marry has long been recognized as one of the vital personal rights essential to the orderly pursuit of happiness by free men.
> judgement in *Loving v. Virginia* 1967

Robert Penn Warren 1905–89
American poet, novelist, and critic

5 Long ago in Kentucky, I, a boy, stood
By a dirt road, in first dark, and heard
The great geese hoot northward.
> *Audubon* (1969) 'Tell Me a Story'

6 They were human, they suffered, wore
   long black coat and gold watch chain.
They stare from daguerrotype with severe
   reprehension,
Or from genuine oil, and you'd never guess
   any pain
In those merciless eyes that now remark
   our own time's sad declension.
> 'Promises' (1957)

Ned Washington 1901–76
American songwriter

7 Hi diddle dee dee (an actor's life for me).
> title of song from the film *Pinocchio* (1940)

8 The night is like a lovely tune,
Beware my foolish heart!
How white the ever-constant moon,
Take care, my foolish heart!
> 'My Foolish Heart' (1949 song)

Keith Waterhouse 1929–
English novelist, dramatist, and screenwriter

9 Jeffrey Bernard is unwell.
> *from the* Spectator's *habitual explanation for the non-appearance of Jeffrey Bernard's column*
> title of play (1989)

James D. Watson 1928–
American biologist. Together with Francis **Crick** he proposed the double helix structure of the DNA molecule
on Watson: see **Medawar 218:7**; see also **Crick and Watson**

10 No *good* model ever accounted for *all* the facts, since some data was bound to be misleading if not plain wrong.
> Francis Crick *Some Mad Pursuit* (1988)

11 Some day a child is going to sue its parents for being born. They will say, my life is so awful with these terrible genetic defects and you just callously didn't find out.
> *on the question of genetic screening of foetuses*
> interview in *Sunday Telegraph* 16 February 1997

Thomas Watson Snr. 1874–1956
American businessman; Chairman of IBM 1914–52

12 Clothes don't make the man . . . but they go a long way toward making a businessman.
> Robert Sobel *IBM: Colossus in Transition* (1981)

13 You cannot be a success in any business without believing that it is the greatest business in the world . . . You have to put your heart in the business and the business in your heart.
> Robert Sobel *IBM: Colossus in Transition* (1981)

Evelyn Waugh 1903–66
English novelist, whose novels of black comedy and social satire were also profoundly influenced by his conversion to Roman Catholicism

14 Charm is the great English blight. It does not exist outside these damp islands. It

spots and kills anything it touches. It kills love, it kills art.
Brideshead Revisited (1945)

1 The sound of English county families baying for broken glass.
Decline and Fall (1928); see **Belloc 27:14**

2 I expect you'll be becoming a schoolmaster, sir. That's what most of the gentlemen does, sir, that gets sent down for indecent behaviour.
Decline and Fall (1928)

3 Any one who has been to an English public school will always feel comparatively at home in prison. It is the people brought up in the gay intimacy of the slums, Paul learned, who find prison so soul-destroying.
Decline and Fall (1928)

4 Only when one has lost all curiosity about the future has one reached the age to write an autobiography.
A Little Learning (1964)

5 In the dying world I come from quotation is a national vice. No one would think of making an after-dinner speech without the help of poetry. It used to be the classics, now it's lyric verse.
The Loved One (1948)

6 He abhorred plastics, Picasso, sunbathing and jazz—everything in fact that had happened in his own lifetime.
The Ordeal of Gilbert Pinfold (1957)

7 *The Beast* stands for strong mutually antagonistic governments everywhere . . . Self-sufficiency at home, self-assertion abroad.
Scoop (1938)

8 Up to a point, Lord Copper.
Scoop (1938)

9 Feather-footed through the plashy fen passes the questing vole.
Scoop (1938)

10 Other nations use 'force'; we Britons alone use 'Might'.
Scoop (1938)

11 To see him fumbling with our rich and delicate language is to experience all the horror of seeing a Sèvres vase in the hands of a chimpanzee.
of Stephen **Spender**
in *Tablet* 5 May 1951

12 I do not aspire to advise my sovereign in her choice of servants.
on why he did not vote
in *Spectator* 2 October 1959

13 A typical triumph of modern science to find the only part of Randolph that was not malignant and remove it.
on hearing that Randolph Churchill's lung, when removed, proved non-malignant
diary, March 1964

14 You have no idea how much nastier I would be if I was not a Catholic. Without supernatural aid I would hardly be a human being.
Noel Annan *Our Age* (1990)

Frederick Weatherly 1848–1929
English songwriter

15 Roses are flowering in Picardy,
But there's never a rose like you.
'Roses of Picardy' (1916 song); Picardy in northern France was also the scene of heavy fighting during the First World War

Beatrice Webb 1858–1943
English socialist, economist, and historian, wife of Sidney **Webb**; they were prominent members of the Fabian Society and helped to establish the London School of Economics (1895)

16 If I ever felt inclined to be timid as I was going into a room full of people, I would say to myself, 'You're the cleverest member of one of the cleverest families in the cleverest class of the cleverest nation in the world, why should you be frightened?'
Bertrand Russell *Autobiography* (1967)

Sidney Webb 1859–1947
English socialist, economist, and historian, husband of Beatrice **Webb**

17 The inevitability of gradualness.
Presidential address to the annual conference of the Labour Party, 26 June 1923

18 Marriage is the waste-paper basket of the emotions.
Bertrand Russell *Autobiography* (1967)

Simone Weil 1909–43
French essayist, philosopher, and mystic. During the Second World War she joined the resistance movement in England and died of tuberculosis while weakened by voluntary starvation in identification with her French compatriots

1 An obligation which goes unrecognized by anybody loses none of the full force of its existence. A right which goes unrecognized by anybody is not worth very much.
   L'Enracinement (The Need for Roots, 1949)
   'Les Besoins de l'âme'

2 All sins are attempts to fill voids.
   La Pesanteur et la grâce (Gravity and Grace, 1948)

3 The authentic and pure values—truth, beauty, and goodness—in the activity of a human being are the result of one and the same act, a certain application of the full attention to the object.
   La Pesanteur et la grâce (Gravity and Grace, 1948)

4 A work of art has an author and yet, when it is perfect, it has something which is essentially anonymous about it.
   La Pesanteur et la grâce (Gravity and Grace, 1948)

5 What a country calls its vital economic interests are not the things which enable its citizens to live, but the things which enable it to make war.
   W. H. Auden A Certain World (1971)

6 At the very best, a mind enclosed in language is in prison.
   'Human Personality' (1943)

Max Weinreich 1894–1969
American Yiddish scholar

7 A language is a dialect with an army and a navy.
   Steven Pinker The Language Instinct (1994)

Victor Weisskopf 1908–2002
American physicist

8 It was absolutely marvellous working for Pauli. You could ask him anything. There was no worry that he would think a particular question was stupid, since he thought all questions were stupid.
   on Wolfgang Pauli
   in American Journal of Physics 1977

Johnny Weissmuller
see Misquotations 224:13

Chaim Weizmann 1874–1952
Russian-born Israeli statesman, President 1949–52

9 Something had been done for us which, after two thousand years of hope and yearning, would at last give us a resting-place in this terrible world.
   of the Balfour declaration; see Balfour 22:2
   speech in Jerusalem, 25 November 1936

Joseph Welch 1890–1960
American lawyer

10 Until this moment, Senator, I think I never really gauged your cruelty or your recklessness . . . Have you no sense of decency, sir? At long last, have you left no sense of decency?
   to Joseph McCarthy, 9 June 1954, defending the US Army against allegations of harbouring subversive activities; the televised confrontation was deeply damaging to McCarthy
   in American National Biography (online edition) 'Joseph McCarthy'

Fay Weldon 1931–
British novelist and scriptwriter
see also Advertising slogans 3:22

11 Natalie had left the wives and joined the women.
   Heart of the Country (1987)

12 The life and loves of a she-devil.
   title of novel (1984)

13 It's very unfashionable to say this, but rape actually isn't the worst thing that can happen to a woman if you're safe, alive and unmarked after the event.
   in Radio Times 4 July 1998

Colin Welland 1934–
English actor and scriptwriter

14 The British are coming.
   speech accepting an Oscar for his Chariots of Fire screenplay, 30 March 1982

Orson Welles 1915–85
American actor and film director
see also **Film lines 114:11**

1 The biggest electric train set any boy ever had!
of the RKO studios
   Peter Noble *The Fabulous Orson Welles* (1956)

2 I hate television. I hate it as much as peanuts. But I can't stop eating peanuts.
   in *New York Herald Tribune* 12 October 1956

3 There are only two emotions in a plane: boredom and terror.
   interview to celebrate his 70th birthday, in *Times* 6 May 1985

H. G. Wells 1866–1946
English novelist. He wrote some of the earliest science-fiction novels, such as *The War of the Worlds* (1898), which combined political satire with warnings about the powers of science
see also **Epitaphs 107:6**

4 'Sesquippledan,' he would say. 'Sesquippledan verboojuice.'
   The History of Mr Polly (1909)

5 The Social Contract is nothing more or less than a vast conspiracy of human beings to lie to and humbug themselves and one another for the general Good. Lies are the mortar that bind the savage individual man into the social masonry.
   Love and Mr Lewisham (1900)

6 Human history becomes more and more a race between education and catastrophe.
   The Outline of History (1920)

7 The shape of things to come.
   title of book (1933)

8 The war that will end war.
   title of book (1914); see also **Lloyd George 201:5**

9 In England we have come to rely upon a comfortable time-lag of fifty years or a century intervening between the perception that something ought to be done and a serious attempt to do it.
   The Work, Wealth and Happiness of Mankind (1931)

Irvine Welsh 1957–
Scottish novelist

10 It's nae good blamin' it oan the English fir colonising us. Ah don't hate the English. They're just wankers. We can't even pick a decent vibrant, healthy culture to be colonised by.
   Trainspotting (1994)

Eudora Welty 1909–2001
American novelist, short-story writer, and critic. Welty's novels chiefly focus on life in the Southern states of the US and contain Gothic elements

11 I am a writer who came of a sheltered life. A sheltered life can be a daring life as well. For all serious daring starts from within.
   One Writer's Beginnings (1984)

12 It was like living near a mountain.
   *on being a writer in Mississippi after **Faulkner***
   On William Faulkner (2003)

Arnold Wesker 1932–
English dramatist, whose writing is associated with the British kitchen-sink drama of the 1950s

13 Chips with every damn thing. You breed babies and you eat chips with everything.
   Chips with Everything (1962)

14 A journalist is somebody who possesses himself of a fantasy and lures the truth towards it.
   Journey into Journalism (1977)

15 The Khomeini cry for the execution of Rushdie is an infantile cry. From the beginning of time we have seen that. To murder the thinker does not murder the thought.
   in *Weekend Guardian* 3 June 1989; see **Khomeini 179:11**

Mae West 1892–1980
American film actress and dramatist. She made her name on Broadway in her own comedies *Sex* (1926) and *Diamond Lil* (1928), memorable for their spirited approach to sexual matters, before embarking on her successful Hollywood career in the 1930s
see also **Film lines 115:3, Military sayings 221:5, Misquotations 225:8**

16 It's better to be looked over than overlooked.
   Belle of the Nineties (1934 film)

1 A man in the house is worth two in the street.
   Belle of the Nineties (1934 film)

2 I always say, keep a diary and some day it'll keep you.
   Every Day's a Holiday (1937 film)

3 Beulah, peel me a grape.
   I'm No Angel (1933 film)

4 I've been things and seen places.
   I'm No Angel (1933 film)

5 When I'm good, I'm very, very good, but when I'm bad, I'm better.
   I'm No Angel (1933 film)

6 It's not the men in my life that counts—it's the life in my men.
   I'm No Angel (1933 film)

7 Give a man a free hand and he'll try to put it all over you.
   Klondike Annie (1936 film)

8 Between two evils, I always pick the one I never tried before.
   Klondike Annie (1936 film)

9 'Goodness, what beautiful diamonds!'
   'Goodness had nothing to do with it.'
   Night After Night (1932 film)

10 I've been in *Who's Who*, and I know what's what, but it'll be the first time I ever made the dictionary.
   letter to the RAF, early 1940s, on having an inflatable life jacket named after her
   Fergus Cashin *Mae West* (1981)

11 Is that a gun in your pocket, or are you just glad to see me?
   usually quoted as, 'Is that a pistol in your pocket . . .'
   J. Weintraub *Peel Me a Grape* (1975)

12 I used to be Snow White . . . but I drifted.
   J. Weintraub *Peel Me a Grape* (1975)

13 A hard man is good to find.
   attributed

14 It's not what I do, but the way I do it. It's not what I say, but the way I say it.
   G. Eells and S. Musgrove *Mae West* (1989)

Rebecca West 1892–1983
English novelist and journalist

15 Were I to . . . take a peasant by the shoulders and whisper to him, 'In your lifetime, have you known peace?' wait for his answer, shake his shoulders and transform him into his father, and ask him the same question, and transform him in his turn to his father, I would never hear the word 'Yes', if I carried my questioning of the dead back for a thousand years.
   of Yugoslavia in the 1930s
   Black Lamb and Grey Falcon (1941) vol. 1

16 There is no such thing as conversation. It is an illusion. There are intersecting monologues, that is all.
   'The Harsh Voice' (1935)

17 Having watched the form of our traitors for a number of years, I cannot think that espionage can be recommended as a technique for building an impressive civilization. It's a lout's game.
   The Meaning of Treason (1982 ed.)

18 The point is that nobody likes having salt rubbed into their wounds, even if it is the salt of the earth.
   The Salt of the Earth (1935)

19 I myself have never been able to find out precisely what feminism is: I only know that people call me a feminist whenever I express sentiments that differentiate me from a doormat or a prostitute.
   in *Clarion* 14 November 1913

20 Just how difficult it is to write biography can be reckoned by anybody who sits down and considers just how many people know the truth about his or her love affairs.
   in *Vogue* 1 November 1952

21 There is, of course, no reason for the existence of the male sex except that sometimes one needs help with moving the piano.
   in *Sunday Telegraph* 28 June 1970

22 Whatever happens, never forget that people would rather be led to *perdition* by a man, than to *victory* by a woman.
   in conversation in 1979, just before Margaret **Thatcher***'s first election victory*
   in *Sunday Telegraph* 17 January 1988

Loelia, Duchess of Westminster
1902–93
English aristocrat

1 Anybody seen in a bus over the age of thirty has been a failure in life.
   Cocktails and Laughter (1983); habitual remark

William C. Westmoreland 1914–2005
American general, commander of United States forces in the Vietnam War, 1964–8

2 Vietnam was the first war ever fought without censorship. Without censorship, things can get terribly confused in the public mind.
   attributed, 1982

R. P. Weston 1878–1936
and **Bert Lee** 1880–1947
British songwriters

3 Good-bye-ee!—Good-bye-ee!
   Wipe the tear, baby dear, from your eye-ee.
   Tho' it's hard to part, I know,
   I'll be tickled to death to go.
   Don't cry-ee—don't sigh-ee!
   There's a silver lining in the sky-ee!
   Bonsoir, old thing! cheerio! chin-chin!
   Nahpoo! Toodle-oo! Good-bye-ee!
   'Good-bye-ee!' (*c.*1915 song)

Alan Wharton 1923–93
English cricketer

4 It's a well-known fact that, when I'm on 99, I'm the best judge of a run in all the bloody world.
   to fellow cricketer Cyril Washbrook; Freddie Trueman *You Nearly Had Me That Time* (1978)

Edith Wharton 1862–1937
American novelist, whose novels are concerned with the conflict between social and individual fulfilment

5 Mrs Ballinger is one of the ladies who pursue Culture in bands, as though it were dangerous to meet it alone.
   Xingu and Other Stories (1916) 'Xingu'

6 To your generation, I must represent the literary equivalent of tufted furniture and gas chandeliers.
   letter to F. Scott Fitzgerald, 8 June 1925

E. B. White 1899–1985
American humorist
see also **Cartoons 56:7**

7 The so-called science of poll-taking is not a science at all but a mere necromancy. People are unpredictable by nature, and although you can take a nation's pulse, you can't be sure that the nation hasn't just run up a flight of stairs.
   in *New Yorker* 13 November 1948

8 Commuter—one who spends his life
   In riding to and from his wife;
   A man who shaves and takes a train,
   And then rides back to shave again.
   'The Commuter' (1982)

Patrick White 1912–90
Australian novelist

9 Conversation is imperative if gaps are to be filled, and old age, it is the last gap but one.
   The Tree of Man (1955)

10 So that, in the end, there was no end.
   The Tree of Man (1955); closing words

11 In all directions stretched the great Australian Emptiness, in which the mind is the least of possessions.
   The Vital Decade (1968) 'The Prodigal Son'

T. H. White 1906–64
English novelist

12 The once and future king.
   taken from Sir Thomas Malory Le Morte d'Arthur: 'Hic iacet Arthurus, rex quondam rexque futurus'
   title of novel (1958)

Theodore H. White 1915–86
American writer and journalist

13 The flood of money that gushes into politics today is a pollution of democracy.
   in *Time* 19 November 1984

Alfred North Whitehead 1861–1947
English philosopher and mathematician

14 Life is an offensive, directed against the repetitious mechanism of the Universe.
   Adventures of Ideas (1933)

15 It is more important that a proposition be interesting than that it be true. This

statement is almost a tautology. For the energy of operation of a proposition in an occasion of experience is its interest, and is its importance. But of course a true proposition is more apt to be interesting than a false one.
Adventures of Ideas (1933)

1 There are no whole truths; all truths are half-truths. It is trying to treat them as whole truths that plays the devil.
Dialogues (1954) prologue

2 Intelligence is quickness to apprehend as distinct from ability, which is capacity to act wisely on the thing apprehended.
Dialogues (1954) 15 December 1939

3 What is morality in any given time or place? It is what the majority then and there happen to like, and immorality is what they dislike.
Dialogues (1954) 30 August 1941

4 Art is the imposing of a pattern on experience, and our aesthetic enjoyment is recognition of the pattern.
Dialogues (1954) 10 June 1943

5 Civilization advances by extending the number of important operations which we can perform without thinking about them.
Introduction to Mathematics (1911)

6 No more impressive warning can be given to those who would confine knowledge and research to what is apparently useful, than the reflection that conic sections were studied for eighteen hundred years merely as an abstract science, without regard to any utility other than to satisfy the craving for knowledge on the part of mathematicians, and that then at the end of this long period of abstract study, they were found to be the necessary key with which to attain the knowledge of the most important laws of nature.
Introduction to Mathematics (1911)

7 The safest general characterization of the European philosophical tradition is that it consists of a series of footnotes to Plato.
Process and Reality (1929)

Katharine Whitehorn 1928–
English journalist

8 Being young is not having any money; being young is not minding not having any money.
Observations (1970)

9 An office party is not, as is sometimes supposed, the Managing Director's chance to kiss the tea-girl. It is the tea-girl's chance to kiss the Managing Director.
Roundabout (1962) 'The Office Party'

10 I wouldn't say when you've seen one Western you've seen the lot; but when you've seen the lot you get the feeling you've seen one.
Sunday Best (1976) 'Decoding the West'

Gough Whitlam 1916–
Australian Labor statesman, Prime Minister 1972–5

11 Well may he say 'God Save the Queen'. But after this nothing will save the Governor-General.
having been dismissed from office by the Governor-General, Sir John Kerr
speech in Canberra, 11 November 1975

12 Maintain your rage and enthusiasm through the campaign for the election now to be held and until polling day.
speech in Canberra, 11 November 1975

Charlotte Whitton 1896–1975
Canadian writer and politician

13 Whatever women do they must do twice as well as men to be thought half as good.
in *Canada Month* June 1963

William H. Whyte 1917–
American writer

14 This book is about the organization man . . . I can think of no other way to describe the people I am talking about. They are not the workers, nor are they the white-collar people in the usual, clerk sense of the word. These people only work for the Organization. The ones I am talking about *belong* to it as well.
The Organization Man (1956)

Ann Widdecombe 1947–
British Conservative politician

1 He has something of the night in him.
of the Conservative politician Michael Howard as a contender for the Conservative leadership (which he subsequently attained in 2003)
in *Sunday Times* 11 May 1997 (electronic edition)

Elie Wiesel 1928–
Romanian-born American writer and Nobel Prize winner; Auschwitz survivor

2 The opposite of love is not hate, it's indifference. The opposite of art is not ugliness, it's indifference. The opposite of faith is not heresy, it's indifference. And the opposite of life is not death, it's indifference.
in *U.S. News and World Report* 27 October 1986

3 Take sides. Neutrality helps the oppressor, never the victim. Silence encourages the tormentor, never the tormented.
accepting the Nobel Peace Prize
in *New York Times* 11 December 1986

4 God of forgiveness, do not forgive those murderers of Jewish children here.
at an unofficial ceremony at Auschwitz on 26 January 1995, commemorating the 50th anniversary of its liberation
in *Times* 27 January 1995

5 600,000 to 800,00 human beings were murdered. We know now, as we knew then, they could have been saved, and they were not.
recalling the genocide in Rwanda
addressing the United Nations Security Council, 14 September 2006, on the situation in Darfur; see also **Clooney 72:9**

Richard Wilbur 1921–
American poet

6 Spare us all word of the weapons, their force and range,
The long numbers that rocket the mind.
'Advice to a Prophet' (1961)

7 We milk the cow of the world, and as we do
We whisper in her ear, 'You are not true.'
'Epistemology' (1950)

8 Mind in its purest play is like some bat

That beats about in caverns all alone,
Contriving by a kind of senseless wit
Not to conclude against a wall of stone.
'Mind' (1956)

9 The good grey guardians of art
Patrol the halls on spongy shoes.
'Museum Piece' (1950)

Billy Wilder 1906–2002
Austrian-born American screenwriter and director
see also **Film lines 116:7, Film lines 116:16**

10 It used to be that we in films were the lowest form of art. Now we have something to look down on.
of television
A. Madsen *Billy Wilder* (1968)

11 What they [critics] call dirty in our pictures, they call lusty in foreign films.
A. Madsen *Billy Wilder* (1968)

12 Hindsight is always twenty-twenty.
J. R. Columbo *Wit and Wisdom of the Moviemakers* (1979)

*on Marilyn **Monroe**'s unpunctuality:*
13 My Aunt Minnie would always be punctual and never hold up production, but who would pay to see my Aunt Minnie?
P. F. Boller and R. L. Davis *Hollywood Anecdotes* (1988)

Thornton Wilder 1897–1975
American novelist and dramatist

14 Even memory is not necessary for love. There is a land of the living and a land of the dead and the bridge is love, the only survival, the only meaning.
The Bridge of San Luis Rey (1927), closing words

15 Marriage is a bribe to make a housekeeper think she's a householder.
The Merchant of Yonkers (1939)

16 Literature is the orchestration of platitudes.
in *Time* 12 January 1953

Robert Wilensky 1951–
American academic

17 We've all heard that a million monkeys banging on a million typewriters will eventually reproduce the entire works of Shakespeare. Now, thanks to the Internet,

we know this is not true.
in *Mail on Sunday* 16 February 1997 'Quotes of
the Week'; see **Eddington 96:7**

Geoffrey Willans 1911–58 and Ronald Searle 1920–
English humorous writers

1 As any fule kno.
Down with Skool! (1953)

2 There is no better xsample of a goody-
goody than fotherington-tomas in the
world in space. You kno he is the one who
sa Hullo Clouds Hullo Sky and skip about
like a girly.
How To Be Topp (1954)

Heathcote Williams 1941–
British dramatist and poet

3 Whales play, in an amniotic paradise.
Their light minds shaped by buoyancy,
unrestricted by gravity,
Somersaulting.
Like angels, or birds;
Like our own lives, in the womb.
Whale Nation (1988)

Kenneth Williams 1926–88
English actor

4 The nice thing about quotes is that they
give us a nodding acquaintance with the
originator which is often socially
impressive.
Acid Drops (1980)

R. J. P. Williams 1926–
British chemist

5 Biology is the search for the chemistry that
works.
lecture in Oxford, June 1996

Robin Williams 1952–
American actor

6 There were a lot of doctors in rehab. It's
rather like being in a fat farm with
nutritionists.
quoted in www.metro.co.uk 29 December
2006 'Quotes of the Year'

Tennessee Williams 1911–83
American dramatist

7 We're all of us guinea pigs in the
laboratory of God. Humanity is just a work
in progress.
Camino Real (1953)

8 What is the victory of a cat on a hot tin
roof?—I wish I knew . . . Just staying on it,
I guess, as long as she can.
Cat on a Hot Tin Roof (1955)

9 I'm not living with you. We occupy the
same cage.
Cat on a Hot Tin Roof (1955)

10 BRICK: Well, they say nature hates a
vacuum, Big Daddy.
BIG DADDY: That's what they say, but
sometimes I think that a vacuum is a hell
of a lot better than some of the stuff that
nature replaces it with.
Cat on a Hot Tin Roof (1955)

11 I didn't go to the moon, I went much
further—for time is the longest distance
between two places.
The Glass Menagerie (1945)

12 We're all of us sentenced to solitary
confinement inside our own skins, for life!
Orpheus Descending (1958)

13 Turn that off! I won't be looked at in this
merciless glare!
A Streetcar Named Desire (1947)

14 BLANCHE: I don't want realism.
MITCH: Naw, I guess not.
BLANCHE: I'll tell you what I want. Magic!
A Streetcar Named Desire (1947)

15 I have always depended on the kindness of
strangers.
A Streetcar Named Desire (1947)

William Carlos Williams 1883–1963
American poet

16 Minds like beds always made up,
(more stony than a shore)
unwilling or unable.
Paterson (1946)

17 so much depends
upon
a red wheel
barrow

glazed with rain
water
beside the white
chickens.
   'The Red Wheelbarrow' (1923)

1 I have eaten
   the plums
   that were in
   the icebox

   and which
   you were probably
   saving
   for breakfast

   Forgive me
   they were delicious
   so sweet
   and so cold.
      'This is Just to Say'

2 Is it any better in Heaven, my friend Ford,
   Than you found it in Provence?
      'To Ford Madox Ford in Heaven' (1944)

Marianne Williamson 1953–
American writer and philanthropist

3 Our deepest fear is not that we are
   inadequate. Our deepest fear is that we are
   powerful beyond measure. It is our light,
   not our darkness, that most frightens us.
      A Return to Love (1992)

Roy Williamson 1936–90
Scottish folksinger and musician

4 O flower of Scotland, when will we see
      your like again,
   that fought and died for your wee bit hill
      and glen
   and stood against him, proud Edward's
      army,
   and sent him homeward tae think again.
   unofficial Scottish Nationalist anthem
      'O Flower of Scotland' (1968)

Wendell Willkie 1892–1944
American lawyer and Republican politician,
presidential candidate in 1940

5 The constitution does not provide for first
   and second class citizens.
      An American Programme (1944)

Angus Wilson 1913–91
English novelist and short-story writer

6 Once a Catholic always a Catholic.
   The Wrong Set (1949)

Charles E. Wilson 1890–1961
American industrialist; President of General Motors,
1941–53
on Wilson: see **Anonymous 10:6**

7 For years I thought what was good for our
   country was good for General Motors and
   vice versa.
      testimony to the Senate Armed Services
      Committee on his proposed nomination for
      Secretary of Defence, 15 January 1953

Colin Wilson 1931–
British writer, whose first book was the best-selling
work of philosophy *The Outsider* (1956)

8 At first sight, the Outsider is a social
   problem. He is the hole-in-corner man.
   The Outsider (1956), opening sentence

9 The Outsider is not a freak, but is only
   more sensitive than the average type of
   man.
   The Outsider (1956)

Earl Wilson 1907–87
American journalist and writer

10 If you think nobody cares if you're alive,
   try missing a couple of car payments.
      attributed

Edward O. Wilson 1929–
American sociobiologist, expert on ants

11 Why do we study insects? Because,
   together with man, hummingbirds and the
   bristlecone pine, they are among the great
   achievements of organic evolution.
   The Insect Societies (1971)

12 Marxism is sociobiology without biology
   ... Although Marxism was formulated as
   the enemy of ignorance and superstition,
   to the extent that it has become dogmatic it
   has faltered in that commitment and is
   now mortally threatened by the discoveries
   of human sociobiology.
   On Human Nature (1978)

1 Wonderful theory, wrong species.
  on Marxism
    in *Los Angeles Times* 21 October 1994

2 Every human brain is born not as a blank tablet (a *tabula rasa*) waiting to be filled in by experience but as 'an exposed negative waiting to be slipped into developer fluid'.
  on the nature v. nurture debate
    attributed; Tom Wolfe in *Independent on Sunday* 2 February 1997

Harold Wilson 1916–95
British Labour statesman, Prime Minister 1964–70, 1974–6
on Wilson: see **Home 156:11, Junor 173:10**; see also **Misquotations 225:7**

3 All these financiers, all the little gnomes in Zurich.
    speech, House of Commons, 12 November 1956

4 I myself have always deprecated . . . in crisis after crisis, appeals to the Dunkirk spirit as an answer to our problems.
    in the House of Commons, 26 July 1961

5 This party is a moral crusade or it is nothing.
    speech at the Labour Party Conference, 1 October 1962

6 If I had the choice between smoked salmon and tinned salmon, I'd have it tinned. With vinegar.
    in *Observer* 11 November 1962

7 The university of the air.
  an early term for the Open University
    in *Glasgow Herald* 9 September 1963

8 A week is a long time in politics.
  probably first said at the time of the 1964 sterling crisis
    Nigel Rees *Sayings of the Century* (1984)

9 [Labour is] the natural party of government.
    in 1965; Anthony Sampson *The Changing Anatomy of Britain*

10 From now the pound abroad is worth 14 per cent or so less in terms of other currencies. It does not mean, of course, that the pound here in Britain, in your pocket or purse or in your bank, has been devalued.
  often quoted as 'the pound in your pocket'
    ministerial broadcast, 19 November 1967

11 Get your tanks off my lawn, Hughie.
  to the trade union leader Hugh Scanlon, at Chequers in June 1969
    Peter Jenkins *The Battle of Downing Street* (1970); see also **Clarke 70:13**

Woodrow Wilson 1856–1924
American Democratic statesman, 28th President of the US 1913–21; he eventually took America into the First World War in 1917 and played a leading role in the peace negotiations and the formation of the League of Nations
on Wilson: see **Clemenceau 71:4**

12 It is like writing history with lightning. And my only regret is that it is all so terribly true.
  on seeing D. W. Griffith's film The Birth of a Nation
    at the White House, 18 February 1915

13 No nation is fit to sit in judgement upon any other nation.
    speech in New York, 20 April 1915

14 There is such a thing as a man being too proud to fight.
    speech in Philadelphia, 10 May 1915

15 We have stood apart, studiously neutral.
    speech to Congress, 7 December 1915

16 It must be a peace without victory . . . Only a peace between equals can last.
    speech to US Senate, 22 January 1917

17 Armed neutrality is ineffectual enough at best.
    speech to Congress, 2 April 1917

18 The world must be made safe for democracy.
    speech to Congress, 2 April 1917

19 Once lead this people into war and they will forget there ever was such a thing as tolerance.
    John Dos Passos *Mr Wilson's War* (1917)

20 Open covenants of peace, openly arrived at.
  first of Wilson's Fourteen Points for a peace treaty to conclude the First World War, which were to be only partially fulfilled by the Treaty of Versailles
    speech to Congress, 8 January 1918

Walter Winchell

see **Catchphrases 59:3**

Duchess of Windsor (Wallis Simpson)

1896–1986

American-born wife of the former **Edward VIII**; her relationship with the king caused a scandal in view of her previous and impending divorces and resulted in the king's abdication in 1936

see also **Anonymous 10:15**

  1 You can never be too rich or too thin.
    attributed

Duke of Windsor

see **Edward VIII**

Oprah Winfrey 1954–

American talk-show host

  2 Luck is preparation meeting opportunity.
    interview, Academy of Achievement, 21
    February 1991

  3 There's no easy way out. If there were, I
    would have bought it. And believe me, it
    would be one of my favourite things!
    of exercise
    in *O: the Oprah Magazine* February 2005

Yvor Winters 1900–68

American poet and critic

  4 The young are quick of speech.
    Grown middle-aged, I teach
    Corrosion and distrust,
    Exacting what I must.
    'On Teaching the Young' (1934)

Jeanette Winterson 1959–

British novelist

  5 Oranges are not the only fruit.
    title of novel, 1985

Ludwig Wittgenstein 1889–1951

Austrian-born British philosopher
see also **Last words 191:5**

  6 Philosophy is a battle against the
    bewitchment of our intelligence by means
    of language.
    Philosophische Untersuchungen (1953)

  7 What is your aim in philosophy?—To
    show the fly the way out of the fly-bottle.
    Philosophische Untersuchungen (1953)

  8 What can be said at all can be said clearly;
    and whereof one cannot speak thereof one
    must be silent.
    Tractatus Logico-Philosophicus (1922)

  9 The world is everything that is the case.
    Tractatus Logico-Philosophicus (1922)

  10 The limits of my language mean the limits
    of my world.
    Tractatus Logico-Philosophicus (1922)

  11 Death is not an event of life.
    Tractatus Logico-Philosophicus (1922)

P. G. Wodehouse 1881–1975

English writer; an American citizen from 1955. His best-known works are humorous stories of the upper-class world of Bertie Wooster and his valet Jeeves, the first of which appeared in 1917
on Wodehouse: see **O'Casey 241:9**

  12 Chumps always make the best husbands
    . . . All the unhappy marriages come from
    the husbands having brains.
    The Adventures of Sally (1920)

  13 It is never difficult to distinguish between a
    Scotsman with a grievance and a ray of
    sunshine.
    Blandings Castle and Elsewhere (1935) 'The
    Custody of the Pumpkin'

  14 There was another ring at the front door.
    Jeeves shimmered out and came back with
    a telegram.
    Carry On, Jeeves! (1925) 'Jeeves Takes Charge'

  15 He spoke with a certain what-is-it in his
    voice, and I could see that, if not actually
    disgruntled, he was far from being
    gruntled.
    The Code of the Woosters (1938)

  16 It is no use telling me that there are bad
    aunts and good aunts. At the core, they are
    all alike. Sooner or later, out pops the
    cloven hoof.
    The Code of the Woosters (1938)

  17 Roderick Spode? Big chap with a small
    moustache and the sort of eye that can
    open an oyster at sixty paces?
    The Code of the Woosters (1938)

  18 To my daughter Leonora without
    whose never-failing sympathy and
    encouragement this book would
    have been finished in half the time.
    The Heart of a Goof (1926) dedication

1 For the first time since sudden love had thrown them into each other's arms, she had found herself beginning to wonder if her Blair was quite the godlike superman she had supposed. There even flashed through her mind a sinister speculation as to whether, when you came right down to it, he wasn't something of a pill.
Hot Water (1932)

2 I turned to Aunt Agatha, whose demeanour was now rather like that of one who, picking daisies on the railway, has just caught the down express in the small of the back.
The Inimitable Jeeves (1923)

3 When Aunt is calling to Aunt like mastodons bellowing across primeval swamps.
The Inimitable Jeeves (1923)

4 It was my Uncle George who discovered that alcohol was a food well in advance of medical thought.
The Inimitable Jeeves (1923)

5 She fitted into my biggest armchair as if it had been built round her by someone who knew they were wearing armchairs tight about the hips that season.
My Man Jeeves (1919) 'Jeeves and the Unbidden Guest'

6 Ice formed on the butler's upper slopes.
Pigs Have Wings (1952)

7 The Right Hon. was a tubby little chap who looked as if he had been poured into his clothes and had forgotten to say 'When!'
Very Good, Jeeves (1930) 'Jeeves and the Impending Doom'

Terry Wogan 1938–
Irish broadcaster

8 Television contracts the imagination and radio expands it.
in *Observer* 30 December 1984

Naomi Wolf 1962–
American writer

9 To ask women to become unnaturally thin is to ask them to relinquish their sexuality.
The Beauty Myth (1990)

Humbert Wolfe 1886–1940
British poet

10 You cannot hope
to bribe or twist,
thank God! the
British journalist.
But, seeing what
the man will do
unbribed, there's
no occasion to.
'Over the Fire' (1930)

Thomas Wolfe 1900–38
American novelist

11 Which of us has not remained forever prison-pent? Which of us is not forever a stranger and alone?
foreword to *Look Homeward, Angel* (1929)

12 Most of the time we think we're sick, it's all in the mind.
Look Homeward, Angel (1929)

13 'Where they got you stationed now, Luke?' . . . 'In Norfolk at the Navy base,' Luke answered, 'm-m-making the world safe for hypocrisy.'
Look Homeward, Angel (1929); see **Wilson 338:18**

14 You can't go home again.
title of book, 1940

Tom Wolfe 1931–
American writer

15 The bonfire of the vanities.
title of novel (1987); deriving from Savonarola's 'burning of the vanities' in Florence, 1497

16 A liberal is a conservative who has been arrested.
The Bonfire of the Vanities (1987); see **Sayings and slogans 286:7**

17 Electric Kool-Aid Acid test.
title of novel on hippy culture (1968)

18 We are now in the Me Decade—seeing the upward roll of . . . the third great religious wave in American history . . . and this one

has the mightiest, holiest roll of all, the beat that goes . . . *Me . . . Me . . . Me . . . Me.*
Mauve Gloves and Madmen (1976) 'The Me Decade'

1 Radical Chic . . . is only radical in Style; in its heart it is part of Society and its tradition—Politics, like Rock, Pop, and Camp, has its uses.
in *New York* 8 June 1970

Lewis Wolpert 1929–
English biologist

2 If Watson and Crick had not discovered the nature of DNA, one can be virtually certain that other scientists would eventually have determined it. With art—whether painting, music or literature—it is quite different. If Shakespeare had not written *Hamlet,* no other playwright would have done so.
The Unnatural Nature of Science (1993)

Kenneth Wolstenholme 1920–2002
English sports commentator

3 They think it's all over—it is now.
television commentary in closing moments of the World Cup Final, 30 July 1966

Victoria Wood 1953–
British writer and comedienne

4 JACKIE: (*very slowly*) Take Tube A and apply to Bracket D.
VICTORIA: Reading it slower does not make it any easier to do.
Mens Sana in Thingummy Doodah (1990)

5 It will be a very traditional Christmas, with presents, crackers, doors slamming and people bursting into tears, but without the big dead thing in the middle.
of a vegetarian Christmas
in *Sunday Times* 24 December 2000

George Woodcock 1912–95
Canadian writer and essayist

6 Canadians do not like heroes, and so they do not have them.
Canada and the Canadians (1970)

Thomas Woodrooffe 1899–1978
British naval officer

7 The whole Fleet's lit up. When I say 'lit up', I mean lit up by fairy lamps.
live outside broadcast, Spithead Review, 20 May 1937
Asa Briggs *History of Broadcasting in the UK* (1965) vol. 2

Harry Woods 1896–1970
American songwriter

8 Oh we ain't got a barrel of money,
Maybe we're ragged and funny,
But we'll travel along
Singin' a song,
Side by side.
'Side by Side' (1927 song)

Tiger Woods 1975–
American golfer

9 Growing up, I came up with this name: I'm a Cablinasian.
explaining his rejection of 'African-American' as the term to describe his Caucasian, Afro-American, Native American, Thai, and Chinese ancestry
interviewed by Oprah Winfrey, 21 April 1997

Virginia Woolf 1882–1941
English novelist, essayist, and critic. A member of the Bloomsbury Group, she gained recognition with *Jacob's Room* (1922). Subsequent novels, such as *Mrs Dalloway* (1925) and *To the Lighthouse* (1927), characterized by their poetic impressionism, established her as an exponent of modernism
on Woolf: see **Laski 189:15**, **Sitwell 295:14**

10 On or about December 1910 human nature changed . . . All human relations have shifted—those between masters and servants, husbands and wives, parents and children. And when human relations change there is at the same time a change in religion, conduct, politics, and literature.
'Mr Bennett and Mrs Brown' (1924)

11 A woman must have money and a room of her own if she is to write fiction.
A Room of One's Own (1929)

12 This is an important book, the critic assumes, because it deals with war. This is an insignificant book because it deals with

the feelings of women in a drawing room.
A Room of One's Own (1929)

1 So that is marriage, Lily thought, a man
and a woman looking at a girl throwing a
ball.
To the Lighthouse (1927)

2 I have lost friends, some by death . . . others
through sheer inability to cross the street.
The Waves (1931)

3 What sort of diary should I like mine to be?
. . . I should like it to resemble some deep
old desk, or capacious hold-all, in which
one flings a mass of odds and ends without
looking them through.
diary, 20 April 1919

4 The scratching of pimples on the body of
the bootboy at Claridges.
*of James **Joyce**'s* Ulysses
letter to Lytton Strachey, 24 April 1922

5 As an experience, madness is terrific . . .
and in its lava I still find most of the things I
write about.
letter to Ethel Smyth, 22 June 1930

6 And now with some pleasure I find that it's
seven; and must cook dinner. Haddock and
sausage meat. I think it is true that one
gains a certain hold on sausage and
haddock by writing them down.
diary, 8 March 1941

Alexander Woollcott 1887–1943
American drama critic

7 She was like a sinking ship firing on the
rescuers.
*of Mrs Patrick **Campbell***
While Rome Burns (1944) 'The First Mrs
Tanqueray'

8 She is so odd a blend of Little Nell and Lady
Macbeth. It is not so much the familiar
phenomenon of a hand of steel in a velvet
glove as a lacy sleeve with a bottle of vitriol
concealed in its folds.
*of Dorothy **Parker***
While Rome Burns (1934) 'Our Mrs Parker'

9 All the things I really like to do are either
illegal, immoral, or fattening.
R. E. Drennan *Wit's End* (1973)

Terry Worrall *fl.* 1991
British spokesman for British Rail

10 We are having particular problems on this
occasion with the type of snow, which is
very dry and powdery and is actually
penetrating all the protection we had on
some of our locomotives.
*explaining disruption on British Rail; popularly
summarized as 'the wrong sort of snow'; see*
Newspaper headlines 237:2
in *Evening Standard* 11 February 1991

Frank Lloyd Wright 1867–1959
American architect, whose 'prairie-style' houses
revolutionized American domestic architecture

11 The physician can bury his mistakes, but
the architect can only advise his client to
plant vines—so they should go as far as
possible from home to build their first
buildings.
in *New York Times* 4 October 1953

James Wright 1927–80
American poet

12 Suddenly I realize
That if I stepped out of my body I would
break
Into blossom.
'A Blessing' (1963)

Kenyon Wright 1932–
Scottish Methodist minister, Chairman of the
Scottish Constitutional Convention

13 What if that other single voice we know so
well responds by saying, 'We say No and
we are the State.' Well, we say Yes and we
are the People!
*of Margaret **Thatcher** as Prime Minister*
speech at the inaugural meeting of the
Scottish Constitutional Convention, 30 March
1989

Harry Wu 1937–
Chinese-born American political activist

14 I want to see the word *laogai* in every
dictionary in every language in the world. I
want to see the laogai ended. Before 1974,
the word 'gulag' did not appear in any
dictionary. Today, this single word
conveys the meaning of Soviet political
violence and its labour camp system.

'Laogai' also deserves a place in our dictionaries.

the laogai *are Chinese labour camps*
in *Washington Post* 26 May 1996

Tammy Wynette 1942–98
and Billy Sherrill *c.*1938–
American singer and American songwriter

1 Stand by your man.
title of song (1968); see also **Clinton 71:10**

y

Isoroku Yamamoto 1884–1943
Japanese admiral, Commander-in-Chief responsible for planning the Japanese attack on Pearl Harbor; he died when his plane was shot down by US forces

1 A military man can scarcely pride himself on having 'smitten a sleeping enemy'; in fact, to have it pointed out is more a matter of shame.

> letter, 9 January 1942; Hirosuki Asawa *The Reluctant Admiral* (1979, tr. John Bester); see **Film lines 114:2**

Minoru Yamasaki 1912–88
American architect, designer of the World Trade Center (1973; destroyed by terrorist attack in September 2001)

2 The World Trade Center should, because of its importance, become a living representation of man's belief in humanity, his need for individual dignity, his belief in the cooperation of men, and through this cooperation his ability to find greatness.

> Paul Heyer *Architects on Architecture* (1967)

W. B. Yeats 1865–1939
Irish poet, whose play *The Countess Cathleen* (1892) and his collection of stories *The Celtic Twilight* (1893) stimulated Ireland's theatrical, cultural, and literary revival
on Yeats: see **Auden 17:9**

3 O body swayed to music, O brightening glance,
How can we know the dancer from the dance?
> 'Among School Children' (1928)

4 Only God, my dear,
Could love you for yourself alone
And not your yellow hair.
> 'Anne Gregory' (1932)

5 The unpurged images of day recede;
The Emperor's drunken soldiery are abed.
> 'Byzantium' (1933)

6 Those images that yet
Fresh images beget,
That dolphin-torn, that gong-tormented sea.
> 'Byzantium' (1933)

7 Now that my ladder's gone
I must lie down where all the ladders start,
In the foul rag-and-bone shop of the heart.
> 'The Circus Animals' Desertion' (1939)

8 We were the last romantics—chose for theme
Traditional sanctity and loveliness.
> 'Coole and Ballylee, 1931' (1933)

9 The intellect of man is forced to choose
Perfection of the life, or of the work,
And if it take the second must refuse
A heavenly mansion, raging in the dark.
> 'Coole Park and Ballylee, 1932' (1933)

10 A woman can be proud and stiff
When on love intent;
But Love has pitched his mansion in
The place of excrement;
For nothing can be sole or whole
That has not been rent.
> 'Crazy Jane Talks with the Bishop' (1932)

11 Nor dread nor hope attend
A dying animal;
A man awaits his end
Dreading and hoping all.
> 'Death' (1933)

12 All changed, changed utterly:
A terrible beauty is born.
> 'Easter, 1916' (1921)

13 Too long a sacrifice

Can make a stone of the heart.
'Easter, 1916' (1921)

1 I write it out in a verse—
MacDonagh and MacBride
And Connolly and Pearse
Now and in time to be,
Wherever green is worn,
Are changed, changed utterly:
A terrible beauty is born.
'Easter, 1916' (1921)

2 The fascination of what's difficult
Has dried the sap of my veins, and rent
Spontaneous joy and natural content
Out of my heart.
'The Fascination of What's Difficult' (1910)

3 Never to have lived is best, ancient writers
say;
Never to have drawn the breath of life,
never to have looked into the eye of day;
The second best's a gay goodnight and
quickly turn away.
'From *Oedipus at Colonus*' (1928) referring to
Sophocles (*c*.496–406 BC) *Oedipus Coloneus*:
'Not to be born is, past all prizing, best'

4 The ghost of Roger Casement
Is beating on the door.
'The Ghost of Roger Casement' (1939)

5 The innocent and the beautiful
Have no enemy but time.
'In Memory of Eva Gore-Booth and Con
Markiewicz' (1933)

6 My country is Kiltartan Cross;
My countrymen Kiltartan's poor.
'An Irish Airman Foresees his Death' (1919)

7 Nor law, nor duty bade me fight,
Nor public men, nor cheering crowds.
'An Irish Airman Foresees his Death' (1919)

8 A shudder in the loins engenders there
The broken wall, the burning roof and
tower
And Agamemnon dead.
'Leda and the Swan' (1928)

9 Did that play of mine send out
Certain men the English shot?
'The Man and the Echo' (1939)

10 We had fed the heart on fantasies,
The heart's grown brutal from the fare.
'Meditations in Time of Civil War' no. 6 'The
Stare's Nest by my Window' (1928)

11 Think where man's glory most begins and
ends
And say my glory was I had such friends.
'The Municipal Gallery Re-visited' (1939)

12 I think it better that at times like these
A poet's mouth be silent, for in truth
We have no gift to set a statesman right;
He has had enough of meddling who can
please
A young girl in the indolence of her youth
Or an old man upon a winter's night.
'On being asked for a War Poem' (1919)

13 Where, where but here have Pride and
Truth,
That long to give themselves for wage,
To shake their wicked sides at youth
Restraining reckless middle-age?
'On hearing that the Students of our New
University have joined the Agitation against
Immoral Literature' (1910)

14 An intellectual hatred is the worst,
So let her think opinions are accursed.
'A Prayer for My Daughter' (1920)

15 Out of Ireland have we come.
Great hatred, little room,
Maimed us at the start.
'Remorse for Intemperate Speech' (1933)

16 That is no country for old men. The young
In one another's arms, birds in the trees—
Those dying generations—at their song.
'Sailing to Byzantium' (1928)

17 An aged man is but a paltry thing,
A tattered coat upon a stick, unless
Soul clap its hands and sing, and louder
sing
For every tatter in its mortal dress.
'Sailing to Byzantium' (1928)

18 And therefore I have sailed the seas and
come
To the holy city of Byzantium.
'Sailing to Byzantium' (1928)

19 All shuffle there; all cough in ink;
All wear the carpet with their shoes;
All think what other people think;
All know the man their neighbour knows.
Lord, what would they say
Did their Catullus walk that way?
'The Scholars' (1919)

20 Things fall apart; the centre cannot hold;
Mere anarchy is loosed upon the world,

The blood-dimmed tide is loosed, and
  everywhere
The ceremony of innocence is drowned;
The best lack all conviction, while the
  worst
Are full of passionate intensity.
  'The Second Coming' (1921)

1 And what rough beast, its hour come
   round at last,
  Slouches towards Bethlehem to be born?
  'The Second Coming' (1921)

2 Romantic Ireland's dead and gone,
  It's with O'Leary in the grave.
  'September, 1913' (1914)

3 O, who could have foretold
  That the heart grows old?
  'A Song' (1919)

4 You think it horrible that lust and rage
  Should dance attendance upon my old age;
  They were not such a plague when I was
   young;
  What else have I to spur me into song?
  'The Spur' (1939)

5 Swift has sailed into his rest;
  Savage indignation there
  Cannot lacerate his breast.
    'Swift's Epitaph' (1933), referring to Jonathan
    Swift (1667–1745) epitaph: '*Ubi saeva
    indignatio ulterius cor lacerare nequit* [Where
    fierce indignation can no longer tear his
    heart]'

6 Was there ever dog that praised his fleas?
    'To a Poet, Who would have Me Praise certain
    bad Poets, Imitators of His and of Mine' (1910)

7 Michaelangelo left a proof
  On the Sistine Chapel roof,
  Where but half-awakened Adam
  Can disturb globe-trotting Madam.
  'Under Ben Bulben' (1939)

8 Irish poets, learn your trade,
  Sing whatever is well made.
  'Under Ben Bulben' (1939)

9 Cast your mind on other days
  That we in coming days may be
  Still the indomitable Irishry.
  'Under Ben Bulben' (1939)

10 Cast a cold eye
   On life, on death.
   Horseman, pass by!
   'Under Ben Bulben' (1939)

of the Anglo-Irish:

11 We ... are no petty people. We are one of
   the great stocks of Europe. We are the
   people of Burke; we are the people of Swift,
   the people of Emmet, the people of Parnell.
   We have created most of the modern
   literature of this country. We have created
   the best of its political intelligence.
     speech in the Irish Senate, 11 June 1925, in the
     debate on divorce

Boris Yeltsin 1931–2007
Russian statesman, President of the Russian
Federation 1991–9

12 You can make a throne of bayonets, but
   you can't sit on it for long.
   *from the top of a tank, during the attempted
   military coup against* **Gorbachev**
     in *Independent* 24 August 1991; see **Inge
     162:9**

13 Europe is in danger of plunging into a cold
   peace.
   *at the summit meeting of the Conference on
   Security and Co-operation in Europe*
     in *Newsweek* 19 December 1994; see **Baruch
     24:13**

14 Today is the last day of an era past.
   *at a Berlin ceremony to end the Soviet military
   presence*
     in *Guardian* 1 September 1994

Sergei Yesenin 1895–1925
Russian poet
see also **Last words 190:10**

15 It's always the good feel rotten.
   Pleasure's for those who are bad.
   'Pleasure's for the Bad' (1923)

Yevgeny Yevtushenko 1933–
Russian poet

16 Over Babiy Yar
   There are no memorials.
   The steep hillside like a rough inscription.
     'Babiy Yar' (1961); in September and October
     1941, Babi Yar in Kiev was the site of a
     massacre of Soviet Jews by Nazi forces

17 Life is a rainbow which also includes black.
     in *Guardian* 11 August 1987

Shoichi Yokoi 1915–97
Japanese soldier

1 It is a terrible shame for me—I came back,
still alive, without having won the war.
on returning to Japan after surviving for 28 years
in the jungles of Guam before surrendering to
the Americans in 1972
　　in *Independent* 26 September 1997

Andrew Young 1932–
American clergyman and diplomat

2 Nothing is illegal if one hundred well-
placed business men decide to do it.
　　Morris K. Udall *Too Funny to be President*
　　(1988)

G. M. Young 1882–1959
English historian

3 Being published by the Oxford University
Press is rather like being married to a
duchess: the honour is almost greater than
the pleasure.
　　Rupert Hart-Davis, letter to George Lyttelton,
　　29 April 1956

Neil Young 1945–
Canadian singer

4 'Heart of Gold' put me in the middle of the
road. Travelling there soon became a bore
so I headed for the ditch. A rougher ride
but I saw more interesting people there.
of the success of this song from his 1972 album
'Harvest'
　　liner notes to *Decade* (1977)

Neil Young 1945–
and Jeff Blackburn
Canadian singer and songwriter

5 It's better to burn out
Than to fade away.
*quoted by Kurt **Cobain** in his suicide note, 8 April*
1994
　　'My My, Hey Hey (Out of the Blue)' (1978 song)

Z

Yevgeny Zamyatin 1884–1937
Russian writer

1 Heretics are the only bitter remedy against the entropy of human thought.
'Literature, Revolution and Entropy' quoted in *The Dragon and other Stories* (1967) introduction

2 Yesterday there was a tsar and there were slaves; today there is no tsar, but the slaves remain; tomorrow there will be only tsars . . . We have lived through the epoch of suppression of the masses; we are living in an epoch of suppression of the individual in the name of the masses; tomorrow will bring the liberation of the individual—in the name of man.
'Tomorrow' (1919) in *A Soviet Heretic* (1970)

Israel Zangwill 1864–1926
Jewish spokesman and writer

3 America is God's Crucible, the great Melting-Pot where all the races of Europe are melting and re-forming!
The Melting Pot (1908)

Emiliano Zapata 1879–1919
Mexican revolutionary, who attempted to implement his programme of agrarian reform by means of guerrilla warfare
see also **Ibarruri 162:2**

4 Many of them, so as to curry favour with tyrants, for a fistful of coins, or through bribery or corruption, are shedding the blood of their brothers.
on the maderistas *who, in Zapata's view, had betrayed the revolutionary cause*
Plan de Ayala 28 November 1911

Frank Zappa 1940–93
American rock musician and songwriter

5 A drug is neither moral or immoral—it's a chemical compound. The compound itself is not a menace to society until a human being treats it as if consumption bestowed a temporary licence to act like an asshole.
The Real Frank Zappa Book (1989)

6 Rock journalism is people who can't write interviewing people who can't talk for people who can't read.
L. Botts *Loose Talk* (1980)

Benjamin Zephaniah 1958–
British poet

7 I've tried Shakespeare, Respect due dere But dis is de stuff I like.
'Dis Poetry' (1992)

8 I think poetry should be alive. You should be able to dance it.
in *Sunday Times* 23 August 1987

Mikhail Zhvanetsky 1934–
Russian writer

9 We enjoyed . . . his slyness. He mastered the art of walking backward into the future. He would say 'After me'. And some people went ahead, and some went behind, and he would go backward.
of Mikhail **Gorbachev**
in *Time* 12 September 1994; attributed

Ronald L. Ziegler 1939–2003
American government spokesman, White House Press Secretary during the Watergate Affair

10 [Mr Nixon's latest statement] is the Operative White House Position . . . and all

previous statements are inoperative.
in *Boston Globe* 18 April 1973

Grigori Zinoviev 1883–1936
Soviet politician

1 Armed warfare must be preceded by a
struggle against the inclinations to
compromise which are embedded among
the majority of British workmen, against
the ideas of evolution and peaceful
extermination of capitalism. Only then will
it be possible to count upon complete
success of an armed insurrection.
*widely reported as a purveyor of 'Red
Propaganda'; it has been suggested that the
'Zinoviev Letter' was deliberately leaked by
British Intelligence prior to the October 1924*
*general election, or that (less probably) it was a
forgery*
letter to the British Communist Party, 15
September 1924

Hiller B. Zobel 1932–
American judge

2 Judges must follow their oaths and do
their duty, heedless of editorials, letters,
telegrams, threats, petitions, panellists and
talk shows.
In this country, we do not administer
justice by plebiscite. A judge . . . is a public
servant who must follow his conscience,
whether or not he counters the manifest
wishes of those he serves; whether or not
his decision seems a surrender to prevalent
demands.
judicial ruling reducing the conviction of
Louise Woodward from murder to
manslaughter, 10 November 1997

Keyword Index

advertisements ideals by its a.   DOUG 92:7
knew a column of a.   HOLM 156:7
advertiser a.'s 'sizzling'   PRIE 262:3
advertisers a. don't object to   SWAF 307:8
A. will advertise   BLIX 36:13
advertising A. is the most   DELL 88:13
A. is the rattling   ORWE 245:11
A. may be described   LEAC 193:12
a. we deserve   SAYE 285:10
invasion of a.   SOLZ 298:8
lust and calls it a.   LAHR 187:4
money I spend on a.   LEVE 198:5
advice integrated a.   ANON 11:2
unsolicited a.   COOL 76:4
wouldn't stoop to giving a.   SNIC 297:15
advise Advisers a.   THAT 313:9
aspire to a.   WAUG 329:12
PLEASE A.   TELE 311:8
aeroplanes it wasn't the a.   FILM 115:17
aesthetic a. enjoyment   WHIT 334:4
degree of my a. emotion   BELL 27:1
affairs his or her love a.   WEST 332:20
taking part in a.   VALÉ 323:4
affection a. you get back   NESB 236:2
affirmative condemn a. action   POWE 260:15
affluent a. society   GALB 128:6
so-called a. society   BEVA 33:11
afloat struggle continually to keep it a.
LA G 187:3
afraid a. of the big bad wolf   CHUR 66:10
a. of Virginia Woolf   ALBE 6:6
Be a.   TAGL 309:1
because she was a. of him   MURD 231:9
I, a stranger and a.   HOUS 158:3
not a. to die   ALLE 7:9
to be a.   FAUL 110:3
were a. to ask   REUB 269:9
Africa A. is a scar   BLAI 36:4
A. than my own body   ORTO 244:11
A. tugs   KISS 183:17
choose between this A.   WALC 326:3
deported A.   GENE 130:16
shape of A.   FANO 109:4
sloggin' over A.   KIPL 181:13
African A. is conditioned   KENY 178:5
A. national consciousness   MACM 209:5
struggle of the A. people   MAND 213:1
Africans A. experience people   KAUN 175:4
after A. the first death   THOM 314:8
A. you, Claude   CATC 58:1
one damned thing a. another   HUBB 159:1
afternoon a. of human life   JUNG 173:6
At five in the a.   LORC 202:14
lose the war in an a.   CHUR 69:8
summer a.   JAME 166:14
again déjà vu all over a.   BERR 31:13
I'll see you a.   COWA 78:4

against a. everything   KENN 178:2
always vote *a*.   FIEL 111:15
anyone who wasn't a. war   LOW 203:7
He was a. it   COOL 76:6
life is 6 to 5 a.   RUNY 277:12
vote a. somebody   ADAM 2:6
Agamemnon And A. dead   YEAT 345:8
When A. cried aloud   ELIO 102:18
age a. shall not weary them   BINY 34:10
a., which forgives itself   SHAW 292:22
dawning of the a. of Aquarius   RADO 265:4
old a. always fifteen years   BARU 24:14
Old a. is the most unexpected   TROT 318:3
unexpectedly great a.   PHIL 253:11
aged a. man is but a paltry thing   YEAT 345:17
learn how to be a.   BLYT 37:9
aggressive see hoodies as a.   CAME 51:10
AGM address the A.   SHUL 294:8
agnosticism all a. means   DARR 84:1
agony it was a., Ivy   CATC 58:19
agree More than three can't a.   HEIN 150:2
agreed you a. to evil   RODR 272:8
agreement blow with an a.   TROT 318:1
ahead a. of your time   MCGO 207:12
get a., get a hat   ADVE 3:29
aids adventure in the world of A.   PERK 252:8
aim forgotten your a.   SANT 283:12
ain't a. necessarily so   HEYW 153:2
air a. becomes uranious   LEHR 195:13
death of a.   ELIO 101:5
lands hatless from the a.   BETJ 32:8
trees are made of a.   FEYN 111:3
university of the a.   WILS 338:7
air conditioning respectability and a.
BARA 23:2
airline a. ticket to romantic   MARV 216:3
world's favourite a.   ADVE 5:13
airplanes feel about a.   KERR 178:8
airport observing a. layouts   PRIC 261:12
Alamein Before A. we never had   CHUR 69:7
Alan A. died suddenly   EPIT 107:1
alas A. but cannot pardon   AUDE 18:15
Albert Went there with young A.   EDGA 97:5
albums bought the Velvets' a.   ENO 105:16
alcohol A. a necessary article   SHAW 292:7
A. didn't cause   BOAZ 37:10
a. doesn't thrill me   PORT 258:16
a. or morphine   JUNG 173:4
a. was a food   WODE 340:4
taken more out of a.   CHUR 68:17
Aldershot burnish'd by A. sun   BETJ 32:15
alibi always has an a.   ELIO 102:12
Alice Pass the sick bag, A.   CATC 60:22
went down with A.   MILN 223:5
alien a. people clutching   ELIO 102:1
damned if I'm an a.   GEOR 131:7
alike all places were a. to him   KIPL 183:4

human beings are more a.	ANGE 9:8	born in A.	MALC 212:4
A-list on every bloody A.	EMIN 105:9	England and A. divided	SHAW 293:17
alive a. and well	ANON 11:8	God bless A.	BERL 30:5
a. and working on	ANON 10:14	I like to be in A.	SOND 298:11
came back, still a.	YOKO 347:1	impresses me about A.	EDWA 97:7
gets out of it a.	FILM 114:13	in the living rooms of A.	MCLU 208:13
If we can't stay here a.	MONT 227:5	I, too, sing A.	HUGH 159:5
Not while I'm a.	BEVI 34:3	love affair with A.	MAIL 211:7
poetry should be a.	ZEPH 348:8	makes A. what it is	STEI 302:10
still a. at twenty-two	KING 181:4	morning again in A.	POLI 257:19
ways of being a.	DAWK 85:3	next to god a.	CUMM 81:3
what keeps us a.	STEI 303:4	what A. did you have	GINS 133:6
what keeps you a.	CAST 57:4	**American** A. as cherry pie	BROW 46:4
all 1066 and a. that	SELL 290:5	A. conscience	KISS 183:17
a. shall be well	ELIO 101:10	A. culture	COLO 74:3
Evening, a.	CATC 58:20	A. Express	ADVE 3:4
That's a. folks	CATC 61:5	A. friends	BLAI 36:3
you've done it a.	MEE 218:8	A. people have spoken	CLIN 72:6
allegiance Any victim demands a.	GREE 137:13	A. white man to find	BALD 21:4
you have pledged a.	BALD 21:6	bad news to the A. people	KEIL 176:4
alley rats' a.	ELIO 103:1	business of the A. people	COOL 76:2
allies no a. to be polite to	GEOR 131:9	changed in A. life	LAHR 187:5
allow a. others to be right	GIDE 132:12	combine A. purity	SZEL 308:6
alone adult is to be a.	ROST 275:11	controlling A. soil	DYLA 95:13
a. against smiling enemies	BOWE 41:14	forget you're an A.	DELI 88:10
dangerous to meet it a.	WHAR 333:5	free man, an A.	JOHN 169:7
go home a.	JOPL 171:6	Greeks in this A. empire	MACM 209:1
I want to be a.	FILM 115:2	I am A. bred	MILL 221:17
never a. with a Strand	ADVE 5:15	in A. politics	MITC 223:12
not sufficiently a.	VALÉ 323:3	in love with A. names	BENÉ 28:12
stranger and a.	WOLF 340:11	justice and the A. way	CATC 59:2
We are not a.	TAGL 309:15	knocking the A. system	CAPO 53:5
When he is a. in the room	KEYN 179:9	Miss A. Pie	MCLE 208:5
You'll never walk a.	HAMM 143:11	point of being an A.	UPDI 321:8
alp a. of unforgiveness	PLOM 255:17	process whereby A. girls	HAMP 143:13
altar high a. on the move	BOWE 41:15	Scratch any A.	RUSK 278:4
alternative Considering the a.	CHEV 65:16	second acts in A. lives	FITZ 118:2
no real a.	THAT 312:9	send A. boys	JOHN 169:13
alternatives decide between a.	BONH 39:2	weakness of A. civilization	PRIE 262:3
exhausted other a.	EBAN 96:5	**Americanism** A. with its sleeves	MCCA 205:9
ignorance of a.	ANGE 9:4	hyphenated A.	ROOS 274:14
always a. be an England	PARK 250:9	**Americans** for A. it is just beyond	KISS 183:18
I a. shall be	LUXE 204:11	keep the A. in	ISMA 163:7
Alzheimer he had A.'s disease	REAG 268:8	my fellow A.	KENN 177:9
amateur a. is a man who can't	AGAT 5:16	new generation of A.	KENN 177:4
amateurs Hell full of musical a.	SHAW 292:11	**Amis** cocoa for Kingsley A.	COPE 77:2
rule by a.	ATTL 16:9	**ammunition** pass the a.	FORG 120:5
ambiguity Seven types of a.	EMPS 105:15	**amniotic** in an a. paradise	WILL 336:3
ambitions fulfilling your a.	DE B 86:6	**amour** c'est l'a.	BOUS 41:9
ambulances a. at the bottom	BOMB 39:1	**amuse** talent to a.	COWA 78:3
America A. is a vast conspiracy	UPDI 321:6	**amused** a. by its presumption	CART 56:6
A. is gigantic	FREU 123:14	**analogies** A. decide nothing	FREU 123:9
A. is God's Crucible	ZANG 348:3	**anarchism** A. is a game	SHAW 292:24
A. is our friend	MERC 219:13	**anarchist** I am an a.	ROTT 276:2
A. is the proof	MCCA 205:10	**anarchy** Mere a. is loosed	YEAT 345:20
A. thus top nation	SELL 290:9	**anatomy** A. is destiny	FREU 123:6
Australia looks to A.	CURT 81:14	**ancient** rivers a. as the world	HUGH 159:8

and a. that's the way — CATC 58:4
  including 'a.' — MCCA 206:3
anecdote a. dehumanizing — EPHR 106:2
angel fallen a. — KELL 176:7
angels A. in jumpers — LEWI 200:1
  herald a. sing — ANON 10:15
  not fallen a. — ARDR 14:4
anger Frozen a. — FREU 123:13
  life of telegrams and a. — FORS 120:13
  Look back in a. — OSBO 246:15
  monstrous a. of the guns — OWEN 247:4
  strike it in a. — SHAW 292:21
angles Offer no a. — TESS 312:1
Anglo-Irishman He was an A. — BEHA 26:17
angry A. young man — PAUL 251:5
angst a. songs for kids — COOP 76:11
anguish going to be howls of a. — HEAL 148:10
animal attend a dying a. — YEAT 344:11
  Be a good a. — LAWR 192:10
  only a. in the world to fear — LAWR 192:14
animals All a. are equal — ORWE 245:2
  at its mercy: a. — KUND 185:14
  takes 40 dumb a. — SAYI 286:20
animation too old for a. — DISN 91:7
Annapurnas other A. — HERZ 152:2
annihilating a. all civilization — SAKH 282:1
annihilation by my own a. — GUNN 140:7
anno domini only a. — HILT 154:6
annoy a. with what you write — AMIS 8:8
annus a. horribilis — ELIZ 104:7
anonymous essentially a. — WEIL 330:4
another a. fine mess — LAUR 191:15
  living in a. country — DELI 88:10
answer a. the phone — CART 57:1
  little English in that a. — HAGU 141:2
  way to a pertinent a. — BRON 44:10
  What *is* the a. — LAST 191:9
answered no one a. — DE L 88:6
answers Love is one of the a. — PAZ 251:11
ant a.'s a centaur — POUN 260:2
Antarctica A. was circled — EISE 99:10
anthology a. is like all — RALE 265:9
anthropomorphic a. view of rat — KOES 184:13
anti-Christ a. of Communism — BUCH 47:8
  I am an A. — ROTT 276:2
anticipation only in the a. of it — HITC 154:12
anti-Fascist premature a. — ANON 13:6
antiwar ecology and a. — HUNT 160:12
anybody Is there a. there — DE L 88:5
anything *a. goes* — FEYE 111:1
  A. goes — PORT 256:11
  A. you can do — BERL 30:3
  believe in a. — CHES 65:15
  nobody tells me a. — GALS 129:4
anywhere get a. in a marriage — MURD 231:13
apart a., studiously neutral — WILS 338:15
apathy a. of human beings — KELL 176:5

ape gorgeous buttocks of the a. — HUXL 161:14
  naked a. — MORR 228:9
apes born of risen a. — ARDR 14:4
aphrodisiac Power is the great a. — KISS 183:15
apologize Never a. — FISH 112:8
apparatus haunted a. sleeps — RAIN 265:6
  mediocrity of the a. — TROT 318:2
appearances exquisitely with a. — MICH 220:4
appearing Television is for a. on — COWA 78:18
appears nothing is what it a. to be — MICH 220:4
applause A. is a receipt — SCHN 287:18
apple make an a. pie — SAGA 281:4
  shaking an a. tree — COLL 74:2
apples moon-washed a. of wonder — DRIN 93:4
appointment a. at the end — DINE 91:1
  a. by the corrupt few — SHAW 292:17
  A. in Samarra — BORR 40:4
  a. with him tonight — MAUG 217:4
apprenticeship a. for freedom — BARA 23:3
appropriate that was not a. — CLIN 72:4
April A. is the cruellest month — ELIO 102:19
  bright cold day in A. — ORWE 245:15
  one A. to another — LONG 202:7
aquarium a. is gone — LOWE 203:9
Aquarius dawning of the age of A. — RADO 265:4
Arab A. world together — ARAF 13:12
  upon the A. population — NEWS 237:12
Arabia spell of far A. — DE L 88:2
Arbeit A. *macht frei* — ANON 10:3
archbishop a. had come to see me — BURG 48:2
  black a. of York — RAMS 266:2
  heart of its A. — RAMS 266:3
  part of an a.'s task — RUNC 277:9
arches Underneath the A. — FLAN 118:5
archipelago Gulag a. — SOLZ 298:5
architect a. can only advise — WRIG 342:11
  A. of the Universe — JEAN 167:10
  artist or an a. — GEHR 130:10
architecture A. is the art — JOHN 170:8
  a. of our future — LAMM 188:1
  dancing about a. — ANON 13:4
  fall of English a. — BETJ 33:2
Arctic future of the A. circle — BROW 46:3
are A. you now — POLI 257:3
arena actually in the a. — ROOS 274:12
Argentina Don't cry for me A. — RICE 270:5
Argentinian young A. soldiers — RUNC 277:7
argument a. of the broken window — PANK 249:1
  This is a rotten a. — ANON 12:13
Ariel Caliban casts out A. — POUN 259:13
Aristotle A. maintained that — RUSS 278:12
ark two by two in the a. — LEVE 198:7
arm did not put your a. around it — BLAC 35:9
Armageddon County Road or A. — DYLA 95:12
  We stand at A. — ROOS 274:13
armaments not a. that cause wars — MADA 210:13

armchairs a. tight about the hips	WODE 340:5
armed a. conflict	EDEN 97:3
A. neutrality	WILS 338:17
A. warfare must be preceded	ZINO 349:1
Armenteers Mademoiselle from A.	ANON 11:15
armful very nearly an a.	GALT 129:5
armistice a. for twenty years	FOCH 119:4
arms a. not spending money alone	EISE 99:12
army contemptible little a.	ANON 10:10
dialect with an a.	WEIN 330:7
Forgotten A.	MOUN 230:1
little ships brought the A.	GUED 140:2
with the A. you have	RUMS 277:6
won't be a bit like the A.	TRUM 319:1
aroma a. of performing seals	HART 146:12
arrange French a.	CATH 57:7
arrested a. one fine morning	KAFK 174:5
conservative been a.	WOLF 340:16
arrive a. where we started	ELIO 101:7
arrived a. and to prove it	CATC 60:8
arrow time's a.	EDDI 96:6
arse a. full of razor blades	KEAT 175:11
politician is an a. upon	CUMM 81:4
Sit on your a.	MACN 210:1
arsenal great a. of democracy	ROOS 274:2
art All a. was modern once	SERO 290:12
A. a revolt against fate	MALR 212:12
A. for art's sake	SAYI 286:1
a. has an author	WEIL 330:4
A. is born of humiliation	AUDE 19:5
A. is meant to disturb	BRAQ 43:1
A. is not a *brassière*	BARN 23:11
a. is not a weapon	KENN 177:16
A. is not truth	PICA 254:8
A. is pattern informed by	READ 267:8
A. is significant deformity	FRY 126:11
A. is the imposing of pattern	WHIT 334:4
A. is the objectification	LANG 188:9
a. is the only thing	BOWE 41:12
A. is vice	DEGA 87:1
A. not reproduce the visible	KLEE 184:1
a. of the impossible	HAVE 147:7
a. of the soluble	MEDA 218:6
a. starts off	BAIL 20:10
creates is a work of a.	GREE 138:4
Deals are my a. form	TRUM 319:4
Dying is an a.	PLAT 255:13
E in A-level a.	HIRS 154:8
enemy of good a.	CONN 75:2
example of modern a.	CHUR 69:12
fascinating kind of a.	WARH 327:10
films the lowest form of a.	WILD 335:10
good grey guardians of a.	WILB 335:9
great religious a.	CLAR 70:8
in the a. world	EMIN 105:9
it is not a.	SCHO 288:2
novel is a.-for-art's-sake	PRIT 262:5
offered you Conflict and A.	PRIE 261:16
only interested in a.	SHAW 293:14
people start on all this A.	HERB 151:15
practical form of a.	COOP 76:13
responsibility is to his a.	FAUL 110:5
symbol of Irish a.	JOYC 172:8
what a. means to me	O'KE 242:21
what great a. removes	BOLA 38:8
where the a. resides	SCHN 288:1
articulate made a. all that I saw	BROW 45:14
artificial a. respiration	BURG 48:3
artisan give employment to the a.	BELL 27:13
artist a. creates through choice, distribution	
	SCHW 289:5
a. is his own fault	O'HA 242:20
a. is someone who	WARH 327:11
a. man and mother woman	SHAW 292:10
a. or an architect	GEHR 130:10
a. remains within	JOYC 172:4
a. will be judged	CONN 75:6
God is only another a.	PICA 254:6
Never trust the a.	LAWR 192:9
portrait of the a.	JOYC 171:13
sign of a true a.	VIDA 325:11
artists A. are not engineers	KENN 177:16
arts interested in the a.	AYCK 19:13
ash a. on an old man's sleeve	ELIO 101:4
empty a. can	CRAN 79:3
Oak, and A., and Thorn	KIPL 182:16
Out of the a.	PLAT 255:14
ashen Your a. hair Shulamith	CELA 62:3
ashes a. for thirty	LAMP 188:5
past is a bucket of a.	SAND 283:7
Asia not in A.	ARDR 14:3
Asian A. boys ought to be	JOHN 169:13
ask a. and cannot answer	SHAW 293:19
a. not what your country	KENN 177:9
could a. him anything	WEIS 330:8
Don't a., don't tell	NUNN 240:7
Don't let's a. for the moon	FILM 113:3
if you gotta a.	MISQ 224:12
never does any harm to a.	KRUT 185:9
To a. the hard question	AUDE 18:16
were afraid to a.	REUB 269:9
Would this man a. why	AUDE 17:4
asking mere a. of a question	FORS 120:19
asphalt a. road	ELIO 102:14
aspidistra biggest a.	HARP 146:4
Keep the a. flying	ORWE 245:10
aspirin a. for a brain tumour	CHAN 63:2
ass kiss my a. in Macy's window	JOHN 170:4
assassin copperheads and the a.	SAND 283:4
you are an a.	ROST 275:12
assassination A. is extreme form	SHAW 293:11
astonish A. me	DIAG 90:3
astonishment Your a.'s odd	KNOX 184:7
astrologers reliability of a.	JONE 170:13

asylum lunatic a. run by lunatics — LLOY 201:10
   taken charge of the a. — ROWL 276:8
ate Freddie Starr a. my hamster — NEWS 237:10
atheist a. is a man — BUCH 47:6
   chic for an a. — RUSS 278:6
   from being an a. — SART 284:9
   I am still an a. — BUÑU 47:14
   remain a sound a. — LEWI 199:5
atheists no a. in the foxholes — CUMM 81:11
Atlantic if I flew the A. — EARH 96:2
atlas blank a. of your body — NERU 235:12
   Look in the a. — AUDE 18:5
atom a. has changed everything — EINS 99:1
   carbon a. possesses — JEAN 167:9
   grasped mystery of the a. — BRAD 42:10
   leads through the a. — EDDI 97:1
   no evil in the a. — STEV 304:8
atomic win an a. war — BRAD 42:9
atoms motions of a. in my brain — HALD 142:2
attack by his plan of a. — SASS 284:20
   terrorist a. against — LIVI 200:15
attacking I am a. — FOCH 119:3
Attenborough David A. has 29 — CONN 74:13
attendant a. lord — ELIO 102:7
attention a. must be paid — MILL 222:5
   a. to the object — WEIL 330:3
   disproportionate amount of a. — GATE 130:7
attic furniture in Tolkien's a. — PRAT 261:9
attractions register competing a. — KNIG 184:5
attractive sexually a. — LURI 204:8
audacity tactful in a. — COCT 72:14
Auden Just a smack at A. — EMPS 105:11
audience looks at the a. — STOC 305:5
audiences two kinds of a. — SCHN 287:17
audio visual full of a. marvels — SMIT 296:12
august A. is a wicked month — O'BR 241:2
aunt Aunt is calling to A. — WODE 340:3
   have the Queen as their a. — MARG 214:11
   pay to see my a. Minnie — WILD 335:13
aunts bad a. and good aunts — WODE 339:16
Auschwitz saved one Jew from A. — AUDE 19:8
   write a poem after A. — ADOR 2:12
   year spent in A. — LEVI 198:9
Austerlitz A. and Waterloo — SAND 283:6
Australia A. looks to America — CURT 81:14
   history of A. — SEDD 289:12
   recession that A. had to have — KEAT 175:12
   take A. right back down — KEAT 175:13
Australian A. republic — MURR 232:1
   A. selfhood — HUGH 159:12
   great A. adjective — BAIL 20:11
   great A. Emptiness — WHIT 333:11
Australians A. wouldn't give — ADVE 3:6
Austria Don John of A. — CHES 64:13
author art has an a. — WEIL 330:4
   a. made a mistake — DIRA 91:5
   a. of *The Satanic Verses* — KHOM 179:11

   death of the A. — BART 24:9
   in search of an a. — PIRA 255:2
   wish the a. was a friend — SALI 282:6
authority make your peace with a. — MORR 228:17
   solely on a. — AYER 19:14
autobiography age to write an a. — WAUG 329:4
   a. is an obituary — CRIS 79:14
   A. is now as common — GRIG 139:6
automobile a. changed our dress — KEAT 176:2
   like an a. — ROOT 275:2
autonomy political a. — GRAY 137:7
autumn a. arrives — BOWE 41:10
   mists of the a. mornings — ORWE 245:13
available I'm the best a. — CLAR 70:7
average a. guy who could carry — EPIT 107:14
   A. made lethal — SHAF 291:7
   lost Mr A. Citizen — JOHN 170:2
averages from th' law of a. — CART 56:4
avoid A. crowds — KAUF 174:10
avoiding a. being — TILL 316:8
awakening moment of a. — COET 72:17
aware a. that you are happy — KRIS 185:6
   be a. of women and children — CARR 54:4
awareness signs of his a. — BLUN 37:7
away WHEN I'M A. — TELE 311:4
awe Shock and A. — ANON 12:5
   Shock and A. — ULLM 321:1
awful Ooh, you are a. — CATC 60:21
   this is an a. place — SCOT 289:10
awfully a. big adventure — BARR 24:2
awhile leave you here a. — ANON 11:3
awoke a. one morning — KAFK 174:4
axes no a. being ground — BROU 45:12
axis a. of evil — BUSH 49:6
   sword the a. of the world — DE G 87:12

babies Ballads and b. — MCCA 206:5
   hates dogs and b. — ROST 275:13
   putting milk into b. — CHUR 68:5
Babiy Yar Over B. there are no — YEVT 346:16
baby b. doesn't understand — KNOX 184:9
   B. in an ox's stall — BETJ 32:5
   Burn, b., burn — POLI 257:9
   one for my b. — MERC 219:11
   Who loves ya, b. — CATC 61:14
Bach B. almost persuades me — FRY 126:12
   of J. S. B. — BEEC 26:14
back B. to the future — FILM 117:1
   b. to the old drawing board — CART 56:13
   b. to the wall — CHRÉ 66:7
   boys in the b. room — LOES 202:1
   boys in the b. rooms — BEAV 25:6
   counted them all b. — HANR 144:1
   Don't look b. — PAIG 248:6
   go b. in the water — TAGL 309:7

I'll be b.   FILM 114:6
in the small of the b.   WODE 340:2
never really works to go b.   LAWS 193:8
on my b.   LAST 190:12
said 'I'll be b.!'   TAGL 309:5
There and b. again   TOLK 316:10
there—but not b. again   JACK 165:4
time to get b. to basics   MAJO 212:1
very good b.-seat driver   THAT 313:14
Winston is b.   ANON 13:3
backing b. into the limelight   BERN 31:7
I'm b. Britain   SAYI 286:19
backside weight of the b.   ADAM 2:8
backward B. ran sentences   GIBB 132:7
walking b. into future   ZHVA 348:9
backwards music b.   SMIT 297:1
backyards clean American b.   MAIL 211:7
bacon b.'s not the only thing   KING 181:5
bad b. against the worse   DAY- 85:12
b. aunts and good aunts   WODE 339:16
b. end unhappily   STOP 306:3
b. times just around   COWA 78:12
B. women never take the blame   BROO 45:6
good, the b., and the ugly   FILM 117:7
no such thing as b. publicity   BEHA 26:20
when I'm b., I'm better   WEST 332:5
badly worth doing b.   CHES 65:13
bag Lays eggs inside a paper b.   ISHE 163:5
baked b. cookies and had teas   CLIN 71:11
balance b. of power   KISS 183:11
bald b., and short of breath   SASS 284:15
Can't act. Slightly b.   ANON 10:7
fight between two b. men   BORG 39:10
Balfour of the B. declaration   WEIZ 330:9
ball Every b. is   BRAD 42:14
girl throwing a b.   WOOL 342:1
way he passed the b.   DOCH 91:10
ballads B. and babies   MCCA 206:5
balls B. will be lost always   BERR 31:15
great b. of fire   BLAC 35:10
Bambi Does B. have teeth   CART 56:2
ban B. the bomb   POLI 257:4
banal awful b. lines   GUIN 140:5
banality b. of evil   AREN 14:5
manufacture of b.   SARR 284:1
banana I am a b.   HISL 154:9
bananas Yes! we have no b.   SILV 294:13
band formed a b.   ENO 105:16
bandage wound, not the b.   POTT 259:4
bands people get into b.   GELD 130:11
bang bigger b. for a buck   ANON 10:6
If the big b. does come   OSBO 246:17
Kiss Kiss B. Bang   KAEL 174:1
no terror in a b.   HITC 154:12
Not with a b. but a whimper   ELIO 101:17
bank b. will lend you money if   HOPE 157:9
cry all the way to the b.   LIBE 200:2

deposit at a Swiss b.   ALLE 7:13
robbing a b.   BREC 43:13
banker as a Scotch b.   DAVI 84:7
banking as much as we value b.   TOYN 317:2
banknotes old bottles with b.   KEYN 179:3
Bantu [B.] has been subjected   VERW 324:11
bar treat if met where any b. is   HARD 145:7
Barabbas always save B.   COCT 72:16
barbarians b. are to arrive today   CAVA 57:11
without the b.   CAVA 57:12
barbarous b. to write a poem   ADOR 2:12
barbie shrimp on the b.   ADVE 4:28
bard goat-footed b.   KEYN 179:2
bark heard a seal b.   CART 56:1
barrel ain't got a b. of money   WOOD 341:8
out of the b. of a gun   MAO 214:5
barricade some disputed b.   SEEG 289:13
baseball B. is very big   GREG 138:12
basics time to get back to b.   MAJO 212:1
bastard all my eggs in one b.   PARK 250:6
we knocked the b. off   HILL 154:4
bastards Keep the b. honest   POLI 257:22
Bastille Voltaire in the B.   DE G 87:15
bat shake a b. at a white man   GREG 138:12
bath Freedom is like taking a b.   KENN 176:12
rather lie in a hot b.   THOM 314:17
test my b. before I sit   NASH 234:18
bathroom revolutionary in a b.   LINK 200:9
bathtub drown it in the b.   NORQ 240:3
bats b. have been broken   HOWE 158:10
batsmen opening b.   HOWE 158:10
battery Rock is like a b.   CLAP 70:4
battle B. of Britain   CHUR 67:7
France has lost a b.   DE G 87:2
we b. for the Lord   ROOS 274:13
battlefield discovered on the b.   LAPI 188:10
battles b. of subsequent wars   ORWE 245:14
mother of all b.   HUSS 161:2
bayonet b. is a weapon   POLI 257:5
bayonets throne of b.   INGE 162:9
throne of b.   YELT 346:12
be Let b. be finale of seem   STEV 303:15
poem should not mean but b.   MACL 208:6
beach On the b.   CHES 65:4
beaches fight on the b.   CHUR 67:6
beam B. me up, Scotty   MISQ 224:1
beans B. meanz Heinz   ADVE 3:7
bear any of us can b.   GIUL 133:10
B. of Very Little Brain   MILN 223:1
Cannot b. very much reality   ELIO 100:12
Grizzly B. is huge and wild   HOUS 158:2
heavy b. who goes with me   SCHW 288:13
so b. ourselves that   CHUR 67:7
teddy b. to the nation   NEWS 237:4
beard man with a b.   JUNO 173:11
bears b. might come with buns   ISHE 163:5
b. the marks of the last   HAIG 141:3

bears (*cont.*)

Teddy B. have their Picnic	KENN 176:13
beast Beauty killed the B.	FILM 115:17
fit night out for man or b.	FIEL 111:14
What rough b.	YEAT 346:1
beastly b. the bourgeois is	LAWR 192:12
b. to the Germans	COWA 78:2
beat b. generation	KERO 178:6
beaten being b. does not matter	STEP 303:9
No Englishman is fairly b.	SHAW 293:9
Beatles B.' first LP	LARK 188:12
beatnik peculiar b. theories	KERO 178:7
beats b. as it sweeps	ADVE 4:2
if anyone b. it	TRUE 318:7
beautiful b. and damned	FITZ 117:15
B.! beautiful!	ALDR 6:9
b. game	PELÉ 252:3
Black is b.	POLI 257:8
hunger to be b.	RHYS 269:14
in a b. way	O'KE 242:21
innocent and the b.	YEAT 345:5
Small is b.	SCHU 288:8
Something b. for God	MUGG 230:9
something b. for God	TERE 311:15
what a b. mornin'	HAMM 143:5
beauty b. cold and austere	RUSS 278:17
B. for some provides	HUXL 161:14
B. in music	IVES 163:10
B. killed the Beast	FILM 115:17
B. momentary in the mind	STEV 304:3
b. of inflections	STEV 304:4
B. vanishes	DE L 88:3
b. without vanity	DUNC 94:2
have b. in one's equations	DIRA 91:4
looked on B. bare	MILL 220:13
terrible b. is born	YEAT 344:12
there is still b.	OFFI 242:18
Where B. was	GALS 129:2
world's b. becomes enough	MORR 229:1
because B. I do not hope to turn	ELIO 100:4
B. it's there	MALL 212:8
B. We're here	ANON 12:17
Becher overcome B.'s Brook	ELIZ 104:9
Beckham Bend it like B.	FILM 117:2
bed b. fell on my father	THUR 316:1
gooseberried double b.	THOM 314:12
in b. with my catamite	BURG 48:2
on the lawn I lie in b.	AUDE 18:3
should of stood in b.	JACO 165:8
Time for b.	CATC 61:7
Who goes to b. with whom	SAYE 285:9
wore in b.	MONR 227:2
bedpost on the b. overnight	ROSE 275:3
bedroom French widow in every b.	
	HOFF 155:13
what you do in the b.	CAMP 51:14
bedrooms in the nation's b.	TRUD 318:4

beds Minds like b. always made up	WILL 336:16
bee b. of sorrow	BABE 20:2
b. produces honey	GOLD 134:12
sting like a b.	ALI 6:13
beef Where's the b.	ADVE 5:12
Where's the b.	MOND 226:12
been B. there, done that	SAYI 286:2
b. things and seen places	WEST 332:4
beer denies you the b. to cry into	MARQ 215:11
only here for the b.	ADVE 4:1
warm b., invincible suburbs	MAJO 211:15
beers other b. cannot reach	ADVE 3:26
three b. and it looks good	FILM 116:5
bees b. do it	PORT 258:20
Beethoven B.'s Fifth Symphony	FORS 120:10
rape, ultra-violence and B.	TAGL 309:2
Roll over, B.	BERR 31:14
beetles special preference for b.	HALD 142:4
begin b. at the beginning	THOM 314:11
b. the Beguine	PORT 256:12
But let us b.	KENN 177:8
Then I'll b.	CATC 58:7
beginning begin at the b.	THOM 314:11
b. is often the end	ELIO 101:8
end of the b.	CHUR 68:3
In my b. is my end	ELIO 100:15
Movies should have a b.	GODA 134:5
pictures didn't have b.	POLL 256:2
begins glory most b. and ends	YEAT 345:11
Beguine begin the B.	PORT 256:12
begun already b. before	CALV 51:5
behave how to b.	LETT 198:1
behaviour studies human b.	ROBB 271:8
behaviourism B. a flat-earth view	KOES 184:13
B. works	AUDE 18:18
behind b. that face	VICK 325:2
no bosom and no b.	SMIT 297:9
beige just my colour: it's *b.*	MEND 219:6
being avoiding b.	TILL 316:8
darkness of mere b.	JUNG 173:3
may not be worried into b.	FROS 126:1
Nothingness haunts b.	SART 284:3
unbearable lightness of b.	KUND 185:13
Belgrano sinking of the B.	DALY 83:6
belief that is B.	SART 284:7
widespread b. more likely	RUSS 278:15
believe b. in life	DU B 93:7
b. in miracles	FOX 122:1
b. in the life to come	BECK 25:10
b. is not necessarily true	BELL 27:2
B. it or not	NEWS 237:1
b. that he exists	HUME 160:9
b. that people are really good	FRAN 122:7
between those who b.	DELO 88:14
don't have to b. that	O'HA 242:19
even if you don't b.	BOHR 38:6
he couldn't b. it	CUMM 81:5

I b. in yesterday — LENN 197:3
I do not b. . . . I know — JUNG 173:8
I don't *b.* it — CATC 60:17
If you b., clap your hands — BARR 24:3
must b. *something* — RUSS 279:7
really b. in themselves — CHES 65:7
Yes, I b. — LAST 191:12
believing stop b. in God — CHES 65:15
stop b. in it — DICK 90:7
bell For whom the b. tolls — BORR 40:10
bellies their b. empty — LOGU 202:4
bells b. of Hell — ANON 12:4
floating many b. down — CUMM 81:2
ring the b. of Heaven — HODG 155:10
belong *b.* to it as well — WHYT 334:14
betray, you must first b. — PHIL 253:7
don't want to b. to any club — MARX 216:5
I b. to Glasgow — FYFF 127:7
man doesn't b. out there — BRAU 43:3
where we really b. — GREE 137:12
belonged once b. somewhere — STEI 302:9
belongs moon b. to everyone — DES 89:6
twentieth century b. — TRUD 318:5
beloved Cry, the b. country — PATO 251:3
bend B. it like Beckham — FILM 117:2
right on round the b. — LAUD 189:16
beneath married b. me — ASTO 15:12
bereaved b. if snobbery died — USTI 322:4
Berkeley sang in B. Square — MASC 216:10
Berlin cross from East to West B. — KOES 184:16
Berliner *Ich bin ein B.* — KENN 177:15
Bernard Jeffrey B. is unwell — WATE 328:9
Bertie Burlington B. — HARG 145:16
best b. lack all conviction — YEAT 345:20
b. of all possible worlds — CABE 50:1
b. Prime Minister we have — BUTL 49:11
b. things in life are free — DES 89:6
b. way out is always through — FROS 125:18
be the b. — HANS 144:3
did the b. we could — UPDI 321:7
I'm the b. — LEWI 199:10
I'm the b. available — CLAR 70:7
Probably the b. — ADVE 4:24
we will do our b. — CHUR 67:12
best-seller b. is the gilded tomb — SMIT 297:3
best-sellers all the great b. — PRIT 262:4
bet You b. your sweet bippy — CATC 61:18
Bethlehem Slouches towards B. — YEAT 346:1
betray b., you must first belong — PHIL 253:7
guts to b. my country — FORS 121:5
whatever you can still b. — LEC 194:16
betrayal any act of b. — RENO 269:8
ecstasy of b. — GENE 131:1
better b. than Man — TAGL 309:13
b. to be looked over — WEST 331:16
can only get b. — PETR 253:6
can only get b. — POLI 258:8

Every day, I am getting b. — COUÉ 77:11
Fail b. — BECK 26:7
go b. with Coke — ADVE 5:5
I can do b. — BERL 30:3
If way to the B. there be — HARD 145:5
nothing b. to do — THAT 313:15
when I'm bad, I'm b. — WEST 332:5
between try to get b. them — STRA 306:5
beware B. my foolish heart — WASH 328:8
bid you b. — KIPL 182:14
bewildered bothered, and b. — HART 146:11
to the utterly b. — CAPP 53:7
bewitched B., bothered — HART 146:11
bewrapt B. past knowing — HARD 145:9
bias impartiality is b. — REIT 269:4
biases critic is a bundle of b. — BALL 22:7
Bible read in de B. — HEYW 153:2
starless and b.-black — THOM 314:11
bicycle arrive by b. — VIER 325:12
fish needs a b. — DUNN 94:8
fish without a b. — SAYI 287:13
so is a b. repair kit — CONN 74:9
bicycle-pump b. the human heart — AMIS 8:6
bicycling old maids b. — MAJO 211:15
bicyclists trouser-clip for b. — MORT 229:8
bidet UNABLE OBTAIN B. — TELE 311:9
big b. enough to take away — FORD 119:13
b. spender — FIEL 111:8
b. tent — POLI 257:7
b. way of doing things — TERE 311:14
born with b. bones — BINC 34:8
fall victim to a b. lie — HITL 155:3
G.O.P.'s b. tent — NEWS 238:1
I am b. — FILM 116:16
bigamy B. is one husband too many — ANON 10:5
biggest b. electric train set — WELL 331:1
bigotry B. tries to keep truth — TAGO 309:17
bike got on his b. — TEBB 310:12
Mind my b. — CATC 60:14
bikini b. is not a bikini — REAR 268:9
[b.] revealed everything about a girl — VREE 325:14
yellow polkadot b. — VANC 323:6
billboard b. lovely as a tree — NASH 235:1
billion a b. here — DIRK 91:6
biography better part of b. — STRA 306:6
B. is about Chaps — BENT 29:13
b. ultimately fiction — MALA 212:2
to write b. — WEST 332:20
biologically b. sound — FREU 123:10
biologist b. passes — ROST 275:10
biology B. is the search for — WILL 336:5
Nothing in b. makes — DOBZ 91:9
bippy You bet your sweet b. — CATC 61:18
birch bringing back the b. — VIDA 325:4
bird catch the b. of paradise — KHRU 180:2
It's a b. — CATC 59:2

bird (*cont.*)

why the caged b. sings — ANGE 9:3

why the caged b. sings — DUNB 94:1

birdcage summer b. — BORR 41:6

birds b. fly through it — HEIS 150:5

b. got to fly — HAMM 142:12

b. trying to communicate — AUDE 19:6

prisoned b. must find — SASS 284:18

Birmingham B. by way of Beachy Head — CHES 64:14

When Jesus came to B. — STUD 307:1

birth B., and copulation — ELIO 102:15

b. of each child — MCWI 210:12

present at the b. — ORTO 244:12

seen b. and death — ELIO 101:19

birthday eighty-first b. — BURG 48:2

Happy b. to you — HILL 154:3

marvel my b. away — THOM 314:7

your 100th b. — TELE 311:7

biscuit cared a b. for it — LAWR 193:6

biscuits hyacinths and b. — SAND 283:9

bisexuality b. doubles your chances — ALLE 7:14

bishop make a b. kick a hole — CHAN 63:1

bitch Gaia a tough b. — MARG 214:12

old b. gone in the teeth — POUN 259:15

bits swallowed their b. — BETJ 32:10

black b. Archbishop of York — RAMS 266:2

B. is beautiful — POLI 257:8

b. kids get an education — POWE 260:15

b. majority rule — SMIT 296:14

B. Panther Party — NEWT 236:5

B. Power — CARM 54:2

b. students had to go — GRAN 136:11

but b. and grey — GREE 137:15

Creature from the B. Lagoon — CRON 80:4

growth of b. consciousness — BIKO 34:6

I am B. — JOHN 169:5

lives of b. and white entwine — NOON 240:1

not b. and white — BOY 42:6

not have the colour b. — MAND 213:9

old b. magic — MERC 219:12

one drop of b. blood — HUGH 159:10

rainbow which includes b. — YEVT 346:17

so long as it is b. — FORD 120:1

with a b. skin — MALC 212:4

young, gifted and b. — HANS 144:2

Young, gifted and b. — IRVI 163:4

blackbird B. has spoken — FARJ 109:6

b. whistling — STEV 304:4

blackbirds B. are the cellos — STEV 304:15

Blackpool seaside place called B. — EDGA 97:5

blacks country is for b. — TSVA 319:6

black widow This is the B., death — LOWE 203:13

Blair if her B. was quite — WODE 340:1

Mrs B.'s knees stiffening — ELIZ 104:10

Sun backs B. — NEWS 238:4

Yo, B. — BUSH 49:9

blame Bad women never take the b. — BROO 45:6

poor wot gets the b. — ANON 12:9

blaming b. it on you — KIPL 182:7

b. on his boots — BECK 25:13

blandness ultimate b. — ROTT 276:4

blast In b.-beruffled plume — HARD 145:3

blatherskite Blatant B. — PHIL 253:12

bleeding instead of b., he sings — GARD 130:4

Blenheim still fighting B. — BEVA 33:5

bless B. 'em all — HUGH 159:4

blessed b. with total recall — GREG 138:9

blew You b. it up — FILM 116:13

blight great English b. — WAUG 328:14

Blighty back to dear old B. — MILL 222:14

blind b. watchmaker — DAWK 85:2

Booth died b. — LIND 200:6

Justice is a b. goddess — HUGH 159:6

splendid work for the b. — SASS 284:16

without science is b. — EINS 98:3

blinds drawing-down of b. — OWEN 247:6

blinked other fellow just b. — RUSK 278:3

bliss Your b. in our hearts — STRU 306:14

blitz b. of a boy — CAUS 57:10

block each b. cut smooth — POUN 259:10

blonde Being b. is definitely — MADO 211:1

b. to make a bishop kick — CHAN 63:1

blondes b. and switchblades — COOP 76:10

Gentlemen prefer b. — LOOS 202:9

blood b. and love without — STOP 305:15

b. come gargling — OWEN 247:7

b. jet is poetry — PLAT 255:12

b. of his followers — EISE 99:11

b. on their hands — SPEN 299:13

B. sport brought to — INGH 162:10

b., toil, tears and sweat — CHUR 67:3

by b. Albanian — TERE 311:17

enough of b. and tears — RABI 265:2

flow of human b. — HUGH 159:8

foaming with much b. — POWE 261:1

for cooling the b. — FLAN 118:7

never run with b. — LEVY 199:1

one drop of black b. — HUGH 159:10

rather have b. on my hands — GREE 137:9

show business with b. — BRUN 46:12

washed in the b. of the Lamb — LIND 200:5

We, your b. family — SPEN 299:15

blood-dimmed b. tide is loosed — YEAT 345:20

bloodshed war without b. — MAO 214:4

bloody Abroad is b. — GEOR 131:10

b. curtain — ELIS 103:16

b. experience of Vietnam — CRON 80:7

B. men like bloody buses — COPE 77:1

Not b. likely — SHAW 293:8

sang within the b. wood — ELIO 102:18

Sunday, b. Sunday — FILM 117:11

under the b. past — AHER 5:20

where the b. hell — ADVE 5:1

blooming b. well dead	SARO 283:16
blossom break Into b.	WRIG 342:12
frothiest, blossomiest b.	POTT 259:3
hundred flowers b.	MAO 214:7
blow B. out, you bugles	BROO 44:12
b. up the other half	LAIN 187:7
b. with an agreement	TROT 318:1
blowing answer is b. in the wind	DYLA 95:1
I'm forever b. bubbles	KENB 176:8
blue b.-eyed devil white man	FARD 109:5
b. guitar	STEV 303:18
b. of the night	CROS 80:8
Her b. body	WALK 326:11
invented b. jeans	SAIN 281:14
last b. mountain	FLEC 118:12
pale b. dot	SAGA 281:8
Space is b.	HEIS 150:5
bluebell Mary, ma Scotch B.	LAUD 191:13
bluebirds There'll be b. over	BURT 48:13
blueprints Genes not like b.	STEW 304:16
blues bury the b. with me	HOOK 157:1
go back to b.	CLAP 70:4
got the Weary B.	HUGH 159:11
in American b.	JAGG 165:9
when the b. started	HOOK 156:12
blunder so grotesque a b.	BENT 29:14
board back to the old drawing b.	CART 56:13
There wasn't any B.	HERB 151:16
boat sank my b.	KENN 177:17
sewer in a glass-bottomed b.	MIZN 226:9
boats passengers off in small b.	LAST 191:7
bodies B. never lie	DE M 88:15
Pile the b. high	SAND 283:6
structure of our b.	STOP 305:8
body Africa than my own b.	ORTO 244:11
b. and the soul know	ROET 272:11
b. building is ritual	PAGL 248:3
b. swayed to music	YEAT 344:3
draw what I feel in my b.	HEPW 151:11
good-will of the b.	RIDI 271:3
i like my b.	CUMM 81:9
interpose my b.	STRA 306:5
my b. and your brains	SHAW 293:15
my useless b.	BROW 45:14
none in the b.	LAWR 192:13
stepped out of my b.	WRIG 342:12
whose b. is this	RODR 272:9
bodyline B. was not an incident	JAME 166:8
bog b.-standard comprehensive	CAMP 51:11
recognize the term b.-standard	BLUN 37:6
Bognor Bugger B.	LAST 190:1
bogus b. god	MACN 209:15
bohemian so-called b. elements	KERO 178:7
boiler ten years in a b. suit	TWEE 320:3
boldly to b. go	RODD 272:3
Bolshevik I must be a B.	MACD 206:13
bomb atom b. is a paper tiger	MAO 214:6

Ban the b.	POLI 257:4
b. on Hiroshima	TRUM 318:9
b. them back into Stone Age	LEMA 195:15
defence against the atom b.	ANON 10:4
'formula' of the atomic b.	MEDA 218:5
bombed glad we've been b.	ELIZ 103:17
bomber b. will always get through	BALD 21:10
bombers b. named for girls	JARR 167:1
bombing b. begins in five minutes	REAG 268:5
bombs Come, friendly b.	BETJ 32:14
bond B. James Bond.	FILM 115:12
bonding male b.	TIGE 316:7
bonds surly b. of earth	MAGE 211:2
surly b. of earth	REAG 268:7
boneless b. wonder	CHUR 66:15
bones b. of one British Grenadier	HARR 146:7
conjuring trick with b.	JENK 167:11
dead men lost their b.	ELIO 103:1
bonfire b. of the vanities	WOLF 340:15
bonjour B. tristesse	ÉLUA 105:6
book b. would have been finished	WODE 339:18
b. you would wish your wife	GRIF 139:4
insignificant b. because	WOOL 341:12
knocks me out is a b.	SALI 282:6
Never judge a b.	EAGA 96:1
one bright b. of life	LAWR 192:7
book-keeping double-entry b.	MULL 231:4
books B. and all forms of writing	SOYI 299:4
b. are either dreams	LOWE 203:8
b. are weapons	ROOS 274:5
B. do furnish a room	POWE 260:9
B. from Boots'	BETJ 32:12
B. say: she did this because	BARN 23:12
b. undeservedly forgotten	AUDE 19:4
his b. were read	BELL 27:17
I don't trust b.	COLB 73:4
If my b. had been any worse	CHAN 63:4
Keeping b. on charity	PERÓ 252:9
made the b. and he died	FAUL 110:2
read any good b. lately	CATC 59:8
study of mankind is b.	HUXL 161:5
boot b. in the face	PLAT 255:10
b. stamping on a human face	ORWE 246:2
bootboy b. at Claridges	WOOL 342:4
Booth B. led boldly	LIND 200:5
boots blaming on his b.	BECK 25:13
Books from B.'	BETJ 32:12
b. are made for walkin'	HAZL 148:8
boots—b.—movin'	KIPL 181:13
doormat in a world of b.	RHYS 270:1
booze fool with b. until he's 50	FAUL 110:6
boozes tell a man who "b."	BURT 48:11
bop Playing 'B.'	ELLI 104:13
bora ring b. is gone	NOON 240:2
border Night Mail crossing the B.	AUDE 18:1
bore healthy male adult b.	UPDI 321:4
Less is a b.	VENT 324:9

bored b. for England	MUGG 230:11
boredom b. and terror	WELL 331:3
first b., then fear	LARK 189:2
perish of despair and b.	FRAN 122:4
Borgias Italy under the B.	FILM 114:11
boring b. kind of guy	BUSH 48:15
Life, friends, is b.	BERR 31:17
born already b. before my lips	MAND 213:11
because you were b. in it	SHAW 292:2
B. in the USA	SPRI 301:2
B. of the sun	SPEN 300:5
b. three thousand years old	DELA 88:9
b. to run	SPRI 301:4
b. with your legs apart	ORTO 244:14
for being b.	WATS 328:11
human beings are b. free	ANON 10:2
I am not yet b.	MACN 210:5
Man is b. to live	PAST 250:18
not to be b. is best	AUDE 17:2
One is not b. a woman	DE B 86:3
bosom no b. and no behind	SMIT 297:9
boss b. there is always	MARQ 215:8
bossing nobody b. you	ORWE 246:4
bossy by the b. for the bully	SELD 290:4
botanist I'd be a b.	FERM 110:12
botch I make a b.	BELL 27:16
bother conscience to b. him	LLOY 201:13
long words B. me	MILN 223:1
young whom I hope to b.	AUDE 18:10
bothered Bewitched, b.	HART 146:11
bottle bothers to buy a b.	DWOR 94:13
way out of the fly-b.	WITT 339:7
bottles old b. with banknotes	KEYN 179:3
bottom at the b. of our garden	FYLE 127:8
forgotten man at the b.	ROOS 273:10
We're on the b.	JOBS 168:2
bought b. the company	ADVE 3:30
b. the Velvets' albums	ENO 105:16
I would have b. it	WINF 339:3
bouquet b. better than the taste	POTT 259:5
bourgeois beastly the b. is	LAWR 192:12
b. prefers comfort	HESS 152:9
bourgeoisie charm of the b.	FILM 117:4
Bovril B. prevents	ADVE 3:8
bovvered Am I b.	CATC 58:2
bowl when I am going to bowl	WARN 327:14
bows got the b. up	LAST 190:12
box fox in the b.	HENR 151:10
life like a b. of chocolates	FILM 115:14
boxes Little b. on the hillside	REYN 269:12
boxing B.'s just show business	BRUN 46:12
boy any b. may become President	STEV 304:9
b. brought in the white sheet	LORC 202:14
b. will ruin himself	GEOR 131:6
Mad about the b.	COWA 78:6
remain a fifteen-year-old b.	ROTH 275:14
sat the journeying b.	HARD 145:9
You silly twisted b.	CATC 62:1
boyfriends Diets are like b.	LAWS 193:8
boys b. in the back room	LOES 202:1
b. in the back rooms	BEAV 25:6
b. not going to be sent	ROOS 274:1
Hello b.	ADVE 3:27
see if the b. are still there	BARU 24:16
send American b.	JOHN 169:13
slower than b.	FRAS 122:11
bra Burn your b.	SAYI 286:3
I want a b.	BLUM 37:1
brain Bear of Very Little B.	MILN 223:1
b. has the consistency	TURI 319:9
b.? It's my second favourite	ALLE 7:8
dry b. in a dry season	ELIO 101:13
fingerprints across his b.	HEND 151:8
hasn't exactly got B.	MILN 223:4
losing your b.	FOX 121:12
motions of atoms in my b.	HALD 142:2
why did He give us a b.	LUCE 204:6
brains feet instead of their b.	SOUS 299:3
my body and your b.	SHAW 293:15
brake invented the b.	NEME 235:9
brandy B. for the parson	KIPL 182:15
b. of the damned	SHAW 292:11
brassière Art is not a b.	BARN 23:11
brave B. new world	BORR 40:5
Brazilian If I were a B.	STIN 305:2
bread made, like b.	LE G 195:9
Royal slice of b.	MILN 223:8
break at the b. of the day	STRU 306:14
b. Into blossom	WRIG 342:12
b. up the play	ACHE 1:9
give a sucker an even b.	FIEL 111:14
Have a b.	ADVE 3:25
if you b. the bloody glass	MACN 210:2
breakdown Madness need not be b.	LAIN 187:9
nervous b.	RUSS 278:7
breakers b. cliffward leaping	CRAN 79:2
breakfast b. three times	MAUG 217:6
committed b. with it	LEWI 199:9
embarrassment and b.	BARN 23:10
intervene—before b.	HESE 152:6
breath drawn the b. of life	YEAT 345:3
last b. of Julius Caesar	JEAN 167:8
brew b. that is true	FILM 116:1
bribe cannot hope to b. or twist	WOLF 340:10
Marriage is a b.	WILD 335:15
bribes open to b.	GREE 137:10
brick b. at a time	HARG 145:17
Follow the yellow b. road	HARB 144:3
Goodbye yellow b. road	JOHN 169:1
bridge b. and the Bradman	ANON 10:12
b. is love	WILD 335:14
b. over troubled water	SIMO 295:2
b. to the future	LAWR 192:8
going a b. too far	BROW 46:7

Women, and Champagne, and B.   BELL 27:15

briefing b. is what *I* do   CALL 50:9

bright future's b.   ADVE 3:21

    young lady named B.   BULL 47:12

brighter women are b. than men   LOOS 202:13

brightness leaking the b. away   SPEN 300:8

bring B. me sunshine   DEE 86:13

brink walked to the b.   DULL 93:9

brinkmanship boasting of his b.   STEV 304:12

bristles my skin b.   HOUS 158:8

Britain Battle of B.   CHUR 67:7

    B. a fit country   LLOY 201:6

    B. will be honoured   HARL 146:1

    B. will still be   MAJO 211:15

    I'm backing B.   SAYI 286:19

    Keep B. tidy   OFFI 242:11

    speak for B.   BOOT 39:4

British bones of one B. Grenadier   HARR 146:7

    B. are coming   WELL 330:14

    B. journalist   WOLF 340:10

    B. nation is unique   CHUR 67:11

    B. would have acted   BART 24:11

    drunken officer of B. rule   WALC 326:3

    I am a B. object   MALO 212:10

    No sex please—we're B.   MARR 215:14

    rather be B.   PAIS 248:7

    We are B., thank God   MONT 227:7

Britons B. alone use 'Might'   WAUG 329:10

broadens travel b. the mind; but   CHES 65:11

broccoli b., dear   CART 56:7

    eat any more b.   BUSH 49:1

broke If it ain't b.   SAYI 286:17

broken bats have been b.   HOWE 158:10

    b. heart and a broken home   HOOK 156:12

    Can it be b.   JENK 167:12

    Morning has b.   FARJ 109:6

    taken up the b. blade   DE G 87:4

brothel b. for the emotions   KOES 184:12

brother be the white man's b.   KING 180:8

    BIG B. IS WATCHING YOU   ORWE 245:16

    B. can you spare a dime   HARB 144:5

    what Big B. is for   KUNZ 185:16

brotherhood freedom and our b.   LAIN 187:7

    table of b.   KING 180:12

brother-in-law brother, not b.   KING 180:8

brothers live together as b.   KING 180:14

    two b. and eight cousins   HALD 142:5

brown Her b. embrace   WALK 326:11

    river Is a strong b. god   ELIO 101:1

Brownie B., you're doing   BUSH 49:7

Browning safety-catch of my B.   JOHS 170:10

brows pallor of girls' b.   OWEN 247:6

Bruce made Adam and B.   BRYA 46:14

brush used as a paint b.   FREN 123:1

brutal heart's grown b.   YEAT 345:10

brute heart of a b. like you   PLAT 255:10

bubbles frill of b.   DUNM 94:4

I'm forever blowing b.   KENB 176:8

buck bigger bang for a b.   ANON 10:6

    b. stops here   TRUM 318:17

bucket anything out of a b.   CONN 74:12

    past is a b. of ashes   SAND 283:7

    stick inside a swill b.   ORWE 245:11

Buckingham Palace guard at B.   MILN 223:5

bugger B. Bognor   LAST 190:1

bugles Blow out, you b.   BROO 44:12

    b. calling from sad shires   OWEN 247:5

building b. works is not sufficient   JOHN 170:7

    stuck in this b.   LAST 190:8

    very old b.   OSBO 246:13

built not what they b.   FENT 110:8

    Who b. Thebes   BREC 43:14

bulbs million light b.   HARP 146:5

bulimia yuppie version of b.   EHRE 97:8

bullet b. through his head   ROBI 271:12

    Faster than a speeding b.   CATC 59:2

bully by the bossy for the b.   SELD 290:4

    such a b. pulpit   ROOS 274:11

bum Indicat Motorem B.   GODL 134:6

bumpy going to be a b. night   FILM 113:8

bungler Man is a b.   SHAW 292:13

bunk History more or less b.   FORD 120:2

burden bear any b.   KENN 177:5

    carry the heavy b.   EDWA 97:6

burdened like being b.   BAIN 21:1

bureaucracy B., the rule of no one   MCCA 206:2

    immobile b.   SAMP 282:12

bureaucrats Guidelines for b.   BORE 39:7

burglars fear of b.   CANE 52:19

burgundy naive domestic B.   CART 56:6

buried b. at midnight   O'BR 241:1

    b. in the rain   MILL 221:13

    b. with me   HEWE 152:13

burlesque b. and the newspapers   STON 305:6

Burlington B. Bertie   HARG 145:16

burn better to b. out   YOUN 347:5

    B., baby, burn   POLI 257:9

    B. your bra   SAYI 286:3

burning b. roof and tower   YEAT 345:8

    b. the rain forest   STIN 305:2

    Is Paris b.   HITL 155:2

    Keep the Home-fires b.   FORD 120:4

    lady's not for b.   FRY 126:7

burnished Furnish'd and b.   BETJ 32:15

burns candle b. at both ends   MILL 220:12

burnt b. at the stake as witches   SMIT 297:8

    if all this was b. cork   GREG 138:11

bury anything we want to b.   MOOR 227:12

    B. my heart at Wounded Knee   BENÉ 28:13

    b. the blues with me   HOOK 157:1

    good day to b. bad news   MISQ 224:7

    physician can b.   WRIG 342:11

    We will b. you   KHRU 180:1

bus Anybody seen in a b.   WEST 333:1

bus (*cont.*)
Can it be a Motor B. GODL 134:6
missed the b. CHAM 62:10
run over by a b. CARR 54:5
stepping in front of a b. OSBO 246:17
buses men are like bloody b. COPE 77:1
more time on the b. STRU 306:12
bush B. wins it NEWS 237:3
bushes like different b. trimmed QUIN 264:8
business Being good in b. WARH 327:10
b. as usual THAT 313:3
B. carried on as usual CHUR 66:12
B. is like a car SAYI 286:4
b. of the American people COOL 76:2
b. practices improve RODD 272:5
b. to get him in trouble ROBI 272:2
do b. together THAT 313:4
heart in the b. WATS 328:13
How to succeed in b. MEAD 218:3
I'm in the hurt b. TYSO 320:8
Liberty is unfinished b. ANON 11:12
Murder is a serious b. ILES 162:4
music b. is not MORR 229:2
no b. like show business BERL 30:9
businessman toward making a b. WATS 328:12
businessmen well-placed b. decide YOUN 347:2
bust dance it b. to bust GREN 138:14
busting June is b. out all over HAMM 143:2
busy b. man has no time MAUR 217:8
Government of the b. SELD 290:4
had a b. day SIGL 294:10
butcher Hog B. for the World SAND 283:3
butler b. did it CATC 58:8
on the b.'s upper slopes WODE 340:6
butter b. for the Royal slice MILN 223:8
guns not with b. GOEB 134:7
no money for b. JOSE 171:7
rather have b. or guns GOER 134:9
Stork from b. ADVE 3:10
butterflies flight of b. SART 284:14
Frogs eat b. STEV 303:16
butterfly breaks a b. on a wheel NEWS 238:7
flap of a b.'s wings LORE 203:2
float like a b. ALI 6:13
buttocks gorgeous b. of the ape HUXL 161:14
butty oul' b. o' mine O'CA 241:6
buy b. a used car POLI 258:12
b. Codham, Cockridden THOM 314:20
b. it like an honest man NORT 240:5
b. me a Mercedes Benz JOPL 171:4
client will beg to b. BURR 48:9
Don't b. a single vote more KENN 177:2
money can't b. me love LENN 196:14
Stop me and b. one ADVE 5:2
by B. and by MCCO 206:8
Byron movement needs a B. POLL 256:1
Byronic think all poets were B. COPE 77:3

bystander never be a b. BAUE 25:2
Byzantium holy city of B. YEAT 345:18

cabinet another to mislead the C. ASQU 15:9
cable little c. cars climb CROS 80:12
Cablinasian I'm a C. WOOD 341:9
cad Cocoa is a c. and coward CHES 65:2
Caesars Sawdust C. NEWS 238:2
worship the C. HUXL 161:7
caff ace c. with a nice museum ADVE 3:2
caftan Iffucan of Azcan in c. STEV 303:13
cage cannot c. the minute MACN 210:7
occupy the same c. WILL 336:9
caged why the c. bird sings ANGE 9:3
why the c. bird sings DUNB 94:1
cake C. or death IZZA 164:1
picked out of a c. RALE 265:9
cakes Exceedingly good c. ADVE 3:19
calamity Oh, c. CATC 60:16
calculating desiccated c. machine BEVA 33:10
Caliban C. casts out Ariel POUN 259:13
California C. is a fine place to live ALLE 7:2
C. to the New York Island GUTH 140:9
Caligula eyes of C. MITT 226:6
call c. it a day COMD 74:4
how you c. to me HARD 145:10
May I c. you 338 COWA 78:16
calling Germany c. JOYC 172:15
callisthenics c. with words PARK 250:3
calls If anybody c. Say BENT 29:15
calm c. and at peace HUME 160:8
Cambridge C. ladies CUMM 81:10
C. people rarely smile BROO 45:2
either Oxford or C. SNAG 297:14
came I c. through MACA 205:3
camel c. is a horse ISSI 163:8
Take my c., dear MACA 205:6
Camelot known as C. LERN 197:5
never be another C. ONAS 243:6
camels More doctors smoke C. ADVE 4:15
camera c. makes everyone SONT 298:17
I am a c. ISHE 163:6
campaign c. in poetry CUOM 81:12
can *c.* nothing but frog-spawn LAWR 192:20
He who c., does SHAW 292:19
know a man who c. ADVE 3:9
Canada all over C. RICH 271:2
C. could have enjoyed COLO 74:3
I see C. DAVI 84:7
Canadian C. content THOM 313:19
definition of a C. BERT 32:1
I'm a C. CRON 80:6
Canadians C. are very reluctant CRON 80:4
C. do not like heroes WOOD 341:6
cancer c. close to the Presidency DEAN 86:1
cut out the c. AITK 6:1

cats (*cont.*)

elderly lady who has two c.	LEWI 199:15
greater c. with golden eyes	SACK 281:2
matchstalk c. and dogs	COLE 73:6
where c. are cats	MARQ 215:6

cattle Actors are c. — HITC 154:10
Catullus C. walk that way — YEAT 345:19
caught man who shoots him gets c. — MAIL 211:12

cause c. may be inconvenient	BENN 29:10
great c. of cheering	BENN 29:9
Rebel without a c.	FILM 117:10
causes aren't any good, brave c.	OSBO 246:17
Tough on the c. of crime	BLAI 35:11

caution c. in love — RUSS 278:10
cavaliers C. (Wrong but) — SELL 290:7
caves c. in which we hide — FITZ 117:16
Ceauşescus C.' execution — O'DO 241:10
Cecilia Blessed C., appear — AUDE 16:13
celebrity C. is a mask — UPDI 321:10
cello of the c. — CASA 55:8
cellos c. of the deep farms — STEV 304:15
cells little grey c. — CHRI 66:8

Celtic C. Tiger	MCAL 205:1
woods of C. antiquity	KEYN 179:2

cement Palestine is the c. — ARAF 13:12
cemetery Help me down C. Road — LARK 189:9

censorship beginning of c.	HARE 145:14
c. is never over	GORD 135:15
extreme form of c.	SHAW 293:11
fought without c.	WEST 333:2

cent did with every c. — FROS 125:6
centaur ant's a c. — POUN 260:2
centre c. cannot hold — YEAT 345:20
centuries Through what wild c. — DE L 88:1

century c. of the common man	WALL 327:4
close the c.	MAND 213:5
sad, glittering c.	BURC 47:15
So the 20th C.	CRAN 79:4
when a new c. begins	MANN 213:14

cerebration unconscious c. — JAME 166:9
ceremony c. of innocence — YEAT 345:20
certain France in a c. way — DE G 87:13
chained probably c. together — HUGH 160:5
chains better to be in c. — KAFK 174:7
chainsaw imagination and a c. — HIRS 154:8
chair speaks of a c. — BISH 35:4
chaise-longue hurly-burly of c. — CAMP 51:13
chalice c. from the palace — FILM 116:1

champagne get no kick from c.	PORT 258:16
like c. or high heels	BENN 29:10
Women, and C., and Bridge	BELL 27:15

chance c. and accident	BACO 20:5
dreams, c., laughter	BUÑU 47:13
Give peace a c.	LENN 196:16
I missed my c.	LAWR 192:17
institutions by c.	HAIL 141:7

in the last c. saloon	MELL 218:11
there is no c.	LAST 190:11
too good to leave to c.	SIMO 295:6

chancy on its c. course — LURI 204:7
chandeliers gas c. — WHAR 333:6
Chanel C. No. 5 — MONR 227:2

change can c. the world	MEAD 218:2
'C.' is scientific	RUSS 279:9
c. the course of history	FILM 113:7
c. the people who teach	BYAT 49:13
c. the world	BARK 23:4
c. we think we see	FROS 124:13
life can c. on a dime	LAHR 187:5
Management that wants to c.	TUSA 319:12
things will have to c.	LAMP 188:4
time for a c.	DEWE 90:2
torrent of c.	CHES 65:9
try to c. things	BOLD 38:10
wind of c. is blowing	MACM 209:5

changed changed, c. utterly	YEAT 344:12
changed, c. utterly	YEAT 345:1
c. upon the blue guitar	STEV 303:18
human nature c.	WOOL 341:10
until I c. myself	MAND 213:6
what cannot be c.	NIEB 238:10

changing c. countries	BREC 43:17
fixed point in a c. age	DOYL 92:13
times they are a-c.	DYLA 95:14

channel Fog in C. — CART 56:3
channels fifty-seven c. — SPRI 301:5

chaos Humour is emotional c.	THUR 316:5
means of overcoming c.	RICH 270:13

chaps Biography is about C. — BENT 29:13
chapter write the next c. — JOHN 169:9

character about a fellow's c.	REAG 268:4
all that's left is c.	SIMP 295:8
content of their c.	KING 180:13
did not have the c.	ROOS 273:8
enormous lack of c.	LEVA 198:3

characters Six c. in search — PIRA 255:2

charge c. of the clattering train	BEAV 25:8
I'm in c.	CATC 60:2

charging marching, c. feet — JAGG 166:4

charity best form of c.	GETT 132:5
Keeping books on c.	PERÓ 252:9
not a gesture of c.	MAND 213:7

charlatan c. is always the pioneer — DOYL 92:14
Charley C. says — OFFI 242:2

charm c. of the bourgeoisie	FILM 117:4
C. the great English blight	WAUG 328:14
Oozing c. from every pore	LERN 197:14
what c. is	CAMU 52:2

Charon C. quit poling — GINS 133:6
Chartres rather sleep in C. Cathedral — JOHN 170:9
chase have to c. after it — KLEE 184:3
chassis worl's in a state o' c. — O'CA 241:7

Chattanooga C. Choo-choo GORD 135:16
Chatterley end of the C. ban LARK 188:12
cheap c. model HOCK 155:8
  how potent c. music is COWA 78:14
  sell it c. SAYI 287:3
  to look this c. PART 250:17
  Words are c. CHAP 63:12
cheaper c. than a prawn sandwich RATN 266:8
  in the c. seats LENN 196:11
cheat cannot c. on DNA WARD 327:7
cheated Old men who never c. BETJ 32:8
cheek dancing c.-to-cheek BERL 30:4
cheer c. when soldier lads march SASS 285:2
  which side do they c. for TEBB 310:13
cheerful It's being so c. CATC 60:6
cheeriness Chintzy, Chintzy c. BETJ 32:6
cheering c. us all up BENN 29:9
cheerio c. my deario MARQ 215:5
cheers Two c. for Democracy FORS 121:6
cheese c.-eating surrender monkeys
    GROE 139:9
  like some valley c. AUDE 18:11
  of c. FADI 109:1
  varieties of c. DE G 87:9
chemical made up of c. elements MULL 231:5
  two c. substances JUNG 173:5
chemistry c. that works WILL 336:5
chemists c.' war DAVI 84:12
cherished My no longer c. MILL 221:15
Chernobyl cultural C. MNOU 226:10
cherries just a bowl of c. BROW 46:5
cherry American as c. pie BROW 46:4
Cheshire smile of a cosmic C. cat HUXL 161:16
Chesterton dared attack my C. BELL 27:12
Chevy Drove my C. to the levee MCLE 208:5
chew can't fart and c. gum JOHN 170:5
chewing gum c. for the eyes ANON 12:10
chianti nice c. FILM 113:15
chic c. for an atheist RUSS 278:6
  Radical C. WOLF 341:1
Chicagowards COCKBURN C. TELE 311:10
chicken c. in every pot HOOV 157:4
  c. shit can turn JOHN 169:6
  fed the c. every day RUSS 278:18
  Some c.! Some neck CHUR 68:1
chickens beside the white c. WILL 336:17
chieftain C. Iffucan of Azcan STEV 303:13
child accused of c. death RICH 270:10
  birth of each c. MCWI 210:12
  c. becomes an adult SZAS 307:12
  c. inherits my body SHAW 293:15
  God bless the c. HOLI 156:2
  has devoured the infant c. HOUS 158:2
  I am to have his c. BURG 48:3
  If you strike a c. SHAW 292:21
  one c. makes you a parent FROS 124:11
  what it is like to be a c. JARR 167:4

childbirth Death and taxes and c. MITC 226:1
childhood C. is the kingdom MILL 220:10
  dolmens round my c. MONT 227:4
  have you seen my c. JACK 165:3
  one moment in c. GREE 137:16
children bellies of his c. STEI 303:3
  by c. to adults SZAS 307:13
  c. are not your children GIBR 132:9
  C. aren't happy with NASH 234:14
  c. are strangers SCHW 288:12
  c. died in the streets AUDE 17:5
  C. have never been very good BALD 21:2
  C.: one is one SAYI 286:5
  c. produce adults DE V 89:11
  C.'s talent to endure ANGE 9:4
  c. to be a credit RUSS 279:3
  c. were lost sight of MOYN 230:3
  c. who leave home SLOV 296:5
  c. who were rough SPEN 300:6
  draw like these c. PICA 254:4
  first class, and with c. BENC 28:7
  get back from c. NESB 236:2
  Goodnight, c. CATC 59:7
  idea that all c. ANNE 9:11
  interest of the c. SHAW 291:17
  made c. laugh EPIT 107:10
  music understood by c. STRA 306:8
  my c. are frightened of me GEOR 131:8
  not much about having c. LODG 201:14
  poor get c. KAHN 174:8
  reasons for having c. RUSS 279:13
  remember the c. you got BROO 45:9
  see his c. fed PUDN 262:13
  some c., in some schools BLUN 37:6
  tiresome for c. SAIN 281:10
  violations committed by c. BOWE 41:13
  We are c. FORS 120:17
  world safer for c. LE G 195:8
Chile Small earthquake in C. COCK 72:12
Chimborazo C., Cotopaxi TURN 319:11
chimpanzee vase in the hands of a c.
    WAUG 329:11
china land armies in C. MONT 227:6
  wall of C. was finished BREC 43:14
Chinese trust the C. DALA 83:1
chintz Chuck out the c. ADVE 3:11
chintzy Chintzy, C. cheeriness BETJ 32:6
chips c. with everything WESK 331:13
Chirac C. would have been happy HAGU 141:2
chivalry law of c. SAYE 285:6
chocolates life like a box of c. FILM 115:14
choice face the c. FILM 113:4
  from fate to c. SACK 281:1
  not your second c. LURI 204:9
choices c. that show what we truly ROWL 276:9
  sum of all the c. DIDI 90:9
choirs c. of wailing shells OWEN 247:5

choo-choo Chattanooga C.   GORD 135:16
choose forced to c.   YEAT 344:9
  I do not c. to run   COOL 76:3
  wisdom to c. correctly   ALLE 7:10
chord just pick a c.   VICI 325:1
choreography c. to the audience   SZEL 308:5
Christ C. follows Dionysus   POUN 259:13
  C. perish in torment   SHAW 293:10
  C. were to return   HARE 145:15
Christian C. ideal not been tried   CHES 65:12
  C. marriage   MARG 214:10
  most C. of worlds   TSVE 319:7
  persuades me to be a C.   FRY 126:12
Christianity C. most materialistic   TEMP 311:12
  Disneyfication of C.   CUPI 81:13
  rock 'n' roll or C.   LENN 196:12
Christmas call off C.   FILM 113:2
  C. is the Disneyfication   CUPI 81:13
  C.-morning bells say 'Come!'   BETJ 32:4
  dreaming of a white C.   BERL 30:11
  just before a hard C.   SMIT 296:7
  Let them know it's C.   GELD 130:12
  not just for C.   SAYI 286:10
  Out of the C. flame   CAUS 57:9
  sack you on C. Eve   HOPE 157:10
  turkeys vote for C.   CALL 51:3
  very traditional C.   WOOD 341:5
Christopher Robin C. has fallen   MORT 229:7
  C. is saying   MILN 223:10
chuck C. it, Smith   CHES 64:5
  C. out the chintz   ADVE 3:11
chucked You're c.   NYE 240:8
chumps C. make the best husbands   WODE 339:12
church C. [of England] should   ROYD 276:11
  C. of England would ask   HARE 145:15
  C.'s Restoration   BETJ 32:11
  Get me to the c. on time   LERN 197:6
  open the windows of the C.   JOHN 168:5
  Railways and the C.   AWDR 19:12
  We are here as a c.   RAMS 266:3
cigar c. called Hamlet   ADVE 3:24
  really good 5-cent c.   MARS 215:16
cigarette c. that bears   MARV 216:3
  smoked my first c.   TOSC 316:13
  than any other c.   ADVE 4:15
cigars roller of big c.   STEV 303:14
cinema c. is truth 24 times   GODA 134:3
circle tightness of the magic c.   MACL 208:7
circuit c. learns your job   MCLU 208:10
circus no right in the c.   MAXT 217:9
cities c., like teeming sores   HOPE 157:7
  c. we had learned about   JARR 167:1
  in the streets of a hundred c.   HOOV 157:5
  shape of our c.   KEAT 176:2
citizens committed c.   MEAD 218:2
  first and second class c.   WILL 337:5

citizenship c. is Indian   TERE 311:17
city c. is not a concrete jungle   MORR 228:8
  c. of perspiring dreams   RAPH 266:6
  felled a c.   THOM 314:4
civil c. to everyone   SISS 295:11
  If this is not c. war   ALLA 7:1
civilization annihilating all c.   SAKH 282:1
  C. advances   WHIT 334:5
  C. and discontents   RIVI 271:7
  c. has from time   ELLI 105:3
  C. nothing more than   ORTE 244:10
  C. the progress   RAND 266:4
  collapse of c.   BELL 28:5
  For a botched c.   POUN 259:15
  history of Western C.   TYNA 320:6
  last product of c.   RUSS 278:11
  life-blood of c.   TREV 317:5
  rottenness of our c.   READ 267:7
  say c. don't advance   ROGE 273:5
  soft resort-style c.   BAUD 25:1
  Speech is c.   MANN 214:3
  stupid of modern c.   KNOX 184:8
  thought of modern c.   GAND 129:12
civilizations clash of c.   HUNT 160:13
civilizes Cricket c. people   MUGA 230:5
civil servant c. doesn't make   IONE 163:1
  Here lies a c.   SISS 295:11
civil servants of c.   BRID 44:4
Civil Service c. has finished   REIT 269:3
  C. is deferential   CROS 80:14
claim c. to one's portion   NAIP 233:10
  last territorial c.   HITL 155:1
claims Extraordinary c.   SAGA 281:7
clamour c. of silence   TAGO 309:18
clan c. and race   MILL 222:8
Clancy C. and Dooley   HEWE 152:12
clap c. your hands   LENN 196:11
  Don't c. too hard   OSBO 246:13
  If you believe, c. your hands   BARR 24:3
  Soul c. its hands and sing   YEAT 345:17
clapped-out c., post-imperial   DRAB 93:1
clash c. between   DELO 88:14
  c. of civilizations   HUNT 160:13
class could have had c.   FILM 113:16
  first and second c. citizens   WILL 337:5
  hands of the ruling c.   STAL 301:9
  use of *force* by one c.   LENI 196:2
  While there is a lower c.   DEBS 86:12
classes capitalism of lower c.   SPEN 300:10
  lower c. had such white   CURZ 82:3
  two c. of travel   BENC 28:7
classical c. mind at work   PIRS 255:5
classics bellyful of the c.   MILL 222:11
classify Germans c.   CATH 57:7
clattering charge of the c. train   BEAV 25:8
Claus ain't no Sanity C.   FILM 114:14
claws pair of ragged c.   ELIO 102:6

clay c. grew tall — OWEN 247:8
C. is the word — KAVA 175:6
had been a lump of c. — POPE 256:3
pure c. of time's mud — MALA 212:2
clean c. American backyards — MAIL 211:7
c. the sky — ELIO 102:11
lie down in c. postures — FOWL 121:9
little gold statue doesn't c. — THER 313:18
New York is so c. now — BOY 42:7
Not a c. & in-between — MCGO 207:11
one more thing to keep c. — FRY 126:8
tragedy is c. — ANOU 13:8
cleans guy who c. the river — PERO 253:1
sweeps as it c. — ADVE 4:2
clear On a c. day — LERN 197:10
clercs trahison des c. — BEND 28:10
clever important to be c. about — MEDA 218:7
Too c. by half — SALI 282:9
cleverest c. member — WEBB 329:16
cliché used every c. except — CHUR 67:9
clichés new c. — GOLD 135:8
click c. with people — EISE 100:3
Clunk, c., every trip — OFFI 242:3
client c. will crawl through — BURR 48:9
cliffs chalk c. of Dover — BALD 21:11
white c. of Dover — BURT 48:13
climate c. change is the most severe — KING 180:7
c. is gentle — MCNE 210:9
whole c. of opinion — AUDE 17:8
climax works its way up to a c. — GOLD 135:10
climb C. ev'ry mountain — HAMM 142:13
clipboards people with c. — LEAR 194:3
clock c. is always slow — SERV 290:14
c. without the pendulum — RUSS 279:11
rock around the c. — DE K 87:17
Stands the Church c. — BROO 45:3
clocks c. were striking thirteen — ORWE 245:15
Stop all the c. — AUDE 17:6
clockwork c. orange — BURG 48:1
cloned successfully c. a lamb — MARC 214:9
Clonmacnoise monks at C. — HEAN 149:3
close C. encounters — FILM 117:3
not c. enough — CAPA 53:2
peacefully towards its c. — DAWS 85:8
closed it was c. — FIEL 112:2
We never c. — VAN 323:7
closer Come c., boys — LAST 190:2
closest c. friends won't tell you — ADVE 3:18
closing c. time in the gardens — CONN 75:6
cloth trick of wearing a c. coat — BALM 22:9
clothes bought his c. with intelligence — AMIE 8:3
C. by a man who doesn't — CHAN 63:8
c. do not make a statement — MUIR 231:2
C. don't make the man — WATS 328:12
C. which make — LURI 204:8
poured into his c. — WODE 340:7

with your c. on — DELL 88:13
clothing sheep in sheep's c. — CHUR 69:14
cloud c. in trousers — MAYA 217:11
Get off my c. — JAGG 166:1
clouds Hullo C. Hullo Sky — WILL 336:2
cloven out pops the c. hoof — WODE 339:16
cloverleaf concrete c. — MUMF 231:7
clowns Send in the c. — SOND 298:14
club don't want to belong to any c. — MARX 216:5
most exclusive c. — NASH 234:6
that terrible football c. — MCGR 207:13
clunk C., click, every trip — OFFI 242:3
clunking big c. fist — BLAI 36:6
clutch c. out of the darkness — CANE 52:19
clutching c. their gods — ELIO 102:1
Clyde poems should be C.-built — DUNN 94:6
coaching C. a football team — LINE 200:7
coachman France is the c. — DE G 87:16
coal island made mainly of c. — BEVA 33:3
coalition real rainbow c. — JACK 165:1
coast c. of Coromandel — SITW 295:15
coat long black c. — WARR 328:6
Coca-Cola blue jeans and C. — GREE 138:6
cocaine C. habit-forming — BANK 22:11
cock c. crowing on its own dunghill — ALDI 6:7
Our c. won't fight — BEAV 25:5
cocktail weasel under c. cabinet — PINT 255:1
cocoa c. for Kingsley Amis — COPE 77:2
C. is a cad and coward — CHES 65:2
coconuts loverly bunch of c. — HEAT 149:13
cod photographer is like the c. — SHAW 293:12
code trail has its own stern c. — SERV 290:13
coffee put poison in your c. — CHUR 69:11
with c. spoons — ELIO 102:5
coffin in a Y-shaped c. — ORTO 244:14
coins for a fistful of c. — ZAPA 348:4
coke go better with C. — ADVE 5:5
cold Cast a c. eye — YEAT 346:10
c. and lonely — PAST 251:2
c. coming we had of it — ELIO 101:18
c. metal of economic theory — SCHU 288:10
c. war — BARU 24:13
c. war warrior — THAT 312:4
fingers of c. are corpse — LAWR 192:22
past the common c. — AYRE 19:19
plunging into a c. peace — YELT 346:13
spy who came in from the c. — LE C 195:1
understand one who's c. — SOLZ 298:7
Without the c. war — UPDI 321:8
cologne diplomatic c. — CRIS 79:12
colonized culture to be c. by — WELS 331:10
colour any c. that he wants — FORD 120:1
by the c. of their skin — KING 180:13
c., culture or ethnic origin — MACP 210:10
C. has taken hold of me — KLEE 184:3
c. purple — WALK 327:1
C. seems to radiate — CLIF 71:9

colour (*cont.*)
I know the c. rose — ABSE 1:2
It's just my c. — MEND 219:6
perceptible through c. — MOND 226:13
problem of the c. line — DU B 93:6
coloured no 'white' or 'c.' signs — KENN 177:14
colourless C. green ideas — CHOM 66:3
colours map-makers' c. — BISH 35:3
nailing his c. — FIEL 111:6
Columbus youth in C., Ohio — THUR 316:1
column Fifth c. — MOLA 226:11
comb two bald men over a c. — BORG 39:10
come believe in the life to c. — BECK 25:10
C. on — CATC 58:11
C. to the edge — LOGU 202:3
c. up and see me sometime — MISQ 225:8
don't want to c. out — BERR 31:12
I go—I c. back — CATC 59:17
nobody will c. — SAND 283:8
shape of things to c. — WELL 331:7
they'll c. out for it — SKEL 296:2
where do they all c. from — LENN 196:15
where you have c. from — CAME 51:7
comeback c. kid — CLIN 72:2
comedy All I need to make a c. — CHAP 63:11
C. is tragedy that happens — CART 54:9
comes Nothing happens, nobody c. — BECK 26:3
comfort bourgeois prefers c. — HESS 152:9
naught for your c. — CHES 64:6
comfortable consider c. or plausible — SAGA 281:5
comfortably Are you sitting c. — CATC 58:7
comforting always a c. thought — MARQ 215:8
cloud of c. convictions — RUSS 279:1
comforts recapture the c. — BRYS 47:2
comical Beautiful c. things — HARV 147:4
coming British are c. — WELL 330:14
cold c. we had of it — ELIO 101:18
c. for us that night — BALD 21:7
Everything's c. up roses — SOND 298:12
Yanks are c. — COHA 73:1
command give a single c. — SCHW 289:1
commandments *Five C.* — DE M 89:1
comment C. is free — SCOT 289:7
C. is free — STOP 305:13
couldn't possibly c. — CATC 61:19
commerce c. in the morning — FILM 114:8
commercial you're labelled c. — MANN 213:12
commission anyone in the C. — ANON 11:7
resigned c. — ANON 10:11
committed c. breakfast with it — LEWI 199:9
c. citizens — MEAD 218:2
committee C.—a group of men — ALLE 7:3
c. a group of unwilling — SAYI 286:6
horse designed by a c. — ISSI 163:8
common century of the c. man — WALL 327:4
c. pursuit — LEAV 194:4

nor lose the c. touch — KIPL 182:9
nothing in c. — PYM 263:6
worth of the c. things of life — SEEG 290:1
commoner persistent c. — BENN 28:14
commons member of the House of C. — POWE 261:5
common sense C. is nothing more — EINS 99:3
communicate birds trying to c. — AUDE 19:6
communism anti-Christ of C. — BUCH 47:8
caused the fall of c. — JOHN 169:2
C. is like prohibition — ROGE 273:4
C. is Soviet power — LENI 196:6
C. the illegitimate child — ATTL 16:7
trouble with C. — LAWR 193:5
communist ain't a c. necessarily — GUTH 140:10
call me a c. — CAMA 51:6
Catholic and the C. — ORWE 246:8
Is he a C. — STAR 302:2
member of the C. Party — POLI 257:3
members of the C. Party — MCCA 205:8
communists came first for the C. — NIEM 238:11
Catholics and C. — GREE 137:9
commuter C.—one who spends — WHIT 333:8
companion gave him a c. — VALÉ 323:3
company bought the c. — ADVE 3:30
c. he chooses — BURT 48:11
soul to the c. store — TRAV 317:3
compassion c. of the healer's art — ELIO 100:19
practise c. — DALA 83:3
compensates c. for the misery — DRAB 93:2
competed when I c. — BLAN 36:11
competing register c. attractions — KNIG 184:5
competition rigour of c. — ANON 10:8
complaint fatal c. of all — HILT 154:6
no cause for c. — SCOT 289:11
complete become c. yourself — FRIE 123:16
complexion schoolgirl c. — ADVE 4:7
complicity Our tribe's c. — HEAN 148:14
composer bad c. writing for society — BRIT 44:6
compound it's a chemical c. — ZAPP 348:5
comprehensible universe is c. — EINS 98:12
comprehensive bog-standard c. — CAMP 51:11
compris Je vous ai c. — DE G 87:5
compromise any c. whatever — SHAR 291:9
Politics without c. — KINN 181:11
computer if it's got a c. — FILM 113:9
modern c. hovers — BREN 44:2
requires a c. — SAYI 287:8
computers C. are anti-Faraday — CORN 77:5
C. are composed of — AUGA 19:9
so many c. — WAŁĘ 326:7
conceit curst c. o' bein' richt — MACD 206:11
concentrating not c. on you — BARN 23:14
conception present at the c. — ORTO 244:12
concepts up the stairs of his c. — STEI 302:14
concert self-imposed torture, the c. — MILL 222:10
concerto C. to be difficult — SCHO 288:3

concrete city is not a c. jungle — MORR 228:8
  c. and tyres — LARK 189:3
  c. cloverleaf — MUMF 231:7
concubine c. of a warlord — JUNG 173:9
concupiscent c. curds — STEV 303:14
condemn c. a little more — MAJO 211:14
condemned c. to be free — SART 284:4
condition c. for freedom — FRIE 124:3
  first c. of humanity — SOYI 299:6
conductors C. must give signals — SZEL 308:5
conference ever born in a c. — FITZ 117:22
  naked into the c. chamber — BEVA 33:9
confinement solitary c. — WILL 336:12
conflict armed c. — EDEN 97:3
  field of human c. — CHUR 67:8
  offered you C. and Art — PRIE 261:16
  tragic c. of loyalties — HOWE 158:11
conform Universe is not obliged to c. — SAGA 281:5
conforms industry applies, man c. — ANON 12:8
confused anyone who isn't c. — MURR 232:6
  C.? You won't be — CATC 58:12
confusion in our sea of c. — GAMO 129:6
Congo C., creeping through — LIND 200:4
conic c. sections were studied — WHIT 334:6
conjuring c. trick with bones — JENK 167:11
conked c. out on November 15th — EPIT 108:2
connect Only c. — FORS 120:14
conqueror you are a c. — ROST 275:12
conscience American c. — KISS 183:17
  C.: the inner voice — MENC 219:1
  c. to bother him — LLOY 201:13
  cruelty with a good c. — RUSS 279:5
  Freedom of c. — JOHN 169:4
  scar on the c. — BLAI 36:4
  will not cut my c. — HELL 150:10
consciences binding on the c. — JOHN 168:3
consciousness c.-expanding drug — CLAR 70:12
  C. the phenomenon — PENR 252:5
  tragic c. — FUEN 126:16
conscription Not necessarily c. — KING 181:3
consent without your c. — ROOS 273:9
consenting only between c. adults — VIDA 325:4
conservation make a speech on c. — STEV 304:14
conservatism c. is based upon — CHES 65:9
conservative become a c. — AREN 14:6
  c. been arrested — WOLF 340:16
  c. is a liberal — SAYI 286:7
  C. is a man — ROOS 273:17
  C. Party always — MACL 208:8
  C. Party at prayer — ROYD 276:11
  is the C. Party leadable — HESE 152:7
  make me c. when old — FROS 125:13
  makes a man more c. — KEYN 178:12
  oldest C. principle — OSBO 246:12
conservatives better with the C. — POLI 258:3
  C. do not believe — HAIL 141:5

night for the C. — PORT 259:2
consoles it c. them — GIDE 132:12
conspicuous Vega c. overhead — AUDE 18:3
conspiracies c. against the laity — SHAW 291:16
conspiracy c. to make you happy — UPDI 321:6
  vast right-wing c. — CLIN 71:12
constituencies go back to your c. — STEE 302:5
constitution c. does not provide — WILL 337:5
  C. has never greatly — BIDD 34:5
  genius of the C. — BREN 43:18
consume more history than they can c. — SAKI 282:4
consumer c. isn't a moron — OGIL 241:12
  c. is the king — SAMU 283:2
  c. society — ILLI 162:5
consumes c. without producing — ORWE 244:15
consuming survive by c. — VANE 324:2
contact c. with this Wild Man — BLY 37:8
  word preserves c. — MANN 214:3
contemplation Has left for c. — BETJ 32:11
contemptible c. little army — ANON 10:10
contender could have been a c. — FILM 113:16
content Canadian content — THOM 313:19
contest not the victory but the c. — COUB 77:10
continent Africa, drifting c. — GENE 130:16
  C. isolated — CART 56:3
  ghost c. — EISE 99:10
continually think c. of those — SPEN 300:4
contraception oral c. — ALLE 7:11
contract Social C. nothing more — WELL 331:5
  verbal c. isn't worth — GOLD 135:3
contradict Never c. — FISH 112:8
contradiction c. is real — LÉVI 198:13
contraire Au c. — BECK 26:10
contrast enjoyment from a c. — FREU 123:5
control Ground c. to Major Tom — BOWI 42:2
  wrong members in c. — ORWE 245:12
controls Who c. the past — ORWE 245:17
controversial what is c. — EPHR 106:3
convalescence enjoy c. — SHAW 291:12
convenience prefers c. to liberty — HESS 152:9
conventional c. wisdom — GALB 128:7
conversation C. is imperative — WHIT 333:9
  no such thing as c. — WEST 332:16
convict c. stain — HUGH 159:12
conviction best lack all c. — YEAT 345:20
convictions cloud of comforting c. — RUSS 279:1
  c. are hills — FITZ 117:16
convinces man who c. the world — DARW 84:4
cook good c., as cooks go — SAKI 282:5
cookies baked c. and had teas — CLIN 71:11
cooking c. of the Mediterranean — DAVI 84:6
cool c. as a mountain stream — ADVE 3:12
  c. web of language — GRAV 137:1
  rather be dead than c. — COBA 72:11
Coolidge admiration for Mr C. — ANON 12:14
cooling for c. the blood — FLAN 118:7

cooperation belief in c. — YAMA 344:2
   partnership and c. — ANON 10:8
copperheads c. and the assassin — SAND 283:4
cops C. are like a doctor — CHAN 63:2
copulating Two skeletons c. — BEEC 26:15
copulation Birth, and c. — ELIO 102:15
coral like c. insects — WARN 328:3
cork c. out of my lunch — FIEL 111:12
   if all this was burnt c. — GREG 138:11
corkscrews crooked as c. — AUDE 17:2
cormorant common c. (or shag) — ISHE 163:5
corn c. is as high — HAMM 143:4
corner At every c., I meet — LOWE 203:12
   c. of a foreign field — BROO 45:5
   just around the c. — COWA 78:12
   mutters away in a c. — CARE 53:10
corny c. as Kansas in August — HAMM 143:10
Coromandel coast of C. — SITW 295:15
coronation King's C. depends — BLUN 37:7
correctness political c. can be — JAME 166:16
correlative objective c. — ELIO 103:10
corridors c. of power — SNOW 297:16
corroboree c. is gone — NOON 240:2
corrupted c. by sentiment — GREE 137:10
cosh c. of the English — STRA 306:10
cosiness c. and irritation — PYM 263:6
cosmetics c. industry is going — RODD 272:6
   tired of the c. — SEXT 291:2
   we make c. — REVS 269:10
cosmologists C. are often in error — LAND 188:7
cost But at what c. — BECK 25:9
   c. of setting him up — NAID 233:7
costs C. merely register — KNIG 184:5
Cotopaxi Chimborazo, C. — TURN 319:11
cotton c. is high — HEYW 153:3
cough all c. in ink — YEAT 345:19
coughing keeping people from c. — RICH 271:1
   one c., and one not — SCHN 287:17
coughs C. and sneezes spread — OFFI 242:4
could someone who c. do it — DE M 88:16
council chaos of a Labour c. — KINN 181:8
count c. everything — CORN 77:5
   Don't c. on me — RICH 270:9
   if you can c. your money — GETT 132:4
   I won the c. — SOMO 298:10
counted c. them all out — HANR 144:1
counterpoint Too much c. — BEEC 26:14
counting it's the c. — STOP 305:9
countries changing c. — BREC 43:17
country ask not what your c. — KENN 177:9
   betraying my c. — FORS 121:5
   Britain a fit c. — LLOY 201:6
   c. and western music — SMIT 297:1
   Cry, the beloved c. — PATO 251:3
   died to save their c. — CHES 64:11
   dying for Queen and c. — THOM 315:9
   dying for your c. — FRAN 122:5

everyday story of c. folk — CATC 58:22
fight for its King and C. — GRAH 136:7
How can you govern a c. — DE G 87:9
King and c. need you — MILI 221:12
living in another c. — DELI 88:10
love to serve my c. — GIBR 132:8
My c. is Kiltartan Cross — YEAT 345:6
My c. is not a country — VIGN 325:13
never let my c. die for me — KINN 181:9
no c. for old men — YEAT 345:16
Once we had a c. — AUDE 18:5
past is a foreign c. — HART 147:3
peace of each c. — JOHN 168:4
quarrel in a far away c. — CHAM 62:7
rather than a c. — PILG 254:10
struck our c. — POWE 260:16
understand the c. — LESS 197:17
vow to thee, my c. — SPRI 301:1
what was good for our c. — WILS 337:7
While there's a c. lane — PARK 250:9
Your c. needs you — MILI 221:11
your King and your C. — RUBE 276:14
You've never seen this c. — PURD 263:2
countryside c. to be laughing — FRIE 124:7
counts only pity that c. — LEVA 198:4
county English c. families — WAUG 329:1
couples chasing the naughty c. — THOM 314:12
courage C. is the thing — BARR 24:6
   C. not simply *one* — LEWI 199:8
   c. of women — RICH 270:11
   c. to change — NIEB 238:10
   C. was mine — OWEN 247:10
   have enough c. — MITC 225:12
   It takes c. — MOWL 230:2
   Pathos, piety, c. — FORS 121:1
   warm c. — BUSH 49:4
   warm c. — ROOS 273:14
courting Are yer c. — CATC 58:6
courtmartialled c. in my absence — BEHA 26:18
cousins two brothers and eight c. — HALD 142:5
couture Haute C. should be fun — LACR 187:1
covenants Open c. of peace — WILS 338:20
cover Duck and c. — OFFI 242:8
cow c. is of the bovine ilk — NASH 234:4
   milk the c. of the world — WILB 335:7
coward sea hates a c. — O'NE 243:13
cowardice C., a lack of ability — HEMI 151:1
cowslip C. and shad-blow — CRAN 79:2
crabs c. in a basket — DURR 94:10
crack C. and sometimes break — ELIO 100:14
   c. in the tea-cup opens — AUDE 17:1
cracked You haven't cracked me yet — BOGA 38:4
cradle c. rocks above an abyss — NABO 233:4
   from the c. to the grave — CHUR 68:4
   rocking the c. — ROBI 272:1
cradling evil c. — BORR 40:9
crane tall as a c. — SITW 295:12

crash car c. as a sexual event   BALL 22:5
   had a c. with a man   CART 56:5
crazed c. with the spell   DE L 88:2
crazy C. like a fox   PERE 252:6
   c. to fly more missions   HELL 150:6
   he's football c.   MCGR 207:13
   Still c. after all   SIMO 295:5
   two c. people together   HART 146:14
create genuinely c. Europe   MONN 226:14
   What I cannot c.   FEYN 111:5
created nothing was c. in the West Indies
     NAIP 233:11
   Nothing will always be c.   WALC 326:4
creates What the chief accountant c.
     GREE 138:4
creation before you think c.'s   FORS 121:4
   I hold C. in my foot   HUGH 159:14
   world since the C.   NIXO 239:3
   your niche in c.   HALL 142:8
creative Deception is not as c.   SAUN 285:4
creator feel at times like the C.   BELL 27:4
   Of the C.   MERW 220:2
creature C. from the Black Lagoon   CRON 80:4
credit children to be a c.   RUSS 279:3
   To c. marvels   HEAN 149:2
credulous Man is a c. animal   RUSS 279:7
crème c. de la crème   SPAR 299:8
Crete people of c.   SAKI 282:4
crevasse like a scream from a c.   GREE 137:14
cricket C.—a game which   MANC 212:13
   c. as organized loafing   TEMP 311:13
   C. civilizes people   MUGA 230:5
   c. test   TEBB 310:13
   c. with their peasants   TREV 317:6
   play Test c.   BRAD 42:13
cried when he c.   AUDE 17:5
crikey C.!   CATC 58:13
crime catalogue of human c.   CHUR 67:4
   C. doesn't pay   SAYI 286:8
   c. rates of the '20s   BOAZ 37:10
   c. you haven't committed   POWE 260:12
   Tough on c.   BLAI 35:11
   UNDULY EMPHASISING C.   TELE 311:10
crimes worst of c.   SHAW 292:3
criminal ends I think c.   KEYN 178:10
   was greed a c. offence   BLAC 35:8
   while there is a c.   DEBS 86:12
criminals squalid c.   REAG 268·6
cringe Australian Cultural C.   PHIL 253:12
   cultural c. where you have   KEAT 175:13
crises age has consisted of c.   ATKI 16:2
crisis cannot be a c. next week   KISS 183:13
   C.? What crisis   MISQ 224:3
   C.? What crisis   NEWS 237:5
   drama out of a c.   ADVE 5:11
   real c. on your hands   THAT 312:12
crisps like eating c.   BOY 42:6

critic c. a man who knows   TYNA 320:5
   c. is a bundle of biases   BALL 22:7
   function of the c.   BELL 27:1
   important book, c. assumes   WOOL 341:12
   in honour of a c.   SIBE 294:9
   not the c. who counts   ROOS 274:12
criticism c.'s motto   FORS 121:4
Cromwell ruin that C. knocked about
     BEDF 26:11
cronies money-grabbing c.   HAGU 141:1
Cronkite lost Walter C.   JOHN 170:2
crook President is a c.   NIXO 239:6
crooked c. as corkscrews   AUDE 17:2
   c. be made straight   ELIO 100:9
crooning c. like a bilious pigeon   SHAW 293:4
cross first at Cradle and the C.   SAYE 285:8
   heaviest has been the C. of Lorraine
     SPEA 299:12
   orgasm has replaced the C.   MUGG 230:10
   There for you to c.   PAUL 251:8
crosses Between the c.   MCCR 206:10
   c. I have had to bear   SPEA 299:12
   with c. of fire   NERU 235:12
crossroads mankind faces a c.   ALLE 7:10
crowd c. will always save   COCT 72:16
crowded Across a c. room   HAMM 143:7
   in a c. theatre   MISQ 225:2
crowds Avoid c.   KAUF 174:10
crown c. of life is neither   HOLT 156:8
   c. of thorns   BEVA 33:7
   C., the symbol of permanence   JUAN 172:16
   neither abdicate the C.   JUAN 172:17
   never wears the c.   HESE 152:3
crucible America is God's C.   ZANG 348:3
crucified choose who is to be c.   COCT 72:16
crucify God they ought to c.   CART 55:3
cruel Such c. glasses   HOWE 158:12
cruellest April is the c. month   ELIO 102:19
cruelty infliction of c.   RUSS 279:5
   main sources of c.   RUSS 279:8
   never really gauged your c.   WELC 330:10
crumb c. falls from the tables   HUGH 159:7
crumpet thinking man's c.   MUIR 230:14
crusade nor is c.   KENN 176:9
   party is a moral c.   WILS 338:5
   this 'c.', this war   BUSH 49:5
cry c. all the way to the bank   LIBE 200:2
   c. at his mother's funeral   CAMU 52:10
   C., the beloved country   PATO 251:3
   denies you the beer to c. into   MARQ 215:11
   Don't c. for me Argentina   RICE 270:5
   Some must c.   RHYS 269:13
crystals growing the c.   HODG 155:9
Cuban C. Missile Crisis   STOC 305:4
cubes sum of two c.   RAMA 266:1
Cubism C. has not been understood   PICA 254:2
cuckoo c. clock   FILM 114:11

cuckoo (*cont.*)
  rainbow and a c.'s song   DAVI 84:9
cuddled c. by a complete stranger   ANNE 9:11
culpable How c. was he   HEAN 148:14
cult c. added to power   ANON 13:2
  c. of the individual   KHRU 179:13
  What's a c.   ALTM 7:17
cultural Australian C. Cringe   PHIL 253:12
  c. autonomy   GRAY 137:7
  c. Chernobyl   MNOU 226:10
  c. Stalingrad   BALL 22:6
  in the C. Revolution   ANON 13:2
culture core of a world's c.   BOLD 38:9
  C. makes life worth   ELIO 103:9
  c. to be colonised by   WELS 331:10
  hear the word c.   JOHS 170:10
  integral part of c.   GOUL 136:5
  pursue C. in bands   WHAR 333:5
  What other c. could   VIDA 325:3
cultures two c.   SNOW 298:1
cunning c. plan   CATC 59:18
  silence, exile, and c.   JOYC 172:5
cup prayed my c. might pass   KIPL 182:5
curate like a shabby c.   AUDE 19:3
curb use the snaffle and the c.   CAMP 51:15
cured c. by hanging from a string   KING 181:5
  c. by more democracy   SMIT 296:6
curiosity c. about the future   WAUG 329:4
  c., freckles, and doubt   PARK 249:7
  Disinterested c.   TREV 317:5
  full of 'satiable c.   KIPL 183:5
currency debauch the c.   KEYN 178:11
curse c. be ended   ELIO 100:9
  C. the blasted, jelly-boned   LAWR 192:20
  c. to this country   CHUR 68:7
  real c. of Eve   RHYS 269:14
curtain bloody c.   ELIS 103:16
  iron c.   CHUR 68:8
  Iron C. did not reach   SOLZ 298:9
customer c. is never wrong   RITZ 271:6
cut we are going to c. it off   POWE 260:14
  will not c. my conscience   HELL 150:10
cutting hand is the c. edge   BRON 44:9
cyclone South Bend c.   RICE 270:4
cyclops view of a paralysed c.   HOCK 155:5
cynicism c. about Parliament   BOOT 39:5
  C. is an unpleasant way   HELL 150:9
Cyprus rings black C.   FLEC 118:14
Cyril Nice one, C.   ADVE 4:19

dabbling d. their fingers   MCGR 208:1
dad fuck you up, your mum and d.   LARK 189:6
  girls in slacks remember D.   BETJ 32:4
  if the d. is present   ORTO 244:12
dada mama of d.   FADI 109:2
daddy D., what did you do   MILI 221:3

  heart belongs to d.   PORT 258:22
  think his d. had trouble   IVIN 163:13
daffodils d. were for Wordsworth   LARK 189:13
daguerrotype stare from d.   WARR 328:6
daintily have things d. served   BETJ 32:9
dairymaid Queen asked the D.   MILN 223:8
damage d. to the earth   COUS 77:14
  seriously d. your health   OFFI 242:15
damaged D. people are dangerous   HART 146:10
dame nothin' like a d.   HAMM 143:9
damn D. you all to hell   FILM 116:13
  d. you England   OSBO 246:19
  don't give a d.   FILM 113:11
  don't give a d.   MITC 226:2
  one d. thing over and over   MILL 221:16
damnation From sleep and from d.   CHES 64:12
damned beautiful and d.   FITZ 117:15
  brandy of the d.   SHAW 292:11
Dan Dangerous D. McGrew   SERV 290:16
dance D., dance, little lady   COWA 78:1
  dancer from the d.   YEAT 344:3
  d. round in a ring   FROS 125:16
  d. to the music of time   BORR 40:8
  Let's face the music and d.   BERL 30:6
  Lord of the D.   CART 55:4
  should be able to d. it   ZEPH 348:8
  too far from the d.   POUN 260:3
danced d. with the Prince of Wales   FARJ 109:7
dancer d. from the dance   YEAT 344:3
dancers d. are all gone   ELIO 100:17
dances Slightly bald. Also d.   ANON 10:7
  truest expression in its d.   DE M 88:15
dancing d. about architecture   ANON 13:4
  [D.] a perpendicular   SHAW 293:16
  d. cheek-to-cheek   BERL 30:4
  D., double-talking   CAUS 57:9
  d. is to walking   WAIN 326:1
  like a Mask d.   ACHE 1:6
  mature women, *d.*   FRIE 124:7
Dane-geld paying the D.   KIPL 183:3
danger clear and present d.   COOK 75:17
  less d. from the wiles   NASH 234:7
  New Labour, new d.   POLI 258:4
  only one thing of d.   NERU 236:1
dangerous Damaged people are d.   HART 146:10
  d. to meet it alone   WHAR 333:5
  desk is a d. place   LE C 194:11
  more d. than an idea   ALAI 6:5
Dante D.'s Inferno   BOGA 38:3
dare It wouldn't d.   CARR 54:5
  Take me if you d.   PANK 248:11
dares Who d. wins   MILI 221:10
daring d. is gone   SCHI 287:14
  d. starts from within   WELT 331:11
dark come out of the d.   MANN 214:1
  D. as the world of man   SITW 295:13
  D. forces   MISQ 224:4

d. for writing	LAST 190:11	he is d., who will not fight	GREN 138:15
d. is light enough	FRY 126:6	If the d. talk to you	SZAS 308:1
d. night of the soul	FITZ 117:21	I see d. people	FILM 114:12
D. side of the moon	PINK 254:12	land of the d.	WILD 335:14
d. world where gods	ROET 272:11	left us our Fenian d.	PEAR 251:14
half the world is always d.	LE G 195:10	more to say when I am d.	ROBI 271:11
His d. materials	BORR 40:15	Not many d.	COCK 72:12
I knew you in the d.	OWEN 247:11	only the d. smiled	AKHM 6:2
In the nightmare of the d.	AUDE 17:12	past is the only d. thing	THOM 314:19
O d. dark dark	ELIO 100:18	President Kennedy was d.	FORS 121:7
Out in the d.	THOM 314:22	quick, and the d.	DEWA 90:1
darker I am the d. brother	HUGH 159:5	rather be d. than cool	COBA 72:11
darkness curse the d.	STEV 304:13	remind me of the d.	SASS 284:17
in the d. bind them	TOLK 316:12	saying 'Lord Jones D.'	CHES 65:14
light in the d. of mere being	JUNG 173:3	simplify me when I'm d.	DOUG 92:4
there is d. everywhere	NEHR 235:7	thirteen men lay d.	HEAN 149:6
time of d.	BREC 43:16	ways of being d.	DAWK 85:3
two eternities of d.	NABO 233:4	we are all d.	KEYN 179:5
darling call you d. after sex	BARN 23:15	you're ten years d.	HAYE 148:7
d. man, a daarlin' man	O'CA 241:6	**deaded** told you I'd be d.	CATC 61:21
data some d. was bound to be	WATS 328:10	**deadener** Habit is a great d.	BECK 26:6
date d. which will live in infamy	ROOS 274:4	**deadlier** d. than the mail	FRY 126:13
doubles your chances for a d.	ALLE 7:14	**deadline** met his own d.	EPIT 107:9
daughter put your d. on the stage	COWA 78:8	**deadlines** multiply d. by pi	RYLE 280:6
to my elder d.	THOM 314:20	**deadlock** Holy d.	HERB 151:18
daughters have three d.	RICH 270:14	**deadly** more d. than the male	KIPL 182:2
David D. wrote the Psalms	NAYL 235:4	**Dead Sea** like a D. fruit	MACM 209:7
day Action this D.	MILI 221:1	**deal** new d.	ROOS 273:11
d. the music died	MCLE 208:4	square d. afterwards	ROOS 274:9
d. war broke out	CATC 58:14	**deals** D. are my art form	TRUM 319:4
Doris D. before she was	MARX 216:7	**dear** D. 338171	COWA 78:16
Just for one d.	BOWI 42:1	**death** accused of child d.	RICH 270:10
long d.'s journey	O'NE 243:11	After the first d.	THOM 314:8
make my d.	FILM 113:12	brooding over d.	HILL 153:10
Mars a d.	ADVE 4:11	Cake or d.	IZZA 164:1
not a second on the d.	COOK 75:15	coming up to d.	SAUN 285:4
tomorrow is another d.	MITC 226:3	consent to my own d.	RODR 272:9
write every other d.	DOUG 92:8	copulation, and d.	ELIO 102:15
days Cast your mind on other d.	YEAT 346:9	D. and taxes and childbirth	MITC 226:1
first 1,000 d.	KENN 177:8	D. destroys a man	FORS 120:15
Ten d. that shook the world	REED 268:12	D. devours all lovely things	MILL 221:14
dazzled Eyes still d.	LIND 200:6	d. hurtling to and fro	HUGH 159:13
dead been d. 10 or 15 years	TRUM 318:13	D. in Venice	MANN 213:13
Better red than d.	POLI 257:6	D. is a master from Germany	CELA 62:5
blooming well d.	SARO 283:16	[D. is] nature's way	SAYI 286:9
cold and pure and very d.	LEWI 199:12	D. is not an event of life	WITT 339:11
d. don't die	LAWR 192:21	d. of air	ELIO 101:5
d. had no speech for	ELIO 101:3	D. of a salesman	MILL 222:3
d. man's town	SPRI 301:3	d. of the Author	BART 24:9
d. men lost their bones	ELIO 103:1	d. shall have no dominion	THOM 314:1
d. writers are remote	ELIO 103:12	D. the most convenient time	LLOY 201:9
declared legally d.	BOMB 38:13	D., where is thy sting-a-ling	ANON 12:4
democracy of the d.	CHES 65:8	d., who had the soldier	DOUG 92:5
Either he's d.	FILM 113:5	D. would summon Everyman	HEAN 148:13
God is d.	FROM 124:10	didn't capture his d.	DREW 93:3
God is not d.	ANON 10:14	died a good d.	ACHE 1:7
Harrow the house of the d.	AUDE 18:13	Even d. is unreliable	BECK 26:9

death (*cont.*)

Finality is d.	STEP 303:7
go on living even after d.	FRAN 122:6
I am become d.	OPPE 243:15
If there wasn't d.	SMIT 297:12
improved by d.	SAKI 282:3
I signed my d. warrant	COLL 73:12
isn't sex but d.	SONT 298:15
Lead me from d. to life	KUMA 185:11
matter of life and d.	SHAN 291:8
much possessed by d.	ELIO 103:8
No d. in my lifetime	HEAN 149:9
nothing but d.	UNAM 321:3
reaction to her d.	ELIZ 104:8
removes Hazard and d.	BOLA 38:8
rendezvous with D.	SEEG 289:13
seen birth and d.	ELIO 101:19
socialism or d.	CHAV 64:4
stars of d.	AKHM 6:3
Swarm over, D.	BETJ 32:14
Ten years after your d.	HUGH 160:4
This is the Black Widow, d.	LOWE 203:13
thoughts so crowded with d.	GUNN 140:7
up the line to d.	SASS 284:15
While there is d.	CROS 80:13
Why fear d.	LAST 191:10

deaths million d. a statistic   STAL 301:12

death sentence d. without a whimper

LAWR 193:2

deathwards plots tend to move d.   DELI 88:11

debt deeper in d.   TRAV 317:3

National D.	SELL 290:8
promise made is a d. unpaid	SERV 290:13

debts so we can pay our d.   NYER 240:10

decade in the same d. with you   ROOS 274:6

Me D.   WOLF 340:18

deceiving nearly d. your friends   CORN 77:9

December May to D.   ANDE 8:11

roses in D.   BARR 24:5

decency Have you no sense of d.   WELC 330:10

deception D. is not as creative   SAUN 285:4

decide ministers d.   THAT 313:9

six people cannot d.   HEIN 150:3

decider I'm the d.   BUSH 49:8

decision make a 'realistic d.'   MCCA 206:1

monologue is not a d.   ATTL 16:4

decisions d. allowed to take   PARK 250:14

decorate painting not made to d.   PICA 254:3

decorum Dulce et d. est   OWEN 247:7

decrees d. may not change   KING 180:9

deduction d. from the smallest   EINS 99:4

deed right d. for the wrong   ELIO 102:10

deep d. sleep of England   ORWE 245:9

defeat d. is an orphan   CIAN 69:16

In d.: defiance	CHUR 69:3
In d. unbeatable	CHUR 68:18

defeated destroyed but not d.   HEMI 151:3

even when he is d.	KUND 185:15
history to the d.	AUDE 18:15

defeats Dewey d. Truman   NEWS 237:6

nobility of his later d.   TAYL 310:8

defence d. against the atom bomb   ANON 10:4

only d. is in offence	BALD 21:10
think of the d. of England	BALD 21:11

defending d. himself   GARC 130:3

defiance In defeat: d.   CHUR 69:3

wilful d. of military   SASS 285:3

definite d. maybe   GOLD 135:7

definition working d. of hell   SHAW 293:2

deformity Art is significant d.   FRY 126:11

dehumanizing anecdote d.   EPHR 106:2

déjà d. vu all over again   BERR 31:13

delegate When in trouble, d.   BORE 39:7

deleted Expletive d.   ANON 10:9

delightful it can be d.   SHAW 291:13

deliver d. us, good Lord   CHES 64:12

demand not a note of d.   SCHN 287:18

democracy cured by more d.   SMIT 296:6

D. is the theory	MENC 218:14
D. is the worst form	CHUR 68:9
d. means government	ATTL 16:8
D. *not* identical	LENI 196:2
d. of the dead	CHES 65:8
D. resumed her reign	BELL 27:15
D. substitutes election	SHAW 292:17
d., tolerance	ANNA 9:10
d. unbearable	PERE 252:7
five hundred years of d.	FILM 114:11
great arsenal of d.	ROOS 274:2
justice makes d. possible	NIEB 236:11
less d. to save	ATKI 16:1
made safe for d.	WILS 338:18
no d. can afford	BEVE 33:14
no d. in physics	ALVA 7:18
not voting that's d.	STOP 305:9
pollution of d.	WHIT 333:13
Russia an empire or d.	BRZE 47:3
Two cheers for D.	FORS 121:6
want to understand d.	STRU 306:12

democrat Senator, and a D.   JOHN 169:7

democratic utterly d. way   GRAH 136:8

demolition d. of a man   LEVI 198:9

denied Justice d.   MILL 220:14

denying they were d.   FREE 122:14

dependent d. on other people's   ELTO 105:4

depends d. what you mean by   CATC 60:4

deposit greater the d.   LAYT 193:9

depression d. when you lose yours

TRUM 318:14

deprivation deliverance from d.   PARI 249:3

D. is for me   LARK 189:13

Derry oak would sprout in D.   HEAN 149:6

desert d. sighs in the bed   AUDE 17:1

my own d. places   FROS 125:2

deserve d. to get it — MENC 218:14
somehow haven't to d. — FROS 125:1
deserves gets what he d. — ANON 11:9
desiccated d. calculating machine — BEVA 33:10
design Good d. is intelligence — PICK 254:9
masterpiece of d. — SMIT 296:8
desire get your heart's d. — SHAW 292:15
desired You who d. so much — CRAN 79:6
desires d. of the heart — AUDE 17:2
desk d. is a dangerous place — LE C 194:15
sleeping under the d. — GATE 130:6
desks school where children sit at d. — NEIL 235:8
desolation D. in immaculate — ROET 272:10
Magnificent d. — ALDR 6:9
despair Do not d. — PUDN 262:12
far side of d. — SART 284:10
one path leads to d. — ALLE 7:10
sins of d. — READ 267:11
Where there is d. — THAT 312:5
despise Government I d. — KEYN 178:10
than to d. — CAMU 52:11
despotism modern form of d. — MCCA 206:2
destination ultimate d. — AWDR 19:12
destined d. to rule — BART 24:12
destiny Anatomy is d. — FREU 123:6
walking with d. — CHUR 69:4
destroy d. the town — ANON 11:6
determined to d. himself — CUMM 81:8
gods wish to d. — CONN 75:1
Whom the mad would d. — LEVI 198:11
destroyed d. but not defeated — HEMI 151:3
destroyer d. of worlds — OPPE 243:15
destruction based on d. — BRUC 46:9
mad d. is wrought — GAND 129:8
means of total d. — SAKH 282:1
to his own d. — FRAM 122:3
details God is in the d. — MIES 220:8
mind which reveres d. — LEWI 199:14
detective d. novel — PRIT 262:5
d. story is about — JAME 166:15
detector shock-proof shit d. — HEMI 151:6
determination d. of a quiet man — SMIT 296:13
de Valera Negotiating with d. — LLOY 201:12
develop suitable person to d. it — DIRA 91:3
developer slipped into d. — WILS 338:2
deviation Without hesitation, d. — CATC 61:15
devil act like a d. — MALC 212:7
believing in the d. — KNOX 184:8
blue-eyed d. white man — FARD 109:5
D. howling 'Ho' — SQUI 301:7
D. knows Latin — KNOX 184:9
d.'s walking parody — CHES 64:9
Old D. Moon in your eyes — HARB 144:7
reference to the d. — CHUR 69:6
white man was *created* a d. — MALC 212:6
devolution d. takes longer — CART 56:9
dialect d. with an army — WEIN 330:7

purify the d. — ELIO 101:6
diamond d. and safire bracelet — LOOS 202:10
d. is forever — ADVE 3:13
diamonds d. a girl's best friend — ROBI 271:9
to give him d. back — GABO 128:1
what beautiful d. — WEST 332:9
Diana D., breathless, hunted — MOTI 229:13
diarist To be a good d. — NICO 236:9
diary discreet d. — CHAN 63:10
keep a d. and some day — WEST 332:2
never kept a d. — LOOS 202:12
secret d. of Adrian Mole — TOWN 316:14
What sort of d. — WOOL 342:3
write a d. every day — POWE 261:2
write in a d. — WARN 328:2
dice God does not play d. — EINS 98:6
dictator Every d. uses religion — BHUT 34:4
dictators D. ride to and fro — CHUR 67:1
weed d. may cultivate — BEVE 33:14
dictatorship d. impossible — PERE 252:7
elective d. — HAIL 141:8
establish a d. — ORWE 246:1
have a d. — TRUM 318:15
dictionary ever made the d. — WEST 332:10
did d. it the hard way — EPIT 108:5
I d. it my way — ANKA 9:9
die all going to d. — BURN 48:7
better to d. on your feet — IBAR 162:2
blues will never d. — HOOK 157:1
did not wish to d. — SHAW 293:19
d. for politicians — THOM 315:9
d. for the industrialists — FRAN 122:5
d. in my week — JOPL 171:5
d. like a true-blue rebel — HILL 154:2
Don't d. of ignorance — OFFI 242:7
faith is something you d. for — BENN 28:15
help you d. peacefully — SAUN 285:5
Hope I d. before — TOWN 316:15
I did not d. — FRYE 126:14
If I should d. — ANON 11:3
If I should d. — BROO 45:5
I'll d. young — BRUC 46:10
last Jews to d. — MEIR 218:9
last man to d. — KERR 178:9
Let me d. a youngman's death — MCGO 207:11
Live and let d. — FLEM 118:18
love one another or d. — AUDE 18:8
never let my country d. for me — KINN 181:9
not afraid to d. — ALLE 7:9
Old soldiers never d. — FOLE 119:5
only let Him d. — STUD 307:1
something he will d. for — KING 180:11
taught us how to d. — BENN 29:2
these who d. as cattle — OWEN 247:4
To d. and know it — LOWE 203:13
To d. will be an awfully big — BARR 24:2
will d. of strangeness — MURR 231:17

died D. some, pro patria — POUN 259:14
  d. to save their country — CHES 64:11
  If you have d. — NERU 235:10
  'I never d.,' says he — HAYE 148:7
  made the books and he d. — FAUL 110:2
  Mother d. today — CAMU 52:9
  question why we d. — KIPL 181:14
dies kingdom where nobody d. — MILL 220:10
  man d. in all — SOYI 299:5
  something in me d. — VIDA 325:5
dietary proper d. laws — RUSH 277:14
dietetics first law of d. — ASIM 15:4
diets D. are like boyfriends — LAWS 193:8
  feel about d. — KERR 178:8
difference d. within the sexes — COMP 74:6
  has made all the d. — FROS 125:15
  makes no d. — MALL 212:9
  What d. does it make — GAND 129:8
differences against small d. — FREU 123:8
different rich are d. — FITZ 117:14
  something completely d. — CATC 58:3
  think d. — ADVE 5:6
  thought they were d. — ELIO 101:19
differently do things d. there — HART 147:3
  one who thinks d. — LUXE 204:10
difficult d.; and left untried — CHES 65:12
  d. takes a little time — NANS 234:1
  D. times lie ahead — FILM 113:4
  D. times lie ahead — TAGL 309:3
  d. we do immediately — MILI 221:4
  fascination of what's d. — YEAT 345:2
difficulties little local d. — MACM 209:4
dig D. for victory — OFFI 242:5
  I could not d. — KIPL 181:15
  I'll d. with it — HEAN 149:1
dignity d. which His Majesty — BALD 21:13
  individual d. — YAMA 344:2
dilly-dally Don't d. on the way — COLL 73:10
dime Brother can you spare a d. — HARB 144:5
  life can change on a d. — LAHR 187:5
dinner asking it to d. — HALS 142:10
  best number for a d. party — GULB 140:6
  eat your d. off its streets — BOY 42:7
  having an old friend for d. — FILM 114:1
  hungry for d. at eight — HART 146:13
dinner-knives with broken d. — KIPL 182:6
diplomatic d. cologne — CRIS 79:12
diplomats D. tell lies — KRAU 185:3
directing D. is really exciting — CLOO 72:8
directors way with these d. — GOLD 135:5
dirt d. doesn't get any worse — CRIS 79:13
dirty call d. in our pictures — WILD 335:11
  d. old town — MACC 206:6
  give pornography a d. name — BARN 23:9
  Is sex d. — ALLE 7:7
  'Jug Jug' to d. ears — ELIO 102:22
  paid to have d. minds — TREV 317:8

  You d. rat — MISQ 225:9
dirty-mindedness journalistic d. — LAWR 193:1
disappoint can't d. — ANDE 8:13
disappointed you have d. us — BELL 27:7
disappointing least d. — BARU 24:15
disappointment bitter d. — HORN 158:1
  d. to children — POWE 260:10
disaster Triumph and D. — KIPL 182:8
disastrous d. and the unpalatable — GALB 128:12
discharge d. for loving one — EPIT 108:9
discontent winter of d. — CALL 51:2
  Winter of d. — NEWS 238:9
discontents Civilization and d. — RIVI 271:7
  source of all our d. — LEAC 193:10
discovered d. the nature of DNA — WOLP 341:2
discovery D. consists of seeing — SZEN 308:7
  invention or d. — CARE 53:13
  Medicinal d. — AYRE 19:19
discreet d. charm — FILM 117:4
  d. diary — CHAN 63:10
discretion D. not the better part — STRA 306:6
discriminated men who are d. — MEIR 218:10
discussion government by d. — ATTL 16:8
disease biggest d. today — TERE 311:16
  D., Ignorance, Squalor — BEVE 33:15
  d. in the family — TREV 317:9
  Life a sexually transmitted d. — ANON 11:13
diseases sneezes spread d. — OFFI 242:4
disenchantment d. for truth — SART 284:6
disestablishment sense of d. — KING 181:1
disgruntled if not actually d. — WODE 339:15
disguise this identical d. — BROO 45:8
dishes who does the d. — FREN 123:3
disinfectants best of d. — BRAN 42:15
disinterested D. curiosity — TREV 317:5
dislike I, too, d. it — MOOR 228:1
Disney Mouse over at Disney — MAYE 217:13
  of Euro D. — BALL 22:6
Disneyfication D. of Christianity — CUPI 81:13
disorder d. in its geometry — DE B 86:5
  put back in d. — CONN 75:5
  there to preserve d. — DALE 83:4
disposable to be d. — MILL 222:7
disproportionate d. amount of attention — GATE 130:7
disproved cannot be d. — RUSS 279:10
disregard Atones for later d. — FROS 125:14
dissolve d. the people — BREC 43:15
dissonances starve on d. — IVES 163:9
distance longest d. between — WILL 336:11
distinction make no d. — BUSH 49:3
distinguished d. thing — JAME 166:13
ditch headed for the d. — YOUN 347:4
diver Don't forget the d. — CATC 58:16
divided d. by a common language — SHAW 293:17
  D. by the morning tea — MACN 210:3
  d. self — LAIN 187:6

divine say that D. providence — JOHN 169:2
divisions How many d. has *he* got — STAL 301:11
DNA cannot cheat on D. — WARD 327:7
  discovered the nature of D. — WOLP 341:2
do as long as they d. what I say — THAT 312:8
  because we know how to d. them — FOX 122:2
  Can I d. you now, sir — CATC 58:9
  d. a girl in — ELIO 102:16
  d. something about it — BURN 48:7
  d. those things which — KEYN 179:1
  D. what thou wilt — CROW 81:1
  he'll say d. this — TRUM 319:1
  Let's d. it — LAST 190:14
  Let's d. it — PORT 258:20
  man got to d. — STEI 303:1
  no-one else will d. — FITZ 118:4
  someone who could d. it — DE M 88:16
  way I d. it — WEST 332:14
doc cards with a man called D. — ALGR 6:11
  What's up, D. — CATC 61:13
doctor D. Spock is worried — POLI 257:11
doctorate This is my second d. — CONN 74:13
doctors d. know a hopeless case — CUMM 81:7
  lot of d. in rehab — WILL 336:6
  More d. smoke Camels — ADVE 4:15
doctrinal On the d. side — QUIN 264:6
doctrine d. something you kill for — BENN 28:15
document Venus becomes a d. — VALÉ 323:5
dodgy d. dossier — NEWS 237:7
does D. she or doesn't she — ADVE 3:14
dog d. is for life — SAYI 286:10
  door is what a d. — NASH 234:5
  drover's d. could lead — HAYD 148:6
  engine of pollution, the d. — SPAR 299:11
  hard d. to keep — CLIN 71:13
  heart to a d. to tear — KIPL 182:14
  lost d. somewhere — ANOU 13:9
  man bites a d. — BOGA 38:5
  nobody knows you're a d. — CART 56:10
  owning a d. — O'RO 244:8
  Was there ever d. — YEAT 346:6
  working like a d. — LENN 196:17
  your wife and your d. — HILL 153:9
doggie How much is that d. — MERR 219:15
dogs D. are Shakespearean — SCHW 288:12
  d. go on with their doggy life — AUDE 17:17
  D. look up to us — CHUR 69:10
  d. of Europe bark — AUDE 17:12
  go to the d. tonight — HERB 151:12
  hates d. and babies — ROST 275:13
  Mad d. and Englishmen — COWA 78:7
  Tom and the other d. — EPIT 107:1
doing stop everyone from d. it — HERB 151:14
dollar costs only a d. — ARDE 14:2
dolls Valley of the d. — SUSA 307:7
dolmens d. round my childhood — MONT 227:4
dolour d. of pad and paper-weight — ROET 272:10

dolphin-torn That d. — YEAT 344:6
domes plump with d. — THWA 316:6
domestic d. establishment — BENN 29:5
dominated d. fraction — BOUR 39:13
domination against white d. — MAND 213:1
  All d. begins — BART 24:10
dominion death shall have no d. — THOM 314:1
domino 'falling d.' principle — EISE 99:14
don D. John of Austria — CHES 64:13
  quiet flows the D. — SHOL 294:5
  Remote and ineffectual D. — BELL 27:12
done Been there, d. that — SAYI 286:2
  could not be d. — DE M 88:16
  decide that nothing can be d. — ALLE 7:3
  d. very well out of the war — BALD 21:8
  ever d. for us — FILM 116:10
  If you want anything d. — THAT 312:3
  Nothing to be d. — BECK 25:12
  Something must be d. — MISQ 225:4
  What is to be d. — LENI 196:4
  you've d. it all — MEE 218:8
donkeys Lions led by d. — MILI 221:8
don't George—d. do that — GREN 138:13
door beating on the d. — YEAT 345:4
  d. is what a dog — NASH 234:5
  d. opens and lets the future — GREE 137:16
  d. we never opened — ELIO 100:11
  opened the d. — DIDD 90:8
  through the d. with a gun — CHAN 63:6
doormat d. in a world of boots — RHYS 270:1
  d. or a prostitute — WEST 332:19
doors close softly the d. — JUST 173:12
  Lock the d. — CAIN 50:6
  no d. or windows — MALA 212:3
  with both d. open — HUGH 159:3
doorstep do this on the d. — JUNO 173:10
dorma Nessun d. — ADAM 2:1
dossier dodgy d. — NEWS 237:7
  draft d. produced — GILL 132:14
dot pale blue d. — SAGA 281:8
double joke with a d. meaning — BARK 23:7
  Labour's d. whammy — POLI 258:2
double-bed peace of the d. — CAMP 51:13
doubles d. your chances for a date — ALLE 7:14
doublethink D. means the power — ORWE 245:20
doubt curiosity, freckles, and d. — PARK 249:7
  d. and good taste — BROD 44:7
  Life is d. — UNAM 321:3
  never in d. — LAND 188:7
Dover white cliffs of D. — BURT 48:13
down born with D.'s syndrome — DE G 87:14
  D. and out in Paris — ORWE 245:7
  d. express in the back — WODE 340:2
  d. into the darkness — MILL 220:11
  meet 'em on your way d. — MIZN 226:5
downhearted Are we d. — KNIG 184:4
  Are we d. — MILI 221:2

dustbin as from a d.   GOLD 134:13
    d. of history   TROT 317:13
duty as much a d. as cooperation   GAND 129:11
    D. is what   FITZ 118:4
    Nor law, nor d.   YEAT 345:7
    sense of d. useful   RUSS 278:9
dying achieve it through not d.   ALLE 7:15
    attend a d. animal   YEAT 344:11
    D. a very dull, dreary   MAUG 217:7
    d. breath of Socrates   JEAN 167:8
    D. is an art   PLAT 255:13
    d. of the light   THOM 314:2
    If this is d.   LAST 190:7
    love to those of the d.   LOWR 204:4
    man's d. is more   MANN 214:2
    nothing new in d.   LAST 190:10
    Those d. generations   YEAT 345:16
dyslexic d. Satanist   SMIT 296:15

e E = mc²   EINS 98:4
eagle E. has landed   ARMS 14:10
eagles Where e. dare   MACL 208:3
ear penetrates the e. with facility   BEEC 26:12
earl e. and a knight   ATTL 16:6
    fourteenth e.   HOME 156:11
earlier Here's one I made e.   CATC 59:11
early as e. in life as possible   RUSS 279:12
    too late or too e.   SART 284:11
earned e. on earth   THAT 312:6
earrings e. for under £1   RATN 266:8
ears Enemy e. are listening   OFFI 242:17
    lets the e. lie back   IVES 163:10
    That man's e.   HUGH 159:3
earth anywhere as nice as E.   HAWK 148:3
    call this planet E.   CLAR 70:11
    damage to the e.   COUS 77:14
    earned on e.   THAT 312:6
    e. glow red-hot   HAWK 148:2
    E., receive an honoured guest   AUDE 17:11
    E.'s the right place   FROS 124:12
    feel the e. move   HEMI 150:13
    he craves the e.   SEXT 291:3
    life on the e.   LURI 204:7
    pilgrims on this e.   RYDE 280:2
    Spaceship E.   FULL 127:3
    surly bonds of e.   MAGE 211:2
    surly bonds of e.   REAG 268:7
earthquake Small e. in Chile   COCK 72:12
    starts with an e.   GOLD 135:10
easier e. job like publishing   AYER 19:17
easing e. the Spring   REED 268:11
east Britain calls the Far E.   MENZ 219:7
    face neither E. nor West   NKRU 239:11
East End look the E. in the face   ELIZ 103:17
Easter E. island statue   KEAT 175:11
eastern E. promise   ADVE 3:20

easy It's not that e.   RAPO 266:7
    Life is not meant to be e.   FRAS 122:12
    Life is not meant to be e.   SHAW 291:13
    No e. problems   EISE 100:1
    no e. way out   WINF 339:3
    what is e.   FILM 113:4
eat e. anything with a face   MCCA 206:4
    e. at a place called Mom's   ALGR 6:11
    E. my shorts   CATC 58:18
eaten e. by missionaries   SPOO 300:13
    He has been e. by the bear   HOUS 158:2
    I have e. the plums   WILL 337:1
eating E. people is wrong   FLAN 118:8
Ebenezer Pale E. thought it wrong   BELL 27:18
echo waiting for the e.   MARQ 215:13
ecology e. and antiwar   HUNT 160:12
economic cold metal of e. theory   SCHU 288:10
    vital e. interests   WEIL 330:5
    when I read e. documents   HOME 156:10
economical e. with the *actualité*   CLAR 70:6
    e. with the truth   ARMS 14:12
economics E. is the science   ROBB 271:8
    knew more about e.   KEYN 179:7
    study of e.   SCHU 288:8
economist greatest e. in the world   SCHU 288:11
    slaves of defunct e.   KEYN 179:4
economists Academic e.   JONE 170:13
economy fear of Political E.   SELL 290:8
    It's the e., stupid   POLI 257:21
ecstasy e. of betrayal   GENE 131:1
edge Come to the e.   LOGU 202:3
edifice e. of modern physics   SNOW 298:2
editor e. did it when I was away   MURD 231:14
Edna Aunt E. is universal   RATT 266:9
educate try to e. people   JAGG 165:9
education black kids get an e.   POWE 260:15
    e. and catastrophe   WELL 331:6
    e., education and education   BLAI 35:13
    [E.] has produced   TREV 317:7
    E. is what survives   SKIN 296:4
    liberal e.   BANK 22:14
    poor e. I have received   BOTT 39:11
    that is e.   ROGE 272:13
    unplanned e. creates   VERW 324:11
effect political e.   HAVE 147:8
efficient have an e. government   TRUM 318:15
effort all wasted e.   AYER 19:15
    redoubling your e.   SANT 283:12
egg e. is a work of art   SMIT 296:8
    e. on our face   BROK 44:8
    Go to work on an e.   ADVE 3:22
    hand that lays the golden e.   GOLD 135:5
    looks like a poached e.   NUFF 240:6
    Wall St. lays an e.   NEWS 238:6
egghead E. weds hourglass   NEWS 237:8
eggs all my e. in one bastard   PARK 250:6
    Lays e. inside a paper bag   ISHE 163:5

ego fulfils a man's e.   ROOT 275:2
egos I like to dress e.   VERS 324:10
eighteen before you reach e.   EINS 99:3
eighty dream you are never e.   SEXT 291:5
ein *E. Reich, ein Volk*   POLI 257:12
Einstein Let E. be   SQUI 301:7
elderly e. lady, who mutters away   CARE 53:10
   trot in an e. fashion   THOM 315:6
elect dissolve the people and e.   BREC 43:15
election e. by incompetent many   SHAW 292:17
   wanted an e.   ROOS 273:8
elections e. are won   ADAM 2:6
   You won the e.   SOMO 298:10
elective e. dictatorship   HAIL 141:8
Electra Mourning becomes E.   O'NE 243:12
electric biggest e. train set   WELL 331:1
   E. Kool-Aid Acid test   WOLF 340:17
   tried to mend the E. Light   BELL 27:13
electricity e. was dripping   THUR 316:2
electrification power plus e.   LENI 196:6
electronic new e. interdependence   MCLU 208:9
elegant Most intelligent, very e.   BUCK 47:9
   so e. So intelligent   ELIO 103:2
elementary E., my dear Watson   MISQ 224:6
elephant as high as an e.'s eye   HAMM 143:4
   can say is 'e.'   CHAP 63:12
   E.'s Child   KIPL 183:5
   herd of e. pacing   DINE 91:1
   sleeping with an e.   TRUD 318:6
elephants golden e. next   SHOR 294:6
   shape of identical e.   QUIN 264:8
elsewhere something that happens e.
      BENN 29:8
Elvis E. was the greatest   LEWI 199:10
email e. of the species   FRY 126:13
embalmer triumph of the e.'s art   VIDA 325:7
embarrassment e. and breakfast   BARN 23:10
embracing e. knowledge   POLA 255:19
emergencies prepared for all e.   FORS 120:12
Emily E., hear   CRAN 79:6
emotion degree of my aesthetic e.   BELL 27:1
   escape from e.   ELIO 103:13
emotional Gluttony an e. escape   DE V 89:10
emotions brothel for the e.   KOES 184:12
   e. were riveted   FOOT 119:7
   gamut of the e.   PARK 249:17
   only two e. in a plane   WELL 331:3
   refusal to admit our e.   RATT 267:2
   waste-paper basket of e.   WEBB 329:18
   world of the e.   COLE 73:8
emperor dey makes you E.   O'NE 243:9
   e. of ice-cream   STEV 303:15
   E.'s drunken soldiery   YEAT 344:5
emperors E. can do nothing   BREC 43:8
empire E. strikes back   FILM 117:5
   e. walking very slowly   FITZ 117:19
   Greeks in this American e.   MACM 209:1

How's the E.   LAST 190:5
ideological e.   NAIP 233:8
liquidation of British E.   CHUR 68:2
lost an e.   ACHE 1:8
Russia an e. or democracy   BRZE 47:3
way she disposed of an e.   HARL 146:1
empires e. of the future   CHUR 68:6
empirical *e. scientific system*   POPP 256:4
employee In a Hierarchy Every E.   PETE 253:5
employment high e. levels   JONE 170:12
emptiness e. The human lack   BOLD 38:9
   great Australian E.   WHIT 333:11
empty Bring on the e. horses   CURT 82:1
enchanted Some e. evening   HAMM 143:7
encore do for an e.   MEE 218:8
encounters Close e.   FILM 117:3
encouraged He e. us   EPIT 107:8
end any beginning or any e.   POLL 256:2
   at the e. of the world   DINE 91:1
   came to an e. all wars   LLOY 201:5
   e. cannot justify the means   HUXL 161:6
   e. is where we start from   ELIO 101:8
   e. of a thousand years   GAIT 128:5
   e. of history   FUKU 126:18
   e. of the beginning   CHUR 68:3
   e. to beginnings of all wars   ROOS 274:7
   e. to the old Britain   BROW 46:1
   evokes the e. of the world   BAUD 25:1
   have the power to e. it   SASS 285:3
   In my beginning is my e.   ELIO 100:15
   on to the e. of the road   LAUD 189:16
   Our e. is Life   MACN 210:8
   there was no e.   WHIT 333:10
   Waiting for the e.   EMPS 105:12
   war that will e. war   WELL 331:8
   where's it all going to e.   STOP 306:2
   world will e. in fire   FROS 125:3
endeavours all my e. are unlucky   DOUG 92:3
ended in 1915 the old world e.   LAWR 192:4
ending Don't tell the e.   TAGL 309:12
   way of e. a war   ORWE 246:9
endogenous neoclassical e. growth
      BROW 45:15
ends e. and scarce means   ROBB 271:8
   It had two e.   SOLZ 298:6
   similar sounds at their e.   LARK 189:14
   way of achieving other e.   BENE 28:11
endure Children's talent to e.   ANGE 9:4
   props to help him e.   FAUL 110:4
endured e. with resignation   RUSS 278:9
enemies alone against smiling e.   BOWE 41:14
   e. of Freedom do not argue   INGE 162:6
   unsavoury e.   RABI 265:1
   you are now our e.   MUGA 230:6
enemy better class of e.   MILL 222:13
   e. of good art   CONN 75:2
   e. to the human race   MILL 222:11

I am the e. you killed	OWEN 247:11
last e.	BORR 40:16
met the e.	CART 56:12
no e. but time	YEAT 345:5
Sir, no man's e.	AUDE 18:12
smitten a sleeping e.	YAMA 344:1
sometimes his own worst e.	BEVI 34:3
energetic e. displaces the passive	BERN 31:4
energy important source of e.	EINS 98:13
enforceable e. safeguards	TRUM 318:10
engine be a Really Useful E.	AWDR 19:11
e. of pollution, the dog	SPAR 299:11
human e. waits	ELIO 103:5
engineering E. with fabric	MUIR 231:1
engineers age of the e.	HOGB 156:1
e. of human souls	STAL 301:10
e. of the soul	GORK 136:2
not e. of the soul	KENN 177:16
England always be an E.	PARK 250:9
bored for E.	MUGG 230:11
damn you E.	OSBO 246:19
deep sleep of E.	ORWE 245:9
E. and America divided	SHAW 293:17
E. is a garden	KIPL 182:6
E. not the jewelled isle	ORWE 245:12
E.'s not a bad country	DRAB 93:1
E. will have her neck	CHUR 68:1
for ever E.	BROO 45:5
Goodbye, E.'s rose	JOHN 168:11
Gott strafe E.	FUNK 127:6
Gott strafe E.	POLI 257:15
History is now and E.	ELIO 101:9
keep your E.	MUGA 230:7
lot that make up E. today	LAWR 192:20
Speak for E.	AMER 8:1
suspended in favour of E.	SHAW 292:2
that will be E. gone	LARK 189:3
think of the defence of E.	BALD 21:11
Wake up, E.	GEOR 131:3
we are the people of E.	CHES 65:1
world where E. is finished	MILL 221:17
English baby doesn't understand E.	KNOX 184:9
Certain men the E. shot	YEAT 345:9
cosh of the E.	STRA 306:10
don't hate the E.	WELS 331:10
E. book is a blank book	PICA 254:2
E. know-how	COLO 74:3
E. language is	WALC 326:5
E. manners more frightening	JARR 167:2
E. may not like music	BEEC 26:13
E. never smash in a face	HALS 142:10
E.-speaking nations	THAT 313:17
E. tongue I love	WALC 326:3
E. unofficial rose	BROO 45:1
E. up with which	CHUR 68:10
fragments of the E. scene	ORWE 245:13
game which the E.	MANC 212:13

great E. blight	WAUG 328:14
in the E. language	JAME 166:14
make them all learn E.	CHUR 69:1
mobilized the E. language	MURR 232:5
prefer their E. sloppy	SAYE 285:10
raped and speaks E.	BORR 40:3
rolling E. road	CHES 64:14
so little E.	HAGU 141:2
You are E.	BECK 26:10
Englishman E., even if alone	MIKE 220:9
E. to open his mouth	SHAW 293:3
No E. is fairly beaten	SHAW 293:9
to be an E.	NASH 234:6
Englishmen E. never will be slaves	SHAW 292:12
Mad dogs and E.	COWA 78:7
Englishwoman E. is so refined	SMIT 297:9
Englishwomen E.'s shoes	HALS 142:9
enigma mystery inside an e.	CHUR 67:2
enjoy e. convalescence	SHAW 291:12
enlisted inspiring the e.	REMN 269:6
enough e. for everyone's need	BUCH 47:7
e. of blood and tears	RABI 265:2
e. to go round	STEA 302:3
meaning of *e.*	AMIS 8:10
Patriotism is not e.	CAVE 62:2
two thousand years is e.	PIUS 255:7
world's beauty becomes e.	MORR 229:1
enoyed doing something you e.	BLAN 36:11
enterprise leave it to private e.	KEYN 179:3
starship E.	RODD 272:3
entertain better to e. an idea	JARR 167:3
entropy e. of human thought	ZAMY 348:1
entwine lives of black and white e.	NOON 240:1
environment humdrum like the e.	THAT 312:12
environmental any e. group	BRUN 46:11
e. history	SEDD 289:12
envy prisoners of e.	ILLI 162:5
epigram Impelled to try an e.	PARK 249:11
purrs like an e.	MARQ 215:12
episode this week's e. of 'Soap'	CATC 58:12
epitaph e. to be my story	FROS 125:8
equal born free and e.	ANON 10:2
law has made him e.	DARR 84:2
more e. than others	ORWE 245:2
talked about e. rights	JOHN 169:9
equality E. for women demands	TOYN 317:2
e. in the servants' hall	BARR 24:1
neither e. nor freedom	FRIE 124:4
not e. or fairness	BERL 30:14
equals peace between e.	WILS 338:16
Pigs treat us as e.	CHUR 69:10
equation e. would halve the sales	HAWK 147:11
equations between politics and e.	EINS 99:7
fire into the e.	HAWK 147:13
have beauty in one's e.	DIRA 91:4
err e. is human	SAYI 287:8

error limit to infinite e. BREC 43:7
  often in e. LAND 188:7
  response to e. GIOV 133:7
errors e. are volitional JOYC 172:11
escape e. from emotion ELIO 103:13
  Gluttony an emotional e. DE V 89:10
Eskimo E. forgets his language OKPI 242:22
espionage e. can be recommended
  WEST 332:17
essential e. ingredient PHIL 253:10
eternity E.'s a terrible thought STOP 306:2
  some conception of e. MANC 212:13
  who love, time is e. VAN 323:10
etherized patient e. upon a table ELIO 102:2
  patient e. upon a table LEWI 199:6
ethical e. dimension COOK 75:16
  e. infants BRAD 42:11
ethnological in the e. section EMPS 105:10
Eton during the holidays from E. SITW 296:1
  playing-fields of E. ORWE 245:14
étonne É.-moi DIAG 90:3
Euclid E. alone has looked MILL 220:13
eunuch Female E. GREE 138:6
  prerogative of the e. STOP 305:10
eunuchs seraglio of e. FOOT 119:8
euphemisms E. are unpleasant truths
  CRIS 79:12
euphoric In an e. dream AUDE 18:7
Euphrates bathed in the E. HUGH 159:9
Europe all the nations of E. SALM 282:10
  create a nation E. MONN 226:15
  dogs of E. bark AUDE 17:12
  E. a continent of mongrels FISH 112:6
  E. has never existed MONN 226:14
  E. in danger of plunging YELT 346:13
  E. of nations DE G 87:8
  E. the unfinished negative MCCA 205:10
  E. will decide DE G 87:6
  from mainland E. THAT 313:17
  get out of E. BOOK 39:3
  going into E. THOM 315:7
  going out all over E. GREY 139:3
  great stocks of E. YEAT 346:11
  keep up with Western E. UPDI 321:5
  Leave this E. FANO 109:3
  map of E. has been changed CHUR 66:13
  that's old E. RUMS 277:4
European E. sense of tradition SZEL 308:6
  green pastures of the E. VERW 324:11
  I'm E. HEWI 152:15
  on E. Monetary Union CHIR 66:2
  policy of E. integration KOHL 185:2
Europeans second-hand E. HOPE 157:7
euthanasia that is e. FUEN 126:15
eve E. ate Adam HUGH 160:2
  real curse of E. RHYS 269:14
  riverrun, past E. and Adam's JOYC 171:9

evening along the road of e. DE L 88:7
  E., all CATC 58:20
  e.—any evening— LEWI 199:6
  five o'clock in an e. BOWE 41:10
  Some enchanted e. HAMM 143:7
event not an e. of life WITT 339:11
events E., dear boy MACM 209:9
  e. overlapping DURR 94:10
  opposition of e. MACM 209:9
ever have you e. been POLI 257:3
  WELL, DID YOU E. PORT 258:23
evermore name liveth for e. EPIT 108:7
every E. day, I am getting better COUÉ 77:11
  E. which way but loose FILM 117:6
everybody E. wants to get inta CATC 58:21
  where is e. FERM 110:11
everyday crashed against the e. LAST 191:2
  e. story of country folk CATC 58:22
everyman Death would summon E.
  HEAN 148:13
everyone E. burst out singing SASS 284:18
  like e. else DE G 87:14
everything against e. KENN 178:2
  chips with e. WESK 331:13
  E.'s goin' my way HAMM 143:5
  e. that is the case WITT 339:9
  Life, the Universe and E. ADAM 2:3
  robbed a man of e. SOLZ 298:4
everywhere children . . . e. CATC 59:7
evidence Extraordinary e. SAGA 281:7
evil axis of e. BUSH 49:6
  banality of e. AREN 14:5
  dealing with pure e. here ROWL 276:10
  Do e. in return AUDE 18:6
  Don't be e. SAYI 286:12
  e. cradling BORR 40:9
  E. visited us yesterday TAYL 310:11
  face of 'e.' BURR 48:10
  good doesn't drive out e. BERN 31:4
  man produces e. GOLD 134:12
  means to fight an e. DAWS 85:7
  no e. in the atom STEV 304:8
  non-cooperation with e. GAND 129:11
  What we call e. FORD 120:3
  willed no e. STEP 303:10
  you agreed to e. RODR 272:8
evils Between two e. WEST 332:8
  greatest of e. SHAW 292:3
  Two e., monstrous RANS 266:5
evolution interested in e. JONE 171:1
  in the light of e. DOBZ 91:9
exaggeration e. is a truth GIBR 132:11
examinations In e., those who do RALE 265:7
examiners Knew more than my e. KEYN 179:7
example teaches by its e. BRAN 42:16
exceedingly E. good cakes ADVE 3:19
exception allowing for e. SPAR 299:7

glad to make an e. — MARX 216:6
excitement share the giddy high e. — KAEL 174:2
exciting films are too e. — BERR 31:18
exclusion cannot be built on e. — ADAM 2:7
e. and prohibition — MILL 222:2
excrement in the place of e. — YEAT 344:10
excursion made an e. to hell — PRIE 262:2
excuse E. My Dust — EPIT 107:4
make a good e. — SZAS 308:4
excuses e. for our failures — FULB 127:1
execute zealous Muslims to e. — KHOM 179:11
execution Ceauşescus' e. — O'DO 241:10
firing squad at his e. — LAST 190:2
public e. — FOOT 119:7
executioners respect their e. — SART 284:12
shouting at her e. — O'DO 241:11
executive e. expression — BRIT 44:5
hold the e. to account — BOOT 39:5
salary of the chief e. — GALB 128:10
exercise E. is the yuppie version — EHRE 97:8
no easy way out [of e.] — WINF 339:3
exhaust e. the little moment — BROO 45:8
exile silence, e., and cunning — JOYC 172:5
exist questioned its right to e. — SCHU 288:9
existence e. is but a brief crack — NABO 233:4
existential crude e. malpractice — FENT 110:9
existing bother of e. — HAWK 147:13
exists Everything e. — FORS 121:1
exit came up with an e. strategy — LENO 197:4
Such a graceful e. — JUNO 173:10
exogenous small e. events — GREE 138:3
ex-parrot THIS IS AN E. — MONT 227:9
expect E. nothing — WALK 326:9
expectations rising e. — CLEV 71:8
talents and our e. — DE B 86:8
expects Nobody e. — MONT 227:10
expediency be sacrificed to e. — MAUG 216:13
expedition abandoning the e. — DOUG 92:3
expenditure E. rises to meet — PARK 250:11
expenses facts are on e. — STOP 305:13
expensive how e. it is to be poor — BALD 21:3
experience e. will teach me the sweetness — SEEG 290:1
had the e. but missed — ELIO 101:2
man of no e. — CURZ 82:2
never had much e. — MARQ 215:4
refuted by e. — POPP 256:4
to be filled in by e. — WILS 338:2
we need not e. it — FRIS 124:8
experienced have e. it — GORD 135:15
experiences e. of our life — MANN 214:1
experiment e. needs statistics — RUTH 279:15
have them fit e. — DIRA 91:4
social and economic e. — HOOV 157:2
expert e. is someone who knows — HEIS 150:4
e. knows more and more — BUTL 49:10
experts 'e.' make the worst Ministers — ATTL 16:9

explain e. why it didn't happen — CHUR 69:9
Never e. — FISH 112:8
explaining forever e. things — SAIN 281:10
explanations uninteresting e. — LEWI 199:3
expletive E. deleted — ANON 10:9
explorers unlucky e. — DOUG 92:3
exploring end of all our e. — ELIO 101:7
exposure public e. — STON 305:6
express down e. in the back — WODE 340:2
expresses music e. itself — STRA 306:9
expressing worth e. in music — DELI 88:12
exterior this flabby e. — LEVA 198:3
exterminate e. a nation — SPOC 300:12
Exterminate! E. — CATC 59:1
extermination e. of capitalism — ZINO 349:1
extinction leads to total e. — ALLE 7:10
extraordinary E. claims — SAGA 281:7
extras don't target e. — ROWL 276:10
extremes E. meet — MACD 206:11
extremism E. in pursuit — JOHN 170:1
e. in the defence — GOLD 135:1
exuberance irrational e. — GREE 138:2
eye Cast a cold e. — YEAT 346:10
close one e. — DOUG 92:6
e.-catching initiatives — BLAI 36:2
e. that can open an oyster — WODE 339:17
if you have the e. — HOLM 156:7
less in this than meets the e. — BANK 22:12
looked into the e. of day — YEAT 345:3
to the e. of God — OLIV 243:3
untrusting e. on all they do — GELL 130:14
eyeball e. to eyeball — RUSK 278:3
eyes bodily hunger in his e. — SHAW 292:5
chewing gum for the e. — ANON 12:10
ever more perfect e. — TEIL 310:14
e. as wide as football-pool — CAUS 57:10
e. of Caligula — MITT 226:6
E. still dazzled — LIND 200:6
good Lord made your e. — LEHR 195:11
Looking into his e. — PURD 263:3
Smoke gets in your e. — HARB 144:4
Stars scribble on our e. — CRAN 79:1

Fabians good man fallen among F. — LENI 196:5
fabric Engineering with f. — MUIR 231:1
face Accustomed to her f. — LERN 197:9
eat anything with a f. — MCCA 206:4
f. looks like a weddding-cake — AUDE 19:7
f. neither East nor West — NKRU 239:11
f. of 'evil' — BURR 48:10
has the f. he deserves — ORWE 246:11
I am the family f. — HARD 145:6
keep your f. — CART 55:7
lose its human f. — DUBČ 93:5
make fun of a f. — VICK 325:2
mask that eats into the f. — UPDI 321:10

face (*cont.*)
never forget a f. — MARX 216:6
stamping on a human f. — ORWE 246:2
touched the f. of God — MAGE 211:3
unacceptable f. — HEAT 149:11
whole life shows in your f. — BACA 20:4
faces not having any f. — PRIE 262:1
Private f. in public places — AUDE 18:2
fact waiting to do away with f. — THOM 315:10
factor Falklands F. — THAT 312:13
facts accounted for *all* the f. — WATS 328:10
f. are lost forever — MAIL 211:11
f. are on expenses — STOP 305:13
f. are sacred — SCOT 289:7
F. do not cease to exist — HUXL 161:11
give you all the f. — AUDE 18:9
not to deny the f. — RYLE 280:4
number of empirical f. — EINS 99:4
That's all the f. — ELIO 102:15
fade just f. away — MACA 205:5
Than to f. away — YOUN 347:5
They simply f. away — FOLE 119:5
fail F. better — BECK 26:7
Others must f. — VIDA 325:6
shall not flag or f. — CHUR 67:6
failed f. miserably — GROE 139:8
they f. before — POLI 258:14
failure Any f. seems so total — QUAN 264:2
different kind of f. — ELIO 100:20
effort nor the f. tires — EMPS 105:14
f. in life — WEST 333:1
f.'s no success at all — DYLA 95:9
formula for f. — SWOP 307:11
Now we are not a f. — VANZ 324:4
political lives end in f. — POWE 261:6
failures f. in love — MURD 231:10
fair F. shares for all — POLI 257:13
follows that it is F. — SWOP 307:10
fairies Do you believe in f. — BARR 24:3
f. at the bottom — FYLE 127:8
fairness excellence as well as f. — ANON 13:1
fairy f. when she's forty — HENL 151:9
myth not a f. story — RYLE 280:4
faith f. and fire within us — HARD 145:8
f. is something you die for — BENN 28:15
f. without doubt — UNAM 321:3
faithless Human on my f. arm — AUDE 17:15
Falklands F. Factor — THAT 312:13
F. thing was a fight — BORG 39:10
fall Life is a horizontal f. — COCT 72:13
Things f. apart — YEAT 345:20
fallen Christopher Robin has f. — MORT 229:7
f. angel — KELL 176:7
good man f. among Fabians — LENI 196:5
people who have never f. — PAST 251:1
planets had f. on me — TRUM 318:8
falling 'f. domino' principle — EISE 99:14

knack of f. without hurting — SCOT 289:9
falls F. the Shadow — ELIO 101:16
falsely testifying f. — CLIN 72:7
falsifiability *f.* of a system — POPP 256:4
fame best f. is a writer's fame — LEBO 194:11
defending himself against f. — GARC 130:3
F. vaporizes — SIMP 295:8
families killed with our f. — BORR 41:8
there are f. — THAT 313:6
these old f. — HUGH 160:5
family disease in the f. — TREV 317:9
f. firm — GEOR 131:11
F. history has — RUSH 277:14
f.—that dear octopus — SMIT 296:9
f. that prays together — SAYI 286:13
f., with its narrow privacy — LEAC 193:10
f. with the wrong members — ORWE 245:12
I am the f. face — HARD 145:6
I have a young f. — FOWL 121:11
Selling off the f. silver — MISQ 225:1
spend more time with f. — THAT 313:10
We, your blood f. — SPEN 299:15
famous by that time I was too f. — BENC 28:8
f. for fifteen minutes — WARH 327:8
F. remarks are very seldom — STRU 306:13
most f. picture — ANON 11:16
of a f. person — WARH 327:9
world f. — RICH 271:2
fan state of the football f. — HORN 158:1
fanatic f. a great leader — BROU 45:13
fanaticism f. consists in — SANT 283:12
fantasies fed the heart on f. — YEAT 345:10
fantasy f., like poetry, speaks — LE G 195:10
Most modern f. — PRAT 261:9
possesses himself of a f. — WESK 331:14
far f. side of despair — SART 284:10
galaxy f., far away — TAGL 309:8
going a bridge too f. — BROW 46:7
how f. one can go too far — COCT 72:14
much too f. out all my life — SMIT 297:7
quarrel in a f. away country — CHAM 62:7
Faraday anti-F. machines — CORN 77:5
still choose to be F. — HUXL 161:15
faraway from f. countries — ATAT 15:13
farce second time as f. — BARN 23:13
wine was a f. — POWE 260:8
farewell F., my friends — LAST 190:3
So f. then — CATC 61:3
farm down on the f. — LEWI 199:11
farmer F. will never be happy — HERB 151:13
farmers inefficient f. — LYNN 204:12
farms cellos of the deep f. — STEV 304:15
farrow old sow that eats her f. — JOYC 172:2
fart can't f. and chew gum — JOHN 170:5
farther only much f. away — FLEM 119:1
fascination f. of what's difficult — YEAT 345:2
fascism form of linguistic f. — JAME 166:16

fiction (*cont.*)
  if she is to write f. — WOOL 341:11
  It's a gift for f. — FILM 115:1
  Poetry is the supreme f. — STEV 303:17
  Reality beats f. — CONR 75:12
fictional My f. project — CARE 53:13
fiddle beyond all this f. — MOOR 228:1
fidelity stone f. — LARK 189:1
field corner of a foreign f. — BROO 45:5
fiend work like a f. — THOM 314:14
fifteen always f. years older — BARU 24:14
  At the age of f. — JUNG 173:9
  famous for f. minutes — WARH 327:8
fifth F. column — MOLA 226:11
fifties tranquillized *F.* — LOWE 203:11
fifty At f., everyone has — ORWE 246:11
  booze until he's f. — FAUL 110:6
  until I was nearly f. — HEAN 149:2
fifty-seven f. channels — SPRI 301:5
fight easier to f. for one's principles — ADLE 2:11
  f. and fight again — GAIT 128:4
  f. for freedom — PANK 248:10
  f. for its King and Country — GRAH 136:7
  f. for what I believe — CAST 57:4
  f. on the beaches — CHUR 67:6
  he is dead, who will not f. — GREN 138:15
  I f. on — THAT 313:12
  must f. to the end — HAIG 141:4
  Never give up the f. — MARL 215:1
  nor duty bade me f. — YEAT 345:7
  those who bade me f. — EWER 106:6
  thought it wrong to f. — BELL 27:18
  too proud to f. — WILS 338:14
  when men refuse to f. — POLI 258:11
fighter f. not a quitter — MAND 213:10
fighting f. for this woman's honour — FILM 116:2
  not fifty ways of f. — MALR 212:11
  not f. does matter — STEP 303:9
  state of affairs worth f. for — ORWE 245:8
  still f. Blenheim — BEVA 33:5
  street f. man — JAGG 166:5
  we keep on f. — HEWE 152:12
figure f. a poem makes — FROS 125:21
  losing her f. or her face — CART 55:7
figures f. in words only — MURR 231:16
fill O f. me — MACN 210:5
  space you f. — COOP 76:14
  trying to f. them — CIOR 70:3
films call lusty in foreign f. — WILD 335:11
  f. the lowest form of art — WILD 335:10
  seldom go to f. — BERR 31:18
filth f. and the fury — NEWS 237:9
  identical, and so is f. — FORS 121:1
final f. solution — HEYD 153:1
  not f. because we are infallible — JACK 165:6
finality F. is death — STEP 303:7
finals This is called F. — LODG 201:15

find f. out for yourself — FITZ 118:3
  Someday I'll f. you — COWA 78:10
fine f. romance with no kisses — FIEL 111:9
  walk a f. line — CLIN 72:7
finest f. hour — CHUR 67:7
finger chills the f. not a bit — NASH 234:18
  f. lickin' good — ADVE 4:3
  little f. to become longer — SCHO 288:3
  points a f. — NIZE 239:9
  Whose f. do you want — NEWS 238:8
fingernails paring his f. — JOYC 172:4
fingerprints f. across his brain — HEND 151:8
fingers cut their own f. — EDDI 97:2
  dabbling their f. — MCGR 208:1
  f. do the walking — ADVE 4:10
  f. of cold are corpse — LAWR 192:22
  pulled our f. out — PHIL 253:8
fingertips Matching lips and f. — ADVE 4:12
finish didn't let me f. — BABE 20:3
  f. the job — CHUR 67:10
  Nice guys. F. last — DURO 94:9
  started so I'll f. — CATC 60:9
finished book would have been f. — WODE 339:18
  f. in the first 100 days — KENN 177:8
  poem is never f. — VALÉ 323:1
  where England is f. — MILL 221:17
finite knowlege can only be f. — POPP 256:9
finned giant f. cars nose forward — LOWE 203:9
fire every time She shouted 'F.' — BELL 27:9
  faith and f. within us — HARD 145:8
  f. and the rose are one — ELIO 101:10
  f. into the equations — HAWK 147:13
  f. of my loins — NABO 233:1
  great balls of f. — BLAC 35:10
  heart is an organ of f. — ONDA 243:7
  light my f. — MORR 228:14
  shouting f. — MISQ 225:2
  tongued with f. — ELIO 101:3
  world will end in f. — FROS 125:3
  You can't f. me — MAHE 211:4
fires Gorse f. — LONG 202:7
  Keep the Home-f. burning — FORD 120:4
firing faced the f. squad — THUR 316:4
firm family f. — GEOR 131:11
first done for the f. time — CORN 77:8
  f. Kinnock in a thousand — KINN 181:10
  f. line — CALV 51:5
  is the f. ball — BRAD 42:14
  men travel f. class — GARC 130:2
  people who got there f. — USTI 322:2
  retaliation in f. — JAME 166:6
fish f. are having their revenge — ELIZ 104:3
  F. are jumpin' — HEYW 153:3
  F. got to swim — HAMM 142:12
  f. needs a bicycle — DUNN 94:8
  f. without a bicycle — SAYI 287:13
  nose forward like f. — LOWE 203:9

No self-respecting f. ROYK 276:12
pretty kettle of f. MARY 216:8
surrounded by f. BEVA 33:3
fishbone monument sticks like f. LOWE 203:10
fishes f. flew and forests walked CHES 64:9
sleeps with the f. FILM 115:5
fish-knives Phone for the f. BETJ 32:9
fist big clunking f. BLAI 36:6
fistful for a f. of coins ZAPA 348:4
fists F. clenched LOGU 202:4
fit isn't f. for humans now BETJ 32:14
not f. for purpose REID 269:1
only the F. survive SERV 290:15
fitness no test of f. for it SHAW 291:17
five At f. in the afternoon LORC 202:14
bombing begins in f. minutes REAG 268:5
Mother of F. Voice PELO 252:4
fix don't f. it SAYI 286:17
fixed f. point in a changing age DOYL 92:13
flabby this f. exterior LEVA 198:3
flag f. to which you have pledged BALD 21:6
High as a f. HAMM 143:10
shall not f. or fail CHUR 67:6
flagellation Not f. RATT 267:2
flame F.-capped, and shout SHAW 293:20
tongues of f. are in-folded ELIO 101:10
When a lovely f. dies HARB 144:4
flames amid fierce f. EPIT 107:3
bursting into f. MORR 228:12
F. for a year LAMP 188:5
Flanders In F. fields MCCR 206:10
flappers London wants f. CAMP 51:12
flash frozen f. of history ANON 10:13
flat Very f., Norfolk COWA 78:13
flattery f. hurts no one STEV 304:5
flavour spearmint lose its f. ROSE 275:3
flaws Psychological f. ANON 12:7
flea literature's performing f. O'CA 241:9
fleas dog that praised his f. YEAT 346:6
educated f. do it PORT 258:20
f. that tease BELL 28:1
fleet whole F.'s lit up WOOD 341:7
flesh F. perishes. I live on HARD 145:6
f. was sacramental ROBI 271:14
world and its shadow, The f. RIDI 271:3
flew and they f. LOGU 202:3
if I f. the Atlantic EARH 96:2
flexible your f. friend ADVE 3:1
flies leave our f. alone ANON 10:17
float f. like a butterfly ALI 6:13
flooded STREETS F. TELE 311:8
floor lie on the f. without MART 216:1
man has just waxed the f. NASH 235:3
repeat on the Golden F. LAST 191:6
flower cracks into furious f. BROO 45:10
drives the f. THOM 314:3
f. of Scotland WILL 337:4

flowers hundred f. blossom MAO 214:7
Say it with f. ADVE 4:26
Where have all the f. gone SEEG 290:2
flutter F. and bear him up BETJ 32:7
fly show the f. the way out WITT 339:7
try to f. by those nets JOYC 172:1
wouldn't hurt a f. LEAC 193:13
flying like a f. saucer landed DYLA 95:16
foaming f. with much blood POWE 261:1
focus one that's in f. WARH 327:9
foe His f. was folly EPIT 107:15
fog f. comes on little cat feet SAND 283:5
F. in Channel CART 56:3
f. that rubs its back ELIO 102:4
fold f., spindle or mutilate SAYI 286:11
Folies-Bergère goes to the F. STOC 305:5
folk all music is f. music ARMS 14:9
trouble with a f. song LAMB 187:10
folk-dancing incest and f. ANON 13:5
folks That's all f. CATC 61:5
follies f. a man regrets most ROWL 276:7
follow F. the money FILM 113:10
followers blood of his f. EISE 99:11
folly His foe was f. EPIT 107:15
lovely woman stoops to f. ELIO 103:7
food advertise f. to hungry GALB 128:9
alcohol was a f. WODE 340:4
f. a tragedy POWE 260:8
F. comes first BREC 43:12
give f. to the poor CAMA 51:6
Good f. is always a trouble DAVI 84:5
problem is f. DONL 92:1
fool As any f. kno WILL 336:1
f. with booze until he's 50 FAUL 110:6
Prove to me that you're no f. RICE 270:6
foolish Beware my f. heart WASH 328:8
more likely to be f. RUSS 278:15
These f. things MARV 216:2
fools flannelled f. at the wicket KIPL 182:10
F.! For I also had my hour CHES 64:10
fools, the fools, the f. PEAR 251:14
perish together as f. KING 180:14
foot foot—f.—sloggin' KIPL 181:13
I hold Creation in my f. HUGH 159:14
silver f. in his mouth RICH 270:12
football Coaching a f. team LINE 200:7
fighting Army f. team RICE 270:4
f. a matter of life SHAN 291:8
F. is a simple game LINE 200:8
F.? the beautiful game PELÉ 252:3
he's f. crazy MCGR 207:13
or play f. CHAR 64:2
owe to f. CAMU 52:17
state of the f. fan HORN 158:1
three games of f. in a row BOMB 38:13
footfalls F. echo in the memory ELIO 100:11
footnotes series of f. to Plato WHIT 334:7

forbidden totally f.   TYNA 320:4
force combines f. with candour   CHUR 69:12
   f. that through the green   THOM 314:3
   f. with a manoeuvre   TROT 318:1
   may the f. be with you   FILM 115:9
   Other nations use 'f.'   WAUG 329:10
   reduce the use of f. to   ORTE 244:10
   use of *f.* by one class   LENI 196:2
forces Dark f.   MISQ 224:4
ford F., not a Lincoln   FORD 119:11
   my friend F.   WILL 337:2
   Nixon gave us F.   ABZU 1:3
foreign any f. assailant   HART 146:9
   call lusty in f. films   WILD 335:11
   corner of a f. field   BROO 45:5
   f. policy   COOK 75:16
   f. policy: I wage war   CLEM 71:3
   into any f. wars   ROOS 274:1
   Life is a f. language   MORL 228:7
   past is a f. country   HART 147:3
foreigners f. are fiends   MITF 226:5
Foreign Secretary attacking the F.   BEVA 33:8
   F. naked into   BEVA 33:9
Foreland Dawn off the F.   KIPL 182:12
foreseen What I had not f.   SPEN 300:8
forest burning the rain f.   STIN 305:2
   Cutting through the f.   LIND 200:4
   In the f.   CHES 65:4
forests fishes flew and f. walked   CHES 64:9
foretell ability to f.   CHUR 69:9
foretold who could have f.   YEAT 346:3
forever diamond is f.   ADVE 3:13
   you can see f.   LERN 197:10
forget do not quite f.   CHES 65:1
   Don't f. the diver   CATC 58:16
   Don't f. the fruit gums   ADVE 3:16
   f. there was such a thing   WILS 338:19
   forgive but do not f.   SZAS 307:14
   never f. a face   MARX 216:6
forgets f. sooner   CAMU 52:5
forgetting consist in merely f.   MAND 213:4
forgive do not f. those murderers   WIES 335:4
   F. my little jokes   FROS 124:14
   f. those who were right   MACL 208:8
   until we f.   PATO 251:4
   wise f. but do not forget   SZAS 307:14
   woman can f. a man   MAUG 217:2
forgiven f. everything   SHAW 292:22
forgiveness what f.   ELIO 101:12
forgot f. about them   AMIE 8:3
   just f. to duck   DEMP 89:2
forgotten books undeservedly f.   AUDE 19:4
   F. Army   MOUN 230:1
   f. man at the bottom   ROOS 273:10
   learned has been f.   SKIN 296:4
   things one has f.   CANE 52:20
fork pick up mercury with a f.   LLOY 201:12

form F. follows function   SULL 307:4
formed small, but perfectly f.   COOP 76:12
formula 'f.' of the atomic bomb   MEDA 218:5
forty fairy when she's f.   HENL 151:9
   Life begins at f.   PITK 255:6
   Men at f.   JUST 173:12
forty-five At f., what next   LOWE 203:12
forum on the way to the F.   SHEV 294:1
forward nothing to look f. to   FROS 124:15
   to push things f.   MOWL 230:2
fought to have f. well   COUB 77:10
foul all f., of course   RYDE 280:3
found certainly f. them   BLIX 36:12
founding f. a bank   BREC 43:13
   inspiration of the f. fathers   HARD 144:11
four At the age of f.   USTI 322:3
   F. legs good   ORWE 245:1
   f. of his fingers   NIZE 239:9
   f.-year-old child could   FILM 116:11
   two plus two make f.   ORWE 245:18
four-legged f. friend   BROO 45:11
fourteenth f. earl   HOME 156:11
fox Crazy like a f.   PERE 252:6
   f. in the box   HENR 151:10
   F. who was my friend   READ 267:9
   sharp hot stink of f.   HUGH 160:3
   They've shot our f.   BIRC 34:11
foxes second to the f.   BERL 30:13
foxholes no atheists in the f.   CUMM 81:11
   signs on the f.   KENN 177:14
fox-hunting prefer f.   HAIL 141:5
fraction dominated f.   BOUR 39:13
fragrance Has she f.   CAUL 57:8
France F. has lost a battle   DE G 87:2
   F. in a certain way   DE G 87:13
   F. is the coachman   DE G 87:16
   F. wants you to take part   CHIR 66:2
   F. will say   EINS 98:8
   I now speak for F.   DE G 87:3
   wield the sword of F.   DE G 87:4
frankly F., my dear   FILM 113:11
fraud not f. or foolishness   DAY- 85:11
freak Outsider is not a f.   WILS 337:9
freaks F. born with their trauma   ARBU 13:14
freckles curiosity, f., and doubt   PARK 249:7
free as soon write f. verse   FROS 126:3
   best things in life are f.   DE S 89:6
   born f. and equal   ANON 10:2
   but it's f.   KRIS 185:7
   Comment is f.   SCOT 289:7
   condemned to be f.   SART 284:4
   Ev'rything f. in America   SOND 298:11
   favours f. speech   BROU 45:12
   f. again   SOLZ 298:4
   F. at last   EPIT 107:5
   F. by '93   POLI 257:14
   f. man, an American   JOHN 169:7

f. society is a society	STEV 304:10	**friend** America is our f.	MERC 219:13
F. speech not to be regulated	DOUG 92:10	betraying my f.	FORS 121:5
Give a man a f. hand	WEST 332:7	diamonds a girl's best f.	ROBI 271:9
I am a f. man	CATC 59:12	four-legged f.	BROO 45:11
I am not f.	DEBS 86:12	having an old f. for dinner	FILM 114:1
in chains than to be f.	KAFK 174:7	I lose a f.	SARG 283:14
Love is f.	BENE 28:11	lay down his wife for his f.	JOYC 172:12
Mother of the F.	BENS 29:11	Little F. of all the World	KIPL 183:7
no such thing as a f. lunch	SAYI 287:6	Phone a f.	CATC 60:23
not only to be f.	PANK 248:10	Reagan for his best f.	WARN 328:1
truth makes men f.	AGAR 2:13	'Strange f.,' I said	OWEN 247:9
Universe is a f. lunch	GUTH 140:8	than make a f.	CURT 81:15
Was he f.	AUDE 18:17	think of him as a f.	SMIT 297:10
you are still f.	OFFI 242:18	To find a f.	DOUG 92:6
freedom apprenticeship for f.	BARA 23:3	Whenever a f. succeeds	VIDA 325:5
conditioned to a f.	KENY 178:5	wish the author was a f.	SALI 282:6
condition for f.	FRIE 124:3	**friends** closest f. won't tell you	ADVE 3:18
enemies of f. do not argue	INGE 162:6	don't make peace with f.	RABI 265:1
first is f. of speech	ROOS 274:3	f. are necessarily	USTI 322:2
F. and slavery are mental	GAND 129:9	glory was I had such f.	YEAT 345:11
f. for the one who thinks	LUXE 204:10	I have lost f.	WOOL 342:2
F. is like taking a bath	KENN 176:12	lay down his f. for his life	THOR 315:12
F. is not a gift	NKRU 239:10	little help from my f.	LENN 197:1
F. is the freedom to say	ORWE 245:18	Money couldn't buy f.	MILL 222:13
F. of conscience	JOHN 169:4	nearly deceiving your f.	CORN 77:9
F. of the press	SWAF 307:8	no absent f.	BOWE 41:11
F. of the press guaranteed	LIEB 200:3	no true f. in politics	CLAR 70:5
F.'s just another word	KRIS 185:7	win f. and influence	CARN 54:3
f. to marry	WARR 328:4	**friendship** F. without envy	DUNC 94:2
f. to offend	RUSH 278:1	**frighten** f. the horses	CAMP 51:14
F., what liberties	GEOR 131:2	**frightened** children are f. of me	GEOR 131:8
gave my life for f.	EWER 106:6	Why should you be f.	WEBB 329:16
I gave them f.	GORB 135:14	**frightening** never more f.	VAN 323:8
neither equality nor f.	FRIE 124:4	**fringe** form the lunatic f.	ROOS 275:1
no easy walk-over to f.	NEHR 235:5	**frog** f. remains	ROST 275:10
peace from f.	MALC 212:5	**frogs** F. eat butterflies	STEV 303:16
Perfect f. is reserved	COLL 73:9	**frontier** f. of my Person	AUDE 18:4
riches and f.	WAŁĘ 326:7	new f.	KENN 177:3
road toward f.	MORR 228:16	**frontiers** old f. are gone	BALD 21:11
there can be no f.	LENI 196:3	rolled back f. of State	THAT 313:7
unless f. is universal	HILL 153:8	**frozen** F. anger	FREU 123:13
freedoms four essential human f.	ROOS 274:3	f. flash of history	ANON 10:13
freeze f. my humanity	MACN 210:5	locked and f.	AUDE 17:12
frei Arbeit macht f.	ANON 10:3	**fruit** like a Dead Sea f.	MACM 209:7
freight literature goes as f.	GARC 130:2	Oranges are not the only f.	WINT 339:5
French F. arrange	CATH 57:7	trees bear strange f.	ALLE 7:4
F./British relationship	MACS 210:11	**frustrating** imagine how f. it is	NOLA 239:12
F. government	COLO 74:3	**fuck** They f. you up	LARK 189:6
F. never care	LERN 197:15	word 'f.' is particularly	TYNA 320:4
F. went in to protect	LYNN 204:12	zipless f.	JONG 171:3
F. widow in every bedroom	HOFF 155:13	**fudging** f. and mudging	OWEN 247:1
F. without tears	RATT 267:1	**fugitive** f. from th' law	CART 56:4
If the F. noblesse	TREV 317:6	**Führer** ein Volk, ein F.	POLI 257:12
We are not F.	MONT 227:7	**fule** As any f. kno	WILL 336:1
Frenchmen Fifty million F.	MILI 221:5	**fun** Ain't we got f.	KAHN 174:8
fresh It's tingling f.	ADVE 4:5	desire to have all the f.	SAYE 285:6
Freud trouble with F. is that	DODD 91:11		

fun (*cont.*)

F. is fun but	LOOS 202:11
f. to be in the same decade	ROOS 274:6
Haute Couture should be f.	LACR 187:1
make f. of a face	VICK 325:2
more f. to be with	NASH 234:7
most f. you can have	DELL 88:13
no reference to f.	HERB 151:19
sex was the most f.	ALLE 7:5
two is f.	SAYI 286:5

function Form follows f.	SULL 307:4
fundament frigid on the f.	NASH 234:18
funeral cry at his mother's f.	CAMU 52:10
heaping up own f. pyre	POWE 260:18
funk take you out of your dull f.	KAEL 174:3
funny f. is subversive	ORWE 246:7
f. old world	FILM 114:13
f. old world	THAT 313:13
f. thing happened	SHEV 294:1
funny-ha-ha Funny-peculiar or f.	HAY 148:5
funny-peculiar F. or funny ha-ha	HAY 148:5
fur to make a f. coat	SAYI 286:20
furious time cracks into f. flower	BROO 45:10
furiously green ideas sleep f.	CHOM 66:3
furnish Books do f. a room	POWE 260:9
furnished F. and burnish'd	BETJ 32:15
furniture don't trip over the f.	COWA 78:17
f. on the deck	MORT 229:10
rearranges the f.	PRAT 261:9
too much of today's f.	LAWR 193:5
fury filth and the f.	NEWS 237:9
fuse through the green f.	THOM 314:3
future architecture of our f.	LAMM 188:1
Back to the f.	FILM 117:1
bridge to the f.	LAWR 192:8
controls the f.	ORWE 245:17
curiosity about the f.	WAUG 329:4
empires of the f.	CHUR 68:6
f. ain't what it used to be	BERR 31:11
f. and the past	BOLA 38:8
f. can be promised	TRUD 318:5
f. not what it was	LEVI 198:10
F. of the Arctic circle	BROW 46:3
f.'s bright	ADVE 3:21
F. shock	TOFF 316:9
He was the f. once	CAME 51:8
It's the f.	KAY 175:9
lets the f. in	GREE 137:16
never think of the f.	EINS 98:9
once and f. king	WHIT 333:12
past, present and f.	EINS 99:6
picture of the f.	ORWE 246:2
promise of a bright f.	AHER 5:20
seen the f. and it works	STEF 302:7
walking backward into f.	ZHVA 348:9

fwowed Tonstant Weader f. up	PARK 249:15

gadget g.-filled paradise	NIEB 236:12
Gaels great G. of Ireland	CHES 64:7
gag tight g. of place	HEAN 149:8
Gaia G. a tough bitch	MARG 214:12
won't accept G.	LOVE 203:6
gaiety only concession to g.	THOM 315:2
gaily G. into Ruislip gardens	BETJ 32:13
gaining Something may be g.	PAIG 248:6
gains no g. without pains	STEV 304:7
galaxy g. far, far away	TAGL 309:8
Galileo G. in two thousand years	PIUS 255:7
status of G. merely	GOUL 136:4
gallant very g. gentleman	EPIT 107:11
gallop G. about doing good	SMIT 297:5
gamble Life is a g.	STOP 306:4
gambles greatest g. in history	ACHE 1:9
game Anarchism is a g.	SHAW 292:24
beautiful g.	PELÉ 252:3
don't like this g.	CATC 59:15
g. is about glory	BLAN 36:10
g. is what counts	ONAS 243:5
how you played the G.	RICE 270:2
urging players to like the g.	SCOL 289:6
games G. people play	BERN 31:6
gamesmanship practice of g.	POTT 259:8
gamut g. of the emotions	PARK 249:17
gangsters nations acted like g.	KUBR 185:10
gap last g. but one	WHIT 333:9
garage to the full g.	HOOV 157:4
garbage G. in, garbage out	SAYI 286:15
Garbo G. talks	TAGL 309:4
garden at the bottom of our g.	FYLE 127:8
Back to the g.	MITC 225:11
England is a g.	KIPL 182:6
g. called Gethsemane	KIPL 182:2
gardenias g. in your hair	HOLI 156:4
garlic clove of g. round my neck	O'BR 241:1
G. bread	KAY 175:9
garter knight of the g.	ATTL 16:6
gas G. smells awful	PARK 249:12
got as far as poison-g.	HARD 144:13
when we met the g.	KIPL 182:5
gasworks by the g. crofts	MACC 206:6
gate Hun is at the g.	KIPL 182:3
man at the g. of the year	HASK 147:5
gates g. to the glorious	FORS 120:9
gauze shoot her through g.	BANK 23:1
gay g. man trapped	BOY 42:5
only g. in the village	CATC 60:20
second best's a g. goodnight	YEAT 345:3
support g. marriage	FRIE 124:1
gazing g. at each other	SAIN 281:12
gear car without a g. box	KINN 181:11
not got a reverse g.	BLAI 36:5
geese great g. honk northward	WARR 328:5
Like g. about the sky	AUDE 16:14
gender tired of the g.	SEXT 291:2

gene selfish g.   DAWK 85:5
General Motors good for G.   WILS 337:7
generals against the law for g.   TRUM 319:2
   we're all G.   USTI 322:3
generalship G. is not about fighting
    REMN 269:6
generation beat g.   KERO 178:6
   best minds of my g.   GINS 133:3
   Every g. revolts   MUMF 231:6
   g. was stolen   FREE 122:14
   G. X   COUP 77:12
   lost g.   STEI 302:12
   never before has a g.   VANE 323:11
generations Those dying g.   YEAT 345:16
generosity exercise our g.   SART 284:8
generously g., if you can   MERE 219:14
genes G. not like blueprints   STEW 304:16
   true of the g.   JONE 171:1
   what males do to g.   JONE 171:2
genetic g. lottery comes up with   PIML 254:11
   mechanism for g. material   CRIC 79:11
   terrible g. defects   WATS 328:11
Genghis to G. Khan   JAY 167:7
genius g. makes no mistakes   JOYC 172:11
   g. of Einstein leads   PICA 254:7
   g. of its scientists   EISE 99:12
   g. of the Constitution   BREN 43:18
   g. with the IQ   VIDA 325:9
   talent and g.   KENN 177:13
   you're a g.   ANDE 8:13
gentle climate is g.   MCNE 210:9
   Do not go g.   THOM 314:2
gentleman g. in Whitehall   JAY 167:5
   very gallant g.   EPIT 107:11
gentlemen G. do not take soup   CURZ 82:4
   G. go by   KIPL 182:15
   G. prefer blondes   LOOS 202:9
   nation of g.   MUGA 230:5
gentleness only a willed g.   THOM 315:4
genuine place for the g.   MOOR 228:1
geography G. is about Maps   BENT 29:13
   like the g. teacher   JAY 167:7
   too much g.   KING 181:2
geometry disorder in its g.   DE B 86:5
George G.—don't do that   GREN 138:13
   G. the Third Ought never   BENT 29:14
Georgia G. on my mind   GORR 136:3
   red hills of G.   KING 180:12
geraniums pot of pink g.   MACN 210:1
geriatric years in a g. home   AMIS 8:9
German language of poems is G.   CELA 62:6
   Waiting for the G. verb   O'BR 241:4
Germans beastly to the G.   COWA 78:2
   G. . . . are going to be squeezed   GEDD 130:9
   G. classify   CATH 57:7
   G. have historic chance   KOHL 185:1
   G. went in to cleanse   LYNN 204:12

G. win   LINE 200:8
keep the G. down   ISMA 163:7
They're G. Don't mention   CLEE 71:2
Germany at war with G.   CHAM 62:9
   Death is a master from G.   CELA 62:5
   G. calling   JOYC 172:15
   G. is the horse   DE G 87:16
   G. will declare   EINS 98:8
   remaining cities of G.   HARR 146:7
   same way as G. has acted   BART 24:11
germs Kills all known g.   ADVE 4:8
   Trap the g.   OFFI 242:4
gerund Save the g.   STOP 305:14
gesture Morality's a g.   BOLT 38:11
get G. a life   SHAT 291:10
   g. what you like   SHAW 292:23
   g. where I am today without   CATC 59:13
   What you see is what you g.   SAYI 287:11
Gethsemane Garden called G.   KIPL 182:4
ghastly G. good taste   BETJ 33:2
ghost g. continent   EISE 99:10
   G. in the Machine   RYLE 280:5
   g. of Roger Casement   YEAT 345:4
   I am the g.   PLAT 255:11
   If the g. cries   RAIN 265:6
ghosts g. outnumber us   DUNN 94:5
ghoul living on another like a g.   HEAD 148:9
giant awaken a sleeping g.   FILM 114:2
giants nuclear g.   BRAD 42:11
   Want one only of five g.   BEVE 33:15
gift Freedom is not a g.   NKRU 239:10
   It's a g. for fiction   FILM 115:1
   through the g. shop   KAY 175:10
gifted vividly g. in love   DUFF 93:8
   young, g. and black   HANS 144:2
   Young, g. and black   IRVI 163:4
gigantic America a g. mistake   FREU 123:14
giggles girls got the g.   ELIZ 104:4
gin G. was mother's milk   SHAW 293:7
   Of all the g. joints   FILM 115:16
   such as g.   WALT 327:6
ginless wicked as a g. tonic   COPE 77:3
Gipper Win just one for the G.   GIPP 133:8
gipsies G. are a litmus test   HAVE 147:9
girdle helps you with your g.   NASH 234:15
girl can't get no g. reaction   JAGG 166:3
   danced with a g.   FARJ 109:7
   diamonds a g.'s best friend   ROBI 271:9
   do a g. in   ELIO 102:16
   g. at an impressionable age   SPAR 299:9
   g. needs good parents   TUCK 319:8
   g. throwing a ball   WOOL 342:1
   If you were the only g.   GREY 139:2
   no g. wants to laugh   LOOS 202:11
   Poor little rich g.   COWA 78:9
   pretty g. is like a melody   BERL 30:7
girls assumption that g.   FRAS 122:11

girls (*cont.*)

bombers named for g.	JARR 167:1
g. who wear glasses	PARK 249:8
It was the g. I liked	BAIL 20:9
nude, giant g.	SPEN 300:7
process whereby American g.	HAMP 143:13
Thank heaven for little g.	LERN 197:12
Treaties like g. and roses	DE G 87:10

given I would have g. gladly — JOHN 169:8
gives never really g. — EAST 96:4
glacier g. knocks in the cupboard — AUDE 17:1
glad just g. to see me — WEST 332:11
gladly I would have given g. — JOHN 169:8
glamour G. is what I sell — DIET 90:11
glance O brightening g. — YEAT 344:3
glare looked at in merciless g. — WILL 336:13
Glasgow G. Empire on a Saturday — DODD 91:11

I belong to G.	FYFF 127:7

glass baying for broken g. — WAUG 329:1

if you break the bloody g.	MACN 210:2
liked the Sound of Broken G.	BELL 27:14
No g. of ours was raised	HEAN 149:4

glasses girls who wear g. — PARK 249:8

g., homosexuality, Watford	JOHN 168:8
Such cruel g.	HOWE 158:12

glittering g. prizes — BORR 40:11

g. prizes	SMIT 296:10

gloaming Roamin' in the g. — LAUD 191:14
global g. thinking — LUCE 204:5

image of a g. village	MCLU 208:9

globally Think g. — SAYI 287:7
globaloney still g. — LUCE 204:5
globe-trotting g. Madam — YEAT 346:7
glorious Mud! G. mud — FLAN 118:7
glory game is about g. — BLAN 36:10

g. was I had such friends	YEAT 345:11
I go to g.	LAST 190:3
Land of Hope and G.	BENS 29:11
What price g.	ANDE 8:12

glove white g. pulpit — REAG 267:13
gloves brandy and summer g. — JOSE 171:7

through the fields in g.	CORN 77:7

glow g. has warmed the world — STEV 304:13
gluttony G. an emotional escape — DE V 89:10
gnomes g. in Zurich — WILS 338:3
go G. ahead, make my day — FILM 113:12

g. anywhere I damn well please	BEVI 34:1
good cook, as cooks g.	SAKI 282:5
G. to jail	SAYI 286:16
Here we g.	ANON 10:16
I can't g. on	BECK 25:11
I g.—I come back	CATC 59:17
I have a g.	OSBO 246:14
In the name of God, g.	AMER 8:2
It's a Rum G.	VAUG 324:8
no place to g.	BURT 48:12
There you g. again	REAG 268:2

Thunderbirds are g.	CATC 61:6
to boldly g.	RODD 272:3
wherever he wants to g.	BRAU 43:3
you can have another g.	QUAN 264:2

goal moving freely, without a g. — KLEE 184:2
goals muddied oafs at the g. — KIPL 182:10
God as G. loved them — GREE 137:11

believe in G.	LAST 191:12
bogus g.	MACN 209:15
by the hand of G.	MARA 214:8
choose a Jewish G.	BROW 46:6
For G.'s sake, look after	LAST 190:4
G. beginning to resemble	HUXL 161:16
G. be thanked	BROO 45:4
G. bless America	BERL 30:5
G. bless the child	HOLI 156:2
G. caught his eye	MCCO 206:8
G. does not play dice	EINS 98:6
G. does not take sides	MITC 223:12
G. gave us memory	BARR 24:5
G. has a soft spot	TUTU 320:2
G. has been replaced	BARA 23:2
G. is a man	NICH 236:7
G. is dead	FROM 124:10
G. is distant, difficult	HILL 153:11
G. is in the details	MIES 220:8
G. is love, but	LEE 195:5
G. is not dead	ANON 10:14
G. is only another artist	PICA 254:6
G. is subtle but not malicious	EINS 98:5
G. loves them	HUME 160:9
G. must think it exceedingly	KNOX 184:7
G. owns heaven	SEXT 291:3
G. paints the scenery	HART 146:14
G. punish England	FUNK 127:6
G. seems to have left	KOES 184:14
G. si Love	FORS 121:3
G. they ought to crucify	CART 55:3
G. this, God that	SQUI 301:8
G. to me is a verb	FULL 127:2
G. will know the truth	EPIT 108:3
G. would give some sign	ALLE 7:13
Had G. on his side	DYLA 95:15
Honest to G.	ROBI 271:13
How odd Of G.	EWER 106:7
if G. talks to you	SZAS 308:1
industry in the G. business	MARC 214:9
In the name of G., go	AMER 8:2
into the Hand of G.	HASK 147:5
known unto G.	EPIT 108:6
like kissing G.	BRUC 46:10
might have become a g.	RUSS 278:6
next to g. america	CUMM 81:3
Not only no G.	ALLE 7:12
only G. can make a tree	KILM 180:5
Only G., my dear	YEAT 344:4
river Is a strong brown g.	ELIO 101:1

gorse G. fires — LONG 202:7
gossip in the g. columns — INGH 162:10
got in our case we have not g. — REED 268:11
  man g. to do — STEI 303:1
gotcha G. — NEWS 237:11
Gott *G. strafe England* — POLI 257:15
gotta g. use words when I talk — ELIO 102:17
Götterdämmerung G. without the gods — MACD 207:2
govern g. in prose — CUOM 81:12
  g. New South Wales — BELL 27:7
government abolish g. — NORQ 240:3
  g. above the law — SCAR 285:13
  G. and public opinion — SHAW 292:12
  g. as an adversary — BRUN 46:11
  g. by discussion — ATTL 16:8
  G. is big enough — FORD 119:13
  g. is the potent — BRAN 42:16
  G. of laws — FORD 119:12
  G. of the busy — SELD 290:4
  g. which robs Peter — SHAW 292:1
  have an efficient g. — TRUM 318:15
  important thing for G. — KEYN 179:1
  Labour G. does — MORR 228:11
  natural party of g. — WILS 338:9
  no British g. should — MACM 209:6
  not get all of the g. — FRIE 124:6
  prepare for g. — STEE 302:5
  wee pretendy g. — CONN 74:10
  work for a G. I despise — KEYN 178:10
  working of local g. — THAT 313:16
  worst form of G. — CHUR 68:9
governments expect g. to be — BLIX 36:13
  g. had better get out — EISE 99:15
  Never believe g. — GELL 130:14
governor *Jimmy Stewart* for g. — WARN 328:1
Governor-General save the G. — WHIT 334:11
grace G. under pressure — HEMI 151:5
  Rain is g. — UPDI 321:9
graces two wonderful g. — HUME 160:8
gracious Goodness g. me — LEE 195:4
gradual g. day weakening — SPEN 300:8
gradualness inevitability of g. — WEBB 329:17
grail g. of laughter — CRAN 79:3
grain rain is destroying his g. — HERB 151:13
grammar destroy every g. school — CROS 80:9
  don't want to talk g. — SHAW 293:5
grand g. to be blooming well dead — SARO 283:16
Grand Canyon down the G. — MARQ 215:13
grandfathers friends with its g. — MUMF 231:6
grandmother We have become a g. — THAT 313:8
grant OLD CARY G. FINE — TELE 311:6
granted taking things for g. — HUXL 161:12
grape peel me a g. — WEST 332:3
grapes g. of wrath — BORR 40:13
grass g. will grow in the streets — HOOV 157:5
  I am the g. — SAND 283:6

grassroots g. revolution — BERN 31:8
gratitude give g. — FAUL 110:1
grave from the cradle to the g. — CHUR 68:4
  into the darkness of the g. — MILL 220:11
  send you to the g. — ORTO 244:14
  shovel a g. in the air — CELA 62:3
  shown Longfellow's g. — MOOR 228:3
  stand at my g. and weep — FRYE 126:14
graves g. of little magazines — PRES 261:10
greasy grey-green, g. Limpopo — KIPL 183:6
great All my shows are g. — GRAD 136:6
  All the world's g. — STEI 302:13
  G. and the Good — SAMP 282:11
  g. balls of fire — BLAC 35:10
  g. life if you don't weaken — BUCH 47:5
  G. Society — JOHN 169:11
  g.—the major novelists — LEAV 194:6
  g. things from the valley — CHES 65:5
  g. tradition — LEAV 194:5
  takes a g. owner — BRAD 42:8
  those who were truly g. — SPEN 300:4
Great Britain G. has lost an empire — ACHE 1:8
greatest Elvis was the g. — LEWI 199:10
  g. living American jurist — CARD 53:9
  I'm not the g. — CLAR 70:7
  I'm the g. — ALI 6:12
greatness g. within them — CAMU 52:7
greed G. is all right — BOES 38:1
  G. is good — FILM 113:13
  not enough for everyone's g. — BUCH 47:7
  was g. a criminal offence — BLAC 35:8
Greek G. as a treat — CHUR 69:1
  G. the language they gave me — ELYT 105:7
  half G., half Latin — SCOT 289:8
Greeks G. had a word — AKIN 6:4
  G. in this American empire — MACM 209:1
green being g. — RAPO 266:7
  Colourless g. ideas — CHOM 66:3
  drives my g. age — THOM 314:3
  G. how I love you — LORC 203:1
  g. shoots of recovery — MISQ 224:8
  Her g. lap — WALK 326:11
  How g. was my valley — LLEW 201:1
  Make it a *g.* peace — DARN 83:8
  My passport's g. — HEAN 149:4
  Wherever g. is worn — YEAT 345:1
greenery In a mountain g. — HART 146:14
greenhouse g. gases — MARG 214:12
Greenpeace G. had a ring to it — HUNT 160:12
greens healing g. — ABSE 1:2
grey but black and g. — GREE 137:15
  little g. cells — CHRI 66:8
grey-green g., greasy Limpopo — KIPL 183:6
grief g. felt so like fear — LEWI 199:2
  G. has no wings — QUIL 264:5
grievance Scotsman with a g. — WODE 339:13
gringo g. in Mexico — FUEN 126:15

groans g. of love · LOWR 204:4
grope Group G. · THOM 315:7
Groucho G. tendency · ANON 11:10
ground G. control to Major Tom · BOWI 42:2
  when I hit the g. · SPRI 301:3
grow never g. out of it · USTI 322:3
  Please help me g. God · BLUM 37:1
  They shall g. not old · BINY 34:10
growing g. the crystals · HODG 155:9
grown-ups facts about g. · JARR 167:4
  G. are always · LEWI 199:3
growth neoclassical endogenous g. · BROW 45:15
grumbling rhythmical g. · ELIO 103:15
gruntled far from being g. · WODE 339:15
guardians good grey g. of art · WILB 335:9
guards Brigade of G. · MACM 209:8
guerrilla g. wins if he does not · KISS 183:12
guest receive an honoured g. · AUDE 17:11
guided g. missiles and misguided · KING 180:17
guile squat, and packed with g. · BROO 45:2
guillotine blade of the g. · PAZ 251:10
guilt assumption of g. · CROS 80:11
  g. of Stalin · GORB 135:12
  put on a dress of g. · MCGO 207:9
guinea g. pigs in laboratory · WILL 336:7
Guinness G. is good for you · ADVE 3:23
  My Goodness, My G. · ADVE 4:16
guitar blue g. · STEV 303:18
gulag G. archipelago · SOLZ 298:5
  word 'g.' did not appear · WU 342:14
gum can't fart and chew g. · JOHN 170:5
gums Don't forget the fruit g. · ADVE 3:16
gun g. in your pocket · WEST 332:11
  Happiness is a warm g. · LENN 196:9
  no g., but I can spit · AUDE 18:4
  out of the barrel of a g. · MAO 214:5
  through the door with a g. · CHAN 63:6
gun-boat answer is to send a g. · BEVA 33:5
gunfire towards the sound of g. · GRIM 139:7
guns G. aren't lawful · PARK 249:12
  g. not with butter · GOEB 134:7
  hundred men with g. · PUZO 263:5
  monstrous anger of the g. · OWEN 247:4
  not the g. that kill · HEST 152:10
  rather have butter or g. · GOER 134:9
gunslinger Hip young g. · ANON 11:1
gut Truth that comes from the g. · COLB 73:3
Gutenberg G. made everybody · MCLU 208:14
guts Mrs Thatcher 'showed g.' · KINN 181:6
  Spill your g. at Wimbledon · CONN 75:9
gutter in the g. with that guy · EISE 99:13
  Journalists belong in g. · PRIE 261:13
guy straight sort of guy · BLAI 36:1
guys Nice g. Finish last · DURO 94:9
gym g. is really depressing · THOM 315:6

habit Growing old a bad h. · MAUR 217:8
  H. is a great deadener · BECK 26:6
  h. is hell for those · HOLI 156:5
habit-forming Cocaine h. · BANK 22:11
haddock hold on sausage and h. · WOOL 342:6
Haig ask for H. · ADVE 3:15
hail one H. Mary · DOYL 92:15
hair And not your yellow h. · YEAT 344:4
  anything with long h. · MASO 216:12
  smoothes her h. · ELIO 103:7
  wash that man right outa my h. · HAMM 143:1
half finished in h. the time · WODE 339:18
  H. dead and half alive · BETJ 32:6
  Too clever by h. · SALI 282:9
half-a-crown help to h. · HARD 145:7
halo What is a h. · FRY 126:8
halt tan with henna hackles, h. · STEV 303:13
Hamlet cigar called H. · ADVE 3:24
  had not written H. · WOLP 341:2
  H. so much paper and ink · PRIE 261:16
  not Prince H. · ELIO 102:7
hamster Freddie Starr ate my h. · NEWS 237:10
hand by the h. of God · MARA 214:8
  Give a man a free h. · WEST 332:7
  h. into the Hand of God · HASK 147:5
  h. is the cutting edge · BRON 44:9
  h. not yet contented · MERW 220:2
  h. that lays the golden egg · GOLD 135:5
  h. that signed the paper · THOM 314:4
  Have still the upper h. · COWA 78:11
  invisible h. in politics · FRIE 124:2
  kiss the h. that wrote · JOYC 172:14
  Left h. down a bit · CATC 60:12
  Put out my h. and touched · MAGE 211:3
  Took me by the h. · TURN 319:11
handbag hitting it with her h. · CRIT 80:2
handclasp h.'s a little stronger · CHAP 63:13
Handel tunes of H. · SITW 295:15
handful fear in a h. of dust · ELIO 102:21
handicap h. her in competition · LURI 204:8
handkerchief scent on a pocket h. · LLOY 201:8
handle can't h. the truth · FILM 116:12
hands blood on their h. · SPEN 299:13
  Holding h. at midnight · GERS 132:2
handstand H. IN SHOWER · TELE 311:9
hang let him h. there · EHRL 97:10
  will not h. myself today · CHES 64:8
hanging cured by h. from a string · KING 181:5
  postcards of the h. · DYLA 95:2
happen poetry makes nothing h. · AUDE 17:10
  what may h. · STEI 303:4
happened after they have h. · IONE 163:3
  funny thing h. · SHEV 294:1
  What h. to the horse · RUBI 277:1
happens h. anywhere · LARK 189:4
  Nothing h., nobody comes · BECK 26:3
  Stuff h. · RUMS 277:5

happiness fatal to true h.	RUSS 278:10
H. is a cigar	ADVE 3:24
H. is an imaginary	SZAS 307:13
H. is a warm gun	LENN 196:9
H. is a warm puppy	SCHU 288:7
H. is finding	CARS 54:7
h. makes up in height	FROS 125:5
h. nor annihilation	HOLT 156:8
h. was a warm puppy	EPHR 106:1
lifetime of h.	SHAW 292:9
or justice or human h.	BERL 30:14
politics of h.	HUMP 160:11
right to h.	RAYN 267:6
happy aware that you are h.	KRIS 185:6
conspiracy to make you h.	UPDI 321:6
H. the hare at morning	AUDE 17:3
prevent from being h.	ANOU 13:9
someone may be h.	MENC 218:13
This is the h. warrior	READ 267:10
want others to be h.	DALA 83:3
Was he h.	AUDE 18:17
harbour h., the bridge	ANON 10:12
those who h. them	BUSH 49:3
hard did it the h. way	EPIT 108:5
h. day's night	LENN 196:17
h. dog to keep	CLIN 71:13
h. man is good to find	WEST 332:13
h. rain's a gonna fall	DYLA 95:5
h. work wins it	ARMS 14:8
How h. it is	FROS 125:7
Look h. at the world	MERE 219:14
To ask the h. question	AUDE 18:16
hard-faced h. men who look as if	BALD 21:8
hard-sell h. or soft-sell TV push	NASH 234:13
hardship time of h. starts	NEWS 238:5
hare Happy the h. at morning	AUDE 17:3
h. sitting up	LAWR 192:11
harlot Prerogative of the h.	KIPL 183:10
Harlow t is silent, as in H.	ASQU 15:10
harm at least do no h.	DALA 83:2
What h. have I ever done	TAWN 310:4
harpsichord describing the h.	BEEC 26:15
harrow H. the house of the dead	AUDE 18:13
Harvard glass flowers at H.	MOOR 228:3
hat get ahead, get a h.	ADVE 3:29
puttin' on my top h.	BERL 30:10
think without his h.	BECK 26:4
way you wear your h.	GERS 132:3
hate h. a song that has sold	BERL 30:12
h. myself in the morning	LARD 188:11
h. the things you hate	GROE 139:10
how much men h. them	GREE 138:5
I h. war	ROOS 273:15
letter of h.	OSBO 246:19
man you love to h.	TAGL 309:10
of love is not h.	WIES 335:2
People must learn to h.	MAND 213:3
players who h. your guts	STEN 303:6
seen much to h. here	MILL 221:17
you h. something in him	HESS 152:8
hated never h. a man enough	GABO 128:1
hates h. dogs and babies	ROST 275:13
hating h., my boy, is an art	NASH 234:16
hatless lands h. from the air	BETJ 32:8
hatred good rancorous h.	WARN 328:3
Great h., little room	YEAT 345:15
intellectual h.	YEAT 345:14
Regulated h.	HARD 144:10
set against the h.	MCEW 207:7
What we need is h.	GENE 130:15
hats working women wore h.	ABZU 1:4
Haughey H. buried at midnight	O'BR 241:1
have with what you h.	HANS 144:3
having h. an old friend for dinner	FILM 114:1
Hays Will H. is my shepherd	FOWL 121:9
haze Purple h. is in my brain	HEND 151:7
he H. would, wouldn't he	RICE 270:7
Who h.	ROSS 275:9
head dark hole of the h.	HUGH 160:3
If you can keep your h.	KIPL 182:7
Inside your h.	HUGH 159:13
Johnny-h.-in-air	PUDN 262:12
keep your h.	PUDN 262:13
purpose of the h.	RIDI 271:3
world in my h.	HEWE 152:13
headstones white linen and h.	CLOO 72:9
healer compassion of the h.'s art	ELIO 100:19
health h. of the whole human race	TOYN 317:1
H. Service is safe	THAT 313:1
seriously damage your h.	OFFI 242:15
toasts to my h.	PHIL 253:11
When you have both, it's h.	DONL 92:1
hear can't h. what they say	SMIT 297:2
Can you h. me, mother	CATC 58:10
h. it through their feet	SOUS 299:3
prefer not to h.	AGAR 2:13
want to h. from your sweater	LEBO 194:8
heard h. it's in the stars	PORT 258:23
You ain't h. nuttin' yet	JOLS 170:11
heart all fact, no h.	COLB 73:4
Beware my foolish h.	WASH 328:8
bicycle-pump the human h.	AMIS 8:6
Bury my h. at Wounded Knee	BENÉ 28:13
committed adultery in my h.	CART 55:2
ease a h. like a satin gown	PARK 249:13
examine my own h.	DE V 89:7
fed the h. on fantasies	YEAT 345:10
Fourteen h. attacks	JOPL 171:1
get your h.'s desire	SHAW 292:15
good at h.	FRAN 122:7
have its heart broken	RAMS 266:3
h. and the intellect	TANS 310:1
h. belongs to Daddy	PORT 258:22
h. grows old	YEAT 346:3

h. in the business	WATS 328:13
h. is a lonely hunter	BORR 40:14
h. is an organ of fire	ONDA 243:7
h. likes a little disorder	DE B 86:5
h. to a dog to tear	KIPL 182:14
h. was warm and gay	HAMM 143:3
h. was with the Oxford men	LETT 198:2
ice in the h.	GREE 138:1
left my h. in San Francisco	CROS 80:12
make a stone of the h.	YEAT 344:13
may not change the h.	KING 180:9
memory of the h.	CAMU 52:5
rag and bone shop of the h.	YEAT 344:7
waters of the h.	THOM 314:5
heart-beat just a h. away	STEV 304:11
hearthstone squats on the h.	QUIL 264:5
heartless h., witless nature	HOUS 158:5
restrain the h.	KING 180:9
hearts queen in people's h.	DIAN 90:5
heat furnace that gives no h.	RAYM 267:5
If you can't stand the h.	TRUM 319:3
white h. of technology	MISQ 225:7
heather bonnie bloomin' h.	LAUD 191:13
cries 'Nothing but h.'	MACD 207:1
heaven any better in H.	WILL 337:2
God owns h.	SEXT 291:3
H. knows I'm miserable	MORR 229:3
H. would be too dull	EPIT 108:11
Imagine there's no h.	LENN 196:10
Pennies don't fall from h.	THAT 312:6
pennies from h.	BURK 48:5
people we find in h.	TUTU 320:2
thirtieth year to h.	THOM 314:6
heaventree h. of stars	JOYC 172:13
heavy h. bear who goes with me	SCHW 288:13
Sob, h. world	AUDE 16:12
Hebrides seas colder than the H.	FLEC 118:10
heck h. of a job	BUSH 49:7
hedgehogs belongs to the h.	BERL 30:13
throwing h. under me	KHRU 180:3
heels like champagne or high h.	BENN 29:10
heigh-ho H., heigh-ho	MORE 228:4
height Happiness makes up in h.	FROS 125:5
Heinz Beanz meanz H.	ADVE 3:7
Helen H.'s face in hell	PARK 249:10
hell bells of H.	ANON 12:4
Damn you all to h.	FILM 116:13
do science in h.	VAUG 324:6
h. for those you love	HOLI 156:5
H. full of musical amateurs	SHAW 292:11
H. is oneself	ELIO 100:7
H. is other people	SART 284:5
If Hitler invaded h.	CHUR 69:6
I'm mad as h.	FILM 114:9
I say the h. with it	CART 56:7
made an excursion to h.	PRIE 262:2
not be H. if you are there	EPIT 108:11

probably redesigned H.	PRIC 261:12
they think it is h.	TRUM 318:12
walked eye-deep in h.	POUN 259:14
War is h., and all that	HAY 148:4
where the bloody h.	ADVE 5:1
why they invented H.	RUSS 279:5
working definition of h.	SHAW 293:2
would be h. on earth	SHAW 292:9
hello H. boys	ADVE 3:27
H., good evening	CATC 59:9
help any belief in h.	MURR 231:15
do something to h. me	LAUR 192:1
h. and support of the woman	EDWA 97:6
little h. from my friends	LENN 197:1
look on and h.	LAWR 192:21
present h. in trouble	ANON 10:1
scream for h. in dreams	CANE 52:20
you can't h. it	SMIT 296:11
helper mother's little h.	JAGG 166:2
Hemingway cannot be H.	LAPI 188:10
hen better take a wet h.	KHRU 180:2
henna tan with h. hackles	STEV 303:13
herald h. angels sing	ANON 10:15
herbs intolerance to h.	WALT 327:6
here H.'s looking at you	FILM 113:14
H. we go	ANON 10:16
If we can't stay h. alive	MONT 227:5
Kilroy was h.	ANON 11:11
only h. for the beer	ADVE 4:1
Well h. I am	SENT 290:10
We're h.	ANON 12:17
heretic oppressor or a h.	CAMU 52:15
heretics H. are the only remedy	ZAMY 348:1
hero Show me a h.	FITZ 118:1
Herod for an hour of H.	HOPE 157:8
H. is his name	CAUS 57:9
heroes Canadians do not like h.	WOOD 341:6
fit country for h.	LLOY 201:6
land that needs h.	BREC 43:6
speed glum h.	SASS 284:15
We can be h.	BOWI 42:1
heroing H. is one of the shortest	ROGE 273:3
herring shoals of h.	MACC 206:7
hesitation Without h., deviation	CATC 61:15
hick Sticks nix h. pix	NEWS 238:3
hidden h. persuaders	PACK 248:1
hide always h. just in the middle	SHAW 293:13
he can't h.	LOUI 203:4
nothing to h.	CHUR 69:13
wise man h. a pebble	CHES 65:4
hiding bloody good h.	GRAN 136:10
high corn is as h.	HAMM 143:4
get h. with a little help	LENN 197:1
Pile it h.	SAYI 287:3
high-tech thing with h.	HOCK 155:7
high-water h. mark of my youth	THUR 316:1
highway each and ev'ry h.	ANKA 9:9

hilarity h. like a scream　GREE 137:14
hill all gone under the h.　ELIO 100:17
　bottom of the h.　BOMB 39:1
　light on the h.　CHIF 65:17
hills convictions are h.　FITZ 117:16
　h. are alive　HAMM 143:8
　red h. of Georgia　KING 180:12
hindsight H. is always twenty-twenty
　　WILD 335:12
hinterland She has no h.　HEAL 148:12
hip H. is the sophistication　MAIL 211:10
　H. young gunslinger　ANON 11:1
hippies h. wanted peace　COOP 76:10
hips armchairs tight about the h.　WODE 340:5
　when your h. stick　NASH 234:15
hipsters angelheaded h. burning　GINS 133:3
hired They h. the money　COOL 76:7
Hiroshima After H.　BOLD 38:10
　bomb on H.　TRUM 318:9
　Einstein leads to H.　PICA 254:7
historians h. left blanks　POUN 259:12
historical h. drama queen　NOON 239:13
history cancer of human h.　SONT 298:16
　change the course of h.　FILM 113:7
　Does h. repeat itself　BARN 23:13
　dustbin of h.　TROT 317:13
　end of h.　FUKU 126:18
　Family h. has　RUSH 277:14
　from the lessons of h.　HUXL 161:4
　frozen flash of h.　ANON 10:13
　h. came to a .　SELL 290:9
　H. gets thicker　TAYL 310:5
　H. is a nightmare　JOYC 172:10
　H. is not what you thought　SELL 290:6
　h. is now and England　ELIO 101:9
　h. is on our side　KHRU 180:1
　H. littered with the wars　POWE 260:17
　h.-making creature　AUDE 19:2
　H. more or less bunk　FORD 120:2
　H. teaches us that men　EBAN 96:5
　h. to the defeated　AUDE 18:15
　h. will record　MORS 229:4
　hope and h. rhyme　HEAN 148:15
　Human h. becomes more　WELL 331:6
　Make poverty h.　SAYI 286:23
　more h. than they can consume　SAKI 282:4
　name is h.　THWA 316:6
　no h. of mankind　POPP 256:7
　not learning from h.　BLAI 35:12
　rattling good h.　HARD 145:12
　reverberates through h.　KOES 184:15
　thousand years of h.　GAIT 128:5
　too much h.　KING 181:2
　writing h. with lightning　WILS 338:12
hit H. the road, Jack　MAYF 217:14
Hitler H.'s level of accuracy　TAYL 310:7
　If H. invaded hell　CHUR 69:6

　If I can't love H.　MUST 232:8
　kidding, Mister H.　PERR 253:2
　like kissing H.　CURT 81:16
　thank heaven for Adolf H.　BUCH 47:8
hitting h. it with her handbag　CRIT 80:2
hobbit there lived a h.　TOLK 316:11
hock weak h. and seltzer　BETJ 32:3
hog Not the whole h.　MILL 222:12
hogs Men eat h.　STEV 303:16
hold love them, and h. on　DUNN 94:7
hole dark h. of the head　HUGH 160:3
　first h. made through　MOOR 227:11
　h.-in-corner man　WILS 337:8
　if you knows of a better h.　CART 57:2
　In a h. in the ground　TOLK 316:11
　making a h. in a sock　EINS 99:9
　mint with the h.　ADVE 4:14
holiday perpetual h.　SHAW 293:2
　to take a h.　RUSS 278:7
holidays during the h. from Eton　SITW 296:1
hollow We are the h. men　ELIO 101:14
Hollywood H. money isn't money　PARK 250:5
　not have been invited to H.　CHAN 63:4
holocaust Somme is like the H.　BARK 23:6
holy H. deadlock　HERB 151:18
　h.-water death　MCGO 207:11
home all the comforts of h.　BRYS 47:2
　can't go h. again　WOLF 340:14
　children who leave h.　SLOV 296:5
　E.T. phone h.　FILM 113:6
　get all that at h.　BENN 29:3
　H. is the place where　FROS 125:1
　H. is where you come to　THAT 313:15
　H. James　HILL 154:5
　I tank I go h.　GARB 129:14
　Keep the H.-fires burning　FORD 120:4
　look as much like h.　FRY 126:10
　no place like h.　LANC 188:6
　those who want to go h.　LAND 188:8
　years in a geriatric h.　AMIS 8:9
Homer had the voice of H.　HALD 142:3
　house on H.'s shores　ELYT 105:7
homes In h., a haunted apparatus　RAIN 265:6
　Stately H. of England　COWA 78:11
homing flock of h. pigeons　HUGH 160:7
homosexuality glasses, h., Watford　JOHN 168:8
　If h. were normal　BRYA 46:14
honest buy it like an h. man　NORT 240:5
　h. and intelligent　ORWE 246:8
　H. to God　ROBI 271:13
　Keep the bastards h.　POLI 257:22
　poor but she was h.　ANON 12:9
honey bee produces h.　GOLD 134:12
　h. still for tea　BROO 45:3
　h. to smear his face　SCHW 288:13
honour Fear God. H. the King　KITC 183:19
　for this woman's h.　FILM 116:2

great peaks of h.   LLOY 201:4
h. almost greater than   YOUN 347:3
peace with h.   CHAM 62:8
signed with their h.   SPEN 300:5
we h. it   SHIE 294:4
years and h. to the grave   KIPL 182:11
hoodie Hug a h.   MISQ 224:9
let's hug a h.   COAK 72:10
hoodies see h. as aggressive   CAME 51:10
hoover onto the board of H.   GREE 138:7
hope h. and history rhyme   HEAN 148:15
H. is definitely not   HAVE 147:6
in the store we sell h.   REVS 269:10
Land of H. and Glory   BENS 29:11
may we bring h.   THAT 312:5
Nor dread nor h. attend   YEAT 344:11
Some blessed H.   HARD 145:4
there is h.   CROS 80:13
tiny ripple of h.   KENN 178:5
two thousand years of h.   WEIZ 330:9
hopeful with a h. heart   LAWR 192:5
hopefulness Lord of all h.   STRU 306:14
hopeless doctors know a h. case   CUMM 81:7
hopes h. of its children   EISE 99:12
horizon just beyond the h.   KISS 183:18
horizontal h. desire   SHAW 293:16
Life is a h. fall   COCT 72:13
horn won't come out of your h.   PARK 249:5
horns memories are hunting h.   APOL 13:10
horribilis annus h.   ELIZ 104:7
horror h. of sunsets   PROU 262:8
h.! The horror   CONR 75:10
horse feeds the h. enough oats   GALB 128:11
h. designed by a committee   ISSI 163:8
never heard no h. sing   ARMS 14:9
torturer's h. scratches   AUDE 17:17
What happened to the h.   RUBI 277:1
where's the bloody h.   CAMP 51:15
horseman greatest h. in Austria   SCHU 288:11
H., pass by   YEAT 346:10
horsemen Four H. rode again   RICE 270:4
horses Bring on the empty h.   CURT 82:1
don't spare the h.   HILL 154:5
frighten the h.   CAMP 51:14
if you cannot ride two h.   MAXT 217:9
I saw the h.   HUGH 160:1
They shoot h. don't they   MCCO 206:9
horseshoe h. over his door   BOHR 38:6
horticulture lead a h.   PARK 250:8
hose out of the turret with a h.   JARR 166:17
host I'd have been under the h.   PARK 250:7
hostile universe is not h.   HOLM 156:6
hot long h. summer   FILM 117:8
On a h., hot day   LAWR 192:16
only in h. water   REAG 267:12
hounds by your own quick h.   MOTI 229:13
hour finest h.   CHUR 67:7

for an h. of Herod   HOPE 157:8
I also had my h.   CHES 64:10
its h. come round at last   YEAT 346:1
matched us with His h.   BROO 45:4
hourglass Egghead weds h.   NEWS 237:8
hours better wages and shorter h.   ORWE 246:4
see the h. pass   CIOR 70:3
house Harrow the h. of the dead   AUDE 18:13
h. a machine for living in   LE C 195:3
H. Beautiful is play lousy   PARK 249:16
h. of the Father   LAST 190:13
man in the h. is worth   WEST 332:1
This H. today is a theatre   BALD 21:13
threshold of a new h.   ATWO 16:10
With usura hath no man a h.   POUN 259:10
houseful three is a h.   SAYI 286:5
householder think she's a h.   WILD 335:15
housekeeper make a h. think   WILD 335:15
housekeeping good h. to the winds   KEYN 179:8
houses h. are all gone   ELIO 100:17
spaces between the h.   FENT 110:8
housework H. expands to fill   CONR 75:14
h., with its repetition   DE B 86:4
no need to do any h.   CRIS 79:13
Houston H., we've had a problem   LOVE 203:5
how H. do they know   PARK 250:4
howls going to be h. of anguish   HEAL 148:10
Howth H. Castle and Environs   JOYC 171:9
huff leave in a h.   FILM 114:4
hug H. a hoodie   MISQ 224:9
let's h. a hoodie   COAK 72:10
hullo H. Clouds Hullo Sky   WILL 336:2
human all h. life is there   ADVE 3:3
all other h. rights   JOHN 169:4
appalling h. beings   CARE 53:14
emptiness. The h. lack   BOLD 38:9
health of the whole h. race   TOYN 317:1
h. beings are more alike   ANGE 9:8
h. beings were murdered   WIES 335:5
H. kind Cannot bear   ELIO 100:12
h. nature changed   WOOL 341:10
H. nature not black and white   GREE 137:15
h., they suffered   WARR 328:6
h. zoo   MORR 228:8
lose its h. face   DUBČ 93:5
love h. beings   GREE 137:11
robot may not injure a h.   ASIM 15:1
To err is h.   SAYI 287:8
ultimate h. mystery   MILL 222:8
wish I loved the H. Race   RALE 265:8
humanity belief in h.   YAMA 344:2
first condition of h.   SOYI 299:6
freeze my h.   MACN 210:5
H. a work in progress   WILL 336:7
Oh, the h.   MORR 228:12
take care of h.   DALA 83:2
humankind answers h. invented   PAZ 251:11

human rights tolerance and h.   ANNA 9:10
humans isn't fit for h. now   BETJ 32:14
humble h. as a tool   FUGA 126:17
Humean H. predicament   QUIN 264:6
humiliation Art is born of h.   AUDE 19:5
  called shame and h.   O'RO 244:5
humility H. must always be   EISE 99:11
humming hear the virus h.   DOTY 92:2
hummy at that word 'h.'   PARK 249:15
  to make it more h.   MILN 222:17
humour H. is emotional chaos   THUR 316:5
  my h. is based   BRUC 46:9
  They have no sense of h.   LEAR 194:3
Hun H. is at the gate   KIPL 182:3
hundred h. flowers blossom   MAO 214:7
  One h. years of solitude   GARC 130:1
hundredth your h. birthday   TELE 311:7
hunger bodily h. in his eyes   SHAW 292:5
  H. allows no choice   AUDE 18:8
  h. is not only in   STEI 303:3
  h. to be beautiful   RHYS 269:14
hungry advertise food to h.   GALB 128:9
  got to be kept h.   DIMA 90:12
hunter heart is a lonely h.   BORR 40:14
  H.'s waking thoughts   AUDE 17:3
Hunter Dunn Miss J. H.   BETJ 32:15
hunters see the first h.   PURD 263:3
hurdles don't really see the h.   MOSE 229:11
hurricane h. on the way   FISH 112:4
hurry H. up please it's time   ELIO 103:3
hurt I'm in the h. business   TYSO 320:8
  never h. a hair   STUD 307:1
  never h. anybody   ELTO 105:5
  wish to h.   BRON 44:11
  Yes it h.   POLI 258:13
hurting If the policy isn't h.   MAJO 211:13
  knack of falling without h.   SCOT 289:9
  once it has stopped h.   BOWE 41:12
  people h. people   MAIL 211:8
hurtling death h. to and fro   HUGH 159:13
husband Bigamy is one h. too many   ANON 10:5
  h. what is left of a lover   ROWL 276:6
  left her h. because   MURD 231:9
  My h. and I   ELIZ 104:6
husbands Chumps make the best h.
       WODE 339:12
  how many h. she had had   GABO 128:3
hush H.! Hush! Whisper who dares
       MILN 223:10
hyacinths h. and biscuits   SAND 283:9
hyphenated h. Americanism   ROOS 274:14
hypochondria h. has always seemed   DIAM 90:4
hypocrisy world safe for h.   WOLF 340:13
hypotheses smallest number of h.   EINS 99:4
hypothesis discard a pet h.   LORE 203:3

I I am a camera   ISHE 163:6
  I plus my surroundings   ORTE 244:9
  My husband and I   ELIZ 104:6
IBM for buying I.   ADVE 4:20
ice after the last i. age   PURD 263:3
  I. formed on the butler   WODE 340:6
  It's fresh as i.   ADVE 4:5
  piece of i. on a hot stove   FROS 126:1
  Some say in i.   FROS 125:3
  splinter of i.   GREE 138:1
iceberg grew the I. too   HARD 145:2
  ill-concealed i.   LAWS 193:7
icebox plums that were in the i.   WILL 337:1
ice-cream emperor of i.   STEV 303:15
  i. out of the container   BRYS 47:1
iceman i. cometh   O'NE 243:10
id PUT THE I. BACK IN YID   ROTH 276:1
idea better to entertain an i.   JARR 167:3
  does get an i.   MARQ 215:9
  good i. but it won't work   ROGE 273:4
  good i.—son   CATC 59:4
  i. And the reality   ELIO 101:16
  i. of death saves him   FORS 120:15
  i. whose time has come   SAYI 287:5
  more dangerous than an i.   ALAI 6:5
  no grand i. was ever born   FITZ 117:22
  originator of a new i.   DIRA 91:3
  to whom the i. first occurs   DARW 84:4
  would be a good i.   GAND 129:12
ideal i. for which I am prepared   MAND 213:1
  i. reader suffering from   JOYC 171:10
idealism morphine or i.   JUNG 173:4
ideals i. of a nation   DOUG 92:7
  shoes with broken high i.   MCGO 207:9
ideas Colourless green i.   CHOM 66:3
  From it our i. are born   GENE 130:15
  genuine i., Bright Ideas   BENT 30:1
  hold two opposed i.   FITZ 117:20
  I don't have i.   RAVE 267:4
identical they exist, but are i.   FORS 121:1
if I. you can keep your head   KIPL 182:7
ignorance Disease, I., Squalor   BEVE 33:15
  Don't die of i.   OFFI 242:7
  evil is simply i.   FORD 120:3
  I. is an evil weed   BEVE 33:14
  i. is never better   FERM 110:13
  i. necessarily infinite   POPP 256:9
  i. so abysmal   MEDA 218:5
  sincere i.   KING 180:16
ignorant become an i. man again   STEV 303:19
  many i. men are sure   DARR 84:1
ignore nothing to i.   NASH 234:14
ignored because they are i.   HUXL 161:11
ignores poetry i. most people   MITC 223:11
Ike I like I.   POLI 257:17
  Poor I.   TRUM 319:1
I'll I. be back   FILM 114:6

ill told you I was i.   EPIT 107:17
  warn you not to fall i.   KINN 181:7
illegal i., immoral, or fattening   WOOL 342:9
  means that it is not i.   NIXO 239:8
  Nothing is i. if   YOUN 347:2
illegitimate no i. children   GLAD 133:11
ill-housed nation i., ill-clad   ROOS 273:16
illness i. the night-side of life   SONT 299:1
  makes i. worthwhile   SHAW 291:12
ill-nourished ill-clad, i.   ROOS 273:16
ills i. of democracy   SMIT 296:6
illuminated i. trouser-clip   MORT 229:8
illusion only an i.   EINS 99:6
  Time is an i.   ADAM 2:4
image just an i.   GODA 134:4
  live without any i.   MURD 231:11
images Fresh i. beget   YEAT 344:6
  i. change as they repeat   WARH 327:12
  I. split the truth   LEVE 198:6
  unpurged i. of day   YEAT 344:5
imagination i. sleeps   CAMU 52:16
  literalists of the i.   MOOR 228:2
  property of the i.   WALC 326:5
  suspend the i.   HEMI 151:1
  takes a lot of i.   BAIL 20:8
  Television contracts i.   WOGA 340:8
  those that have no i.   SHAW 293:10
imagine I. there's no heaven   LENN 196:10
imitate i. each other   HOFF 155:11
  Immature poets i.   ELIO 103:11
  never failed to i. them   BALD 21:2
immanent I. Will that stirs   HARD 145:1
immaturity expression of human i.   BRIT 44:5
immoral illegal, i., or fattening   WOOL 342:9
immorality i. what they dislike   WHIT 334:3
immortal that couldn't be i.   SZYM 308:10
immortality i. can be assured   GALB 129:1
  i. through my work   ALLE 7:15
  Milk's leap toward i.   FADI 109:1
  Millions long for i.   ERTZ 106:4
  organize her own i.   LASK 189:15
impartiality i. is bias   REIT 269:4
impatient growing i. to see him   SMIT 297:10
imperialism I.'s face   AUDE 18:7
  I. the monopoly stage   LENI 196:1
imperialisms prey of rival i.   KENY 178:5
impertinent ask an i. question   BRON 44:10
importance taking decisions of i.   PARK 250:14
important i. book, critic assumes   WOOL 341:12
  i. to be clever *about*   MEDA 218:7
  same as i.   PRAT 261:8
  thing that is i.   SAIN 281:11
importunities life's odious i.   FREU 123:10
impossible art of the i.   HAVE 147:7
  Dream the i.   DARI 83:7
  i. takes little longer   NANS 234:1
  i. takes longer   MILI 221:4

  i. to carry the burden   EDWA 97:6
  says that it is i.   CLAR 70:10
  two words, 'i.'   GOLD 135:4
impostors treat those two i.   KIPL 182:8
impressionable at an i. age   SPAR 299:9
improbability high degree of i.   FISH 112:10
  statistical i.   DAWK 85:4
improbable i. chances   LURI 204:7
improved i. by death   SAKI 282:3
improvisation I. is too good   SIMO 295:6
impure all things are i.   LAWR 192:3
in I'm i. to win   CLIN 71:14
  KNEW YOU HAD IT I. YOU   TELE 311:3
  when it's i. you   FROS 125:7
inadequate how i. intelligence is   EINS 98:11
  not that we are i.   WILL 337:3
inadvertence by chance or i.   HAIL 141:7
incest i. and folk-dancing   ANON 13:5
incident Bodyline was not an i.   JAME 166:8
include i. me out   GOLD 135:2
inclusion Life being all i.   JAME 166:11
income he has i.   NASH 234:9
  rises to meet i.   PARK 250:11
income tax I. made more liars   ROGE 273:1
incompatibility i. is the spice   NASH 234:9
incompetence Rise to His Level of I.   PETE 253:5
  sheer i.   JONE 170:12
incomplete i. until he has married   GABO 128:2
incomprehensible most i. fact   EINS 98:12
inconceivable i. idea of the sun   STEV 303:19
inconvenient cause may be i.   BENN 29:10
  lie even when i.   VIDA 325:11
increased i. by one penny   CART 56:11
incredible i. as if you fired   RUTH 279:16
indecent for i. behaviour   WAUG 329:2
independence i. as dearly   ANON 13:1
  i. of judges   DENN 89:4
  war for i.   MCAL 205:2
India final message of I.   FORS 121:3
  I. will awake to life   NEHR 235:6
  No one can make I. kneel   SING 295:10
  Nothing in I.   FORS 120:19
Indians I. are you   BALD 21:6
indifference it's i.   WIES 335:2
indifferent It is simply i.   HOLM 156:6
indignation Savage i. there   YEAT 346:5
individual cult of the i.   KHRU 179:13
  i. men and women   THAT 313:6
individualism system of rugged i.   HOOV 157:3
individuality had its own i.   RYDE 280:3
individually I. you agreed to evil   RODR 272:8
individuals things i. are doing   KEYN 179:1
indomitable i. Irishry   YEAT 346:9
industrialists die for the i.   FRAN 122:5
industry permit a cottage i.   MARC 214:9
  Science finds, i. applies   ANON 12:8
ineffectual Remote and i. Don   BELL 27:12

inevitability i. of gradualness — WEBB 329:17
inevitable foresee the i. — ASIM 15:2
inexactitude terminological i. — CHUR 66:11
infallible not final because we are i. — JACK 165:6
infamy date which will live in i. — ROOS 274:4
  I., infamy — FILM 114:10
inferior make you feel i. — ROOS 273:9
inferno Dante's I. — BOGA 38:3
  i. of his passions — JUNG 173:2
infinite door to i. wisdom — BREC 43:7
  ignorance necessarily i. — POPP 256:9
  Space is almost i. — QUAY 264:3
infinitive care what a split i. — FOWL 121:10
  when I split an i. — CHAN 63:5
inflation I. one form of taxation — FRIE 124:5
  pay to get i. down — LAMO 188:2
inflections beauty of i. — STEV 304:4
influence i. on human life — MULL 231:4
  i. people — CARN 54:3
  i. to your son — ICE 162:3
information lost in i. — ELIO 102:13
informed badly-i. labrador — NYE 240:9
inhale didn't i. — CLIN 72:1
  if he doesn't i. — STEV 304:5
initiatives eye-catching i. — BLAI 36:2
injury i. is done to us — PATO 251:4
injustice i. makes democracy — NIEB 236:11
ink all cough in i. — YEAT 345:19
inn remember an I., Miranda — BELL 28:1
inner have no I. Resources — BERR 31:17
  It is my i. voice — GAND 129:13
innocence assumption of i. easy — CROS 80:11
  ceremony of i. — YEAT 345:20
  i. is like a dumb leper — GREE 137:17
  I. no earthly weapon — HILL 153:11
  not in i. — ARDR 14:3
innocent i. and the beautiful — YEAT 345:5
  We are i. — ROSE 275:5
innuendoes beauty of i. — STEV 304:4
inoperative statements i. — ZIEG 348:10
inquisition Spanish I. — MONT 227:10
inscription like a rough i. — YEVT 346:16
insect gigantic i. — KAFK 174:4
insects Why do we study i. — WILS 337:11
insecurity international i. — NIEB 236:12
inside i. the tent pissing out — JOHN 170:3
insignificance of the utmost i. — CURZ 82:2
insomnia suffering from ideal i. — JOYC 171:10
inspiring i. the enlisted — REMN 269:6
instincts i. already catered for — BENN 29:5
  true to your i. — LAWR 192:10
institution always an i. — DAY 85:9
  change an i. — TUSA 319:12
  transformed into i. — SART 284:13
institutional i. racism — MACP 210:10
institutions acquiring their i. — HAIL 141:7
instrument i. powerful — MURR 232:4

State is an i. — STAL 301:9
insulted never *hope* to get i. — DAVI 85:1
insurance National compulsory i. — CHUR 68:4
intact is there, i. — TRIM 317:11
integration policy of European i. — KOHL 185:2
intellect i. of man is forced — YEAT 344:9
  Pessimism of the i. — GRAM 136:9
intellectual become an i. — SCHW 289:2
  i. hatred — YEAT 345:14
  i. is someone whose — CAMU 52:8
  'I.' suggests — AUDE 17:18
  i. who underrates — KUND 185:12
intellectuals All i. should — RUSS 279:12
  treachery of the i. — BEND 28:10
intelligence arresting human i. — LEAC 193:12
  bewitchment of i. — WITT 339:6
  bought his clothes with i. — AMIE 8:3
  first-rate i. — FITZ 117:20
  how inadequate i. is — EINS 98:11
  I. is quickness — WHIT 334:2
  i. made visible — PICK 254:9
  underestimating i. — MENC 219:3
intelligent honest and i. — ORWE 246:8
  Most i., very elegant — BUCK 47:9
  rule of i. tinkering — EHRL 97:9
  so i. — ELIO 103:2
intensity full of passionate i. — YEAT 345:20
intentions only had good i. — THAT 312:7
interact do not i. at all — UPDI 321:12
intercourse positions in i. — KEAT 176:2
interest compete for her i. — LEWI 199:15
  gives them an i. — BAIN 21:1
interested i. in the arts — AYCK 19:13
  only i. in art — SHAW 293:14
interesting more i. people — YOUN 347:4
  proposition be i. — WHIT 333:15
  Very i. . . . . but — CATC 61:9
international I. life — DEBR 86:10
  i. wrong — AUDE 18:7
Internet I. is an élite — CHOM 66:4
  On the I., nobody — CART 56:10
  thanks to the I. — WILE 335:17
interpose i. my body — STRA 306:5
interrupt i. yourself in a minute — CAME 51:9
intersecting i. monologues — WEST 332:16
intervene i.—before breakfast — HESE 152:6
intolerance I. of groups — FREU 123:8
intolerant not to tolerate the i. — POPP 256:6
invent i. the universe — SAGA 281:4
invented extraordinarily well i. — FULL 127:4
  i. blue jeans — SAIN 281:14
  i. the brake — NEME 235:5
  only lies are i. — BRAQ 43:2
invention i. of a mouse — DISN 91:8
  i. or discovery — CARE 53:13
  Marriage a wonderful i. — CONN 74:9
invisible i. hand in politics — FRIE 124:2

i., refined out of	JOYC 172:4
no i. means of support	BUCH 47:6
priest of the i.	STEV 303:12
Iraq creating I.	BELL 27:4
Ireland coming to I. today	GEOR 131:4
great Gaels of I.	CHES 64:7
I. holds these graves	PEAR 251:14
I. hurt you into poetry	AUDE 17:9
I. is the old sow	JOYC 172:2
I. we dreamed of	DEV 89:9
Out of I. have we come	YEAT 345:15
Romantic I.'s dead	YEAT 346:2
what I have got for I.	COLL 73:12
Irish I. poets, learn your trade	YEAT 346:8
Let the I. vessel lie	AUDE 17:11
symbol of I. art	JOYC 172:8
what the I. people wanted	DEV 89:7
Irishman secondarily, I'm an I.	HEWI 152:15
Irishmen appeal to all I.	GEOR 131:4
Irishry indomitable I.	YEAT 346:9
iron he's got i. teeth	GROM 139:11
i. curtain	CHUR 68:8
I. Curtain did not reach	SOLZ 298:9
i. lady	ANON 11:5
I. Lady	THAT 312:4
irrational i. exuberance	GREE 138:2
i. is rational	STEV 304:1
irrigation numerical i. system	AUGA 19:9
irritation cosiness and i.	PYM 263:6
is what the meaning of 'i.' is	CLIN 72:5
Islam I. has established them	KHOM 179:10
island at this i. now	AUDE 17:14
i. made mainly of coal	BEVA 33:3
soggy little i.	UPDI 321:5
isolated Continent i.	CART 56:3
isolationist you'll find an i.	RUSK 278:4
it It's just I.	KIPL 183:8
Italy I. under the Borgias	FILM 114:11
itsy I. bitsy teenie weenie	VANC 323:6
ivy it was agony, I.	CATC 58:19
Iwo Jima Marines took I.	ROSE 275:7
jack news of my boy J.	KIPL 182:13
jack-knife j. has Macheath	BREC 43:11
jail dey gits you in j.	O'NE 243:9
Go to j.	SAYI 286:16
jamais j. triste archy	MARQ 215:7
James Bond. J. Bond	FILM 115:12
Home J.	HILL 154:5
J. I, James II	GUED 140:3
J. James Morrison Morrison	MILN 223:6
Jane J., Jane, tall as a crane	SITW 295:12
Me Tarzan, you J.	MISQ 224:13
Japan to J.'s advantage	HIRO 154:7
Japanese reconcile J. action	CHUR 67:13
jaw-jaw To j. is always better	CHUR 68:13

jazz If you're in j.	MANN 213:12
J. is the only music	COLE 73:7
J. music is to be played	MORT 229:9
J. will endure	SOUS 299:3
Picasso, sunbathing and j.	WAUG 329:6
jealousy J. is feeling alone	BOWE 41:14
To j. nothing is more	SAGA 281:9
jeans blue j. and Coca-Cola	GREE 138:6
invented blue j.	SAIN 281:14
jeepers J. Creepers	MERC 219:10
Jeeves J. shimmered out	WODE 339:14
Jefferson when J. ate alone	KENN 177:13
Jellicoe J. was the only man	CHUR 69:8
jelly blasted, j.-boned swines	LAWR 192:20
shivers like the j.	PIRO 255:3
jellybeans way of eating j.	REAG 268:4
jest laughing at some j.	KIPL 182:1
Jesus J. loves you more	SIMO 295:3
j. told him; he wouldn't	CUMM 81:5
J. wants me for a sunbeam	TALB 309:19
more popular than J. now	LENN 196:12
thinks he is J. Christ	CLEM 71:4
to the heart of J.	TERE 311:17
When J. came to Birmingham	STUD 307:1
jet blood j. is poetry	PLAT 255:12
Jew declare that I am a J.	EINS 98:8
J. and the language	CELA 62:6
Just J.-*ish*	MILL 222:12
saved one J. from Auschwitz	AUDE 19:8
jewellery just rattle your j.	LENN 196:11
Jewish don't have to be J.	ADVE 5:14
J. man with parents alive	ROTH 275:14
murderers of J. children	WIES 335:4
national home for the J. people	BALF 22:2
solution of J. question	GOER 134:10
Jews all poets are J.	TSVE 319:7
But spurn the J.	BROW 46:6
came for the J.	NIEM 238:11
condition of the J.	SART 284:14
last J. to die	MEIR 218:9
To choose The J.	EWER 106:7
jigsaw piece in a j. puzzle	FILM 115:13
Jim It's life, J.	MISQ 224:11
worried about J.	CATC 60:3
job circuit learns your j.	MCLU 208:10
do his j. when he doesn't feel	AGAT 5:16
easier j. like publishing	AYER 19:17
finish the j.	CHUR 67:10
heck of a j.	BUSH 49:7
he's doing a grand j.	CATC 60:24
j. working-class parents	ABBO 1:1
looking for a j.	MORR 229:3
neighbour loses his j.	TRUM 318:14
jobs create j.	TSVA 319:6
phoney-baloney j.	FILM 116:9
jockey j. retires	ARCA 14:1
jogging alternative to j.	FITT 112:11

John King J. was not a good man   MILN 223:7
Johnnies between the J. and the Mehmets
                                        ATAT 15:13
Johnny J.-head-in-air   PUDN 262:12
joints Of all the gin j.   FILM 115:16
joke every j. a custard pie   ORWE 246:7
  j. with a double meaning   BARK 23:7
  not seen the j.   VIDA 325:3
jokes doesn't make j.   IONE 163:1
  Forgive my little j.   FROS 124:14
journal page of your j.   HUGH 160:4
journalism J. largely consists   CHES 65:14
  nearest thing to j.   CAPA 53:3
  rule of j.   HERS 151:20
journalist British j.   WOLF 340:10
  never was a j.   DAY 85:9
  No first-class j.   JUNO 173:11
journalistic j. dirty-mindedness   LAWR 193:1
journalists J. belong in gutter   PRIE 261:13
  j. dabbling   MCGR 208:1
  tell lies to j.   KRAU 185:3
journey j. *really* necessary   OFFI 242:9
  long day's j.   O'NE 243:11
  now begin the j.   REAG 268:8
journeying sat the j. boy   HARD 145:9
joy oh! weakness of j.   BETJ 33:1
  shock of your j.   HUGH 160:4
  Strength through j.   POLI 257:23
  tables of j.   HUGH 159:7
Judas Whether J. Iscariot   DYLA 95:15
judge Before you j. me   JACK 165:3
  best j. of a run   WHAR 333:4
  Here come de j.   CATC 59:10
  Never j. a book   EAGA 96:1
  not j. this movement kindly   READ 267:7
judged nation is j.   LÉVE 198:8
judgement j. of your parents   UPDI 321:7
  nation fit to sit in j.   WILS 338:13
  wait for the last j.   CAMU 52:4
judges independence of j.   DENN 89:4
  j. can tap   MARS 215:17
  J. must follow their oaths   ZOBE 349:2
jug 'J. Jug' to dirty ears   ELIO 102:22
juggle how to j. work, love, home   FRIE 123:17
July on the Fourth of J.   HAMM 143:10
jumpers Angels in j.   LEWI 200:1
June J. is bustin' out all over   HAMM 143:2
jungle city is not a concrete j.   MORR 228:8
  monkeys in the j.   CASH 55:11
  wise primitive in giant j.   MAIL 211:10
juniper under a j.-tree   ELIO 100:6
junk J. is the ideal product   BURR 48:9
jurist living American j.   CARD 53:9
just be British than j.   PAIS 248:7
  j. an image   GODA 134:4
  J. like that   CATC 60:10
  j. one of those things   PORT 258:19

J. say no   OFFI 242:10
may not be a j. peace   IZET 163:14
talk of a j. war   SORL 299:2
justice act of j.   MAND 213:7
  I don't want j.   HUGH 160:6
  If this is j.   HISL 154:9
  j. and the American way   CATC 59:2
  J. denied   MILL 220:14
  J. is a blind goddess   HUGH 159:6
  J. is not to be taken   CARD 53:8
  J. is the first condition   SOYI 299:3
  j. makes democracy possible   NIEB 236:11
  J. should not only be done   HEWA 152:11
  ounce of j.   TANS 309:20
  pursuit of j.   GOLD 135:1
  victors' j.   SHAW 293:18
justifiable not a j. act of war   BELL 27:3

Kaiser put the kibosh on the K.   ELLE 104:12
Kane of *Citizen K.*   THOM 315:10
Kansas corny as K. in August   HAMM 143:10
  not in K. any more   FILM 116:6
keep If you can k. your head   KIPL 182:7
  K. the bastards honest   POLI 257:22
  k. your England   MUGA 230:7
  some day it'll k. you   WEST 332:2
keeps gave it us for k.   AYRE 19:19
Kennedy President K. was dead   FORS 121:7
  you're no Jack K.   BENT 30:2
Kensal Green by way of K.   CHES 64:15
Kentucky Long ago in K.   WARR 328:5
kept I k. my word   DE L 88:6
kettle k.'s breath   HILL 153:10
  pretty k. of fish   MARY 216:8
Khrushchev not have married Mrs K.
                                        VIDA 325:8
kibosh put the k. on the Kaiser   ELLE 104:12
kick first k. I took   SPRI 301:3
  Nixon to k. around   NIXO 239:2
kid comeback k.   CLIN 72:2
  have one k.   O'RO 244:8
  Here's looking at you, k.   FILM 113:14
kiddies k. have crumpled   BETJ 32:9
kidding k., Mister Hitler   PERR 253:2
kids don't have any k. yourself   LARK 189:7
  how many k. did you kill   POLI 257:16
  just a couple of k.   HOLI 156:5
  K. and water   OFFI 242:12
  K. are the best   GROE 139:10
  leave his k.   BUFF 47:11
kill bombers to k. the babies   LE G 195:8
  get out and k. something   LEAC 193:13
  how many kids did you k.   POLI 257:16
  k. a mockingbird   LEE 195:6
  k. animals and stick in   NICO 236:10
  K. millions of men   ROST 275:12

knowing Bewrapt past k.   HARD 145:9
knowingly Never k. undersold   ADVE 4:18
knowledge After such k.   ELIO 101:12
 k. can only be finite   POPP 256:9
 k. they cannot lose   OPPE 244:1
 k. we have lost   ELIO 102:13
 make k. available   BLAC 35:9
 never better than k.   FERM 110:13
 search for k.   RUSS 278:5
 show of k.   DOUG 92:9
known k. and the unknown   PINT 254:14
 k. unto God   EPIT 108:6
 there are k. unknowns   RUMS 277:3
knows if you k. of a better 'ole   CART 57:2
 K. Things   MILN 223:4
 sits in the middle and k.   FROS 125:16
Knox John K. in Paradise   PARK 249:10
Korea doing in K.   TRUM 318:11

laboratory guinea pigs in l.   WILL 336:7
labour chaos of a L. council   KINN 181:8
 done to the L. Party   TAWN 310:4
 Don't let L. ruin it   POLI 258:3
 important to the L. Party   BROW 46:2
 is L.'s call   POLI 257:13
 L. Government does   MORR 228:11
 L. isn't working   POLI 258:1
 L. Party owes more   PHIL 254:1
 L.'s double whammy   POLI 258:2
 [L.] the natural party   WILS 338:9
 leader for the L. Party   BEVA 33:10
 New L., new danger   POLI 258:4
 to live without l.   TAWN 310:3
labrador badly-informed l.   NYE 240:9
lace Nottingham l.   BETJ 32:3
lacy l. sleeve with vitriol   WOOL 342:8
ladder l. of important things   STIP 305:3
ladders where all the l. start   YEAT 344:7
ladies l., God bless them   SAYE 285:8
 L., just a little more   TREE 317:4
 l. who lunch   SOND 298:13
 worth any number of old l.   FAUL 110:5
lady elderly l., who mutters away   CARE 53:10
 for the old l. in Dubuque   ROSS 275:8
 iron l.   ANON 11:5
 L., be good   GERS 131:13
 l. loves Milk Tray   ADVE 3:5
 l.'s not for burning   FRY 126:7
 l.'s not for turning   THAT 312:10
 l. that's known as Lou   SERV 290:16
 little l. comes by   GAY 130:8
 talk like a l.   SHAW 293:5
 why the l. is a tramp   HART 146:13
Lafayette L., *nous voilà*   STAN 301:13
lager pint of l. would be nice   STEW 305:1
laid l. end to end   PARK 250:2

laity conspiracies against the l.   SHAW 291:16
lake meal on a l.   MEND 219:5
lame without religion is l.   EINS 98:3
lamp post leaning on a l.   GAY 130:8
lamps l. are going out   GREY 139:3
land L. of Hope and Glory   BENS 29:11
 l. of my fathers   THOM 314:15
 L. that I love   BERL 30:5
 l. that needs heroes   BREC 43:6
 l. was ours before   FROS 125:4
 more precious than l.   SADA 281:3
 One Law, one L., one Throne   KIPL 183:1
 seen the promised l.   KING 180:15
 This l. is your land   GUTH 140:9
landing fight on the l. grounds   CHUR 67:6
landmarks fewer l. in space   CAMU 52:5
landslide pay for a l.   KENN 177:2
language by means of l.   WITT 339:6
 cool web of l.   GRAV 137:1
 divided by a common l.   SHAW 293:17
 growing up in the same l.   QUIN 264:8
 In such lovely l.   LAWR 192:19
 l. charged with meaning   POUN 260:6
 L. is a form of human reason   LÉVI 198:12
 L. is conceived in sin   QUIN 264:7
 l. of Shakespeare   SHAW 293:4
 l. of the unheard   KING 180:18
 L. tethers us   LIVE 200:13
 laogai in every l.   WU 342:14
 laughter in a l.   GOLD 134:11
 Life is a foreign l.   MORL 228:7
 limits of my l.   WITT 339:10
 mind enclosed in l.   WEIL 330:6
 mobilized the English l.   MURR 232:5
 mystery of l.   KELL 176:6
 Political l. is designed   ORWE 246:5
 prohibiting l.   BART 24:10
 rich and delicate l.   WAUG 329:11
 Slang is a l.   SAND 283:10
 suicides have a special l.   SEXT 291:6
 without a l.   CAPA 53:3
languages between and across l.   CRAW 79:7
 'primitive' l.   CHAT 64:3
 speaks eighteen l.   PARK 250:1
laogai want to see l. ended   WU 342:14
lascivious l. gloating   STOP 305:8
lash sodomy, prayers, and the l.   CHUR 68:12
lassie I love a l.   LAUD 191:13
last Free at l.   EPIT 107:5
 l. breath of Julius Caesar   JEAN 167:8
 l. day of an era past   YELT 346:14
 l. enemy   BORR 40:16
 l. man to die   KERR 178:9
 L. night I dreamt   DU M 93:10
 l. person who has sat on him   HAIG 141:3
 l. time I saw Paris   HAMM 143:3
 l. while they last   DE G 87:10

Look thy l.   DE L 88:4
Nice guys. Finish l.   DURO 94:9
wait for the l. judgement   CAMU 52:4
We were the l. romantics   YEAT 344:8
won the l. war   ROOS 273:7
Las Vegas loathing in L.   THOM 315:8
late rather l. for me   LARK 188:12
This is a l. parrot   MONT 227:9
too l. or too early   SART 284:11
later l. than you think   SERV 290:14
lateral l. thinking   DE B 86:7
Latin Devil knows L.   KNOX 184:9
half Greek, half L.   SCOT 289:8
learn L. as an honour   CHUR 69:1
latrine mouth used as a l.   AMIS 8:4
laugh no girl wants to l.   LOOS 202:11
Others may be able to l.   RHYS 269:13
why people l.   FIEL 111:16
laughing fun I ever had without l.   ALLE 7:5
killed while l.   KIPL 182:1
l. at us   FRIE 124:7
laughter L. . . . civilized music   USTI 322:1
l. in a language   GOLD 134:11
L. would be bereaved   USTI 322:4
more frightful than l.   SAGA 281:9
laurel oppressors l. you   WALC 326:2
lava in its l. I still find   WOOL 342:5
law against the l. for generals   TRUM 319:2
fear of the L.   JOYC 171:11
government above the l.   SCAR 285:13
had people not defied the l.   SCAR 285:12
judgement of the l.   JACK 165:5
keystone of the rule of l.   DENN 89:4
l. has made him equal   DARR 84:2
l. not supported by people   HUMP 160:10
l. of the Yukon   SERV 290:15
Nor l., nor duty   YEAT 345:7
One L., one Land, one Throne   KIPL 183:1
whole of the L.   CROW 81:1
lawn Get your tanks off my l.   WILS 338:11
on the l. I lie in bed   AUDE 18:3
scooters off my l.   CLAR 70:13
laws Government of l.   FORD 119:12
If l. are needed   KHOM 179:10
l. of God will be suspended   SHAW 292:2
neither l. made   JOHN 168:3
lawyer freely as a l. interprets   GIRA 133:9
l. with his briefcase   PUZO 263:5
lay L. your sleeping head   AUDE 17:15
layout Perfection of planned l.   PARK 250:13
LBJ All the way with L.   POLI 257:2
Hey, L., how many kids   POLI 257:16
lead can't see who's in the l.   SNAG 297:14
couldn't l. a flock   HUGH 160:7
l. a horticulture   PARK 250:8
leadable is the Conservative Party l.
    HESE 152:7

leader fanatic a great l.   BROU 45:13
Take me to your l.   CATC 61:4
test of a l.   LIPP 200:10
Wanna be the l.   MCGO 207:10
leadership L. is not about being   KEAT 176:1
L. means making   CHRÉ 66:6
leaf wise man hide a l.   CHES 65:4
leaguer become a big l.   DIMA 90:12
leaking L. is what you do   CALL 50:9
leap giant l. for mankind   ARMS 14:11
learn clever ones l. Latin   CHUR 69:1
l. how to be aged   BLYT 37:9
People must l. to hate   MAND 213:3
learned l. has been forgotten   SKIN 296:4
learning not l. from history   BLAI 35:12
leave forever taking l.   RILK 271:4
If you can't l. in a taxi   FILM 114:4
if you l. things alone   CHES 65:9
l. our flies alone   ANON 10:17
l. the country   NEWS 237:13
l. without the King   ELIZ 104:1
You better l.   DYLA 95:3
leaves l. will fall on my breast   NERU 235:10
lecture first to l. you   ELTO 105:4
lectures hissed my mystery l.   SPOO 300:14
led l. in Mesopotamia   LAWR 193:4
left L. hand down a bit   CATC 60:12
position was on the l.   MOSL 229:12
leftovers nothing but l.   ULLM 321:2
left-wing social contract is l.   DEBR 86:10
leg does not resemble a l.   APOL 13:11
legacies l. of empire   SAMP 282:12
legend L. ON THE LICENCE   HERS 151:20
Your l. ever did   JOHN 168:9
Your l. ever will   JOHN 168:12
legends Men must have l.   MURR 231:17
legs born with your l. apart   ORTO 244:14
Four l. good   ORWE 245:1
leisure fill l. intelligently   RUSS 278:11
length for what it lacks in l.   FROS 125:5
Lenin L. was right   KEYN 178:11
leopards three white l. sat   ELIO 100:6
leper innocence is like a dumb l.   GREE 137:17
Lesbia L. with her sparrow   MILL 221:14
less about l. and less   MAYO 217:15
l. in this than meets the eye   BANK 22:12
L. is a bore   VENT 324:9
L. is more   MIES 220:7
l. than $10,000   EVAN 106:5
more about l. and less   BUTL 49:10
One square foot l.   BENC 28:9
lessons from the l. of history   HUXL 161:4
l. to be drawn   ELIZ 104:8
let L. me go   LAST 190:13
L.'s go to work   FILM 115:4

let (*cont.*)

L.'s roll	LAST 190:15
Lethe waters of L.	GINS 133:6
letter Someone wants a l.	ADVE 4:29
letters can't write l.	BISH 35:5
l. get in wrong places	MILN 223:3
l. to a non-existent	LEWI 199:7
levee Drove my Chevy to the l.	MCLE 208:5
levers shan't be pulling the l.	THAT 313:14
Levis sold a million pairs of L.	BURR 48:8
Levy to love L.'s	ADVE 5:14
lexicons We are walking l.	LIVE 200:14
liar answered 'Little L.'	BELL 27:9
knows the man to be a l.	UPDI 321:11
proved l.	HAIL 141:6
liars Income Tax made more L.	ROGE 273:1
liberal first L. leader	STEE 302:5
l. education	BANK 22:14
l. employer	HOPE 157:10
l. is a conservative who	WOLF 340:16
L. is a man who uses	ROOS 273:17
l. who has been mugged	SAYI 286:7
liberals l. can understand	BRUC 46:8
liberation Women's L. is just	MEIR 218:10
liberationists furious about the l.	LOOS 202:13
liberties Freedom, what l.	GEOR 131:2
liberty defence of l.	GOLD 135:1
holy name of l.	GAND 129:8
L. is liberty, not	BERL 30:14
L. is precious	LENI 196:8
L. is unfinished business	ANON 11:12
L. means responsibility	SHAW 292:18
safeguards of l.	FRAN 122:8
survival and success of l.	KENN 177:5
library less time in the l.	STRU 306:12
l. is thought in	SAMU 283:1
you have a public l.	BENN 29:1
licence LEGEND ON THE L.	HERS 151:20
l. to act like an asshole	ZAPP 348:5
l. to print your own money	THOM 315:11
licensed l. to kill	FILM 114:5
L. to kill	FLEM 118:15
licking finger l. good	ADVE 4:3
lie Bodies never l.	DE M 88:15
definition of a l.	ANON 10:1
Every word she writes is a l.	MCCA 206:3
fall victim to a big l.	HITL 155:3
home to a l.	POUN 259:14
It's not a l.	FILM 115:1
l. even when inconvenient	VIDA 325:11
l. that makes us realize truth	PICA 254:8
l. to them remorselessly	FORS 120:16
old L.: Dulce et decorum	OWEN 247:7
possible to l. for the truth	ADLE 2:10
Well, that's a l.	MISQ 225:6
lied because our fathers l.	KIPL 181:14
I l. to please the mob	KIPL 181:15

We l. morning, noon and night	GYUR 140:11
lies Castle of lies	BOOK 39:3
Here l. Groucho Marx	EPIT 107:12
l. about the Democrats	STEV 304:6
L. are the mortar	WELL 331:5
l. of tongue and pen	CHES 64:12
make l. sound truthful	ORWE 246:5
Matilda told such Dreadful L.	BELL 27:8
only l. are invented	BRAQ 43:2
Without l. humanity would	FRAN 122:4
life actor's l. for me	WASH 328:7
afternoon of human l.	JUNG 173:6
all human l. is there	ADVE 3:3
believe in l.	DU B 93:7
believe in the l. to come	BECK 25:10
can be a daring l.	WELT 331:11
captured part of his l.	DREW 93:3
contempt for l.	VANE 323:11
content to manufacture l.	BERN 30:17
discovered the secret of l.	CRIC 79:10
dog is for l.	SAYI 286:10
essence of l.	DAWK 85:4
frontiers of l.	HERZ 152:1
Further sacrifice of l.	DE V 89:8
gave my l. for freedom	EWER 106:6
Get a l.	SHAT 291:10
goes through l. holding on	ELLI 105:1
great l. if you don't weaken	BUCH 47:5
isn't l. a terrible thing	THOM 314:13
It's l., Jim	MISQ 224:11
I've had a wonderful l.	LAST 191:5
lay down his friends for his l.	THOR 315:12
lay down my l. for	HALD 142:5
Lead me from death to l.	KUMA 185:11
l. a glorious cycle of song	PARK 249:6
l. and loves of a she-devil	WELD 330:12
l. a series of images	WARH 327:12
L. a sexually transmitted disease	ANON 11:13
L. begins at forty	PITK 255:6
L. being all inclusion	JAME 166:11
l. exists in the universe	JEAN 167:9
L., friends, is boring	BERR 31:17
l. had been ruined	BROO 45:7
l. in the village	LEE 195:7
l. is 6 to 5 against	RUNY 277:12
L. is a foreign language	MORL 228:7
L. is a gamble	STOP 306:4
L. is a great surprise	NABO 233:3
L. is a horizontal fall	COCT 72:13
L. is an offensive	WHIT 333:14
L. is a rainbow which	YEVT 346:17
L. is Colour and Warmth	GREN 138:15
L. is doubt	UNAM 321:3
L. is first boredom	LARK 189:2
l. is generally something	BENN 29:8
L. is just one damned	HUBB 159:1
L. is not having been told	NASH 235:3

L. is nothing much to lose	HOUS 158:6	dying of the l.	THOM 314:2
L. is not meant to be easy	FRAS 122:12	Give me a l.	HASK 147:5
L. is not meant to be easy	SHAW 291:13	gives a lovely l.	MILL 220:12
l. is one damn thing	MILL 221:16	l. at the end of the tunnel	LOWE 204:2
L. is the other way round	LODG 201:14	L. breaks where no sun	THOM 314:5
l. is the thing	SMIT 297:4	l. has gone out	NEHR 235:7
L. is too short to stuff	CONR 75:13	l. in the darkness	JUNG 173:3
l. is washed in the speechless	BARZ 24:17	l. my fire	MORR 228:14
L. just a bowl of cherries	BROW 46:5	l. one candle	HARP 146:5
l. like a box of chocolates	FILM 115:14	l. on the hill	CHIF 65:17
l. of any important person	PRIE 261:14	speed far faster than l.	BULL 47:12
L. says: she did this	BARN 23:12	tried to mend the Electric L.	BELL 27:13
L.'s better with	POLI 258:3	waited for the l.	ROBI 271:12
l. sentence goes on	CONL 74:7	while the l. fails	ELIO 101:9
l.'s rich pageant	MARS 215:15	**lightest** poor tread the l.	HARR 146:8
L., the Universe and Everything	ADAM 2:3	**lightness** unbearable l. of being	KUND 185:13
l. till my work is done	EPIT 107:7	**lightning** known the l.'s hour	DAY- 85:10
l. till the end of my work	SWAN 307:9	writing history with l.	WILS 338:12
live out my l. talking	VANZ 324:4	**lights** glare of l.	CHRÉ 66:7
looked at l. from both sides	MITC 225:10	turn out the l.	NEWS 237:13
makes l. worth living	ELIO 103:9	watching the tail l.	CRAN 79:4
matter of l. and death	SHAN 291:8	**like** but I l. you	CATC 60:21
matters in your l.	RUSH 277:13	but you'll l. it	CATC 61:20
measured out my l.	ELIO 102:5	don't know whether I l. it	VAUG 324:7
more a way of l.	ANON 12:3	don't l. this game	CATC 59:15
Music is l.	IVES 163:11	I know what I l.	BEER 26:16
no l. that couldn't be	SZYM 308:10	I L. Ike	POLI 257:17
not an event of l.	WITT 339:11	l. everyone else	DE G 87:14
not in giving l.	DE B 86:2	l. everyone else	SHIE 294:2
not the men in my l. that counts	WEST 332:6	l. is not necessarily good	BELL 27:2
one's own l. lacks	BARK 23:5	l. what you get	SHAW 292:23
On l., on death	YEAT 346:10	man you don't l.	THOM 314:16
Our end is L.	MACN 210:8	**liked** l. it so much	ADVE 3:30
outer l. of telegrams	FORS 120:13	wish to be l.	RUSS 278:9
Perfection of the l.	YEAT 344:9	would have l. to be Perón	PERÓ 252:10
priceless gift of l.	ROSE 275:5	**likely** Not bloody l.	SHAW 293:8
remaining years of l.	MAND 213:2	**likes** does know what she l.	RATT 266:9
Reverence for L.	SCHW 289:3	does what he l. to do	GILL 132:13
shilling l. will give you	AUDE 18:9	**lilacs** breeding L.	ELIO 102:19
sketchy understanding of l.	CRIC 79:9	**Lilibet** this special day. L.	TELE 311:7
some problems with my *l.*	SIMO 295:1	**limbs** deck your lower l. in pants	NASH 235:2
sons and daughters of L.	GIBR 132:9	**limelight** backing into the l.	BERN 31:7
taking l. by the throat	FROS 126:2	in the middle of the l.	SHAW 293:13
There is l., but not for you	MORT 229:6	**limited** so whizzed the L.	CRAN 79:4
there would be no l.	UPDI 321:9	**limits** l. of my language	WITT 339:10
university of l.	BOTT 39:11	**limousine** One perfect l.	PARK 249:9
Water is l.'s *mater*	SZEN 308:8	**Limpopo** grey-green, greasy L.	KIPL 183:6
What is this l.	DAVI 84:11	**Lincoln** Ford, not a L.	FORD 119:11
whole l. shows in your face	BACA 20:4	L. County Road	DYLA 95:12
Who owns my life	RODR 272:9	L. was shovelled	SAND 283:4
Without work, l. goes rotten	CAMU 52:18	L. went to New Orleans	HUGH 159:9
you lived your l.	JOHN 168:9	**line** active l. on a walk	KLEE 184:2
lifeless virtue is l.	PAST 251:1	first l.	CALV 51:5
life sentence escape the l.	LAWR 193:2	playing on the l.	FORS 120:17
lifetime l. of happiness	SHAW 292:9	problem of the colour l.	DU B 93:6
light brief crack of l.	NABO 233:4	through colour and l.	MOND 226:13
dark is l. enough	FRY 126:6	**lines** awful banal l.	GUIN 140:5

lines (*cont.*)

I plant l.	WALC 326:6
Just say the l.	COWA 78:17
sentiment in short l.	LARK 189:14

linguistic form of l. fascism — JAME 166:16
l. philosophy — RUSS 279:11
link You are the weakest l. — CATC 61:17
linoleum shoot me through l. — BANK 23:1
lion nation that had l.'s heart — CHUR 68:16
lions L. led by donkeys — MILI 221:8
lips already born before my l. — MAND 213:11

Loose l. sink ships	MILI 221:9
Matching l. and fingertips	ADVE 4:12
My l. are sealed	MISQ 224:14
Read my l.	BUSH 48:16
Watch my l.	BLUN 37:4
Watch my l.	BLUN 37:5

lipstick bears a l.'s traces — MARV 216:3
too much l. — NASH 234:15
liquid Cats, no less l. — TESS 312:1
liquidation l. of British Empire — CHUR 68:2
liquor l. is quicker — NASH 234:17
listen don't want to l. to *you* — LEBO 194:8
Stop-look-and-l. — OFFI 242:16
listening ain't l. — GLAS 134:1

hearing without l.	SIMO 295:4
l., lying in wait	THOM 314:21

lit whole Fleet's l. up — WOOD 341:7
literalists l. of the imagination — MOOR 228:2
literary l. equivalent — WHAR 333:6
Of all the l. scenes — PRES 261:10
literature as for l. — POUN 260:1

Great l. is	POUN 260:6
life ruined by l.	BROO 45:7
like their l. clear	LEWI 199:12
l. can and should do	BYAT 49:13
l. goes as freight	GARC 130:2
L. is mostly about	LODG 201:14
L. is news	POUN 260:5
l.'s performing flea	O'CA 241:9
L. the orchestration	WILD 335:16
real l. can exist only	MACD 206:13
Remarks are not l.	STEI 302:8
rest is l.	VALÉ 323:2
Russian l. saved	RATU 267:3

litmus Gypsies are a l. test — HAVE 147:9
little another l. man — ARCA 14:1

L. boxes on the hillside	REYN 269:12
l. boys who wanted	STEI 302:13
l. grey cells	CHRI 66:8
L. man, you've had a busy	SIGL 294:10
L. one! Oh, little one	STEP 303:8
l. people pay taxes	HELM 150:11
l. ships of England	GUED 140:2

live enable its citizens to l. — WEIL 330:5
find a way to l. — CRON 80:5
he isn't fit to l. — KING 180:11

If you don't l. it	PARK 249:5
L. and let die	FLEM 118:18
l. at all is miracle	PEAK 251:12
l. in an unlivable situation	LAIN 187:8
l. on your knees	IBAR 162:2
l. our lives	RILK 271:4
l. this long	BLAK 36:8
l. through someone else	FRIE 123:16
l. together as brothers	KING 180:14
l. until you die	SAUN 285:5
l. without mirrors	ATWO 16:11
Man is born to l.	PAST 250:18
might as well l.	PARK 249:12
Sacco's name will l.	VANZ 324:3
stories in order to l.	DIDI 90:10
taught us how to l.	BENN 29:2
than to l. up to them	ADLE 2:11
to l. long enough	ELIZ 104:11
work while I may l.	EPIT 107:7

lived Never to have l. is best — YEAT 345:3
liver ate his l. — FILM 113:15
lives Careless talk costs l. — OFFI 242:1
l. to be sacrificed — NEWS 237:12
woman who l. for others — LEWI 199:4
liveth name l. for evermore — EPIT 108:7
living go on l. even after death — FRAN 122:6

I *love* l.	SIMO 295:1
I shall go on l.	NERU 235:10
land of the l.	WILD 335:14
L. and partly living	ELIO 102:9
l. in a time	BREC 43:16
l. in Philadelphia	EPIT 107:13
L. is abnormal	IONE 163:2
Look to the l.	DUNN 94:7
machine for l. in	LE C 195:3
not learning from but l.	BLAI 35:12
not l. with you	WILL 336:9
way of l. with the Negro	BALD 21:4
well and l. in	ANON 11:8
world does not owe us a l.	PHIL 253:8

Lloyd George L. knew my father — ANON 11:14
loafing cricket as organized l. — TEMP 311:13
loathing Fear and l. — THOM 315:8
local little l. difficulties — MACM 209:4
working of l. government — THAT 313:16
locally act l. — SAYI 287:7
lock L. the doors — CAIN 50:6
logic l. of our times — DAY- 85:12
nothing more than l. gates — AUGA 19:9
logical l. positivists — AYER 19:16
loins shudder in the l. engenders — YEAT 345:8
Lolita kept by a little girl named L. — NABO 233:5
L., light of my life — NABO 233:1
London 1938 in L. — MIDL 220:6

L. Pride handed down to us	COWA 78:5
L. spread out in the sun	LARK 189:10
L. Transport diesel-engined	FLAN 118:9

love (*cont.*)

If I can't l. Hitler	MUST 232:8
I'll l. you	AUDE 16:14
I l. the smell	FILM 114:7
I l. the smell	FILM 114:8
I l. you	BURN 48:7
I l. you	LAST 190:8
It's so simple, l.	PRÉV 261:11
Land that I l.	BERL 30:5
Let's fall in l.	PORT 258:20
longing for l.	RUSS 278:5
l. affair with America	MAIL 211:7
l. and work	FREU 123:12
l. boat has crashed	LAST 191:2
L. consists in this	RILK 271:5
L., curiosity, freckles	PARK 249:7
l. does not consist in	SAIN 281:12
L. doesn't just sit there	LE G 195:9
L. Flames for a year	LAMP 188:5
L. has pitched his mansion	YEAT 344:10
l. human beings	GREE 137:11
l. in another's soul	LAYT 193:9
l. is a thing that can never	PARK 249:6
L. is a universal migraine	GRAV 137:3
L. is free	BENE 28:11
L. is given	HUGH 159:7
l. is given over-well	PARK 249:10
L. is here to stay	GERS 132:1
L. is just a system	BARN 23:15
L. is mutually feeding	HEAD 148:9
L. is one of the answers	PAZ 251:11
L. is the delusion	MENC 218:12
L. makes the world go round	MACK 208:2
L. means not ever having	TAGL 309:9
L.? Most natural painkiller	LAST 191:3
l. one another or die	AUDE 18:8
L. set you going	PLAT 255:15
l. that asks no question	SPRI 301:1
L. the Beloved Republic	FORS 121:6
l. them, and hold on	DUNN 94:7
L.-thirty, love-forty	BETJ 33:1
l. . . . whatever that may	CHAR 63:15
l. will steer the stars	RADO 265:4
l. without the rhetoric	STOP 305:15
l. you for yourself alone	YEAT 344:4
make l. in a canoe	BERT 32:1
Make l. not war	SAYI 286:22
man in l. is incomplete	GABO 128:2
Man's l. is of man's life	AMIS 8:6
man you l. to hate	TAGL 309:10
money can't buy me l.	LENN 196:14
Most people l. love	PAST 250:19
Need we say it was not l.	MILL 221:15
never l. a stranger	BENS 29:12
no l. for such	THOM 315:4
Onstage I make l.	JOPL 171:6
opposite of l.	WIES 335:2

people they l.	ADVE 4:22
revolution where l. not allowed	ANGE 9:7
right place for l.	FROS 124:12
search for l.	WAŁĘ 326:7
support of the woman I l.	EDWA 97:6
There is only l.	MCEW 207:7
they're in l.	TAGL 309:14
thought that l. would last	AUDE 17:7
tired of L.	BELL 27:11
to l. Levy's	ADVE 5:14
vividly gifted in l.	DUFF 93:8
When l. congeals	HART 146:12
Where l. rules	JUNG 173:7
who l., time is eternity	VAN 323:10
wilder shores of l.	BLAN 36:9
will survive of us is l.	LARK 189:1
Work is l. made visible	GIBR 132:10
You can only l. one war	GELL 130:13

loved l. you, so I drew these tides | LAWR 193:3

thirst to be l.	RHYS 269:14
wish I l. the Human Race	RALE 265:8

lovely l. woman stoops to folly | ELIO 103:7

on all things l.	DE L 88:4
Wouldn't it be l.	LERN 197:13

lover best l. in Vienna | SCHU 288:11

l. and killer are mingled	DOUG 92:5
l.'s quarrel with the world	FROS 125:8
what is left of a l.	ROWL 276:6

lovers l. and tribes | ONDA 243:8

Though l. be lost	THOM 314:1
wonder if it's l.	MULD 231:3

loves God l. them | HUME 160:9

lady l. Milk Tray	ADVE 3:5
life and l. of a she-devil	WELD 330:12
Who l. ya, baby	CATC 61:14
woman whom nobody l.	CORN 77:7

loving Can't help l. dat man | HAMM 142:12

discharge for l. one	EPIT 108:9

lowbrow first militant l. | BERL 30:16

lower capitalism of l. classes | SPEN 300:10

l. classes had such white	CURZ 82:3
l. than vermin	BEVA 33:4
While there is a l. class	DEBS 86:12

loyal Lousy but l. | SAYI 286:21

loyalties l. which centre upon | CHUR 69:5

tragic conflict of l.	HOWE 158:11

loyalty I want l. | JOHN 170:4

L. is the Tory's secret	KILM 180:6
l. we feel to unhappiness	GREE 137:12

LSD L.? Nothing much happened | AUDE 19:6

L. reminds me of minks	GRAV 137:6
PC is the L. of the '90s	LEAR 194:2

luck believes in l. | STEA 302:4

but it is l.	FORS 120:17
Good night, and good l.	BORR 40:12
Good night and good l.	CATC 59:6
L. is preparation	WINF 339:2

watching his l.	SERV 290:16
lucky l. if he gets out of it	FILM 114:13
lugubrious l. man in a suit	ELIZ 104:4
lullaby Once in a l.	HARB 144:8
lump had been a l. of clay	POPE 256:3
lumps l. in it	STEP 303:7
lunatic all in l. asylums	CHES 65:7
form the l. fringe	ROOS 275:1
lunatics lunatic asylum run by l.	LLOY 201:10
l. have taken charge	ROWL 276:8
lunch cork out of my l.	FIEL 111:12
ladies who l.	SOND 298:13
L. is for wimps	FILM 115:6
no such thing as a free l.	SAYI 287:6
unable to l. today	PORT 258:21
Universe is a free l.	GUTH 140:8
luncheon do not take soup at l.	CURZ 82:4
lunchtime L. doubly so	ADAM 2:4
lungs from froth-corrupted l.	OWEN 247:7
lures l. the truth	WESK 331:14
lust despair rather than l.	READ 267:11
horrible that l. and rage	YEAT 346:4
l. and calls it advertising	LAHR 187:4
l. and rape and incest	BENN 29:3
L., REVENGE, SEX	LEIS 195:14
to l. after it	LEWI 199:9
lusty call l. in foreign films	WILD 335:11
luxury To trust people is a l.	FORS 120:11
lying branch of the art of l.	CORN 77:9
listening, l. in wait	THOM 314:21
One of you is l.	PARK 249:14
Lyonnesse When I set out for L.	HARD 145:11
lyric now it's l. verse	WAUG 329:5
lyrics Writing song l.	PARI 249:3
M dreaded four M.'s	STRE 306:11
Macavity M. WASN'T THERE	ELIO 102:12
Macbeth I appeared as M.	HARG 145:17
Little Nell and Lady M.	WOOL 342:8
Macheath jack-knife has M.	BREC 43:11
machine desiccated calculating m.	BEVA 33:10
Ghost in the M.	RYLE 280:5
m. for living in	LE C 195:3
m. for turning red wine	DINE 91:2
sausage m.	CHRI 66:9
machines M. are the new proletariat	ATTA 16:3
M. are worshipped	RUSS 279:4
M. have less problems	WARH 327:13
whether m. think	SKIN 296:3
macht Arbeit m. frei	ANON 10:3
mad Everybody's a m. scientist	CRON 80:5
I'm m. as hell	FILM 114:9
M. about the boy	COWA 78:6
M. dogs and Englishmen	COWA 78:7
men that God made m.	CHES 64:7
Whom the m. would destroy	LEVI 198:11

madam globe-trotting M.	YEAT 346:7
made Here's one I m. earlier	CATC 59:11
I m. it	FILM 113:1
m., like bread	LE G 195:9
m. us what we were	BALL 22:4
Madeira M., m'dear	FLAN 118:6
madeleine little piece of m.	PROU 262:10
Madelon Ce n'est que M.	BOUS 41:9
mademoiselle M. from Armenteers	ANON 11:15
madhouse don't want m.	EMPS 105:13
madmen M. in authority	KEYN 179:4
madness destroyed through m.	GINS 133:3
m. is terrific	WOOL 342:5
M.! Madness	FILM 115:7
M. need not be breakdown	LAIN 187:9
m. of TV	PAGL 248:4
moment of m.	DAVI 84:8
magazines graves of little m.	PRES 261:10
magic indistinguishable from m.	CLAR 70:9
m. of Shaw's words	TAYL 310:9
mistake medicine for m.	SZAS 308:2
old black m.	MERC 219:12
tell you what I want. M.	WILL 336:14
tightness of the m. circle	MACL 208:7
magical it is a m. event	PRIE 261:15
magistrate shocks the m.	RUSS 279:6
magnificent M. desolation	ALDR 6:9
Mean, Moody and M.	TAGL 309:11
maid old m. is like death	FERB 110:10
maidens laughter of comely m.	DE V 89:9
maids Old m. biking	ORWE 245:13
mail deadlier than the m.	FRY 126:13
Night M. crossing the Border	AUDE 18:1
maimed M. us at the start	YEAT 345:15
maintain M. your rage	WHIT 334:12
maintenance art of motorcycle m.	PIRS 255:4
major change from m. to minor	PORT 258:15
Ground control to M. Tom	BOWI 42:2
With M. Major it had been	HELL 150:7
majority black m. rule	SMIT 296:14
m. are wrong	DEBS 86:11
silent m.	NIXO 239:4
what m. happen to like	WHIT 334:3
majors live with scarlet M.	SASS 284:15
make M. do and mend	OFFI 242:13
M. love not war	SAYI 286:22
m. my day	FILM 113:12
Scotsman on the m.	BARR 24:4
wrote M. IT NEW	POUN 259:11
maker Whether my M. is prepared	CHUR 68:15
making ways of m. you talk	CATC 61:11
maladjusted m. kids	HEST 152:10
male Every modern m.	BLY 37:8
existence of the m. sex	WEST 332:21
M. bonding	TIGE 316:7
m., middle class, middle-aged	STRE 306:11

male (*cont.*)

m. of the species	LAWR 192:12
more deadly than the m.	KIPL 182:2

malicious subtle but not m. EINS 98:5
malignant not m. and remove it WAUG 329:13
mama M. may have HOLI 156:2

m. of dada	FADI 109:2

mammon authentic m. MACN 209:15
man Any m. has to, needs to ELIO 102:16

better than M.	TAGL 309:13
century of the common m.	WALL 327:4
contact with this Wild M.	BLY 37:8
demolition of a m.	LEVI 198:9
everyone has sat except a m.	CUMM 81:4
fit night out for m. or beast	FIEL 111:14
from pig to m.	ORWE 245:3
Give a m. a free hand	WEST 332:7
God is a m.	NICH 236:7
had a crash with a m.	CART 56:5
hard m. is good to find	WEST 332:13
It's that m. again	NEWS 237:15
know a m. who can	ADVE 3:9
landing a m. on the Moon	KENN 177:10
led to *perdition* by a m.	WEST 332:22
m. at the gate of the year	HASK 147:5
m. bites a dog	BOGA 38:5
m. could ease a heart	PARK 249:13
m. got to do	STEI 303:1
M. grows beyond his work	STEI 302:14
M. hands on misery to man	LARK 189:7
m. in the house is worth	WEST 332:1
m. is dead	FROM 124:10
M. is the only creature	ORWE 244:15
m. you love to hate	TAGL 309:10
met a m. who wasn't there	MEAR 218:4
more like a m.	LERN 197:7
never done talking of M.	FANO 109:3
one small step for a m.	ARMS 14:11
said, ask a m.	THAT 312:3
saw a m. this morning	SHAW 293:19
Sir, no m.'s enemy	AUDE 18:12
Stand by your m.	WYNE 343:1
standing by my m.	CLIN 71:10
the m. who	CART 56:8
woman without a m.	SAYI 287:13
You'll be a M., my son	KIPL 182:9

management Australia's current m.

	JONE 170:12
m. of a balance of power	KISS 183:11
M. that wants to change	TUSA 319:12

manager No m. ever got fired ADVE 4:20
managing director M.'s chance WHIT 334:9
man-appeal gives a meal m. ADVE 4:21
mandarin M. style CONN 75:3
Manderley went to M. again DU M 93:10
mangrove together by m. roots BISH 35:2
manhood m. an opportunity KEIL 176:3

manifesto first powerful plain m. SPEN 300:3
man-in-the-street To the m. AUDE 17:18
mankind giant leap for m. ARMS 14:11

M. has done more damage	COUS 77:14
M. is on the move	SMUT 297:13
M. must put an end to war	KENN 177:11
M.'s moral test	KUND 185:14
no history of m.	POPP 256:7
not in Asia, was m. born	ARDR 14:3
study of m. is books	HUXL 161:5

manner All m. of thing shall be ELIO 101:10
manners automobile changed our m.

	KEAT 176:2
English m. more frightening	JARR 167:2

manoeuvre force with a m. TROT 318:1
mansion Love has pitched his m. YEAT 344:10
manufacture content to m. life BERN 30:17
manunkind busy monster, m. CUMM 81:6
manure liquid m. from the West SOLZ 298:9
many so much owed by so m. CHUR 67:8
map make a m. JONE 171:1

m.-makers' colours	BISH 35:3
showed a m. of the world	JAY 167:7

maps Dreams are m. SAGA 281:6

Geography is about M.	BENT 29:13

marathon fought near M. GRAV 137:2
march do not m. on Moscow MONT 227:6

don't m. as alternative	FITT 112:11
m. my troops towards	GRIM 139:7
m. towards it	CALL 51:1
Men who m. away	HARD 145:8

marching m., charging feet JAGG 166:4
Margaret It's me, M. BLUM 37:1
Marie I am M. of Roumania PARK 249:6
marijuana experimented with m. CLIN 72:1
marines M. took Iwo Jima ROSE 275:7
market enterprise of the m. ANON 10:8

m. has no morality	HESE 152:4
on m. research	RODD 272:7

Market Harborough AM IN M. TELE 311:1
market-place gathered in the m. CAVA 57:11
Marlowe quoting from this M. STAR 302:2
marriage Christian m. MARG 214:10

get anywhere in a m.	MURD 231:13
M. a wonderful invention	CONN 74:9
M. is a bribe	WILD 335:15
M. isn't a word	FILM 115:10
M. is popular because	SHAW 292:20
M. is waste-paper basket	WEBB 329:18
m. on the rocks	MERR 219:17
So that is m.	WOOL 342:1
support gay m.	FRIE 124:1
three of us in this m.	DIAN 90:6
value of m. is not	DE V 89:11

marriages All the unhappy m. WODE 339:12
married can't get m. at all FILM 116:7

getting m. in the morning	LERN 197:6

Getting you m. is not easy   SETH 291:1
incomplete until he has m.   GABO 128:2
m. beneath me   ASTO 15:12
m.—to be the more together   MACN 210:3
Onassis would not have m.   VIDA 325:8
trendy Smug M.   FIEL 111:7
usually m. to each other   LAND 188:8
very old m. couple   MACS 210:11
when they got m.   HOLI 156:3
marry freedom to m.   WARR 328:4
m. your mistress   GOLD 134:14
men we wanted to m.   STEI 303:5
Mars between the Earth and M.   RUSS 279:10
Martha had enough of M.   MACM 209:10
Martians understand than M.   SOLZ 298:3
Martini into a dry M.   FILM 115:3
martini olives in your m.   CARS 54:7
martyr regarded as a m.   KHOM 179:11
martyrdom m. must run its course   AUDE 17:17
marvel m. my birthday away   THOM 314:7
marvels to credit m.   HEAN 149:2
Marx illegitimate child of Karl M.   ATTL 16:7
in M.'s pages   SCHU 288:10
Marxism M. is sociobiology   WILS 337:12
more to Methodism than M.   PHIL 254:1
Marxist M.—Groucho tendency   ANON 11:10
Mary one Hail M.   DOYL 92:15
time for some M.   MACM 209:10
Mary Jane matter with M.   MILN 223:9
mascot best m. is a good mechanic   EARH 96:3
mask like a M. dancing   ACHE 1:6
m. that eats into the face   UPDI 321:10
masochistic m. form   OLIV 243:4
masons Where did the m. go   BREC 43:14
mass two thousand years of m.   HARD 144:13
Massachusetts denied in M.   MILL 220:14
masses calling 'em the m.   PRIE 262:1
If it is for the m.   SCHO 288:2
master Death is a m. from Germany   CELA 62:5
masterpiece knows, at sight, a m.   POUN 260:1
masters never wrong, the Old M.   AUDE 17:16
We are not the m.   BLAI 35:14
We are the m. now   MISQ 225:5
mastery I had m.   OWEN 247:10
mastodons like m. bellowing   WODE 340:3
masturbation Don't knock m.   ALLE 7:6
M. is the thinking   HAMP 143:12
m. of war   RAE 265:5
matched m. us with His hour   BROO 45:4
matches have a box of m.   HOME 156:10
with that stick of m.   MAND 213:8
matching M. lips and fingertips   ADVE 4:12
matchstalk painted m. men   COLE 73:6
materialistic m. of religions   TEMP 311:12
materials His dark m.   BORR 40:15
mateship as dearly as m.   ANON 13:1

mathematician appear as a pure m.   JEAN 167:10
mathematics avoid pregnancy by m.   MENC 219:2
In m. you don't   NEUM 236:3
M. may be defined   RUSS 278:16
M., rightly viewed   RUSS 278:17
no place for ugly m.   HARD 144:12
Matilda M. told such Dreadful Lies   BELL 27:8
matter Does it m.   SASS 284:16
not fighting does m.   STEP 303:9
position of m.   RUSS 278:13
What is the m.   MILN 223:9
You m.   SAUN 285:5
mattering can go on m.   BOWE 41:12
matters m. in your life   RUSH 277:13
Nobody that m.   MILL 220:10
What can I do that m.   SPEN 300:9
mattress crack it open on a m.   MILL 222:4
maturing mind is m. late   NASH 234:12
mausoleum used as its m.   AMIS 8:4
may M. to December   ANDE 8:11
maybe definite m.   GOLD 135:7
M., just maybe   ADVE 4:13
mayor watch the m.   LETT 198:1
MBEs looking for your M.   KEAT 175:13
McCarthyism M. [cartoon text]   CART 57:3
M. is Americanism   MCCA 205:9
McNamara M.'s War   MCNA 209:11
me For you but not for m.   ANON 12:4
M. Decade   WOLF 340:18
meal building a m.   MEND 219:5
gives a m. man-appeal   ADVE 4:21
m. was never found   ULLM 321:2
mean depends what you m. by   CATC 60:4
Down these m. streets   CHAN 63:3
even if you don't m. it   TRUM 318:16
Know what I m., Harry   BRUN 46:13
M., Moody and Magnificent   TAGL 309:11
poem should not m. but be   MACL 208:6
whatever that may m.   CHAR 63:15
meaning emptied of m.   CAMU 52:16
Is there a m. to music   COPL 77:4
joke with a double m.   BARK 23:7
language charged with m.   POUN 260:6
m. doubtless objectionable   ANON 12:12
missed the m.   ELIO 101:2
real m. lies underneath   CARE 53:12
meaningless money is m.   ONAS 243:5
meanings With words and m.   ELIO 100:16
means decide all m. are permitted   DAWS 85:7
end cannot justify the m.   HUXL 161:6
ends and scarce m.   ROBB 271:8
Whatever 'in love' m.   DUFF 93:8
meant it's what I m.   VAUG 324:7
'w-a-t-e-r' m. the wonderful   KELL 176:6
measles m. of the human race   EINS 99:8

measured m. out my life   ELIO 102:5
measurements easier to make m.   SULL 307:3
mechanic best mascot is a good m.   EARH 96:3
mechanized m. slaughterhouses   VANE 324:1
medal m. for killing two men   EPIT 108:9
media exposed to the m.   BOWI 42:4
  m. It sounds like   STOP 305:11
medical in advance of m. thought   WODE 340:4
medicinal M. discovery   AYRE 19:19
medicine mistake m. for magic   SZAS 308:2
mediocre middle-aged and m.   STRE 306:11
  Some men are born m.   HELL 150:7
mediocrity m. of the apparatus   TROT 318:2
  m. thrust upon them   HELL 150:7
Mediterranean cooking of the m.   DAVI 84:6
medium best m. of all   BERN 31:3
  call it a m. because   ACE 1:5
  m. is the message   MCLU 208:11
  mother and m.   SZEN 308:8
meet m. 'em on your way down   MIZN 226:7
  We'll m. again   PARK 250:10
meeting great ordeal of m. me   CHUR 68:15
megalith M.-still   HUGH 160:1
Mehmets between the Johnnies and the M.
                               ATAT 15:13
melody m. lingers on   BERL 30:8
  pretty girl is like a m.   BERL 30:7
melting-pot M. where all races   ZANG 348:3
member accept me as a m.   MARX 216:5
memoirs write m. is to speak ill   PÉTA 253:4
memorandum m. is written   ACHE 1:10
memorials there are no m.   YEVT 346:16
memories m. are card-indexes   CONN 75:5
  m. are hunting horns   APOL 13:10
memory Footfalls echo in the m.   ELIO 100:11
  God gave us m.   BARR 24:5
  m. revealed itself   PROU 262:10
  M. says: Want   RICH 270:9
  no force can abolish m.   ROOS 274:5
  No m. of having starred   FROS 125:14
  Poor people's m.   CAMU 52:5
  quits the m. with difficulty   BEEC 26:12
  sense them like a m.   MOSE 229:11
  stay in a man's m.   KIPL 183:8
  Thanks for the m.   ROBI 271:10
men all m. are rapists   FREN 123:2
  how much m. hate them   GREE 138:5
  I eat m. like air   PLAT 255:14
  If m. could get pregnant   KENN 176:10
  m. are like bloody buses   COPE 77:1
  M. are so honest   LERN 197:7
  M. at forty   JUST 173:12
  M. eat hogs   STEV 303:16
  m. hurrying back   MULD 231:3
  M. seldom make passes   PARK 249:8
  M.! the only animal to fear   LAWR 192:14
  m. we wanted to marry   STEI 303:5

  m. who are discriminated   MEIR 218:10
  M. who march away   HARD 145:8
  m. with the muck-rakes   ROOS 274:10
  not the m. in my life that counts   WEST 332:6
  treat m. like possessions   COLL 73:11
  war between m. and women   THUR 316:3
  We are the hollow m.   ELIO 101:14
menace m. to be defeated   SCAR 285:13
mend Make do and m.   OFFI 242:13
mental Freedom and slavery are m.   GAND 129:9
  m. processes   HALD 142:2
Mercedes buy me a M. Benz   JOPL 171:4
merciless looked at in m. glare   WILL 336:13
mercury pick up m. with a fork   LLOY 201:12
mercy I want m.   HUGH 160:6
mermaids heard the m. singing   ELIO 102:8
merrygoround It's no go the m.   MACN 209:16
Mesopotamia led in M.   LAWR 193:4
mess Another fine m.   LAUR 191:15
  m. we have made of things   ELIO 100:8
message if there is a m.   PAXM 251:7
  medium is the m.   MCLU 208:11
  m. of your play   BEHA 26:19
messages m. should be delivered   GOLD 135:9
messenger m.-boy Presidency   SCHL 287:15
met m. his own deadline   EPIT 107:9
  m. the enemy   CART 56:12
  We m. at nine   LERN 197:8
metaphor it's a lovely m.   LOVE 203:6
metaphysical m. brothel   KOES 184:12
Methodism more to M. than Marxism
                               PHIL 254:1
Mexico gringo in m.   FUEN 126:15
mice as long as it catches m.   DENG 89:3
  slept with m.   COWA 78:19
Michelangelo M. left a proof   YEAT 346:7
  Talking of M.   ELIO 102:3
microphone paid for this m.   REAG 268:1
middle in the m. of the road   BEVA 33:6
  m. of the road   YOUN 347:4
  Secret sits in the m.   FROS 125:16
middle age dead centre of m.   ADAM 2:5
  pleasures of m.   POUN 260:4
  reckless m.   YEAT 345:13
middle-aged Grown m.   WINT 339:4
Middle Ages go and live in the M.   SMIT 297:8
middle class m. morality   SHAW 293:6
midnight Holding hands at m.   GERS 132:2
  M. Without Pity   JOHN 169:5
  stroke of the m. hour   NEHR 235:6
might Britons alone use 'M.'   WAUG 329:10
migraine Love is a universal m.   GRAV 137:3
miles m. to go before I sleep   FROS 125:20
militant first m. lowbrow   BERL 30:16
  m. pacifist   EINS 98:10
military close my m. career   MACA 205:5
  entrust to m. men   CLEM 71:7

m. man approaches	SHAW 292:14	**Mineworkers** National Union of M.	
milk end is moo, the other, m.	NASH 234:4		MACM 209:8
Gin was mother's m.	SHAW 293:7	**minister** Yes, M.! No, Minister	CROS 80:14
lady loves M. Tray	ADVE 3:5	**ministers** 'experts' make the worst M.	
m. and the yoghurt	TRIL 317:10		ATTL 16:9
M.'s leap toward immortality	FADI 109:1	how much my M. talk	THAT 312:8
m. the cow of the world	WILB 335:7	m. decide	THAT 313:9
putting m. into babies	CHUR 68:5	**mink** trick of wearing m.	BALM 22:9
milka Drinka Pinta M. Day	ADVE 3:17	**minks** LSD reminds me of m.	GRAV 137:6
million Fifty m. Frenchmen	MILI 221:5	**minor** change from major to m.	PORT 258:15
make a m.	ANON 11:4	**minorities** treats its m.	LÉVE 198:8
m. deaths a statistic	STAL 301:12	**minority** not enough to make a m.	ALTM 7:17
m. million spermatozoa	HUXL 161:13	**mint** m. with the hole	ADVE 4:14
millionaire I am a M.	SHAW 292:4	**minute** cannot cage the m.	MACN 210:7
old-fashioned m.	FISH 112:9	fill the unforgiving m.	KIPL 182:9
Who wants to be a m.	PORT 259:1	**minutes** famous for fifteen m.	WARH 327:8
millions I will be m.	EPIT 108:1	have the seven m.	COLL 74:1
M. long for immortality	ERTZ 106:4	**miracle** is m. enough	PEAK 251:12
that of m. of others	LOEW 202:2	m. of sorts	GRAH 136:8
mimic we m. men	NAIP 233:12	**miracles** believe in m.	FOX 122:1
minarets Fretted with m.	THWA 316:6	**Miranda** remember an Inn, M.	BELL 28:1
mind all in the m.	WOLF 340:12	**mirror** in the rear m.	RODD 272:7
beat at your m.	HECH 149:14	m. to national attitudes	KUNZ 185:16
Cast your m. on other days	YEAT 346:9	**mirrors** live without m.	ATWO 16:11
could not make up his m.	OLIV 243:2	**miserable** Heaven knows I'm m.	MORR 229:3
cutting edge of the m.	BRON 44:9	m. as the rest of us	FRIE 124:1
don't m. if I do	CATC 59:16	**misery** Man hands on m. to man	LARK 189:7
empires of the m.	CHUR 68:6	**misfits** m., Looney Tunes	REAG 268:6
Georgia on my m.	GORR 136:3	**misguided** missiles and m. men	KING 180:17
losing your m.	FOX 121:12	**mislead** one to m. the public	ASQU 15:9
m. begins to roam	SOLZ 298:3	**misleading** bound to be m.	WATS 328:10
m. enclosed in language	WEIL 330:6	**misquotation** M. is the privilege	PEAR 252:1
M. in its purest play	WILB 335:8	**misrule** Thirteen years of Tory m.	POLI 258:9
m. is just like a spin-dryer	NOLA 239:12	**missed** m. the bus	CHAM 62:10
m. is maturing late	NASH 234:12	Woman much m.	HARD 145:10
M. my bike	CATC 60:14	**misses** m. family and friends	EPIT 108:2
m. of the oppressed	BIKO 34:7	**missiles** guided m. and misguided	KING 180:17
m. the least of possessions	WHIT 333:11	**missing** m. a couple of car payments	
m. watches itself	CAMU 52:8		WILS 337:10
m. which reveres details	LEWI 199:14	**missionaries** eaten by m.	SPOO 300:13
not to have a m.	QUAY 264:4	**Mississippi** singing of the M.	HUGH 159:9
no way out of the m.	PLAT 255:9	**mistake** America a gigantic m.	FREU 123:14
out of my m.	BELL 28:4	author made a m.	DIRA 91:5
sex in the m.	LAWR 192:13	have made a great m.	MORS 229:4
travel broadens the m.	CHES 65:11	make a m., it's a beaut	LA G 187:2
Until reeled the m.	GIBB 132:7	m. shall not be repeated	EPIT 108:4
violence in the m.	ALDI 6:8	Shome m., shurely	CATC 61:1
Why m. being wrong	AYER 19:18	**mistakes** genius makes no m.	JOYC 172:11
would know the m. of God	HAWK 148:1	If he makes m.	CHUR 69:5
mindful M. of the Church's teaching		M. are a fact	GIOV 133:7
	MARG 214:10	some of the worst m.	HEIS 150:4
minds M. like beds always made up	WILL 336:16	**mistress** marry your m.	GOLD 134:14
m. of ordinary men	BRON 44:11	m. knows the man	UPDI 321:11
paid to have dirty m.	TREV 317:8	**misunderstood** don't want to be m.	
mine lovin' dat man of m.	HAMM 142:12		FRUM 126:5
she is m. for life	SPAR 299:9	through being m.	COCT 72:15
mines m. reported in the fairway	KIPL 182:12	**mites** with m. of stars	MAYA 217:12

Mitty Walter M., the undefeated   THUR 316:4
moanday m., tearsday, wailsday   JOYC 171:11
mob I lied to please the m.   KIPL 181:15
mockingbird kill a m.   LEE 195:6
model provide logical m.   LÉVI 198:13
   you are a m.   HOCK 155:8
moderate person of m. means   EAST 96:4
   white m. devoted to   KING 180:10
moderation m. in the pursuit   GOLD 135:1
   M. the highest virtue   JOHN 170:1
modern All art was m. once   SERO 290:12
   spirit of m. life   CLIF 71:9
modernity M. is the transition   SACK 281:1
modest good deal to be m. about   CHUR 68:14
molecule inhales one m. of it   JEAN 167:8
molecules without understanding m.
     CRIC 79:9
moll King's M. Reno'd   NEWS 237:17
mom place called M.'s   ALGR 6:11
moment Exhaust the little m.   BROO 45:8
   if only for a m.   SZYM 308:10
   m. of awakening   COET 72:17
   m. of madness   DAVI 84:8
   one brief shining m.   LERN 197:5
momentary Beauty m. in the mind   STEV 304:3
Mona Lisa reaction to the M.   ROYK 276:13
monarch m. of the road   FLAN 118:9
monarchy US presidency a Tudor m.   BURG 48:4
money ain't got a barrel of m.   WOOD 341:8
   bank will lend you m. if   HOPE 157:9
   Capitalism is using its m.   CAST 57:6
   corrupted by m.   GREE 137:10
   costs a lot of m.   PART 250:17
   divided up their m.   STEA 302:3
   Follow the m.   FILM 113:10
   hain't the m., but th' principle   HUBB 159:2
   haven't got the m.   RUTH 280:1
   He had m. as well   THAT 312:7
   Hollywood m. isn't money   PARK 250:5
   if you can count your m.   GETT 132:4
   licence to print your own m.   THOM 315:11
   listen to m. singing   LARK 189:11
   long enough to get m. from   LEAC 193:12
   lost m. by underestimating   MENC 219:3
   m. can't buy me love   LENN 196:14
   M. couldn't buy friends   MILL 222:13
   M. doesn't talk, it swears   DYLA 95:6
   M. gives me pleasure   BELL 27:11
   m. goes with the wind   SIMP 295:8
   m.-grabbing cronies   HAGU 141:1
   m. gushes into politics   WHIT 333:13
   M. is like a sixth sense   MAUG 217:3
   m. is meaningless   ONAS 243:5
   m. I spend on advertising   LEVE 198:5
   M., money, money   ANDE 9:2
   M. was exactly like sex   BALD 21:5
   Never ask of m. spent   FROS 125:6

   not having any m.   WHIT 334:8
   not spending m. alone   EISE 99:12
   only interested in m.   SHAW 293:14
   poet can earn more m.   AUDE 19:1
   poetry in m.   GRAV 137:5
   possible to make m.   BLAN 36:11
   rub up against m.   RUNY 277:17
   Show me the m.   FILM 116:3
   Sound m. is the oldest   OSBO 246:12
   Take the m. and run   FILM 117:13
   talking real m.   DIRK 91:6
   they have more m.   FITZ 117:14
   They hired the m.   COOL 76:7
   use the m. for the poor   PERÓ 252:9
   voice is full of m.   FITZ 117:17
   voter who uses his m.   SAMU 283:2
   Weapons are like m.   AMIS 8:10
   When you have m., it's sex   DONL 92:1
mongrels energetic m.   FISH 112:6
monkey attack the m.   BEVA 33:8
   make a m. of a man   BENC 28:6
monkeys cheese-eating surrender m.
     GROE 139:9
   m. banging on typewriters   WILE 335:17
   m. in the jungle   CASH 55:11
   m. strumming on typewriters   EDDI 96:7
   of the Arctic M.   BROW 46:3
   you get m.   SAYI 286:18
monks m. at Clonmacnoise   HEAN 149:3
monogamy M. is the same   ANON 10:5
monologue m. is not a decision   ATTL 16:4
monologues Intersecting m.   WEST 332:16
monopoly best of all m. profits   HICK 153:5
   m. stage of capitalism   LENI 196:1
Monroe mouth of Marilyn M.   MITT 226:6
monster busy m., manunkind   CUMM 81:6
monstrous m. carbuncle   CHAR 63:16
   M. carbuncles   SPEN 300:1
month April is the cruellest m.   ELIO 102:19
   m. of tension   LESS 197:18
monument m. sticks like fishbone   LOWE 203:10
monuments smashing m.   LEC 194:13
moo One end is m.   NASH 234:4
   Silly m.   CATC 61:2
moocow m. coming down along the road
     JOYC 171:14
moody Mean, M. and Magnificent   TAGL 309:11
moon Dark side of the m.   PINK 254:12
   Don't let's ask for the m.   FILM 113:3
   landing a man on the M.   KENN 177:10
   land on the m.   KOES 184:16
   looking at the full m.   GINS 133:4
   m. belongs to everyone   DE S 89:6
   m. in lonely alleys   CRAN 79:3
   m. is in the seventh house   RADO 265:4
   m. shone bright   ELIO 103:4
   m., the stars   TRUM 318:8

m. walks the night	DE L 88:8	m. of all battles	HUSS 161:2
Old Devil M. in your eyes	HARB 144:7	m. of all treachery	PAIS 248:8
only a paper m.	HARB 144:6	M. of Five Voice	PELO 252:4
Only you beneath the m.	PORT 258:18	M. of the Free	BENS 29:11
wanted the m.	STEI 302:13	m.'s little helper	JAGG 166:2
moonlight m. and music	BERL 30:6	m. will be there	HERB 151:12
M. behind you	COWA 78:10	my father and my m.	JENN 168:1
moonlit Knocking on the m. door	DE L 88:5	rob his m.	FAUL 110:5
moral don't have a m. plan	CRON 80:6	Took great care of his M.	MILN 223:6
It *is* a m. issue	NEWS 237:14	**mothers** Come m. and fathers	DYLA 95:14
Mankind's m. test	KUND 185:14	m. who sent their sons	ATAT 15:13
No m. system can rest	AYER 19:14	**mothers-in-law** m. and Wigan Pier	BRID 44:4
party is a m. crusade	WILS 338:5	**Mother Teresa** Hemingway and M.	LAPI 188:10
purely m. act	HAVE 147:8	**motion** poetry in m.	KAUF 175:3
moralists delight to m.	RUSS 279:5	**motorcycle** art of m. maintenance	PIRS 255:4
morality Goodbye, m.	HERB 151:15	**mould** frozen in an out-of-date m.	JENK 167:12
know about m.	CAMU 52:17	**mountain** Climb ev'ry m.	HAMM 142:13
market has no m.	HESE 152:4	go up to the m.	KING 180:15
middle-class m.	SHAW 293:6	In a m. greenery	HART 146:14
M.'s a gesture	BOLT 38:11	last blue m.	FLEC 118:12
two kinds of m.	RUSS 279:2	living near a m.	WELT 331:12
What is m.	WHIT 334:3	**mountains** For us, the m.	HERZ 152:1
morals Food first, then m.	BREC 43:12	**mourn** no cause to m.	OWEN 247:9
more knows m. and more	MAYO 217:15	**mourners** let the m. come	AUDE 17:6
Less is m.	MIES 220:7	**mourning** Don't waste time in m.	HILL 154:2
m. and more about less	BUTL 49:10	M. becomes Electra	O'NE 243:12
m. equal than others	ORWE 245:2	**mouse** invention of a m.	DISN 91:8
m. Piglet wasn't there	MILN 222:16	that damned M.	MAYE 217:13
m. than somewhat	RUNY 277:11	**mouth** Englishman to open his m.	SHAW 293:3
M. will mean worse	AMIS 8:7	Keep your m. shut	OFFI 242:17
morning arrested one fine m.	KAFK 174:5	m. of Marilyn Monroe	MITT 226:6
autumn arrives in the m.	BOWE 41:10	m. used as a latrine	AMIS 8:4
getting married in the m.	LERN 197:6	My m. went across	NERU 235:12
Good m., sir	CATC 59:5	poet's m. be silent	YEAT 345:12
hate myself in the m.	LARD 188:11	silver foot in his m.	RICH 270:12
m. again in America	POLI 257:19	Word of m. is the best	BERN 31:3
M. has broken	FARJ 109:6	z is keeping your m. shut	EINS 99:2
take you in the m.	BALD 21:7	**mouthful** filling in a m. of decay	OSBO 246:18
We lied m., noon and night	GYUR 140:11	**mouths** examining his wives' m.	RUSS 278:12
what a beautiful m.	HAMM 143:5	stuffed their m. with gold	BEVA 33:13
Mornington M. Crescent	HARG 145:17	**movable** Paris is a m. feast	HEMI 151:2
Morocco we're M. bound	BURK 48:6	**move** feel the earth m.	HEMI 150:13
moron consumer isn't a m.	OGIL 241:12	**moved** We shall not be m.	SAYI 287:9
IQ of a m.	VIDA 325:9	**moves** If it m., salute it	MILI 221:6
Morris M. Minor prototype	NUFF 240:6	**movie** book by its m.	EAGA 96:1
mortar Lies are the m.	WELL 331:5	good m. can take you out of	KAEL 174:3
Moscow do not march on M.	MONT 227:6	m. was shot in 3B	FILM 116:5
mosquito just another m.	OKPI 242:22	**movies** able to talk about m.	KAEL 174:2
moss Kate M. would be used as	FREN 123:1	M. should have a beginning	GODA 134:5
mother artist man and m. woman	SHAW 292:10	pay to see bad m.	GOLD 135:6
Can you hear me, m.	CATC 58:10	thing that can kill the m.	ROGE 272:13
cry at his m.'s funeral	CAMU 52:10	**Mozart** no female M.	PAGL 248:5
Did this happen to your m.	WALK 326:8	**MP** Being an M.	ABBO 1:1
have a beautiful m.	WALK 326:11	Being an M.	PARR 250:16
I have been a m. to you	O'DO 241:11	**much** so m. owed by so many	CHUR 67:8
m. and medium	SZEN 308:8	**muckrakes** men with the m.	ROOS 274:10
M. died today	CAMU 52:9	**mud** M.! Glorious mud	FLAN 118:7

mud (*cont.*)

  pure clay of time's m.　MALA 212:2
mudging fudging and m.　OWEN 247:1
mugged liberal who has been m.　SAYI 286:7
Mulligan plump Buck M.　JOYC 172:6
multiply m. deadlines by pi　RYLE 280:6
multitude m. of tongues　HAND 143:15
mum fuck you up, your m. and dad　LARK 189:6
  oafish louts remember M.　BETJ 32:4
mumble When in doubt, m.　BORE 39:7
mumbo-jumbo enough of the m.　GUIN 140:5
murder about a m.　ORWE 245:6
  brought m. into the home　HITC 154:11
  commit a m.　VAN 323:9
  decided to m. his wife　ILES 162:4
  m. by the throat　LLOY 201:7
  m. men everywhere　FANO 109:3
  m. respectable　ORWE 246:5
  m. the thinker　WESK 331:15
  not m. but the restoration　JAME 166:15
  to m., for the truth　ADLE 2:10
  We hear war called m.　MACD 207:3
murdered human beings were m.　WIES 335:5
murderer m. for fancy prose style　NABO 233:2
  shoot your m.　ACHE 1:7
murderers m. of Jewish children　WIES 335:4
Murdoch wrapped in a M. newspaper　ROYK 276:12
muscles M. better and nerves more　CUMM 81:9
muse Why does my M. only speak　SMIT 297:6
museum ace caff with a nice m.　ADVE 3:2
  m. inside our heads　LIVE 200:14
mush m. and slush　OWEN 247:1
mushroom supramundane m.　LAUR 192:2
  too short to stuff a m.　CONR 75:13
music all m. is folk music　ARMS 14:9
  Beauty in m.　IVES 163:10
  body swayed to m.　YEAT 344:3
  country and western m.　SMIT 297:1
  dance to the m. of time　BORR 40:8
  day the m. died　MCLE 208:4
  don't like my m.　LOEW 202:2
  English may not like m.　BEEC 26:13
  Good m. is that which　BEEC 26:12
  how potent cheap m. is　COWA 78:14
  I got m.　GERS 131:12
  Is there a meaning to m.　COPL 77:4
  Jazz is the only m.　COLE 73:7
  Let's face the m. and dance　BERL 30:6
  most civilized m.　USTI 322:1
  M. begins to atrophy　POUN 260:3
  m. business is not　MORR 229:2
  m. expresses itself　STRA 306:9
  M. is feeling, then　STEV 304:2
  M. is life　IVES 163:11
  M. is your own experience　PARK 249:5
  m. that survives is　ROSE 275:4

  m. the brandy of the damned　SHAW 292:11
  m. was pretty phenomenal　JOHN 168:8
  My m. is best understood　STRA 306:8
  sound of m.　HAMM 143:8
  twang, and you've got m.　VICI 325:1
  What do you think about m.　VAUG 324:8
  What m. is more enchanting　SMIT 297:2
  What the m. says　BOWI 42:3
  worth expressing in m.　DELI 88:12
  Writing about m.　ANON 13:4
musician m., if he's a messenger　HEND 151:8
Muslims zealous M. to execute　KHOM 179:11
must you m. go on　BECK 25:11
mutilate fold, spindle or m.　SAYI 286:11
myriad There died a m.　POUN 259:15
mystery grasped m. of the atom　BRAD 42:10
  I had m.　OWEN 247:10
  riddle wrapped in a m.　CHUR 67:2
myth m. not a fairy story　RYLE 280:4
  purpose of m.　LÉVI 198:13
  thing itself and not the m.　RICH 270:8
myths Science must begin with m.　POPP 256:8

nabobs nattering n.　AGNE 5:19
nagging N. is the repetition　SUMM 307:6
nail I n. my pictures together　SCHW 289:4
nailing n. his colours　FIEL 111:6
naive n. domestic Burgundy　CART 56:6
  n. forgive and forget　SZAS 307:14
naked n. ape　MORR 228:9
  n. into the conference chamber　BEVA 33:9
  swimming n.　BUFF 47:10
name except her mother's maiden n.　VREE 325:14
  In the n. of God, go　AMER 8:2
  know, yet can't quite n.　LARK 189:5
  n. at the top of the page　CHUR 68:19
  n. is history　THWA 316:6
  n. liveth for ever　SASS 285:1
  n. liveth for evermore　EPIT 108:7
  Not in my n.　SAYI 287:1
  prefer a self-made n.　HAND 143:16
  problem that has no n.　FRIE 123:15
  problem that has no n.　FRIE 123:17
  state with the prettiest n.　BISH 35:2
named N. Shamed　NEWS 237:18
names confused things with n.　SART 284:7
  in love with American n.　BENÉ 28:12
  n. of all these particles　FERM 110:12
naming n. of parts　REED 268:10
napalm n. in the morning　FILM 114:7
Napoleon thinks he is N.　CLEM 71:4
Napoleons Caesars and N.　HUXL 161:7
narrative descriptive n.　EPHR 106:2
nastier how much n. I would be　WAUG 329:14
nasty n. in the woodshed　GIBB 132:6

new (*cont.*)

New Labour, n. danger	POLI 258:4
n. world order	BUSH 49:2
nothing n. in dying	LAST 190:10
pulse of this n. day	ANGE 9:5
shock of the n.	DUNL 94:3
so quite n. a thing	CUMM 81:9
threshold of a n. house	ATWO 16:10
wrote MAKE IT N.	POUN 259:11
Youth is something very n.	CHAN 63:9

New England charge against N. — KRUT 185:8

news good day to bury bad n. — MISQ 224:7

good n. yet to hear	CHES 64:15
HERE IS THE N.	HEAN 149:7
how much n. there is	DOUG 92:8
man bites a dog, that is n.	BOGA 38:5
news that STAYS n.	POUN 260:5
told bad n. to American	KEIL 176:4

New South Wales govern N. — BELL 27:7

newspaper make a great n. — BRAD 42:8

Murdoch n.	ROYK 276:12
n. is a nation talking	MILL 222:9
n. is to be Accurate	SWOP 307:10
n. touches a story	MAIL 211:11

newspapers burlesque and the n. — STON 305:6

n. I can't stand	STOP 305:12
N., television networks	STEW 304:17
read the n. avidly	BEVA 33:12
writing for the n.	LEWI 199:15

New York kind of N. — USTI 322:5

N. is so clean now	BOY 42:7
N. makes one think	BELL 28:5
present in N.	CHAP 63:14
three o'clock in N.	MIDL 220:6

New Yorker N. will be — ROSS 275:8

next n. to god america — CUMM 81:3

used to be the n. president	GORE 136:1

nice all the n. people — SPAR 299:7

involving not very n. people	FRAN 122:8
Naughty but n.	ADVE 4:17
N. guys. Finish last	DURO 94:9
N. one, Cyril	ADVE 4:19
n. to people on your way up	MIZN 226:7
N. to see you	CATC 60:15
N. work if you can get it	GERS 132:2
not about being n.	KEAT 176:1
thoroughly n. people	PYM 263:6

nicely That'll do n. — ADVE 3:4

nicens n. little boy — JOYC 171:14

niche your n. in creation — HALL 142:8

Nigeria daughter of N. — EMEC 105:8

nigger n. of the world — ONO 243:14

night blue of the n. — CROS 80:8

dark n. of the soul	FITZ 117:21
fit n. out for man or beast	FIEL 111:14
gentle into that good n.	THOM 314:2
hard day's n.	LENN 196:17

Illness the n.-side of life	SONT 299:1
journey into n.	O'NE 243:11
language of the n.	LE G 195:10
moon walks the n.	DE L 88:8
N. and day	PORT 258:18
N. Mail crossing the Border	AUDE 18:1
n. of the long knives	HITL 154:13
N., snow, and sand	NERU 235:11
n. starvation	ADVE 3:28
something of the n.	WIDD 335:1
terrible n.	PORT 259:2
We lied morning, noon and n.	GYUR 140:11

nightclubs able to pass n. — DOCH 91:10

nightgowns tweed n. — GING 133:1

nightingale n. sang in Berkeley — MASC 216:10

nightingales n. are singing near — ELIO 102:18

nightmare History is a n. — JOYC 172:10

In the n. of the dark	AUDE 17:12
national n. is over	FORD 119:12

nightmares Don't have n. — CATC 58:17

n. about two things	STOC 305:4

ninety n.-minute patriots — SILL 294:11

nix Sticks n. hick pix — NEWS 238:3

Nixon N. impeached himself — ABZU 1:3

no can't say N. in any of them — PARK 250:1

It's n. go the merrygoround	MACN 209:16
Just say n.	OFFI 242:10
man who says n.	CAMU 52:12
N.! No! No	THAT 313:11
she said 'n.'	ALLE 7:11
We say N.	WRIG 342:13
Yeah but n. but	CATC 61:16

Noah N. he often said to his wife — CHES 65:3

one poor N.	HUXL 161:13

Nobel dinner for N. Prizewinners — KENN 177:13

nobility n. without pride — DUNC 94:2

noble days of the N. Savage — BIKO 34:6

nobody N. came — GINS 133:2

n. knows you're a dog	CART 56:10
n.'s going to stop 'em	BERR 31:12
n.'s perfect	FILM 116:7
n. tells me anything	GALS 129:4
n. will come	SAND 283:8
Nothing happens, n. comes	BECK 26:3
there is n. there	KEYN 179:9

nod Old N., the shepherd — DE L 88:7

one great n. after the other	NOLA 239:12

noise Go placidly amid the n. — EHRM 98:1

loud n. at one end	KNOX 184:10
love the n. it makes	BEEC 26:13
n.! And the people	ANON 12:1
n. is an effective means	GOEB 134:8

noisy into the n. crowd — TAGO 309:18

non-being avoiding n. — TILL 316:8

non-cooperation n. with evil — GAND 129:11

nonexistent obsolescent and n. — BREN 44:2

non-violence N. the first article — GAND 129:10

no one rule of n.   MCCA 206:2
Norfolk bear him up the N. sky   BETJ 32:7
  Very flat, N.   COWA 78:13
normal N. is the good smile   SHAF 291:7
north answer from the N.   KIPL 183:1
  heart of the N. is dead   LAWR 192:22
  He was my N., my South   AUDE 17:7
  to us the near n.   MENZ 219:7
North America Mr and Mrs N.   CATC 59:3
northern N. reticence   HEAN 149:8
nose run up your n. dead against   BALD 22:1
  thirty inches from my n.   AUDE 18:4
  very shiny n.   MARK 214:13
noses turn up our n.   SHIE 294:4
  where the n. would go   HEMI 150:12
nostalgia N. isn't what it used   ANON 12:2
not n. I, but the wind   LAWR 192:18
  N. in my name   SAYI 287:1
  N. so much a programme   ANON 12:3
  N. while I'm alive   BEVI 34:3
  say 'Why n.'   SHAW 291:11
note longest suicide n.   KAUF 175:2
  same n. can be played   COLE 73:7
notebook in a little n.   LASK 189:15
notes n. I handle no better   SCHN 288:1
nothing and n. on   SPRI 301:5
  don't believe in n.   CHES 65:15
  Emperors can do n.   BREC 43:8
  individually can do n.   ALLE 7:3
  like n. one has seen before   WALC 326:4
  men who are n.   NAIP 233:9
  not enough to do n.   BUFF 47:11
  N. ain't worth nothin'   KRIS 185:7
  n. forces itself on me   RAVE 267:4
  N. gold can stay   FROS 125:12
  N. happens, nobody comes   BECK 26:3
  N. is ever done   SHAW 292:8
  N. is more dangerous   ALAI 6:5
  N., like something   LARK 189:4
  N. to be done   BECK 25:12
  n. to look backward to   FROS 124:15
  n. to say   CAGE 50:4
  n. was created in the West Indies   NAIP 233:11
  say n.   HEAN 149:8
  You ain't heard n. yet   JOLS 170:11
nothingness N. haunts being   SART 284:3
notice not escaped our n.   CRIC 79:11
  taken no n. of   HARE 145:13
noun verb not a n.   FULL 127:2
novel n. is the one bright book   LAWR 192:7
  n. tells a story   FORS 120:6
novelists great—the major n.   LEAV 194:6
  n. are often appalling   CARE 53:14
novels you lose two n.   MCWI 210:12
now not right n.   JAY 167:6
  We are the masters n.   MISQ 225:5
nowness n. of everything   POTT 259:3

nuclear n. giants   BRAD 42:11
nudge nudge n., snap snap   MONT 227:8
nuisance exchange of one n.   ELLI 105:2
  n. in time of war   CHUR 68:7
nuisances small n. of peace-time   HAY 148:4
NUM against the Pope or the N.   BALD 22:1
number best n. for a dinner party   GULB 140:6
  called the wrong n.   CART 57:1
  I am not a n.   CATC 59:12
  n. of the question   CHUR 68:19
  very interesting n.   RAMA 266:1
numbers n. that rocket the mind   WILB 335:6
numerical n. irrigation system   AUGA 19:9
Nuremberg of the N. trials   SHAW 293:18
  prosecution at N.   JACK 165:5
nurse always keep a-hold of N.   BELL 27:6
  N. UNUPBLOWN   TELE 311:5
nutritionists in a fat farm with n.   WILL 336:6
nuts N.   MCAU 205:7

oafs muddied o. at the goals   KIPL 182:10
oak O., and Ash, and Thorn   KIPL 182:16
  o. would sprout in Derry   HEAN 149:6
oaths Judges must follow their o.   ZOBE 349:2
oats feeds the horse enough o.   GALB 128:11
obedience life of o.   EICH 98:2
obey people would immediately o.   SCHW 289:1
obituary except your own o.   BEHA 26:20
  o. in serial form   CRIS 79:14
object I am a British o.   MALO 212:10
objectification o. of feeling   LANG 188:9
objectionable meaning doubtless o.

                                                ANON 12:12
objective have a great o.   CHIF 65:17
  o. correlative   ELIO 103:10
obligation o. goes unrecognized   WEIL 330:1
obliteration policy is o.   BELL 27:3
oblivion love, and then o.   MCEW 207:7
obscenity 'o.' is not a term   RUSS 279:6
obsolescence planned o.   STEV 303:11
obsolescent o. and nonexistent   BREN 44:2
obsolete war is o. or men are   FULL 127:5
obstacles knew no o.   SEGR 290:3
obvious in o. distress   BALF 22:3
occurred Ought never to have o.   BENT 29:14
ocean drop in the o.   TERE 311:14
  Earth when it is clearly O.   CLAR 70:11
  like being in the o.   JOBS 168:2
October O., that ambiguous month

                                                LESS 197:18
octopus dear o.   SMIT 296:9
odd But not so o.   BROW 46:6
  How o. Of God   EWER 106:7
  must think it exceedingly o.   KNOX 184:7
odds mass of o. and ends   WOOL 342:3
off I want to be o. it   PAXM 251:9

offence I was like to give o. — FROS 125:11
  only defence is in o. — BALD 21:10
offend freedom to o. — RUSH 278:1
offensive extremely o. — SMIT 296:11
  Life is an o. — WHIT 333:14
  what is merely o. — EPHR 106:3
offer o. he can't refuse — PUZO 263:4
office in o. but not in power — LAMO 188:3
  o. party is not — WHIT 334:9
official No sane local o. — SMIT 296:7
  This high o., all allow — HERB 151:16
officialism Where there is o. — FORS 121:2
oil foreign o. controlling — DYLA 95:13
  Scotland's o. — POLI 257:20
oiled O. his way around the floor — LERN 197:14
Okie O. means you're scum — STEI 303:2
old Anyone can get o. — ELIZ 104:11
  attendance on my o. age — YEAT 346:4
  die before I get o. — TOWN 316:15
  first sign of o. age — HICK 153:6
  getting too o. — DISN 91:7
  Growing o. a bad habit — MAUR 217:8
  Growing o. is like — POWE 260:12
  heart grows o. — YEAT 346:3
  HOW O. CARY GRANT — TELE 311:6
  I grow o. . . . I grow old — ELIO 102:8
  know they're o. — JENN 168:1
  make me conservative when o. — FROS 125:13
  no country for o. men — YEAT 345:16
  now am not too o. — BLUN 37:3
  o. age always fifteen years — BARU 24:14
  O. age is the most unexpected — TROT 318:3
  O. age should burn — THOM 314:2
  o. age, the last gap but one — WHIT 333:9
  o. heads on young shoulders — SPAR 299:8
  o. is having lighted rooms — LARK 189:5
  o. man in a dry month — ELIO 101:11
  O. man river — HAMM 143:6
  O. soldiers never die — FOLE 119:5
  planned by o. men — RICE 270:3
  that's o. Europe — RUMS 277:4
  They shall grow not o. — BINY 34:10
  too o. to rush up to the net — ADAM 2:5
  until they're o. — BINC 34:8
  warn you not to grow o. — KINN 181:7
  When I am an o. woman — JOSE 171:7
older ask somebody o. than me — BLAK 36:7
  grow o. and older — SAYE 285:9
  O. men declare war — HOOV 157:6
  O. women treat men — COLL 73:11
  so much o. then — DYLA 95:11
old-fashioned o. millionaire — FISH 112:9
olives o. in your martini — CARS 54:7
omelette o. all over our suits — BROK 44:8
omelettes make o. properly — BELL 28:2
omnibus horse power o. — FLAN 118:9
Onassis O. would not have married — VIDA 325:8

once o. and future king — WHIT 333:12
  O. we had a country — AUDE 18:5
one But the O. was Me — HUXL 161:13
  centre upon number o. — CHUR 69:5
  How to be o. up — POTT 259:6
  o. for my baby — MERC 219:11
  square root of minus o. — BECK 26:9
oneself Hell is o. — ELIO 100:7
only If you were the o. girl — GREY 139:2
  It's the o. thing — SAND 283:11
  O. connect — FORS 120:14
  o. gay in the village — CATC 60:20
  O. the lonely — ORBI 244:4
onstage O. I make love — JOPL 171:6
ooh O., you are awful — CATC 60:21
oozing O. charm from every pore — LERN 197:14
open in the great o. spaces — MARQ 215:6
  O. covenants of peace — WILS 338:20
opened o. the door — DIDD 90:8
opera o. ain't over — SAYI 287:2
  O. is when a guy gets — GARD 130:4
operatic so romantic, so o. — PROU 262:8
operations o. we can perform — WHIT 334:5
opinion form a clear o. — BONH 39:2
  Government and public o. — SHAW 292:12
  o. has been widely held — RUSS 278:15
  what is my o. — LOEW 202:2
  whole climate of o. — AUDE 17:8
opponents o. eventually die — PLAN 255:8
opportunity maximum of o. — SHAW 292:20
  o. for achievement — KEIL 176:3
  preparation meeting o. — WINF 339:2
  when he had the o. — ROWL 276:7
opposite o. of people — STOP 306:1
  walk in the o. direction — RODD 272:6
opposition effective means of o. — GOEB 134:8
oppressed mind of the o. — BIKO 34:7
oppression violence and o. — SOLZ 298:8
  war against o. — MCAL 205:2
oppressor ends as an o. — CAMU 52:15
  Neutrality helps the o. — WIES 335:3
  weapon in hands of o. — BIKO 34:7
oppressors Your former o. — WALC 326:2
opprobrium term of o. — MOYN 230:3
optimism not the same as o. — HAVE 147:6
  o. and pessimism — GREE 138:3
  o. of the will — GRAM 136:9
optimist o. is a guy — MARQ 215:4
  o. proclaims — CABE 50:1
opulence private o. — GALB 128:8
oral o. contraception — ALLE 7:11
orange clockwork o. — BURG 48:1
  future's O. — ADVE 3:21
  happen to be an o. — ALLE 7:2
oranges O. are not the only fruit — WINT 339:5
orchestra signals to the o. — SZEL 308:5
orchestration o. of platitudes — WILD 335:16

order new world o.   BUSH 49:2
  not necessarily in that o.   GODA 134:5
  restoration of o.   JAME 166:15
orders led by o.   EICH 98:2
ordinary learn to see the o.   BAIL 20:8
  O. made beautiful   SHAF 291:7
  see God in the o. things   EPIT 107:10
  warn you not to be o.   KINN 181:7
organ heart is an o. of fire   ONDA 243:7
  o. grinder is present   BEVA 33:8
organization about the o. man   WHYT 334:14
  o. is and must be   MILL 222:2
  o. of forms   CART 55:6
organize o. her own immortality   LASK 189:15
  waste time mourning—o.   HILL 154:2
organized it's got to be o.   HOCK 155:6
organizing Only an o. genius   BEVA 33:3
orgasm o. has replaced the Cross   MUGG 230:10
original o. is unfaithful   BORG 39:9
  saves o. thinking   SAYE 285:7
originality O. is deliberate   HOFF 155:11
originator o. of a new idea   DIRA 91:3
orphan defeat is an o.   CIAN 69:16
Oscar assume that O. said it   PARK 249:11
other happens to o. people   CART 54:9
  o. Annapurnas   HERZ 152:2
  O. voices, other rooms   CAPO 53:6
  Prudence is the o. woman   ANON 12:6
  wonderful for o. people   KERR 178:8
others woman who lives for o.   LEWI 199:4
Otis Miss O. regrets   PORT 258:21
ought something o. to be done   WELL 331:9
out best way o. is always through   FROS 125:18
  counted them all o.   HANR 144:1
  get o. while we're young   SPRI 301:4
  include me o.   GOLD 135:2
  truth is o. there   CATC 61:8
outcast o. on the world   HEWI 152:14
outer o. life of telegrams   FORS 120:13
outlaw attacks from o. states   REAG 268:6
outlaws o. Russia forever   REAG 268:5
outside just going o.   LAST 190:6
  just going o.   MAHO 211:5
  nothing o. of the text   DERR 89:5
  observed from o.   BARK 23:5
outsider I'm not an o.   EMIN 105:9
  O. is a social problem   WILS 337:8
  O. is not a freak   WILS 337:9
Ovaltineys We are the O.   ADVE 5:9
over ain't o. till it's over   BERR 31:10
  censorship is never o.   GORD 135:15
  oversexed, and o. here   TRIN 317:12
  O. there   COHA 73:1
  They think it's all o.   WOLS 341:3
overcoat only its o.   CARE 53:12
overcome We shall o.   SAYI 287:10
overlapping events o.   DURR 94:10

overlooked looked over than o.   WEST 331:16
overpaid O., overfed, oversexed   TRIN 317:12
oversexed o., and over here   TRIN 317:12
overstated save by being o.   BERL 30:15
owed so much o. by so many   CHUR 67:8
own apart from my o.   GABO 128:3
  money and a room of her o.   WOOL 341:11
  only to those who o. one   LIEB 200:3
  To each his o.   ANON 11:9
owner takes a great o.   BRAD 42:8
ownership common o.   ANON 12:15
Oxford either O. or Cambridge   SNAG 297:14
  heart was with the O. men   LETT 198:2
  secret in the O. sense   FRAN 122:9
  sends his son to O.   STEA 302:4
Oxford University Press by the O.   YOUN 347:3
oxygen o. of publicity   THAT 313:5
oyster eye that can open an o.   WODE 339:17
  world is an o.   MILL 222:4

paces open an oyster at sixty p.   WODE 339:17
pacifist absolute p.   EINS 98:7
  militant p.   EINS 98:10
  quietly p. peaceful   WALK 326:10
pack p. up your troubles   ASAF 14:14
packaging brilliant p.   SMIT 296:8
  my product and her p.   RUBI 277:2
page allowed P. 3 to develop   MURD 231:14
  never know on what p.   STON 305:7
pageant life's rich p.   MARS 215:15
paid attention must be p.   MILL 222:5
  p. for this microphone   REAG 268:1
pain intoxication with p.   BRON 44:11
  she hasn't a p.   MILN 223:9
painkiller most natural p.   LAST 191:3
pains no gains without p.   STEV 304:7
paint can't pick it up, p. it   MILI 221:6
  painter than the p.   CLOO 72:8
  p. objects as I think them   PICA 254:5
  p. sunlight   HOPP 157:12
  p. with my prick   MISQ 224:10
painted unreality of p. people   UPDI 321:13
painter I am a p.   SCHW 289:4
  more fun to be the p.   CLOO 72:8
painting essence of p.   MOND 226:13
  marvellous p.   BACO 20:5
  no matter what you're p.   HOCK 155:6
  P. became everything   BROW 45:14
  P. is saying 'Ta'   SPEN 300:2
  p. not made to decorate   PICA 254:3
  start p. yourself   HOCK 155:8
palate steps down the p.   NABO 233:1
pale p. blue dot   SAGA 281:8
  whiter shade of p.   REID 269:2
Palestine establishment in P.   BALF 22:2
  P. is the cement   ARAF 13:12

pallor p. of girls' brows — OWEN 247:6
palms p. before my feet — CHES 64:10
paltry aged man is but a p. thing — YEAT 345:17
Pandora open that P.'s Box — BEVI 34:2
pangs free of any p. — CURT 81:14
panic Don't p. — ADAM 2:2
  with wonderful p. — HECH 149:14
panther Black P. Party — NEWT 236:5
pants deck your lower limbs in p. — NASH 235:2
paper at a piece of tissue p. — RUTH 279:16
  keep the p. work down — ORTO 244:13
  only a p. moon — HARB 144:6
  ran the p. for propaganda — BEAV 25:7
  reactionaries are p. tigers — MAO 214:6
  scrap of p. — BETH 32:2
  worth the p. it is written — GOLD 135:3
papers He's got my p. — PINT 254:13
  what I read in the p. — ROGE 273:2
parades produce victory p. — HOBS 155:4
paradise catch the bird of p. — KHRU 180:2
  gadget-filled p. — NIEB 236:12
  P. by way of — CHES 64:15
  paved p. — MITC 223:16
paradises true p. are — PROU 262:11
paralysed view of a p. cyclops — HOCK 155:5
paranoid Only the p. survive — GROV 140:1
pardon Alas but cannot p. — AUDE 18:15
  thousand Ta's and P.'s — BETJ 32:13
pardons p. him for writing well — AUDE 17:13
parent one child makes you a p. — FROS 124:11
  p. who could see his boy — LEAC 193:11
parentage P. important — SHAW 291:17
parenthood means valuing p. — TOYN 317:2
parents girl needs good p. — TUCK 319:8
  In mine it was the p. — SLOV 296:5
  Jewish man with p. alive — ROTH 275:14
  judgment of your p. — UPDI 321:7
  lost to his p. — BOWI 42:4
  only illegitimate p. — GLAD 133:11
  P.—especially step-parents — POWE 260:10
  p. kept me from children — SPEN 300:6
  p. obey their children — EDWA 97:7
  p. were created for — NASH 234:14
  produce bad p. — MORS 229:5
  sue its p. — WATS 328:11
Paris after they've seen P. — LEWI 199:11
  Down and out in P. — ORWE 245:7
  Is P. burning — HITL 155:2
  last time I saw P. — HAMM 143:3
  P. is a movable feast — HEMI 151:2
park come out to the ball p. — BERR 31:12
  p., a policeman — CHAP 63:11
  Poisoning pigeons in the p. — LEHR 195:12
parking put up a p. lot — MITC 223:16
parley-voo Hinky, dinky, p. — ANON 11:15
parliament enables P. to do — SHAW 292:7
  function of P. — BOOT 39:5

modern P. — CONN 74:8
[p.] a lot of hard-faced men — BALD 21:8
p. of whores — O'RO 244:6
P. would not exist — SCAR 285:12
right of P. to decide on war — EPIT 107:16
Scottish P. — EWIN 106:8
shall be a Scottish p. — ANON 12:11
shall be a Scottish p. — DEWA 89:12
parliamentarian pleasure for a p. — CRIT 80:1
parody devil's walking p. — CHES 64:9
parrot This is a late p. — MONT 227:9
parsley P. is gharsley — NASH 234:8
part still p. of the people — BALL 22:4
  What isn't p. of ourselves — HESS 152:8
particles names of all these p. — FERM 110:12
partly Living and p. living — ELIO 102:9
parts naming of p. — REED 268:10
  refreshes the p. — ADVE 3:26
  save all the p. — EHRL 97:9
party great p. is not to be — HAIL 141:6
  nasty p. — MAY 217:10
  natural p. of government — WILS 338:9
  office p. is not — WHIT 334:9
  p.'s over — COMD 74:4
  p.'s over — CROS 80:10
  p. there are two kinds of people — LAND 188:8
  save the P. we love — GAIT 128:4
pasarán No p. — IBAR 162:1
pass Do not p. go — SAYI 286:16
  p. the ammunition — FORG 120:5
  prayed my cup might p. — KIPL 182:5
  They shall not p. — IBAR 162:1
  They shall not p. — MILI 221:1
passed That p. the time — BECK 26:5
  Timothy has p. — EPIT 108:8
  way he p. the ball — DOCH 91:10
passengers p. off in small boats — LAST 191:7
passeront Ils ne p. pas — MILI 221:7
passes beauty p. — DE L 88:3
  Men seldom make p. — PARK 249:8
passing-bells p. for these — OWEN 247:4
passion p. to which he has always — POWE 260:7
  prose and the p. — FORS 120:14
  vows his p. is infinite — PARK 249:14
passionate full of p. intensity — YEAT 345:20
passions inferno of his p. — JUNG 173:2
passive energetic displaces the p. — BERN 31:4
passport My p.'s green — HEAN 149:4
past always praising the p. — SMIT 297:8
  cannot remember the p. — SANT 283:13
  last day of an era p. — YELT 346:14
  neither repeat his p. — AUDE 19:2
  nothing but the p. — KEYN 178:12
  p., brittle with relics — THOM 315:5
  p. exudes legend — MALA 212:2
  p. is a bucket of ashes — SAND 283:7
  p. is a foreign country — HART 147:3

p. is lost	CHAP 63:14	no p. is truly safe	ANNA 9:10
p. is the only dead thing	THOM 314:19	not a p. treaty	FOCH 119:4
p. not getting any better	LEVI 198:10	no way to p.	MUST 232:9
p., present and future	EINS 99:6	Open covenants of p.	WILS 338:20
Remembrance of things p.	BORR 41:1	p. between equals	WILS 338:16
Time present and time p.	ELIO 100:10	P. cannot be built	ADAM 2:7
under the bloody p.	AHER 5:20	p. for our time	CHAM 62:8
Utopia is a blessed p.	KISS 183:18	p. from freedom	MALC 212:5
Who controls the p.	ORWE 245:17	P. is indivisible	LITV 200:12
pathless Truth is a p. land	KRIS 185:5	P. is much more precious	SADA 281:3
pathos P., piety, courage	FORS 121:1	P. is poor reading	HARD 145:12
patience other people's p.	UPDI 321:4	p. like retarded pygmies	PEAR 252:2
patient p. etherized upon a table	ELIO 102:2	p. of the double-bed	CAMP 51:13
p. etherized upon a table	LEWI 199:6	P., political p.	MITC 223:13
patria Died some, pro p.	POUN 259:14	p. there may be in silence	EHRM 98:1
patries *Europe des p.*	DE G 87:8	p. will guide the planets	RADO 265:4
patriotism knock the p. out	SHAW 293:1	p. with honour	CHAM 62:8
P. is a lively sense	ALDI 6:7	people want p. so much	EISE 99:15
P. is not enough	CAVE 62:2	plunging into a cold p.	YELT 346:13
patriots ninety-minute p.	SILL 294:11	potent advocates of p.	GEOR 131:5
patrol P. the halls	WILB 335:9	prefers a negative p.	KING 180:10
pattable she is p.	NASH 234:9	speak p. unto nation	REND 269:7
pattern Art is p. informed by	READ 267:8	tell me p. has broken out	BREC 43:9
Art is the imposing of p.	WHIT 334:4	than to make p.	CLEM 71:5
Pauli P. [exclusion] principle	GAMO 129:6	victory of the p.	HOPK 157:11
pause eine kleine P.	LAST 191:4	war and p. in 21st century	KOHL 185:2
pauses p. between the notes	SCHN 288:1	**peaceful** p. revolution impossible	KENN 177:12
paved p. paradise	MITC 223:16	quietly pacifist p.	WALK 326:10
paw ear on its p.	MAYA 217:12	**peacefully** p. towards its close	DAWS 85:8
pay Can't p., won't pay	POLI 257:10	**peach** dare to eat a p.	ELIO 102:8
Crime doesn't p.	SAYI 286:8	**peaches** p. and what penumbras	GINS 133:5
Not a penny off the p.	COOK 75:15	**peacock** till night like a p.	O'CA 241:5
p. any price	KENN 177:5	**peak** small things from the p.	CHES 65:5
p. to see my Aunt Minnie	WILD 335:13	**peanuts** become like salted p.	KISS 183:14
p. us, pass us	CHES 65:1	hate it as much as p.	WELL 331:2
sum of things for p.	HOUS 158:4	If you pay p.	SAYI 286:18
we are made to p. for	FRIE 124:6	**pear** go round the prickly p.	ELIO 101:15
We won't p.	FO 119:2	**pearl** splendid p.	SEXT 291:4
paycock till night like a p.	O'CA 241:5	**peas** ability to sort p.	HOLU 156:9
paying p. the Dane-geld	KIPL 183:3	**peasant** cross woman's p. origins	O'DO 241:11
price well worth p.	LAMO 188:2	p. by the shoulders	WEST 332:15
payments missing a couple of car p.		**peasants** cricket with their p.	TREV 317:6
	WILS 337:10	**pebble** wise man hide a p.	CHES 65:4
payroll art of meeting a p.	GETT 132:5	**pederasty** not p.	RATT 267:2
pays *Mon p. ce n'est pas un pays*	VIGN 325:13	**pedestal** save the p.	LEC 194:13
PC P. is the LSD of the '90s	LEAR 194:2	**pedestrians** two classes of p.	DEWA 90:1
peace curse in time of p.	CHUR 68:7	**peel** orange p. picked out	RALE 265:9
don't make p. with friends	RABI 265:1	p. me a grape	WEST 332:3
Give p. a chance	LENN 196:16	**peepers** where you get them p.	MERC 219:10
hard and bitter p.	KENN 177:4	**peepshow** ticket for the p.	MACN 209:16
have you known p.	WEST 332:15	**peer** Not a reluctant p.	BENN 28:14
In p.: goodwill	CHUR 69:3	**peerage** When I want a p.	NORT 240:5
In the arts of p.	SHAW 292:13	**pellet** p. with the poison	FILM 116:1
Let p. fill our heart	KUMA 185:11	**pen** had a rainbow p.	BAEZ 20:7
Make it a *green* p.	DARN 83:8	spark-gap mightier than p.	HOGB 156:1
make your p. with authority	MORR 228:17	squat p. rests	HEAN 149:1
may not be a just p.	IZET 163:14	**pencils** sadness of p.	ROET 272:10

penicillin trials of p.   HODG 155:9
pennies P. don't fall from heaven   THAT 312:6
  p. from heaven   BURK 48:5
penny Not a p. off the pay   COOK 75:15
pension hang your hat on a p.   MACN 210:1
  spend my p. on brandy   JOSE 171:7
people American p. have spoken   CLIN 72:6
  as if p. mattered   SCHU 288:8
  law not supported by p.   HUMP 160:10
  look after our p.   LAST 190:4
  Most p. ignore most poetry   MITC 223:11
  noise! And the p.   ANON 12:1
  no petty p.   YEAT 346:11
  Not many p. know that   CAIN 50:7
  p. are the masters   BLAI 35:14
  P. die, but books never   ROOS 274:5
  p. hurting people   MAIL 211:8
  P.'s Princess   BLAI 35:15
  P. take pictures   ADVE 4:22
  p. were a kind of solution   CAVA 57:12
  People who need p.   MERR 219:16
  Power to the p.   POLI 258:6
  still part of the p.   BALL 22:4
  voice of the p.   BALD 21:12
  we are the p. of England   CHES 65:1
  What kind of a p.   CHUR 67:13
Peoria It'll play in P.   POLI 257:18
pepper Sergeant P.   TYNA 320:6
percentage reasonable p.   BECK 26:1
perdition led to *p.* by a man   WEST 332:22
perestroika [p.] combines   GORB 135:13
  started the process of p.   GORB 135:14
perfect ever more p. eyes   TEIL 310:14
  It's not p.   BINC 34:9
  nobody's p.   FILM 116:7
  Nothing is p.   STEP 303:7
  One p. rose   PARK 249:9
perfection P. of planned layout   PARK 250:13
  P. of the life   YEAT 344:9
perfectly small, but p. formed   COOP 76:12
perform p. without thinking   WHIT 334:5
period p. of silence on your part   ATTL 16:5
periphrastic p. study   ELIO 100:16
perish p. together as fools   KING 180:14
perished Now that love is p.   MILL 221:15
Perón not been born P.   PERÓ 252:10
perpendicular p. expression   SHAW 293:16
perpetrator thou shalt not be a p.   BAUE 25:2
persecuted because he is p.   GOUL 136:4
persecution certain amount of p.   RUSS 279:12
Pershing 58% Don't Want P.   SAYI 286:14
Persians Truth-loving P.   GRAV 137:2
persistence take the place of p.   COOL 76:8
person no more than a p.   AUDE 17:8
  P. from Porlock   SMIT 297:10
  third p. was in the room   POPE 256:3
personal P. isn't the same   PRAT 261:8

  p. is political   POLI 258:5
  P. relations   FORS 120:13
  warm p. gesture   GALB 128:10
personalities meeting of two p.   JUNG 173:5
  p. of the two sexes   MEAD 218:1
personality good p.   TUCK 319:8
  product of his own p.   FROM 124:9
personally should be p. associated   BLAI 36:2
perspiring city of p. dreams   RAPH 266:6
persuaders hidden p.   PACK 248:1
persuasive p. argument   FRAM 122:3
pertinent way to a p. answer   BRON 44:10
perversion War the universal p.   RAE 265:5
pervert loophole through which p.   BRON 44:11
pessimism P. of the intellect   GRAM 136:9
pessimist p. fears this is true   CABE 50:1
  p. waiting for rain   COHE 73:2
pestilence learn in a time of p.   CAMU 52:11
petal dropping a rose p.   MARQ 215:13
Peter government which robs P.   SHAW 292:1
  P. Principle   PETE 253:5
petrol price of p. has been increased CART 56:11
pettiness to expiate: a p.   LAWR 192:17
petty no p. people   YEAT 346:11
phagocytes stimulate the p.   SHAW 291:15
phallic P. and ambrosial   POUN 259:13
phallus future is the p.   LAWR 192:8
Philadelphia living in P.   EPIT 107:13
  went to P., but   FIEL 112:2
philistinism our yawning P.   PRIT 262:5
philosophical p. tradition   WHIT 334:7
philosophy linguistic p.   RUSS 279:13
  P. is a battle   WITT 339:6
phone answer the p.   CART 57:1
  call him up on the p.   SALI 282:6
  E.T. p. home   FILM 113:6
  never even made a p. call   CHOM 66:4
  P. a friend   CATC 60:23
  P. for the fish-knives   BETJ 32:9
  p. has not rung   MITC 226:4
  p. is for you   LEBO 194:10
phoney p.-baloney jobs   FILM 116:9
photo I took the p.   ROSE 275:7
photograph p. is a secret   ARBU 13:15
photographed I p. them   ARBU 13:13
photographer p. is like the cod   SHAW 293:12
  to be a good p.   BAIL 20:8
photographing reflection p. other reflections
                                                             MICH 220:3
photography P. deals exquisitely   MICH 220:4
  p. is all right if   HOCK 155:5
  P. is truth   GODA 134:3
  p. of an event   CART 55:6
physical lightly called p.   COLE 73:8
physician p. can bury mistakes   WRIG 342:11
physicists p. have known sin   OPPE 244:1
  p.' war   DAVI 84:12

physics edifice of modern p.	SNOW 298:2
no democracy in p.	ALVA 7:18
p. or stamp collecting	RUTH 279:14
p. was more interesting	PULL 263:1
pi multiply deadlines by p.	RYLE 280:6
pianists no better than many p.	SCHN 288:1
piano help with moving the p.	WEST 332:21
Picardy in P. it was	KIPL 182:4
Roses are flowering in P.	WEAT 329:15
Picasso abhorred plastics, P.	WAUG 329:6
pick p. it up	MILI 221:6
p. out the plums	HARM 146:3
P. yourself up	FIEL 111:11
pickle weaned on a p.	ANON 12:14
picnic Teddy Bears have their P.	KENN 176:13
picture idea of a good p.	WARH 327:9
most famous p.	ANON 11:16
no go the p. palace	MACN 210:1
One p. is worth	BARN 23:8
pictures I nail my p. together	SCHW 289:4
people take p.	ADVE 4:22
P. are for entertainment	GOLD 135:9
p. aren't good enough	CAPA 53:2
p. didn't have beginning	POLL 256:2
p. that got small	FILM 116:16
pie make an apple p.	SAGA 281:4
Miss American P.	MCLE 208:5
p. in the sky when you die	HILL 154:1
pig from p. to man	ORWE 245:3
p. got up and walked away	BURT 48:11
pigeon crooning like a bilious p.	SHAW 293:4
pigeons flock of homing p.	HUGH 160:7
Poisoning p.	LEHR 195:12
pigs P. treat us as equals	CHUR 69:10
Pilate water like P.	GREE 137:9
pile P. it high	SAYI 287:3
P. the bodies high	SAND 283:6
pilgrims land of the p.	CUMM 81:3
We are all p.	RYDE 280:2
We are the P.	FLEC 118:12
pill little yellow p.	JAGG 166:2
sleeping p. is white	SEXT 291:4
something of a p.	WODE 340:1
women may take the p.	THOM 315:3
pillars p. of the nation state	PROD 262:6
seven p. of wisdom	BORR 41:3
pillow like the feather p.	HAIG 141:3
pilot What do I tell the p.	LAST 191:8
pimples scratching of p.	WOOL 342:4
pink bright p. dress	SHUL 294:8
p. right down to	NIXO 239:1
pinko-grey really p.	FORS 120:18
pinstripe come in a p. suit	FEIN 110:7
pint p. of plain	O'BR 241:3
p.—that's very nearly	GALT 129:5
pinta Drinka P. Milka Day	ADVE 3:17
pioneer always the p.	DOYL 92:14
pips until the p. squeak	GEDD 130:9
piranha p. strikes	SZYM 308:9
piss worth a pitcher of warm p.	GARN 130:5
pissed p. in our soup	BENN 29:4
pissing inside the tent p. out	JOHN 170:3
pistol I reach for my p.	JOHS 170:10
p. in your pocket	WEST 332:11
pistons black statement of p.	SPEN 300:3
pit work in the p.	CHAR 64:2
pitchfork use my wit as a p.	LARK 189:8
pity Midnight Without P.	JOHN 169:5
only p. that counts	LEVA 198:4
P. the feeling which arrests	JOYC 172:3
p. this busy monster	CUMM 81:6
Poetry is in the p.	OWEN 247:2
unbearable p.	RUSS 278:5
pix Sticks nix hick p.	NEWS 238:3
place at the wrong p.	BRAD 42:12
have no p. in it	NAIP 233:9
In p. of strife	CAST 57:5
in the wrong p.	DYLA 95:3
places all p. were alike to him	KIPL 183:4
been things and seen p.	WEST 332:4
distance between two p.	WILL 336:11
placidly Go p. amid the noise	EHRM 98:1
plagiarism one author, it's p.	MIZN 226:8
plagiarist No p. can excuse	HAND 143:14
plagiarize P.! Let's no one	LEHR 195:11
plain no p. women on television	FORD 119:10
pint of p.	O'BR 241:3
plan by his p. of attack	SASS 284:20
cunning p.	CATC 59:18
don't have a moral p.	CRON 80:6
plane It's a p.	CATC 59:2
only two emotions in a p.	WELL 331:3
planet hanging from a round p.	EDDI 96:9
planets stars and all the p.	TRUM 318:8
plank landing on a p. travelling	EDDI 96:9
planned p. obsolescence	STEV 303:11
planning p. is indispensable	EISE 100:2
plans p. are useless	EISE 100:2
plant I p. lines	WALC 326:6
plantation still working on a p.	HOLI 156:4
planter Ulsterman, of p. stock	HEWI 152:15
plants talk to the p.	CHAR 64:1
plasticine playing with P.	PARK 249:4
plastics abhorred p., Picasso	WAUG 329:6
platitude longitude with no p.	FRY 126:9
p. is simply a truth	BALD 21:9
stroke a p. until	MARQ 215:12
platitudes orchestration of p.	WILD 335:16
Plato p. told him: he couldn't	CUMM 81:5
series of footnotes to P.	WHIT 334:7
play Did that p. of mine send out	YEAT 345:9
every time I p. it	JOHN 168:6
Games people p.	BERN 31:6
It'll p. in Peoria	POLI 257:18

play (*cont.*)
musicians want to p.	ROSE 275:4
P. it again, Sam	FILM 114:3
P. it again, Sam	MISQ 224:15
p. it over again	LAMB 187:10
P. it tough	BRAD 42:13
p. things as they are	STEV 303:18
work, rest and p.	ADVE 4:11
y is p.	EINS 99:2

player We need a p. HENR 151:10

players p. who hate your guts STEN 303:6
| urging p. to like the game | SCOL 289:6 |

playing p. on the frontiers HERZ 152:1
p. on the line	FORS 120:17
p. with Plasticine	PARK 249:4
stood like a p. card	MAIL 211:9

plays enjoyed going to p. UPDI 321:13
| Shaw's p. | AGAT 5:17 |

please *try to p. everyone* SWOP 307:11

pleased 'p.' is pronounced MURR 231:15

pleasure give that sort of p. GLEN 134:2
greater than the p.	YOUN 347:3
No p. worth giving up	AMIS 8:9
P.'s for those who are bad	YESE 346:15

pleats witty little p. BAIL 20:9

plebiscite justice by p. ZOBE 349:2

plots p. tend to move deathwards DELI 88:11

plumber choose to be a p. EINS 99:5
getting a p. on weekends	ALLE 7:12
I can't get a p.	SCHW 289:1
p. comes to unblock	GLEN 134:2

plume in blast-beruffled p. HARD 145:3

plums I have eaten the p. WILL 337:1
| pick out the p. | HARM 146:3 |
| p. and orange peel | RALE 265:9 |

pocket gun in your p. WEST 332:11
| pound in your p. | WILS 338:10 |

poem figure a p. makes FROS 125:21
p. is never finished	VALÉ 323:1
p. lovely as a tree	KILM 180:4
p. must ride on its own melting	FROS 126:1
p. should not mean but be	MACL 208:6
write a p. after Auschwitz	ADOR 2:12

poems P. are made by fools KILM 180:5
| p. should be Clyde-built | DUNN 94:6 |

poet All a p. can do is warn OWEN 247:3
ask a p. to sing	BOLD 38:10
hate what every p. hates	KAVA 175:7
No p. ever interpreted	GIRA 133:9
p. can earn more money	AUDE 19:1
p. is the priest	STEV 303:12
p.'s hope: to be	AUDE 18:11
p.'s inward pride	DAY- 85:10
p.'s mouth be silent	YEAT 345:12
p.'s voice need not merely	FAUL 110:4
p. will give up writing	CELA 62:6
p. with a poem	MCGI 207:8

| worst tragedy for a p. | COCT 72:15 |

poetry blood jet is p. PLAT 255:12
campaign in p.	CUOM 81:12
danger to you here. P.	NERU 236:1
Ireland hurt you into p.	AUDE 17:9
no more define p.	HOUS 158:7
p. begins to atrophy	POUN 260:3
p. ignores most people	MITC 223:11
p. in money	GRAV 137:5
p. in motion	KAUF 175:3
P. is a way to taking life	FROS 126:2
[P.] is capable of saving	RICH 270:13
P. is in the pity	OWEN 247:2
P. is not most important	THOM 314:17
P. is the achievement	SAND 283:9
P. is the supreme fiction	STEV 303:17
P. is to prose	WAIN 326:1
P. is what is lost	FROS 126:4
p. makes nothing happen	AUDE 17:10
P. not a turning loose	ELIO 103:13
p. should be alive	ZEPH 348:8
p. strays into my memory	HOUS 158:8
saying it and that is p.	CAGE 50:4
Writing a book of p.	MARQ 215:13

poets all p. are Jews TSVE 319:7
Irish p., learn your trade	YEAT 346:8
mature p. steal	ELIO 103:11
No death has hurt p. more	HEAN 149:9
Nor till the p. among us	MOOR 228:2
Should p. bicycle-pump	AMIS 8:6
think all p. were Byronic	COPE 77:3

point rather make a p. CURT 81:15
| Up to a p., Lord Copper | WAUG 329:8 |

points p. a finger NIZE 239:9

pointy shiny, p. things KAY 175:8

poison got as far as p.-gas HARD 144:13
| put p. in your coffee | CHUR 69:11 |
| Slowly the p. | EMPS 105:14 |

poisoning P. pigeons LEHR 195:12

polecat semi-house-trained p. FOOT 119:9

police among p. officers ORTO 244:13
p. are those who arrest	HARR 146:6
p. can beat you	SHAW 292:24
p. were to blame	GRAN 136:10

policeman little p. MURR 232:2
p. and a pretty girl	CHAP 63:11
p. is there to preserve	DALE 83:4
terrorist and the p.	CONR 75:11

policemen aren't enough p. LEC 194:12
| how young the p. look | HICK 153:6 |
| sadists become p. | CONN 74:14 |

policy foreign p. COOK 75:16
home p.: I wage war	CLEM 71:3
If the p. isn't hurting	MAJO 211:13
instrument of national p.	BRIA 44:3
My [foreign] p.	BEVI 34:1
p. of the good neighbour	ROOS 273:13

polite no allies to be p. to — GEOR 131:9
politeness suave p. — KNOX 184:6
political fear of P. Economy — SELL 290:8
  half your p. life — THAT 312:12
  personal is p. — POLI 258:5
  p. autonomy — GRAY 137:7
  p. correctness can be — JAME 166:16
  P. language is designed — ORWE 246:5
  p. lives end in failure — POWE 261:6
  p. mind — COOL 76:5
  p. significance — HAVE 147:8
  p. will — LYNN 204:13
politician judge a p. — IVIN 163:12
  my life as a p. — POWE 261:5
  p. does get an idea — MARQ 215:9
  p. is an arse upon — CUMM 81:4
  p. to complain about — POWE 261:3
  p. was a person — LLOY 201:11
  statesman is a p. — TRUM 318:13
politicians die for p. — THOM 315:9
  tanks of the p. — NEWS 238:5
  to be left to the p. — DE G 87:7
politics between p. and equations — EINS 99:7
  do not go in for p. — CAMU 52:7
  In p., if you want anything — THAT 312:3
  invisible hand in p. — FRIE 124:2
  no true friends in p. — CLAR 70:5
  p. and little else — CAMP 52:1
  P., executive expression — BRIT 44:5
  P. is not the art — GALB 128:12
  P. is the Art — BUTL 49:12
  P. is war without bloodshed — MAO 214:4
  p. making us unhappy — FILI 112:3
  p. of happiness — HUMP 160:11
  P. supposed to be — REAG 268:3
  p. the art of impossible — HAVE 147:7
  P. the art of preventing — VALÉ 323:4
  P. too serious a matter — DE G 87:7
  P. without compromise — KINN 181:11
  week is a long time in p. — WILS 338:8
poll-taking science of p. — WHIT 333:7
poll tax of the p. — THAT 313:16
pollution engine of p., the dog — SPAR 299:11
  p. of democracy — WHIT 333:13
polyester p. sheets — FARR 109:9
ponies Five and twenty p. — KIPL 182:15
  p. have swallowed — BETJ 32:10
pony nice little Shetland p. — LARK 189:12
poodle right hon. Gentleman's p. — LLOY 201:2
Pooh in 'The House at P. Corner' — PARK 249:15
pool Walk across my swimming p. — RICE 270:6
poor For the urban p. the police — HARR 146:6
  give food to the p. — CAMA 51:6
  help the many who are p. — KENN 177:6
  how expensive it is to be p. — BALD 21:3
  I've been p. — KAUF 174:9
  My countrymen Kiltartan's p. — YEAT 345:6

nice people were p. — SPAR 299:7
  p. but she was honest — ANON 12:9
  p. don't know that — SART 284:8
  p. get children — KAHN 174:8
  P. little rich girl — COWA 78:9
  p. tread the lightest — HARR 146:8
  p. who die — SART 284:2
  p. wot gets the blame — ANON 12:9
  undeserving p. — SHAW 293:6
Pope against the P. or the NUM — BALD 22:1
  P.! How many divisions — STAL 301:11
poppies In Flanders fields the p. — MCCR 206:10
population world p. would be — HAWK 148:2
porch keep on the p. — CLIN 71:13
porcupines throw p. under you — KHRU 180:3
Porlock Person from P. — SMIT 297:10
pornography give p. a dirty name — BARN 23:9
  p. is really about — SONT 298:15
  p. of war — RAE 265:5
  P. the attempt to — LAWR 192:6
porridge consistency of cold p. — TURI 319:9
Porsches friends all drive P. — JOPL 171:4
porter shone bright on Mrs P. — ELIO 103:4
portion claim to one's p. — NAIP 233:10
portrait Every time I paint a p. — SARG 283:14
  p. of the artist — JOYC 171:13
portraits wish my p. to be — FREU 123:4
position altering the p. — RUSS 278:13
  Every p. must be held — HAIG 141:4
  only p. for women — CARM 54:1
positive ac-cent-tchu-ate the p. — MERC 219:9
  power of p. thinking — PEAL 251:13
positivists logical p. — AYER 19:16
possessions how little p. count — ELTO 105:4
  least of p. — WHIT 333:11
possibility p. of suicide — CIOR 70:2
possible Art of the P. — BUTL 49:12
  not the art of the p. — GALB 128:12
  says that something is p. — CLAR 70:10
possum said the Honourable P. — BERR 31:18
postal p. districts packed — LARK 189:10
postcards p. of the hanging — DYLA 95:2
poster Kitchener is a great p. — ASQU 15:5
postman p. always rings twice — CAIN 50:5
  think I am, a bloody p. — BEHA 26:19
postulating 'p.' what we want — RUSS 278:14
postures lie down in clean p. — FOWL 121:9
pot chicken in every p. — HOOV 157:4
  Look at p. — NASH 234:13
potato p.-gatherers like — KAVA 175:6
  You like p. — GERS 131:14
potatoes Stuffing insead of p.? — ADVE 5:3
potent how p. cheap music is — COWA 78:14
potential p. you actually have — BROW 46:1
pottery P. is a practical — COOP 76:13
pound p. in your pocket — WILS 338:10
  Save the p. — POLI 258:7

poured p. into his clothes — WODE 340:7
poverty languishing in p. — MAND 213:5
  Make p. history — SAYI 286:23
  Overcoming p. is not a gesture — MAND 213:7
  setting him up in p. — NAID 233:7
  struggled with p. — BALD 21:3
  war on p. — JOHN 169:10
  worst of crimes is p. — SHAW 292:3
power All p. to the Soviets — POLI 257:1
  balance of p. — KISS 183:11
  Black P. — CARM 54:2
  corridors of p. — SNOW 297:16
  cult added to p. — ANON 13:2
  have the p. to end it — SASS 285:3
  in office but not in p. — LAMO 188:3
  no will to p. — JUNG 173:7
  only have p. over people — SOLZ 298:4
  p. grows out of the barrel — MAO 214:5
  P. is not a means — ORWE 246:1
  P. is the great aphrodisiac — KISS 183:15
  P.? It's a Dead Sea fruit — MACM 209:7
  p. of suppress — NORT 240:4
  p.-state — TEMP 311:11
  P. to the people — POLI 258:6
  P. without responsibility — KIPL 183:10
  responsibility without p. — STOP 305:10
  rob it of its p. — SZAS 308:3
  Sitting tight is p. — BELL 28:3
  source of p. — MARS 215:17
  they confer p. — RUSS 279:4
  What p. have you got — BENN 28:16
powerful fear is that we are p. — WILL 337:3
powers high contracting p. — BRIA 44:3
  p. at work in this country — MISQ 224:4
  real separation of p. — DENN 89:4
practical p. form of art — COOP 76:13
  P. men, who believe — KEYN 179:4
practise preach but do not p. — RUSS 279:2
praise P. the Lord — FORG 120:5
  spoiled with p. — COOL 76:5
praised dog that p. his fleas — YEAT 346:6
pram p. in the hall — CONN 75:2
pray Often when I p. — LEWI 199:7
  Work and p. — HILL 154:1
prayer Conservative Party at p. — ROYD 276:11
  wing and a p. — ADAM 2:9
  wish for p. is a prayer — BERN 31:1
prayers saying his p. — MILN 223:10
prays family that p. together — SAYI 286:13
preach p. but do not practise — RUSS 279:2
precedent dangerous p. — CORN 77:8
precious p. it must be rationed — LENI 196:8
predicament human p. — QUIN 264:6
  It is a p. — BENN 29:7
predict only p. things after — IONE 163:3
prefaces Shaw's p. — AGAT 5:17
preference special p. for beetles — HALD 142:4

pregnancy avoid p. by mathematics — MENC 219:2
pregnant If men could get p. — KENN 176:10
prejudices deposit of p. laid — EINS 99:3
  proprietor's p. — SWAF 307:8
preliminary in the p. stages — HUXL 161:8
premature p. anti-Fascist — ANON 13:6
preparation p. meeting opportunity — WINF 339:2
prepare not to p. for life — PAST 250:18
prepared BE P. — BADE 20:6
  p. for all emergencies — FORS 120:12
prerogative p. of the eunuch — STOP 305:10
  P. of the harlot — KIPL 183:10
presence posted p. of the watcher — JAME 166:10
present know nothing but the p. — KEYN 178:12
  no p. in Wales — THOM 315:5
  past, p. and future — EINS 99:6
  perpetuates the p. — DE B 86:4
  p. in New York — CHAP 63:14
  Time p. and time past — ELIO 100:10
  who controls the p. — ORWE 245:17
preserve do not p. myself — ORTE 244:9
  there to p. disorder — DALE 83:4
  Whom God P. — MORT 229:8
presidency cancer close to the P. — DEAN 86:1
  heart-beat from the P. — STEV 304:11
  messenger-boy P. — SCHL 287:15
  pursuit of the P. — JOHN 170:1
  Teflon-coated P. — SCHR 288:5
  US p. a Tudor monarchy — BURG 48:4
  vice-p. isn't worth — GARN 130:5
president All the P.'s men — BERN 31:9
  anybody could become p. — DARR 84:3
  any boy may become P. — STEV 304:9
  any wartime P. — BIDD 34:5
  choose to run for P. — COOL 76:3
  going to be your next p. — CART 55:1
  in an American p. — NOON 239:13
  P. is a crook — NIXO 239:6
  security around the p. — MAIL 211:12
  to hide from the P. — CHUR 69:13
  used to be the next p. — GORE 136:1
  We are the P.'s men — KISS 183:16
  When the P. does it — NIXO 239:8
presidents about to change p. — GRAH 136:8
press complain about the p. — POWE 261:3
  Freedom of the p. — SWAF 307:8
  Freedom of the p. guaranteed — LIEB 200:3
  independent p. — STEW 304:17
  Let's go to p. — CATC 59:3
  lose your temper with the P. — PANK 248:9
  popular p. is drinking — MELL 218:11
  power of the p. — NORT 240:4
  p. still hounded you — JOHN 168:10
  p. would kill her — SPEN 299:13
  with you on the free p. — STOP 305:12
pressed p. out of shape — FROS 125:17

pressure Grace under p.   HEMI 151:5
presumption amused by its p.   CART 56:6
pretended p. to be real   NAIP 233:12
pretender Old P.   GUED 140:3
pretendy wee p. government   CONN 74:10
pretty lived in a p. how town   CUMM 81:2
   policeman and a p. girl   CHAP 63:11
   p. girl is like a melody   BERL 30:7
   p. straight sort   BLAI 36:1
   We're so p.   ROTT 276:3
prevent not knowing how to p.   RUSS 279:13
preventing Politics the art of p.   VALÉ 323:4
price love that pays the p.   SPRI 301:1
   pay any p.   KENN 177:5
   p. of petrol has been increased   CART 56:11
   p. well worth paying   LAMO 188:2
   What p. glory   ANDE 8:12
   Wot p. Selvytion nah   SHAW 292:6
prices reduce the rise in p.   HEAT 149:10
prick paint with my p.   MISQ 224:10
prickly go round the p. pear   ELIO 101:15
pride here have P. and Truth   YEAT 345:13
   London P. handed down to us   COWA 78:5
   look backward to with p.   FROS 124:15
priest p. of the invisible   STEV 303:12
priggish p. schoolgirl   GRIG 139:5
prime One's p. is elusive   SPAR 299:10
Prime Minister best P. we have   BUTL 49:11
   HOW DARE YOU BECOME P.   TELE 311:4
   next P. but three   BELL 27:7
   No woman will be P.   THAT 312:2
   P. has nothing to hide   CHUR 69:13
   Unknown P.   ASQU 15:8
primitive call it a 'p. society'   GREG 138:10
   'p.' languages   CHAT 64:3
   wise p. in giant jungle   MAIL 211:10
prince Advise the p.   ELIO 102:7
   danced with the P. of Wales   FARJ 109:7
   P. of Wales not a position   BENN 29:7
princess People's P.   BLAI 35:15
   P. of Wales was   DOWD 92:11
Principle *Peter P.*   PETE 253:5
principle hain't the money, but th' p.

    HUBB 159:2
   little of the p. left   REIT 269:3
   useful thing about a p.   MAUG 216:13
principles easier to fight for one's p.   ADLE 2:11
print licence to p. your own money

    THOM 315:11
priorities p. have gone all wrong   BEVA 33:11
prison at home in p.   WAUG 329:3
   born in p.   MALC 212:4
   enclosed in language is in p.   WEIL 330:6
   forever p.-pent   WOLF 340:11
   while there is a soul in p.   DEBS 86:12
prisoner your being taken p.   KITC 183:20
prisoners p. of addiction   ILLI 162:5

privacy society of p.   RAND 266:4
   You have zero p.   MCNE 209:13
private P. faces in public places   AUDE 18:2
   p. opulence   GALB 128:8
   p. . . . secret . . . intimate   STOP 306:1
privilege only extended p.   HILL 153:8
privileges p. you were born with   BROW 46:1
prized local, but p. elsewhere   AUDE 18:11
prizes glittering p.   BORR 40:11
   glittering p.   SMIT 296:10
   winners of the big p.   ORWE 245:19
probably P. the best   ADVE 4:24
problem can't see the p.   CHES 65:10
   Houston, we've had a p.   LOVE 203:5
   most severe p. we are facing   KING 180:7
   Outsider is a social p.   WILS 337:8
   p.-solving minds   KAUN 175:4
   p. that has no name   FRIE 123:15
   p. that has no name   FRIE 123:17
   p. to be overcome   KEIL 176:3
   you're part of the p.   CLEA 71:1
problems all our p.   THAT 313:17
   Machines have less p.   WARH 327:13
   No easy p.   EISE 100:1
procrastination p. is the art   MARQ 215:3
producing consumes without p.   ORWE 244:15
product bad p. fail faster   BERN 31:2
   my p. and her packaging   RUBI 277:2
production means of p.   ANON 12:15
products p. people really want   NASH 234:13
profession important p.   SHAW 291:17
   second oldest p.   REAG 268:3
professional p. is a man who can   AGAT 5:16
professionalism there is so much p.

    SCOL 289:6
professions p. are conspiracies   SHAW 291:16
   shortest-lived p.   ROGE 273:3
profits best of all monopoly p.   HICK 153:5
programme Not so much a p.   ANON 12:3
progress Humanity a work in p.   WILL 336:7
   illusion of p.   ANON 12:18
   p. if a cannibal uses   LEC 194:14
   P. is a comfortable disease   CUMM 81:6
   'p.' is ethical   RUSS 279:9
   'p.' is the exchange   ELLI 105:2
   social p., order   JOHN 168:4
prohibiting p. language   BART 24:10
prohibition Communism is like p.   ROGE 273:4
   enacting P.   HOOV 157:2
   exclusion and p.   MILL 222:2
   P. makes you want   MARQ 215:11
project less ambitious p.   ANON 10:14
proletariat new p.   ATTA 16:3
prolonged deliberately p.   SASS 285:3
promise Eastern p.   ADVE 3:20
   p. made is a debt unpaid   SERV 290:13
   p. of their early years   POWE 260:10

promised reach the p. land · · · CALL 51:1
seen the p. land · · · KING 180:15
promises have p. to keep · · · FROS 125:20
man who p. least · · · BARU 24:15
promising first call p. · · · CONN 75:1
prone position for women is p. · · · CARM 54:1
pronounce p. it properly · · · LERN 197:15
pronounced 'please' is p. · · · MURR 231:15
pronunciation p. reigned · · · HEAN 149:7
proof America is the p. · · · MCCA 205:10
propaganda on p. · · · CORN 77:9
purely for p. · · · BEAV 25:7
triumphs of p. · · · HUXL 161:3
property Private p. is necessary · · · TAWN 310:2
p. of the imagination · · · WALC 326:5
Thieves respect p. · · · CHES 65:6
through p. that we shall · · · PANK 248:11
prophet not as a p. · · · MAND 213:2
prophets ceased to pose as its p. · · · POPP 256:5
proposition meaning of a p. · · · SCHL 287:16
proprietor p.'s prejudices · · · SWAF 307:8
props p. to help him endure · · · FAUL 110:4
prose Good p. like a window-pane · · · ORWE 245:4
govern in p. · · · CUOM 81:12
Poetry is to p. · · · WAIN 326:1
p. and the passion · · · FORS 120:14
prose-song Gertrude Stein's p. · · · LEWI 199:16
prosperous p. or caring society · · · HESE 152:5
prostitute doormat or a p. · · · WEST 332:19
made into a p. · · · BOWI 42:3
prostitutes small nations like p. · · · KUBR 185:10
protect p. our phoney-baloney · · · FILM 116:9
two solitudes p. · · · RILK 271:5
protection calls mutely for p. · · · GREE 137:17
Protestant P. counterpoint · · · BEEC 26:14
P. with a horse · · · BEHA 26:17
White-Anglo Saxon-P. · · · BALT 22:10
proud too p. to fight · · · WILS 338:14
prove I could p. everything · · · PINT 254:13
to p. it I'm here · · · CATC 60:8
Provence found it in P. · · · WILL 337:2
proverbs Solomon wrote the P. · · · NAYL 235:4
providence way that P. dictates · · · HITL 154:14
provinces Brought up in the p. · · · BENN 29:8
prudence P. is the other woman · · · ANON 12:6
prurient p. curiosity · · · STOP 305:8
psalms David wrote the P. · · · NAYL 235:4
psychiatrist p. is a man who goes · · · STOC 305:5
psychological P. flaws · · · ANON 12:7
psychopath p. is the furnace · · · RAYM 267:5
pub could do with a p. here · · · STEW 305:1
public admired in p. life · · · ROOS 273:8
give the p. something · · · SKEL 296:2
I and the p. know · · · AUDE 18:6
immaculate p. places · · · ROET 272:10
one to mislead the p. · · · ASQU 15:9
Private faces in p. places · · · AUDE 18:2

p. rallies around an idea · · · ASIM 15:3
p. squalor · · · GALB 128:8
respect p. opinion · · · RUSS 278:8
tell the p. which way · · · SULZ 307:5
publications previous p. · · · HILB 153:7
publicity no such thing as bad p. · · · BEHA 26:20
now called p. · · · O'RO 244:5
oxygen of p. · · · THAT 313:5
P. is justly commended · · · BRAN 42:15
public relations precedence over p. · · · FEYN 111:4
public school to an English p. · · · WAUG 329:3
publish p. and be sued · · · INGR 162:11
publisher makes everybody a p. · · · MCLU 208:14
publishers become p. · · · CONN 74:14
publishing easier job like p. · · · AYER 19:17
p. faster · · · PAUL 251:6
puck p. is going to be · · · GRET 139:1
pulpit such a bully p. · · · ROOS 274:11
white glove p. · · · REAG 267:13
pulse p. of this new day · · · ANGE 9:5
take a nation's p. · · · WHIT 333:7
two people with the one p. · · · MACN 210:4
punch I'll just p. him · · · RODD 272:4
p. above its weight · · · HURD 161:1
punctual Aunt Minnie always p. · · · WILD 335:13
punk p. was a good idea · · · COLL 74:2
punt better fun to p. · · · SAYE 285:6
puppy Happiness is a warm p. · · · SCHU 288:7
happiness was a warm p. · · · EPHR 106:1
pure p. as the driven slush · · · BANK 22:13
purify p. the dialect · · · ELIO 101:6
Puritan to the P. all things are · · · LAWR 192:3
Puritanism not P. but February · · · KRUT 185:8
P. The haunting fear · · · MENC 218:13
purple colour p. · · · WALK 327:1
deep p. falls · · · PARI 249:2
I shall wear p. · · · JOSE 171:7
P. haze is in my brain · · · HEND 151:7
p. to lavender · · · WALK 327:2
purpose not fit for p. · · · REID 269:1
purrs p. like an epigram · · · MARQ 215:12
pursuit common p. · · · LEAV 194:4
pushed and he p. · · · LOGU 202:3
put up with which I will not p. · · · CHUR 68:10
pygmies peace like retarded p. · · · PEAR 252:2
pyjamas in p. for the heat · · · LAWR 192:16
pylons P., those pillars bare · · · SPEN 300:7
pyramid economic p. · · · ROOS 273:10
pyre heaping up own funeral p. · · · POWE 260:18

quack q. of yesterday · · · DOYL 92:14
quacks q. like a duck · · · CARE 53:11
quad No one about in the Q. · · · KNOX 184:7
quality Never mind the q. · · · POWE 261:7
quarks Three q. for Muster Mark · · · JOYC 171:12
quarrel lover's q. with the world · · · FROS 125:8

no q. with the Viet Cong	ALI 6:14	**radio** had the r. on	MONR 227:1
q. in a far away country	CHAM 62:7	R. and television	SARR 284:1
takes one to make a q.	INGE 162:7	r. expands it	WOGA 340:8
Quebec Long Live Free Q.	DE G 87:11	**rag** foul r. and bone shop	YEAT 344:7
queen choice of a Q.	BALD 21:12	Shakespeherian R.	ELIO 103:2
dying for Q. and country	THOM 315:9	**rage** horrible that lust and r.	YEAT 346:4
have the Q. as their aunt	MARG 214:11	Maintain your r.	WHIT 334:12
historical drama q.	NOON 239:13	r. to live	VANE 323:11
Q. has the quality	PHIL 253:10	**ragged** pair of r. claws	ELIO 102:6
q. in people's hearts	DIAN 90:5	**railway** by r. timetables	TAYL 310:6
To toast *The* Q.	HEAN 149:4	R. termini	FORS 120:9
queerer q. than we suppose	HALD 142:1	**railways** R. and the Church	AWDR 19:12
questing passes the q. vole	WAUG 329:9	**rain** buried in the r.	MILL 221:13
question Answer to the Great Q.	ADAM 2:3	glazed with r. water	WILL 336:17
ask an impertinent q.	BRON 44:10	hard r.'s a gonna fall	DYLA 95:5
asked any clear q.	CAMU 52:2	r. in Spain	LERN 197:11
mere asking of a q.	FORS 120:19	r. is destroying his grain	HERB 151:13
q. is absurd	AUDE 18:17	R. is grace	UPDI 321:9
q. why we died	KIPL 181:14	real sad r.	CASH 55:12
To ask the hard q.	AUDE 18:16	Singin' in the r.	FREE 122:13
very simple q.	LARD 188:11	Still falls the r.	SITW 295:13
what is the q.	LAST 191:9	waiting for it to r.	COHE 73:2
questions *all* q. were stupid	WEIS 330:8	waiting for r.	ELIO 101:11
ask q. of those	RALE 265:7	wedding-cake in the r.	AUDE 19:7
queue orderly q. of one	MIKE 220:9	**rainbow** Follow ev'ry r.	HAMM 142:13
quick q., and the dead	DEWA 90:1	had a r. pen	BAEZ 20:7
quiet determination of a q. man	SMIT 296:13	Lord survives the r.	LOWE 204:1
is a q. life	HICK 153:5	no r. nation	MAND 213:9
never have a q. world	SHAW 293:1	r. and a cuckoo's song	DAVI 84:9
q. flows the Don	SHOL 294:5	R. gave thee birth	DAVI 84:10
q. on the western front	REMA 269:5	r. which includes black	YEVT 346:17
should be kept very q.	LOOS 202:13	real r. coalition	JACK 165:1
quietly q. pacifist peaceful	WALK 326:10	Somewhere over the r.	HARB 144:8
quit I q.	MAHE 211:4	**rains** r. pennies from heaven	BURK 48:5
try again. Then q.	FIEL 112:1	**raise** practically r. themselves	GROE 139:10
quitter fighter not a q.	MAND 213:10	**Ramsbottom** Mr and Mrs R.	EDGA 97:5
quotation always have a q.	SAYE 285:7	**rape** procrastinated r.	PRIT 262:4
get a happy q. anywhere	HOLM 156:7	r. isn't the worst thing	WELD 330:13
q. is a national vice	WAUG 329:5	r., ultra-violence and Beethoven	TAGL 309:2
quotations heaps of q.	DOUG 92:9	you r. it	DEGA 87:1
read books of q.	CHUR 69:2	**raped** r. and speaks English	BORR 40:3
quote man is to q. him	BENC 28:6	**Raphael** draw like R.	PICA 254:4
quoted very seldom q. correctly	STRU 306:13	**rapist** r. bothers to buy a bottle	DWOR 94:13
quotes q. give us acquaintance	WILL 336:4	**rapists** all men are r.	FREN 123:2
		rapper to your son as a r.	ICE 162:3
		rappers first r. of Europe	BJÖR 35:6
rabbit r. in a snare	STEP 303:8	**rat** anthropomorphic view of r.	KOES 184:13
race clan and r.	MILL 222 8	Anyone can r.	CHUR 66:14
r. between education	WELL 331:6	giant r. of Sumatra	DOYL 92:12
white r. *is* the cancer	SONT 298:16	terrier can define a r.	HOUS 158:7
races so-called white r.	FORS 120:18	You dirty r.	MISQ 225:9
racism institutional r.	MACP 210:10	**rational** irrational is r.	STEV 304:1
racket Once in the r.	CAPO 53:4	make life more r.	AYER 19:15
radar writer's r.	HEMI 151:6	only r. position	DIAM 90:4
radical dared be r. when young	FROS 125:13	**rationed** precious it must be r.	LENI 196:8
R. Chic	WOLF 341:1	**rats** r.' alley	ELIO 103:1
R. is a man	ROOS 273:17	**rattle** Shake, r. and roll	CALH 50:8

ray r. of sunshine   WODE 339:13
razor arse full of r. blades   KEAT 175:11
  mirror and a r.   JOYC 172:6
  r. rusting   PLAT 255:11
reach I r. for my pistol   JOHS 170:10
  other beers cannot r.   ADVE 3:26
  r. the promised land   CALL 51:1
reaction can't get no girl r.   JAGG 166:3
  if there is any r.   JUNG 173:5
reactionaries r. are paper tigers   MAO 214:6
reactionary R. is a somnambulist   ROOS 273:17
read his books were r.   BELL 27:17
  not r. Eliot, Auden   RICH 270:15
  people who can't r.   ZAPP 348:6
  r. any good books lately   CATC 59:8
  r., much of the night   ELIO 102:20
  R. my lips   BUSH 48:16
  r. the life of any important   PRIE 261:14
  r. too widely   PEAR 252:1
  superfluous to r.   HILB 153:7
  what I r. in the papers   ROGE 273:2
  who don't r. the books   BYAT 49:13
  Why r.   FITZ 118:3
reader birth of the r. must be   BART 24:9
  ideal r. suffering from   JOYC 171:10
  not to inform the r.   ACHE 1:10
reading careful of his r.   LEWI 199:5
  lie in a hot bath r.   THOM 314:17
  Like R., only farther   FLEM 119:1
  Peace is poor r.   HARD 145:12
  prefer r.   SMIT 297:4
  R. isn't an occupation   ORTO 244:13
  R. it slower   WOOD 341:4
  what is worth r.   TREV 317:7
readmission r. to the human race   LYNN 204:12
real Be r.   CONN 74:11
  event is r.   SHIE 294:4
  home to a r. world   TURK 319:10
  r. slow walk   CASH 55:12
  talking r. money   DIRK 91:6
  washed in the speechless r.   BARZ 24:17
realism I don't want r.   WILL 336:14
realistic make a 'r. decision'   MCCA 206:1
reality Cannot bear very much r.   ELIO 100:12
  currency of all r. shows   TRUS 319:5
  other people's r.   SONT 298:17
  principal part of r.   BORG 39:8
  R. beats fiction   CONR 75:12
  R. is that which   DICK 90:7
  r. take precedence   FEYN 111:4
  they are a r.   DEWA 89:12
really be a R. Useful Engine   AWDR 19:11
  what I r. really want   ROWB 276:5
reaping No, r.   BOTT 39:12
reason form of human r.   LÉVI 198:12
  for the wrong r.   ELIO 102:10
reasons We want better r.   RUSS 279:13

rebel die like a true-blue r.   HILL 154:2
  R. without a cause   FILM 117:10
  What is a r.   CAMU 52:12
rebellion r. and revivalism   THOM 315:1
recall blessed with total r.   GREG 138:9
receipt Applause is a r.   SCHN 287:18
receiver left the r. off the hook   KOES 184:14
recession r. that Australia had to have   KEAT 175:12
  r. when your neighbour   TRUM 318:14
  spend way out of a r.   CALL 50:10
recherche À la r. du temps perdu   PROU 262:7
recipes like r. in a cookbook   STEW 304:16
  r. always successful   VALÉ 323:2
recirculation commodious vicus of r.   JOYC 171:9
reckless r. with our government   SHOR 294:7
recognize only a trial if I r. it   KAFK 174:6
reconciliation bridge of r.   RUNC 277:7
  stability and r.   MITC 223:13
  True r. does not   MAND 213:14
reconvened hereby r.   EWIN 106:8
record as fast as the world r.   COLE 73:5
  look at the r.   IVIN 163:12
  not merely be the r.   FAUL 110:4
recover never r. until   PATO 251:4
red been in the r. all my life   GUTH 140:10
  Better r. than dead   POLI 257:6
  not even r. brick   OSBO 246:16
  r. wheel barrow   WILL 336:17
  rise with my r. hair   PLAT 255:14
reds honour the indomitable R.   DUNN 94:6
redundancy handing out r. notices   KINN 181:8
redwood From the r. forest   GUTH 140:9
reeled Until r. the mind   GIBB 132:7
referee having two you are a r.   FROS 124:11
refined Englishwoman is so r.   SMIT 297:9
reflection r. photographing other reflections   MICH 220:3
refreshes r. the parts   ADVE 3:26
refrigerator advertise a r.   BLIX 36:13
refuse offer he can't r.   PUZO 263:4
regicides r. of earlier times   CAMU 52:13
regret perfunctory r.   SAKI 282:2
regrets I have no r.   CRES 79:8
  Miss Otis r.   PORT 258:21
  no r.   VAUC 324:5
regrette Je ne r. rien   CRES 79:8
  je ne r. rien   VAUC 324:5
regulated R. hatred   HARD 144:10
  speech is not to be r.   DOUG 92:10
rehab lot of doctors in r.   WILL 336:6
Reich Ein R., ein Volk   POLI 257:12
reindeer Red-nosed R.   MARK 214:13
rejoice r. at that news   THAT 312:11
  r., rejoice   HEAT 149:12
relations in personal r.   RUSS 278:9

not have sexual r. — CLIN 72:3
Personal r. — FORS 120:13
relationship human r. suffers — FORS 121:2
r. that was not — CLIN 72:4
relationships R., relationships — FISH 112:5
relative Success is r. — ELIO 100:8
religion can't talk r. to — SHAW 292:5
Every dictator uses r. — BHUT 34:4
r. has always been to me — POTT 259:4
R. is the frozen thought — KRIS 185:4
r. weak — SZAS 308:2
r. without science — EINS 98:3
starting a new r. — ORWE 246:10
start your own r. — ANON 11:4
That is my r. — SHAW 292:4
Theme is my r. — REVS 269:11
tourism is their r. — RUNC 277:8
wisest r. — HAIL 141:5
religions materialistic of r. — TEMP 311:12
they who found r. — PROU 262:9
religious great r. art — CLAR 70:8
reluctant Not a r. peer — BENN 28:14
remarkable anything r. about it — PAST 250:19
remarks Famous r. are very seldom — STRU 306:13
R. are not literature — STEI 302:8
remember cannot r. the past — SANT 283:13
I r. it well — LERN 197:8
r. for ever — WARN 328:2
R. me when I am dead — DOUG 92:4
r. the children you got — BROO 45:9
r. this, a kiss is — HUPF 160:14
We will r. them — BINY 34:10
what you can r. — SELL 290:6
Yes; I r. Adlestrop — THOM 314:18
yet never can, r. — THOM 314:21
remembered like to be r. — POWE 261:4
r. around the world — DISN 91:8
remembrance R. of things past — BORR 41:1
remind foolish things r. me — MARV 216:2
remorse doesn't understand r. — SZYM 308:9
remove not malignant and r. it — WAUG 329:13
rendezvous r. with Death — SEEG 289:13
Reno'd Kings Moll R. — NEWS 237:17
renounce I r. war — FOSD 121:8
rent r. we pay for our room — CLAY 70:14
reorganized we would be r. — ANON 12:18
repeat condemned to r. it — SANT 283:13
images change as they r. — WARH 327:12
neither r. his past — AUDE 19:2
repeated mistake shall not be r. — EPIT 108:4
simply a truth r. — BALD 21:9
repetition deviation, or r. — CATC 61:15
Nagging is the r. — SUMM 307:6
repetitious r. mechanism — WHIT 333:14
republic Australian r. — MURR 232:1
destroyed the R. — DE V 89:8

Love the Beloved R. — FORS 121:6
repulsive Right but R. — SELL 290:7
reputation don't need a r. — MITC 225:12
re-rat takes ingenuity to r. — CHUR 66:14
rescuers firing on the r. — WOOL 342:7
research Basic r. is what — BRAU 43:4
r. the art of the soluble — MEDA 218:6
steal from many, it's r. — MIZN 226:8
resign r. from the Government — COOK 75:17
resigned I am not r. — MILL 220:11
r. commission — ANON 10:11
resistance break the r. — STAL 301:9
resistible r. rise of Arturo Ui — BREC 43:10
resort-style soft r. civilization — BAUD 25:1
resources Have no Inner R. — BERR 31:17
respect r. due dere — ZEPH 348:7
r. for women — NYE 240:8
r. of the people — MARS 215:17
respectability r. and air conditioning — BARA 23:2
save a shred of r. — READ 267:7
respiration artificial r. — BURG 48:3
response r. to error — GIOV 133:7
responsibility Liberty means r. — SHAW 292:18
no sense of r. — KNOX 184:10
Power without r. — KIPL 183:10
r. without power — STOP 305:10
slightest sense of r. — ANON 11:7
rest Swift has sailed into his r. — YEAT 346:5
work, r. and play — ADVE 4:11
restaurant table at a good r. — LEBO 194:11
resting-place give us a r. — WEIZ 330:9
restoration Church's R. — BETJ 32:11
restraint praise the firm r. — CAMP 51:15
restructuring r. combines — GORB 135:13
retaliation r. in first — JAME 166:6
reticence Northern r. — HEAN 149:8
retire don't r. in this business — MITC 226:4
retires jockey r. — ARCA 14:1
retiring r. at high speed toward — HALS 142:11
retreating my right is r. — FOCH 119:3
seen yourself r. — NASH 235:2
return I shall r. — MACA 205:3
I will r. — EPIT 108:1
r. of democratic control — STEE 302:6
revealed r. everything about a girl — VREE 325:14
revelation first hole is a r. — MOOR 227:11
revelations offers stupendous r. — HOFF 155:13
revenge fish are having their r. — ELIZ 104:3
gave us Ford as his r. — ABZU 1:3
r. by the culture — PADE 248:2
tribal, intimate r. — HEAN 149:5
reverence R. for Life — SCHW 289:3
reverse not got a r. gear — BLAI 36:5
revisited r. ideas — OLDF 243:1
revivalism rebellion and r. — THOM 315:1
revolt r., disorder — MORR 228:16

revolution after the r.   AREN 14:6
   grassroots r.   BERN 31:8
   most important r. the first   TANS 310:1
   peaceful r. impossible   KENN 177:12
   R.'s delightful   HUXL 161:8
   r. where love not allowed   ANGE 9:7
   r. will raise its head   LUXE 204:11
   safeguard a r.   ORWE 246:1
   volcano of r.   ELLI 105:3
revolutionary Every r. ends   CAMU 52:15
   forge his r. spirit   GUEV 140:4
   his r. triumph   TAYL 310:8
   r. in a bathroom   LINK 200:9
revolutions modern r. have ended   CAMU 52:14
revolver resembles a r.   FANO 109:4
reward r. is when we die   RYDE 280:2
rhetoric love without the r.   STOP 305:15
Rhine think of the R.   BALD 21:11
Rhodesia majority rule in R.   SMIT 296:14
rhyme hope and history r.   HEAN 148:15
   still more tired of R.   BELL 27:11
rhythm I got r.   GERS 131:12
   sweet, soft, plenty r.   MORT 229:9
rhythmical r. grumbling   ELIO 103:15
Ribstone Pippin Right as a R.   BELL 27:10
rice r. pudding for dinner   MILN 223:9
rich all the r. people   STEA 302:3
   by chance grow r.   THOM 314:20
   can't spend ourselves r.   BLAC 35:7
   In the r. man's world   ANDE 9:2
   never be too r. or too thin   WIND 339:1
   no boy from a r. family   DIMA 90:12
   not really a r. man   GETT 132:4
   parish of r. women   AUDE 17:9
   people r. enough to pay   HEAL 148:10
   Poor little r. girl   COWA 78:9
   r. are different   FITZ 117:14
   r. get rich   KAHN 174:8
   r. is better   KAUF 174:9
   r. man never really gives   EAST 96:4
   r. person should leave   BUFF 47:11
   r. wage war   SART 284:2
   r. wot gets the gravy   ANON 12:9
   save the few who are r.   KENN 177:6
   sincerely want to be r.   CORN 77:6
   to tax r. people   LLOY 201:9
richness r. of lovers and tribes   ONDA 243:8
riddle r. of the sands   CHIL 66:1
   r. wrapped in a mystery   CHUR 67:2
ride if you cannot r. two horses   MAXT 217:9
   She's got a ticket to r.   LENN 196:19
ridiculous heart of the r.   MAHO 211:5
rien je ne regrette r.   VAUC 324:5
right allow others to be r.   GIDE 132:12
   convinced that they are r.   VAN 323:8
   curst conceit o' bein' r.   MACD 206:11
   exclusively in the r.   HUXL 161:10

forgive those who were r.   MACL 208:8
   just not r.   PARK 250:15
   man of the r.   MOSL 229:12
   no r. in the circus   MAXT 217:9
   not only to be r.   SZAS 307:12
   not r. now   JAY 167:6
   one WAS r.   POUN 260:4
   questioned its r. to exist   SCHU 288:9
   R. as a Ribstone Pippin   BELL 27:10
   R. but Repulsive   SELL 290:7
   r. deed for the wrong   ELIO 102:10
   r. goes unrecognized   WEIL 330:1
   R. Now is a lot better   BINC 34:9
   r. of Parliament to decide on war   EPIT 107:16
   r. to happiness   RAYN 267:6
   scientists are probably r.   ASIM 15:3
   Self-government is our r.   CASE 55:9
   timing was r.   MURR 232:4
   Two wrongs don't make a r.   SZAS 308:4
   vast r.-wing conspiracy   CLIN 71:12
   Want to do r.   RICH 270:9
   what is r.   FILM 113:4
righteous seen the r. forsaken   BLUN 37:3
rights equal in dignity and r.   ANON 10:2
   sick had no r.   FORS 120:16
   Stand up for your r.   MARL 215:1
   talked about equal r.   JOHN 169:9
   vital personal r.   WARR 328:4
   your r. become only   CASE 55:10
right-wing life is r.   DEBR 86:10
rime r. was on the spray   HARD 145:11
ring One R. to rule them all   TOLK 316:12
   pulled through a wedding r.   REAR 268:9
   R. of bright water   BORR 41:2
rings postman always r. twice   CAIN 50:5
riot r. is the language of   KING 180:18
ripper no female Jack the R.   PAGL 248:5
ripple tiny r. of hope   KENN 178:3
rise And still I r.   BORR 40:2
   into this world to r. above   FILM 115:15
   resistible r. of Arturo Ui   BREC 43:10
   r. at ten thirty   HARG 145:16
   still, like air, I'll r.   ANGE 9:6
risen r. without trace   MUGG 230:8
rises sun also r.   HEMI 151:4
rising r. expectations   CLEV 71:8
risks just one of the r. he takes   STEV 304:9
   We took r.   SCOT 289:11
ritual body building is r.   PAGL 248:3
river Across the r.   BORR 40:1
   guy who cleans the r.   PERO 253:1
   Ol' man r.   HAMM 143:6
   r. Is a strong brown god   ELIO 101:1
   Sleepless as the r.   CRAN 79:5
riverrun r., past Eve and Adam's   JOYC 171:9
rivers I've known r.   HUGH 159:8
   r. in this country   LEVY 199:1

streets are r. of blood   MURR 232:2
road ads and not the r.   NASH 234:11
   Follow the yellow brick r.   HARB 144:9
   Golden R. to Samarkand   FLEC 118:13
   Goodbye yellow brick r.   JOHN 169:1
   Hit the r., Jack   MAYF 217:14
   in the middle of the r.   BEVA 33:6
   one more for the r.   MERC 219:11
   on to the end of the r.   LAUD 189:16
   r. through the woods   KIPL 183:2
   r. toward freedom   MORR 228:16
   rolling English r.   CHES 64:14
roads How many r.   DYLA 95:1
   Two r. diverged   FROS 125:15
   without fear the lawless r.   MUIR 230:12
roam mind begins to r.   SOLZ 298:3
roaming R. in the gloamin'   LAUD 191:14
roar called upon to give the r.   CHUR 68:16
   r. of London's traffic   CATC 60:19
roareth that r. thus   GODL 134:6
roast R. beef and Yorkshire   ORWE 245:6
rob r. his mother   FAUL 110:5
robbed We was r.   JACO 165:7
robbing r. a bank   BREC 43:13
robin r. with a worm   MCGI 207:8
Robinson here's to you, Mrs R.   SIMO 295:3
robot r. may not injure a human   ASIM 15:1
robotics Rules of R.   ASIM 15:1
robs government which r. Peter   SHAW 292:1
robust r. exchange of ideas   BREN 44:1
rock being in a r. band   STIP 305:3
   like the R. of Gibraltar   GAMO 129:6
   r. around the clock   DE K 87:17
   R. is like a battery   CLAP 70:4
   R. journalism is people   ZAPP 348:6
   Sex and drugs and r. and roll   DURY 94:12
   simple r. and roll reasons   GELD 130:11
rocked r. the system   ROBI 272:1
rocket not r. science   LINE 200:7
   numbers that r. the mind   WILB 335:6
Rockies R. may crumble   GERS 132:1
rocks marriage on the r.   MERR 219:17
   r. remain   HERB 151:17
role not yet found a r.   ACHE 1:8
roll Let's r.   LAST 190:15
   R. over, Beethoven   BERR 31:14
   Shake, rattle and r.   CALH 50:8
rolled bottoms of my trousers r.   ELIO 102:8
rolling jus' keeps r. along   HAMM 143:6
   Like a r. stone   DYLA 95:8
   r. English road   CHES 64:14
Roman Before the R. came to Rye   CHES 64:14
romance fine r. with no kisses   FIEL 111:9
   music and love and r.   BERL 30:6
Romans R. ever done   FILM 116:10
romantic R. Ireland's dead   YEAT 346:2
   ticket to r. places   MARV 216:3

Wrong but R.   SELL 290:7
romantics We were the last r.   YEAT 344:8
romping r. of sturdy children   DE V 89:9
roof cat on a hot tin r.   WILL 336:8
room about to enter a r.   EDDI 96:9
   All I want is a r.   LERN 197:13
   Books do furnish a r.   POWE 260:9
   boys in the back r.   LOES 202:1
   Great hatred, little r.   YEAT 345:1
   money and a r. of her own   WOOL 341:11
   smoke-filled r.   SIMP 295:7
rooms boys in the back r.   BEAV 25:6
   lighted r. inside your head   LARK 189:5
   Other voices, other r.   CAPO 53:6
rope see a piece of r.   DALA 83:1
rose English unofficial r.   BROO 45:1
   fire and the r. are one   ELIO 101:10
   Goodbye, England's r.   JOHN 168:11
   I know the colour r.   ABSE 1:2
   Into the r.-garden   ELIO 100:11
   One perfect r.   PARK 249:9
   R. is a rose   STEI 302:11
   Roves back the r.   DE L 88:1
   white r. of Scotland   MACD 206:12
rosebud R. is just a piece   FILM 115:13
roses ash the burnt r. leave   ELIO 101:4
   Everything's coming up r.   SOND 298:12
   R. are flowering in Picardy   WEAT 329:15
   r. in December   BARR 24:5
   Treaties like girls and r.   DE G 87:10
rot it must be all r.   NICH 236:7
rotted simply r. early   NASH 234:12
rotten good to feel r.   YESE 346:15
   tree was already r.   JOHN 169:3
   You r. swines   CATC 61:21
rottenness r. of our civilization   READ 267:7
rough children who were r.   SPEN 300:6
round R. and round the circle   ELIO 100:9
   R. up the usual suspects   FILM 115:8
Roundheads R. (Right but)   SELL 290:7
Rousseau R. was the first   BERL 30:16
royal If you have a R. Family   PIML 254:11
   My children are not r.   MARG 214:11
   needed no r. title   SPEN 299:14
royalty R. the gold filling   OSBO 246:18
rub r. up against money   RUNY 277:10
rubbish show so far? R.   CATC 61:12
Rubens If I were alive in R.'s time   FREN 123:1
rubs fog that r. its back   ELIO 102:4
Rudolph R., the Red-nosed   MARK 214:13
rugby R. Union which is   THOM 315:1
rugged system of r. individualism   HOOV 157:3
rugs like a million bloody r.   FITZ 117:19
ruin r. himself in twelve months   GEOR 131:6
   r. that Cromwell knocked about   BEDF 26:11
Ruislip Gaily into R. gardens   BETJ 32:13
rule golden r. is   SHAW 292:16

rule (*cont.*)

One Ring to r. them all	TOLK 316:12
R. 1, on page 1	MONT 227:6
r. by amateurs	ATTL 16:9
r. the world	BART 24:12
rules keep making up these sex r.	SALI 282:7
make the r.	BAVA 25:3
R. of Robotics	ASIM 15:1
rum It's a R. Go	VAUG 324:8
r., sodomy, prayers	CHUR 68:12
run All you need to r.	RADC 265:3
best judge of a r.	WHAR 333:4
born to r.	SPRI 301:4
He can r.	LOUI 203:4
In the long r.	KEYN 179:5
Now Teddy must r.	KENN 178:4
Take the money and r.	FILM 117:13
They get r. down	BEVA 33:6
What makes Sammy r.	SCHU 288:6
runaway r. Presidency	SCHL 287:15
rung phone has not r.	MITC 226:4
runner long-distance r.	SILL 294:12
Russia forecast the action of R.	CHUR 67:2
From R. with love	FLEM 118:17
innocent R. squirmed	AKHM 6:3
outlaws R. forever	REAG 268:5
R. an empire or democracy	BRZE 47:3
Russian R. literature saved	RATU 267:3
Russians keep the R. out	ISMA 163:7
rye Before the Roman came to R.	CHES 64:14
catcher in the r.	BORR 40:7
comin' through the r.	SALI 282:8

Sacco S.'s name will live	VANZ 324:3
sack S. the lot	FISH 112:7
s. you on Christmas Eve	HOPE 157:10
sacrament abortion would be a s.	KENN 176:10
sacramental flesh was s.	ROBI 271:14
sacrifice final s.	SPRI 301:1
Further s. of life	DE V 89:8
great pinnacle of S.	LLOY 201:4
Too long a s.	YEAT 344:13
you refused a lesser s.	MARY 216:9
sacrificed be s. to expediency	MAUG 216:13
lives to be s.	NEWS 237:12
sacrifices forgive him for the s.	MAUG 217:2
sad It's very s.	CURT 81:15
real s. rain	CASH 55:12
sadists repressed s.	CONN 74:14
safe Health Service is s.	THAT 313:1
made s. for democracy	WILS 338:18
s. to be unpopular	STEV 304:10
s. to go back in the water	TAGL 309:7
world s. for hypocrisy	WOLF 340:13
safeguards enforceable s.	TRUM 318:10
safer world s. for children	LE G 195:8

safety strike against public s.	COOL 76:1
sagas frosty s.	CRAN 79:1
peoples who memorized s.	BJÖR 35:6
said if you want anything s.	THAT 312:3
sailed I have s. the seas	YEAT 345:18
saint call me a s.	CAMA 51:6
Sloane turned secular s.	BURC 47:15
sake Art for art's s.	SAYI 286:1
salad turn to chicken s.	JOHN 169:6
salary s. depends on not understanding	SINC 295:9
s. of the chief executive	GALB 128:10
sales equation would halve the s.	HAWK 147:11
salesman Death of a s.	MILL 222:3
s. is got to dream	MILL 222:6
salmon smoked s. and tinned	WILS 338:6
saloon in the last chance s.	MELL 218:11
salt s. rubbed into their wounds	WEST 332:18
salute If it moves, s. it	MILI 221:6
salvation Wot prawce s. nah	SHAW 292:6
Sam Play it again, S.	FILM 114:3
Play it again, S.	MISQ 224:15
Samaritan remember the Good S.	THAT 312:7
Samarkand Golden Road to S.	FLEC 118:13
Samarra Appointment in S.	BORR 40:4
tonight in S.	MAUG 217:4
Sammy What makes S. run	SCHU 288:6
sand Night, snow, and s.	NERU 235:11
sands riddle of the s.	CHIL 66:1
sandwich cheaper than a prawn s.	RATN 266:8
raw-onion s.	BARN 23:13
sane if he was s. he had to fly	HELL 150:6
San Francisco left my heart in S.	CROS 80:12
sanity ain't no S. Claus	FILM 114:14
sank s. my boat	KENN 177:17
Sighted sub, s. same	MASO 216:11
Santa shoot S. Claus	SMIT 296:7
sap dried the s. out of my veins	YEAT 345:2
new s. running	HEWE 152:12
sardines s. will be thrown	CANT 53:1
sat everyone has s. except a man	CUMM 81:4
I s. down and wept	BORR 40:6
She s. down	JACK 165:2
Satan casting out S. by Satan	SORL 299:2
Satanic Verses author of *The S.*	KHOM 179:11
Satanist dyslexic S.	SMIT 296:15
satellite With s. TV	O'DO 241:10
satiable full of s. curtiosity	KIPL 183:5
satin ease a heart like a s. gown	PARK 249:13
satire S. is what closes Saturday	KAUF 174:11
satisfaction can't get no s.	JAGG 166:3
satisfied can't be s.	HUGH 159:11
Saturday closes S. night	KAUF 174:11
Glasgow Empire on a S.	DODD 91:11
saucer like a flying s. landed	DYLA 95:16
sausage hold on s. and haddock	WOOL 342:6
s. machine	CHRI 66:9

savage days of the Noble S. — BIKO 34:6
savaged s. by a dead sheep — HEAL 148:11
save destroy the town to s. it — ANON 11:6
  God s. the King — MOYN 230:4
  helped s. the world — KEYN 179:8
  s. the Governor-General — WHIT 334:11
  S. the pound — POLI 258:7
  through life trying to s. — ROGE 273:6
  To s. your world — AUDE 17:4
saved could have been s. — WIES 335:5
  could have s. sixpence — BECK 25:9
  only s. the world — CHES 64:11
saving capable of s. us — RICH 270:13
saw I s. you do it — STOP 306:1
sawdust S. Caesars — NEWS 238:2
say anything good to s. — LONG 202:8
  has nothing to s. — TAYL 310:9
  more to s. when I am dead — ROBI 271:11
  nothing to s. — CAGE 50:4
  S. it with flowers — ADVE 4:26
  s. nothing — HEAN 149:8
  see what I s. — FORS 120:7
  see what I s. — WALL 327:5
  way I s. it — WEST 332:14
  wink wink, s. no more — MONT 227:8
says Charley s. — OFFI 242:2
scaffolding s. has hardly gone up — LAMM 188:1
scandal because of a s. — HAIL 141:6
scar s. on the conscience — BLAI 36:4
scare can't s. him — STEI 303:3
  s. myself with my own — FROS 125:2
scarlet His sins were s. — BELL 27:17
scarves underneath its s. — CARE 53:12
scenery among savage s. — HOFF 155:13
  God paints the s. — HART 146:14
scent s. on a pocket handkerchief — LLOY 201:8
scepticism s. kept her — SART 284:9
schedule my s. is already full — KISS 183:13
schizophrenic s. is a special — LAIN 187:8
  you are a s. — SZAS 308:1
school destroy every grammar s. — CROS 80:9
  Let us think of a bad s. — NEIL 235:8
schoolchildren What all s. learn — AUDE 18:6
schoolgirl priggish s. — GRIG 139:5
  s. complexion — ADVE 4:7
schoolmaster becoming a s. — WAUG 329:2
schoolmasters bunch of s. — JAGG 165:9
schools some children, in some s. — BLUN 37:6
science after learning s. — FEYN 111:3
  aim of s. — BREC 43:7
  All s. is either physics — RUTH 279:14
  do s. in hell — VAUG 324:6
  essence of s. — BRON 44:10
  fear s. — POLA 255:19
  grand aim of all s. — EINS 99:4
  In s. the credit goes — DARW 84:4
  redefined the task of s. — HAWK 147:12

  S. aggregate of recipes — VALÉ 323:2
  S. doesn't interest me — BUÑU 47:13
  S. finds, industry applies — ANON 12:8
  S. is an edged tool — EDDI 97:2
  s. is its redemption — QUIN 264:7
  S. is part of culture — GOUL 136:5
  s. is strong — SZAS 308:2
  S. may have found a cure — KELL 176:5
  S. must begin with myths — POPP 256:8
  s. reassures — BRAQ 43:1
  S. without religion — EINS 98:3
  separation of state and s. — FEYE 111:2
  triumph of modern s. — WAUG 329:13
science fiction S. writers foresee — ASIM 15:2
scientific empirical s. system — POPP 256:4
  importance of s. work — HILB 153:7
  new s. truth — PLAN 255:8
scientist distinguished s. says — CLAR 70:10
  Everybody's a mad s. — CRON 80:5
  exercise for research s. — LORE 203:3
  not try to become a s. — EINS 99:5
scientists best s. aren't — CHOM 66:5
  in the company of s. — AUDE 19:3
  s. are probably right — ASIM 15:3
  than most young s. — MEDA 218:7
scissors end up using s. — HOCK 155:7
scooters s. off my lawn — CLAR 70:13
scorer One Great S. — RICE 270:2
scorpion like a demented s. — RUNC 277:9
Scotch as a S. banker — DAVI 84:7
  Mary, ma S. Bluebell — LAUD 191:13
Scotland flower of S. — WILL 337:4
  In S. we live between — CRAW 79:7
  lives in a castle in S. — SNIC 297:15
  our infinite S. — MACD 207:1
  S.'s oil — POLI 257:20
  S.'s rightful heritage — CONN 74:8
  sing Flower of S. — SILL 294:11
  white rose of S. — MACD 206:12
Scotsman S. on the make — BARR 24:4
  S. with a grievance — WODE 339:13
Scottish S. Parliament — EWIN 106:8
  shall be a S. parliament — ANON 12:11
  shall be a S. parliament — DEWA 89:12
Scotty Beam me up, S. — MISQ 224:1
scouts s.' motto — BADE 20:6
scrabble s. with all the vowels — ELLI 104:13
scrap s. of paper — BETH 32:2
scrape s. your strings darker — CELA 62:4
scratching s. of pimples — WOOL 342:4
scream like a s. from a crevasse — GREE 137:14
  no one can hear you s. — TAGL 309:6
  s. till I'm sick — CROM 80:3
screw seek the right s. — HOLU 156:9
scum Okie means you're s. — STEI 303:2
  They are s. — MAUG 217:5
scuttling S. across the floors — ELIO 102:6

sea complaining about the s.   POWE 261:3
  In a solitude of the s.   HARD 144:14
  in our s. of confusion   GAMO 129:6
  Put out to s.   MACN 210:8
  s.-change in politics   CALL 51:4
  s. curling Star-climbed   MERW 220:2
  s. hates a coward   O'NE 243:13
  s. is the universal   COUS 77:13
  serpent-haunted s.   FLEC 118:11
  snotgreen s.   JOYC 172:7
seagulls When s. follow a trawler   CANT 53:1
seal heard a s. bark   CART 56:1
sealed My lips are s.   MISQ 224:14
seals aroma of performing s.   HART 146:12
seams Amusing little s.   BAIL 20:9
search in s. of an author   PIRA 255:2
seas floors of silent s.   ELIO 102:6
  s. colder than the Hebrides   FLEC 118:10
  s. of pity lie   AUDE 17:12
  s. roll over   HERB 151:17
season dry brain in a dry s.   ELIO 101:13
  man has every s.   FOND 119:6
seasons man for all s.   BORR 40:17
seat-belts Fasten your s.   FILM 113:8
second grow a s. tongue   MONT 227:3
  not a s. on the day   COOK 75:15
  not your s. choice   LURI 204:9
  s. best's a gay goodnight   YEAT 345:3
  s. oldest profession   REAG 268:3
  This is my s. doctorate   CONN 74:13
second-best s. is anything but   LESS 197:16
second-hand s. Europeans   HOPE 157:7
secret discovered the s. of life   CRIC 79:10
  girls that have no s.   SPEN 300:7
  neurosis is a s.   TYNA 320:7
  photograph is a s.   ARBU 13:15
  s. diary of Adrian Mole   TOWN 316:14
  s. in the Oxford sense   FRAN 122:9
  S. sits in the middle   FROS 125:16
secretary being S. of State   STIP 305:3
secretive make sex less s.   SZAS 308:3
secrets privacy and tawdry s.   LEAC 193:10
  throw their guilty s.   PRIE 261:13
security otherwise styled s.   MADA 210:13
  s. around the president   MAIL 211:12
seduction In s., the rapist   DWOR 94:13
see come up and s. me sometime   MISQ 225:8
  I'll s. you again   COWA 78:4
  I s. dead people   FILM 114:12
  I shall never s.   KILM 180:4
  Nice to s. you   CATC 60:15
  nobody would s.   ARBU 13:13
  s. and hear nothing   THOM 314:21
  s. the hours pass   CIOR 70:3
  s. things and say 'Why'   SHAW 291:11
  s. what I say   WALL 327:5
  wait and s.   ASQU 15:6

  What you s. is what you get   SAYI 287:11
seeing s. what everybody has seen   SZEN 308:7
seem Let be be finale of s.   STEV 303:15
seen being s. for what one is   DRAB 93:2
  I have s. war   ROOS 273:15
  nobody's ever s.   ANON 11:16
  s. one city slum   AGNE 5:18
  should be s. to be done   HEWA 152:11
  thing that is not s.   SAIN 281:11
  when you've s. one Western   WHIT 334:10
  You've never s. this country   PURD 263:2
segregation S. now   WALL 327:3
  walls of s. came down   JACK 165:2
selection discrimination and s.   JAME 166:11
  Natural s. a mechanism   FISH 112:10
  no more s.   BLUN 37:5
  no s. by examination   BLUN 37:4
self divided s.   LAIN 187:6
  inner silent s.   MERT 220:1
  live without the s.   ATWO 16:11
  S.-pity? It's the only pity   LEVA 198:4
self-assertion s. abroad   WAUG 329:7
self-contempt S., well-grounded   LEAV 194:7
self-defence it was in s.   MARL 215:2
self-exhaustion S. in war   HART 146:9
self-government S. is our right   CASE 55:9
selfish accept the s. gene   LOVE 203:6
  s. gene   DAWK 85:5
  small and s. is sorrow   ELIZ 104:2
self-knowledge S. does not   CARE 53:14
self-made s. man is one who   STEA 302:4
  s. man may prefer   HAND 143:16
self-respect starves your s.   PARR 250:16
self-revelation s., whether it be   LANC 188:6
self-sufficiency S. at home   WAUG 329:7
sell could s. her words for money   LOOS 202:12
  I'll s. him   LEAC 193:11
  s. it cheap   SAYI 287:3
  s. Jack like soapflakes   KENN 178:1
  to s. time   TAWN 310:3
selling S. off the family silver   MISQ 225:1
  s. postcards   DYLA 95:2
seltzer weak hock and s.   BETJ 32:3
semi-attention constant s.   MERT 220:1
semi-house-trained s. polecat   FOOT 119:9
senator S., and a Democrat   JOHN 169:7
sensations easy prey to s.   TREV 317:7
sense good when it makes s.   MCEW 207:6
  Have you no s. of decency   WELC 330:10
  in biology makes s.   DOBZ 91:9
  Money is like a sixth s.   MAUG 217:3
  something makes s.   HAVE 147:6
  talk s. to American people   STEV 304:7
senseless kind of s. wit   WILB 335:8
sensibility dissociation of s.   ELIO 103:14
  informed by s.   READ 267:8
sensitive more s. than the average   WILS 337:9

shares Fair s. for all — POLI 257:13
shark s. has pretty teeth — BREC 43:11
sharks s. circling, and waiting — CLAR 70:5
Shaw S.'s plays — AGAT 5:17
shed disused s. in Co. Wexford — MAHO 211:6
she-devil life and loves of a s. — WELD 330:12
sheep savaged by a dead s. — HEAL 148:11
  s. in sheep's clothing — CHUR 69:14
  s. to pass resolutions — INGE 162:7
sheepdog if it was a s. — MASO 216:12
sheet brought in the white s. — LORC 202:14
sheets polyester s. — FARR 109:9
shelf s. life of the modern — TRIL 317:10
shell aggressive s. — MCLU 208:12
  fired a 15-inch s. — RUTH 279:16
shells choirs of wailing s. — OWEN 247:5
sheltered s. life can be — WELT 331:11
shepherd Old Nod, the s. — DE L 88:7
sheriff I shot the s. — MARL 215:2
shift s. in what the public wants — CALL 51:4
shilling s. life will give you — AUDE 18:9
shimmered Jeeves s. out — WODE 339:14
shimmy s. like my sister Kate — PIRO 255:3
shiny s., pointy things — KAY 175:8
ship as the smart s. grew — HARD 145:2
  captain of a broken s. — LA G 187:3
  like a sinking s. — WOOL 342:7
  on board a s. — FULL 127:4
  s. appeared in the air — HEAN 149:3
ships all the s. at sea — CATC 59:3
  little s. of England — GUED 140:2
  Loose lips sink s. — MILI 221:9
  s. have been salvaged — HALS 142:11
  s. sail like swans asleep — FLEC 118:14
  wrong with our bloody s. — BEAT 25:4
shires bugles calling from sad s. — OWEN 247:5
shit chicken s. can turn — JOHN 169:6
  ocean of s. — TANS 309:20
  shock-proof s. detector — HEMI 151:6
shivering s. human soul — PAST 251:2
shivers s. like the jelly — PIRO 255:3
shoals s. of herring — MACC 206:7
shock characterized by s. — FRAN 122:10
  Future s. — TOFF 316:9
  S. and Awe — ANON 12:5
  S. and Awe — ULLM 321:1
  s. of the new — DUNL 94:3
  s. of your joy — HUGH 160:4
shocked not s. by this subject — BOHR 38:7
shocking something s. — PORT 256:11
shocks s. the magistrate — RUSS 279:6
shoe other s. to drop — MURR 232:1
shoes changing s. — BREC 43:17
  Englishwomen's s. — HALS 142:9
  s. with broken high ideals — MCGO 207:9
  to run is good s. — RADC 265:3
shoeshine smile and a s. — MILL 222:6

shook Ten days that s. the world — REED 268:12
shoot s. me in my absence — BEHA 26:18
  s. me through linoleum — BANK 23:1
  s. Santa Claus — SMIT 296:7
  s. your murderer — ACHE 1:7
  They s. horses don't they — MCCO 206:9
  they shout and they s. — INGE 162:6
  You'd s. a fellow down — HARD 145:7
shooting Stop s. — DE M 89:1
  war minus the s. — ORWE 246:6
shoots green s. of recovery — MISQ 224:8
  man who s. him gets caught — MAIL 211:12
shop foul rag and bone s. — YEAT 344:7
shopping main thing today—s. — MILL 222:7
  Whole families s. — GINS 133:5
shore To the other s. — PAUL 251:8
shores wilder s. of love — BLAN 36:9
short long and the s. — HUGH 159:4
shorts Eat my s. — CATC 58:18
shot Certain men the English s. — YEAT 345:9
  I s. the sheriff — MARL 215:2
  They've s. our fox — BIRC 34:11
shoulder keep looking over his s. — BARU 24:16
  standing s. to shoulder — HAWK 148:2
  stand s. to shoulder — BLAI 36:3
shoulders City of the Big S. — SAND 283:3
  old heads on young s. — SPAR 299:8
  s. held the sky — HOUS 158:4
shout they s. and they shoot — INGE 162:6
shovels need men with s. — CLOO 72:9
show S. me the money — FILM 116:3
  s. you a loser — LOMB 202:5
  think of the s. so far — CATC 61:12
  wrong if someone can s. you — AYER 19:18
show business no business like s. — BERL 30:9
  s. with blood — BRUN 46:12
shower HANDSTAND IN S. — TELE 311:9
  sweetness of a s. — THOM 314:23
showman great s. whose technique — TAYL 310:10
shows All my s. are great — GRAD 136:6
  currency of all reality s. — TRUS 319:5
shrimp s. learns to whistle — KHRU 179:12
  s. on the barbie — ADVE 4:28
shrink discussed it with his s. — FARR 109:9
shroud stiff dishonoured s. — ELIO 102:18
  striped s. — THOM 315:2
shudder s. in the loins engenders — YEAT 345:8
shuffle All s. there — YEAT 345:19
shutter click the s. — EISE 100:3
sick kingdom of the s. — SONT 299:1
  Pass the s. bag, Alice — CATC 60:22
  scream till I'm s. — CROM 80:3
  s. had no rights — FORS 120:16
  think we're s. — WOLF 340:12
Sid Tell S. — ADVE 5:4
Sidcup get down to S. — PINT 254:13
side Dark s. of the moon — PINK 254:12

skin (*cont.*)

my s. bristles	HOUS 158:8
skull beneath the s.	ELIO 103:8
skins such white s.	CURZ 82:3
skirmish trivial s. fought	GRAV 137:2
skull s. beneath the skin	ELIO 103:8
sky clean the s.	ELIO 102:11
held the s. suspended	HOUS 158:4
Hullo Clouds Hullo S.	WILL 336:2
pie in the s. when you die	HILL 154:1
slacks girls in s. remember Dad	BETJ 32:4
slag-heap post-industrial s.	DRAB 93:1
slamming doors s.	WOOD 341:5
slang S. is a language	SAND 283:10
slap Slip, slop, s.	OFFI 242:14
slaughterhouses mechanized s.	VANE 324:1
slave moment the s. resolves	GAND 129:9
slave of that s.	CONN 75:8
slavery they impose s.	RUSS 279:4
slaves millions of royal s.	GENE 130:16
never will be s.	SHAW 292:12
s. remain	ZAMY 348:2
sons of former s.	KING 180:12
sleep deep s. of England	ORWE 245:9
Do s. well	CATC 58:17
from my mother's s.	JARR 166:17
green ideas s. furiously	CHOM 66:3
have to go to s.	LAST 190:9
Let us s. now	OWEN 247:12
miles to go before I s.	FROS 125:20
None shall s.	ADAM 2:1
put the world to s.	MUIR 230:13
rather s. in Chartres Cathedral	JOHN 170:9
S. is when all	GOLD 134:13
wake to s.	ROET 272:12
when you s. you remind me	SASS 284:17
sleeping Lay your s. head	AUDE 17:15
s. pill is white	SEXT 291:4
s. under the desk	GATE 130:6
s. with an elephant	TRUD 318:6
smitten a s. enemy	YAMA 344:1
waken a s. giant	FILM 114:2
sleepless S. as the river	CRAN 79:5
sleeps s. with the fishes	FILM 115:5
while the world s.	NEHR 235:6
sleepwalker assurance of a s.	HITL 154:14
sleepy I'm not s.	DYLA 95:10
sleeve Ash on an old man's s.	ELIO 101:4
lacy s. with vitriol	WOOL 342:8
sleeves Americanism with its s.	MCCA 205:9
rolls up its s.	SAND 283:10
slept s. with mice	COWA 78:19
slick Don't be s.	BERN 31:5
slip S. another shrimp	ADVE 4:28
S., slop, slap	OFFI 242:14
slitty-eyed you'll all be s.	PHIL 253:9
Sloane S. turned secular saint	BURC 47:15

slogans instead of principles, s.	BENT 30:1
slogged s. up to Arras	SASS 284:20
slop Slip, s., slap	OFFI 242:14
slopes on the butler's upper s.	WODE 340:6
slouches S. towards Bethlehem	YEAT 346:1
Slough friendly bombs, fall on S.	BETJ 32:14
slow telling you to s. down	SAYI 286:9
tend to s. you down	CARR 54:4
Time is too s.	VAN 323:10
slower had to be s.	FRAS 122:11
Reading it s.	WOOD 341:4
slowly twist s. in the wind	EHRL 97:10
slum In almost any s.	HARR 146:6
seen one city s.	AGNE 5:18
slums gay intimacy of the s.	WAUG 329:3
slush mush and s.	OWEN 247:1
pure as the driven s.	BANK 22:13
smack give them such a s.	MERC 219:13
Just a s. at Auden	EMPS 105:11
small pictures that got s.	FILM 116:16
s., but perfectly formed	COOP 76:12
S. is beautiful	SCHU 288:8
s. states—Israel, Athens	INGE 162:8
s.-talking world	FRY 126:9
they are very s.	UPDI 321:12
smallest even the s. person	FILM 113:7
smash English never s. in a face	HALS 142:10
smashing s. monuments	LEC 194:13
smell sense of s.	KELL 176:7
s. and hideous hum	GODL 134:6
s. of commerce	FILM 114:8
s. of napalm	FILM 114:7
Sweet s. of success	FILM 117:12
smile Cambridge people rarely s.	BROO 45:2
faint fleeting s.	THUR 316:4
good s. in a child's eyes	SHAF 291:7
has a nice s.	GROM 139:11
It's OK to s.	OFFI 242:18
s. and a shoeshine	MILL 222:6
S. at us, pay us	CHES 65:1
s. dwells a little longer	CHAP 63:13
s. of a cosmic Cheshire cat	HUXL 161:16
s., smile, smile	ASAF 14:14
smiled only the dead s.	AKHM 6:2
smith Chuck it, S.	CHES 64:5
smitten s. a sleeping enemy	YAMA 344:1
smoke rise then as s. to the sky	CELA 62:4
S. gets in your eyes	HARB 144:4
smoked s. my first cigarette	TOSC 316:13
smoke-filled s. room	SIMP 295:7
smoking S. can seriously damage	OFFI 242:15
smug s.-faced crowds	SASS 285:2
trendy S. Married	FIEL 111:7
snake bitten by a s.	DALA 83:1
s. came to my water-trough	LAWR 192:16
snakes S. eat frogs	STEV 303:16
snare rabbit in a s.	STEP 303:8

sneaky snouty, s. mind	NICO 236:9
sneezes Coughs and s. spread	OFFI 242:4
snipe could shoot s. off him	POWE 260:11
snobbery bereaved if s. died	USTI 322:4
S. with Violence	BENN 29:6
snotgreen s. sea	JOYC 172:7
snouty s., sneaky mind	NICO 236:9
snow congealed s.	PARK 250:5
dark over the s.	THOM 314:22
first fall of s.	PRIE 261:15
like the s. geese	OKPI 242:22
Night, s., and sand	NERU 235:11
s. falling faintly	JOYC 171:8
type of s.	WORR 342:10
woods fill up with s.	FROS 125:19
wrong sort of s.	NEWS 237:2
snowed s. for six days	THOM 314:9
snows more it s., *tiddely pom*	MILN 222:17
Snow White used to be S.	WEST 332:12
soaked s. to the skin	COHE 73:2
soap mouths out with s.	NEZ 236:6
this week's episode of 'S.'	CATC 58:12
soapflakes sell Jack like s.	KENN 178:1
sob S., heavy world	AUDE 16:12
sober tomorrow I shall be s.	CHUR 69:15
social s. and economic experiment	HOOV 157:2
S. Contract nothing more	WELL 331:5
s. progress, order	JOHN 168:4
socialism S. can only arrive	VIER 325:12
S. does not mean	ORWE 246:4
S. is what	MORR 228:11
S. nothing but capitalism	SPEN 300:10
s. or death	CHAV 64:4
s. would not lose	DUBČ 93:5
socialists s. throw it away	CAST 57:6
socially often s. impressive	WILL 336:4
society affluent s.	GALB 128:6
bad composer writing for s.	BRIT 44:6
call it a 'primitive s.'	GREG 138:10
good s. is one	MCEW 207:6
Great S.	JOHN 169:11
litmus test of civil s.	HAVE 147:9
nature of our s.	POWE 260:16
no such thing as S.	THAT 313:6
prosperous or caring s.	HESE 152:5
so-called affluent s.	BEVA 33:11
S. is built on	MAIL 211:8
S. needs to condemn	MAJO 211:14
s. of privacy	RAND 266:4
s. where it is safe	STEV 304:10
sociobiology Marxism is s.	WILS 337:12
sock making a hole in a s.	EINS 99:9
socks have to wash your s.	DE B 86:6
soda wash their feet in s. water	ELIO 103:4
Sodom S. and Gomorrah	BELL 28:5
sodomy rum, s., prayers	CHUR 68:12
sofa s. upholstered in panther	PLOM 255:18

soft s. under-belly of Europe	MISQ 225:3
softly S. along the road	DE L 88:7
soggy s. little island	UPDI 321:5
soldier British s. stand up to	SHAW 291:14
s. exchanged for the heart	TANS 310:1
s. of the Great War	EPIT 108:6
s.'s life is terrible hard	MILN 223:5
s. trying to violate	STRA 306:5
who had the s. singled	DOUG 92:5
soldiers Old s. never die	FOLE 119:5
old s. never die	MACA 205:5
young Argentinian s.	RUNC 277:7
soldiery Emperor's drunken s.	YEAT 344:5
solidity appearance of s.	ORWE 246:5
solitary s. confinement	WILL 336:12
solitude feel his s. more keenly	VALÉ 323:3
One hundred years of s.	GARC 130:1
solitudes Two s.	BORR 41:7
two s. protect	RILK 271:5
Solomon S. wrote the Proverbs	NAYL 235:4
soluble art of the s.	MEDA 218:6
solution can't see the s.	CHES 65:10
either part of the s.	CLEA 71:1
final s.	HEYD 153:1
people were a kind of s.	CAVA 57:12
total s.	GOER 134:10
solutions all the s.	THAT 313:17
s. are not	ASIM 15:2
some S. mishtake, shurely	CATC 61:1
someday S. I'll find you	COWA 78:10
someone s. may be happy	MENC 218:13
S. wants a letter	ADVE 4:29
something s. completely different	CATC 58:3
S. may be gaining	PAIG 248:6
S. must be done	MISQ 225:4
s. of the night	WIDD 335:1
Time for a little s.	MILN 223:2
was there s.	CATC 59:5
sometime come up and see me s.	MISQ 225:8
woman is a s. thing	HEYW 153:4
somewhat more than s.	RUNY 277:11
somewhere S. over the rainbow	HARB 144:8
Somme S. is like the Holocaust	BARK 23:6
son good idea—s.	CATC 59:4
My s. is home and dry	ELIZ 104:9
s. was killed while laughing	KIPL 182:1
would I tell you, s. of mine	NOON 240:1
song carcase of an old s.	THOM 315:5
hate a s. that has sold	BERL 30:12
only s. where I get	JOHN 168:6
s. is ended (but the melody)	BERL 30:8
s. was wordless	SASS 284:19
trouble with a folk s.	LAMB 187:10
Writing s. lyrics	PARI 249:3
songs angst s. for kids	COOP 76:11
s. were brilliant	BAEZ 20:7
sons for my own s.	RICH 270:11

sons (*cont.*)

s. and daughters of Life   GIBR 132:9
they have become our s.   ATAT 15:13
sophistication Hip is the s.   MAIL 211:10
Sorbonne one day at the S.   STEV 304:1
sorrow bee of s.   BABE 20:2
small and selfish is s.   ELIZ 104:2
sorry having to say you're s.   TAGL 309:9
S. for itself   LAWR 192:15
sort ability to s. peas   HOLU 156:9
soteriological In s. terms   FENT 110:9
sought least s. for   CRAN 79:6
soul dark night of the s.   FITZ 117:21
engineers of the s.   GORK 136:2
give his own s.   BOLT 38:12
literature saved my s.   RATU 267:3
Lord take my s.   LAST 191:1
love in another's s.   LAYT 193:9
not engineers of the s.   KENN 177:16
owe my s. to the company store   TRAV 317:3
shivering human s.   PAST 251:2
S. clap its hands and sing   YEAT 345:17
s. swooned slowly   JOYC 171:8
soulless when work is s.   CAMU 52:18
souls engineers of human s.   STAL 301:10
furnished s.   CUMM 81:10
only in men's s.   STEV 304:8
stuff of other people's s.   MCGR 208:1
sound feeling, then, not s.   STEV 304:2
S. money is the oldest   OSBO 246:12
s. of music   HAMM 143:8
s. of surprise   BALL 22:8
sounds similar s. at their ends   LARK 189:14
soup do not take s. at luncheon   CURZ 82:4
pissed in our s.   BENN 29:4
south go s. in the winter   ELIO 102:20
I want to go s.   LAWR 192:22
Yes, but not in the S.   POTT 259:7
South Africa S., renowned   CAMP 52:1
southern S. trees bear strange   ALLE 7:4
souvenirs *s. sont cors de chasse*   APOL 13:10
sovereign advise my s.   WAUG 329:12
change for a s.   NESB 236:2
sovereignties addition of s.   MONN 226:14
Soviet S. power plus electrification   LENI 196:6
Soviets All power to the S.   POLI 257:1
Soviet Union S. has indeed   FULB 127:1
S. was playing   ACHE 1:9
sow old s. that eats her farrow   JOYC 172:2
space art of how to waste s.   JOHN 170:8
cantos of unvanquished s.   CRAN 79:1
Filling a s.   O'KE 242:21
In s., no one can hear you   TAGL 309:6
more s. where nobody is   STEI 302:10
S. is almost infinite   QUAY 264:3
S. is blue   HEIS 150:5
S. isn't remote   HOYL 158:13

s. you leave behind   COOP 76:14
untrespassed sanctity of s.   MAGE 211:3
spaces s. between the houses   FENT 110:8
spaceship S. Earth   FULL 127:3
S. Earth   FULL 127:4
spade pick up a s.   FITZ 118:3
Spain Go to S. and get killed   POLL 256:1
nor leave S.   JUAN 172:17
permanence and unity of S.   JUAN 172:16
spain rain in S.   LERN 197:11
spanner their throats with a s.   BETJ 32:10
spare Brother can you s. a dime   HARB 144:5
do in his s. time   GILL 132:13
spark-gap s. mightier than pen   HOGB 156:1
sparrow Lesbia with her s.   MILL 221:14
sparrows pass through for the s.   GALB 128:11
speak I didn't s. up   NIEM 238:11
I now s. for France   DE G 87:3
s. before you think   FORS 121:4
s. for Britain   BOOT 39:4
S. for England   AMER 8:1
s. ill of everybody except   PÉTA 253:4
S. softly   ROOS 274:8
s. when they are spoken to   NEIL 235:8
whereof one cannot s.   WITT 339:8
speaking talking without s.   SIMO 295:4
speaks s. of a chair   BISH 35:4
spearmint s. lose its flavour   ROSE 275:3
special all s. cases   CAMU 52:3
specialist definition of a s.   MAYO 217:15
spectacle global s.   DEBO 86:9
spectacular assured by a s. error   GALB 129:1
spectators anything more than s.   ASQU 15:7
speech dead had no s. for   ELIO 101:3
gift of articulate s.   SHAW 293:4
make a s. on conservation   STEV 304:14
our concern was s.   ELIO 101:6
quick of s.   WINT 339:4
s. from Ernest Bevin   FOOT 119:7
S. is civilization   MANN 214:3
speechless washed in the s. real   BARZ 24:17
speed s. far faster than light   BULL 47:12
s. glum heroes   SASS 284:15
Unsafe at any s.   NADE 233:6
spelling s. is Wobbly   MILN 223:3
spend can't s. ourselves rich   BLAC 35:7
s., and spend, and spend   NICH 236:8
s. more time with my family   FOWL 121:11
s. your way out   CALL 50:10
spender big s.   FIEL 111:8
spent Never ask of money s.   FROS 125:6
spermatozoa million million s.   HUXL 161:13
spider s. trying to hide   NERU 235:12
spill let them not s. me   MACN 210:6
S. your guts at Wimbledon   CONN 75:9
spin Sob, as you s.   AUDE 16:12
spinach I say it's s.   CART 56:7

spindle fold, s. or mutilate	SAYI 286:11	**Stalingrad** cultural S.	BALL 22:6
spin-dryer mind is just like a s.	NOLA 239:12	**stall** Baby in an ox's s.	BETJ 32:5
spinner S. of the Years	HARD 145:2	**stallions** bared teeth of s.	CRAN 79:2
spires grey s. of Oxford	LETT 198:2	**stamp** physics or s. collecting	RUTH 279:14
spirit appeals to the Dunkirk s.	WILS 338:4	**stamps** stick in s.	NICO 236:10
forge his revolutionary s.	GUEV 140:4	**stand** all might s. up	JACK 165:2
sacramental of the s.	ROBI 271:14	Get up, s. up	MARL 215:1
spirits S. of well-shot woodcock	BETJ 32:7	no time to s. and stare	DAVI 84:11
spiritual Music is s.	MORR 229:2	S. by your man	WYNE 343:1
not being a s. people	MANC 212:13	s. up to anything except	SHAW 291:14
spiritualist you are a s.	SZAS 308:1	supposed to s. on that?	CART 57:3
spiritualists convention of s.	STOP 305:11	**standing** s. by my man	CLIN 71:10
spit no gun, but I can s.	AUDE 18:4	**star** Being a s. made it possible	DAVI 85:1
You s. on your people	WALC 326:2	By a high s. our course	MACN 210:8
splinter s. of ice	GREE 138:1	go to another s. system	HAWK 148:3
splinters teeth like s.	CAUS 57:10	*got* to come back a s.	FILM 116:14
split care what a s. infinitive	FOWL 121:10	guiding s.	CARS 54:6
Images s. the truth	LEVE 198:6	S. captains glow	FLEC 118:10
when I s. an infinitive	CHAN 63:5	**stardust** We are s.	MITC 225:11
Spock Dr. S. is worried	POLI 257:11	**stare** dead s. in a million adults	SHAF 291:7
spoiled s. with abuse	COOL 76:5	never to s. at people	BALF 22:3
spoken American people have s.	CLIN 72:6	no time to stand and s.	DAVI 84:11
spongy on s. shoes	WILB 335:9	**staring** S. at the sun	BORR 41:5
spoons world locks up its s.	SHAW 292:14	**starless** s. and bible-black	THOM 314:11
sport owe to s.	CAMU 52:17	**starred** No memory of having s.	FROS 125:14
participate in any s.	BOMB 39:1	**stars** heard it's in the s.	PORT 258:23
Serious s.	ORWE 246:6	heaventree of s.	JOYC 172:13
thing about s.	GREA 137:8	knowledge of the s. leads	EDDI 97:1
sportsman s. is a man who	LEAC 193:13	reaches for the s.	KOES 184:16
spray rime was on the s.	HARD 145:11	seven s. go squawking	AUDE 16:14
spring easing the S.	REED 268:11	s. of death	AKHM 6:3
first hour of s.	BOWE 41:10	S. scribble on our eyes	CRAN 79:1
only the right to s.	FOND 119:6	We have the s.	FILM 113:3
s. breaks through again	COWA 78:4	We've got more s.	MAYE 217:13
s. is wound up tight	ANOU 13:7	with mites of s.	MAYA 217:12
s. now comes unheralded	CARS 54:8	**starship** s. Enterprise	RODD 272:3
s. summer autumn winter	CUMM 81:2	**start** end is where we s. from	ELIO 101:8
spur s. me into song	YEAT 346:4	S. all over again	FIEL 111:11
spy s. who came in from the cold	LE C 195:1	s. in the streets	KENN 176:11
squalor public s.	GALB 128:8	s. your own religion	ANON 11:4
square S. deal afterwards	ROOS 274:9	wholly new s.	ELIO 100:20
squat s., and packed with guile	BROO 45:2	**started** arrive where we s.	ELIO 101:7
squats s. on the hearthstone	QUIL 264:5	s. so I'll finish	CATC 60:9
squawking seven stars go s.	AUDE 16:14	**starter** few thought he was a s.	ATTL 16:6
squeak until the pips s.	GEDD 130:9	Your s. for ten	CATC 61:22
stab No iron can s. the heart	BABE 20:1	**starting** s. a new religion	ORWE 246:10
saw him s.	READ 267:10	**starvation** night s.	ADVE 3:28
stability political s.	MITC 223:13	**starve** let our people s.	NYER 240:10
stage put your daughter on the s.	COWA 78:8	s. on dissonances	IVES 163:9
stain bright s. on the vision	GRAV 137:3	**state** no such thing as the S.	AUDE 18:8
convict s.	HUGH 159:12	reinforcement of the S.	CAMU 52:14
s. upon the silence	BECK 26:8	rolled back frontiers of S.	THAT 313:7
stained hole in a s. glass window	CHAN 63:1	separation of s. and science	FEYE 111:2
stake s. driven through his heart	O'BR 241:1	s. has no place	TRUD 318:4
stalemate end in a s.	CRON 80:7	S. is an instrument	STAL 301:9
Stalin guilt of S.	GORB 135:12	s. with the prettiest name	BISH 35:2
S. himself rose	TROT 318:2	While the S. exists	LENI 196:3

stately S. Homes of England	COWA 78:11
S., plump Buck Mulligan	JOYC 172:6
statement black s. of pistons	SPEN 300:3
woman makes the s.	MUIR 231:2
statements s. inoperative	ZIEG 348:10
statesman he was a s.	LLOY 201:11
set a s. right	YEAT 345:12
s. is a politician	TRUM 318:13
station By Grand Central S.	BORR 40:6
statistic million deaths a s.	STAL 301:12
statistical s. improbability	DAWK 85:4
s. possibilities	DIAM 90:4
statistics experiment needs s.	RUTH 279:15
statue little gold s. doesn't clean	THER 313:18
s. has never been set up	SIBE 294:9
status quo restored the s.	SQUI 301:7
stay If we can't s. here alive	MONT 227:5
love is here to s.	GERS 132:1
Nothing gold can s.	FROS 125:12
s. up all night	BRYS 47:1
things to s. as they are	LAMP 188:4
stays prays together s. together	SAYI 286:13
steak not the meat of the s.	PRIE 262:3
steal s. from many, it's research	MIZN 226:8
s. more than a hundred men	PUZO 263:5
stealing For de little s.	O'NE 243:9
steamers little holiday s.	PRIE 262:2
steaming wealth of s. phrases	SCHU 288:10
steamroller Fermi was a s.	SEGR 290:3
steel surgeon plies the s.	ELIO 100:19
steeples dreary s. of Fermanagh	CHUR 66:13
step One more s. along	CART 55:5
one small s. for a man	ARMS 14:11
step-parents especially s.	POWE 260:10
sterilized thoroughly s.	SAKI 282:2
stick carry a big s.	ROOS 274:8
rattling of a s. inside	ORWE 245:11
should s. together	HUGH 160:5
Work was like a s.	SOLZ 298:6
sticks S. nix hick pix	NEWS 238:3
stiffening Mrs Blair's knees s.	ELIZ 104:10
still And s. I rise	BORR 40:2
S. crazy after all	SIMO 295:5
S. falls the rain	SITW 295:13
s., like air, I'll rise	ANGE 9:6
s. point	ELIO 100:13
stimulate s. the phagocytes	SHAW 291:15
sting s. itself to death	RUNC 277:9
s. like a bee	ALI 6:13
where is thy s.-a-ling-a-ling	ANON 12:4
stir Add sex, and s.	CILA 70:1
stirred Shaken and not s.	FLEM 118:16
stock It's my s.-in-trade	DIET 90:11
stocking glimpse of s.	PORT 256:11
stole son of a bitch s. my watch	FILM 116:4
stolen generation was s.	FREE 122:14
s. his wits away	DE L 88:2

stone bomb them back into S. Age	LEMA 195:15
caught the first s.	POWE 260:13
Let them not make me a s.	MACN 210:6
Like a rolling s.	DYLA 95:8
make a s. of the heart	YEAT 344:13
through a piece of s.	MOOR 227:11
stood should of s. in bed	JACO 165:8
stop full s. at the right place	BABE 20:1
nobody's going to s. 'em	BERR 31:12
S. all the clocks	AUDE 17:6
s. believing in it	DICK 90:7
s. everyone from doing it	HERB 151:14
S.-look-and-listen	OFFI 242:16
S. me and buy one	ADVE 5:2
S. shooting	DE M 89:1
S. the world	NEWL 236:4
stops buck s. here	TRUM 318:17
storage thought in cold s.	SAMU 283:1
store in the s. we sell hope	REVS 269:10
stories tell ourselves s.	DIDI 90:10
stork S. from butter	ADVE 3:10
storm not to be taken by s.	CARD 53:8
Stormont Ulster Parliament at S.	GEOR 131:4
stormy S. weather	KOEH 184:11
story novel tells a s.	FORS 120:6
page-one s.	STON 305:7
s. is ephemeral and doomed	FAUL 110:3
St Paul's Say I am designing S.	BENT 29:15
strafe Gott s. England	POLI 257:15
straight nothing ever ran quite s.	GALS 129:2
pretty s. sort	BLAI 36:1
strain train take the s.	ADVE 4:9
Words is	ELIO 100:14
strand never alone with a S.	ADVE 5:15
walk down the S.	HARG 145:16
strange 'S. friend,' I said	OWEN 247:9
strangeness will die of s.	MURR 231:17
stranger by a complete s.	ANNE 9:11
I, a s. and afraid	HOUS 158:3
Look, s.	AUDE 17:14
never love a s.	BENS 29:12
s. and alone	WOLF 340:11
wiles of the s.	NASH 234:7
You may see a s.	HAMM 143:7
strangers kindness of s.	WILL 336:15
s. in the Capitol	HEWI 152:14
strappy s. sandals	SHUL 294:8
strategy came up with an exit s.	LENO 197:4
straw Headpiece filled with s.	ELIO 101:14
strawberry S. fields forever	LENN 196:18
stream cool as a mountain s.	ADVE 3:12
street don't do it in the s.	CAMP 51:14
inability to cross the s.	WOOL 342:2
s. fighting man	JAGG 166:5
sunny side of the s.	FIEL 111:10
talking at s. corners	VANZ 324:4
worth two in the s.	WEST 332:1

streets children died in the s.	AUDE 17:5	
Down these mean s.	CHAN 63:3	
grass will grow in the s.	HOOV 157:5	
start in the s.	KENN 176:11	
S. FLOODED	TELE 311:8	
strength S. through joy	POLI 257:23	
stretch s. the human frame	SCAR 285:11	
strife In place of s.	CAST 57:5	
step towards an end of s.	GEOR 131:4	
strike s. against public safety	COOL 76:1	
s. it in anger	SHAW 292:21	
when to s.	HEIN 150:2	
string wire netting, s. and cotton wool		
	SCHW 289:5	
strings scrape your s. darker	CELA 62:4	
striped s. shroud	THOM 315:2	
stroke at a s., reduce the rise	HEAT 149:10	
strong nature of s. people	BONH 39:2	
only the S. shall thrive	SERV 290:15	
realize how s. she is	REAG 267:12	
river Is a s. brown god	ELIO 101:1	
struck s. regularly like gongs	COWA 78:15	
struggle s. between artist man	SHAW 292:10	
s. continues	LAST 191:1	
s. towards the heights	CAMU 52:6	
to-day the s.	AUDE 18:14	
struggled s. against tyranny	TUTU 320:1	
stuck s. in this building	LAST 190:8	
students black s. had to go	GRAN 136:11	
studiously apart, s. neutral	WILS 338:15	
study proper s. of mankind	HUXL 161:5	
stuff de s. I like	ZEPH 348:7	
S. happens	RUMS 277:5	
too short to s. a mushroom	CONR 75:13	
stuffing S. instead of potatoes?	ADVE 5:3	
stumbles how the strong man s.	ROOS 274:12	
stump mount the s.	STEV 304:14	
stupid *all* questions were s.	WEIS 330:8	
interesting . . . but s.	CATC 61:9	
It's the economy, s.	POLI 257:21	
on the part of the s.	WARN 328:3	
pretend to be more s.	STAR 301:14	
s. neither forgive nor	SZAS 307:14	
style has no real s.	PICA 254:6	
Mandarin s.	CONN 75:3	
murderer for fancy prose s.	NABO 233:2	
sub Sighted s., sank same	MASO 216:11	
subject not shocked by this s.	BOHR 38:7	
sublime most s. noise	FORS 120:10	
ridiculous, the s.	MAHO 211:5	
submarine yellow s.	LENN 197:2	
substitute no s. for talent	HUXL 161:9	
no s. for victory	MACA 205:4	
substitutes Ours is the age of s.	BENT 30:1	
subtle s. but not malicious	EINS 98:5	
subversive funny is s.	ORWE 246:7	
subway in a New York s.	STRA 306:7	

succeed How to s. in business	MEAD 218:3
If at first you don't s.	FIEL 112:1
not enough to s.	VIDA 325:6
not going to s.	MORT 229:6
possible to s.	RENO 269:8
succeeds Whenever a friend s.	VIDA 325:5
success If *A* is a s. in life	EINS 99:2
no s. like failure	DYLA 95:9
S. is relative	ELIO 100:8
Sweet smell of s.	FILM 117:12
successful recipes always s.	VALÉ 323:2
sucker give a s. an even break	FIEL 111:13
sue s. its parents	WATS 328:11
sued publish and be s.	INGR 162:11
suet-pudding cold, black s.	LEWI 199:16
Suez S. Canal flowing through	EDEN 97:4
suffering About s. they were	AUDE 17:16
not true that s. ennobles	MAUG 217:1
sufferings constant in human s.	JOYC 172:3
sufficient building works is not s.	JOHN 170:7
S. conscience	LLOY 201:13
sugar no s. cane for miles	HOLI 156:4
suicide infamous s.	PLAT 255:11
it is s.	MACD 207:3
longest s. note	KAUF 175:2
possibility of s.	CIOR 70:2
S. is our way	MAHE 211:4
s. kills two people	MILL 222:1
suicides s. have a special language	SEXT 291:6
suit lugubrious man in a s.	ELIZ 104:4
times will s. me	HOWA 158:9
suitable s. case for treatment	MERC 219:8
suites get to the s.	KENN 176:11
suits omelette all over our suits	BROK 44:8
people in s.	CAME 51:10
sum s. of all the choices	DIDI 90:9
Sumatra giant rat of S.	DOYL 92:12
summer long hot s.	FILM 117:8
on a hot s. afternoon	ANON 12:13
s. afternoon	JAME 166:14
s. birdcage	BORR 41:6
S. time and the livin'	HEYW 153:3
sun At the going down of the s.	BINY 34:10
Born of the s.	SPEN 300:5
inconceivable idea of the s.	STEV 303:19
staring at the s.	BELL 27:5
Staring at the s.	BORR 41:5
s. also rises	HEMI 151:4
S. backs Blair	NEWS 238:4
S. Wot Won It	NEWS 237:16
watched the s. going down	VAN 323:9
where no s. shines	THOM 314:5
sunbathing Picasso, s. and jazz	WAUG 329:6
sunbeam Jesus wants me for a s.	TALB 309:19
Sunday Never on S.	FILM 117:9
rainy S. afternoon	ERTZ 106:4
S., bloody Sunday	FILM 117:11

Sunday (*cont.*)

S. go-to-meeting clothes	SHIE 294:3
working week and S. best	AUDE 17:7
sundial s., and I make a botch	BELL 27:16
sunlight paint s.	HOPP 157:12
S. is said to be	BRAN 42:15
s. on the garden	MACN 210:7
sunlit broad, s. uplands	CHUR 67:7
sunny some s. day	PARK 250:10
s. side of the street	FIEL 111:10
sunset s. of my life	REAG 268:8
sunsets Autumn s. exquisitely	HUXL 161:14
horror of s.	PROU 262:8
sunshine Bring me s.	DEE 86:13
ray of s.	WODE 339:13
superior S. people never make	MOOR 228:3
superman godlike s.	WODE 340:1
It's S.	CATC 59:2
superstition main source of s.	RUSS 279:8
supplies just bought fresh s.	BREC 43:9
support depend on the s. of Paul	SHAW 292:1
no invisible means of s.	BUCH 47:6
s. of the woman I love	EDWA 97:6
suppose queerer than we s.	HALD 142:1
suppress power of s.	NORT 240:4
supreme isn't *on* the S. Court	CARD 53:9
S. God	EMPS 105:10
surely Shome mishtake, s.	CATC 61:1
surface looks dingy on the s.	PIRS 255:5
surfaces queen of s.	DOWD 92:11
surgeon s. plies the steel	ELIO 100:19
surprise Life is a great s.	NABO 233:3
Live frugally on s.	WALK 326:9
sound of s.	BALL 22:8
surrealism S. has been the drunken flame	PAZ 251:10
surrender cheese-eating s. monkeys	GROE 139:9
we shall never s.	CHUR 67:6
surroundings I plus my s.	ORTE 244:9
survival s. game	CHRÉ 66:7
there is no s.	CHUR 67:5
we are their s. machines	DAWK 85:6
survive know they can s.	HART 146:10
Only the paranoid s.	GROV 140:1
s. to consume	VANE 324:2
will s. of us is love	LARK 189:1
survives music that s. is	ROSE 275:4
survivors more the s.' affair	MANN 214:2
suspects Round up the usual s.	FILM 115:8
swallow speed of a s.	BETJ 33:1
swamps across primeval s.	WODE 340:3
swans ships sail like s. asleep	FLEC 118:14
swearing s. is part of it	GREA 137:8
swears Money doesn't talk, it s.	DYLA 95:6
sweat blood, toil, tears and s.	CHUR 67:3
s. of its labourers	EISE 99:12

sweater want to hear from your s.	LEBO 194:8
sweeps beats as it s.	ADVE 4:2
sweet dead thing that smells s.	THOM 314:19
S. smell of success	FILM 117:12
S., soft, plenty rhythm	MORT 229:9
technically s.	OPPE 244:2
sweetness experience will teach me the s.	SEEG 290:1
s. of a shower	THOM 314:23
sweets bag of boiled s.	CRIT 80:1
swell Thou s.! Thou witty	HART 147:1
What a s. party	PORT 258:23
swift S. has sailed into his rest	YEAT 346:5
swimmers as s. into cleanness	BROO 45:4
swimming s. naked	BUFF 47:10
swines You rotten s.	CATC 61:21
swing ain't got that s.	MILL 222:15
s. for it	KING 181:4
Swiss operated by the S.	USTI 322:5
switchblades blondes and s.	COOP 76:10
Switzerland In S. they had	FILM 114:11
sword I gave them a s.	NIXO 239:7
s. and the currency	PROD 262:6
s. of truth	AITK 6:1
s. the axis of the world	DE G 87:12
wield the s. of France	DE G 87:4
swords paper hats and wooden s.	USTI 322:3
sympathy messages of s.	AYCK 19:13
Tea and s.	ANDE 9:1
symphony Beethoven's Fifth S.	FORS 120:10
system rocked the s.	ROBI 272:1

t t. is silent, as in *Harlow*	ASQU 15:10
ta saying 'T.' to God	SPEN 300:2
table patient etherized upon a t.	ELIO 102:2
tablet keep taking The T.	THOM 315:3
tactful t. in audacity	COCT 72:14
tails Brushin' off my t.	BERL 30:10
Taisez-vous T.! Méfiez-vous	OFFI 242:17
take big enough to t. away	FORD 119:13
can't t. it with you	HART 147:2
can't t. that away from me	GERS 132:3
not going to t. this	FILM 114:9
t. it back	LE C 195:2
T. me to your leader	CATC 61:4
t. you in the morning	BALD 21:7
takes t. just like a woman	DYLA 95:7
talcum bit of t. is always walcum	NASH 234:3
tale most tremendous t. of all	BETJ 32:5
Trust the t.	LAWR 192:3
talent no substitute for t.	HUXL 161:9
no t. for writing	BENC 28:8
t. to amuse	COWA 78:3
tomb of a mediocre t.	SMIT 297:3
talents t. and our expectations	DE B 86:8
talk Careless t. costs lives	OFFI 242:1

good to t.	ADVE 4:4
how much my Ministers t.	THAT 312:8
If you t. to God	SZAS 308:1
Money doesn't t., it swears	DYLA 95:6
people who can't t.	ZAPP 348:6
t. like a lady	SHAW 293:5
t. to the plants	CHAR 64:1
use words when I t. to you	ELIO 102:17
ways of making you t.	CATC 61:11
talking ain't t. about him	GLAS 134:1
nation t. to itself	MILL 222:9
opposite of t. is waiting	LEBO 194:9
stop people t.	ATTL 16:8
t. without speaking	SIMO 295:4
You t. to me?	FILM 116:15
talks Garbo t.	TAGL 309:4
tall short and the t.	HUGH 159:4
t. as a crane	SITW 295:12
tambourine Mr T. Man	DYLA 95:10
tango Takes two to t.	HOFF 155:12
tank tiger in your t.	ADVE 4:25
tanks Get your t. off my lawn	WILS 338:11
t. of the politicians	NEWS 238:5
tanstaafl acronym т.	SAYI 287:6
target don't t. extras	ROWL 276:10
tarnished neither t. nor afraid	CHAN 63:3
Tarot readers of T. cards	JONE 170:13
tarted should be t. up	BOWI 42:3
tarts action of two t.	MACM 209:6
Tarzan Me T., you Jane	MISQ 224:13
tasks dear unfinished t.	ANON 11:3
taste bouquet better than the t.	POTT 259:5
doubt and good t.	BROD 44:7
ghastly good t.	BETJ 33:2
tasted I've t. it	KAY 175:9
t. your worm	SPOO 300:14
tastes if it t. good, it's bad	ASIM 15:4
tattered t. coat upon a stick	YEAT 345:17
taught t. us how to live	BENN 29:2
t. what is	BRUC 46:9
tax power to t.	BLAC 35:7
to t. rich people	LLOY 201:9
taxation Inflation one form of t.	FRIE 124:5
taxes Death and t. and childbirth	MITC 226:1
little people pay t.	HELM 150:11
no new t.	BUSH 48:16
Sex and t.	JONE 171:2
taxi If you can't leave in a t.	FILM 114:4
t. throbbing waiting	ELIO 103:5
taxi-cab look like a t.	HUGH 159:3
taxis hiring t. to scuttle round	KINN 181:8
taxpayer at the t.'s expense	MENC 219:4
Tchaikovsky better sort of T.	SCHO 288:4
tea honey still for t.	BROO 45:3
T., although an Oriental	CHES 65:2
T. and sympathy	ANDE 9:1
t. for two	CAES 50:2
teabag woman is like a t.	REAG 267:12
teach change the people who t.	BYAT 49:13
T. us to care	ELIO 100:5
teacher omnipresent t.	BRAN 42:16
teaches He who cannot, t.	SHAW 292:19
tea-cup crack in the t. opens	AUDE 17:1
tea-girl t.'s chance to kiss	WHIT 334:9
teapot china t. revolving	RUSS 279:10
tear Wipe the t., baby dear	WEST 333:3
tears blood, toil, t. and sweat	CHUR 67:3
bursting into t.	WOOD 341:5
enough of blood and t.	RABI 265:2
French without t.	RATT 267:1
t. I cannot hide	HARB 144:4
tearsday moanday, t., wailsday	JOYC 171:11
tease fleas that t.	BELL 28:1
technical few t. details	NYE 240:9
technically t. sweet	OPPE 244:2
Technik *Vorsprung durch T.*	ADVE 5:8
technique t. improved as the real	TAYL 310:10
technology advanced t.	CLAR 70:9
new t. imposed	SEDD 289:12
T. . . . the knack	FRIS 124:8
white heat of t.	MISQ 225:7
teddy Now T. must run	KENN 178:4
T. Bears have their Picnic	KENN 176:13
t. bear to the nation	NEWS 237:4
teenager as a t.	LEBO 194:10
teenie Itsy bitsy t. weenie	VANC 323:6
teeth Does Bambi have t.	CART 56:2
he's got iron t.	GROM 139:11
old bitch gone in the t.	POUN 259:15
shark has pretty t.	BREC 43:11
women have fewer t.	RUSS 278:12
Teflon T.-coated Presidency	SCHR 288:5
telegrams life of t. and anger	FORS 120:13
telephones Tudor monarchy with t.	BURG 48:4
television first law of t.	ADAM 2:8
I hate t.	WELL 331:2
no plain women on t.	FORD 119:10
of t.	WILD 335:10
Radio and t.	SARR 284:1
see bad t. for nothing	GOLD 135:6
Some t. programmes	ANON 12:10
T. brought brutality	MCLU 208:13
T. closer to reality	PAGL 248:4
T. contracts imagination	WOGA 340:8
T. has brought murder	HITC 154:11
T. has made dictatorship	PERE 252:7
T. is for appearing on	COWA 78:18
T. is simultaneously	JAME 166:7
T.? word is half Greek	SCOT 289:8
thinking man's t.	HAMP 143:12
tell closest friends won't t. you	ADVE 3:18
Don't ask, don't t.	NUNN 240:7
Don't t. the ending	TAGL 309:12
t. ourselves stories	DIDI 90:10

tell (cont.)

T. Sid	ADVE 5:4
T. them I came	DEL 88:6
t. them of us and say	EPIT 108:10
T. the truth	BERN 31:5
What do I t. the pilot	LAST 191:8
telling t. you something	DUNM 94:4
tells nobody t. me anything	GALS 129:4
t. the truth	MUNR 231:8
temper Never lose your t. with	PANK 248:9
never to lose me t.	O'CA 241:8
truth that has lost its t.	GIBR 132:11
temperature acquire a t.	SCHU 288:10
temporary t. thing I took on about	
	MCNE 209:14
temps À la recherche du t. perdu	PROU 262:7
temptation maximum of t.	SHAW 292:20
t. to be good	BREC 43:5
ten less than $10,000	EVAN 106:5
t.-sixty-six and all that	SELL 290:5
Your starter for t.	CATC 61:22
tenants T. of the house	ELIO 101:13
tendency Groucho t.	ANON 11:10
tender I'll be irreproachably t.	MAYA 217:11
tennis Anyone for t.	CATC 58:5
play t. with the net down	FROS 126:3
tent big t.	POLI 257:7
G.O.P.'s big t.	NEWS 238:1
inside the t. pissing out	JOHN 170:3
tents t. have been struck	SMUT 297:13
terminological t. inexactitude	CHUR 66:11
terrible isn't life a t. thing	THOM 314:13
t. beauty is born	YEAT 344:12
T. is the temptation	BREC 43:5
t. night	PORT 259:2
terrier t. can define a rat	HOUS 158:7
territorial last t. claim	HITL 155:1
terror boredom and t.	WELL 331:3
From all that t. teaches	CHES 64:12
no t. in a bang	HITC 154:12
objects of t.	SOYI 299:4
T. arises from a sense	KING 181:1
T. the feeling which	JOYC 172:3
unity against t.	BUSH 49:4
victory in spite of all t.	CHUR 67:5
terrorism democratic world and t.	BLAI 36:3
even than the threat of t.	KING 180:7
this war on t.	BUSH 49:5
terrorist t. and the hijacker	THAT 313:5
t. and the policeman	CONR 75:11
t. attack against	LIVI 200:15
terrorists t. who committed	BUSH 49:3
terrorize t. a whole nation	MURR 232:3
test cricket t.	TEBB 310:13
play T. cricket	BRAD 42:13
testing virtue at the t. point	LEWI 199:8
text nothing outside of the t.	DERR 89:5

thank terrible thing, t. God	THOM 314:13
T. heaven for little girls	LERN 197:12
thanks T. for the memory	ROBI 271:10
that t.'s the way it is	CATC 58:4
Thatcher it is for Mrs T.	CALL 51:4
people like Mrs T.	BROW 46:2
thcream t. till I'm sick	CROM 80:3
theatre goes with slipping into a t.	KAEL 174:3
in a crowded t.	MISQ 225:2
only regret in the t.	BARR 24:7
problems of the modern t.	RATT 266:9
t. to be entertained	BENN 29:3
This House today is a t.	BALD 21:13
theft t. over honest toil	RUSS 278:14
theme T. is my religion	REVS 269:11
theories T. pass	ROST 275:10
theory t. against the second law	EDDI 96:8
Wonderful t.	WILS 338:1
there Because it's t.	MALL 212:8
I am not t.	FRYE 126:14
MACAVITY WASN'T T.	ELIO 102:12
met a man who wasn't t.	MEAR 218:4
Over t.	COHA 73:1
T. and back again	TOLK 316:10
t.—but not back again	JACK 165:4
T. you go again	REAG 268:2
thermodynamics second law of t.	EDDI 96:8
thicker History gets t.	TAYL 310:5
thieves One of the t. was saved	BECK 26:1
T. respect property	CHES 65:6
thin become unnaturally t.	WOLF 340:9
never be too rich or too t.	WIND 339:1
t. man inside every fat man	ORWE 245:5
t. one wildly signalling	CONN 75:4
thing Courage is the t.	BARR 24:6
one damned t. after another	HUBB 159:1
one damn t. over and over	MILL 221:16
t. itself and not the myth	RICH 270:8
t. that is not seen	SAIN 281:11
things been t. and seen places	WEST 332:4
confused t. with names	SART 284:7
just one of those t.	PORT 258:19
T. ain't what they used	PERS 253:3
T. can only get better	PETR 253:6
T. can only get better	POLI 258:8
T. fall apart	YEAT 345:20
t. they didn't know	POUN 259:12
think able to t.	KUND 185:15
can't make her t.	PARK 250:8
Don't t. twice	DYLA 95:4
easier to act than to t.	AREN 14:4
faster than you t.	PAUL 251:6
I don't t. much of it	LAST 190:7
know what I t.	WALL 327:5
might very well t. that	CATC 61:19
not so t. as you drunk	SQUI 301:6
paint objects as I t. them	PICA 254:5

people do they t. we are	CHUR 67:13
speak before you t.	FORS 121:4
tell what I t.	FORS 120:7
t. different	ADVE 5:6
t. globally	SAYI 287:7
t. of yourself one way	HEDR 150:1
t. what other people think	YEAT 345:19
t. with our wombs	LUCE 204:6
t. without his hat	BECK 26:4
we've got to t.	RUTH 280:1
whether machines t.	SKIN 296:3
You know more than you t.	SPOC 300:11
thinker murder the t.	WESK 331:15
thinking lateral t.	DE B 86:7
our modes of t.	EINS 99:1
power of positive t.	PEAL 251:13
saves original t.	SAYE 285:7
t. is diminished	EICH 98:2
t. man's crumpet	MUIR 230:14
t. what nobody has thought	SZEN 308:7
third t. of my life over	ALLE 7:16
T. World is an artificial	NAIP 233:8
thirteen clocks were striking t.	ORWE 245:15
T. years of Tory misrule	POLI 258:9
thirtieth t. year to heaven	THOM 314:6
thirty bus over the age of t.	WEST 333:1
t. pieces of silver	BEVA 33:7
thorn Oak, and Ash, and T.	KIPL 182:16
thorns crown of t.	BEVA 33:7
thou T. swell! Thou witty	HART 147:1
Through the T.	BUBE 47:4
thought beautiful clean t.	LAWR 192:11
forced into a state of t.	GALS 129:3
frozen t. of men	KRIS 185:4
t. in a concentration camp	ROOS 274:5
t. in cold storage	SAMU 283:1
What was once t.	DÜRR 94:11
where a t. might grow	MAHO 211:6
thoughts bring my t. to an end	SMIT 297:10
One has to multiply t.	LEC 194:12
thousand first t. days	KENN 177:8
lasts for a t. years	CHUR 67:7
not in a t. years	SMIT 296:14
t. years of history	GAIT 128:5
three breakfast t. times	MAUG 217:6
More than t. can't	HEIN 150:2
Though he was only t.	MILN 223:6
t. beers and it looks good	FILM 116:5
t. is a houseful	SAYI 286:5
T. o'clock always too late	SART 284:11
t. o'clock in the morning	FITZ 117:21
t. of us in this marriage	DIAN 90:6
threshold t. of a new house	ATWO 16:10
thriftily men who left them t.	KIPL 182:11
throat in the city's t.	LOWE 203:10
murder by the t.	LLOY 201:7
taking life by the t.	FROS 126:2

t. 'tis hard to slit	KING 181:4
throne One Law, one Land, one T.	KIPL 183:1
t. could remain empty	CAMU 52:13
t. of bayonets	INGE 162:9
t. of bayonets	YELT 346:12
through best way out is always t.	FROS 125:18
live t. someone else	FRIE 123:16
thrown t. it back	POWE 260:13
thrush aged t., frail, gaunt	HARD 145:3
thunderbirds T. are go	CATC 61:6
Tiananmen tanks into T. Square	ANON 13:2
Tiber River T. foaming	POWE 261:1
ticket She's got a t. to ride	LENN 196:19
take a t. at Victoria	BEVI 34:1
tickled t. to death to go	WEST 333:3
tiddely more it snows, t. pom	MILN 222:17
tide Not this t.	KIPL 182:13
when the t. goes out	BUFF 47:10
tides drew these t. of men	LAWR 193:3
Push in their t.	THOM 314:5
tidy Keep Britain t.	OFFI 242:11
tiger atom bomb is a paper t.	MAO 214:6
Celtic T.	MCAL 205:1
t. in your tank	ADVE 4:25
tigers ride to and fro upon t.	CHUR 67:1
tamed and shabby t.	HODG 155:10
tight Sitting t. is power	BELL 28:3
t. gag of place	HEAN 149:8
tile not red brick but white t.	OSBO 246:16
tilt We do not t. on either side	GAND 129:7
time As t. goes by	HUPF 160:14
at the wrong t.	BRAD 42:12
dance to the music of t.	BORR 40:8
devote more t. to them	FOWL 121:11
expands to fill the t.	CONR 75:14
Get me to the church on t.	LERN 197:6
given t. to prepare	HUME 160:8
good t. was had by all	SMIT 297:11
Hurry up please it's t.	ELIO 103:3
idea whose t. has come	SAYI 287:5
leave exactly on t.	MUSS 232:7
may be some t.	LAST 190:6
no enemy but t.	YEAT 345:5
peace for our t.	CHAM 62:8
something to do with the t.	ROGE 273:6
spend more t. with family	THAT 313:10
That passed the t.	BECK 26:5
t. cracks into furious flower	BROO 45:10
t. for a change	DEWE 90:2
T. for a little something	MILN 223:2
T. for bed	CATC 61:7
T. has no divisions	MANN 213:14
T. has transfigured them	LARK 189:1
T. is an illusion	ADAM 2:4
t. is running out	KOES 184:14
t. is the longest distance	WILL 336:11
T. is too slow	VAN 323:10

time (*cont.*)

t. of darkness	BREC 43:16
T. present and time past	ELIO 100:10
t.'s arrow	EDDI 96:6
T.'s up	BOOT 39:6
T. was away and somewhere	MACN 210:4
to fill the t. available	PARK 250:12
to sell t.	TAWN 310:3
very good t. it was	JOYC 171:14

time-lag comfortable t. — WELL 331:9

times bad t. just around — COWA 78:12

difficult t. lie ahead	TAGL 309:3
t. they are a-changin'	DYLA 95:14
t. will suit me	HOWA 158:9
Top people take *The T.*	ADVE 5:7

timetables by railway t. — TAYL 310:6

timid inclined to be t. — WEBB 329:16

timing real bad sense of t. — MCGO 207:12

t. was right — MURR 232:4

Timothy T. has passed — EPIT 108:8

T. Winters comes — CAUS 57:10

tin cat on a hot t. roof — WILL 336:8

on a corrugated t. roof — BEEC 26:15

Tina acronym T. — THAT 312:9

ting bells of Hell go t.-a-ling — ANON 12:4

tingling It's t. fresh — ADVE 4:5

tinkering rule of intelligent t. — EHRL 97:9

tinned smoked salmon and t. — WILS 338:6

Tipperary long way to T. — JUDG 173:1

tipster racing t. who only — TAYL 310:7

tired I'm t. — LAST 190:9

I was t. of it	PARK 250:15
they'll be bloody t.	TRUE 318:7
t. of being a woman	SEXT 291:2
t. of Love	BELL 27:11

Tiresias T., old man — ELIO 103:6

tiring Shakespeare is so t. — KAUF 175:1

tit get her t. caught — MITC 223:14

titanic deck of the T. — MORT 229:10

title needed no royal t. — SPEN 299:14

titter T. ye not — CATC 60:18

toad Give me your arm, old t. — LARK 189:9

let the t. work — LARK 189:8

toads gardens with real t. — MOOR 228:2

toast accumulation of t. — PHIL 253:11

today get where I am t. without — CATC 59:13

standing here t.	JOHN 169:8
T. is the last day	YELT 346:14
t. the struggle	AUDE 18:14
T. we have naming of parts	REED 268:10
we gave our t.	EPIT 108:10
will not hang myself t.	CHES 64:8

toe big t. ends up making a hole — EINS 99:9

toil blood, t., tears and sweat — CHUR 67:3

theft over honest t. — RUSS 278:14

toilet nearest t. two blocks away — JOHN 170:9

told I think we should be t. — CATC 59:14

I t. you so	EPIT 107:6
like to be t. the worst	CHUR 67:11
plato t. him: he couldn't	CUMM 81:5
t. you I was ill	EPIT 107:17

tolerance such a thing as t. — WILS 338:19

T. the essential — PHIL 253:10

tolerant being t. for nothing — GREG 138:11

tolerate not to t. the intolerant — POPP 256:6

tolerated women not merely t. — AUNG 19:10

tolls For whom the bell t. — BORR 40:10

Tom gone to join T. — EPIT 107:1

Ground control to Major T. — BOWI 42:2

tomato You like t. — GERS 131:14

tomb t. of a mediocre talent — SMIT 297:3

tombs in the cool t. — SAND 283:4

tomorrow For your t. we gave — EPIT 108:10

Leave t. behind	COWA 78:1
T. for the young	AUDE 18:14
t. is another day	MITC 226:3
t. we will be killed	BORR 41:8
what to see t.	STEI 303:4

tongue grow a second t. — MONT 227:3

lies of t. and pen	CHES 64:12
tip of the t.	NABO 233:1

tongues multitude of t. — BREN 44:1

multitude of t. — HAND 143:15

tons Sixteen t. — TRAV 317:3

tool humble as a t. — FUGA 126:17

Science is an edged t. — EDDI 97:2

tools Give us the t. — CHUR 67:10

toothaches underrates t. — KUND 185:12

toothpaste t. is out of the tube — HALD 142:6

top made it to the t. — MALL 212:9

people at the t.	HUXL 161:8
T. of the world	FILM 113:1
T. people	ADVE 5:7

topography T. displays — BISH 35:3

torch t. passed to new generation — KENN 177:4

tornado set off a t. in Texas — LORE 203:2

Toronto T. is a kind — USTI 322:5

torture self-imposed t. — MILL 222:10

So does t. — AUDE 18:18

torturer t.'s horse scratches — AUDE 17:17

Tory hatred for the T. Party — BEVA 33:4

Thirteen years of T. misrule	POLI 258:9
T.'s secret weapon	KILM 180:6

total t. solution — GOER 134:10

totalitarianism name of t. — GAND 129:3

totem t.-symbol in his hand — KOES 184:16

Toto T., I've a feeling — FILM 116:6

totter t. towards the tomb — SAYE 285:7

tough in t. joints — RUNY 277:11

t. get going	SAYI 287:12
T. on crime	BLAI 35:11

toughness T. doesn't have to come — FEIN 110:7

tour Vive le T. — ARMS 14:8

tourism t. is their religion — RUNC 277:8

What an odd thing t. is	BRYS 47:2	**treason** Shakespeare the word t.	BENN 29:4
tourist makes everyone a t.	SONT 298:17	**treasury** T. to fill old bottles	KEYN 179:3
town destroy the t.	ANON 11:6	**treaties** T. like girls and roses	DE G 87:10
Dirty old t.	MACC 206:6	**treatment** suitable case for t.	MERC 219:8
go down to the end of the t.	MILN 223:6	**treaty** not a peace t.	FOCH 119:4
lived in a pretty how t.	CUMM 81:2	**tree** billboard lovely as a t.	NASH 235:1
trace risen without t.	MUGG 230:8	cut down a redwood t.	STEV 304:14
tracing fitful t. of a portal	STEV 304:3	finds that this t.	KNOX 184:7
tracks hungry on the t.	CRAN 79:4	only God can make a t.	KILM 180:5
trade Irish poets, learn your t.	YEAT 346:8	poem lovely as a t.	KILM 180:4
There isn't any T.	HERB 151:16	t. was already rotten	JOHN 169:3
tradition great t.	LEAV 194:5	**trees** apple t. will never get	FROS 125:10
T. means giving votes	CHES 65:8	into the t.	BORR 40:1
traduced t. Joseph K.	KAFK 174:5	t. are made of air	FEYN 111:3
traffic reckless motor t.	DEWA 90:1	t. bear strange fruit	ALLE 7:4
roar of London's t.	CATC 60:19	t. that grow so fair	KIPL 182:16
tragedies two t. in life	SHAW 292:15	**trenches** t. in the Great War	STOC 305:4
tragedy comedy is t. that happens	CART 54:9	**trespass** t. there and go	HOUS 158:5
convenient in t.	ANOU 13:7	**trial** only a t. if I recognize it	KAFK 174:6
first time as t.	BARN 23:13	**tribal** t., intimate revenge	HEAN 149:5
food a t.	POWE 260:8	**tribalism** It is pure t.	FITT 112:11
I will write you a t.	FITZ 118:1	**tribe** dialect of the t.	ELIO 101:6
t. has struck	POWE 260:16	Our t.'s complicity	HEAN 148:14
t. is clean	ANOU 13:8	**tribes** lovers and t.	ONDA 243:8
t. of a man	OLIV 243:2	**trick** conjuring t. with bones	JENK 167:11
what t. means	STOP 306:3	**trickle-down** T. theory	GALB 128:11
tragic I acted so t.	HARG 145:17	**tried** Christian ideal not been t.	CHES 65:12
t. consciousness	FUEN 126:16	one I never t. before	WEST 332:8
trahison t. des clercs	BEND 28:10	t. your best	GROE 139:8
trail t. has its own stern code	SERV 290:13	**trigger** do you want on the t.	NEWS 238:8
train biggest electric t. set	WELL 331:1	**trip** Clunk, click, every t.	OFFI 242:3
charge of the clattering t.	BEAV 25:8	don't t. over the furniture	COWA 78:17
light of the oncoming t.	LOWE 204:2	**triste** jamais t. archy	MARQ 215:7
like a runaway t.	CONL 74:7	**tristesse** Bonjour t.	ÉLUA 105:6
Runs the red electric t.	BETJ 32:13	**triumph** his revolutionary t.	TAYL 310:8
shaves and takes a t.	WHIT 333:8	our career and our t.	VANZ 324:4
t. is arriving on time	MUSS 232:7	T. and Disaster	KIPL 182:8
t. take the strain	ADVE 4:9	t. of the embalmer's art	VIDA 325:7
trained We t. hard	ANON 12:18	**trivial** such t. people	LAWR 192:19
traitors form of our t.	WEST 332:17	**Trojan** T. 'orses will jump out	BEVI 34:2
tramp why the lady is a t.	HART 146:13	**troops** t. towards the sound	GRIM 139:7
tranquillity remembered in t.	THUR 316:5	Withdrawal of US t.	KISS 183:14
T. Base here	ARMS 14:10	**trot** t. in an elderly fashion	THOM 315:6
tranquillized t. Fifties	LOWE 203:11	**trouble** business to get him in t.	ROBI 272:2
translated T. Daughter, come	AUDE 16:13	it is not our t.	MARQ 215:8
translation unfaithful to the t.	BORG 39:9	present help in t.	ANON 10:1
what is lost in t.	FROS 126:4	t. with 'the vision thing'	IVIN 163:13
trap into a t. from which	LAWR 193:4	When in t., delegate	BORE 39:7
trauma Freaks born with their t.	ARBU 13:14	**troubled** bridge over t. water	SIMO 295:2
travel t. broadens the mind; but	CHES 65:11	**troubles** From t. of the world	HARV 147:4
t. in the direction of	BERR 31:16	pack up your t.	ASAF 14:14
two classes of t.	BENC 28:7	t. seemed so far away	LENN 197:3
travelled took the one less t.	FROS 125:15	**trousers** bottoms of my t. rolled	ELIO 102:8
traveller said the T.	DE L 88:5	cloud in t.	MAYA 217:11
trawler When seagulls follow a t.	CANT 53:1	**trucking** Keep on t.	CATC 60:11
treachery mother of all t.	PAIS 248:8	**trucks** learn about t.	AWDR 19:11
t. of the intellectuals	BEND 28:10	**true** always t. to you, darlin'	PORT 256:10

true (*cont.*)
And is it t. — BETJ 32:5
believe is not necessarily t. — BELL 27:2
than that it be t. — WHIT 333:15
what we are saying is t. — RUSS 278:16
would like to be t. — HARE 145:14
You are not t. — WILB 335:7
trumpets blaze of t. — LUXE 204:11
trust gives his t. slowly — LE C 195:2
I don't t. books — COLB 73:4
Never t. a man — JUNO 173:11
Never t. the artist — LAWR 192:9
To t. people is a luxury — FORS 120:11
truth Art is not t. — PICA 254:8
Believing T. is staring — BELL 27:5
can't handle the t. — FILM 116:12
economical with the t. — ARMS 14:12
forsake this t. — ROSE 275:5
here have Pride and T. — YEAT 345:13
how many people know the t. — WEST 332:20
Images split the t. — LEVE 198:6
just tell the t. — TRUM 318:12
keep t. safe in its hand — TAGO 309:17
know the t. at last — EPIT 108:3
lawyer interprets the t. — GIRA 133:9
lures the t. — WESK 331:14
mistook disenchantment for t. — SART 284:6
new scientific t. — PLAN 255:8
possesses not only t. — RUSS 278:17
seek to suppress t. — SOYI 299:4
silence about t. — HUXL 161:3
simply a t. repeated — BALD 21:9
stop telling the t. — STEV 304:6
sword of t. — AITK 6:1
Tell the t. — BERN 31:5
to lie for the t. — ADLE 2:10
t. 24 times per second — GODA 134:3
t. about herself — MUNR 231:8
t., beauty, and goodness — WEIL 330:3
t. cannot be told — SOLZ 298:3
T. exists, only lies — BRAQ 43:2
T. is a pathless land — KRIS 185:5
t. is out there — CATC 61:8
t., justice and the American way — CATC 59:2
T.-loving Persians — GRAV 137:2
t. makes men free — AGAR 2:13
t. 'out of a multitude' — BREN 44:1
T. that comes from the gut — COLB 73:3
t. that has lost its temper — GIBR 132:11
unpleasant way of saying t. — HELL 150:9
truthiness definition of 't.' — COLB 73:3
truths all t. are half-truths — WHIT 334:1
Few new t. have ever won — BERL 30:15
old universal t. — FAUL 110:3
repetition of unpalatable t. — SUMM 307:6
t. being in and out — FROS 124:13
try never t. — GROE 139:8

t., try again — FIEL 112:1
We t. harder — ADVE 5:10
trying I am t. to be — SMIT 296:11
just goes on t. — PICA 254:6
without really t. — MEAD 218:3
tsar no t., but the slaves — ZAMY 348:2
T-shirt got the T. — SAYI 286:2
tube toothpaste is out of the t. — HALD 142:6
Tudor US presidency a T. monarchy — BURG 48:4
tumour aspirin for a brain t. — CHAN 63:2
ripens in a t. — ABSE 1:2
tune guy who could carry a t. — EPIT 107:14
turn on, t. in and drop out — LEAR 194:1
tunes know my t. and whistle them — SCHO 288:4
t. of Handel — SITW 295:15
tunnel back down the time t. — KEAT 175:13
light at the end of the t. — LOWE 204:2
turkeys t. vote for Christmas — CALL 51:3
turn and quickly t. away — YEAT 345:3
Because I do not hope to t. — ELIO 100:4
t. on, tune in and drop out — LEAR 194:1
T. that off — WILL 336:13
turning lady's not for t. — THAT 312:10
point of the t. world — ELIO 100:13
turnip candle in that great t. — CHUR 68:11
turret washed me out of the t. — JARR 166:17
turtle t. lives 'twixt plated — NASH 234:2
TV blight has hit the T. industry — STRE 306:11
by T. stupor — SOLZ 298:8
T.—a clever contraction — ACE 1:5
twang t., and you've got music — VICI 325:1
tweed t. nightgowns — GING 133:1
twelve snowed for t. days — THOM 314:9
twentieth half of the t. century — QUAN 264:1
language of the t. century — BEVA 33:5
t. century belongs — TRUD 318:5
t. century will be — TOYN 317:1
twenty at T. I tried to vex — AUDE 18:10
twenty-twenty Hindsight is always t. — WILD 335:12
twice Don't think t. — DYLA 95:4
must do t. as well as men — WHIT 334:13
postman always rings t. — CAIN 50:5
twist t. slowly in the wind — EHRL 97:10
twisted You silly t. boy — CATC 62:1
two Takes t. to tango — HOFF 155:12
tea for t. — CAES 50:2
t. by two in the ark — LEVE 198:7
t. cultures — SNOW 298:1
t. glasses and two chairs — MACN 210:4
t. is fun — SAYI 286:5
t. plus two make four — ORWE 245:18
We're number t. — ADVE 5:10
worth t. in the street — WEST 332:1
type t. of snow — WORR 342:10
types Seven t. of ambiguity — EMPS 105:15
typewriters banging on million t. — WILE 335:17

monkeys strumming on t. — EDDI 96:7
tyranny against a monstrous t. — CHUR 67:4
conditions of t. — AREN 14:7
silent in the face of t. — SOYI 299:5
struggled against t. — TUTU 320:1
unnecessary t. — RUSS 278:8
tyres concrete and t. — LARK 189:3

ugly beautiful and becomes u. — BAIL 20:10
Bessie, you're u. — CHUR 69:15
good, the bad, and the u. — FILM 117:7
no place for u. mathematics — HARD 144:12
UK within the U. — STRA 306:10
Ulsterman U., of planter stock — HEWI 152:15
ultimate u. blandness — ROTT 276:4
umbrella where I left my u. — GREG 138:9
UN won't need the U. — CLOO 72:9
unable u. to find work — COOL 76:9
unacceptable u. face — HEAT 149:11
unaccommodated unnecessary and u.
— NAIP 233:10
unaware And I was u. — HARD 145:4
unbearable in victory u. — CHUR 68:18
u. lightness of being — KUND 185:13
unbeatable In defeat u. — CHUR 68:18
unbeautiful are u. and have — CUMM 81:10
unborn possible to talk to the u. — BARZ 24:17
unbroken part of u. stream — HAWK 147:10
uncertainty u. principle — HAWK 147:12
Uncle Sam U. came along — NEZ 236:6
unconscious royal road to the u. — MISQ 224:5
u. cerebration — JAME 166:9
uncool U. people — ELTO 105:5
undecided five who are u. — STEN 303:6
under got you u. my skin — PORT 258:17
I'd have been u. the host — PARK 250:7
under-belly soft u. of Europe — MISQ 225:3
underestimating u. intelligence — MENC 219:3
underneath U. the Arches — FLAN 118:5
underrates u. toothaches — KUND 185:12
undersold Never knowingly u. — ADVE 4:18
understand child could u. — FILM 116:11
don't u. things — NEUM 236:3
don't u. too hot — SALI 282:7
failed to u. it — BOHR 38:7
Grown-ups never u. — SAIN 281:10
I do not u. — FEYN 111:5
liberals can u. — BRUC 46:8
much that I did not u. — ORWE 245:8
u. a little less — MAJO 211:14
u. nothing — CORN 77:5
u. the situation — MURR 232:6
What you can't u. — DYLA 95:14
understanding it is u. — HOLT 156:8
salary depends on not u. — SINC 295:9
sketchy u. of life — CRIC 79:9

understate u. the situation — MURR 232:2
understood don't care if I'm u. — FRUM 126:5
I have u. you — DE G 87:5
music u. by children — STRA 306:8
undertaking no such u. — CHAM 62:9
underwear right down to her u. — NIXO 239:1
undeservedly books u. forgotten — AUDE 19:4
undeserving u. poor — SHAW 293:6
uneconomic shown it to be 'u.' — SCHU 288:9
uneducated u. man to read books — CHUR 69:2
unemployment leave it to u. — KEYN 179:3
rising u. — LAMO 188:2
u. results — COOL 76:9
unexpected most u. of all things — TROT 318:3
unexplained you're u. as yet — HALL 142:8
unfaithful original is u. — BORG 39:9
unfinished Liberty is u. business — ANON 11:12
unfit chosen from the u. — SAYI 286:6
unforgiveness alp of u. — PLOM 255:17
unforgiving fill the u. minute — KIPL 182:9
unfree Ireland u. shall never be at peace
— PEAR 251:14
unhappily bad end u. — STOP 306:3
unhappiness loyalty we feel to u. — GREE 137:12
U. is best defined — DE B 86:8
vocation of u. — SIME 294:14
unhappy making us u. — FILI 112:3
only speak when she is u. — SMIT 297:6
U. the land that needs — BREC 43:6
unheard language of the u. — KING 180:18
unhurt U. people not much good — STAR 302:1
uniform I love the u. — MIDD 220:5
uninspiring may be u. — GEOR 131:7
uninteresting u. explanations — LEWI 199:3
union Act of U. is there — TRIM 317:11
u. has been guiding star — CARS 54:6
U. is important — BROW 46:2
unity national u. — BUSH 49:4
national u. — ROOS 273:14
u. of our fatherland — KOHL 185:1
universal u. sewer — COUS 77:13
universe Architect of the U. — JEAN 167:10
fact about the u. — EINS 98:12
good u. next door — CUMM 81:7
Life, the U. and Everything — ADAM 2:3
mechanism of the U. — WHIT 333:14
Somewhere in the u. — TAGL 309:13
u. go to all the bother — HAWK 147:13
U. is a free lunch — GUTH 140:8
u. is not hostile — HOLM 156:6
U. is not obliged to conform — SAGA 281:5
u. is not only queerer — HALD 142:1
u.'s existence made known — PENR 252:5
u. sleeps — MAYA 217:12
universities men who go to the u. — MAUG 217:5
university able to get to a u. — KINN 181:10
u. of life — BOTT 39:11

university (*cont.*)

u. of the air — WILS 338:7

u. training — AMIS 8:7

unjoined *u.* system — ANON 11:2

unknown glorious and the u. — FORS 120:9

known and the u. — PINT 254:14

tread safely into the u. — HASK 147:5

U. Prime Minister — ASQU 15:8

unknowns also unknown u. — RUMS 277:3

unluckily good u. — STOP 306:3

unlucky so u. that he runs into — MARQ 215:10

unmaking things are in the u. — KING 181:1

unnatural only u. sex act — KINS 181:12

unnecessary to do the u. — SAYI 286:6

unofficial English u. rose — BROO 45:1

unpalatable disastrous and the u. — GALB 128:12

unplayable another u. work — SCHO 288:3

unpopular safe to be u. — STEV 304:10

unprincipled sold by the u. — CAPP 53:7

unreality u. of painted people — UPDI 321:13

unreliable Even death is u. — BECK 26:9

unsafe U. at any speed — NADE 233:6

unsayable say the u. — RUSH 278:2

unsolicited u. advice — COOL 76:4

unsorted all the u. stuff — GOLD 134:13

unspeakable speak the u. — RUSH 278:2

untalented product of the u. — CAPP 53:7

unthinking thoughts upon the u. — KEYN 179:6

unthought never be u. — DÜRR 94:11

untried difficult; and left u. — CHES 65:12

untrue man who's u. to his wife — AUDE 17:18

unupblown NURSE U. — TELE 311:5

unwanted feeling of being u. — TERE 311:16

unwell Jeffrey Bernard is u. — WATE 328:9

unwilling group of the u. — SAYI 286:6

u. or unable — WILL 336:16

up nice to people on your way u. — MIZN 226:7

U. to a point, Lord Copper — WAUG 329:8

uplands broad, sunlit u. — CHUR 67:7

upper Like many of the U. Class — BELL 27:14

prove the u. classes — COWA 78:11

upright we walk u. — GAND 129:7

upstanding clean u. chap like you — KING 181:4

upwards car could go straight u. — HOYL 158:13

uranious air becomes u. — LEHR 195:13

uranium element u. may be turned — EINS 98:13

urine red wine of Shiraz into u. — DINE 91:2

us he is u. — CART 56:12

USA Born in the U. — SPRI 301:2

used ain't what they u. to be — PERS 253:3

buy a u. car — POLI 258:12

get u. to them — NEUM 236:3

useful be a Really U. Engine — AWDR 19:11

what is apparently u. — WHIT 334:6

useless plans are u. — EISE 100:2

usual Business carried on as u. — CHUR 66:12

usura With u. hath no man a house — POUN 259:10

usury u. is contrary to Scripture — TAWN 310:3

uterus what your u. looks like — EPHR 106:1

Utopia U. is a blessed past — KISS 183:18

utterance such a door of u. — MACD 206:13

U-turn media catchphrase, the U. — THAT 312:10

vacancy create a job v. — GOLD 134:14

vacant v. interstellar spaces — ELIO 100:18

We're v. — ROTT 276:3

vacuum behind the v. cleaner — GREE 138:7

v. a hell of a lot better — WILL 336:10

vague don't be v. — ADVE 3:15

valley great things from the v. — CHES 65:5

How green was my v. — LLEW 201:1

V. of the dolls — SUSA 307:7

value Nothing has v. — FORS 121:1

values authentic and pure v. — WEIL 330:3

Victorian v. — THAT 313:2

van Follow the v. — COLL 73:10

vanished this v. woman — HAWK 147:10

vanities bonfire of the v. — WOLF 340:15

vanity feeds your v. — PARR 250:16

vase Sèvres v. in the hands — WAUG 329:11

vast v. right-wing conspiracy — CLIN 71:12

vaulting V. the sea — CRAN 79:5

Vega V. conspicuous overhead — AUDE 18:3

vengeance stay the hands of v. — JACK 165:5

Venice Death in V. — MANN 213:13

Venus V. becomes a document — VALÉ 323:5

verb God to me is a v. — FULL 127:2

Waiting for the German v. — O'BR 241:4

verbal v. contract isn't worth — GOLD 135:3

verboojuice Sesquippledan v. — WELL 331:4

verifiability not the *v.* — POPP 256:4

verification method of its v. — SCHL 287:16

vermin lower than v. — BEVA 33:4

vernacular It is our v. — BAIL 20:11

verse as soon write free v. — FROS 126:3

died to make v. free — PRES 261:10

give up v., my boy — POUN 260:1

No subject for immortal v. — DAY- 85:12

write it out in a v. — YEAT 345:1

very Be v. afraid — TAGL 309:1

V. interesting . . . but — CATC 61:9

vessel v. with the pestle — FILM 116:1

vice Art is v. — DEGA 87:1

defence of liberty is no v. — GOLD 135:1

English v. — RATT 267:2

quotation is a nation v. — WAUG 329:5

vices V. are general — MURD 231:12

victim Any v. demands allegiance — GREE 137:13

oppressor, never the v. — WIES 335:3

thou shalt not be a v. — BAUE 25:2

victims v. of American Fascism — ROSE 275:6

walk (*cont.*)

never learned to w. forward	ROOS 273:17
no easy w.-over to freedom	NEHR 235:5
W. across my swimming pool	RICE 270:6
w. on the wild side	ALGR 6:10
You'll never w. alone	HAMM 143:11

walked Cat w. by himself · KIPL 183:4

W. day and night	LOGU 202:4

walking boots are made for w. · HAZL 148:8

dancing is to w.	WAIN 326:1
empire w. very slowly	FITZ 117:19
fingers do the w.	ADVE 4:10
w. with destiny	CHUR 69:4

walks w. like a duck · CARE 53:11

w. through a wall	MALA 212:3

wall against a w. of stone · WILB 335:8

doesn't love a w.	FROS 125:9
walks through a w.	MALA 212:3
Watch the w., my darling	KIPL 182:15

walling What I was w. in · FROS 125:11

Wall St. W. lays an egg · NEWS 238:6

waltz dance a second w. · SHIE 294:3

goes out of a beautiful w.	GREN 138:14

wanna W. be the leader · MCGO 207:10

want get what you w. · LURI 204:9

people know what they w.	MENC 218:14
something they w. to see	SKEL 296:2
third is freedom from w.	ROOS 274:3
W. one only of five giants	BEVE 33:15
we w. it now	MORR 228:15
What does a woman w.	FREU 123:11
what I really really w.	ROWB 276:5
what we all w.	SHIE 294:2

war After each w. · ATKI 16:1

ain't gonna be no w.	MACM 209:2
anyone who wasn't against w.	LOW 203:7
at w. with Germany	CHAM 62:9
beating of w. drums	KOES 184:15
Britain should to to w.	COOK 75:17
bungled, unwise w.	PLOM 255:17
cold w.	BARU 24:13
cold w. warrior	THAT 312:4
condemn recourse to w.	BRIA 44:3
day w. broke out	CATC 58:14
done very well out of the w.	BALD 21:8
Don't mention the w.	CLEE 71:2
easier to make w.	CLEM 71:5
enable it to make w.	WEIL 330:5
first w. fought without	WEST 333:2
First World W. had begun	TAYL 310:6
for w. like precocious giants	PEAR 252:2
France has not lost the w.	DE G 87:2
going to the w.	CHES 64:13
go to w. with the Army	RUMS 277:6
home policy: I wage w.	CLEM 71:3
if someone gave a w.	GINS 133:2
If this is not civil w.	ALLA 7:1

I hate w.	ROOS 273:15
I have seen w.	ROOS 273:15
involve us in the wrong w.	BRAD 42:12
In w.: resolution	CHUR 69:3
I renounce w.	FOSD 121:8
killed in the w.	POWE 261:4
live under the shadow of a w.	SPEN 300:9
lose the w. in an afternoon	CHUR 69:8
Make love not w.	SAYI 286:22
Mankind must put an end to w.	KENN 177:11
McNamara's W.	MCNA 209:11
no declaration of w.	EDEN 97:3
not a justifiable act of w.	BELL 27:3
nuisance in time of w.	CHUR 68:7
Older men declare w.	HOOV 157:6
Once lead this people into w.	WILS 338:19
page 1 of the book of w.	MONT 227:6
quaint and curious w. is	HARD 145:7
rich wage w.	SART 284:2
right of Parliament to decide on w.	
	EPIT 107:16
seek no wider w.	JOHN 169:12
seven days w.	MUIR 230:13
so vehemently against w.	FREU 123:10
subject is W.	OWEN 247:2
talk of a just w.	SORL 299:2
tempered by w.	KENN 177:4
they'll give a w.	SAND 283:8
third world w.	TRUM 318:11
this w. on terrorism	BUSH 49:5
understood this liking for w.	BENN 29:5
Vietnam as a w.	PILG 254:10
wage w. against	CHUR 67:4
w. and peace in 21st century	KOHL 185:2
W. being deliberately prolonged	SASS 285:3
w. between men and women	THUR 316:3
w. for independence	MCAL 205:2
w. has used up words	JAME 166:12
w. in which everyone	CONN 75:7
W. is hell, and all that	HAY 148:4
W. is not the word	KENN 176:9
w. is obsolete or men are	FULL 127:5
w. is politics with bloodshed	MAO 214:4
W. is too serious a matter	CLEM 71:7
W. makes good history	HARD 145:12
w. minus the shooting	ORWE 246:6
w. on poverty	JOHN 169:10
w. situation has developed	HIRO 154:7
w. that will end war	WELL 331:8
W. the universal perversion	RAE 265:5
w. which existed to produce	HOBS 155:4
W. will cease when	POLI 258:11
waste of God, w.	STUD 307:2
way of ending a w.	ORWE 246:9
We hear w. called murder	MACD 207:3
what a lovely w.	LITT 200:11
what did you do in the W.	MILI 221:3

win an atomic w.	BRAD 42:9	go back in the w.	TAGL 309:7
without having won the w.	YOKO 347:1	Kids and w.	OFFI 242:12
won the last w.	ROOS 273:7	Ring of bright w.	BORR 41:2
You can only love one w.	GELL 130:13	That stretch of w.	PAUL 251:8
warfare Armed w. must be preceded	ZINO 349:1	W. is life's *mater*	SZEN 308:8
warlord concubine of a w.	JUNG 173:9	w. like Pilate	GREE 137:9
warm man who's w. to understand	SOLZ 298:7	'w.' meant the wonderful	KELL 176:6
w. courage	BUSH 49:4	where the w. goes	CHES 65:3
w. courage	ROOS 273:14	**Waterloo** battle of W. won	ORWE 245:14
warn All a poet can do is w.	OWEN 247:3	**watermelons** down by the w.	GINS 133:5
w. you not to be ordinary	KINN 181:7	**Watson** Elementary, my dear W.	MISQ 224:6
War Office except the British W.	SHAW 291:14	Good old W.	DOYL 92:13
warrior cold war w.	THAT 312:4	**waves** w. of optimism	GREE 138:3
This is the happy w.	READ 267:10	**waving** not w. but drowning	SMIT 297:7
wars brought us to these w.	DAY- 85:11	**waxed** man has just w. the floor	NASH 235:3
came to an end all w.	LLOY 201:5	**way** All the w. with LBJ	POLI 257:2
end to beginnings of all w.	ROOS 274:7	did it the hard w.	EPIT 108:5
History littered with the w.	POWE 260:17	Every which w. but loose	FILM 117:6
how do w. start	KRAU 185:3	have it your own w.	CART 56:1
into any foreign w.	ROOS 274:1	I did it my w.	ANKA 9:9
not armaments that cause w.	MADA 210:13	If w. to the Better there be	HARD 145:5
w. planned by old men	RICE 270:3	more a w. of life	ANON 12:3
wartime any w. President	BIDD 34:5	no w. out of the mind	PLAT 255:9
this w. atmosphere	CONR 75:12	on the w. to the Forum	SHEV 294:1
war-war better than to w.	CHUR 68:13	see no other w.	DAY- 85:11
was picked the w. of shall	CUMM 81:8	that's the w. it is	CATC 58:4
wash have to w. your socks	DE B 86:6	w. I do it	WEST 332:14
w. that man right outa my hair	HAMM 143:1	**ways** w. of making you talk	CATC 61:11
w. the wind	ELIO 102:11	**we** W.'re here	ANON 12:17
washed w. in the blood	LIND 200:5	**weak** w. always have to decide	BONH 39:2
washes Persil w. whiter	ADVE 4:23	w. from your loveliness	BETJ 33:1
washing w. on the Siegfried Line	KENN 177:1	W. shall perish	SERV 290:15
wasp everything about the w.	THOM 314:10	**weaken** great life if you don't w.	BUCH 47:5
White-Anglo Saxon-Protestant (w.)		**weakening** w. the will	SPEN 300:8
	BALT 22:10	**weakest** You are the w. link	CATC 61:17
waste art of how to w. space	JOHN 170:8	**weakling** seven-stone w.	ADVE 4:6
Don't w. time in mourning	HILL 154:2	**weakness** oh! w. of joy	BETJ 33:1
w. it is to lose one's mind	QUAY 264:4	one major w.	KAY 175:10
W. of Blood	STUD 307:2	**weaned** w. on a pickle	ANON 12:14
w. remains and kills	EMPS 105:14	**weapon** art is not a w.	KENN 177:16
wasted all w. effort	AYER 19:15	his w. wit	EPIT 107:15
spend on advertising is w.	LEVE 198:5	Innocence no earthly w.	HILL 153:11
waste-paper file your w. basket	BENN 29:1	offensive and dangerous w.	PICA 254:3
w. basket of emotions	WEBB 329:18	Tory's secret w.	KILM 180:6
watch done far better by a w.	BELL 27:16	w. in hands of oppressor	BIKO 34:7
like a fat gold w.	PLAT 255:15	w. with worker at each end	POLI 257:5
or my w. has stopped	FILM 113:5	would call a w.	KAY 175:8
sit out front and w. me	BARR 24:7	**weapons** all word of the w.	WILB 335:6
son of a bitch stole my w.	FILM 116:4	books are w.	ROOS 274:5
W. my lips	BLUN 37:4	W. are like money	AMIS 8:10
W. my lips	BLUN 37:5	**weary** got the W. Blues	HUGH 159:11
w. the mayor	LETT 198:1	**weasel** w. under cocktail cabinet	PINT 255:1
W. the wall, my darling	KIPL 182:15	w. word	ROOS 274:15
watcher posted presence of the w.	JAME 166:10	**weather** doesn't matter what the w. is	
watching BIG BROTHER IS W. YOU	ORWE 245:16		JOBS 168:2
watchmaker *blind* w.	DAWK 85:2	Stormy w.	KOEH 184:11
water bridge over troubled w.	SIMO 295:2	w. turned around	THOM 314:7

weather (*cont.*)

  you won't hold up the w.   MACN 210:2

web cool w. of language   GRAV 137:1

  W. is a tremendous   BERN 31:8

Webster Like W.'s Dictionary   BURK 48:6

  W. was much possessed   ELIO 103:8

wedding pulled through a w. ring   REAR 268:9

wedding-cake face looks like a w.   AUDE 19:7

weds Egghead w. hourglass   NEWS 237:8

wee w. pretendy government   CONN 74:10

weed Ignorance is an evil w.   BEVE 33:14

weeds grubbing w. from gravel   KIPL 182:6

week die in my w.   JOPL 171:5

  greatest w. in the history   NIXO 239:3

  That was the w. that was   BIRD 35:1

  w. is a long time in politics   WILS 338:8

weekend long w.   FORS 120:8

  w. starts here   CATC 61:10

weekends getting a plumber on w.   ALLE 7:12

weep stand at my grave and w.   FRYE 126:14

weight lose a bit of w.   CONN 74:12

  one and half times own w.   UPDI 321:4

  punch above its w.   HURD 161:1

  w. of the backside   ADAM 2:8

welcome good evening, and w.   CATC 59:9

welfare W. became a term   MOYN 230:3

  w.-state   TEMP 311:11

well alive and w.   ANON 11:8

  all shall be w.   ELIO 101:10

  Didn't she do w.   CATC 58:15

  Do sleep w.   CATC 58:17

  W. here I am   SENT 290:10

  w. of loneliness   HALL 142:7

wept I sat down and w.   BORR 40:6

west construction of the W.   NAIP 233:8

  face neither East nor W.   NKRU 239:11

  in the gardens of the W.   CONN 75:6

  liquid manure from the W.   SOLZ 298:9

  W. Lothian   DALY 83:5

  where the W. begins   CHAP 63:13

western delivered by W. Union   GOLD 135:9

  quiet on the w. front   REMA 269:5

  When you've seen one W.   WHIT 334:10

Westerners W. have aggressive   KAUN 175:4

West Indies created in the W.   WALC 326:4

  nothing was created in the W.   NAIP 233:11

wet out of these w. clothes   FILM 115:3

  so w. you could shoot snipe   POWE 260:11

Wexford disused shed in Co. W.   MAHO 211:6

whale Save the w.   SAYI 287:4

  screw the w.   STOP 305:14

whales W. play   WILL 336:3

whammy Labour's double w.   POLI 258:2

what know what's w.   WEST 332:10

  W. is to be done   LENI 196:4

  W.'s up, Doc   CATC 61:13

  w., when and why   WARN 327:14

wheat packed like squares of w.   LARK 189:10

wheel breaks a butterfly on a w.   NEWS 238:7

  created the w.   APOL 13:11

  invented the w.   NEME 235:9

  red w. barrow   WILL 336:17

wheels w. of black Marias   AKHM 6:3

when forgotten to say 'W.!'   WODE 340:7

  what, w. and why   WARN 327:14

where w. do they all come from   LENN 196:15

  w. is everybody   FERM 110:11

  W. OUGHT I TO BE   TELE 311:1

  w. the bloody hell   ADVE 5:1

  W. were you?   TAGL 309:16

  w. you are going   CAME 51:7

whereof w. one cannot speak   WITT 339:8

whimper Not with a bang but a w.   ELIO 101:17

whin three w. bushes rode across   KAVA 175:5

whisky good old boys drinkin' w.   MCLE 208:5

  W. makes it go round   MACK 208:2

whisper my w. was already born   MAND 213:11

  W. who dares   MILN 223:10

whispering just w. in her mouth   MARX 216:4

whistle know my tunes and w. them   SCHO 288:4

  shrimp learns to w.   KHRU 179:12

  W. while you work   MORE 228:5

  You know how to w.   FILM 115:11

white American w. man to find   BALD 21:4

  be the w. man's brother   KING 180:8

  blue-eyed devil w. man   FARD 109:5

  dreaming of a w. Christmas   BERL 30:11

  fat w. woman   CORN 77:7

  no 'w.' or 'coloured' signs   KENN 177:14

  say this for the w. race   GREG 138:10

  shake a bat at a w. man   GREG 138:12

  so-called w. races   FORS 120:18

  W.-Anglo Saxon-Protestant   BALT 22:10

  w. heat of technology   MISQ 225:7

  w. man's cruelties   MALC 212:7

  w. man was *created* a devil   MALC 212:6

  w. race does not really   STEI 302:9

  w. race *is* the cancer   SONT 298:16

  w. students were sent   GRAN 136:11

white-collar not the w. people   WHYT 334:14

Whitehall gentleman in W.   JAY 167:5

White House imported the W.   ANON 11:2

  whitewash at the W.   NIXO 239:5

whiter Persil washes w.   ADVE 4:23

  w. shade of pale   REID 269:2

whites need the knowledge of w.   TSVA 319:6

whitewash w. at the White House   NIXO 239:5

Whitman tonight, Walt W.   GINS 133:4

  Walt W.—   CRAN 79:2

who W. he   ROSS 275:9

  w. the hell are you   CATC 60:1

  W.? Whom   LENI 196:7

whom Who? W.   LENI 196:7

whores parliament of w.	O'RO 244:6	**windbeaten** w. verbs	ELYT 105:7
Who's Who been in *W*.	WEST 332:10	**window** argument of the broken w.	PANK 249:1
why about the wasp, except w.	THOM 314:10	back upon the w.-panes	ELIO 102:4
see things and say 'W.'	SHAW 291:11	doggie in the w.	MERR 219:15
W. not? Why not? Yeah	LAST 191:11	Good prose like a w.-pane	ORWE 245:4
w. people laugh	FIEL 111:16	has not one w.	JAME 166:10
Would this man ask w.	AUDE 17:4	hole in a stained glass w.	CHAN 63:1
wicked August is a w. month	O'BR 241:2	kiss my ass in Macy's w.	JOHN 170:4
wicket flannelled fools at the w.	KIPL 182:10	**windows** open the w. of the Church	JOHN 168:5
wider seek no w. war	JOHN 169:12	**windscreen** through the w.	DUNM 94:4
w. still and wider	BENS 29:11	**wine** doesn't get into the w.	CHES 65:3
widow French w. in every bedroom		red sweet w. of youth	BROO 44:12
	HOFF 155:13	red w. of Shiraz into urine	DINE 91:2
W. The word consumes itself	PLAT 255:16	w. was a farce	POWE 260:8
width feel the w.	POWE 261:7	**wing** w. and a pray'r	ADAM 2:9
wields He who w. the knife	HESE 152:3	**wings** Grief has no w.	QUIL 264:5
wife decided to murder his w.	ILES 162:4	on laughter-silvered w.	MAGE 211:2
If I were your w.	CHUR 69:11	**wink** wink w., say no more	MONT 227:8
lay down his w. for his friend	JOYC 172:12	**winner** frightful Grand National w.	LARK 189:12
man who's untrue to his w.	AUDE 17:18	**winning** W. is everything	HILL 153:9
riding to and from his w.	WHIT 333:8	w. isn't everything	SAND 283:11
she is your w.	OGIL 241:12	**wins** Who dares w.	MILI 221:10
w. only guesses	UPDI 321:11	w. if he does not lose	KISS 183:12
wish your w. or servants	GRIF 139:4	**Winston** W. is back	ANON 13:3
your w. and your dog	HILL 153:9	**winter** furious w. blowing	RANS 266:5
Wigan mothers-in-law and W. Pier	BRID 44:4	go south in the w.	ELIO 102:20
road to W. Pier	ORWE 246:3	not a country, it is w.	VIGN 325:13
wild never saw a w. thing	LAWR 192:15	W. is icummen in	POUN 259:9
to be a little w.	KEYN 179:6	w. of discontent	CALL 51:2
walk on the w. side	ALGR 6:10	W. of discontent	NEWS 238:9
wilder w. shores of love	BLAN 36:9	**wire** w. netting, string and cotton wool	
wilderness Women have no w.	BOGA 38:2		SCHW 289:5
will Immanent W. that stirs	HARD 145:1	**wisdom** conventional w.	GALB 128:7
political w.	LYNN 204:13	door to infinite w.	BREC 43:7
settled w.	STEE 302:6	seven pillars of w.	BORR 41:3
w. to carry on	LIPP 200:10	W. was mine	OWEN 247:10
wrote my w. across the sky	LAWR 193:3	w. we have lost	ELIO 102:13
willed only a w. gentleness	THOM 315:4	**wise** w. forgive but do not forget	SZAS 307:14
wilt Do what thou w.	CROW 81:1	**wisecracking** w. and wit	PARK 250:3
Wimbledon Spill your guts at W.	CONN 75:9	**wisely** nations behave w. once	EBAN 96:5
wimps Lunch is for w.	FILM 115:6	**wish** If otherwise w. I	SHAW 293:19
win From w. and lose	MITC 225:10	want or w. to have	RUMS 277:6
Germans w.	LINE 200:8	w. for prayer is a prayer	BERN 31:1
I'm in to w.	CLIN 71:14	w. I loved the Human Race	RALE 265:8
that's to w.	MALR 212:11	**wit** his weapon w.	EPIT 107:15
To w. in Vietnam	SPOC 300:12	W. has truth in it	PARK 250:3
w. an atomic war	BRAD 42:9	**witch-doctors** Accountants are w.	HARM 146:2
W. just one for the Gipper	GIPP 133:8	**witches** burnt at the stake as w.	SMIT 297:8
wind answer is blowin' in the w.	DYLA 95:1	convinced there were w.	BLIX 36:12
candle in the w.	JOHN 168:9	**withdrawal** W. of US troops	KISS 183:14
how the w. doth ramm	POUN 259:9	**without** get where I am today w.	CATC 59:13
not I, but the w.	LAWR 192:18	**witnessed** worst thing I've ever w.	
Not with this w. blowing	KIPL 182:13		MORR 228:13
solidity to pure w.	ORWE 246:5	**witnesses** w. to the desolation	GEOR 131:5
twist slowly in the w.	EHRL 97:10	**wits** stolen his w. away	DE L 88:2
wash the w.	ELIO 102:11	**witty** Thou swell! Thou w.	HART 147:1
w. of change is blowing	MACM 209:5	**wives** left the w. and joined	WELD 330:11

wobbly spelling is W.   MILN 223:3
wolf afraid of the big bad w.   CHUR 66:10
  w. of a different opinion   INGE 162:7
Wolsey W.'s Home Town   NEWS 237:17
woman artist man and mother w.   SHAW 292:10
  comfort about being a w.   STAR 301:14
  done, ask a w.   THAT 312:3
  Every w. adores a Fascist   PLAT 255:10
  fat white w.   CORN 77:7
  just like a w.   DYLA 95:7
  like a beautiful w.   CASA 55:8
  No w. will be Prime Minister   THAT 312:2
  One is not born a w.   DE B 86:3
  one w. differs from another   MENC 218:12
  prime truth of w.   CHES 65:13
  Prudence is the other w.   ANON 12:6
  there is no w.   CHAN 63:7
  tired of being a w.   SEXT 291:2
  trapped in a w.'s body   BOY 42:5
  victory by a w.   WEST 332:22
  What does a w. want   FREU 123:11
  Why can't a w. be   LERN 197:7
  w. can be proud and stiff   YEAT 344:10
  w. can forgive a man   MAUG 217:2
  w. he loves   ELIZ 104:9
  w. is a sometime thing   HEYW 153:4
  w. is like a teabag   REAG 267:12
  w. makes the statement   MUIR 231:2
  W. much missed   HARD 145:10
  w. must have money   WOOL 341:11
  w. only the right to spring   FOND 119:6
  W. the nigger of the world   ONO 243:14
  w. who lives for others   LEWI 199:4
  w. without a man   SAYI 287:13
womanist W. is to feminist   WALK 327:2
womankind packs off its w.   SHAW 292:14
wombs think with our w.   LUCE 204:6
women all these surplus w.   RICH 270:14
  be aware of w. and children   CARR 54:4
  blame the w.'s movement   TWEE 320:3
  Certain w. should be struck   COWA 78:15
  claim our right as w.   PANK 248:10
  courage of w.   RICH 270:11
  designs to please w.   CLIF 71:9
  Equality for w. demands   TOYN 317:2
  feelings of w. in drawing room   WOOL 341:12
  fight to get w. out   GREE 138:7
  Good w. always think   BROO 45:6
  joined the w.   WELD 330:11
  man who doesn't know w.   CHAN 63:8
  no plain w. on television   FORD 119:10
  position for w. is prone   CARM 54:1
  Some w.'ll stay   KIPL 183:8
  turn into American w.   HAMP 143:13
  Votes for w.   POLI 258:10
  war between men and w.   THUR 316:3
  Whatever w. do   WHIT 334:13

W., and Champagne, and Bridge   BELL 27:15
  w. are brighter than men   LOOS 202:13
  w. become unnaturally thin   WOLF 340:9
  w. come and go   ELIO 102:3
  w., God help us   SAYE 285:8
  w. have fewer teeth   RUSS 278:12
  W. have no wilderness   BOGA 38:2
  W. have very little idea   GREE 138:5
  W. never have young minds   DELA 88:9
  w. not merely tolerated   AUNG 19:10
  W.'s Liberation is just   MEIR 218:10
  w. were first at the Cradle   SAYE 285:8
  working w. wore hats   ABZU 1:4
won I w. the count   SOMO 298:10
  No one w.   ROOS 273:7
  not that you w. or lost   RICE 270:2
  not to have w.   COUB 77:10
  Sun Wot W. It   NEWS 237:16
wonder boneless w.   CHUR 66:15
  moon-washed apples of w.   DRIN 93:4
wonderful I've had a w. life   LAST 191:5
  W. theory   WILS 338:1
  Yes, w. things   CART 54:10
won't administrative w.   LYNN 204:13
woodcock Spirits of well-shot w.   BETJ 32:7
woods go down in the w. today   KENN 176:13
  road through the w.   KIPL 183:2
  Whose w. are whose   O'RO 244:7
  Whose w. these are   FROS 125:19
  w. against the world   BLUN 37:2
  w. are lovely, dark   FROS 125:20
woodshed nasty in the w.   GIBB 132:6
Woodstock W. rises from his pages   BURR 48:8
wooed w. by slow advances   CARD 53:8
Woolf afraid of Virginia W.   ALBE 6:6
word Every w. she writes is a lie   MCCA 206:3
  for whom the w. 'fuck'   TYNA 320:4
  Greeks had a w.   AKIN 6:4
  I kept my w.   DE L 88:6
  most contradictory w.   MANN 214:3
  War is not the w.   KENN 176:9
  weasel w.   ROOS 274:15
  W. of mouth is the best   BERN 31:3
words answer you in two w.   GOLD 135:4
  could sell her w. for money   LOOS 202:12
  dreamed out in w.   MURR 231:16
  fear those big w.   JOYC 172:9
  few w. of my own   EDWA 97:6
  gotta use w. when I talk   ELIO 102:17
  long w. Bother me   MILN 223:1
  magic of Shaw's w.   TAYL 310:9
  may w. matter to you   SMIT 296:12
  shoot me with your w.   ANGE 9:6
  threw w. like stones   SPEN 300:6
  Trying to learn to use w.   ELIO 100:20
  war has used up w.   JAME 166:12
  W. are cheap   CHAP 63:12

w. are emptied	CAMU 52:16	w. like a dog	LENN 196:17
w. cascade down into my lap	NOLA 239:12	w. women wore hats	ABZU 1:4
w. for moral ideas	CHAT 64:3	**working-class** job w. parents want	ABBO 1:1
W. ought to be	KEYN 179:6	**working classes** worst fault of w.	MORT 229:6
W. strain	ELIO 100:14	**works** building w. is not sufficient	JOHN 170:7
W. the most powerful drug	KIPL 183:9	seen the future and it w.	STEF 302:7
worth ten thousand w.	BARN 23:8	w. even if you don't	BOHR 38:6
wrestle With w.	ELIO 100:16	**world** adventure in the w. of Aids	PERK 252:8
you can drug, with w.	LOWE 203:8	all the towns in all the w.	FILM 115:16
Wordsworth daffodils were for W.	LARK 189:13	along the W. I go	CART 55:5
work doesn't look like w.	ARNO 14:13	blamed for worsening the w.	JAME 166:7
good idea but it won't w.	ROGE 273:4	Brave new w.	BORR 40:5
got my w. cut out	SQUI 301:8	decide the fate of the w.	DE G 87:6
Go to w. on an egg	ADVE 3:22	Feed the w.	GELD 130:12
immortality through my w.	ALLE 7:15	funny old w.	THAT 313:13
in w. does what he wants	COLL 73:9	Hog Butcher for the W.	SAND 283:3
Let's go to w.	FILM 115:4	in 1915 the old w. ended	LAWR 192:4
let the toad w.	LARK 189:8	In a w. I never made	HOUS 158:3
looked for w.	TEBB 310:12	In the rich man's w.	ANDE 9:2
love and w.	FREU 123:12	limits of my w.	WITT 339:10
Man grows beyond his w.	STEI 302:14	Little Friend of all the W.	KIPL 183:7
men think. Sex, w.	FISH 112:5	loosed upon the w.	YEAT 345:20
men w. more and dispute less	TAWN 310:2	Love makes the w. go round	MACK 208:2
Nice w. if you can get it	GERS 132:2	new w. order	BUSH 49:2
off to w. we go	MORE 228:4	only girl in the w.	GREY 139:2
of the life, or of the w.	YEAT 344:9	only saved the w.	CHES 64:11
slaughterhouses of w.	VANE 324:1	point of the turning w.	ELIO 100:13
unable to find w.	COOL 76:9	put the w. to sleep	MUIR 230:13
watch them at work	BARN 23:14	rule the w.	BART 24:12
Whistle while you w.	MORE 228:5	Sob, heavy w.	AUDE 16:12
Without w., life goes rotten	CAMU 52:18	Stop the w.	NEWL 236:4
W. and pray	HILL 154:1	sword the axis of the w.	DE G 87:12
W. expands	PARK 250:12	Ten days that shook the w.	REED 268:12
W. is love made visible	GIBR 132:10	third w. war	TRUM 318:11
W. is of two kinds	RUSS 278:13	Top of the w.	FILM 113:1
w. is terribly important	RUSS 278:7	way the w. ends	ELIO 101:17
W. is the call	MORR 228:10	We want the w.	MORR 228:15
W. is *x*	EINS 99:2	woods against the w.	BLUN 37:2
W. liberates	ANON 10:3	w. beauty becomes enough	MORR 229:1
w. like a fiend	THOM 314:14	w. empty of people	LAWR 192:11
w., rest and play	ADVE 4:11	w. famous	RICH 271:2
w. till the end of my life	SWAN 307:9	w. in my head	HEWE 152:13
W. to survive	VANE 324:2	w. is an oyster	MILL 222:4
W. was like a stick	SOLZ 298:6	w. is becoming like asylum	LLOY 201:10
w. while I may live	EPIT 107:7	w. is everything that is	WITT 339:9
wouldn't know how to w. it	FILM 113:9	w. is what it is	NAIP 233:9
worked So on we w.	ROBI 271:12	w. like a Mask dancing	ACHE 1:6
yes it w.	POLI 258:13	w. must be made safe	WILS 338:18
worker weapon with w. at each end	POLI 257:5	w. of silence	EPIT 107:2
w. is the slave	CONN 75:8	w. safe for hypocrisy	WOLF 340:13
workers not the w.	WHYT 334:14	w.'s favourite airline	ADVE 5:13
secure for the w.	ANON 12:15	w.'s in a state o' chassis	O'CA 241:7
working in his w. time	GILL 132:13	w. stood like a playing card	MAIL 211:9
it isn't w.	MAJO 211:13	w.'s worst wound	SASS 285:1
killin' meself w.	O'CA 241:5	W. War III	DAVI 84:12
kind of like w.	BISH 35:5	w. will end in fire	FROS 125:3
Labour isn't w.	POLI 258:1	**World Cup** it's for the W.	LENO 197:4

worlds best of all possible w.   CABE 50:1
  destroyer of w.   OPPE 243:15
worm robin with a w.   MCGI 207:8
  tasted your w.   SPOO 300:14
worms diet of w.   FENT 110:9
worried Dr. Spock is w.   POLI 257:11
  may not be w. into being   FROS 126:1
  w. about Jim   CATC 60:3
worrying What's the use of w.   ASAF 14:14
worse bad against the w.   DAY- 85:12
  fear of finding something w.   BELL 27:6
  If my books had been any w.   CHAN 63:4
  More will mean w.   AMIS 8:7
  w. off for having known   STEP 303:10
worsening blamed for w. the world   JAME 166:7
worship second is freedom to w.   ROOS 274:3
worst full look at the w.   HARD 145:5
  intellectual hatred the w.   YEAT 345:14
  like to be told the w.   CHUR 67:11
  rape isn't the w. thing   WELD 330:13
  While the w. are full   YEAT 345:20
  world's w. wound   SASS 285:1
  w. form of Government   CHUR 68:9
  w. is yet to come   JOHN 170:6
  w. thing I've ever witnessed   MORR 228:13
  w. time of the year   ELIO 101:18
  You do your w.   CHUR 67:12
worth confident of their own w.   AUNG 19:10
  makes life w. living   ELIO 103:9
  w. doing badly   CHES 65:13
Worthington on the stage, Mrs W.   COWA 78:8
wotthehell w. archy   MARQ 215:7
would He w., wouldn't he   RICE 270:7
wound world's worst w.   SASS 285:1
  w., not the bandage   POTT 259:4
Wounded Knee Bury my heart at W.
                                              BENÉ 28:13
wounds salt rubbed into their w.   WEST 332:18
wrath grapes of w.   BORR 40:13
wreck w. and not the story   RICH 270:8
wrestled w. for perhaps too long   HOWE 158:11
wringer big fat w.   MITC 223:14
wrings at last w. its neck   RUSS 278:18
write I w. lousy   CAES 50:3
  love to w. them   BISH 35:5
  people who can't w.   ZAPP 348:6
  w. all the books   EDDI 96:7
  w. every other day   DOUG 92:8
writer best fame is a w.'s fame   LEBO 194:11
  I'm a w.   WALC 326:6
  modern hardback w.   TRIL 317:10
  No w. can give that   GLEN 134:2
  protect the w.   ACHE 1:10
  things a w. is for   RUSH 278:2
  w. must refuse   SART 284:13
  w.'s only responsibility   FAUL 110:5
  w.'s radar   HEMI 151:6

writers dead w. are remote   ELIO 103:12
writing able to live by my w.   NABO 233:5
  continue w.   GARC 130:3
  get it in w.   LEE 195:5
  little point in w.   AMIS 8:8
  live and despise w.   SMIT 297:6
  no talent for w.   BENC 28:8
  thought *nothing* of her w.   SITW 295:14
  W. is not a profession   SIME 294:14
wrong but also to be w.   SZAS 307:12
  called the w. number   CART 57:1
  customer is never w.   RITZ 271:6
  different kinds of w.   COMP 74:5
  Eating people is w.   FLAN 118:8
  excuse the w. by showing   HAND 143:14
  Fifty million Frenchmen can't be w.
                                              MILI 221:5
  Had anything been w.   AUDE 18:17
  in the w. place   DYLA 95:3
  involve us in the w. war   BRAD 42:12
  majority are w.   DEBS 86:11
  never w., the Old Masters   AUDE 17:16
  not even w.   PAUL 251:7
  only an accumulated w.   CASE 55:10
  ran w. through all the land   MUIR 230:12
  right deed for the w.   ELIO 102:10
  something has gone w.   POTT 259:6
  thought it w. to fight   BELL 27:18
  very probably w.   CLAR 70:10
  We were w.   MCNA 209:12
  Why mind being w.   AYER 19:18
  W. but Wromantic   SELL 290:7
  w. members in control   ORWE 245:12
  w. sort of snow   NEWS 237:2
  w. species   WILS 338:1
  w. with our bloody ships   BEAT 25:4
wrongs Two w. don't make a right   SZAS 308:4
wysiwyg shortened to w.   SAYI 287:11

X Generation X.   COUP 77:12
xerox X. makes everybody   MCLU 208:14
XXXX wouldn't give a X.   ADVE 3:6

Yale libel on a Y. prom   PARK 250:2
Yanks Y. are coming   COHA 73:1
yeah Y. but no but   CATC 61:16
year man at the gate of the y.   HASK 147:5
  thirtieth y. to heaven   THOM 314:6
years after all these y.   SIMO 295:14
  One hundred y. of solitude   GARC 130:1
  two thousand y. of hope   WEIZ 330:9
yellow And not your y. hair   YEAT 344:4
  Follow the y. brick road   HARB 144:9
  Goodbye y. brick road   JOHN 169:1
  y. polkadot bikini   VANC 323:6

y. submarine	LENN 197:2	voices of y. people	SMIT 297:2
yes getting the answer y.	CAMU 52:2	Women never have y. minds	DELA 88:9
never hear the word 'Y.'	WEST 332:15	y. are quick of speech	WINT 339:4
We say Y.	WRIG 342:13	y., gifted and black	HANS 144:2
Y., but not in the South	POTT 259:7	Y., gifted and black	IRVI 163:4
Y., I believe	LAST 191:12	y. men think it is	HOUS 158:6
Y.; I remember Adlestrop	THOM 314:18	y. whom I hope to bother	AUDE 18:10
Y. it hurt	POLI 258:13	**younger** like y. men	COLL 73:11
Y., Minister! No, Minister	CROS 80:14	y. than that now	DYLA 95:11
Y.! we have no bananas	SILV 294:13	y. with time	CASA 55:8
yesterday Evil visited us y.	TAYL 310:11	**youngster** going out a y.	FILM 116:14
I believe in y.	LENN 197:3	**yourself** interrupt y. in a minute	CAME 51:9
keeping up with y.	MARQ 215:3	**youth** belongs to Y.	QUAN 264:1
perhaps it was y.	CAMU 52:9	it is y. who must fight	HOOV 157:6
Y.'s men	POLI 258:14	not just a y.	SARK 283:15
yid PUT THE ID BACK IN Y.	ROTH 276:1	red sweet wine of y.	BROO 44:12
yo Y., Blair	BUSH 49:9	shake their wicked sides at y.	YEAT 345:13
York black Archbishop of Y.	RAMS 266:2	y. and laughter go	SASS 285:2
you For y. but not for me	ANON 12:4	Y. is something very new	CHAN 63:9
Your country needs y.	MILI 221:11	Y., which is forgiven	SHAW 292:22
young angry and defrauded y.	KIPL 181:15	**yuppie** y. version of bulimia	EHRE 97:8
Being y. is not minding	WHIT 334:8		
Being y. is overestimated	QUAN 264:2		
get out while we're y.	SPRI 301:4	**Zaire** Z. is the trigger	FANO 109:4
Hip y. gunslinger	ANON 11:1	**zeal** tempering bigot z.	KNOX 184:6
how y. the policemen look	HICK 153:6	**Zen** Z. and the art	PIRS 255:4
I have been y.	BLUN 37:3	**zero** You have z. privacy	MCNE 209:13
I'll die y.	BRUC 46:10	**Zimbabwe** keep my Z.	MUGA 230:7
resolute, the y.	KIPL 182:11	**zipless** z. fuck	JONG 171:3
They're y.	TAGL 309:14	**zoo** human z.	MORR 228:8
too y. to fall asleep	SASS 284:17	running a z.	O'RO 244:8
too y. to take up golf	ADAM 2:5	**Zurich** gnomes in Z.	WILS 338:3

Thematic Index

Administration

Age

America

Art

Britain

Business

Business (cont.)

green shoots of recovery	MISQ 224:8
guided by 'feminine' principles	RODD 272:5
ideals of nation by advertisements	DOUG 92:7
in the store we sell hope	REVS 269:10
looking in the rear view mirror	RODD 272:7
Lunch is for wimps	FILM 115:6
market has no morality	HESE 152:4
not run by itself except downhill	SAYI 286:4
Only the paranoid survive	GROV 140:1
put your heart in the business	WATS 328:13
really want to make a million	ANON 11:4
riding on a smile and a shoeshine	MILL 222:6
romantic sleeping under the desk	GATE 130:6
salary of the chief executive	GALB 128:10
smell of commerce in the morning	FILM 114:8
vital economic interests	WEIL 330:5
What the chief accountant creates	GREE 138:4

Computing

count everything	CORN 77:5
email of the species is deadlier	FRY 126:13
Internet is an élite organization	CHOM 66:4
logic gates stretched out to the horizon	
	AUGA 19:9
LSD of the '90s	LEAR 194:2
nobody knows you're a dog	CART 56:10
obsolescent and nonexistent	BREN 44:2
to really foul things up	SAYI 287:8
tremendous grassroots revolution	BERN 31:8
use them in the search for love	WAŁĘ 326:7
voyager in virtuality can return	TURK 319:10
You have zero privacy anyway	MCNE 209:13

Drinks

bouquet is better than the taste	POTT 259:5
Cocoa is a cad and coward	CHES 65:2
discovered that alcohol was a food	WODE 340:4
naïve domestic Burgundy	CART 56:6
Probably the best lager	ADVE 4:24
Shaken and not stirred	FLEM 118:16
took the cork out of my lunch	FIEL 111:12
wine was a farce	POWE 260:8

Education

able to read but unable to	TREV 317:7
education, education and education	BLAI 35:13
gained in the university of life	BOTT 39:11
He who cannot, teaches	SHAW 292:19
Ignorance is an evil weed	BEVE 33:14
knew more than examiners	KEYN 179:7
More will mean worse	AMIS 8:7
not even red brick but white tile	OSBO 246:16

read Shakespeare and shoot dice	BANK 22:14
Watch my lips: no selection	BLUN 37:4
When you have nothing to live up to	ANDE 8:13

Environment

cherish that pale blue dot	SAGA 281:8
done more damage	COUS 77:14
government as an adversary	BRUN 46:11
have met the enemy	CART 56:12
I am the grass; I cover all	SAND 283:6
I would be burning the rain forest	STIN 305:2
Make it a *green* peace	DARN 83:8
most severe problem we are facing	KING 180:7
remains will be concrete and tyres	LARK 189:3
silent spring	CARS 54:8
Spaceship Earth	FULL 127:3
standing shoulder to shoulder	HAWK 148:2
They paved paradise	MITC 223:16
Think globally, act locally	SAYI 287:7
won't accept Gaia	LOVE 203:6

Europe

all our problems	THAT 313:17
continent of energetic mongrels	FISH 112:6
Europe des patries	DE G 87:8
instead of a nation France	MONN 226:15
open that Pandora's box	BEVI 34:2
sword and the currency	PROD 262:6
thousand years of history	GAIT 128:5
war and peace in the 21st century	KOHL 185:2

Family

children produce adults	DE V 89:11
did the best we could	UPDI 321:7
fundamental defect of fathers	RUSS 279:3
Kids are the best	GROE 139:10
running a zoo	O'RO 244:8
source of all our discontents	LEAC 193:10
they fuck you up	LARK 189:6
two is fun, three is a houseful	SAYI 286:5
you are a referee	FROS 124:11

Fashion

Chuck out the chintz	ADVE 3:11
ease a heart like a satin gown	PARK 249:13
fun, foolish and almost unwearable	LACR 187:1
I don't really like knees	SAIN 281:13
I like to dress egos	VERS 324:10
make a woman's life difficult	LURI 204:8
revisited ideas	OLDF 243:1
starts off beautiful and becomes ugly	BAIL 20:10
to look this cheap	PART 250:17

trick of wearing mink	BALM 22:9
wish I had invented blue jeans	SAIN 281:14

Film

biggest electric train set	WELL 331:1
Directing is really exciting	CLOO 72:8
Glamour is what I sell in my act	DIET 90:11
invention of a mouse	DISN 91:8
Kiss Kiss Bang Bang	KAEL 174:1
lie down in clean postures	FOWL 121:9
park, a policeman and a pretty girl	CHAP 63:11
pictures that got small	FILM 116:16
playing with Plasticine	PARK 249:4
seen one Western you've seen them all	
	WHIT 334:10
too old for animation	DISN 91:7
truth 24 times per second	GODA 134:3
We've got more stars	MAYE 217:13
writing history with lightning	WILS 338:12

Fitness

All you need to run	RADC 265:3
Fat is a feminist issue	ORBA 244:3
if it tastes good	ASIM 15:4
Modern body building is ritual	PAGL 248:3
pint . . . very nearly an armful	GALT 129:5
There's no easy way out	WINF 339:3
to become unnaturally thin	WOLF 340:9
trot in an elderly fashion	THOM 315:6
useful knack of falling	SCOT 289:9
wonderful for other people	KERR 178:8
yuppie version of bulimia	EHRE 97:8

Food

any more broccoli	BUSH 49:1
best number for a dinner party	GULB 140:6
Candy is dandy	NASH 234:17
Diets are like boyfriends	LAWS 193:8
don't eat anything with a face	MCCA 206:4
Exceedingly good cakes	ADVE 3:19
Good food is always a trouble	DAVI 84:5
I say it's spinach	CART 56:7
Milk's leap toward immortality	FADI 109:1
Naughty but nice	ADVE 4:17
Time for a little something	MILN 223:2

Future

ain't what it used to be	BERR 31:11
bad times just around the corner	COWA 78:12
belongs to those who will build it	TRUD 318:5
boot stamping on a human face	ORWE 246:2
It comes soon enough	EINS 98:9

I've seen the promised land	KING 180:15
pie in the sky	HILL 154:1
seen the future and it works	STEF 302:7
tomorrow is another day	MITC 226:3

Health

health of the whole human race	TOYN 317:1
I am getting better and better	COUÉ 77:11
I told you I was ill	EPIT 107:17
journey into the sunset of my life	REAG 268:8
makes illness worthwhile	SHAW 291:12
More doctors smoke Camels	ADVE 4:15
only rational position	DIAM 90:4
sick had no rights	FORS 120:16
straight past the common cold	AYRE 19:19
this great adventure	PERK 252:8
without losing your mind	FOX 121:12

Language

dialect with an army and a navy	WEIN 330:7
great Australian adjective	BAIL 20:11
He mobilized the English language	MURR 232:5
language lacks words to express	LEVI 198:9
language that rolls up its sleeves	SAND 283:10
mystery of language was revealed	KELL 176:6
nobody's special property	WALC 326:5
so little English in that answer	HAGU 141:2
such force as a full stop	BABE 20:1
Summer afternoon	JAME 166:14
two countries divided by a common language	
	SHAW 293:17
We are walking lexicons	LIVE 200:14
What can be said at all	WITT 339:8

Law

independence of judges	DENN 89:4
Islam has established them	KHOM 179:10
lawyer with his briefcase	PUZO 263:5
menace to be defeated	SCAR 285:13
not enough jails	HUMP 160:10
Our Constitution works	FORD 119:12
Parliament itself would not exist	SCAR 285:12
those who arrest you	HARR 146:6

Literature

All a poet can do today is warn	OWEN 247:3
best-seller is the gilded tomb	SMIT 297:3
daring starts from within	WELT 331:11
Good prose is like a window-pane	ORWE 245:4
If a writer has to rob his mother	FAUL 110:5
monkeys banging on typewriters	WILE 335:17
mostly about having sex	LODG 201:14
news that STAYS news	POUN 260:5

Literature (*cont.*)

novel tells a story	FORS 120:6
objects of terror	SOYI 299:4
only one thing of danger	NERU 236:1
principle of procrastinated rape	PRIT 262:4
Self-knowledge does not necessarily help	
	CARE 53:14
shelf life of the modern hardback writer	
	TRIL 317:10
shock-proof shit detector	HEMI 151:6
splinter of ice in the heart	GREE 138:1
way of taking life by the throat	FROS 126:2
We tell ourselves stories	DIDI 90:10
wish your wife or servants to read	GRIF 139:4
world full of audio visual marvels	SMIT 296:12

Love

All you need is love	LENN 196:13
Birds do it, bees do it	PORT 258:20
disorder in its geometry	DE B 86:5
give him diamonds back	GABO 128:1
Love, and then oblivion	MCEW 207:7
Love is a universal migraine	GRAV 137:3
Love is free	BENE 28:11
love is of man's life a thing apart	AMIS 8:6
money can't buy me love	LENN 196:14
most natural painkiller	LAST 191:3
my North, my South	AUDE 17:7
not ever having to say you're sorry	TAGL 309:9
one of the answers	PAZ 251:11
someone to call you darling after sex	BARN 23:15
two solitudes protect and touch	RILK 271:5
whatever that may mean	CHAR 63:15

Marriage

Bigamy is having one husband too many	
	ANON 10:5
deep peace of the double-bed	CAMP 51:13
Get me to the church on time	LERN 197:6
I married beneath me	ASTO 15:12
isn't a word . . . it's a sentence	FILM 115:10
maximum of temptation	SHAW 292:20
never again so much together	MACN 210:3
not a public conveyance	MURD 231:13
right to be just as miserable	FRIE 124:1
three of us in this marriage	DIAN 90:6
trendy Smug Married	FIEL 111:7
waste-paper basket	WEBB 329:18
When you marry your mistress	GOLD 134:14

Men and Women

all men are rapists	FREN 123:2
desire to have all the fun	SAYE 285:6
do twice as well as men	WHIT 334:13

Every woman adores a Fascist	PLAT 255:10
food, sports and last, relationships	FISH 112:5
help with moving the piano	WEST 332:21
how much men hate them	GREE 138:5
juggle work, love, home	FRIE 123:17
like a fish without a bicycle	SAYI 287:13
men we wanted to marry	STEI 303:5
more like a man	LERN 197:7
no wilderness in them	BOGA 38:2
Older men treat women like possessions	
	COLL 73:11
only the right to spring	FOND 119:6
opportunity for achievement	KEIL 176:3
Toughness not in a pinstripe suit	FEIN 110:7
who does the dishes	FREN 123:3

Money

better class of enemy	MILL 222:13
billion here and a billion there	DIRK 91:6
If you can actually count your money	
	GETT 132:4
I've been rich and I've been poor	KAUF 174:9
leave his kids enough to do anything	BUFF 47:11
Money doesn't talk, it swears	DYLA 95:6
Money gives me pleasure all the time	BELL 27:11
Money is like a sixth sense	MAUG 217:3
Money, money, money	ANDE 9:2
Money was exactly like sex	BALD 21:5
Pennies don't fall from heaven	THAT 312:6
pound in your pocket	WILS 338:10
principle o' th' thing	HUBB 159:2
spend, and spend, and spend	NICH 236:8
tell you about the very rich	FITZ 117:14
try to rub up against money	RUNY 277:10

Music

bought the Velvets' albums	ENO 105:16
brandy of the damned	SHAW 292:11
children starve on his dissonances	IVES 163:9
He always had a rainbow pen	BAEZ 20:7
hear it through their feet	SOUS 299:3
how potent cheap music is	COWA 78:14
if you gotta ask you'll never know	MISQ 224:12
jazz the sound of surprise	BALL 22:8
just pick a chord, go twang	VICI 325:1
Let's face the music and dance	BERL 30:6
lie back in an easy chair	IVES 163:10
Music is feeling, then, not sound	STEV 304:2
pauses between the notes	SCHN 288:1
scrabble with the vowels missing	ELLI 104:13
should be tarted up	BOWI 42:3
sweet, soft, plenty rhythm	MORT 229:9
to get laid, to get fame	GELD 130:11
too good to leave to chance	SIMO 295:6

truest expression of a people   DE M 88:15
Writing about music   ANON 13:4

Past

go and live in the Middle Ages   SMIT 297:8
Hindsight is always twenty-twenty   WILD 335:12
human nature changed   WOOL 341:10
in 1915 the old world ended   LAWR 192:4
only dead thing that smells sweet   THOM 314:19
past is a bucket of ashes   SAND 283:7
Stands the Church clock at ten to three
                                       BROO 45:3

Photography

camera makes everyone a tourist   SONT 298:17
cod which produces a million eggs   SHAW 293:12
famous picture nobody's ever seen   ANON 11:16
frozen flash of history   ANON 10:13
in a fraction of a second   CART 55:6
learn to see the ordinary   BAIL 20:8
more important to click with people   EISE 100:3
one that's in focus   WARH 327:9
point of view of a paralysed cyclops   HOCK 155:5
reflection photographing other reflections
                                       MICH 220:3
secret about a secret   ARBU 13:15
you aren't close enough   CAPA 53:2

Politics

argument of the broken window pane
                                       PANK 249:1
Art of the Possible   BUTL 49:12
can take a nation's pulse   WHIT 333:7
election by the incompetent many   SHAW 292:17
expression of human immaturity   BRIT 44:5
feeds your vanity   PARR 250:16
government by discussion   ATTL 16:8
have been twice spoiled   COOL 76:5
Instead of rocking the cradle   ROBI 272:1
man who promises least   BARU 24:15
must have an ethical dimension   COOK 75:16
ninety-minute patriots   SILL 294:11
not the voting that's democracy   STOP 305:9
only safe pleasure   CRIT 80:1
Politics without compromise   KINN 181:11
second oldest profession   REAG 268:3
start in the streets   KENN 176:11
too serious to be left to politicians DE G 87:7
war without bloodshed   MAO 214:4
week is a long time in politics   WILS 338:8
Women, and Champagne   BELL 27:15
Wonderful theory, wrong species   WILS 338:1

Popular Culture

Add sex, and stir   CILA 70:1
anything with long hair   MASO 216:12
currency of all reality shows   TRUS 319:5
decisive moment   TYNA 320:6
famous for fifteen minutes   WARH 327:8
first rappers of Europe   BJÖR 35:6
I think of it as a cultural Stalingrad BALL 22:6
It's like kissing God   BRUC 46:10
more popular than Jesus   LENN 196:12
more than ten people like you   MANN 213:12
no hard-sell or soft-sell TV push   NASH 234:13
pay to see bad movies   GOLD 135:6
shaking an apple tree   COLL 74:2
turn on, tune in, drop out   LEAR 194:1
want to hear from your sweater   LEBO 194:8
what Big Brother is for   KUNZ 185:16
Whole families shopping at night   GINS 133:5

Present

controls the past   ORWE 245:17
Exhaust the little moment   BROO 45:8
gadget-filled paradise   NIEB 236:12
Ours is the age of substitutes   BENT 30:1
past is lost   CHAP 63:14
We are now in the Me Decade   WOLF 340:18

Press

cut out the cancer   AITK 6:1
drinking in last chance saloon   MELL 218:11
editor did it when I was away   MURD 231:14
elderly lady in Hastings   LEWI 199:15
facts are lost forever   MAIL 211:11
facts are on expenses   STOP 305:13
facts are sacred   SCOT 289:7
find a page-one story   STON 305:7
Go to where the silence is   GOOD 135:11
if a man bites a dog, that is news   BOGA 38:5
It takes a great owner   BRAD 42:8
men with the muck-rakes   ROOS 274:10
my one form of continuous fiction   BEVA 33:12
nation talking to itself   MILL 222:9
None of this was made up   HERS 151:20
omelette all over our suits   BROK 44:8
saying 'Lord Jones Dead'   CHES 65:14
such of the proprietor's prejudices   SWAF 307:8
When seagulls follow a trawler   CANT 53:1

Quotations

achieve unexpected felicities   HOLM 156:7
for an uneducated man to read   CHUR 69:2
make a monkey out of a man   BENC 28:6
make quite a fair show of knowledge   DOUG 92:9

Quotations (*cont.*)

plums and orange peel picked out   RALE 265:9
privilege of the learned   PEAR 252:1

Religion

conjuring trick with bones   JENK 167:11
Conservative Party at prayer   ROYD 276:11
cosmic Cheshire cat   HUXL 161:16
Disneyfication of Christianity   CUPI 81:13
elderly lady, who mutters away   CARE 53:10
frozen thought of men   KRIS 185:4
How many divisions has *he* got   STAL 301:11
how much nastier I would be   WAUG 329:14
I am still an atheist   BUÑU 47:14
I do not pretend to know   DARR 84:1
most materialistic of all great religions
                                          TEMP 311:12
no atheists in the foxholes   CUMM 81:11
not been tried and found wanting   CHES 65:12
scandal and glory of the Church   RAMS 266:2
throw open the windows   JOHN 168:5
We may be surprised   TUTU 320:2
When men stop believing in God   CHES 65:15
why they invented Hell   RUSS 279:5
wish for prayer is a prayer itself   BERN 31:1
women were first at the Cradle   SAYE 285:8
wound, not the bandage   POTT 259:4

Royalty

could do with a pub here   STEW 305:1
genetic lottery comes up with   PIML 254:11
glad we've been bombed   ELIZ 103:17
gold filling in a mouthful of decay   OSBO 246:18
have the Queen as their aunt   MARG 214:11
kill animals and stick in stamps   NICO 236:10
My husband and I   ELIZ 104:6
only five kings left   FARO 109:8
People's Princess   BLAI 35:15
queen in people's hearts   DIAN 90:5
She needed no royal title   SPEN 299:14
support of the woman I love   EDWA 97:6
The family firm   GEOR 131:11

Science

art of the soluble   MEDA 218:6
ask an impertinent question   BRON 44:10
either physics or stamp collecting   RUTH 279:14
Genes not like engineering blueprints
                                          STEW 304:16
grand aim of all science   EINS 99:4
most incomprehensible fact   EINS 98:12
not be content to manufacture life   BERN 30:17

often in error, but never in doubt   LAND 188:7
ones who know what they're looking for
                                          CHOM 66:5
physicists have known sin   OPPE 244:1
says that something is possible   CLAR 70:10
set a limit to infinite error   BREC 43:7
shocked by this subject   BOHR 38:7
There is no democracy in physics   ALVA 7:18
when I don't know what I'm doing   BRAU 43:4
world looks so different after   FEYN 111:3

Sex

buy a bottle of wine   DWOR 94:13
did thee feel the earth move   HEMI 150:13
girls who wear glasses   PARK 249:8
Give a man a free hand   WEST 332:7
If men could get pregnant   KENN 176:10
in the street and frighten the horses   CAMP 51:14
Is that a pistol in your pocket   WEST 332:11
It's just It   KIPL 183:8
most fun I ever had without laughing   ALLE 7:5
not got your niche in creation   HALL 142:8
only unnatural sex act   KINS 181:12
orgasm has replaced the Cross   MUGG 230:10
Sexual intercourse began in 1963   LARK 188:12
something I really don't understand   SALI 282:7

Society

condemn a little more   MAJO 211:14
help the many who are poor   KENN 177:6
no such thing as Society   THAT 313:6
prisoners of addiction and envy   ILLI 162:5
To give employment to the artisan   BELL 27:13
where it is safe to be unpopular   STEV 304:10

Sport

22 men chase a ball for 90 minutes   LINE 200:8
don't really see the hurdles   MOSE 229:11
Football? It's the beautiful game   PELÉ 252:3
game is about glory   BLAN 36:10
get to shake a bat at a white man   GREG 138:12
hard tour and hard work wins it   ARMS 14:8
I'm the greatest   ALI 6:12
more serious than that   SHAN 291:8
my *business* to get him in trouble   ROBI 272:2
Nice guys finish last   DURO 94:9
not as fast as the world record   COLE 73:5
show business with blood   BRUN 46:12
Spill your guts at Wimbledon   CONN 75:9
swearing is very much part of it   GREA 137:8
war minus the shooting   ORWE 246:6